# Shakespeare's
# Christian Dimension

# Shakespeare's Christian Dimension

*An Anthology of Commentary*

*edited by*

## Roy Battenhouse

INDIANA UNIVERSITY PRESS
*Bloomington & Indianapolis*

The paper used in this publication meets the minimum requirements of American National Standard for Information Sciences—Permanence of Paper for Printed Library Materials, ANZI Z39.48-1984.

 ™

Manufactured in the United States of America


Library of Congress Cataloging-in-Publication Data

Shakespeare's Christian dimension : an anthology of commentary /
    edited by Roy Battenhouse.
        p.    cm.
    Includes bibliographical references and index.
    ISBN 0-253-31122-5
    1. Shakespeare, William, 1564–1616—Religion. 2. Christian drama,
English—History and criticism. 3. Drama—Religious aspects—Christianity.
4. Christianity and literature.   I. Battenhouse, Roy W. (Roy Wesley), 1912– .
PR 3011.S48   1994
822.3'3—dc20                                                            93-31520


1 2 3 4 5 99 98 97 96 95 94

*This book is for*

Anna & John

# CONTENTS

# PREFACE

Commentary on Christian dimensions in Shakespeare has been accumulating over the years. Beginning in the nineteenth century with a noticing of his biblical allusions and of passages reminiscent of Bible themes, it has deepened to include attention to his echoings of liturgical language and theological concepts. Increasingly, the relation of his plays to medieval mystery and morality drama has been probed and illustrated, and also his indebtedness to the world-views of Augustine, Boethius, Aquinas, Dante, and Erasmus. Observations on these matters, along with interpretations of Shakespeare's works in the light of Christian lore, have been substantive enough to warrant now a scholarly overview for public attention. A bringing together of pertinent excerpts from the commentary of the last fifty years can provide, especially if the selections are read in conjunction with each other, an impressive challenge to reappreciate the Christian roots of Shakespeare's art.

The present anthology reprints ninety-two pieces of commentary on twenty-six of the plays. In addition, it provides a supplementary bibliography of more than two hundred fifty further items. These features taken together make it a useful research manual, especially if readers consult its Index. Yet it is not exhaustive in its coverage; it is simply a sifting out of what seems to me chiefly valuable. My guiding purpose has been to provide both for scholars and for the general reader a reliable sampling of the influence of Shakespeare's Christian heritage on the shaping of his plays.

The collection can be a timely resource for today's college teachers, I believe, since it focuses attention on a perspective quite different from various of the modern ones nowadays widely used—for instance, the "cultural materialism" which proceeds to question whether Shakespeare's art is "for all time" as Ben Jonson supposed. Our students, I think, deserve the option of an alternative to such an approach. Let the present volume serve this classroom need, so that informed debate may be possible.

My title "Christian Dimension" is intended to indicate that more than local color is involved when Shakespeare puts biblical allusions or echoes into the speech of persons in his plays. Such references point us often to paradigms by which the action can be evaluated. For even when a speaker misapplies Scripture, his distortion exposes a blind spot in his character. A biblical norm, so to speak, puts him under judgment. Drama has, underneath its value of entertainment, a logic of design that gives it a core of parable—so Sidney insisted in his Elizabethan defense of poetry. Thus the reader is challenged to be a seeker of wisdom such as Ecclesiasticus 39 describes: "He will be conversant with dark parables" and "travel through strange countries." Jesus used parables to challenge in auditors their capacity to distinguish between good and evil. May not Shakespeare's stories have a similar purpose, evident in the shape they give to the paths of human felicity or folly?

A well known New Testament parable tells of a sower whose seed produced a proper harvest only when it met with good soil. Shakespeare undoubtedly knew this parable, and it is likely that he understood its four kinds of soil as representing the diverse kinds of listener response his own plays would receive. In any case the response of auditors over the centuries, both to the Bible and to Shakespeare, has varied in accord with each reader's capacities of heart and mind. Often the capacity has been shallow. But a kind of good-soil responsiveness to the seminal potential of Shakespeare's artwork seems to me evident in the commentaries the present anthology contains. At least their attention to biblical themes and patterns, it can be said, offers us eyes for seeing and ears for hearing dimensions of meaning which usually go unrecognized by other schools of criticism. Patrick Murray could remark in his *The Shakespearian Scene* (1969) that "the volume of distinctly Christian ideas, implied or expressed in Shakespeare's work as a whole, has not yet received anything like its due share of attention." Toward remedying this situation I have prepared the present book.

I am indebted and grateful to many publishers and authors for their permissions to reprint the excerpts here assembled. All the essays have been abridged, and many of their footnotes (sometimes all) have been eliminated. I have had to prune severely in order to present essential insights from a large array of commentators. Their fuller texts should be looked into by painstaking readers. I have not tried to standardize the line references to Shakespeare, which here are always those of each essayist to his chosen text.

Finally, let me record that I have received invaluable help from my wife Marian and from my daughter Anna and her husband John Kolts, to each of whom I feel a deep gratitude.

Roy Battenhouse
Bloomington, Indiana

# Shakespeare's Christian Dimension

The jewell that we find, we stoop and take't
Because we see it, but what we do not see
We tread upon, and never think of it.

— *Measure for Measure*

Let those who think I have said too little, or those
who think I have said too much forgive me, and let
those who think I have said just enough join me in
giving thanks to God.

— Augustine, *City of God*

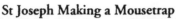

**St Joseph Making a Mousetrap**

Robert Campin, Triptych of the Annunciation, ca. 1428
By permission of the Metropolitan Museum of Art
The Cloisters Collection, 1956

# INTRODUCTION

## An Overview of Christian Interpretation

Many ordinary readers have felt instinctively that Shakespeare and the Bible belong together. Yet inevitably there have been others who claim for the poet their own reductive beliefs, despite his burial in a church and a Last Will that names Christ his savior. At the turn of the present century, for instance, we find Shakespeare described by Churton Collins as a "theistical agnostic," and A. C. Bradley saying that he painted the world "without regard to anyone's beliefs." John Robertson (a celebrated Disintegrator) declared that Shakespeare was groping his way toward the "sanity" of Auguste Comte. And England's poet laureate John Masefield, when writing on *Shakespeare and the Spiritual Life* (1924), was confident that to the dramatist "orthodox religion" meant almost nothing, since he "held to no religion save that of humanity and his own great nature." A follow-up to this contention was voiced by D. G. James in his *Dream of Learning* (1951), where Christianity is equated with "a fierce censorship" and we are assured that Shakespeare "did not write as a Christian." Even more skeptical are some of today's deconstructionists who seem to say that any author's personal belief is irrelevant and also irrecoverable.

Nevertheless a growing body of scholarship tying Shakespeare's plays to Christian insights has been accumulating since the mid-nineteenth century, and so an overview of this history will be helpful as a background to some summary observations on the achievements the present anthology catalogs.

The religious contexts of action in Shakespearean drama are the focus of our anthology. They may help us recall that in Elizabethan England religion was considered the anchor of morals, and the God of Christian faith was generally believed to be the creator, sustainer, and judge of all mankind. The guidebook for understanding good and evil in all sorts and conditions of life was Holy Scripture, a capstone to testimonies provided universally in the Book of Nature. In such a context everyone's history could be one of journey toward self-knowledge and health, or else of opportunities squandered. Do not Shakespeare's stories imply this sense of history? Historical criticism in our time should be open to perceptions that a drama's horizons of understanding can be ultimately Christian in their outreach.

Of signal importance has been Hermann Ulrici's *Shakespeare's Dramatic Art*, which appeared in English translation in 1846 and grew to a third edition by 1880. Ulrici read Shakespeare as "a Christian in the truest sense" with a "Christian view of life." He saw the dramatist's achievement as a blending of the "idealistic art" of the Middle Ages with the realism of modern history; and with this perspective he had no difficulty in accepting the ending of *King Lear* as a salvation of soul for Lear and Gloucester in their coming to see the true nature of love after undergoing a purification. Similarly, Ulrici read *The Merchant of Venice* and *Measure for Measure* as showing that human virtue is possible only in and through an inner love that combines strictness with mercy. In all of Shakespeare's comedies he saw what he called a "dialectics of irony" employed to neutralize one-sided obsessions, and he defended Shakespeare's puns as intrinsic to this comic method. Thus a portrait of the poet as moral philosopher replaced the wild genius presumed by eighteenth-century critics.

In this altered context, English writers began to speak of Shakespeare as Christian, and studies soon appeared in tribute to the national poet's congruence with the Good Book. Of these the most substantial were Bishop Charles Wordsworth's *Shakespeare's Knowledge and Use of the Bible* (1864) written for the Anniversary ceremonies and expanded in a third edition of 1880; J. B. Selkirk's (*pseud.* for James Brown) *Bible Truths with Shakespearian Parallels* (1872), which had a sixth edition by 1888; and, in America, William Burgess's *The Bible in Shakespeare* (Chicago, 1903; later reprints). Wordsworth devoted a long chapter to Shakespeare's biblical allusions and another to his "Religious Principles and Sentiments derived from the Bible." He disagreed with Mr. Bowdler's excising from *The Family Shakespeare* the clown's speech in *All's Well* about the narrow gate and the porter's speech in *Macbeth* about the primrose way. He noted that in the tragedies the catastrophe results from sinful passions such as revenge and jealousy. He concluded his book by saying that no other Elizabethan "has paid homage to Christianity as effectually as Shakespeare." Selkirk arranged parallel quotations from Shakespeare and the Bible on more than a hundred topics. He concluded that Shakespeare's genius had so assimilated and reproduced the Bible's great truths that his words seem to renew its authority. Burgess proclaimed Shakespeare a sincere believer of "the main doctrines of the Christian religion" and offered in evidence from the plays parallels filling 16 pages and 150 pages of quotations on topics such as Conscience, God's Attributes, Thankfulness, etc. He found eight references to Cain, a confused memory of the 23rd Psalm by Mistress Quickly, and "the very likeness of Ahab and Jezebel" in the Macbeths (here citing Thomas Eaton's *Shakespeare and the Bible*, 1857).

Are there shortcomings in these studies? By hindsight we can observe that some of the moral sentiments cited are less genuinely Christian than they sound. For instance, Iago's discourse on free will is listed by Selkirk among Shakespeare's Bible truths. Actually, however, Iago was here using a Pelagian language to lure Roderigo to enslave himself to his lustful passion. In other passages, even when the moral idea expressed is indeed Christian and may reflect Shakespeare's own faith, Selkirk fails to note that the speaker who voices it was actually using it hypocritically to mislead his listeners—as is the case, surely, in King Henry IV's reference to "Those blessed feet.... nailed / For our advantage to the bitter cross." Here the king puts piety on display when, for his political advantage, he is about to postpone the crusade he had promised his feet would make. This truth of the drama can be overlooked by readers who look to Shakespeare simply as a storehouse of moral sentiments.

Let me discern also a misapprehension by Burgess when noting Canterbury's reference in *Henry V* to the Book of Numbers. This indicates, says Burgess, Shakespeare's versatility in using Scripture. A wiser inference would be that the Archbishop is being characterized as an irresponsible exegete, who cites from Numbers a text which (a canny reader might know) is a half-truth since it omits the more pertinent passage in Numbers where Moses disallowed a daughter the right to inherit land from her father if she marries a foreigner. Shakespeare's ironic point, wholly missed by Burgess, is that Henry V has no valid claim to France. A bigger mistake regarding Henry V is made by Wordsworth. He misreads the whole character of this king's piety by failing to see the irony in Shakespeare's having him fulsomely ascribe his Agincourt victory to God's arm alone, right after we have seen the battle won by Henry's order to cut the throats of prisoners. The Victorian Bishop's uncritical feelings of patriotism along with his liking for moral sentiment have left a blindspot in his ability to see. When tabulating Bible allusions he can point us to Matthew 2 as the source for Henry's mention of "Herod's bloody-hunting slaughtermen" but without perceiving in Henry a kinship with Herod. This blindspot, I must add, was also in Ulrici's vision and caused his declaring that Henry's career stands for "the moral purification and amendment of man." Indeed, it can be said that the deceitfulness of this monarch's piety remained largely unexposed by literary critics until around 1950, when Professor Goddard focused his Quaker intelligence on the specifics of the action in Shakespeare's play. Only then did the possibility arise that our "country" poet might have viewed history with the irony of an Erasmus.

A disillusionment with romantic idealism emerged after World War I and was signalled by T. S. Eliot's *The Waste Land.* While this poem got its popularity from its truth-telling vignettes of hollow love quest, its anthropological diggings encompassed a scope of history from Agamemnon's times to the present day. And its author was eventually discovered to be, surprisingly, an apologist for Christian orthodoxy. His essays in appreciation of Lancelot Andrewes and Dante, while at the same time he questioned Arnold's humanism and Lambeth's churchmanship, made possible a revived scholarly attention to the history of religion and to medieval drama in particular, along with some modern experiments in churchyard drama, and some stageplays that hinted of Christian mysteries hidden in secular experience. Eliot himself proceeded not only to tell us that literary criticism needed to be "completed" by recourse to theological truths, but also to provide avenues to those truths in his *Four Quartets* begun in the 30s and concluded during World War II in the 40s.

Those two decades are usually described by historians of Shakespeare criticism as an era of "historical" approaches. That is true; but the wide range of history that was reinvigorating scholarship needs to be more fully appreciated. While some students were delving into the history of theatre in general, or of Elizabethan acting companies, or of medieval story conventions, others were looking into schoolbooks and Stratford schoolmasters (two of them of Catholic sympathies) during Shakespeare's boyhood, or assessing the extent of his familiarity with the Bible (42 of its books by R. Noble's count) and the Prayerbook, or reviewing the contents of the Elizabethan *Homilies* appointed for church use. The history of ideas became important with the publication of Lily B. Campbell's *Shakespeare's Tragic Heroes* (1930) and Howard Patch's *The Tradition of Boethius* (1935) and Willard Farnham's *The Medieval Heritage of Elizabethan Tragedy* (1936). And concurrently, scholars of Old English literature and the medieval poets began to re-estimate the Christian ingredients of *Beowulf* and the works of Cynewulf, Langland, and Chaucer. All this, when accompanied by the proddings from T.S. Eliot I have mentioned, provided challenging horizons for those of us who underwent our graduate training in the mid-30s.

Historic religion received an increasing attention during World War II when the B.B.C. put on the air some talks by C.S. Lewis, known for his witty *Screwtape Letters* but now offering the public a core of "mere Christianity." His *The Case for Christianity* appeared in 1946. Almost everybody in those years seemed interested in Christianity's relation to culture. A stream of books around that topic issued from both Protestant and Catholic scholars, but was fed especially by Maritain's *True Humanism* (1938), *Ransoming the Time* (1941), and *Christianity and Democracy* (1945), along with Gilson's various expoundings of the medieval philosophers. De Lubac launched his multi-volume *Exégèse Médiévale* in 1941; and after a while Protestant and Catholic presses alike were publishing each a series of translations from the Church Fathers. Also new journals cropped up with titles such as *The Christian Scholar* and *Christendom*, college courses on the metaphysical poets flourished, and literary critics were shown by Erich Auerbach's *Mimesis* (Eng. tr., 1953) the special qualities characteristic of Judaeo-Christian stylistics.

Shakespeare's relation to Catholic tradition was first probed in the mid-nineteenth century by Richard Simpson, whose papers were assembled and amplified in Henry S. Bowden's *The Religion of Shakespeare* (1899). The contention of this book was the probability of a personal sympathy for the Old Faith by Shakespeare. Bowden began with some distinctions between Catholic and Protestant doctrines, and then showed how biographical documents relating to Shakespeare can have a hidden religious explanation. His coverage of the plays was chiefly impressionistic, noting the Catholic tone of lines such as "Unhousel'd, disappointed, unanel'd" in

*Hamlet*, or the reference by the Countess in *All's Well* to "her prayers, whom Heaven delights to hear," or Prospero's allusion to "her help, of whose soft grace" he has had aid. An overconcern for pious wording, however, misled Bowden to eulogize Henry V as an "ideal" king and to misattribute compassion to Pandulph in *King John*. His best insights are his likening the persecuted Catholics under Queen Elizabeth to the plight of Edgar in *King Lear*, and his reply to Harsnett by quoting Thomas More to the effect that occasional fraudulent miracles should not blind us to the reality of true miracles—the kind Bowden finds in the conversion of Lear, in the healing of the King of France by Helena, and in the cures by King Edward in *Macbeth*.

The argument that Shakespeare "retained a genuine esteem for certain aspects" of Catholicism was renewed by John Henry de Groot in his *The Shakespeares and "The Old Faith"* (1946). To Bowden's culling of Catholic phrases he added others; and as evidence of Shakespeare's familiarity with the Rheims *New Testament* he cited the words *cockle, narrow* gate, and not a hair *perished*, unique to that translation. But De Groot's important contribution was his convincing argument, based centrally on discoveries made by Herbert Thurston in 1923 and subsequently, that the Last Will and Testament of John Shakespeare, the poet's father, was indeed no forgery but reliable evidence of his probable contact with the Jesuit missioners, since the Will follows a formula for Testaments drawn up by St Charles Borromeo and imported into England by them. This historical evidence justified De Groot in postulating a home training of young William which could have included Catholic lore and its continuing witness in iconography, such as the wall tapestries referred to by Falstaff. Moreover, John Speed's reference in 1611 to the "papist" Robert Persons and "his poet" implies that the dramatist retained Catholic sympathies.

Mutschmann and Wentersdorf's *Shakespeare and Catholicism* (1952) explained why "religion mattered supremely to Shakespeare" and concluded, on the basis of a large array of evidence both historical and dramatic, that he was a secret Catholic all his life and may have died a papist. M.D.H. Parker in her *The Slave of Life* (1955) devoted an Appendix to capsulizing and reinforcing the biographical interpretations of Mutschmann and Wentersdorf, and in her earlier chapters she drew on doctrines in Augustine and Aquinas to account for the idea of justice that undergirds Shakespeare's dramaturgy. More recently, Peter Milward has summarized the biographical problem in his *Shakespeare's Religious Background* (1973), and in *Shakespeare Yearbook 1* (1990) has written of Shakespeare's affinities with Thomas More, and has termed the plays "a synthesis of tradition and reform" in which allusions to the contemporary religious scene "cry out from between the lines."

The horizons of history uncovered by the scholars I have just mentioned, it should be noted, are larger than those entertained by E.M.W. Tillyard in his *Elizabethan World Picture* (1943) and his *Shakespeare's History Plays* (1944). For although he attempted in the latter book a providential view of history, the sense of providence he relied on was that of Edward Hall's Protestant overview rather than that of Augustine's *City of God* (the textbook of More and Erasmus). Tillyard's unawareness of the difference can be seen to be, in retrospect, the cause of the difficulty he got into when interpreting Henry V. In following Hall's portrait of Henry as an ideal king, Tillyard complains, Shakespeare ends with a copybook hero whose platitudes depress us and whose coarseness suggests that the dramatist was "writing up something he had begun to hate." The play's "slack construction" suggests that its author "had written his epic of England and had no more to say on the matter." But are these remarks consistent with Tillyard's overall claim that the eight plays constitute a unified chain of moral interpretation? At odds with this is also his comment that in *3 Henry VI* Shakespeare failed to make his material significant because he got tired or bored. It seems to me Tillyard approximates a satisfactory reading only when he views Henry Richmond as a godly minister of England's deliverance from Richard's tyranny. Yet, even here, he does not see that Hall's tracing of the happy outcome to a "policy" suggested by Buckingham has been replaced by Shakespeare's scene of the Queen's rejecting of Richard's "policy" pleas. Is not Shakespeare revising Hall's sense of providence by relying on Thomas More's sense of it in the material Hall borrowed from More and tried to overlay with moralizing on the glory of national unity?

Richmond's prayer to the "gracious" eye of God is not recorded by Hall. And when Tillyard cites it, his surrounding commentary reveals a twentieth-century fear of identifying Shakespeare with any settled beliefs:

> If one were to say that in *Richard III* Shakespeare pictures England restored to order through God's grace, one gravely risks being lauded or execrated for attributing to Shakespeare personally the full doctrine of prevenient grace according to Calvin. When therefore I say that *Richard III* is a very religious play, I want to be understood as speaking of the play and not of Shakespeare. For the purposes of the tetralogy and most obviously for this play Shakespeare accepted the prevalent belief that God had guided England into her haven of Tudor prosperity. And he accepted it with his whole heart, as later he did not accept the supposed siding of God with the English against the French he so loudly proclaimed in *Henry V*. (p. 204)

This passage leaves unexplained what Shakespeare did "accept" (believe?) regarding Henry V's status within a providential order, and also it seems to say that Tillyard thinks Calvin the only available interpreter of divine providence, and that "Tudor prosperity" is its goal. If Tillyard had consulted Augustine or Boethius, however, he could have learned that political prosperity is not identical with divine blessing, and that providence punishes a sinner centrally with his own sin and the interior weariness it entails (as in the vanity of "idol ceremony" confessed by Henry). But instead Tillyard supposes a Shakespeare of shifting belief, one who put his heart into Hall's (implicitly Calvinist?) belief when writing *Richard III* but lost enthusiasm for it subsequently.

Understandably, many readers of Tillyard have been unsatisfied with his explanations. Yet what warrants our skepticism, I would say, is not the premise that Shakespeare's histories reflect a divine providence but rather Tillyard's version of providence. Moreover, to grasp Shakespeare's chain we need to read the eight plays in the order given them in the folio's text rather than in their order of composition. Beginning with Richard's disowning of the balm of grace and ending with Henry Richmond's turning to grace and sacrament, the cycle places Henry V at a midpoint in the downward spiraling, a place in England's history analogous to Julius Caesar's in Rome's history, whereas the later Henry Tudor is analogous to Rome's Constantine.

The historical approaches I have associated with post-Bradleyan criticism were accompanied by a concurrent attention to Shakespeare's language of symbolism. One may regard this development as an amplifying of Romanticism's focus on the poet as a questing Seer, and perhaps as a continuation of Keats's idea that "Shakespeare lived a life of allegory" on which his works comment. G. Wilson Knight became its spokesman in 1930 with his metaphorically titled *Wheel of Fire,* for which T. S. Eliot provided a Prefatory Note. Eliot here wrote of the need to grasp the "whole design" of a poetic drama and to read both character and plot with an understanding of the work's "subterrene or submarine music." He also emphasized that the greatest poetry speaks "on two planes at once," a sensory experience within which there moves a pattern of deeper meaning. Eliot was perhaps remembering Augustine's analysis of a logic we listen for under time-borne sounds.

Knight saw Shakespeare's plays as having a spatial-temporal patterning of Tempest and Music set forth in a language of parable. And the most striking essay in Knight's many volumes was his early "*Measure for Measure* and the Gospels." Here he uncovered the affinity of Shakespeare's drama to the parables of Jesus and defended the Duke of this play as embodying in his actions the ethical wisdom of Jesus. Knight was writing not from any knowledge of the history of theology but rather as a post-Romantic who valued human imagination as the key to insight into life; he found in Shakespeare a poet whose genius coincided here with that of Christ—each being, as Knight explained elsewhere, an independent pioneer who challenged "orthodox" morality. Knight's reliance simply on imaginative genius was later to betray him into uncritical admiration for the transrational poetry of Nietzsche, by the light of which his comments on the mystical humanism of Shakespeare became questionable. Nevertheless his emphasis on symbolism has done much to reinvigorate Shakespeare criticism. It has directed attention to dimensions of myth and miracle in Shakespeare's plays, besides encouraging the efforts of Northrop Frye to associate literary genres with seasonal phases in the cycle of human experience.

S. L. Bethell in *The Winter's Tale: A Study* (1947) probed more radically than either Knight or Frye. Noting this play's atmosphere of supernatural religion, he stated his conviction that Shakespeare wrote "from the standpoint of orthodox Christianity" while using archaic dramatic methods to put his audience into an experiencing of symbolic meanings. Bethell's earlier *Shakespeare and the Popular Dramatic Tradition* (1944) had called attention to a multiconsciousness in Shakespeare's language, tracing its source to medieval popular drama. Then in his *Literary Criticism and the English Tradition* (1948) he proceeded to emphasize that a poem's most significant level is the sequence of events it re-creates in the mind, a narrative that conveys by its author's attitude a criticism of life, for the grasping of which the real world must be co-present with the play world in the minds of the audience. Anticipating some of today's theorists, Bethell insisted that a work's quality of *insight* into human experience is what critics ultimately judge, and that in this matter

> there is no critical neutrality; there are only Christian critics and Marxist critics and Moslem critics—and critics who think themselves disinterested but who are really swayed unconsciously by the beliefs they have necessarily acquired by being members of a particular society in a particular place and time. . . . The 'pure critics' of today adhere in fact to the dogmatic position of nineteenth-century humanism, which has been for so long the atmosphere of English academic circles that it is taken for granted like the air itself. . . . The Christian, on the other hand, knows that . . . assumptions, unexamined because scarcely realized as assumptions, are part of the lot of fallen man. Such dogma, untrue or unclear, reflects the curse of Adam, and against it we have only to set the revealed dogma which we experience as a partial clearing of vision. . . . The Christian critic has little reason for arrogance, and if he should fail to do justice in his calling the fault lies with him and not the Cause he has espoused. (pp. 25–26)

A similarly Christian response to the special quality of Shakespeare's narrative language may be seen in Nevill Coghill's ground-breaking essay of 1950 on the medieval "Basis of Shakespearian Comedy." Citing Dante's explanation of the four levels of meaning possible in a story of human journey, Coghill defined Shakespearean comedy as a journey from misery to joy and illustrated the presence of an allegorical import in several of Shakespeare's comedies.

Meanwhile in 1946 there appeared in PMLA my essay arguing that Shakespeare's *Measure for Measure* was informed by Christianity's doctrine of Atonement. The Duke's role, I explained, is a secular analogue of St Luke's "He hath visited and redeemed his people" and is replete with imagery of a star-led shepherd and king of love who rescues the lost and ransoms the guilty by a conquest such as the Church Fathers describe when explicating the Atonement story. The play's whole action, as I read it, participates by analogy in the biblical cycle of sin, law, sentence, intervention, faith, suffering, and reconciliation. This reading was curtly dismissed by Tillyard, who preferred to view the play as an artistic failure. Yet other scholars—notably Barbara Lewalski, J. A. Bryant, and R. G. Hunter—turned to biblical typology as an under-structure of Shakespeare's art; and by 1969 I was able to argue that biblical "premises" (a baptised Aristotelianism) governed his depicting of tragedy. "Typological Criticism" was the label David Bevington aptly used when discussing Christian interpretations in the Introduction to his textbook *Shakespeare* (3rd edition, 1980). He credited it, however, only with serving the cause of "image" study and remarked that its dissenters had made it assume "a defensive posture." True, it has been elbowed to the sidelines during our post-Vietnam era. But in fact its leaven of insight has been quietly enlarging, as will be evident in the range of selections in my present anthology. Arthur C. Kirsch, for instance, has recently invoked the Atonement motif when explaining the structure of *Much Ado* and also of *Cymbeline*, while Frances Pearce has invoked it in her commentary on *All's Well*.

Crosscurrents among Christian interpreters do of course sometimes muddle its impact. Their variety needs to be taken into account. Roland M. Frye, for instance, brought a narrowly Protestant cast of mind to his book on *Shakespeare and Christian Doctrine* (1963), in which he assailed "The School of Knight," his label for followers of G. Wilson Knight, especially J.A. Bryant. In Frye's view they were translating Shakespeare "out of dramatic into theological terms" not allowed by Luther and Calvin for secular drama. He therefore spoke of "blatant abuses of criticism" in theological analyses of Shakespeare and insisted that the plays should be read as employing Christian doctrine only for local characterizations and not as "essential" to his art. This argument, while it gave a welcome handle to anti-Christian readers, ignored the use of typology by Elizabethan poets such as Spenser. It also raised the hackles of Professor Knight, who proceeded to charge Frye with grossly misrepresenting him as medieval whereas in fact he regarded Shakespeare as looking "ahead to Ibsen and Nietzsche," and Knight's phrase "miniature Christs" was a "passing analogy" only. (See his *Shakespeare and Religion* [1967], pp.293–303.) One can see in Knight's reply his own muddling of a Dionysian with a Christian ethic. Frye, on the other hand, was supposing that Christian typology is essentially irrelevant to everyday life. Barbara Lewalski, herself of Protestant sympathies, has commented on the error of Frye's stance (in a footnote to her essay on *Twelfth Night, infra*).

But did Bryant's treatment of Shakespeare's tragedies harbor sometimes an ambiguity akin to Knight's? One of Frye's objections was to Bryant's finding "redemptions" in the love-deaths of Antony and Cleopatra. Bryant describes the death of these lovers as a "selfless" expenditure which enabled them to achieve "the distinctively Christian ideal of humanity." May not some readers question whether the suicides are really "selfless" and resemble a Christian sacrifice? Bryant qualifies by saying they "never really see the parallel" between their human action and "that perfect action which might have saved them." Does he mean they grasped imperfectly the Christian ideal? I proposed rather, in 1969, that theirs is a parody version of true sacrifice. That is, they unwittingly enact a grotesque analogy to the Christian ideal. Swayed by Wilson Knight's view of Cleopatra, Bryant admired her "strong toil of grace" without noticing that hers is a "riggish" kind of grace beloved by worshipers of Isis. David Kastan, more recently, has commented on the tragic deceptiveness of Cleopatra's grace (see *infra*).

When interpreting Shakespeare's comedies Bryant made good use of biblical analogy, as have other subsequent critics alert to typology. Applying this approach to tragedy, however, can be more complex. For here an interpreter is tempted to go beyond seeing in the tragic hero a likeness to Saul or Jezebel or some other type of sinful Adamkind and imagine a change in the hero that results in a quasi-Christian serenity. A frequent divergence among practitioners of Christian criticism has been over whether Othello or Hamlet or Richard II can be supposed to have died a saved soul. While skeptics would simply rule out this question as irrelevant, the critics who tackle it do so sometimes unconvincingly.

Pertinent to this issue is some considering of a tragedy's traditional function of catharsis. Can a tragedy exercise our pity and fear if it ends with its hero triumphant? Critics such as O.B. Hardison and John Andrews discussed this. A purging of pity and fear, they argued, depends on our seeing some great failure or failures unintended by the tragic actor but fated by his mischoices. I myself agreed with this interpretation and proposed that ideally a spectator needs to be brought to say at the end of a tragedy, "There but for the grace of God go I." The auditor needs to arrive at a valid state of pity and fear through the story's cleansing us of muddied or crude modes of pity and fear. In a similar way, a comedy should exercise our emotion of laughter and bring us to a purged mode of joy. Both comedy and tragedy, if thus viewed, are intended to be educative in a therapeutic way—not chiefly in a moralistic or didactic way. Drama is properly an invitation to self-discovery. It is the telling of a story which engages our emotions and minds in their unpurged condition (what Bethell referred to as the crude assumptions of our fallen nature). Then it proceeds to refine these as we react to the story itself, unless we resist or obstruct that process. Do not our best theologians (both nowadays and in early church history) engage us with a story, a "narrative theology," and does not the dramatist Shakespeare make his appeal through some "old tale" of perennial relevance?

Francis Fergusson has been a critic helpful especially for understanding what Aristotle meant by the imitation of an action. Very simply, according to Fergusson, Aristotle was referring to a basic action of the human psyche, imitated by six means, plot being the foremost. Fergusson's essay on *Macbeth*, in 1951, defined the basic action of that play as a psychic impulse to "outrun the pauser, reason"—which we see the hero persist in to his own downward destruction. But also, in this unusual tragedy with dimensions more than Aristotelian, we see a counter-movement when Malcolm outruns the pauser reason in an upward and saving direction. Through an engraced faith he overcomes his rational hesitancy regarding the trustworthiness of Macduff, and then with him undertakes a rescue of Scotland under the aegis of "powers above." A restoring of civic health "by the grace of Grace" closes the action. Supplementing Fergusson, other critics have elaborated on how sin and grace condition the two contrasting directions of psychic action imitated in this drama. It is as if the dramatist were aware of St Paul's providential view of history in Rom 5:20, that where sin increases, grace abounds all the more, since we see an Adam-like tragic fall by Macbeth followed by a grace of intervention by Malcolm (whose mother on her knees "Died every day she lived") and by England's Edward, the Confessor-king.

For Christian critics there is significance in the fact that a typological reading of history was provided by St Paul's interpretation of the Red Sea crossing. Our forefathers, says Paul, were baptized in the cloud and in the sea (1 Cor 10:2) and drank of the Rock which is Christ. This means that they began to participate in Christian mystery when they escaped from Egyptian values and committed themselves to the faith of Moses. It means that the sea-experience of these pre-Christians was a washing analogous to Christian baptism. It means, by implication, that a washing or purgation can happen anywhere or anytime when a nation or a person undergoes some ordeal that dissolves an old orientation and gives birth to a new. In short, every tempest-moment in human experience can either drown or baptize, either wreck or educate. History is our schoolhouse, not a treadmill. Around that truth Shakespeare constructed his dramas.

*King Lear* is a foremost example. The spouting hurricanoes to which Lear bares his head serve to drown his pride. They dissolve it, as we see, into a madness like that of Nebuchadnezzar, who had to eat grass in order to discover grace. Critics who find in this play's hero an earnest of redemption—and there are today still many who do—see the saving process as under way but incomplete when the story closes tragic and open-ended. They see a purgation that involves his dying to a blind self and being raised out of that grave by a Cordelia who foreshadows Christ's role. And one recent critic, significantly, has outlined the logic of this story by invoking as its gloss the church's liturgy for the eve on which candidates are prepared for Easter baptism. That liturgy, as reviewed by John Cunningham (in 1984 in *Christianity and Literature*) rehearses mankind's journey toward the Light in four stages: 1) into the wilderness; 2) into the baptistry; 3) out of the baptistry in new garments; and 4) at the gate of death, where the soul pants for a higher life. These are the stages Lear experiences analogously in his pagan Britain.

But if historical experience itself mediates baptisms, moments when an old order of life is replaced by a new, can we not apply this framework of understanding to our reading of England's history as dramatized in *Richard III*? By the end of *3 Henry VI* Shakespeare has depicted a national history reduced to a swirl; imagery of wind and tide predominate. At this point the Machiavel Richard turns those waters into a vortex of fraud that drowns almost the whole community in an ordeal of bloodshed. A nadir is reached when innocent babes are massacred, as if by a biblical Herod. But this very outrage causes the warring queens to unite in a sisterhood of weeping mothers, so to speak. Together they renounce their addiction to Fortune's favors and turn to a rescuer from overseas. A secret supporter of this conversion is Lord Stanley (ancestor of the Lord Derby who in Shakespeare's day was suspected of Catholic sympathies), and another supporter is the Bishop of Ely (from whom Thomas More acquired his sense of history). Ely's desertion worries Richard with an anxiety comparable, say, to that felt by ancient Pharaoh when Moses escaped. And in the final showdown at Bosworth, the famous cry of the defeated Richard, "A horse, my kingdom for a horse," echoes, I think, the Bible's tribute to God in Ex 15:21: "the horse and his rider he hath thrown into the sea." Shakespeare has a biblical sense of history. Critics such as Tom Driver, Edward Berry, and Emrys Jones have articulated this point with various kinds of evidence.

Even in Shakespeare's lighter comedies it can be seen that the Bible's Red Sea crossing has a secular analogy in the purgation that precedes a lover's achieving of an adult maturity. "True lovers have been ever crossed," says Hermia in *A Midsummer Night's Dream*, and in that comedy the cross is their night of misadventures in a moonlit woods. Idolatrous fancies enbondage them in follies until a corrective ointment frees their eyes and they escape from dotage into a daylight understanding. The barking dogs and hunters' horns which help them wake up have a function here like that in Shakespeare's *The Tempest*, where Ariel sings of watchdogs and chanticleer's cry when directing young Ferdinand's education. In both plays a cleansing of eyes and heart is a necessary preparation for marriage festival. This is the case also in the comedy of *Much Ado*, which depicts the victimization of lovers to ego-serving fashions until their folly is exposed and they repent it. Figuratively they must undergo a death and rebirth, as is emphasized in each of the plays I have mentioned. Until that crossing is made, the story in each play turns about the wayward antics of deluded questers—for instance, the trashing of marriage by Claudio in *Much Ado*, or the treacheries plotted by Antonio's party and Caliban's, or Titania's monstrous obsession and Bottom's dream.

Bottom's dream, by the way, has been discovered by Christian critics to be Shakespeare's travesty analogy of St Paul's experience. That is, Paul's report in 1 Cor 2:9 and 2 Cor 12:4 of experiencing a mystery that transcended his daily routine has its parody parallel in the experience Bottom reports in befuddled amazement over having experienced what "the ear of man hath not seen" and his tongue is "not able to conceive." Bottom's wondrous perception that "Man is but an ass" has its exemplification in the absurd Pyramus and Thisbe story, which ends with pathetic suicides. By contrast, the lovers in Shakespeare's main plot are able to substitute self-mockery for suicide, make a successful transition from self-love to self-knowledge, and then join in wedding festivities which conclude with a hallowing of the household. In metaphoric terms, they have had a crossover experience, a kind of sacramental transformation.

Imagery of death and rebirth, as a little reflection can tell us, is basic to the structure of Shakespeare's romances. In *All's Well* Helena pretends a death as part of her St Francis strategy for shaming Bertram to death while offering him a rebirth into true love. Hermione in *The Winter's Tale* simulates death in order to become in due time the disguised bearer of new life for Leontes; and at that play's very middle we hear an old shepherd say, "Now bless thyself: thou mett'st with things dying, I with things new-born." In *Cymbeline* Imogen must fall asleep in a grave and emerge as a disguised Fidele in order to re-win her husband while also converting Britain's king. In *The Tempest* Alonzo must be brought to a mudded state of guilty despair, and Caliban to a literal quagmire, before each of them can receive grace or become wise enough to seek it.

*Pericles* is the most spacious of Shakespeare's romances, traversing as it does a lifetime journey on the part of its hero, in voyages that involve two episodes of storm at sea and then a calm of melancholy before his being visited by a voice that touches on the music of the spheres and directs him to a temple of joy. The structure of this play—so Cynthia Marshall has recently argued (in 1991)—is a capsulized story of the human race through the Seven Ages of History discerned by St Augustine in the Bible and publicized in The *Golden Legend*, the people's manual of heroic adventure in medieval times. Thus, for instance, the first storm encountered by Pericles corresponds to that in the biblical Age of Noah; Pericles emerges from it with a recovered armor that symbolizes faith. A second storm accompanies his departure from Pentapolis and entails the seeming loss of a family member, as in the Age of Abraham. Many years later, however, a visiting of Pericles by Marina parallels the biblical Age of the Prophets that brings news of salvation. The poet Gower is the play's Chorus to guide us through what Marshall appropriately calls a Cosmic Overview.

We know that *Pericles*, along with *King Lear*, was on the repertoire of some touring actors who performed these plays in the country house of a Yorkshire Catholic family in 1610. Evidently, neither play in such circles was thought to be, as some moderns suppose, haphazardly episodic or destructive of Christian faith. Many evangelical Protestants, also, are likely to have welcomed these plays, since the biblical typology of *Pericles* is akin to that of those Protestants who chose to risk their lives in voyages to America, and we know (as pertinent to *King Lear*) that exorcism was practised in Puritan circles as well as Catholic ones (to the dismay of Samuel Harsnett, who had objected to exorcisings by the puritan John Darrell before turning his attack on the "papists"). These parties, alongside many Christians in general in the early seventeenth century, are not likely to have regarded *The Tempest*, as some of today's critics do, as a recording of European despotism, but rather to have perceived in it a meaning such as James Walter has expounded in an essay in PMLA (1983) which invokes Augustine's allegorical interpretation of Genesis as a key to the metaphors Shakespeare uses in telling the Tempest story of providence in history. As Kenneth Muir has remarked, contemporary voyage literature included William Strachey's account of a shipwreck in Bermuda which carried memories of Paul's shipwreck on an island in which not a hair perished (Acts 27:34).

There is abundant evidence, much more than I have here touched on, for taking seriously the Christian contexts of Shakespeare's dramatic art. But can it nowadays receive a fair hearing? Much of recent critical opinion is not encouraging. Near my desk is a series of books called "The Critics Debate" published by Humanities Press International. T. F. Wharton on *Measure for Measure* (1989) begins debate by saying that this play's "imperfections are obvious." When he gets around to summarizing Christian interpretations he does this inaccurately and reductively, and then proceeds to cite with approval critics who help him argue that the Duke is a meddlesome manipulator with no holiness whatever. Bill Overton's review of *The Winter's Tale* (1989) avoids Wharton's dogmatic skepticism. Overton is painstaking in all his summaries of critics, and he praises Traversi, Bethell, and Knight for helping establish that the play is "worth the fullest attention." But he objects to their letting the play become a "symbolic vehicle for ultimate truths about life." He feels that Bethell has "imposed" a Christian perspective on the play. He believes more attention should be paid to "political questions" so as not to abstract the play from the processes of history. What he means by this is implied in his honest confession at the beginning of his study: "I practise no religion, and my politics are socialist." Plainly, his hermeneutical circle conditions his range of appreciation.

We can expect the Christian dimension of Shakespeare's work to be downplayed or misrepresented by readers whose habit patterns of sensibility resist the acknowledgment of Christian mystery. St Paul recognized that to rationalists the cross would seem scandalous, while to legalistic moralists it was a stumbling block. He had to appeal beyond these obstacles to a latent capacity in human beings to learn through crisis-experience the reality of a divinely reasonable love and its higher moral law. Shakespeare's plays still exercise occasionally a similar function for some of their spectators today. Insofar as this is the case, should we not be grateful that they serve both a timely need and a timeless value? There is after all within today's culture some "good soil" capable of bringing forth a thirtyfold harvest so to speak, and occasionally a hundredfold.

# Part I

# Some Key Assessments

*Comment and bibliography*
*Robert Speaight*
*J. A. Bryant, Jr.*
*L. A. Cormican*
*Nevill Coghill*
*Glynne Wickham*
*Francis Fergusson*
*Tom F. Driver*
*M. D. H. Parker*
*Roy Battenhouse*
*Charles Huttar*

# Tragic Heroism Displayed

THE DEATHS OF ANTONY AND CLEOPATRA

From Laurent de Premierfait's translation of Boccaccio's *De casibus*,
MS Royal 14 E v, late fifteenth century.
By permission of The British Library

# SOME KEY ASSESSMENTS

## Comment and bibliography

The assessments presented in this section are all concerned to declare that a true appreciation of Shakespeare requires an allowing of habits of art and thought which Elizabethans inherited from Christian tradition.

Our anthology's first item is by a British scholar-actor who played Becket's role a thousand times in Eliot's *Murder in the Cathedral.* Robert Speaight says bluntly that Shakespeare is unintelligible without an understanding of Christian doctrine. He supports this with remarks on *Hamlet* and *All's Well* which fly in the face of Romantic views. We should not suppose that Shakespeare approved an ethic of revenge, Speaight says. And instead of agreeing with critics who have faulted Helena, he speaks of the "humility" of the bed-trick and terms her a suffering mediator of redemption.

Next, J. A. Bryant ably explains why biblical allusions in Shakespeare are more than decorative. They witness to an artist who uses Scripture typologically. They call attention to depths in the meaning of the story Shakespeare is telling, an allegorical figuration which adds up to something more strange and constant than fancy's images.

Several selections on Shakespeare's affinity with Dante follow. L. A. Cormican's essay explains to modern readers the value of the concept of hell: it intensifies our attention to the importance of human choices. It is part of an idiom for examining the human will's inclination to wink at truth and shut out the light and thus flee from "the good of the intellect." By showing us the "restless ecstasy" that results, *Macbeth* corroborates Augustine's dictum that the human heart is restless until it rests in God.

Nevill Coghill's remarks on the medieval basis of Shakespearean comedy have contributed greatly toward clarifying why Shakespeare's sense of form differs from Ben Jonson's. Shakespeare had Dante's habit of thinking in allegory, a figurative method that points to a spiritual dimension beyond the naturalistic meaning of events. Shakespeare is concerned with the accuracy of his narrative taken as a whole to convey in comedy how human life can move from a harsh situation to a prosperous ending.

Glynne Wickham endorses Coghill's view of Shakespearean comedy and adds that in tragedy the medieval fall-of-princes is modeled on Adam's fall, where catastrophe's causes are traced to enemies within and without. Moreover, Shakespeare can mingle literary styles and genres because he does not have a neoclassicist's sense of plot dominating character.

Francis Fergusson assures us that Dante and Shakespeare share the classical-Christian view of human nature and destiny that is grounded in Aristotelian philosophy, Christian theology, and a heritage of allegory. Shakespeare wished to imitate human action in a way that reveals its God-given meanings. A realism of the kind Auerbach described in his *Mimesis* as distinctly Christian is characteristic of Shakespeare.

Tom Driver in comparing Shakespeare's sense of history with that of Greek drama also cites Auerbach's analysis. A biblical and Augustinian sense of time is operative; the present is compounded of memory and anticipation, and the future is open. Man is seen as undergoing a sequence in which later events clarify earlier ones, a principle of typological understanding. A belief that temporal process is ordered by a divine purpose undergirds Shakespeare's plays. No separation of styles is observed, since his sense of history roots in that of the Mystery cycles of English drama.

M. D. H. Parker highlights the themes of providence and grace in Shakespeare's romances. The redemption these plays enact arises from a supernatural restorative power present in heroines such as Marina, Hermione, Perdita, Imogen, and Miranda. In restoring Pericles, Marina is likened to the Virgin Mary who "begett'st him that did thee beget." Miranda, who prompts Prospero's action of forgiveness, has a fortitude "infused by heaven." Hermione accepts suffering "for my better grace," and her daughter Perdita when "grown in grace" does all things well. Parker summarizes by saying that for Shakespeare nature without grace is "unnatural" but becomes fully natural with divine aid—a Christian doctrine to which David and the pagan sibyls also witness. *The Tempest* is an allegory of sin and redemption spiced with analogues to Adam and Eve; it concludes with a golden joy that echoes the *exultet* of Easter liturgy.

Roy Battenhouse holds that Shakespeare, like Dante, grounds his depiction of tragedy on the Augustinian principle that sinful action has a perverted likeness to salvific action. A misdirected love, said Augustine, unwittingly mimics a divine love and obtains a maimed liberty. Exemplifications of this can be seen in *Antony and Cleopatra* and in *Hamlet*. Antony's supper with his followers has a parody likeness to the Last Supper of Christ; and his offering up to Egypt his self-stabbed body parodies Christ's offering to God his wounded body. Cleopatra's demonstration of "immortal longings" by putting an asp to her breast has a perverted likeness to the Virgin Mary's nursing. In *Hamlet* the Ghost's visitation, contrary to Christ's, makes "night hideous"; and when Hamlet and Claudius minister to each other a poisoned cup, a perversion of holy communion is manifest.

Charles Huttar defends a Christian reading of Shakespeare's sonnet 146 against a recent critic who would read it as reflecting an ironic humanism. This critic, Huttar explains, has misrepresented the tenets of traditional Christianity. When these are grasped correctly the sonnet's meaning is clearly Christian. The "poore soul" we are asked to pity is a victim of its own self-deception that allows an excessive spending on its "fading mansion." The admonition to "feed on death" is the remedy of swallowing up death as Christ did (according to 1 Cor 15:54).

In the supplementary bibliography the works of S. L. Bethell, M. D. H. Parker, and Peter Milward are particularly noteworthy. Bethell's book in 1944 called attention to Shakespearean drama's inclusion of figurative meanings along with the literal. Parker's book aimed to uncover the "formative metaphysical pattern" (p. 11) beneath the artistic surfaces of Shakespeare's mirror; she found sources in Augustine and Aquinas and devoted a long chapter to "The Idea of Justice in the Orthodox Tradition." Milward's *Shakespeare's Religious Background* finds echoes of or affinity with Shakespeare's language in a wide spectrum of sources: Elizabethan Bible translations, the Prayerbook and the sermons of popular Anglican preachers, and (what will surprise some readers) the writings of Catholic recusants. Milward's other works reveal his expert awareness of biblical allusions latent in Shakespeare's plays.

L. A. Cormican on the liturgy makes several splendid points. Recommending the book of Psalms as a "very practical" introduction to Shakespeare, he remarks that for the dramatist the facts of history are not so much an account of things once done as they are "a parable of what people continue to do." Shakespeare's distinctive dramatic structure, Cormican says, comes from an urge to "exhaust the meaning of the opening situation" in a language having several levels of intelligibility. Margreta De Grazia points out that for Elizabethans the corruption of language was associated with a pride like that of Babel in Genesis, whereas healthful language depended on a gift of the Holy Spirit. Honor Matthews comments well on Shakespeare's use of the motifs of false-seeming and false-naming that are prominent in medieval drama.

Robert G. Hunter, Emrys Jones, René Fortin, and Cherrell Guilfoyle are scholarly critics who have made important contributions to an appreciation of Shakespeare's religious dimension, and our anthology will reprint some of their insights as we proceed to individual plays.

## Supplementary bibliography

Battenhouse, Roy. "Tragedy and Biblical Analogues," in *Shakespearean Tragedy* (Indiana University Press, 1969), pp. 88–95.

_____. "Shakespeare's Re-Vision of Lucrece," pp. 3–41, and "The Reshaped Meaning of *Coriolanus*," pp. 303–10, in *Shakespearean Tragedy* (1969).

Bethell, S. L. *Shakespeare and the Popular Dramatic Tradition* (Westminster: King and Staples, 1944), pp. 43–67, 104–16.

Bryant, J. A., Jr. *Hippolyta's View* (University Press of Kentucky, 1961), esp. pp. 1–18, 109–15.

Cormican, L. A. "Medieval Idiom: Shakespeare and the Liturgy," *Scrutiny* 17 (1950), 186–202.

Cunningham, J. V. *Woe or Wonder: The Emotional Effect of Shakespearean Tragedy* (University of Denver Press, 1951).

De Grazia, Margreta. "Shakespeare's View of Language: An Historical Perspective," *Shakespeare Quarterly* 29 (1978), 374–88.

De Groot, John H. *The Shakespeares and "The Old Faith"* (New York: King's Crown Press, 1946). See also F. W. Brownlow, "John Shakespeare's Recusancy," *Shakespeare Quarterly* 40 (1989), 186–91.

Fortin, René. "The Two Voices of Shakespearean Tragedy," *Shakespeare Quarterly* 32 (1981), 80–94.

Frye, Roland M. *Shakespeare and Christian Doctrine* (Princeton University Press, 1963), pp. 215–19 ("Nature" in *AYL* and *R&J*).

Guilfoyle, Cherrell. *Shakespeare's Play within Play: Medieval Imagery and Scenic Form* (Kalamazoo: Medieval Institute Publications, 1990).

Hunter, Robert G. *Shakespeare and the Comedy of Forgiveness* (Columbia University Press, 1965).

Jones, Emrys. *The Origins of Shakespeare* (Oxford University Press, 1977), Ch. 2 ("The Mystery Cycles").

Livermore, Ann. "Shakespeare and St Augustine," *Quarterly Review* 303 (1965), 181–93.

Matthews, Honor. *Character & Symbol in Shakespeare's Plays: A Study of Certain Christian and Pre-Christian Elements in Their Structure and Imagery* (Cambridge University Press, 1962).

Milward, Peter, S. J. *Shakespeare's Religious Background* (Indiana University Press, 1973).

_____. "Shakespeare's Medieval Inheritance," *Shakespeare Studies* (Japan) 2 (1963), 49–62.

_____. "Three Essays on Shakespeare and Religion," *Shakespeare Yearbook* 1 (1990), 117–40.

Murray, Patrick J. *The Shakespearian Scene: Some Twentieth-Century Perspectives* (New York: Barnes & Noble, 1969), Ch. 3 ("The Religious Aspect").

Mutschmann, H., and Wentersdorf, K. *Shakespeare and Catholicism* (New York: Sheed and Ward, 1952).

Myrick, Kenneth. "The Theme of Damnation in Shakespeare's Tragedies," *Studies in Philology* 38 (1941), 221–45.

Noble, Richmond. *Shakespeare's Biblical Knowledge and Use of the Book of Common Prayer* (London: S. P. C. K., 1935).

Parker, M. D. H. *The Slave of Life* (London: Chatto & Windus, 1955), esp. Chs. 2, 7.

Sims, James H. *Dramatic Uses of Biblical Allusion in Marlowe and Shakespeare* (University of Florida Press, 1966).

Spivack, Bernard. *Shakespeare and the Allegory of Evil* (Columbia University Press, 1958), pp. 151–205.

Toole, William B. *Shakespeare's Problem Plays: Studies in Form and Meaning* (New York: Humanities Press, 1966), Ch. 2 ("The Divine Comedy, The Morality Play, The Mystery Cycle," pp. 39–97).

Velz, John W. "From Jerusalem to Damascus: Biblical Dramaturgy in Medieval and Shakespearian Conversion Plays," *Comparative Drama* 16 (1982), 311–26.

_____. "Medieval Dramatic Eschatology in Shakespeare," *Comparative Drama* 26 (1992), 312–29.

Williams, Charles. "Forgiveness in Shakespeare," in *He Came Down From Heaven* (London: Faber & Faber, 1950), pp. 111–18.

*Robert Speaight (1960)*

## Christianity in Shakespeare

No one but the most reactionary agnostic any longer thinks it paradoxical to assert that Shakespeare's plays are penetrated through and through by Christianity. Indeed, without an understanding of Christian doctrine, they are quite unintelligible. But of course they approximate in varying degrees to anything we can formally describe as a Christian theatre. His themes are Justice and Mercy, and they can be heard, *en sourdine*, even through the comedies. Duke Frederick, in *As You Like It*, is converted by meeting a hermit in the Forest of Arden (the least of its improbabilities) and thus the banished Duke has his rule restored to him. Oliver is converted when Orlando mercifully saves him from the snake. Jaques, refusing the natural happiness of his companions, wanders off to learn from the hermit a wisdom which is not of this world. In *Twelfth Night* Antonio is pardoned by Orsino, and Malvolio, though he leaves his persecutors determined on revenge, is still entreated "to a peace." *The Merchant of Venice* may be described as a comedy of mercy; the Doge's "I pardon thee thy life before thou ask it," taking its cue from Portia's celebrated plea, rings in contrast to Shylock's "I stand here for justice; answer, shall I have it?"

The tragedy of Hamlet is not that he fails, until the penultimate instant, to kill Claudius, but that a nature made for love should have turned itself to hatred. The fact that every man is aware of much of Hamlet in himself, and that Shakespeare may have put himself more directly into the character than into any other of his creations, should not lead us to suppose that Hamlet has his moral approval. Hamlet's temptation was not to neglect the ghost's instructions but to carry them out.

[In Denmark] the time is indeed "out of joint," but in so far as Hamlet tries to set it right, he sets it wrong. Even his single victory, in the Play Scene, is Pyrrhic. So far from exposing Claudius' guilt to the eyes of all, he only seals the sentence of his own exile. . . . The logic of revenge was popular with an Elizabethan audience, but Shakespeare saw through it. Followed half-heartedly by Hamlet and wholeheartedly by Laertes, it littered the stage with corpses.

What Shakespeare [in *Macbeth*] interprets with miraculous skill, both in the sleep-walking scene and in the last defiance on the ramparts, is the essential loneliness of damnation. It has not needed death to separate Macbeth from the partner and instigator of his crime. Each walks or wanders to their end in an atrocious solitude. Macbeth, in a sudden quiet which is only broken by the cry of women, is beyond the reach of remorse but not of self-pity. The loveless "tomorrows" stretch out before him into the infinite future until they mingle with an eternity which he is now too insensitive to fear. Neither Macbeth nor Lady Macbeth can minister to themselves; they are fixed, already, in the state of damnation as Christian theology has conceived it.

Helena carries through in *All's Well* the regenerative task which Isabella [in *Measure for Measure*] had left incomplete. It is important to notice that in both cases virginity is a necessary and initiating force. . . . [Helena] goes after her man and gets him; but she gets him by the grace of God. She is the direct medium of divine power. Moreover, it is only when she has miraculously cured the sick King that she wins the right to choose Bertram for her husband. [The scene in which] she prevails on the King to accept her cure has the scriptural allusions and incantatory rhythm of liturgy; the rhymed couplets put it in a parenthesis as clearly marked as the "play within the play" of *Hamlet* .

> He that of greatest works is finisher
> Oft does them by the weakest minister:
> So holy writ in babes hath judgement shown,
> When judges have been babes; great floods have flown
> From simple sources; and great seas have dried
> When miracles have by the greatest been denied.

The King is sceptical:

> Art thou so confident? Within what space
> Hopest thou my cure?

and Helena replies:

> The great'st grace lending grace.

We are led at last to Lafeu's comment, which has lost no jot or tittle of its relevance: "They say miracles are past: and we have our philosophical persons to make modern and familiar things supernatural and causeless. Hence it is that we make trifles of terrors; ensconcing ourselves into seeming knowledge, when we should submit ourselves to an unknown fear."

The miracle that heals the King is also the miracle that, indirectly, brings Bertram to his senses. . . . But the second cure was more costly to Helena than the first. Like another Mediator, she has to empty herself of pride in order that she may work redemption. That is the significance of the bed-trick. Helena stands against Bertram as the Middle Ages against the Renaissance; she is the old wisdom against the new flashiness. . . . Through all her pursuit of Bertram she remains the "suffering servant," and it is important to notice that she never condemns him. Judgement is not blind; but judgement is swallowed up in love.

From *Christian Theatre* (New York: Hawthorn Books, 1960), pp. 64–81, excerpts abridged.

*J. A. Bryant, Jr. (1961)*

# Typology in Shakespeare [editor's title]

The average Elizabethan (who was religious and Christian, whatever his doctrinal persuasions may have been) would probably have sat, or stood, through a Shakespeare play without noticing the astonishing number of allusions to Scripture, Prayer Book, and dogma generally. He would have missed them because to him they were commonplace; we miss them because to us they are almost completely foreign, and their strangeness seems but a part of the general strangeness of an unfamiliar language. With all our learning, we are likely to be unaware until it is pointed out to us that Shakespeare more than any other popular playwright of his time had absorbed the language of Prayer Book and Geneva Bible. Fortunately, that much at least has been pointed out to us by Richmond Noble. What remains to be examined is the way this assimilated material worked in his art.

The solution most likely to gain acceptance in our time is one roughly analogous to the position taken by Theseus in *A Midsummer Night's Dream*: Shakespeare *used* Scripture as contemporary humanists used their classical allusions, to ornament a tale or to point to some abstract value. It was simply another way of giving a "habitation" and a "name" to something not readily apprehended by the senses. Scripture was familiar to his audiences; therefore Shakespeare used Scripture. This was one reason why he managed to be popular for as long as he did: he had his finger on the pulse of the audience; he himself was uncommitted. Modern interpreters frequently offer us something like this as the objective point of view—the really "safe" one—but it leaves too much unexplained. For example, Miss Helen Gardner, who is well aware of the presence of typology in Elizabethan devotional literature, argues at some length that its importance in secular literature is negligible (*The Limits of Literary Criticism*, pp. 46–55). She points to a flourishing interest in the literal sense of Scripture, both in Shakespeare's time and earlier, and adds revealingly, "Neither comedy nor tragedy can exist if the individual is only valued as illustrative of the general." Of course, it is quite true that typology could, and occasionally did, degenerate into little more than an ingenious game of signs and illustrations; but genuine typology is never merely illustrative. A genuine typologist regards Scriptural history as sacramental and looks upon the individual in it as incorporating meaning rather than pointing to it; and consciously or unconsciously, Shakespeare was a genuine typologist in his use of Scriptural allusion and analogy. If he had used Scriptural material only in the way Miss Gardner thinks it possible for a poet to use such material, then his allusions to Adam, Cain, Abel, God, and Christ might have served merely as ornamental signs, illustrative examples, things to be seen through, pointers to something else. Actually, they seldom operate merely in this way.

It should be noted that practically all of Shakespeare's allusions, like the allusions of any good poet, tend to earn their way in the context in which they appear. They extend the depth of the play itself; they do not merely point to depths outside the play in philosophy, theology, politics, or some other more abstract realm of knowledge. The critic who has the courage to remain in contact with Shakespeare's text usually finds that the resources of the metaphors operating within the play are difficult to exhaust. Instead of representing outlets into other realms, they are tributaries flowing in, so that whatever they bring to the play from other literatures or other disciplines becomes known in a new and unique way in the work of art itself. The result is indeed "transfigured so together" that it "more witnesseth than fancy's images, /And grows to something of great constancy." It is, in short, a kind of knowledge that defies restatement in any other terms, but knowledge nevertheless—"howsoever, strange and admirable."

Shakespeare's references to the data of Elizabethan Christianity and his frequent recourse to Biblical analogies have in addition to this ordinary power of metaphor the extraordinarily vital shaping power of typology.

From *Hippolyta's View: Some Christian Aspects of Shakespeare's Plays*, pp. 15–17.
Copyright 1961, University Press of Kentucky; renewed 1989, J. A. Bryant, Jr.

*L. A. Cormican (1951)*

## Medieval Idiom in Shakespeare

Among [Shakespeare's] unobtrusive triumphs is the use he makes of the belief in hell. This notion is so foreign to modern thought that it requires more than ordinary detachment from self to see its importance in relation to Shakespearean tragedy. But, even keeping within reasonably simple limits, we may see its dramatic usefulness.... The belief in hell habituated the mind of the audience to the notion that the consequences of some actions, some choices, are endless. Belief in such tremendous consequences fixed a particular kind of attention and interest on temporal action, an intenser insight into motives and inclinations which precede, as well as consequences which follow, deliberate choice.... Dante was most faithful to the medieval spirit when he ascribed the creation of hell to the *Sommo Amore*. For hell was looked on not so much as a willful punishment inflicted from outside man, but rather as the natural result of ultimate refusal to meet God on terms of love.

As agents in human affairs, the medieval mind also accepted angels and demons; these were never looked on, even by as sceptical and querying a mind as Scotus, as mere personifications or mental embodiments of the powers of good and evil within man; they were thought of as real, intelligent substances, . . . as able to communicate some of their powers to men, as able to league themselves to men to accomplish certain forms of good or evil. The fullest use of this belief is made in *Macbeth*, perhaps the most sensible treatise on demonology in the language. It is Banquo who speaks for the more sane and balanced medieval view on man's dealings with the demons:

> Oftentimes to win us to our harms,
> The instruments of darkness tell us truths,
> Win us with honest trifles, to betray us
> In deepest consequence.

The "instruments of darkness" (a biblical allusion) are not only the witches, but also the "murdering ministers," and "metaphysical aid" which Macbeth and his wife believe to be as real as themselves.

*Macbeth* is not the only, but it is the most extensive and the most interesting example of fusing deep psychology, wide theology, with dramatic talent. The special quality of the play lies largely in the poet's power to make *night* mean so many things, to make it so rich in suggestiveness. . . . The settling of the final gloom is appropriately expressed as the extinction of light: "out, out, brief candle." Night's candles are indeed burnt out for Macbeth; the savage pessimism is worded far more effectively than any pessimist has managed to word it; the previous prayer that heaven might not peep through the blanket of the dark has been granted in full to Macbeth as well as to his wife. Convention required that Macbeth should die at the end of the play; dramatic neatness required that his wife should die before him. But through the constant reference to the more than human powers that are at work, their deaths are given a vaster significance than could be attained by any mere convention or technical skill; their deaths are the final answer to their double prayer: "Come, thick night, and pall thee in the dunnest smoke of hell," "Come, seeling night, scarf up the tender eye of pitiful day." The final agony is the infernal agony of realizing that they have brought their misery upon themselves. . . . So well is the traditional philosophy fitted into the dramatic scheme that it is transformed into the dramatic situation; hardly a word of the traditional language of morality appears, but the whole concept of the corruption of Macbeth and his wife is essentially moral. His mental gloom and her madness are the inevitable revenge of nature on the evil doer, the recoil of a nature which rebels against abuse.

The special tragic quality of the play draws constantly on three principles essential to the medieval ethic: the connection between the moral and the intellectual orders, the objectivity of the moral order, and the notion of impenitence as the supreme moral evil. In the medieval conception, morality is essentially intellectual. The play as a whole may be considered as a commentary on

> *le genti dolorose*
> *c'hanno perduto il ben dell' intelletto*
>
> (the wretched people
> who have sacrificed the good of the intellect.)

For *"il vero e lo bene dello intelletto"* (Conv. II 13); the special good or perfection of the intellect is truth. The desire of Macbeth and his wife for darkness, for the aid of night in their wickedness, is really a desire for moral blindness ("let not light see my black and deep desires"); the whole strenuous effort to "screw their courage to the sticking place" is really an attempt to pervert their moral sense so that what is foul may appear fair; they reject the "good of the intellect."

Shakespeare's great effort was to present human choices in their most profound aspects. The medieval ethic saw all human actions as replicas either of Adam sinning or of Christ redeeming. The *Imitation of Christ* is particularly based on the doctrine of the "old Adam" who lives on in every human being. The principle that "no man liveth to himself or dieth to himself" meant not only the practice of brotherly love towards neighbors, it implied the vast reverberations of actions, both good and evil. Some of the basic elements in the Adam story and in the Macbeth story (in Shakespeare's version, rather than in Holinshed's) are very similar: the suggestion of evil from outside demonic forces, the fully deliberate choice of evil which seems good for the time being, the tremendous, though unseen, consequences of the desire for power—"you shall be as gods" in the Adam story is parallel to the hope that their act

> Shall for all our nights and days to come
> Give solely sovereign sway and masterdom.

The dramatic irony here supposes that we link the desire for power with both the increasing hold of evil on Macbeth's mind (and the consequent diminution of power over himself) and with the madness which robs Lady Macbeth of reason, the very source of power over oneself. This is almost exactly the medieval doctrine that the power of concupiscence over man (the lust of the eyes, the lust of the flesh, the pride of life) comes from Adam's rejection of the objective divine law.

Where the Shakespearean and the Dantesque lines of thought meet is in the conception of peace which is as cosmic as sin. "Our peace is in the Divine Will" (Par. III 85) from which comes all harmony and all law; the attempt to violate that harmony destroys peace within the sinner. Macbeth in his ambition "puts rancours in the vessel of his peace," and while he lives must "on the torture of the mind lie in restless ecstasy." It can hardly be by pure accident that the language here is almost exactly the opposite of Dante's description of the joy of heaven,

> *vita integra d'amore and di pace,*
> *senza brama sicura ricchezza.* (Par. XXVII 8)

(a life compact of love and peace,
secure abundance which stays all further longing.)

Both Macbeth's restless ecstasy and Dante's peaceful ecstasy are echoes (very probably deliberate in Dante) of the great phrase of Augustine: *"Fecisti nos ad te, et inquietum est cor nostrum donec requiescat in te."*

From "Medieval Idiom in Shakespeare," *Scrutiny* 17 (1951), 303–14 abridged.

*Nevill Coghill (1950)*

# The Basis of Shakespearian Comedy

Vincent de Beauvais flourished a century later than Matthieu de Vendome and his aphorism on the nature of Comedy is quoted by Sir Edmund Chambers in the second volume of his work *The Medieval Stage* (p. 209n):

> *Commoedia poesis exordium triste laeto fine commutans.*
> (Comedy is a poem changing a sad beginning into a happy ending.)

If Boethius was right in defining Tragedy as a story in which a flourishing prosperity was cast down by the deeds of fortune to a miserable end, then Comedy must be precisely the reverse, a story that started in sorrow and danger and, by a happy turn of fortune, ended in felicity. It was a tale of trouble that turned to joy.

This simple formula is the true basis of Shakespearian Comedy. It is not, however, so simple as it looks. It was claimed to be not merely the shape of comic form but also the shape of ultimate reality. That, at least, was the claim that Dante made for it and in virtue of which was fashioned the greatest of all imaginative and philosophical structures in poetry, *The Divine Comedy*. The story of the Universe was to be a Comedy as defined.

As well as a lofty poet, Dante was a lofty lecturer, and in dedicating the *Paradiso* to Can Grande he set forth a lengthy and explicit account of how his Comedy was to be understood. It contains two passages of special interest to this inquiry, one dealing with comic form itself and its supposed origins, the other with the various planes of meaning upon which it may be proper to interpret a Comedy. I shall later attempt to apply both passages to the understanding of Shakespeare. In setting them forth I have reversed the order in which they occur in Dante's epistle, so that I may deal with the question of form, which is the easier, first. The more difficult question of allegory will be considered later.

Dante: Epistle to Can Grande
    10.   The title of this book is: "Here begins the Comedy of Dante Alighiere a Florentine by nation, not by manners." As a note to which it should

be known that the word Comedy derives from *comos*, a village, and *oda*, a song, whence Comedy, a sort of rustic song. Comedy is moreover a kind of poetical narrative, differing from all others. It differs therefore from Tragedy in its matter thus, that Tragedy is calm and noble to start with, but in its ending or outcome stinking and terrifying (*foetida et horribilis*); and it is named for that reason after *tragos*, that is, a goat, and *oda*, a goatish song, so to speak; that is, it stinks like a goat, as appears by Seneca in his Tragedies. Comedy on the other hand begins with the harshness of some affair (*asperitatem alicuius rei*) but its matter ends happily (*prospere*) as appears by Terence and his Comedies... similarly it differs in its manner of speech: Tragedy, lofty and sublime; Comedy negligent and humble... and hence it appears that the present work is called a Comedy. For if we look at the matter, it stinks and is terrifying to begin with, being *Infernus*, in the end it is happy, pleasing and to be desired (*prospera, desiderabilis et grata*), being *Paradisus*.

This shows what the vision of genius can make of a truism, even when it is expressed in lecturer's language. It transforms the simple formula of Vincent de Beauvais into a true and total picture of ultimate reality. Dante, however, did more than this for our comprehension. He laid it down how his Comedy was to be understood; here he was only explaining for the benefit of Can Grande principles also laid down in the first chapter of the Second Treatise of the *Convivio*; and there these principles are stated to be valid for all poetry, not merely for his own. These are the terms in which he expounds them to Can Grande:

> 7.  ... Be it known that the meaning of this work is not single (*simplex*), indeed it can be called *polysemos*, that is of several meanings; for there is first the meaning to be had from the letter; another is to be had from what is signified by the letter. And the first is called the literal (meaning); the second, however, is called the allegorical, or the moral, or the anagogical. This method of analysis, that it may seem the clearer, may be considered in these verses: "*In exitu Israel de Aegypto, domus Iacob de populo barbaro, facta est Iudaea sanctificatio eius, Israel potestas eius.*" Now if we only look at the letter, the meaning to us is the exodus of the Children of Israel from Egypt, at the time of Moses; if to the allegory, the meaning to us is our redemption made though Christ; if to the moral meaning, there is signified the conversion of the soul from the grief and misery of sin into a state of grace; if to the anagogical, the departure of the holy soul from this servitude of corruption into the liberation (*libertatem*) of eternal glory. And although these mystical senses are called by various names, they can all be generally called allegorical, since they differ from the literal or historical. In view of these things it is clear that the subject should be double (*duplex*) round which should flow alternate meanings.

Dante has thus taken over and expanded (but with what enlargement!) the hints of the fourth-century grammarians, including the hint that love is a theme in Comedy. In the *Divine Comedy* it is the theme of themes, though it is no longer merely human love but love absolute, the power and the glory of God, seen by created souls as the Beatific Vision, for which indeed they were created.

Dante, as I have said, saw the formula for Comedy as the pattern or picture of ultimate reality, and applied it to the state of the soul after death. That application may be extended to include life on earth; there was trouble in Eden, the knot was untied on Calvary, there is bliss in Heaven. The course of human life well-lived is a Comedy as defined. These realities, then unquestioned, could be figured in an earthly tale that followed the same pattern. Any human harmony achieved out of distress can awaken overtones of joy on higher planes. It is a proof how strongly [Dante] held to a view of life as harmony that he learnt how to stretch Comedy to contain sorrow and evil, and yet to show them capable of resolution in love and joy. *Measure for Measure* and *The Winter's Tale* are the extreme examples of this vision and power.

I now come, with diffidence, to the most conjectural part of this essay, namely the development of a theme which of its nature can only be treated with the dangerous help of subjective intuition; but I will cling to such facts as I can. The first is the fact of the medieval tradition of allegory. I will not pretend that Shakespeare read either the *Epistle to Can Grande* or the *Convivio*. But I think it reasonable to suppose that an age that had produced *The Faerie Queene* felt more at home in allegory than we do. It was an age that found no difficulty in accepting *The Song of Songs* as a figure of the love of Christ for His Church, and the act of holy matrimony as a signification of that same love. Thinking in allegory is to us an unaccustomed habit of mind, but to those in a medieval tradition, second nature. It only means a habit of power to draw simultaneous meanings on parallel planes of experience. In proportion as materialist ways of life encroach upon us, other more spiritual planes withdraw and are lost to view. Ceasing to think of them, we lose the faculty to do so and at last deny that such a faculty can have had genuine part in a poetry which we think can be well enough understood without it.

Yet in recent years much has been done to enlarge our apprehensions of imagery in poetry, especially in the poetry of Shakespeare. For the most part this new study of imagery has been devoted to the study of the detail of poetry; that *a narrative itself, taken as a whole, may be an image* is an idea that has received too little attention.

Let us, however, begin with a detail, taken from *Cymbeline*. It is from the speech of Posthumus (5.3) describing a panic flight in battle; he interjects this parenthesis about panic:

> (Oh a sinne in Warre
> Damn'd in the first beginners)

How easily familiar with Christian thought an audience must have been to catch this fugitive allusion to Adam and Eve, those "first beginners" in the sin that brought damnation in its train! Yet it is there, and can allude to nothing else. It is to be caught as an overtone in an exciting battlepiece, packed with other imagery.

[What] is true of the detail of this poetry I hold to be often true of the narrative as a whole.

If I use the word "allegory" in connection with Shakespeare I do not mean that the characters are abstractions representing this or that vice or virtue (as they do in some allegories, say *The Roman de la Rose* or *The Castle of Perseverance* itself). I mean that they contain and adumbrate certain principles, not in a crude or neat form, but mixed with other human qualities; but that these principles taken as operating in human life do in fact give shape and direction to the course, and therefore to the meaning, of the play.

Let us turn to the Trial scene [of *The Merchant of Venice*]. The principle here mainly adumbrated in Shylock is justice, in Portia, mercy. He stands, and says he stands, for the Law, for the notion that a man must be as good as his bond. It is the Old Law. As Piers Plowman has it:

> the olde lawe graunteth
> That gylours be bigiled. and that is gode resoun.
> *Dentem pro dente, & oculum pro oculo.*

Before Shylock's uncompromising demand for justice, mercy is in the posture of a suppliant refused. Thrice his money is offered him and rejected. He is begged to supply a surgeon at his own cost. But no, it is not in the bond.

From the technical point of view the scene is constructed on a sudden reversal of situation, a traditional dramatic dodge to create surprise and *dénouement*. The verbal trick played by Portia is not a part of her "character," but a device to turn the tables and show justice in the posture of a suppliant before mercy. The reversal is instantaneous and complete, as it is also unexpected for those who do not know the story in advance. Portia plants the point firmly: "Downe, therefore, and beg mercy of the Duke." And, in a twinkling, mercy shows her quality [in the words of the Duke]:

> That thou shalt see the difference of our spirit,
> I pardon thee thy life before thou aske it:
> For halfe thy wealth, it is Anthonio's,
> The other halfe comes to the generall state,
> Which humblenesse may driue vnto a fine.

Out of this there comes the second reversal. Shylock, till then pursuing Anthonio's life, now has to turn to him for favour; and this is Anthonio's response:

> So please my Lord the Duke, and all the Court
> To quit the fine for one halfe of his goods,
> I am content; so he will let me haue
> The other halfe in vse, to render it
> Vpon his death, vnto the Gentleman
> That lately stole his daughter.
> Two things prouided more, that for this fauour
> He presently become a Christian:

> The other, that he doe record a gift
> Heere in the Court of all he dies possest
> Unto his sonne Lorenzo, and his daughter.

Evidently Anthonio recognizes the validity of legal deeds as much as Shylock does, and his opinion of Jessica's relationship with Lorenzo is in agreement with Shakespeare's, namely that the bond between husband and wife overrides the bond between father and daughter. Cordelia and Desdemona would have assented. Nor is it wholly alien to Shylock who is himself a family man. For him to provide for Jessica and Lorenzo is not unnaturally harsh or vindictive.

It is Anthonio's second condition that seems to modern ears so harshly vindictive. In these days all good humanitarians incline to the view that a man's religion is his own affair, that a religion imposed is a tyranny, and that one religion is as good as another, if sincerely followed.

But the Elizabethans were not humanitarians in this sense. Only in Utopia, where it was one of "the auncientest lawes among them that no man shall be blamed for reasonynge in the mayntenaunce of his owne religion" (and Utopia was not in Christendom) would such views have seemed acceptable. Whether we dislike it or not, Shylock had no hope, by Elizabethan standards, of entering a Christian eternity of blessedness; he had not been baptized.

It will, of course, be argued that it is painful for Shylock to swallow his pride, abjure his racial faith, and receive baptism. But then Christianity is painful. Its centre is crucifixion, nor has it ever been held to be equally easy for all natures to embrace. If we allow our thoughts to pursue Shylock after he left the Court we may well wonder whether his compulsory submission to baptism in the end induced him to take up his cross and follow Christ. But from Anthonio's point of view, Shylock has at least been given his chance of eternal joy, and it is he, Anthonio, that has given it to him. Mercy has triumphed over justice, even if the way of mercy is a hard way.

Once this aspect of the Trial scene is perceived, the Fifth Act becomes an intelligible extension of the allegory (in the sense defined); for we return to Belmont to find Lorenzo and Jessica in each other's arms. Christian and Jew, New Law and Old, are visibly united in love. And their talk is of music, Shakespeare's recurrent symbol of harmony.

From English Association *Essays and Studies* 3 (1950), 4–6, 17, 21–23, excerpts abridged. Permission from John Murray Ltd.

*Glynne Wickham (1969)*

## Shakespeare's "Small Latine and Less Greeke"

In comedy Shakespeare is primarily concerned with telling a story. He gives the emphasis, as also in history and tragedy, to narrative that Jonson reserves for form. To the neo-classical enthusiast Shakespeare's plays inevitably appear shapeless. No shred of concern about "the unities," about "the rules"! Flagrant anachronisms and absurdities! Seas crossed with the aid of Chorus: generations bridged by Time! Yet if Jonson's realism had no room for Shakespeare's romance, Shakespeare's romance was but slightly concerned with Jonson's realism. Accused of wanting art or form, anyone writing within the mediaeval tradition would have replied, "my narrative is my form. I am telling a story and that story, for those with eyes to see, ears to hear and hearts to feel, has several meanings. Besides the letter of my narrative, there is what is signified by the letter; and in this significance lies my art." The matter is summed up by Jonson's latest and best editors (Herford & Simpson) as concisely as can be.

> We must not seek in the hard, categorical veracity of Jonson's art, the kind of truth by which supreme artists like Dante or Shakespeare in interpreting a country and an age interpret also universal humanity. (i, 126)

Jonson, with his great Latin and considerable Greek, modelling himself deliberately upon the ancients, is essentially a satirist in comedy. His sense of form and the economy of means which that implies enable him, at his best, to sweep away all bounds of incredulity in his audience and present them with visions of human greed, hypocrisy and guile so extravagant as to dazzle and delight.

Nowhere is the difference between the classical and mediaeval conception of comedy better exemplified than in *The Comedy of Errors*. As Mr. Nevill Coghill first demonstrated, Shakespeare borrowed Plautus' *Menaechmi* for his plot, but then altered the story drastically to conform with accepted custom.

> Few comedies, one might suppose [I quote Mr. Coghill], could reach a preposterous conclusion that started with a man being seriously led out to execution. Yet this is what happens to the Merchant Egeon in the first scene of *The Comedy of Errors*; and Egeon is the father of the Antipholus twins, a major character in fact. This gambit is not in Plautus, and the style in which it is introduced is as high as tragedy could wish it to be. Execution on Egeon is deferred; but it is not remitted. He remains (albeit off-stage) in anticipation of immediate death until the last scene. That death is then about to be inflicted on him when from an improbable Abbey (in Ephesus) an even more improbable Abbess appears and is most improbably discovered to be Egeon's long-lost wife, and the means of his deliverance. She is also Shakespeare's invention, and turns the catastrophe to general joy. (*Essays and Studies*, 1950, p. 9)

Death and laughter, ever strangers on the classical stage, had been companions on the English stage long before Shakespeare wrote for it. In the Wakefield Miracles, Mak the Shepherd steals a sheep on the night of the Nativity and Roman "torturers" jest with one another as Christ dies. This mingling of genre, the purist Jonson could not abide. But for those to whom it was acceptable, as it was to Shakespeare, the proportions could be varied within the formula. Hence the wrangling about the "dark" or "tragi"-comedies. For Shakespeare and his like they were simply comedies with rather more emphasis upon the sorrow than the joy. For Sidney, Jonson and their like they were bastard products without classical precedent, neither comedy nor tragedy but "mongrel tragi-comedy." Echoes of such argument come to us in Polonius' introduction of the players to Hamlet.

The difference of approach to comedy, thus far considered, applies with equal force to tragedy. If we accept tragedy to mean what Jonson, Dryden, Boileau or their classical masters define it as meaning, then Shakespeare never wrote a tragedy: he wrote melodramas. In classical tragedy, according to its theorists, plot precedes character so that the inevitability of the action may be apparent. A compact action was of paramount importance and the poet ought to discipline himself in terms of locality and time-span to this end. To Jonson this self-discipline was "arte." Christian thinking, however, tended to reverse this order of precedence. Tragedy, to the mediaeval mind, was quite simply the Fall of Princes. Responsibility for the fall was of course complicated by the idea of what I may call "a suffering to the point of death" and hence concerned pain. Why do we have to suffer pain? How ought we to suffer it? What do we get out of it? How can we rise above it? These, surely, are the fundamental questions which provoke the desire to write, to act, to read or to see tragedies at any time anywhere. In the Middle Ages they were answered in terms of Sin, the archetypal patterns being supplied by the Book of Genesis, and to some extent still, in classical terms of Fate—usually thought of as Dame Fortune with her Wheel, but increasingly as Divine Providence. The two are easily mingled. Chaucer makes the point explicitly in the opening stanzas of "The Monkes Tale."

> 1)  I wol biwayle in maner of Tragedie. . . .

> 2)  At Lucifer, though he an angel were,
> And nat a man, at him I wol biginne;
> For, thogh fortune may non angel dere,
> From heigh degree yet fel he for his sinne
> Down in-to helle, wher he yet is inne.
> Now artow Sathanas, that maist nat twinne
> Out of miserie, in which that thou art falle.

> 3)  Lo Adam, in the feld of Damassene,
> With goddes owene finger wroght was he,
> And nat bigeten of mannes sperme unclene,
> And welte al Paradys, saving o tree.

> Had never worldly man so heigh degree
> As Adam, til he for misgovernaunce
> Was drive out of his hye prosperitee
> To labour, and to helle, and to meschaunce.

The Fall of Princes, therefore, could be attributed either to enemies within or to enemies without or to both in combination. Emphasis could vary in any given story, a factor which differentiates the mediaeval theory of tragedy from its classical antecedents—Shakespeare's from Jonson's. Thus, as with comedy, classical tragic theory was inherited as a literary tradition, transformed by Christian theology and pressed by Elizabethans into the service of the native drama. Tragedy still tells the story of the fall of a Prince, but with a difference. The Prince is shown to be personally responsible for his Fall. Lucifer fell by pride and so does Lear. The inevitability of the catastrophe is transferred from the plot to the character of the central protagonist.

From *Shakespeare's Dramatic Heritage* (London: Routledge, 1969), pp. 93–96. Used by permission.

*Francis Fergusson (1977)*

## Dante and Shakespeare

There are plenty of differences between Dante and Shakespeare. But it is clear to anyone who reads them carefully that they share the classical-Christian vision of human nature and destiny which was composed of Aristotelian philosophy, Christian theology, and the heritage of pagan and biblical literature made relevant to their time by allegorical interpretation. That of course was the accepted "world picture," as Tillyard called it; and it was available to any poet of the time. But so far as I know only Dante at the beginning of the Renaissance and Shakespeare at the end were able to use it in all its harmonious complexity to mirror earthly life.

Dante was writing in the *Commedia* the unified epic of his own journey of enlightenment, while Shakespeare in the course of his twenty-eight years of playwriting was presenting a great variety of versions of human comedy and tragedy. Nevertheless their conceptions of the art and the purpose of poetry were similar. When Hamlet tells the players that the purpose of their art is "to hold, as 'twere, the mirror up to nature; to show virtue her own feature, scorn her own image, and the very age and body of the time his form and pressure," and Dante tells Can Grande that his aim in the *Commedia* was to show "man, as by good or ill deserts, in the exercise of the freedom of his choice, he becomes liable to punishing or rewarding justice," they are in essential agreement. Dante adopts the make-believe of the postmortem journey, while Shakespeare always creates an earthly setting, but both wished to imitate human action as we learn to recognize it on earth, and to reveal its God-given meaning.

That is partly because they were both brought up on that Aristotelian ethics, metaphysics, and psychology which was the standard philosophy from Dante's Aquinas to Shakespeare's Hooker. In the *Poetics* Aristotle writes: "Life consists in action, and its end [or aim] is a mode of action"; action is at the base of his philosophy of man. When Hamlet speaks of mirroring nature and when Dante names "man ... in the exercise of the freedom of his choice" they both assume Aristotle's view. And they both (though they did not know the *Poetics*) have the Aristotelian idea that poetry is the imitation of action.

Both poets are responsible for the meanings of the actions they imitate.... Dante is quite clear about the meanings he built into the *Commedia*: in his Letter 10 to Can Grande he associates them with the four meanings traditionally found in biblical narrative: Letter, Allegory, Trope (or moral meaning), and Anagoge.... Shakespeare does not always employ the traditional allegory (as he did in *The Merchant of Venice*, labelling its elements), but he saw the meanings of his plays as moral and religious, and sometimes points that out.... In considering the allegory of Dante or Shakespeare it is essential to remember that it is far more realistic than the allegory we are more familiar with. The three meanings are thought of as contained in the letter, as Dante and his masters frequently remind us. In Dante's example the actual journey of the Hebrews to the promised land comes first, with all its dust and noise and fatigue and terror, and only by realizing that can we get its moral, religious, or mystic meanings. This feature was plain to the exegetes from before Dante to Shakespeare. Thomas Aquinas put it this way: "In Holy Writ no confusion results, for all the interpretations are founded on one, the literal." William Whitaker, an Anglican divine contemporary with Shakespeare, is in agreement: "We concede such things as allegory, anagoge and tropology in Scripture," he writes, "but meanwhile we deny that there are many and various senses. We affirm that there is but one true, proper and genuine sense of Scripture, arising from the words rightly understood, which we call the literal: and we contend that allegories, tropologies and anagoges are not various senses, but various collections from one sense, or various applications and accommodations of that one meaning." Shakespeare writes in that tradition: he gives us his story as real, but as having the moral and religious meanings that make it significant.

Shakespeare's realism distinguishes him from most of his contemporaries and assimilates him to Dante and to certain medieval doctrines. Auerbach in his *Mimesis* studied this medieval realism, the basis of the fourfold allegory of Dante; and he enabled us to distinguish it sharply from the kind that C. S. Lewis studied in his *Allegory of Love*, which is more familiar to readers of English than the full medieval variety. Lewis's allegory is essentially a matter of personifying such abstract concepts as Peace, War, the Virtues, the Vices. Lewis finds it in Bunyan, the *Roman de la Rose*, Spenser, and many other places. He excludes Dante from his "allegory of love" explicitly, and Shakespeare by simple omission. In that he is right, for though Dante and Shakespeare can use personification when they need it—as well as icons, liturgical symbols, pagan gods—their allegory rises essentially out of the dramatic interplay of "real" people. Their fictions are intended to reflect not our concepts but the actual world, in which God's own meaning was supposed to be embodied (if we could only learn to see it) just as it was supposed to be in the events recorded in Scripture.

From *Trope and Allegory*, pp. 1–6, excerpts abridged. Copyright 1977, University of Georgia Press. Used by permission.

*Tom F. Driver (1960)*

## Shakespeare's Sense of History [editor's title]

The roots of Shakespeare's dramatic form are primarily in the domestic English drama, running back through the chronicle-histories to the Morality plays and the Mysteries based on the universal grandeur of biblical history. This is the drama Shakespeare saw as a boy, in all probability. At any rate, it was the popular drama. If we compare Shakespeare's drama with the Mystery plays, we see that the dramatic power is heightened, the artistry much refined, and the situations secularized and universalized. But we do not find that the pattern has changed very much; for that pattern was designed to show the development of historical events in sequence, from the first things to the last, as if man is to be known only through his history.

In addition to seeing man in the sequence of historical events and immersed in a sea of mundane detail, the medieval religious plays also provided an overarching interpretation of history which gave meaning to time and to the apparent trivialities of daily existence. It is this combination of meaning and triviality, event and interpretation, now and eternity, which is the primary key to the understanding of Shakespeare's dramatic form. The problem in understanding Shakespearean form, as in the Christian interpretation of man's existence, is not the quantitative one of relating the parts to the whole but rather that of relating events in time to a controlling purpose.

In Shakespeare the action is one which moves from knowledge to event, or rather from event to knowledge to new event, and such revelations as there are come about through the power of later events to fulfill and clarify earlier ones. In

*Richard III* all the action tends toward a final day of judgment in which a climactic battle reveals the former evil in all its horror and vindicates the good. Here parallels with biblical history and eschatological *motifs* give meaning to the history of the English throne.... *Macbeth* reveals the immoral as, among other things, an attempt to usurp time and control the future, the play representing a war between sin and that beneficent power which ultimately controls history. *The Winter's Tale* also focuses upon sin, demonstrating it to be the act of a violent will over which reconciliation triumphs through grace and the fullness of time. In every case, the problems arise in the course of historical existence and the conclusion is a return to orderly succession in the state.

[The] action of the Shakespearean play is expressed through the sense of passing time. The reason for that has not so much to do with mere "realism" as with the expression of the nature of the action. In moments of crisis and decision, the Shakespearean hero reminds himself and his audience of his history—past, present and anticipated future—because that is the only way he has of seeing the meaning in his act. The moments when the present is most keenly felt are like the "historical present" of biblical thought and like Augustine's reflections on present time: they are compounds of memory and expectation. The past in Shakespeare is very important because it aids in the definition of the present. It is madmen who behave "as the world were now but to begin" (*Hamlet* 4.5.103). Yet the past does not, as in the Greek plays, dominate the present and bind it in the grip of necessity. The difference lies in the understanding of the future. In Shakespeare the future is open. It contains the possibility of the new, both as a result of action which man may take and as result of growth and the providential shaping of events which lie outside man's control. The future is open in Shakespeare in the same way that it is in the Bible—not totally uncharted and free for any type of action whatsoever, but full of beneficent promise and tending toward a final culmination which robs the past of its terror and gives significance to the choices of the present. Shakespeare's belief in history is not that of some present-day existentialists, to whom the moment of present choice is everything and an order in history nothing except anathema (and who therefore have no notion of history at all); rather he believes in an ordering purpose above the temporal process, indistinguishable in form from the Christian idea of Providence, which imposes the burden of choice upon man without abandoning history to chaos.

It goes hand in hand with the temporal nature of the Shakespearean action that it should be in some degree internalized. The present which is compounded of memory and anticipation cannot be adequately presented except from "the inside." The importance of time in Judaeo-Christian thought has accompanied an emphasis upon personal responsibility; for in this view the present is meaningless apart from act, choice, and will. History, as [R. G.] Collingwood says, is the study of the "inside" and the "outside" of the event; in the Christian era history became the history of passion (*The Idea of History*, p. 57). In line with this tradition, Shakespeare attempts the fusion of the inner and the outer. The effect on dramatic form is to be found in the close interdependence of character and action, in the depiction of moments when decisive choice is made, in the many ways (of which soliloquy is one) by means of which the interior thought of the character is revealed, and in the sense of involvement and identification which the audience is made to feel for the people and situations on stage.

The fusion of inner and outer—not only interdependence but also correspondence between what character experiences and what the total action reveals—this fusion leads to the adoption of nature into the realm of the historical. Professor Tillich has reminded us that in Hebraism and Christianity "history tends to absorb nature into itself" (*Biblical Religion*, p. 40), and Professor Auerbach has pointed out the New Testament prototypes for the upheavals in nature which accompany the moral outrages and spiritual crises of the Shakespearean characters (*Mimesis*, p. 323). In Shakespeare the action is not the result of disturbances in nature, nor is nature in itself the final arbiter of human action; rather, disturbances in nature are the result of action taken by men in the course of historical existence. Even in such a nature-drenched play as *The Winter's Tale*, nature is but a grand metaphor to describe the history of sin and reconciliation in human life. The Shakespearean tragic hero is guilty of sin, rather than *hybris*, which means his offense originates in the will and is directed not against nature, but against that unnamed sovereign who orders nature and against persons actually confronted in the course of the action. Shakespeare does not believe in a capricious control over the universe, and therefore the medieval idea of Natural Law may be used accurately to describe what the plays represent; but the simple term nature and the word *hybris* are alike too impersonal to do justice to the reality he presents—a reality which is rooted in a personal center making choices in a situation defined by its unique history.

Among the many ways in which Shakespeare imitates action in which time is fundamentally important is the technique of anticipation and fulfillment. I have already noted that the action itself is such as reaches its full development and resolution in temporal events—usually in a battle or a duel, or a scene of reconciliation. Shakespeare has not been content to let only the plot represent such action, he also worked into the poetic structure itself a principle whereby early events and lines achieve their full meaning only in later ones. The opening lines of *Richard III*,

> Now is the winter of our discontent
> Made glorious summer by this sun of York

have an apparent meaning when first spoken, but they are subject to a variety of interpretations as the play progresses and are finally seen to have been prophetic of the play's action, in which England's winter of discontent is truly dispelled. Similarly, the line in the opening scene of *The Winter's Tale*, "shook hands, as over a vast; and embrac'd, as it were, from the ends of opposed winds" (33), is not fully expounded until the last scene, in which Leontes is shown embracing his friends over the "wide gap" created by sin and time. The nearest equivalent in Greek tragedy is Sophoclean irony, such as Oedipus' pronouncement of the curse which later turns out to have been directed against himself. But here the irony is dependent on a change from ignorance to knowledge, a lifting of a veil, whereas in Shakespeare the full meaning actually does not exist at the beginning but must be brought into being through the events of the play, the process usually being not one in which the later event negates the former but in which early potentialities are deepened, explored, and brought to full fruition. In other words, the later insights of the Shakespearean play often stand in the same relation to its early ones as do the New Testament events to those of the Old Testament in Christian exegesis. The earlier is a "type" of the later, and the full depth of the former is not seen except in the light of the latter, as Moses the deliverer from bondage is a prefiguring "type" of Christ the Redeemer, or the destruction of Jerusalem a prefiguration of the Divine Wrath in the Last Days.

When we come to language, [we encounter] Shakespeare's mixture of styles. Shakespeare does not mind moving from poetry to prose and back again when it suits him, or from the most elevated language of the court to the plain speech of porters and gravediggers. The language of his plays more often achieves unity through continuing images and themes than through consistent adherence to a "tone" or "style" throughout. This fact is a reflection of his devotion to concrete reality. At great moments the high and the low are bound together in the same events, the drunken Porter with the virtuous Macduff. No more can the comic and tragic be rigidly separated. Shakespeare is in these matters the heir of the medieval religious plays, which had found the most sublime religious events so imbedded in the common stuff of life that the humorous and the momentous played together. The rigid separation of styles depends upon *a priori* principles which cannot be maintained where the starting point is historical reality.

Matters affecting theatrical presentation and divisions between the acts and scenes also reflect, ideally in each case, the types of action which they are meant to assist in imitating. The externalized action of the Greek drama can be well expressed by an actor wearing a mask and cothurnus, standing upon a probably shallow stage above a well-trained chorus and in a great open theater before several thousand spectators. The internalized, flowing action of the Shakespearean play could not be represented well in such surroundings. Shakespeare required, in comparison, a more intimate theater where actor and audience were in close rapport, where the mask gave way to the human face, where the actors themselves, instead of a chorus, provided the physical movement, where entrances and exits were facilitated so that action might turn again and again from the reflective word to the immediate event.

The multiplicity of scenes in the Shakespearean play is designed to maintain the flow of events and to be able to show the action from more than one side, as is also the lengthy *dramatis personae* list. It is likely that Shakespeare did not think of act and scene divisions as his editors have impressed them upon our minds; but he certainly thought of a continuous procession of episodes and dialogues so that a freely flowing motion might be maintained, within which a rhythm of acceleration and retardation could be achieved. It is this procession of images that gives the spectator the sense of being on a journey and thus reinforces the notion of movement through time. The Shakespearean play is an account of departure and arrival.

If the division of scenes in the Shakespearean play expresses a principle of motion, the alternation of ode and episode in the Greek play expresses a principle of balance. Parados, when the Chorus enters, balances exodus, when it leaves. Between, song and scene follow one another so regularly that there is generated a sense of poise, which corresponds faithfully to the intent of the action, which is to celebrate the fundamental equilibrium of nature.

Another view was possible, however—one which was being prepared in Palestine even before the time of Athens' glory. In Israel there developed a belief, in spite of one national calamity after another, that in history itself there was revealed a divine purpose which would in time be brought to fulfillment. When, in that tradition, the crucifixion and resurrection of Christ was declared to be the very center of history, the story of mankind was turned into an historical drama. This is the tradition which bequeaths to Shakespeare his basic understanding of man. He seldom expresses it in overt religious language. His plays are not to be read as models of Christian doctrine. Yet it is true that the form of his plays is consistent with the biblical interpretation of man and the universe. Shakespearean man is imbedded in the ambiguities and moral demands of history, while the Shakespearean dramatic action seeks its resolution in the fulfilling events of time.

From *The Sense of History in Greek and Shakespearean Drama* (Columbia University Press, 1960), pp. 201–11 abridged. Used by permission.

*M. D. H. Parker (1955)*

## Nature and Grace in the Romances [editor's title]

The last three acts [of *Pericles*] illustrate the theme of providence and Grace.... Marina, "born in a tempest" to what seems "a lasting storm," is above all "grace." She is "absolute Marina," whose contrast "darks in Philoten, all graceful marks."

She preaches "divinity" in a brothel, and sends Lysimachus away "saying his prayers." She sings "like one immortal," and "deep clerks she dumbs." Yet she is "flesh and blood," she has "a working pulse," she is "no fairy." If we ask:

> What country-woman?
> Here of these shores?

she replies:

> No, nor of any shores;
> Yet I was mortally brought forth, and am
> No other than I appear.

She lives where she is "but a stranger." ... Marina, fraught with her paradisal but human perfections, suggests Mary, "the second Eve," the "stella maris" of Latin hymn and English lyric, immaculate in the midst of corruption, "blessed," virgin, restorative of life: "Thou that begett'st him that did thee beget."

*Pericles* has reminiscences of *Lear*, which underpin what is, largely through the work of Professor Wilson Knight, its acknowledged resurrection theme. The unnatural vice of Antiochus, like the unnatural vice of Goneril, evokes the image of dust blown in the face; and Thaisa's actual restoration ... is a "present kindness" which makes his "past miseries sport." ... In all the last comedies there is a child who is in a crucial position in the plot, and the word which echoes in *Pericles* is the word "born":

> When I was born the wind was north. ...
>     When I was born
> Never were waves or wind more violent. ...
> Born in a tempest, when my mother died. ...

What is born in Marina, as it is to be born in Perdita and Miranda and in Cymbeline's lost sons, is a new humanity, from which redemption flows back to the old. ... Behind grace again lies the supernatural world out of which it comes, the "immortal Dian" of Pericles, the gods by whatever name they go, the "heaven" which "infuses" Miranda. "*Teste David cum Sibylla*," says the Roman sequence in the Mass for All Souls' Day, calling pagan as well as Jewish witness for Christian doctrine; and the *Act Against Abuses*, which made it illegal to use the words "God," "Christ" or "Jesus" on the stage, made Sibylline theology a necessity in the theatre, if one were to have theology there at all.

*Cymbeline*, though it has this metaphysical background, is the most explicitly moral of the last four plays. ... The suffering of the innocent with and for the guilty wrests from Cymbeline his pride in mere power, so that he acknowledges, though still free in will and body, the justice of his bond to the Emperor, which he had wished to put to the arbitrament of force. From Posthumus, "to himself unknown," who was "without seeking to find," and who was to be saved by suffering and knowledge, Cymbeline learns mercy. For Posthumus has learnt justice long before this, and mercy from his own forgiveness. He talked in prison of "the penitent instrument" which must loose the fetters of conscience and make him "free for ever," and found it not enough. "Gods are more full of mercy"; they offer to "satisfy," to give life for life. That offer made, Posthumus, saved by forgiveness, learns the use of power:

> The power that I have on you is to spare you;
> The malice toward you to forgive you. Live,
> And deal with others better.

"A sad tale's best for winter," says Mamillius, and for three acts *The Winter's Tale* bears him out. From the wilful damnation of his choice in the teeth of the oracle, Leontes is plucked by suffering, but it is for Time that tries all, "the joy and terror of good and bad," to turn the winter tragedy of guilty and guiltless suffering into a summer comedy of resurrection and life, "now grown in grace, equal with wondering." . . . The pagan Hermione talks much of grace even before her accusation, and goes to her undeserved suffering with a devotion strikingly Christian: "This action I now go on / Is for my better grace." So Perdita, "grown in grace," does all things well, and at her feast offers to her guests "grace and remembrance," rosemary and rue. Of her discovery to the "penitent" and "reconciled" Leontes, the first gentleman remarks:

> Who would be thence that has the benefit of access?
> Every wink of an eye, some new grace will be born.

Paulina again speaks to her royal visitors in a paraphrase of traditional devotion: "My poor house to visit / It is a surplus of your grace." This is more than a verbal echo of the Missal's antecommunion prayer: "*Domine, non sum dignus ut intres sub tectum meum.*" The scene is a chapel, and Paulina, changing like a priest from one receiving, to one conferring a benefit, announces Hermione's resurrection in the words: "It is requir'd / That you awake your faith." To Hermione, she says: "Bequeath to death your numbness, for from him / Dear life redeems you."

*The Tempest* makes a different emphasis. As nature without grace, apparent nature, is unnatural ("I do forgive thee, unnatural though thou art"), the new, redeemed nature, real nature, is, even in being nature, supernatural in the old sense. This is quite a different contrast from the contrast with artificial:

> Nothing nature I ever saw so noble.
> These are not natural events.

> There is in this business more than nature
> Was ever conduct of.

Nature indeed "makes the mean," but behind nature, even behind the "great creating nature" of *The Winter's Tale*, lies another power, as behind the Platonic *natura naturans* lies "the one and the good." So in the orthodox theology, it is only through the Incarnation that man regains not only that lost gift of supernatural grace which raised him to communion with God and fitted him for eternal life, but the integrity of his unfallen nature itself.

*The Tempest* has been called "Shakespeare's miracle play," and Sebastian, the doubter to Antonio's plain atheist, exclaims at the last and crowning mercy of Ferdinand's restoration, "A most high miracle." Yet.... there is no mention of Christ, not even an anachronistic allusion like that of Leontes to Judas's betrayal, the only specific reference to Christ's Person in the last four plays. It is, of course, as untrue to say that "there is no word of God" as to say "there is not a hint of immortality." Of God there is talk enough—by the only three good men in the play.

> Miranda:    How came we ashore?
> Prospero:   By Providence divine.
> Ferdinand: Sir, she is mortal;
>      But by immortal Providence she's mine.
> Gonzalo:   Look down, you gods.

Alonzo, the best of the bad, appeals to the "heavens," a common substitute for "God" or "Christ" or "Jesus" after the *Act Against Abuses*.

*The Tempest* is more complex than any parable, in that it is not one allegory but several, which cross and interact; the recessional allegory of being, summed up in the famous speech (4.1.147), and murmured in the typical sea-image of Ariel's song; the allegory of sin and redemption which constitutes the story of Antonio and Sebastian; and the allegory in which the quasi-symbolic figures of Ariel and Caliban shade off the parable into the morality.

The story of Antonio and Sebastian has frequent analogies with the story of Satan and Adam and Eve, analogies not coherent and consecutive, but fluctuating and reiterative, in the way artistic as opposed to didactic analogies typically are. For the artist does not set out to expound a doctrine or metaphysic; he creates in the context of doctrine and metaphysic, which are the mould of the experience he is to express, rather than the end of his expression. The function of ideas in poetry is not to be created, but to create.

Of all, innocent and guilty, Prospero can say from the beginning what was true of neither *Cymbeline* nor *The Winter's Tale*:

>   Tell your piteous heart
> There's no harm done
>
>   There is no soul—
> No, not so much perdition as an hair—
> Betid to any creature in the vessel

"But the very hairs of your head are numbered," said Christ in St Matthew (10:30), and Prospero's lines to Miranda, even in manner reminiscent of mystic revelation, to which the soul is typically feminine and sometimes also a daughter, are certainly reminiscent in sense:

>   No harm.
> I have done nothing but in care of thee,

Of thee, my dear one, thee, my daughter, who
Art ignorant of what thou art.

So though the seas (and Ariel as a Dantesque harpy of justice) may "threaten, they are merciful," and this mercy lies behind Prospero as well as in him: "By foul play as thou say'st, were we heav'd thence / But blessedly holp hither." *The Tempest's* God is indeed the god of St Augustine and St Thomas, who is so powerful that he can even make good of evil, the evil of sin for which he is not responsible. It is his omniscience which has "chalked forth the way," and Gonzalo goes on to sum up the end of that way in a speech which transfers into other terms, curiously reminiscent in cadence and image, the doctrine of natural *in* supernatural perfection:

Was Milan thrust from Milan, that his issue
Should become kings of Naples? O! rejoice
Beyond a common joy, and set it down
With gold on lasting pillars. In one voyage
Did Claribel her husband find at Tunis,
And Ferdinand, her brother, found a wife
Where he himself was lost; Prospero his dukedom
In a poor isle; and all of us ourselves,
When no man was his own.

"*O certe necessarium Adae peccatum, quod Christi morte deletum est! O felix culpa, quae talem ac tantum meruit habere Redemptorem!*" (O truly necessary sin of Adam, which by Christ's death is blotted out! O happy fault, that deserved to have such and so great a Redeemer!) This, the most famous cry of the Exultet from the Blessing of the Paschal Candle in the Roman Missal, passes into Shakespeare's "pillar" image, "glittering like gold": "*Sed jam columnae hujus praeconia novimus, quam in honorem dei rutilans ignis accendit.*" (And now we know the tidings of this pillar, which the fire, glittering like gold, lights to the glory of God.)

From *The Slave of Life: A Study of Shakespeare and the Idea of Justice* (London: Chatto & Windus, 1955), pp. 176–92, excerpts abridged.

*Roy Battenhouse (1986)*

## Shakespeare's Augustinian Artistry [editor's title]

One of the significant features of Shakespearean tragedy is imagery that frequently echoes Bible language or paradigm, even when the play's setting is pagan. A striking instance of this is Antony's "Last Supper," as Middleton Murry in 1936 termed it when noting how Antony's fellowship in 4.2 carries echoes of Christ's. When Antony requests, "Well my good fellows, wait on me tonight. / Scant not my cups"; and again, "Tend me tonight, ... Haply you shall not see me more";

and again, "Tend me tonight two hours," do we not have an analogy to Christ's Passover and Gethsemane? Antony concludes by saying that "tomorrow.... I'll expect victorious life." The parallel in Plutarch is only this:

> So being at supper (as it is reported) he commanded his officers and household servants that waited on him at his bord, that they should fill his cuppes full, and make as much of him as they could: for said he, you know not whether you shall do so much for me tomorrow or not.... it may be you shall see me no more, but a dead bodie. [But to "salve" their grief he added that he thought "safely to return with victory."] (Bullough, V, 307–08)

Shakespeare has evidently enlarged Plutarch's story with overtones of a Christian Passion unknown to Antony and his world. Why so? Is the dramatist asking us to see Antony as a prefigurer of Christian redemption? This is not likely since Antony's "gaudy night" is far from being a godly night; he has proposed his "bounteous" meal to "mock the midnight bell" and drown consideration.

A more likely explanation of this supper's double-level language is that Shakespeare is inviting us to recall a theological aphorism of Augustine, namely, that "souls in their very sins seek but a sort of likeness to God, in a proud and perverted, and so to say, slavish freedom" (*On the Trin.* I.xi.5). In other words, Antony is enacting unwittingly a perverted likeness to Christ, a dark analogy to divine love. Only in a grotesque way is he prefiguring Christ; his action is a parody of Christ's.

This implication is the more evident if we notice in a preceding scene a biblical echo Shakespeare puts in Antony's mouth when Cleopatra seems to be forsaking Antony by betraying him into the hands of Caesar, his enemy. With a kind of godly jealousy Antony cries out:

> O that I were
> Upon the hill of Basan, to outroar
> The horned herd (3.8.126–28)

For Elizabethan auditors this language would serve to recall that of the troubled godly man in Psalm 22, who cried out:

> My God, my God, why hast thou forsaken me? ... Many oxen are come about me; fat bulles of Basan close me in on every side. They gape upon me with their mouths. (Prayerbook tr.)

This is the well-known Messianic psalm, in which the sufferer, while besieged by wicked men, puts his trust in God to deliver him. But in Shakespeare's play the reference to Basan carries a contrast to the biblical analogy it evokes, since Antony has placed his trust not in God but in a valued-as-god Cleopatra, a boggler and Egyptian charmer; hence his response to the "herd" that encompasses him is a desire to "outroar" them. What the situation thus presents is an ironic parallel to Christian paradigm. We are asked to see, at one and the same time, an analogy to godly suffering and a perverse likeness of it.

All sins, in Augustine's view, are modes of misdirected love. They are caused by a soul's immoderate inclination to some mutable good. Goods such as bodily pleasure, or worldly fame and honor, or even human souls themselves are misloved unless loved for the sake of God. By straying from Him, the soul substitutes a perverse similitude of the divine—pride for exaltedness, or prodigality for true liberality, or a wanton tenderness in place of charity. Yet no soul can altogether escape God's law, since (as Augustine says, quoting Ps 139) even "if I make my bed in hell, behold, thou art there." Darkened traces of the Creator remain in sinners. Hence Augustine in his *Confessions* (II.[vi.].14) observes: "All pervertedly imitate Thee, who remove far from Thee. . . . Behold, thy servant, fleeing from his Lord, and obtaining a shadow." A "darkened likeness of Thy Omnipotency" was what Augustine came to see in the "maimed liberty" of misdirected love.

An illustration of maimed liberty is provided by Shakespeare in the scene of Antony's suicide in the name of "nobleness." The awkward facts are in Plutarch, but Shakespeare has amplified them with typological overtones—e.g., Antony's likening himself to a bridegroom (a metaphor in Ps 19:5 applied to Christ by Augustine in *Confessions* IV.[xxi.].19) as he offers his pierced body to "Egypt" and proclaims himself "the greatest Prince of the world." Such details, for an Elizabethan auditor, could evoke the memory of Christ who made his claim to a kingdom not of this world by offering redemptive wounds in hands, feet, and side. The reader, says Andrew Fichter, is continually made aware of "the parody the play will become in the light of Christian revelation." (*Sh. Survey* 33 [1980], 110).

Cleopatra's suicide in imitation of Antony's exhibits this moral parody in a feminine mode. The asp at her breast is as monstrous a proof of queenliness as is Antony's self-stabbed belly a proof of princeliness. Shakespeare's Cleopatra has a repugnance (not mentioned in Plutarch) to being made a public spectacle in Caesar's Rome. A private "gibbet" within her pyramid is her substitute for allowing "Mechanic slaves / With greasy aprons, rules and hammers [to] / Uplift us to the view" (5.4.209–11). Her scorn for rules and hammers, however, would suggest to a Christian auditor a contrast to Christ's enduring such a shame because "If I be lifted up, I will draw all men unto me" (Jn 12:32). One of the episodes in mystery-cycle drama depicted hammerers nailing Christ to a cross on which he was uplifted. That paradigm has its dark or perverse analogy in Cleopatra's applying an asp to her arm to display *her* triumph. She becomes more specifically a parody of the Virgin Mary when she puts an asp to her breast and describes this serpent as the "baby" she nurses to give suck to "immortal longings."

Shakespeare has signalled parody through details not found in Plutarch. Plutarch mentioned no asp at Cleopatra's breast or "heaven" in her mouth. He did tell, in two sentences, of a basket of figs brought to her by a laughing countryman. But Shakespeare has made specific the quality of this countryman's laughter. The "joy of the worm," he clownishly tells her, has "no goodness" in it and "it is not worth the feeding." Then he jests about a woman "something given to lie" who made "a good report of the worm" but is not to be believed. He that believes her saying, this clown remarks, will never be saved by what she does—here echoing the story in Genesis of Adam's straying from salvation by believing Eve's report and copying her deed. Thus through a jest Cleopatra is being identified typologically by Shakespeare with "old Eve," the "eastern star" of Charmian's Egyptian imagination, a twisted version of the Christian star of Mary the Virgin.

And alongside Shakespeare's echo of Genesis, the Bible's first book, is an echo of its last book. Cleopatra's cry, "Husband, I come" is her unintended parody of Rv 22:17, "The Spirit and the bride say, Come," in reference to a heavenly marriage to Jesus the Lamb who provides "a new heaven, and a new earth." Quest for a new heaven and a new earth has characterized Antony and Cleopatra from their first meeting (see 1.2.17). Indeed, as Ethel Seaton pointed out (in *RES*, 1946), many echoes of St John's Apocalypse punctuate Shakespeare's play from beginning to end, serving as "sunken bells" sounding under the tide and swell of the poetry. What these echoes amount to can not be dismissed as "local color" as some critics would evasively suppose. Rather, the dramatist's imagery is signaling a more-than-Plutarchan perspective for viewing the Roman world's most famous lovers.

Dolora Cunningham (in *SQ*, 1955), when studying the means by which Cleopatra prepares for death, found an odd similarity to penitential disciplines of Christian preparation for immortality. Each of the stages prescribed by medieval theologians for repentance—conviction of sin, contrition of heart, faith that God will forgive, and a purpose to amend one's life—have a kind of shadowy parallel in Cleopatra's resolve to begin to make "A better life." But since Antony is her god and his lips her heaven, the analogy to Christian penance is misleading, says Cunningham, unless used for placing Cleopatra's different version of transcendence. "The lovers' perverse location of the absolute in themselves and their love amounts to an easily recognizable parody of the Christian life" (p. 13). I think Augustine would have said so too, although he would also say that whether or not one's outlook is Christian, humane understanding must recognize in these tragic lovers a misdirected love that achieves not "liberty" but its maimed version. Shakespeare and Augustine understand the mimicking of "new heaven" that accompanies prodigal imaginings.

So, likewise, did Dante. A recent book by Anthony K. Cassell (*Dante's Fearful Art of Justice*, Toronto, 1984) points out that the tragedies which Dante and Virgil together view inside the walls of the City of Dis are those caused by sin against Reason but also (as the imagery of punishment shows) by a perverse mimicking of God. The damned, Cassell explains, "remain in some way images of the Godhead whom they rejected":

> In *Inferno* v, Francesca buffeted like a dove figures a lustful counterpart of the loving symbol of the Holy Spirit. . . . Farinata's punishment (in *Inferno* x) points ironically to Christ upright in his tomb . . . Caiaphas lies crucified like

Christ (but nailed to the ground among the hypocrites). The thieves in *Inferno* xxiv–xxv metamorphose into . . . inversions of the crucified Christ as prefigured, familiarly, by the brazen, healing serpent hung on Moses' staff . . . God's image prevails even to the depths where Satan's triune heads dripping tears and bloody drool are a clear, intentionally banal, parody. In this Dante follows the Augustine tradition which held that sin itself was but a perverse imitation of the Deity. (pp. 9–10)

Dante's poetic art, Cassell argues, has figural "secondary" meanings which as "sunken metaphor" blend intermittently into the literal story to structure an interplay between levels of significance (pp. 6–7). "The literal level of the *Inferno* is not reducible to its secondary senses but is deeply dependent on them; these other levels are . . . vertical meanings which go above and beyond" (p. 14).

I find particularly interesting Cassell's comments on Dante's depiction of Farinata, a great war-chief of Italy's Ghibelline faction. Dante the wayfarer encounters the ghost of this historical personage among the heretics of the City of Dis, Augustine's Earthly City of discord, where dwell typologically at various levels those souls who have turned from God to serve human glory. Here Farinata is seen rising from a hot tomb, erect above the flames from the waist up. The iconography suggests an analogy to Christ rising out of his sepulchre, and since Dante also terms the tomb an "ark," a further analogy to Noah's voyaging above the flood is suggested. But Farinata's attitude, by contrast to those paradigms, is one of pride and contempt for his enemies; and the smoke from the flames dims his light and sight. The situation is thus a dark analogy to faith and resurrection. While Dante the wayfarer sees Farinata as a "great soul," Dante the poet places such "magnanimity" as an Earthly City's valiancy. The scene's imagery illustrates, as Cassell notes, St Paul's saying that "though I give my body to be burned, and have not charity, it profiteth me nothing," and St Gregory's gloss that in such a case the fire of fining only "afflicts torment and not cleansing." Dante's scene conveys a "profound moral parody... of the liturgical *visitatio sepulchri*"; the "He is not here, For he is risen!" is parodied and reversed in Farinata's appearance (p. 24).

It seems to me one can speak similarly of Shakespeare's depiction in *Hamlet* of the warlike ghost whose appearance arouses in young Hamlet an eagerness to know "why the sepulchre / Wherein we saw thee quietly inurned / Hath oped his ponderous and marble jaws / To cast thee up again." This imagery suggests an analogy to Jonah or to Christ's resurrection, but at the same time in a dark version that makes "night hideous" and horridly shakes Hamlet's disposition. This ghost is like Farinata in having his abode in sulphurous flames, and in speaking pridefully with contempt. To Horatio and Marcellus, earlier, he has seemed to have "majesty" but yet to be an "extravagant and erring" spirit if judged by Christian lore. Cherrell Guilfoyle (in *Comp. Drama* 14 [1980]) has described the opening scene of *Hamlet* as an antithesis to the angelic visitation in the Coventry nativity play. This ghost's visitation amounts to a parody of divine visitation.

Whereas Dante was protected from Farinata's speech by relying on Virgil to guide him, we see Hamlet self-victimized by a rash idolizing of his father's ghost, with the result that he resolves to wipe away all "saws of books" to serve revenge. Here Hamlet's vow is presented by Shakespeare in language that suggests a perverse likeness to that of Moses. Hamlet calls for "tablets" to write down a "one commandment" that inverts the "Thou shalt have no other gods before me" which Moses received from God. Then the action moves to Hamlet's demanding three times a covenant-swearing that pledges his friends to "secrecy" on a sword-hilt. Editors who notice that Hamlet speaks of "grace and mercy" as he presents the sword-hilt have suggested that it is being used as a Christian cross. But if so, is not Shakespeare asking us to see the irony of sealing with the cross a secret message of revenge? While Hamlet's triple invocation imitates biblical form, the content of his request perverts grace and mercy. The iconography is that of analogy, but in a parody version of holy covenant.

In a similar way, the iconography of the ending of *Hamlet* is that of sacrament debased. A rapier "anointed" with poison and a wine-cup spiced with a "pearl" of poison symbolize an unholy warfare and unholy communion. Christ as pearl is grotesquely present. A kind of Black Mass is being celebrated, its ministers a Claudius and a Hamlet divided against each other (as typical of Earthly City factionalism), yet joined in ministering a cup of death and damnation. None of this symbolic imagery was in the story Shakespeare inherited from Saxo and Belleforest. Has not the dramatist invented it to give us an Augustinian perspective on the mimicking of God that characterizes misdirected human loves? For Augustine, all human mistaking falls within a divine order that permits wayward souls to fight against each other for temporal dominion, yet binds them fast in a fellowship that flings them "headlong by an equal weight of desire into the same abyss," united in their ways and deserts (quoted by Cassell, p. 22).

Analogy as a principle of dramatic construction was inherited by Shakespeare from his medieval predecessors. Its reflection in his art has been illustrated in Joan Hartwig's recent *Shakespeare's Analogical Scene: Parody as Structural Syntax* (1983). Hartwig rightly defines parody as a reductive mimicking. But I think we need to distinguish two rather different kinds of parody. We can all recognize in the Porter scene of *Macbeth,* for instance, a reduction of Macbeth's tragic plight to comic terms. This is a case of linear parody; it mimics the story's literal level. But if we examine an earlier scene in which Macbeth commits himself to celebrating "Pale Hecate's offerings," is there not evident another level of reductionism? That scene, which begins by his saying "When my drink is ready, ... strike upon the bell" and ends by his saying "The bell is sounded," parodies a Christian Mass, in which traditionally a bell is sounded to mark Christ's offering to God of his body and blood as a Saving sacrifice. Macbeth's vision of the handle of a dagger as emblem of his mission is an evident perversion of devotion to the Cross. Macbeth's ending the scene with "It is done" is like that of Dr. Faustus in Marlowe's play, where the hero ritualizes his commitment to fantasies of power through a pact sealed with *consummatum est*, Christ's words from the Cross. Parody of this kind involves what we may call an upside-down analogy or vertical parody, distinguishable from the kind of linear analogy to Faustus's behavior presented comically by the yokels Robin and Dick in Marlowe's subplot.

Hartwig's book focuses on parody presented on a horizontal plane of literal story, whereas I am urging that we pay attention to a vertical plane as well, since the art of Shakespeare, like Marlowe's, includes both. If I may cite an example, it seems to me Hartwig observes with fine insight the comic parody of Romeo's plight provided by the Nurse's blubbering of woe. But unnoticed by Hartwig is the parody of holy communion which Romeo presents us by his drinking a poisoned cup with the words, "Here's to my love!" on a Thursday night which, for Christian auditors, carries memories of Christ's Last Supper and a love higher than that of "paramour" devotion. Here Romeo's action amounts to a mimicking of divine sacrifice; it involves a religious reductionism. The nurse's woe, on the other hand, is simply a reducing of Romeo's level of heroic emotion to its analogy at a level of domestic farce. Both cases call for audience perception through analogy. But the one kind invites theological reflection, while the other parodies upper-class folly in lower-class versions.

From "Augustinian Roots in Shakespeare's Sense of Tragedy," *The Upstart Crow: A Shakespeare Journal* 6 (1986), 1–7, revised.

*Charles Huttar (1968)*

## The Christian Basis of Sonnet 146

In a recent article Mr. B. C. Southam saw reflected in Sonnet 146 an ironic humanism directly opposed to the traditional Christian interpretation of the poem[1].... Southam implicitly or explicitly assumes the following tenets to be representative of Christianity: 1) that soul and body are at odds, the soul and its desires being good and the body and its desires evil; 2) that "rigorous asceticism" or "bodily subjugation" is the best rule of life; 3) that "the gentleness of Christian charity" requires a master to allow his servant to exploit him; 4) that "Beatitudo non est virtutis praemium, sed ipsa virtus ... is the Christian ethic"; and 5) that, in keeping with the "rigorous asceticism," "eternity of life in heaven is the reward for bodily privation on earth." He finds among these tenets an inner contradiction: the third, in the metaphorical orientation of the poem (master-soul, servant-body), is opposed to the first two, and the fifth is opposed to the fourth. Shakespeare, he says, is calling attention to these contradictions and asserting a human-istic ethic in which such contradictions do not exist.

There is one small mistake: these doctrines are not typical Christianity at all. The first two are neo-Platonism. The third grossly distorts Christian charity, whose function is to ennoble human relationships (such as that of master and servant), not to abolish them. The fourth is Stoicism. The second and fifth contain phrases reminiscent of Christianity, but the Bible and majority Christian opinion use these phrases in a far subtler way than has been grasped in the interpretation in question.

It is not necessary, therefore, to discover in this sonnet a humanism which avoids the supposed contradictions of Christianity. For Christianity itself avoids these contradictions. The critics who for decades agreed in calling this a Christian poem were not mistaken. Only by so viewing it can one appreciate its full density.

> Poore soule the center of my sinfull earth,
> My sinfull earth these rebbell powres that thee array,
> Why dost thou pine within and suffer dearth
> Painting thy outward walls so costlie gay?

The center of an object is that in which its essential characteristics are *concentrated*. The soul is what gives life to the fleshly part, and it shares the body's characteristics, including sinfulness. As the headquarters of the body, the proper source of commands, the soul cannot take refuge in a Platonic dichotomy between it and the body, or claim to be an alien imprisoned in "sinful earth." The soul must share in responsibility for the sin. The irony is heightened by the fact that of the two partners, the soul, being eternal, has more to lose by its actions than the body, and nothing to gain. This is a commonplace in Christian doctrine and there is every reason to suppose that a sixteenth-century poet could take it for granted as an un-derlying part of his argument.[2] Nor is it entirely hidden. Shakespeare's acceptance of "sinful" as the proper epithet for the microcosm's "earth" (including soul as its "center") comes near to being an explicit endorsement of the Christian way of de-scribing the situation. The pity we are encouraged to feel ("Poore soule") is not for the soul victimized, but for the soul self-deceived—or at least deceived[3] and self-destroying. The figure in line three is not of the soul as ascetic. Self-privation may be explained on other grounds than asceticism: stupidity, for instance, or willful-ness. The pining of the soul is not at all that spiritual humility enjoined by Christ in the Beatitudes and rendered in the Geneva Bible which Shakespeare knew by the word "poore" (Mt 5:3). It is just what it says, dearth, spiritual starvation, lack of the kind of nourishment which is proper to the soul.

An effective siege cuts off provisions and reduces the inmates of the fortress to starvation. This metaphor not only is prominent in the first quatrain, but domi-nates the entire poem. This lends support to the proposed emendation of line two, correcting an apparent printer's error, to read: "Feeding these rebbell powres that thee array."[4] The soul, in its deceived and self-destroying career, is feeding its very enemies and as a result is pining away (the word has associations of starving and of being consumed) and suffers dearth (famine). Spiritual nourishment and its opposite constitute the subject of the entire sonnet.

The main shift in line four, though, is to the imagery of real estate which will continue to appear in lines five through eight and line eleven.

> Why so large cost hauing so short a lease,
> Doest thou vpon thy fading mansion spend?
> Shall wormes inheritors of this excesse
> Eate vp thy charge? is this thy bodies end?

In the "fading mansion" we have another of those commonplaces, too universal to be tagged as specifically Christian, yet in fullest harmony with Christian thought and with the practice of Christian writers contemporary with Shakespeare. There are, of course, numerous biblical parallels.[5] But the symbolism of the body as a house is probably even older; undoubtedly so is the awareness that this house fades. The sentiment of the second quatrain is quite ordinary. . . . In lines seven and eight the image of expenditure is continued. The soul's outlay upon its "mansion" has become excessive, and it is destined to lose all its "charge" to the worms at the body's "end." Read another way, however, these ambivalent lines continue the moral judgment of the soul begun in the opening quatrain. "Excess" can have associations of sin as well as extravagance, and the body may be the soul's "charge" in the sense of being its protégé for whose welfare the soul is responsible. Allowing the body to become nothing more than food for worms, is the soul's fault, for neglecting its salvation. If we understand "end" as meaning "purpose," then the answer invited to the question, "Is this thy bodies end?" is not the obvious Yes, but rather No; metamorphosis and not decay is the purpose for which the body was created. Both readings, the expenditure image and the moral judgement, are valid.

> Then soule liue thou vpon thy seruants losse,
> And let that pine to aggrauat thy store;
> Buy tearmes diuine in selling houres of drosse:
> Within be fed, without be rich no more,
>     So shalt thou feed on death, that feeds on men,
>     And death once dead, ther's no more dying then.

There is no notion of revenge in the sestet. Neither the poet nor the soul addressed is under any illusion as to who is responsible for the soul's plight: it is the soul. Hence it is meaningless to speak of vengeance in connection with the soul's coming to itself and asserting its rightful superiority over the body. It was Hooker who said, "the soule ... ought to conduct the bodie,"[6] and Erasmus asserted that when the mind dominates the body "it does so to the great advantage of the latter."[7]

Thus in the soul's action recommended in this sonnet there is no violation of the Christian master's obligation to his servant. The superiority of the soul over body and the obligation of soul to achieve life at the expense of immediate bodily pleasures is precisely the only way in which the metaphor of soul as master and body as servant has any meaning. . . . The reason that the soul, the master, is in trouble in the octave of Shakespeare's sonnet is that it has abdicated its magistracy. The advice the sestet offers to remedy this situation is, "Live thou upon thy servant's loss": since the "lease" is "short," since the body must die, save the expense which would go only to the feeding of worms and instead devote it to pursuits productive of life for the soul. The servant will pine anyhow, but no need for the master to starve with it; hence the soul must cease futile efforts to preserve the body ("let that pine," with "let" meaning "allow" rather than having a jussive force) and turn the inevitable to its own advantage ("aggrauat thy store").[8] This is, of course, very close to the words of Jesus, "Lay up for yourselves treasures in heaven, where neither moth nor rust doth corrupt, and where thieves do not break through and steal" (Mt 6:20). With these words, which are part of the Gospel lesson for Ash Wednesday in the Anglican Church, Shakespeare must surely have been familiar.

In line eleven we return to the legal imagery of line five. A "term" was the period of time for which a lease was granted. The contrast between "hours" and "tearmes" represents the contrast between the body's lease and eternity. And these "tearmes" are "diuine," unlike anything earthly; they are eternal. They can be purchased at small price: dross will buy them. Mr. Southham calls this "a transaction that is starkly simonious . . . concluded in grossly commercial terms." It is nothing of the sort, but rather a metaphor in the finest scriptural tradition. "Sell that thou hast, and give to the poor, and thou shalt have treasure in heaven," Jesus tells the rich young ruler (Mt 19:21). "Again, the kingdom of heaven is like unto treasure hid in a field; the which when a man hath found, he hideth, and for joy thereof goeth and selleth all that he hath, and buyeth that field" (Mt 13:44). Simony is the sin of perverting spiritual gifts for worldly gain. Shakespeare's advice is just the opposite. We should not let the commercial metaphor lead us astray.

The advice of lines nine through eleven is summarized in the twelfth with its picture of the soul, now nourished, no longer starved as in line three. Like the other key words in the sonnet, "death" may be taken in two senses, both relevant. The obvious meaning, of course, is eventual loss of life and the subsequent decay of the body, to which the poem has already alluded in lines seven and eight. But "death" is also the name for the principle of mortality itself, the process of the fading of the mansion which takes place even during life. There is some justification for identifying this idea of death with "sin."[9] Taken thus, to "feed on death" is to derive spiritual nourishment from the very principle of starvation, to turn the Destroyer of men to one's own advantage in building up. (See note 9 above.) The idea of death being dead lent itself to the word play in which the Elizabethan age so delighted. Shakespeare toyed with it elsewhere: "And fight and die is death destroying death" (*Rd II*, 3.2.184). In more of a theological vein, a popular textbook of the time said: "Now then seeing death is dead to them that beleeue in him, there is nothing in death which a man ought to feare. . . . So our death dieth, and is not able in any sort to hurt vs. . . ." [10] If Shakespeare went to church on Easter he heard of the "Paschal Lambe, . . . who by his death hath destroyed death." If he attended an Anglican funeral service he heard in these words from 1 Cor 15:54 the very image of feeding on death: "Death is swallowed up in victory."

We see that in Sonnet 146 Shakespeare used ideas and even phrases closely associated with Christian thought. We must add—unless we are to deny him the artist's self-consciousness—that he knew he was using them. To argue that he used them ironically requires certain presuppositions indicating that Christianity is susceptible to such satire; and I have shown that these presuppositions are mistaken.

## Notes

1  "Shakespeare's Christian Sonnet? Number 146," *Shakespeare Quarterly* 11 (1960), 67–71.
2  Cf. Donne's Holy Sonnet:
   I am a little world made cunningly
   Of Elements, and an Angelike spright,
   But black sinne hath betraid to endlesse night
   My worlds both parts, and (oh) both parts must die. . . .
3  Cf. Malone's emendation (1780) of line two: "Fool'd by. . . ."
4  C. Knox Pooler, ed., *Sonnets* in Arden, 2d ed. rev. (London, 1931), p. 138.
5  E.g., 2 Cor 5:4; Ps 90:5–6; Is 40:6–7; 64:6; I Pet 1:24.
6  *Of the Lawes of Ecclesiasticall Politie. Eyght Bookes* (London, [1594]), p. 65 (1.8.6).
7  *The Education of a Christian Prince*, tr. Lester Born (New York, 1936), p. 175.
8  "For which cause we faint not; but though the outward man perish, yet the inward man is renewed day by day" (2 Cor 4:16).
9  "In the day that thou eatest thereof thou shalt die" (Gn 2:17). "Who shall deliver me from the body of this death?" (Rom 7:24). "To be carnally minded is death" (Rom 8:6).
10  Peter de la Primaudaye, *The French Academie*, tr. T. B. [Part One] (London, 1586) p. 102.

From "The Christian Basis of Shakespeare's Sonnet 146," *Shakespeare Quarterly* 19 (1968), 355–65 abridged.

# Part II

# On Shakespeare's Comedies

## Die To Live

Death *is no* Loſſe, *but rather,* Gaine ;
*For wee by* Dying, Life *attaine.*

MORS VITÆ INITIVM.

ILLVSTR. XXI.

*Book.* I.

From George Wither,
*A Collection of Emblems, Ancient and Moderne* (1635), pl. 21.
By permission of The Folger Shakespeare Library

# ON SHAKESPEARE'S COMEDIES

## Introduction

The plays that various of today's critics have described as Shakespeare's "festive" comedies, "problem" comedies, and final "romances" appear with no categorizing distinction in the Folio's collection of fourteen comedies. The occasions of folly and mishap differ, yet all the plays end with a festivity that celebrates some problem overcome. Each accords with the traditional definition of comedy as an action that begins in trouble and ends in joy. The initial trouble in each case is not only some outward misfortune but also an anxiety of soul, and the final resolution cures both, including as it typically does for Shakespeare, a good fortune overarched with blessedness, a prospective happiness in grace which Christian hymnody would call a "joy of heaven to earth come down." Romance crowns a communal discovery that is associated often with religion's mystery of at-one-ment. Shakespearean comedy has as its dimensions a range of human journey that begins usually in something like Dante's dark woods and culminates in a providential coming to self-knowledge and light.

The story invites laughter—but always of two kinds. One kind is a profane laughter at the folly of persons unaware of their own natural foolishness as postlapsarian human beings. The antics of human misunderstanding or whim can be funny to a distanced observer, and exhibits of flagrant behavior allow us the amusement of pondering human absurdity and fallibility. The laughter can be turned on oneself by adopting some ritual of mock rule. A second kind of laughter is that of the joy discovered when the ridiculous is converted into a happiness of communion-in-grace. Some token of blessedness then concludes the action. An exercising and purging of our capacity for the risible is the therapeutic benefit of Shakespearean comedy.

A mingling of clowns with kings is characteristic of Shakespeare's art. No other dramatist has so persistently included a jester among the personages in society. Because such a figure has no social pretensions he can serve flexibly as a mediator between parties and a humorous dissolver of animosities. His very marginality to worldly enterprises frees him to offer sly comments. He thus becomes a licensed example of earthy realism amid the human delusions he deflates, and often also a spokesman of conundrums that hide spiritual mysteries. Unexpected theological truths crop up in the seemingly inconsequential palaver of Shakespeare's "fools"— not only in Touchstone and Lavatch in the comedies, but also in Falstaff the commentator on history, and in anonymous persons in a typical tragedy, for instance, the gravedigger in *Hamlet* and the "rural fellow" who jests with Cleopatra. Clowns and fools are Shakespeare's unadvertised supporters of biblical insights.

# THE COMEDY OF ERRORS

## Comment and bibliography

This shortest and possibly earliest of Shakespeare's comedies anticipates his late and most mature comedies by concluding with a family reunion, while also along the way it entertains us, as does *The Tempest*, with a good deal of slapstick comedy. The Dromio twins, by which Shakespeare doubles the comic motif of mistaken identity taken over from the *Menaechmi* of Plautus, have a Christian wit for clownishly making light of ass-like buffetings. And Dromio of Syracuse, in a low comedy contrast to his master's mysterious meeting with the wondrous Luciana, encounters belowstairs a kitchen wench, Nell, all grease and no grace, whose body is a bawdy globe of "countries." Thus a paralleling of fool *vis à vis* holy fool adventuring replaces the kind of romance one finds in Plautus's *Amphitruo*. The Ephesus of Shakespeare's story mirrors St Paul's Ephesus (and contemporary London too?) in being troubled by cozening spirits at odds with the biblical piety of a Luciana. By adding to this the frame-story of a fatherly Egeon seeking for his lost kinfolk, Shakespeare provides an envelope of Christian quest that enables discoveries of "identity" to take place at a religious house. There a whole city's liberation from estranging illusions occurs and is celebrated with a concluding baptismal feast.

Chris Hassel's commentary calls our attention to a recorded performance of this comedy on the night of Holy Innocents Day, a customary time for mockingly celebrating human errors. Then he quotes from the Innocents Day church lessons the promise of Jeremiah that the Lord will regather the scattered members of families. These contexts suggest that liturgy influenced the timing of the play's staging and its theme.

Glyn Austen's essay comments on the "sacramental" significance of the play's action as it moves toward a comic catharsis. The sick legal system of Ephesus is reflected more generally in a social disorder that becomes farcically sinister until its victims flee to a holy priory. Here an exorcism attempted earlier by Dr. Pinch is miraculously superseded. The redemption in Act 5 is a gift of grace, a healing transformation for everyone. It involves a casting off of the "old Adam" and the gaining of a new humanity in a restoration of personal identity and social cohesion. The concluding invitation to a baptismal feast extends by implication to us, the play's auditors.

Notable in our supplementary bibliography is Arthur Kinney's showing of the pervasiveness of Mystery cycle form and features in *The Comedy of Errors*. The play's New Testament sources have been tabulated by R. A. Foakes. The essay by T. W.

Baldwin traces the Old Testament sources of Luciana's advice to Adriana as she elaborates on the shamefulness of adultery (2.1.104–15) and its effect on the innocent wife (2.2.132–48). Persistent in self-justification, Adriana does not realize that her own actions are betraying her into a complicity in the evil she complains of, making her deserving of the reproof the Abbess will give her.

Sanderson reviews the play's twelve mentionings of "patience," including the counseling of patience by Luciana, Balthazar, Dr. Pinch, and the officer who interrupts the beating of Dromio E by his master. Dromio's witty reply states a major theme of the play: "Nay, 'tis for me to be patient; I am in adversity" (4.4.20). The play's ostensible models of patience in adversity are Egeon and Emilia.

## Supplementary bibliography

Baldwin, T. W. "Three Homilies in *The Comedy of Errors*," in Richard Hosley, ed., *Essays on Shakespeare and Elizabethan Drama* (University of Missouri Press, 1962), pp. 137–47.

Foakes, R. A. Arden edition, *The Comedy of Errors* (Methuen, 1962), pp. 113–15 ("Sources: The Bible").

Kinney, Arthur. "Shakespeare's *Comedy of Errors* and the Nature of Kinds," *Studies in Philology* 85 (1988), 29–52.

Sanderson, James. "Patience in *The Comedy of Errors*," *Texas Studies in Literature and Language* 16 (1975), 603–18.

Weld, John S. "Old Adam New Apparelled," *Shakespeare Quarterly* 7 (1956), 453–56.

*R. Chris Hassel, Jr. (1979)*

## The Liturgical Context of *Errors* [editor's title]

The account of Gray's Inn Christmas revels for 1594 includes almost unmistakable references to the performance of *The Comedy of Errors* as part of the festivity "upon Innocents-Day at night." We learn that after great confusion and revelry upon the stage of mock ceremony and misrule, and in the face of

> Throngs and Tumults . . . able to disorder and confound any good Inventions whatsoever, it was thought good not to offer any thing of Account, saving Dancing and Revelling with Gentlewomen; and after such Sports, a Comedy of Errors (like to *Plautus* his *Menechmus*) was played by the Players. So that Night was begun, and continued to the end, in nothing but Confusion and Errors; whereupon, it was ever afterwards called, *The Night of Errors*. (*Gesta Greyorum*, ed W. W. Greg, pp. 20, 22)

The secular festival's traditions of misrule and universal confusion are combined in the play and the *Gesta Greyorum* with a more profound celebration of universal human absurdity, a celebration with liturgical overtones. That combination gives us an unusually complete understanding of the general and specific context of the play's festival performance.

Error seems to have been the traditional hallmark of Innocents' celebrations, as well as the badge of their successes. The following night mock charges are brought against the Master of Revels, charges which ironically celebrate the appropriateness of the play to its festival occasion: "And Lastly, that he had foisted a Company of base and common Fellows, to make up our Disorders with a Play of Errors and Confusions; and that that Night had gained to us Discredit, and it self a Nickname of Errors" (p. 23). Discredit is credit in the topsy-turvy Kingdom of Purpoole. The reason, of course, is the centuries-old tradition of beginning the Feast of Fools on Childermas or Innocents' Day. Until the time of the *Spectator*, Innocents was considered for this reason "the most unlucky day in the calendar"; it certainly is so to the inhabitants of Ephesus. Even the abundance of ass and ass-head jokes in the play may have had elusive connections to the festival tradition. In the culminating ceremony of the Feast of Fools, on 1 January, the ass was sometimes led in honor up the aisles of the cathedral. This tradition recalled, of course, the ass's close association with Christ's humility in Bethlehem as well as Jerusalem. Although the Feast of Fools was more common in France than in England, and although it was fairly well suppressed by the middle of the sixteenth century, its survival in the revelry at Gray's Inn suggests that it had not yet been completely forgotten. The subsequent performance of the play at Whitehall before James I on Innocents' Night 1604 reinforces the intimate association of the play and its festive occasion.

A glance at the liturgical tradition of Innocents' Day makes it even less likely that mere nostalgia or coincidence explains the dual performance of the play on that religious festival. The repetition of *nativitie* in the final lines of the play seems to suggest a general awareness of the Christmas season. More specifically, as soon as we read the "proper" Lesson prescribed for Holy Innocents' Day in the *Book of Common Prayer*, we are struck by relationships to the framing story of Egeon and Emilia, Shakespeare's unique addition to his sources. Jer 31:1–17, like the framework of *The Comedy of Errors*, is about the dispersal and reunion of families. In fact, from such other prescribed passages as Bar 4:21–30, Mt 2:13–18, Rv 14:1–5, and Is 60, we realize that this theme was a central motif of the liturgical festival.

Dealing as it does with the Lord's promise to reunite the dispersed and weeping families of Israel, Jeremiah 31 is insistently parallel to the first and final scene of *Errors*. After the Lord's several promises to gather the remnant of Israel from the coasts of the world, verses 15–17, on the ultimate deliverance of all innocents, seem particularly close to the situation and the sensibility of Egeon and Emilia, parents of their own lost children:

> 15  A voice was heard on hie, a mourning and bitter weping, Ra[c]hel weping for her children, . . . because thei were not.

16  Thus saith the Lord, Refraine thy voice from weping, and thine eyes from teares: for thy worke shal be rewarded, saith ye Lord, and thei shal come againe from the land of the enemie.

17  And there is hope in thine end, saith the Lord, that thy children shal come againe to their owne borders.

In the other prescribed passages the theme remains the same: innocents have been scattered or displaced by their enemies, but they will eventually be returned home, even if that home is with the Lamb in heaven. Such strong parallels in narrative, theme, and tone suggest that Shakespeare expected his audience to perceive and appreciate the similarities as part of their dramatic experience.

From *Renaissance Drama & the English Church Year*, pp. 38–41. Copyright 1979 by the University of Nebraska Press. Used by permission.

*Glyn Austen (1987)*

## Redemption in *The Comedy of Errors*

The Early Comedies of Shakespeare, disparate as they are in terms of plot and style, are bound together by fundamental common elements in their dramatic structure, and in their thematic content. Their essential unity is to be seen in structural development by Shakespeare's constant use of a cycle of Redemption moving from tragedy to renewal; and this process is supported thematically by repetitive allusions to "religious" themes—the fall of man, judgement, baptism, penance, exorcism, blessing, to name but some. Shakespeare's purpose throughout is to construct a movement towards a comic catharsis, which operates on two levels. In the context of the play itself, order is restored, tragedy averted, the balance between appearance and reality re-introduced, and ritual celebration made possible. On a secondary level the audience / reader is brought through a process of emotional disorder and tension to release and well-being, so that the play may reasonably be said to have a "sacramental" significance; it is a means by which those who participate in it find a sense of grace and re-creation.

*The Comedy of Errors* begins with Egeon, hapless victim of cruel fate, and of forces over which he has no control. Ephesus and Syracuse are in dispute, apparently due to the shedding of the blood of Ephesian merchants by the Duke of Syracuse, and now any Syracusan unfortunate enough to fall into Ephesian hands is in mortal danger, literally. Duke Solinus stands, ostensibly, as the voice of Law and Justice, which is immutable. For Egeon the prospect is bleak as Solinus declares:

> Thy substance, valued at the highest rate,
> Cannot amount unto a hundred marks;
> Therefore by law thou art condemn'd to die. (1.1.23–5)

He has the rest of the day to raise the necessary ransom, else he must pay the penalty the law requires.

Shakespeare is here creating an outwardly paradoxical conflict between Law and Justice. He causes a schism between the two aspects of judgement which should be inseparable, and which were ideally presented as such by his great contemporary, Richard Hooker, in his *Lawes of Ecclesiastical Politie*, the first four books of which were published in 1593. For Hooker there is an essential harmony between law itself, whose "seat is the bosom of God," and the temporal Prince, who is its executor, and is described as a father-figure. Shakespeare, however, undermines this unity at the outset by revealing the law, in this case, as unjust. Egeon has committed no crime worthy of death, yet die he must. Hooker's father-prince has graphically become two people: Solinus the Duke, and Egeon the father. There is a sickness at the heart of Ephesus in this schism which gives a structural impetus in the play for the confusions which are to follow. The sickness of an unmitigable and merciless legal system is clearly reflected in the disordered society we are soon to behold.

Egeon's fate is starkly revealed in this first scene as a fall from grace, which reflects significantly on the direction the plot of *Errors* will take, and the conclusion it will reveal. In the very first line we hear the words:

> Proceed, Solinus, to procure my fall. . . . (1.1.1)

"Fall" and the subsequent reference to the "doom of death" (1.1.2) are deliberately evocative of the Creation story of Genesis; and this point is underlined soon after when Egeon speaks of his wife "almost at fainting under / The pleasing punishment that women bear" (1.1.46)—an unmistakable allusion to the childbirth pains imposed on Eve as a penalty for sin. Sin and judgement, grace and redemption, form the thematic context of *The Comedy of Errors*. The Christian cycle from Fall to Redemption is continuously injected, by allusion, into the tale so as to underpin, and reflect upon, the working out of the comic structure.

If we turn, briefly, to the final Act, we see that the comic process has indeed brought about an entirely different complexion on events for Egeon. By now the conflict between Law and Justice has been resolved—or rather bypassed—by the interposition of what can only be termed as grace. When the son of the condemned prisoner, Antipholus of Ephesus, offers the required ransom, the Duke replies,

> It shall not need, thy father hath his life. (5.1.390)

This sea-change has become possible because of the sacramental nature of the denouement. Egeon has been literally redeemed: bought out of his fate within and by the dramatic structure of the comedy; and his judgement and redemption form both a frame for the comic action and a commentary upon it. On the very road to execution he finds life, and it is life bought not by money, but by the experience of the drama itself.

The festival joy of the conclusion has its value only as an adjunct to, and a reversal of, the misery of the first scene. Comedy itself as a renewing force only has potency if there is a clear alternative of disorder and unhappiness, and the fact that we know that all will be well does not diminish our ability to enter into Egeon's experience of tragedy.

Beneath the farcical hilarity of the Ephesian world, Shakespeare constructs a framework of evil, corruption and disorder that is simultaneously comic and sinister. On the surface is a typical mercantile society of merchants and tradesmen, cargo ships and inns—a model, indeed, of the dramatist's London. Yet Ephesus is nonetheless fully itself in the occult associations which Shakespeare stresses, and which have their root in a familiar passage from The Acts of the Apostles. We read in Acts Chapter 19 of the effect of the preaching of St Paul on the Ephesian people, showing the extent of the interest in the black arts:

> Many also of those who were now believers came, confessing and divulging their practices. And a number of those who practiced magic arts brought their books together and burned them in the sight of all; and they counted the value of them and found it came to fifty thousand pieces of silver. (Acts 19:18–19, RSV)

Shakespeare's primary reason for shifting the setting from the Epidamnum of his Plautine source to Ephesus would have been to capitalize on the proverbial quality of the latter as a disordered society.

Shakespeare takes every available opportunity to build on the theme of the connection between Ephesus and witchcraft, by continuously alluding to the presence of evil, and by counterbalancing these associations of sin (elaborated by Antipholus in 1.2.97–100) with subtle Christian elements. The farce, then, is built upon a religious conflict, and it will lead to an ending with deep religious significance. By the end of Act 2 poor Antipholus of Syracuse, bewildered by the "wife" he has acquired, cries out:

> O for my beads; I cross me for a sinner
> This is the fairy land; O spite of spites,
> We talk with goblins, elves and sprites. (2.2.188–90)

And the following lines are reminiscent of the antics of morality play devils:

> If we obey them not this will ensue—
> They'll suck our breath, or pinch us black and blue. (2.2.191–2)

The references to the prayer-beads, and to crossing oneself, show Antipholus clinging to Christian symbols of redemption; yet equally his nightmare world is one born out of a popular superstitious awareness which borders on the pagan. "Fallenness" has been established as the state of Egeon, and Shakespeare is painting in the backcloth of a world order which is fallen, with good ranged against evil, God against devil, and conflict the crucible from which renewal will emerge. The objective credibility of the supernatural is, frankly, not under debate here—it is irrelevant to the dramatist's purpose. What matters is that it is becoming more and more real for the protagonists.

In the person of Pinch, the "Schoolmaster"—presumably learned in the Latin tongue, and therefore able to address evil spirits—we encounter a figure who has both Christian and pagan antecedents. Adriana calls him a "conjurer" (4.4.45), and Antipholus of Ephesus cries, "Peace, doting wizard, peace" (4.4.56). Yet he seems to be on the right side in the good / evil contest. Encountering the enraged Antipholus of Ephesus, Pinch is in no doubt that his "ecstasy" is of diabolic origin, and launches into an immediate exorcism, which is, indeed, an overtly Christian rite:

> I charge thee, Satan, hous'd within this man,
> To yield possession to my holy prayers,
> And to thy state of darkness hie thee straight;
> I conjure thee by all the saints in heaven. (4.4.52–55)

This exorcism is structurally most important, coming as it does at a climactic point prior to the restoration of order of Act 5; and it is thematically crucial, for exorcism is a symbol of deliverance that the play's society increasingly craves.

Again and again Ephesus is depicted as hellish in its disorder. For example, when Adriana asks Dromio of Syracuse how his master is (meaning, naturally, the other Antipholus), he responds that "he's in Tartar Limbo, worse than hell." Tartar, or the Mohammedan, Limbo is presumably worse than the Christian one! And the officer who has arrested Antipholus of Ephesus is "A devil in an everlasting garment" (4.2.31–32). Later Dromio is to call the officer "old Adam new-apparelled" (4.3.13–14), suggestive of the fall of Man in the Genesis myth, and yet also recalling Ephesians 4:22–24, in which St Paul writes of casting off the old man and putting on the new, i.e. the new man created in Christ. Dromio is making a theological pun,

> . . . translating the whole action of Antipholus' arrest in the terms of bondage
> to sin, damnation, and redemption. (J. S. Weld, *SQ* 7, 455)

I have argued that the renewal and redemption of the final Act is presented as "grace"—in other words, not earned, or struggled through to, but, to define the term, freely given. Grace is the antithesis of something bought. So it is that the grace which the comic structure is to provide, and always provides, is made all the more stark and significant by the manifest failure of the protagonists to buy or trade order and contentment. Again and again the motifs of confusion are monetary in nature: money is passed by Antipholus of Syracuse to his servant; a precious chain is intended to be given to Adriana by her husband Antipholus of Ephesus; the Courtesan has a ring; Adriana gives more money to bail out her spouse.

Trade is the concern of Ephesus, based on financial profit and loss, and the value-symbols of that financial world are catalysts of failure and disorder throughout, just as trade has failed Egeon. And so matters proceed, until the Abbess intervenes, until brother meets brother, until unearned pardon for Egeon—all of which transforms Ephesus, like sacramental grace.

[Egeon] stands, to a degree, as a representative of humanity, worn and beaten by life's vicissitudes—a victim, in terms of the play's own "fall" language of a world order renewable only by external grace. His own loss of identity is constantly echoed in the experience of his sons and their men; for this is the personal fruit of a cosmic confrontation between order and evil. As the play progresses, the protagonists come to know themselves less and less, until the point arrives, is imposed, when self-knowledge becomes a possibility. Theologically, the process of the play draws on the Pauline concept of casting off the old man and putting on the new (i.e., the new man re-created in Christ); and it is valid for us to make this connection since the ethos of *Errors* is so manifestly a Christian one. The new man is literally put on in Act 5 when redemption comes, as we move from tragedy to comedy, disorder to order, fall to grace. It is surely no coincidence that we find this image developed in Paul's *Letter to the Ephesians*. The changed man (in Christ) is exhorted to

> ... be renewed in the spirit of your mind; and that ye put on the new man, which after God is created in righteousness and true holiness. (Eph 4:23–24, AV)

These verses formed part of the Epistle read at Holy Communion for the Nineteenth Sunday after Trinity in the *Book of Common Prayer*. We may presume Shakespeare's knowledge of this passage.

Structurally, the most important entrance in the entire play is Emilia's, in 5.1. Her exclusion has allowed the Ephesian world to draw close to death, madness, violence, and the disintegration of personality. The social order has become "possessed," and Act 5 serves as a general exorcism, with Emilia as the officiant. We have been prepared for this process of deliverance by the exorcist Pinch, and by several other references in the course of the main plot, such as when Antipholus of Syracuse cries out to the Courtesan as if she were an evil spirit:

> Avoid then, fiend, what tellest thou me of supping?
> Thou art, as you are all, a sorceress;
> I conjure thee to leave me and be gone. (4.3.63–5)

The dramatist is, I would argue, utilizing a familiar Christian setting (from Acts and Ephesians) together with a dependence on the Christian "myth"—the story of the world's cycle from fall to redemption—to underpin his primary aim in the play, which is to allow the comic structure to be seen as re-creative, sacramental in its effect. The Abbess Emilia is the (long-hidden) means by which the play-structure leads through to new life, to a new order.

The abbess's first words express her role as the calmer of the storm: "Be quiet, people; wherefore throng you hither?" (5.1.32) And immediately afterwards she instructs Adriana in what becomes a wifely catechism: the broken marriage-bond is being addressed, not without irony as mother-protectress confronts wife. Emilia's priory offers a womb-like security, within which the Syracusan pair enter "for sanctuary" (5.1.94); and Emilia claims that she will treat Antipholus herself with "wholesome syrups, drugs and holy prayers," since

> It is a branch and parcel of mine oath.
> A charitable duty of my order (5.1.106–7)

She is identified as a nursing sister, minister of healing and wholeness, and the only character able to restore order, even rivalling the Duke as a symbol of effective power. He is at a loss to unravel all the confusions following the entry of the Ephesian master and man, and orders helplessly, "Why, this is strange; go, call the abbess hither." (5.1.281) Emilia emerges, bringing with her the Syracusans, and thus we find both sets of twins on stage for the first time. The restorative process has begun, with a concomitant return to the romance theme. Again we hear of "the fatal raft" (5.1.354), and "rude fisherman of Corinth" (5.1.357), and the first scene is recalled, save that the tragic has become the comic.

Identity may now be rediscovered: wives find husbands, brothers are reunited, social cohesion is restored. For Egeon death is no more, since the penalty of the law is remitted at a stroke. In short, grace has come to Ephesus, and the "new man" has come to being. Throughout this final Act Christian references and allusions are numerous—to provide a philosophical (even theological) undergirding for the plot structure. The redemption which has come to Ephesus (as in Paul's Ephesus) is presented with a deliberately Christian vocabulary which underlines again and again the sacramental nature of what is happening.

The conclusions of *Errors* are manifestly a new birth, for society and individuals. Emilia declares:

> Thirty-three years have I but gone in travail
> Of you, my sons, and till this present hour
> My heavy burden ne'er delivered. (5.1.400–2)

It is not coincidence that her gestation period parallels the traditional view of Christ's earthly span, surely. Her deliverance from travail, also, recalls the possession theme deep-rooted in the central action, and, as I have noted, shows the exorcistic nature of the play's resolution. Yet it is in the last words of the Abbess that the relationship between the action of the play and the Christian cycle from fall to grace is finally cemented:

> Go to a gossips' feast with me,
> After so long grief such felicity. (5.1.405–6)

The gossips' feast is a baptismal feast, a celebration of the primary Christian sacrament of regeneration and resurrection. More is going on here than simply a happy ending: the play is revealing Comedy as fundamentally linked with religious experience, and is, in effect, a religious experience itself. As R. C. Hassel remarks:

> Communion in Shakespearian comedy transcends the literal feast to become a sharing of psychological, aesthetic and perhaps even religious insight. (*Shakespeare-Jahrbuch* 106 [1970], 161)

The baptism allusion recalls the water of the sea-journey in Act 1 scene 1, and here, at the play's end, it serves to stress the purgative and redemptive nature of events. Baptism, a sacramental act, stands at the absolute climax of *Errors* as a symbol of the grace which has been bestowed. The process from death to rebirth is skillfully sealed by its appearance, and the grace-bestowing essence of the comic form is given a perfect thematic conclusion.

From "Ephesus Restored: Sacramentalism and Redemption in *The Comedy of Errors*," *Journal of Literature & Theology* 1 (1987), 54–69 abridged. Used by permission of Oxford University Press.

# THE MERCHANT OF VENICE

## Comment and bibliography

Central to this play is the test of the three caskets, a parable about the Christian paradox of losing things worldly to gain things heavenly. No suitor for the virtuous beauty of the Lady of Belmont can succeed without being willing to "give and hazard" all he has. In particular, he must be able to subordinate all love of gold (external shows for the "eye") and all love of silvery self-justification (rewards for the "I") and give first of all an open ear to Portia's words: "I stand for sacrifice." Bassanio's preparation for meeting this test includes a knowledge of his prior loss of fortune through prodigality and his present dependence on a friend's sacrificial loan. He can therefore listen well to Portia's admonition to "Pause a day or two before you *hazard*," and to her "Beshrew your eyes" so that "If you do love me you will *find me* out." Portia, although bound by her father's will not to teach any suitor how to choose right, may nevertheless favor with means for learning how whoever has a heart with open ears. Grace and law are not exclusive of each other, and grace is given when an aptitude for it is evident. "Let music sound," says Portia, thus enabling Bassanio to make his choice amid a background of old song that invites the hearer to "ring fancy's knell."

But if law and grace need not be mutually exclusive, neither are justice and mercy, or the letter of the law and the spirit hidden behind the letter. Just as the law of Moses depends on a God who mercifully delivered Israel from Egypt, so also that law's purpose or end is charitable love, and likewise the law of Venice in this drama requires not solely the keeping of sworn bonds but also a recognizing of the purpose of protecting life that validates bonds. It is therefore not by mere quibbling or trickery, as some critics of the play would suppose, that Portia defeats Shylock, but rather by revealing the heart of the law within its literal demands. She herself embodies the mercy of intercession, which was the spirit of the God of Moses. And it is because Antonio hears the call for mercy in her legal presentation that he can subsequently offer Shylock both mercy and justice, and thus return good for evil, and indeed now offer brotherhood to a neighbor he formerly treated as an outsider.

The superiority of the law-of-the-spirit to the bond of the letter is the theme underlying the business of the rings which concludes the play. Bassanio when aided by Antonio can be moved to give his wedding ring as a debt of gratitude to the "Doctor" who deserves this—and who, he will discover, gave it him to begin with as an outward token of a larger and spiritual commitment. Portia's secret intervention as a Daniel-like Balthazar is the inner truth of her pretended retirement to a monastery and her stopping at wayside "crosses" to pray during her journey away from Belmont.

Shakespeare's great achievement in this play is his integration of major motifs inherited from Christian story—the three caskets; a ring given and returned and given again; and a pound of flesh sought for, confounded, and then bestowed in a transformed sense. Shylock is the secretly malicious seeker for a pound of flesh, his hoped-for means of revenge. He thinks it a just payment for his abused dignity, which he values even more than his ducats. But his greed gets confounded by his blindness to true justice, evident in his bewildered cry "Is this the law?" and then he is given a humane sentence that incorporates him into a community of recon- cilement. Thus he receives "a pound of flesh" in the sense of "a measure of human love"—a flesh of spiritual brotherhood.

Those critics who nowadays complain that the play's final festivities do not include Shylock have overlooked his presence by proxy. He has signed a will and sent it for the occasion. A will is in legal parlance a deed. Shylock is present indeed at the feast of joy in which he is said to drop "manna." The story concludes, as in other of Shakespeare's comedies, with a new beginning in token form that is open to enlargement.

Selected for our anthology are seven pieces of pertinent commentary. J. A. Bryant views Antonio and Portia as the two saviors of Bassanio, representing sym- bolically the human and the divine aspects of Christ, whose role of ransoming they enact figuratively. Barbara Lewalski uses categories from Dante for expound- ing levels of meaning in Shakespeare's drama. John Cooper points out usefully that Shylock's eloquent defense of revenge appeals to a common humanity that Shakespeare's audience would have recognized as our "fallen" humanity. Joan Holmer notices that Shylock's preference for Barabbas fits his symbolic role of the "faithless" Jew, and that his appreciation of Jacob's increase in wealth adheres to the letter rather than the spirit of Bible story. Lawrence Danson develops two im- portant points: 1) a *puer senex* paradox is manifest in Portia's rescuing role as Bal- thazar; and 2) Shylock's conversion is symbolic of the conversion of the Jews hoped for by St Paul and predicted by him as the gift the Gentiles would bring the Jews. Jewish obstinacy can be viewed paradoxically as a *felix culpa* that benefits all man- kind (Rom 11:28).

Austin Dobbins and Roy Battenhouse bring out the significance of the sub- plot story of Jessica's elopement. It is she, they point out, who embodies the spirit of the founders of Judaism since, in her exodus from a house of bondage compa- rable to Pharaoh's Egypt, she takes with her as Israel did the "spoils" of Egyptian gold. Mark Gnerro notes in justification of Jessica's elopement the evidence pro- vided in her love duet with Lorenzo in Act 5, which as Gnerro points out echoes the "night" at the Red Sea celebrated in the Christian liturgy of Holy Saturday.

In supplementary essays, the significance of the doctrines of *felix culpa* and of the "blessed night" of Israel's deliverance is developed further by Gary Grund's documented references to Ambrose, Hooker, Andrewes, and Donne. The Paschal liturgy, Grund explains, "serves as a unifying cultural framework for the play and organizes a series of redemptions—Portia's, Bassanio's, Antonio's and Jessica's—into a coherent and vital pattern of meaning easily recognizable by Shakespeare's audience" (p. 64). Grund also aptly quotes Jessica's seeing in Portia the "joys of heaven here on earth" (3.5.70).

The function of Launcelot Gobbo, as explained in René Fortin's essay, is to focus our attention on the theme of filial piety and on the play's allegory of the transference of divine favor from the "old" Jewish dispensation to the Christian dispensation. Old Gobbo, Launcelot's sandblind father, is analogous to the spiritually blind Isaac of biblical story, who had to be tricked into transferring to Jacob the family birthright, a blessing far more important than material wealth. Jacob (as Paul explains in Romans 9–11) is a figure of Israel's "child of promise," the Jew of "faith." Ironically, in the play, Shylock begins as a "faithless" Jew who has to be deceived by a Rebecca-like daughter (Jessica). Her righteousness of faith embraces the Gentile Lorenzo, and subsequently Shylock is prompted by Antonio to make Lorenzo (with Jessica) his heir. His early reference to the "wise mother" Rebecca (in 1.3.69) illustrates St Paul's point that "hardened" Jews cite Scripture without understanding it (Rom 10:8). Providentially, the Gentiles become God's instrument for restoring the Jews to the "election" promised them by grace.

John Coolidge, after citing Tyndale's comment that the Jews have lost the spiritual knowledge "of all the Scripture," suggests that the play can be read as reflecting a "contest between Christian and Jew for the possession of the Hebrew Scriptures." The meaning to be chosen in the caskets is that of Christian love hidden beneath a forbidding exterior. Various passages in the play accord with Jesus' rebuke of the legalists and with the implication of Dt 23:20 that usury is an estrangement, for which the remedy is Lk 6:35, "Lend, looking for nothing again." Coolidge says the play may be called "a work of Christian apologetics."

Joan Holmer's second essay elaborates on the point that Antonio and Shylock, who begin as persons blinded by pride and hatred respectively, are both educated by painful reverses in the course of the play. Nevill Coghill was the earliest critic after Gollancz to sketch the play's allegorical meaning. John Doebler reviews its "iconic" imagery, and Allan Holaday the influence of the Parliament-in-Heaven motif. Benjamin Nelson and Celeste Wright both discuss theological views of usury. Frank McCombie finds in Portia the characteristics ascribed to Wisdom in Old Testament literature. Lonnell Johnson explores the likeness of Portia to Daniel. Warren Smith defends the play against the charge of anti-semitism.

## Supplementary bibliography

Coghill, Nevill. "The Theme of *The Merchant of Venice*," rptd. in *Twentieth Century Interpretations*, ed. Sylvan Barnet (Englewood Cliffs: Prentice Hall, 1970).

Coolidge, John S. "Law and Love in *The Merchant of Venice*," *Shakespeare Quarterly* 27 (1976), 243–63. Cf. Coolidge's *The Pauline Renaissance in England: Puritanism and the Bible* (Cambridge University Press, 1970).

Doebler, John. "*The Merchant of Venice*: Divine Comedy," in *Shakespeare's Speaking Pictures* (University of New Mexico Press, 1974), pp. 39–65.

Fortin, René. "Launcelot and the Uses of Allegory in *The Merchant of Venice*," *Studies in English Literature* 14 (1974), 259–70.

Fowler, David. *The Bible in Early English Literature* (University of Washington Press, 1976), p. 52, on the meaning of Jacob's mottled rods in 1.3.

Grund, Gary R. "The Fortunate Fall and Shakespeare's *Merchant of Venice*," *Studia Neophilologica* 55 (1983), 153–65.

Holaday, Allan. "Antonio and the Allegory of Salvation," *Shakespeare Studies* 4 (1968), 109–18.

Holmer, Joan O. "The Education of the Merchant of Venice," *Studies in English Literature* 25 (1985), 307–35.

Johnson, Lonnell E. "Shylock's Daniel," *College Language Association Journal* 35 (1992), 353–66.

Levitsky, Ruth. "Shylock as Unregenerate Man," *Shakespeare Quarterly* 28 (1977), 58–64.

McCombie, Frank. "Wisdom as Touchstone in *The Merchant of Venice*," *New Blackfriars* 64 (1983), 113–23.

Milward, Peter. "The Religious Implications of *The Merchant of Venice*," in *Shakespeare's Other Dimension* (Tokyo, 1989), pp. 29–46.

Nelson, Benjamin. *The Idea of Usury* (Princeton University Press, 1949), pp. 141–54.

Smith, Warren D. "Shakespeare's Shylock," *Shakespeare Quarterly* 15 (1964), 193–99.

Taylor, Myron. "The Passion of Antonio: A Reply to Recent Critics," *Christian Scholar* 49 (1966), 127–31.

Wright, Celeste. "The Usurer's Sin in Elizabethan Literature," *Studies in Philology* 35 (1938), 178–94.

*J. A. Bryant, Jr. (1961)*

## Bassanio's Two Saviors [editor's title]

Sir Israel Gollancz in some delightfully informal essays justified the *Merchant of Venice* as a Christian allegory after the manner of the late medieval morality plays.[1] He cited two texts as fundamental to the interpretation of the play. The first, "Greater love hath no man than this, that a man should lay down his life for his friend" (Jn 15:13), relates obviously to the business of the bond; and the second, taken from Ephesians, "Christ also loved the Church and gave himself for it" (Eph 5:25), has in addition some applicability to the love making, the caskets and

Portia's successful attempt to resolve the moral indebtedness of her husband. Along with J. D. Rea and Hope Traver, Gollancz also saw the bond element of the story as deriving from the medieval versions of the debate of the four heavenly daughters (based on Ps 85) and the medieval stories about Satan's arraignment of the Redeemer.[2]

Benjamin N. Nelson, acknowledging Gollancz's work, finds that it makes the play a minor document in the history of the idea of usury. "Antonio's heroic suretyship to Shylock for Bassanio," he writes, "finds its prototype in Christ's act in serving as 'ransom' to the Devil for all mankind."[3] And Nevill Coghill, who has undertaken to develop some of the implications of Gollancz's essays about the medieval background of *The Merchant*, has found the play more fundamentally Christian even than its medieval prototypes. Coghill describes the play as "an *exemplum* in modern dress" on the theme of Justice and Mercy, the Old Law and the New; it asserts the rightness of both principles, he believes, and the need for some sort of compromise between them—justice yielding a little to mercy, and mercy yielding a little to justice.[4]

Gollancz, Nelson, and Coghill, who have all seen Antonio as a figure of Christ, the perfect friend who so loved man that he gave himself for him, may be accused of unwarranted spiritualizing or allegorizing; but the analogy that leads them on is substantially supported by Antonio's letter, which Bassanio reads aloud to Portia at the close of the second scene in Act 3:

> Sweet Bassanio, my ships have all miscarried, my creditors grow cruel, my estate is very low, my bond to the Jew is forfeit; and since in paying it, it is impossible I should live, all debts are cleared between you and I, if I might but see you at my death. Notwithstanding, use your pleasure; if your love do not persuade you to come, let not my letter. (2.3.318–25)

We might dismiss as something demanded by the plot Antonio's observation, "my bond to the Jew is forfeit; and . . . in paying it, it is impossible I should live." Nevertheless, it would be difficult to find in all the Renaissance literary examples of perfect friendship a neater statement of a neater parallel to Christ's voluntary assumption of the debt that was death to repay. And one does not find among such examples a satisfactory parallel to Antonio's demand upon Bassanio, which follows immediately: "all debts are cleared between you and I, if I might but see you at my death." Here we are beyond Platonism and completely within the realm of Christian dogma, which holds that the sinner is not ransomed by the death of the Saviour unless he witnesses that death.

Taking Antonio as a figure of Christ, however, raises the question of what to do with Portia; for in the *Gesta* version of the casket story Portia is the Christ, "which the chosen men choose," and in the bond story she is the "daughter" of Christ, "the sowle I-made to the similitude of god." A good deal of this is retained in *The Merchant of Venice*. As the Prince of Morocco so eloquently testifies, Portia is the bride whom all the world desires: "From the four corners of the earth they come" (2.7.39). But, more important, she is the bride-intended only for the elect. "O me, the word choose!" she complains to Nerissa. "I may neither choose who I would nor refuse who I dislike." Nerissa's reply could stand for the reply of almost any theologian, Calvinist or Catholic, to a catechumen disturbed by the doctrine of election:

> Your father was ever virtuous, and holy men at their death have good inspirations; therefore the lott'ry that he hath devised in these three chests of gold, silver, and lead, whereof who chooses his meaning chooses you, will, no doubt, never be chosen by any rightly but one who you shall rightly love. (1.2.30–36)

And, indeed, when the casket story reaches its climax, we are hard put to say who really does choose, so ardent are they both, Bassanio and Portia, in desiring one another. When she discovers, however, that her husband is not really free and cannot be hers until Antonio's debt is paid, she offers "To pay the petty debt twenty times over," and sends him away with "Since you are dear bought, I will love you dear."

The triumph of mercy in this play comes not in Act 4 but in the disposition of Bassanio in Act 5, where a young man who has seemingly deserved nothing at last comes to merit and get everything, all because two people love him and are willing to give and hazard all they have for him. What we need to keep clearly in mind throughout the trial scene is that Portia is as much Bassanio's savior as Antonio is. Her whole objective in coming to the trial, as her trick about the ring at the close of that scene shows, is to snare Bassanio, her means to rescue Antonio from Shylock's grasp, and her reason for tolerating in "godlike amity" Antonio's claim upon her husband's affections is that she sees in Antonio the image of herself (3.4.16–21). Antonio, as the play has it, is saved principally for the sake of Bassanio. For without Antonio's initial willingness to give himself, Bassanio could never have come to the lady in the first place; and without the lady's willingness to rescue Antonio from the consequences of his awful hazard, Bassanio, untested by the lady's device at the trial, would have remained unregenerate, simply another adventurer, not worth much to anybody.

The debate of the Heavenly Daughters can help us understand Portia's part in the play provided we do not lean exclusively on late medieval representations of it. In the year of Shakespeare's death the Anglican John Boys published an exposition of Psalm 85, proper for Christmas Day morning prayer, which is much more relevant to *The Merchant of Venice* than are *Piers Plowman* and *The Castle of Perseverance*. Boys begins with the traditional explanation:

> In Christ aduent, *Mercy and truth are met together,* righteousnesse and peace haue kissed each other. Bernard hath a prettie dialogue to his purpose, betweene *righteousnesse* and *truth* on the one side, *mercy* and *peace* on the other part, contending about the redemption of mankinde. Christ our blessed Mes-

sias and Mediator ended the quarrell at his coming, and made them all exceeding kinde kissing friends: for in giuing himselfe a ransome for all men, he did at once pay both vnto *Iustice* her debt, and grant vnto *Mercy* her desire.[5]

Then he proceeds to amplify, first, with the suggestion that Coghill worked into his interpretation of *The Merchant*: "Righteousness and peace meet in Christ, God and man: for by these two, some Diuines vnderstand the Old Testament and the New." After this, Boys advances a totally new suggestion, which illuminates the play better than any that has been made so far:

> Or by these two vertues vnderstand Christs two natures, his diuine nature by *mercie*, hauing power to forgiue sinnes, and to heale all manner of sicknesse; by *truth* his humane nature.... And this exposition is more probable by the next verse [Ps 85:11]: *Truth shall flourish out of the earth, and righteousness hath looked down from heauen.* Christ is *truthe*, as he saith of himselfe, *I am the way, the truth, etc.* and Christ is our righteousness, 1 Cor 1:30. Now Christ as man, and borne of the Virgin Mary, *budded out of the earth:* and as God, he looked down from *heauen.* That men might be iustified by grace from heauen, it pleased him on this day to *bud out of the earth.*[6]

Whether or not one accepts as relevant the analogy suggested by Boys' exposition (Antonio representing Christ's physical nature, which offered a physical body as sacrifice; and Portia representing Christ's divine nature, offering forgiveness), one is almost bound, it seems to me, to accept the functional identity of Antonio and Portia. They are united in opposition to Shylock and united in their effort to claim Bassanio for their side; they are united, moreover, in their method, which as John R. Brown has pointed out in his recent edition of the play,[7] is that of "giving and hazarding" all they have and expecting nothing in return. They are opposed, however, as truth and mercy are opposed, or as any two halves of a whole may be said to be opposed. Each is a partial manifestation of what, according to the Christian idea of human regeneration, it takes to save a man.... It takes both friend and bride, working together, each for the other and jointly for Bassanio, to bring about a transformation in the young man.

Bassanio, like Gianetto in *Il Pecorone*, is asked to give up his ring, and like Gianetto he refuses on the ground that his wife gave it to him. The differences here are two. Gianetto in refusing speaks eloquently of his love for his wife ("I love her better than I love myself.... I would not exchange her for any woman in the world"), yet he gives up the ring without any outside prompting (the bondsman is not even present) in apparent recognition of the supreme obligation that he has to the savior of his friend. Bassanio, free and clear, recognizes no supreme obligation. He would give a present of three thousand ducats, but he is by no means prepared to give and hazard all he has until Antonio shames him into it by saying, "Let his deservings and my love withal / Be valued 'gainst your wife's commandment." Worse still, he gives no indication that he cherishes the ring as anything more than a pledge of his newly acquired wealth:

> Good sir, this ring was given me by my wife;
> And when she put it on, she made me vow
> That I should neither sell nor give nor lose it. (4.1.441–43)

Portia's reply is precise and to the point: "That 'scuse serves many men to save their gifts." The important point, however, is that he does surrender the ring. Nevill Coghill, in defending the conversion of Shylock as an act of mercy, comments, "Mercy has triumphed over justice, even if the way of mercy is a hard way." He might have said something like this about Bassanio with equal propriety. Bassanio comes into his reward in the hardest possible way. He gives up his old nature with diffidence and pain. He is among those elect who make it to the table only because they are pushed.

At the table, however, the feast is the same for everybody, and Bassanio takes his seat at it, with his eyes, for the first time, wide open. When Portia charges him with his sin, which properly motivated would have been no sin at all, he shows an understanding of honor and gratitude that were completely lacking at the time of the event:

> I was enforc'd to send it after him;
> I was beset with shame and courtesy;
> My honour would not let ingratitude
> So much besmear it. (5.1.216–19)

Most important of all, however, is his recognition of what it is that justifies his seat at Belmont:

> Bassanio    Portia, forgive me this enforced wrong;
> And in the hearing of these many friends
> I swear to thee, even by thine own fair eyes,
> Wherein I see myself—
> Portia            Mark you but that!
> In both my eyes he doubly sees himself,
> In each eye, one. Swear by your double self,
> And there's an oath of credit. (240–46)

And instantly Bassanio complies, swearing by his true "double self" the oath that cannot be broken:

> Pardon this fault, and by my soul I swear
> I never more will break an oath with thee. (247–48)

Beyond this Bassanio cannot go, and Antonio steps in with a reminder that his sacrifice for Bassanio is as eternal as his friendship:

> I once did lend my body for his wealth,
> Which, but for him that had your husband's ring,
> Had quite miscarried. I dare be bound again,
> My soul upon the forfeit, that your lord
> Will never more break faith advisedly. (249–53)

"Then," says Portia, tying the whole matter up, "you shall be his surety," and she returns the ring to her husband. Bassanio, having acknowledged both agents of his redemption, his friend and his bride, is at last entitled to wear it.

## Notes

1   *Allegory and Mysticism in Shakespeare* (London, 1931).
2   See Hope Traver, "Four Daughters of God," *PMLA*, 40 (1925), 44–92, and J. D. Rea, "Shylock and the *Processus Belial*," *Philological Quarterly* 7 (1929), 311–13.
3   *The Idea of Usury* (Princeton, 1949), 144 n.
4   "The Governing Idea. Essays in Stage Interpretation of Shakespeare," *Shakespeare Quarterly* (Vienna), 1 (1947), 12.
5   *The Works of John Boys, Doctor in Diuinitie and Deane of Canterburie* (London, 1622), 803.
6   *Boys*, 804.
7   *The Merchant of Venice* (1957), pp. lvii-lviii.

From *Hippolyta's View: Some Christian Aspects of Shakespeare's Plays*, pp. 34–47 abridged. Copyright 1961, the University Press of Kentucky; renewed 1989 by J. A. Bryant, Jr.

*Barbara K. Lewalski (1962)*

## Allegory in *The Merchant of Venice*

The allegorical aspects of *The Merchant of Venice* can, I believe, be greatly illuminated by the medieval allegorical method exemplified by Dante.... In contrast to personification allegory wherein a particular is created to embody an insensible, Dante's symbolic method causes a particular real situation to suggest a meaning or meanings beyond itself. In *MV* Shakespeare, like Dante, is ultimately concerned with the nature of the Christian life, though as dramatist he is fully as interested in the way in which the allegorical dimensions enrich the particular instance as in the use of the particular to point to higher levels of meaning. The various dimensions of allegorical significance in *MV*, though not consistently maintained throughout the play and not susceptible of analysis with schematic rigor, are generally analogous to Dante's four levels of allegorical meaning: a literal or story level; an allegorical significance concerned with truths relating to humanity as a whole and to Christ as head of humanity; a moral or tropological level dealing with factors in the moral development of the individual; and an anagogical significance treating the ultimate reality, the Heavenly City. Moreover, comprehension of the play's allegorical meanings leads to a recognition of its fundamental unity, discrediting the common critical view that it is a hotchpotch which developed contrary to Shakespeare's conscious intention.

The use of Biblical allusion to point to such allegorical meanings must now be illustrated in relation to the various parts of the work.

At what would correspond in medieval terminology to the "moral" level, the play is concerned to explore and define Christian love and its various antitheses. As revealed in the action, Christian love involves both giving and forgiving: it demands an attitude of carelessness regarding the things of this world founded upon a trust in God's providence; an attitude of self-forgetfulness and humility founded upon recognition of man's common sinfulness; a readiness to give and risk everything, possessions and person, for the sake of love; and a willingness to forgive injuries and to love enemies. In all but the last respect, Antonio is presented throughout the play as the very embodiment of Christian love, and Shylock functions as one (but not the only) antithesis to it.

Antonio's practice of Christian love is indicated throughout the play under the metaphor of "venturing," and the action begins with the use of this metaphor in a mock test of his attitude toward wealth and worldly goods. The key scripture text opposing love of this world to the Christian love of God and neighbor is Mt 6:19–21:

> Lay not up treasures for your selves upon the earth, where the moth and canker corrupt, & where theeves dig through, and steale. / But lay up treasures for your selves in heaven....

The quality of Antonio's love is shown in the positive forms of charity and benevolence.... Though his first loan to Bassanio has not been repaid, Antonio is willing to "venture" again for his friend "My purse, my person, my extremest means" (1.1.138), even to the pledge of a pound of his flesh. And when this pledge (and with it his life) is forfeit, he can still release Bassanio from debt: "debts are clear'd between you and I" (3.2.317). Furthermore, Antonio lends money in the community at large without seeking interest, and often aids victims of Shylock's usurious practices.

Shylock's "thrift" poses the precise contrast to Antonio's "ventures." His is the worldliness of niggardly prudence, well-characterized by his avowed motto, "Fast bind, fast find, / A proverb never stale in thrifty mind" (2.5.53–54). He locks up house and stores before departing, he begrudges food and maintenance to his servant Launcelot, he demands usurious "assurance" before lending money. This concern with the world poisons all his relations with others and even his love for Jessica: the confused cries, "My daughter! O my ducats! O my daughter!" after Jessica's departure (2.8.15), reveal, not his lack of love for his daughter, but his laughable and pitiable inability to determine what he loves most.

Antonio at the outset of the play is rather in the position of the publican described as friendly to his brethren only—he loves and forgives Bassanio beyond all measure, but hates and reviles Shylock. For evidence of this we have not only Shylock's indictment. "You call me misbeliever, cut-throat dog, / And spet upon my Jewish gaberdine, / . . . And foot me as you spurn a stranger cur" (1.3.106–7, 113), but also Antonio's angry reply promising continuation of such treatment: "I am as like to call thee so again, / To spet on thee again, to spurn thee too." (1.3.125–6) Indeed, the moral tension of the play is lost if we do not see that Shylock, having been the object of great wrongs, must make a difficult choice between forgiveness and revenge—and that Antonio later finds himself in precisely the same situation.

Ironically, Shylock poses at first as the more "Christian" of the two in that, after detailing his wrongs, he explicitly proposes to turn the other cheek. Of course it is merely pretence: Shylock has declared for revenge at the first sight of Antonio (1.3.41–42), and according to Jessica's later report, he eagerly planned for the forfeit of Antonio's flesh long before the bond came due (3.2.283–87). And in this fixed commitment to revenge, this mockery of forgiveness, lies I believe the reason for the often deplored change from the "human" Shylock of the earlier scenes to the "monster" of Act 4. At the level of the moral allegory Shylock undergoes (rather like Milton's Satan) the progressive deterioration of evil; he turns by his own choice into the cur that he has been called. Conversely, Antonio in the trial scene suffers hatred and injury but forgoes revenge and rancor, manifesting a genuine spirit of forgiveness—for Shylock's forced conversion is not revenge, as will be seen. Thus, his chief deficiency surmounted, Antonio becomes finally a perfect embodiment of Christian love.

The Shylock-Antonio opposition functions also at what the medieval theorists would call the "allegorical" level; in these terms it symbolizes the confrontation of Judaism and Christianity as theological systems—the Old Law and the New—and also as historic societies. In their first encounter, Shylock's reference to Antonio as a "fawning publican" and to himself as a member of the "sacred nation" (1.3.36–43) introduces an important aspect of this contrast. The reference is of course to the parable of the Pharisee and the Publican (Lk 18:9–13) which was spoken "unto certayne which trusted in themselves, that they were ryghteous, and despised other." The contemporary interpretation of this parable is suggested in Tomson's note [to his edition of the New Testament]: "Two things especially make our prayers voyde and of none effect: confidence of our owne ryghteousnesse, and the contempts of other."

Several allusions to Shylock's future conversion suggest the Christian expectation of the final, pre-millennial conversion of the Jews. The first such reference occurs, most appropriately, just after Shylock's feigned offer to forgo usury and forgive injury. Antonio salutes Shylock's departure with the words, "The Hebrew will turn Christian, he grows kind" (1.3.173). "Kind" in this context implies both "natural" (in forgoing unnatural interest) and "charitable"; thus Antonio suggests that voluntary adoption of these fundamental Christian principles would lead to the conversion of the Jew. The second prediction occurs in Lorenzo's declaration, "If e'er the Jew her father come to heaven, / It will be for his gentle daughter's sake" (2.4.33–4)—again with the pun on gentle-gentile. As Shylock's daughter and as a voluntary convert to Christianity, Jessica may figure forth the filial relationship of the New Dispensation to the Old, and Lorenzo's prediction may carry an allusion to Paul's prophecy that the Jews will ultimately be saved through the agency of the Gentiles. At any rate, the final conversion of the Jews is symbolized in just such terms in the trial scene: because Antonio is able to rise at last to the demands of Christian love, Shylock is not destroyed, but, albeit rather harshly, converted. Interestingly enough, however, even after Portia's speeches at the trial have reminded Antonio and the court of the Christian principles they profess, Gratiano yet persists in demanding revenge. This incident serves as a thematic counterpoint to the opposition of Old Law and New, suggesting the disposition of Christians themselves to live rather according to the Old Law than the New. Such a counterpoint is developed at various points throughout the play—in Antonio's initial enmity to Shylock, in the jeers of the minor figures, in Shylock's statements likening his revenge to the customary vengeful practices of the Christians and his claim to a pound of flesh to their slave trade in human flesh (4.1.90–100). Thus the play does not present arbitrary, black-and-white moral estimates of human groups, but takes into account the shadings and complexities of the real world.

As Shylock and Antonio embody the theological conflicts and historical interrelationships of Old Law and New, so do they also reflect, from time to time, the ultimate sources of their principles in a further allegorical significance. Antonio, who assumes the debts of others (rescuing Bassanio, the self-confessed "Prodigal," from a debt due under the law), reflects on occasion the role of Christ satisfying the claim of Divine Justice by assuming the sins of mankind.... And Shylock, demanding the "bond" which is due him under the law, reflects the role of the devil, to whom the entire human race is in bondage through sin—an analogy which Portia makes explicit when she terms his hold upon Antonio a "state of hellish cruelty."

The story of Bassanio and the casket choice also appears to incorporate a "moral" and an "allegorical" meaning. At the moral level, the incident explores the implications of Christian love in the romantic relationship, whereas Antonio's story deals with Christian love in terms of friendship and social intercourse. Morocco, in renouncing the leaden casket because it does not offer "fair advantages," and in choosing the gold which promises "what many men desire," exemplifies the confusion of love with external shows: like most of the world, he values Portia not for herself but for her beauty and wealth. However, the death's head within the golden casket indicates the common mortality to which all such accidents as wealth and beauty are finally subject. Aragon, by contrast, represents love of self so strong that it precludes any other love. He renounces the gold because he considers himself superior to the common multitude whom it attracts; he disdains the lead as not "fair" enough to deserve his hazard; and in choosing the silver which promises "as much as he deserves" he declares boldly, "I will assume desert" (2.9.51). But the blinking idiot in the casket testifies to the folly of him who supposes that love can be bargained for in the pitiful coin of human merit. Bassanio, on the other hand, chooses the lead casket which warns, "Who chooseth me, must give and hazard all he hath" (2.9.21) thus signifying his acceptance of the self-abnegation, risk, and venture set up throughout the play as characteristics of true Christian love. And the metaphor of the "venture" is constantly used with reference to Bassanio and Portia just as it is with Antonio.

At the "allegorical" level, the caskets signify everyman's choice of the paths to spiritual life or death. This analogy is explicitly developed in the "Moral" appended to the casket story in the *Gesta Romanorum* which is almost certainly Shakespeare's source for this incident. In the *Gesta* the casket choice tests the worthiness of a maiden (the soul) to wed the son of an Emperor (Christ). The moral declares, "The Emperour sheweth this Mayden three vessells, that is to say, God putteth before man life & death, good and evil, & which of these he chooseth hee shall obtaine." This passage carries a reference to Dt 30:15–20. That Shakespeare intended . . . to make the caskets symbolize the great choices of spiritual life and death is evident by the constant references in the lovers' conversation to "life" and "death" just before Bassanio's venture. . . . That the casket choice represents Everyman's choice among values is further emphasized by the multitude at Portia's door: some of them refuse to choose (like the inhabitants of the vestibule of Hell in Dante); others choose wrongly and, having demonstrated by this that they are already wedded to false values, are forbidden to make another marriage.

The meaning of the symbolic caskets is further illuminated by Jas 5:2–3: "Your riches are corrupt; Your golde and silver is cankered." Morocco, the pagan, with his boasts is a fit type of worldliness, Mammon. . . . Aragon, the Spaniard, is the type of Pharisaical self-righteousness: his sonorously complacent language about the "barbarous multitudes" and the faults of others (2.9.19–52) rather suggests the "sounding brasse" and "tinckling cymbale" of Paul's image (1 Cor 13:1), and certainly recalls the Pharisee's prayer. But through its first line, "The fire seven times tried this," the scroll refers Aragon to the twelfth Psalm, which denounces vanity and proud speaking. . . . [The] lessoning of Morocco and Aragon foreshadows the defeat and conversion of Shylock, for he represents in somewhat different guise these same antichristian values of worldliness and self-righteousness.

The trial scene climaxes the action at all the levels of meaning that have been established. As has been suggested, it portrays at the moral level Shylock's degradation to a cur and a monster through his commitment to revenge, and by contrast, Antonio's attainment of the fullness of Christian love through his abjuration of revenge. Allegorically, the scene develops the sharpest opposition of Old Law and New in terms of their respective theological principles, Justice and Mercy, Righteousness and Faith; it culminates in the final defeat of the Old Law and the symbolic conversion of the Jew.

Antonio's predicament in the courtroom of Venice is made to suggest traditional literary and iconographical presentations of the "Parliament of Heaven" in which fallen man was judged. Both sides agree that Antonio's bond (like the sinner's) is forfeit according to the law, and that the law of Venice (like that of God) cannot be abrogated. Shylock constantly threatens, "If you deny me, fie upon your law" (4.1.101) and Portia concurs, "there is no power in Venice / Can alter a decree established" (4.1.214–15). The only question then is whether the law must be applied with strictest justice, or whether mercy may somehow temper it. In the traditional allegory of the Parliament of Heaven, Justice and Mercy, as the two principal of the four "daughters" of God, debate over the judgment to be meted out to man. . . . So in the trial scene Shylock as the embodiment of the Old Law represents Justice: "I stand for Judgment. . . . I stand here for Law" (4.1.103, 142), whereas Portia identifies herself with that "Quality of Mercy" enthroned by the New Law. Also, another conception of the Heavenly Court is superadded to this by means of several references during the trial to Shylock as Devil (4.1.213, 283). The scene takes on something of the significance of the trial described in the medieval drama, the *Processus Belial*, in which the Devil claims by justice the souls of mankind due him under the law, and the Virgin Mary intercedes for man by appealing to the Mercy of God.

In either formulation, the demands of Justice and Mercy are reconciled only through the sacrifice of Christ, who satisfies the demands of justice by assuming the debts of mankind, and thus makes mercy possible. Therefore it is not surprising that the courtroom scene also evokes something of the crucifixion scene—as the moment of reconciling these opposed forces, as the time of defeat for the Old Law, as the prime example of Christian Love and the object of Christian Faith. Both plot situation and language suggest a typical killing of Christ by the Jew. Antonio, baring his breast to shed his blood for the debt of another, continues the identification with Christ occasionally suggested at other points in the play. Shylock's cry, "My deeds upon my head" clearly suggests the assumption of guilt by the Jews at Christ's crucifixion . . . and his later remark, "I have a daughter—/ Would any of the stock of Barrabas / Had been her husband, rather than a Christian" recalls the Jews' choice of the murderer Barrabas over Christ as the prisoner to be released at Passover (Mt 27:16–21).

Throughout the action thus far described, Shylock has persistently denied pleas to temper justice with mercy—to forgive part of the debt, to accept three times the value of the debt rather than the pound of flesh, or even to supply a doctor "for charity" to stop Antonio's wounds. His perversity is rooted in his explicit denial of any need to "deserve" God's mercy by showing mercy to others, for he arrogates to himself the perfect righteousness which is the standard of the Old Law—"What judgment shall I dread doing no wrong?" (4.1.89). Accordingly, after Portia's "Tarry a little," the action of the scene works out a systematic destruction of that claim of righteousness.

The stipulation for Shylock's conversion, though it of course assumes the truth of Christianity, is not antisemitic revenge: it simply compels Shylock to avow what his own experience in the trial scene has fully "demonstrated"—that the Law leads only to death and destruction, that faith in Christ must supplant human righteousness. In this connection it ought to be noted that Shylock's pecuniary punishment under the laws of Venice precisely parallels the conditions imposed upon a Jewish convert to Christianity throughout most of Europe and also in England during the Middle Ages and after. All his property and goods, as the ill-gotten gain of usury, were forfeit to the state upon his conversion, but he was customarily allotted some proportion (often half) of his former goods for his maintenance, or else given a stipend or some other means of support.

There is some evidence that Shylock himself in this scene recognizes the logic which demands his conversion, though understandably he finds this too painful to admit explicitly. His incredulous question "Is that the law?" (4.1.309) when he finds the law invoked against him, shows a new and overwhelming consciousness of the defects of legalism. Also, he does not protest the condition that he become a Christian as he protested the judgment (soon reversed) which would seize all his property: his brief "I am content" suggests, I believe, not mean-spiritedness but weary acknowledgement of the fact that he can no longer make his stand upon the discredited Law.

The ring episode is, in a sense, a comic parody of the trial scene—it provides a means whereby Bassanio may make at least token fulfillment of his offer to give "life itself, my wife, and all the world" (4.1.280) to deliver Antonio. The ring is his token of his possession of Portia and all Belmont: in offering it Portia declared, "This house, these servants, and the same myself / Are yours ... I give them with this ring, / Which when you part from, lose, or give away, / Let it presage the ruin of your love, / And be my vantage to exclaim on you" (3.2.170–74). So that in giving the ring to the "lawyer" Balthasar—which he does only at Antonio's bidding—Bassanio surrenders his "claim" to all these gifts, even to Portia's person, and is therefore taunted at his return with his alleged infidelity. But Belmont is the land of the spirit, not the letter, and therefore after Bassanio has been allowed for a moment to feel his loss, the whole crisis dissolves in laughter and amazement as Antonio again binds himself (his soul this time the forfeit) for Bassanio's future fidelity, and Portia reveals her own part in the affair. At the moral level, this pledge and counter pledge by Bassanio and Antonio continue the "venture" metaphor and further exemplify the willingness to give all for love.

Belmont functions chiefly at the anagogical level (if one may invoke the term): it figures forth the Heavenly City.... Here Gentile and Jew, Lorenzo and Jessica, are united in each other's arms, talking of the music of the spheres:

> Look how the floor of heaven
> Is thick inlaid with patens of bright gold,
> There's not the smallest orb which thou behold'st
> But in his motion like an angel sings,
> Still quiring to the young-eye'd cherubins;
> Such harmony is in immortal souls. (5.1.58–63)

In Belmont all losses are restored and sorrows end: Bassanio wins again his lady and all Belmont; Antonio is given a letter signifying that three of his argosies are returned to port richly laden; and Lorenzo receives the deed naming him Shylock's future heir. Lorenzo's exclamation, "Fair ladies, you drop manna in the way of starving people," together with the reference to "patens" in the passage quoted above, sets up an implied metaphor of the heavenly communion. Here all who have cast their bread upon the waters in the "ventures" of Christian love receive the reward promised.

From "Biblical Allusion and Allegory in *The Merchant of Venice*," *Shakespeare Quarterly* 13 (1962), 327–43, excerpts abridged.

*John R. Cooper (1970)*

## Shylock's Humanity

Perhaps the chief piece of evidence for the sympathetic interpretation of Shylock is the familiar speech, or rather the familiar fragment of a speech, that Shylock makes to Salanio and Salarino in Act 3, scene 1:

> I am a Jew. Hath not a Jew eyes? hath not a Jew hands, organs, dimensions, senses, affections, passions? fed with the same food, hurt with the same weapons, subject to the same diseases, healed by the same means, warmed and cooled by the same winter and summer, as a Christian is? If you prick us, do we not bleed? if you tickle us, do we not laugh? if you poison us, do we not die? and if you wrong us, shall we not revenge? If we are like you in the rest, we will resemble you in that. If a Jew wrong a Christian, what is his humility? Revenge. If a Christian wrong a Jew, what should his sufferance be by Christian example? Why, revenge. The villainy you teach me, I will execute, and it shall go hard but I will better the instruction.

To say that this speech gives dignity to Shylock is not to say that it amounts to a genuine defense or provides a real excuse for him. It is a matter of interest, however, that some critics have thought that it did or was intended to.

For us, the heirs of the Enlightenment, the Romantic movement, and the century of the Common Man, acts often seem justified merely by being recognizable as the consequence of emotions we have felt ourselves. *"Tout comprendre, c'est tout pardonner"* is a recognizably modern idea. It was, of course, far otherwise for Shakespeare's audience and presumably for Shakespeare himself. For them the human nature that Shylock describes and correctly says is shared by Jew and Christian was fallen, both in its biological weakness and in its unruly passions and, far from excusing his behavior, it was rather the fundamental reason why men sinned and so needed forgiveness, grace, and redemption. The speech provides a brief summary of the state of fallen man, who feels "The penalty of Adam, / The seasons' difference." He is subject to pain, injury, and disease. Most important, his passions are unruly and not controlled by reason. When he is wronged, he wants revenge. Shylock, in seeking revenge against Antonio, is not justified. He is merely acting as fallen human beings tend to act.

It is a critical commonplace that *The Merchant of Venice* is concerned with the familiar theme of the conflict of law or, less precisely, justice with mercy. In the trial scene, the Christians continually urge Shylock to be merciful only to be rebuffed by his appeals to justice and the letter of the law.

> Bassanio    This is no answer, thou unfeeling man,
> To excuse the current of thy cruelty.
> Shylock    I am not bound to please thee with my answers.
> ["Bound" has here the sense of "required by law."]
> . . . .
> Duke    How shalt thou hope for mercy, rendering none?
> Shylock    What judgement shall I dread, doing no wrong?

The Duke's question echoes the Lord's Prayer ("Forgive us our trespasses as we forgive those who trespass against us") and the parable of the unmerciful servant (Mt 28:21–35). Shylock's answer shows a moral assurance based on the law, the letter of which seems to justify his demands.... The important point is the theological one. With hardness of heart he rejects the new law of mercy, and with the pride of the Pharisees he is confident that he is justified by obedience to the letter of the law. His is the ironical situation in which St Paul, in the epistle to the Romans, sees the Jews who have made the great rejection. They are condemned by the very Law in which they place their trust. So Portia tries to make Shylock see the real implication of his statement that Jews and Christians are alike men and are similarly vengeful:

> Though justice be thy plea, consider this,
> That, in the course of justice, none of us
> Should see salvation: we do pray for mercy;

> And that same prayer doth teach us all to render
> The deeds of mercy.

Though his forced conversion to Christianity seems to us to be cruel and insulting, we are meant, I think and as many critics have said, to see this as the altogether kindly conversion of Shylock to the new rule of mercy and thus his liberation from the dilemma of the old Law.

From "Shylock's Humanity," *Shakespeare Quarterly* 21 (1970), 117–21 abridged.

*Joan Ozark Holmer (1978)*

## Shylock and the Leaden Casket [editor's title]

Although Shakespeare dramatically explains Shylock's antipathy towards Christians in his development of the Jew figure from his source materials, he does not justify Shylock's revenge; two wrongs do not equal a right. Shylock's mention of Barabbas in the trial scene is another version of the Jewish choice of Barabbas over Christ: "Would any of the stock of Barabbas / Had been her husband, rather than a Christian" (4.1.292–93). Moreover, Shylock's very naming of Barabbas in the trial scene is significant since Barabbas was a murderer (Mk 14:8; Lk 23:20), and Shylock wants to murder Antonio.

I suggest that Shylock's rejection of Christ may be figuratively seen as a rejection of the leaden casket. The choice of the leaden casket symbolizes the wisdom which understands the paradoxical nature of love as gaining only in giving and hazarding all. As we have noted regarding the leaden casket's motto, love as the gift or sacrifice of one's self is basic to the New Law as fulfilled in Christ: "Greater love then this hathe no man, when any man bestoweth his life for his friends" (Jn 15:13, Geneva). Antonio's offer of life emulates this ideal during the trial, while Shylock's intention of taking life is the moral opposite. It is deeply ironic that the unwise Shylock calls Antonio and Bassanio fools because they value giving which Shylock negatively terms "prodigality." Mercy or generosity of spirit, like generosity with wealth, Shylock brands as foolish: "I'll not be made a soft and dull-ey'd fool, / To shake the head, relent, and sigh, and yield" (3.3.14–15).

The choice of the leaden casket, which separates the merely cunning from the truly wise, may also allegorically represent the choice of Christ as Wisdom, wisdom being one of the manifestations of the divine nature in Christ and one of Christ's titles as the second person of the Trinity. Man's knowledge of spiritual things comes from the Spirit of God and not from the spirit of the world "which teacheth things wherewith the worlde is delited, and which men understand by nature" (1 Cor 2:12, Geneva gloss). Paul claims that the natural man "whose knowledge and judgement is not cleared by Gods Spirit" (1 Cor 2:14) considers spiritual things foolish because without spiritual discernment he cannot know them. The idea of the foolishness of the worldly wise, demonstrated in Shylock's downfall in the trial when he is caught in the very trap he laid for Antonio (snared by the letter of the law), appears in *Il Pecorone* but is Biblical in origin; the *Geneva Bible* states it most clearly: "He catcheth the wise in their owne craftines . . . when they them selves are entangled in the same snares, which they laid for others" (1 Cor 3:19 and gloss). Shylock's rejection of Christ is analogous to the rejection of the leaden casket because he considers the true wisdom of giving and hazarding mere foolishness, insisting rather on personal gain, whether of earthly treasure or flesh.

Shylock's swearing "by Jacob's staff" (2.5.36) recalls his earlier misinterpretation of Jacob's "way to thrive" (1.3.84) as the result of human craftiness, because in the source for this allusion Jacob demonstrates the proper attitude by humbly extolling God's omnipotent goodness as the cause of his rich blessings (Gn 32:10). Moreover, the Geneva gloss on Jacob's staff ("that is, poore, and without all provision") indicates that it is symbolic of Jacob's former poverty before God's beneficence to him, because earlier he passed over Jordan with only his staff and now he comes with two companies. Shylock's appreciation of Jacob's vast increase in wealth adheres to the letter and not the spirit of the text. Likewise, when Shylock hails Balthazar as "a Daniel come to judgment (4.1.219), it is as a "wise young judge" (220) that he honors him, and yet Shylock seems not to penetrate the merely literal resemblances of his comparison. Daniel is indeed described as "a yong childe" (Susanna, 5.45), not unlike the youthful Portia disguised as Balthazar, but Daniel's wisdom lay in judging those seeking judgment and finding them unworthy, significantly convicting them "by their owne mouth" (5.61) much as Portia does when she uses Shylock's own demands for justice against him. Shylock's literalism chiefly characterizes his attitude toward the law and himself; he stands on the letter of the law and self-righteousness. The election of Christ, however, frees man from dependence on the law and self-righteousness and signifies his dependence on God through faith and grace (Gal 3; Rom 10:3–4). The spirit of the New Law betokened by Portia's statement prior to Bassanio's casket choice, "I stand for sacrifice" (3.2.57), is twice purposefully parodied in Shakespeare's characterization of Shylock during the trial scene: "I stand for judgment" (4.1.103) and "I stand here for law" (4.1.142). Thus, the spirit of the New Law as expressed through Christ and implicitly signified by the leaden casket motto, designed to temper the letter with the spirit, self-reliance with God-reliance, is rejected by Shylock overtly in his words and deeds and implicitly in his attitude of literalism.

Shylock does not get what he *desires*, the pound of flesh nor thrice the bond (5.1.314). He does not get what he *deserves*, the bare principal (4.1.332). Instead,

Shylock is made to *give and hazard* all he has, his life, his faith, and his wealth (4.1.343–86), this very sentence constituting his opportunity for salvation in terms of the values generated by the play. Indeed, Shylock's incredulous response, "Is that the law?" (4.1.309), also has the ring of disillusionment. Shylock's dramatic hesitation when Portia insists on using the letter of the law against him— "Why doth the Jew pause? Take thy forfeiture" (4.1.331)—recalls the Prince of Arragon's hesitant silence when he unlocks the wrong casket—"Too long a pause for that which you find there" (2.9.53). Shakespeare's purpose in making Shylock give and hazard all is illuminated by the fact that none of his sources for the flesh-bond story require any giving or hazarding beyond the bond. The sources end the trial with simple defeat; Shakespeare alone attempts to educate and save his Jewish usurer.

From "Loving Wisely and the Casket Test: Symbolic and Structural Unity in *The Merchant of Venice*," *Shakespeare Studies* 11(1978), 64–66.

*Lawrence Danson (1978)*

## Shylock's Trial [editor's title]

The most common charge against Portia is that she leads Shylock on. Repeatedly she affirms the "justice" of his suit ("the Venetian law / Cannot impugn you as you do proceed" [4.1.174–75]), only to turn on him at the end with the objection that "This bond doth give thee here no jot of blood" (302). And now Portia seems to have discovered some previously unmentioned laws, against shedding "one drop of Christian blood" (306) or against any alien's "direct, or indirect attempts / To seek the life of any citizen" (346–47). There have of course been many other criticisms of Portia's procedures, for instance that she seems to act simultaneously as judge and counsel for the defense, or that the suit ought to have been dismissed immediately since the flesh-bond would have been unenforceable in any court in Europe. But the more legalistic the criticism the further we are from the play's essential fictional shape and spirit.

Portia quite plainly states a part of that spirit, and an aspect of the play's parabolic significance, when she tells Shylock "as thou urgest justice, be assur'd / Thou shalt have justice more than thou desir'st" (4.1.311–12). Thus the lesson she stated earlier in discursive terms—

> That in the course of justice, none of us
> Should see salvation: we do pray for mercy,

> And the same prayer, doth teach us all to render
> The deeds of mercy— (195–98)

she now contrives to have enacted in a fully dramatic way. The spiritual truth is embodied in a secular analogue.

An important clue to Portia's pedagogic function—as well as to another of the play's rings of reconciled opposites—is found in the related epithets applied to her in her role as Balthazar. The Duke says that Bellario has recommended "A young and learned doctor to our court" (4.1.144); and when the actual letter is read, again we hear "'I never knew so young a body with so old a head'" (4.1.160–61). Shylock praises this young "Daniel come to Judgment" as a "wise young judge," (4.1.22) and again: "O wise and upright judge, / How much more elder art thou than thy looks!" (246–47). Along with these various allusions to the combination in Balthazar of youth's vigor and age's wisdom, we may recall from an earlier scene the message found by Morocco in a death's head:

> Had you been as wise as bold,
> Young in limbs, in judgment old,
> Your answer had not been inscroll'd. (2.7.70–72)

The reiterated paradoxical image, combining in one person what is best both in youth and in age, alludes to a Renaissance moral commonplace: "A man who could display his vitality with caution was called *puer senex* or *paedogeron*, that is, a 'hoary youth.'"[1] The ideal of the *puer senex* has been traced by Ernst Curtius to origins in "late pagan Antiquity," when it was popular as a topos of praise:

> It is [Curtius continues] all the more significant, then, that the Bible had something corresponding to show. Of Tobias we read that he was the youngest of all, but never acted childishly: "Cumque esset junior omnibus . . . nihil tamen puerile gessit in opere" (1:4). The Wisdom of Solomon 4:8 ff. declares that age is honorable but is not to be measured by years: "Wisdom is the grey hair unto men." The Vulgate has: "Cani sunt sensus hominis." The old man's grey hair, then, serves as a figurative expression for the wisdom which old age should possess. But this wisdom of old age can also be the portion of youth. . . . The topos *puer senex* was impressed on the memory of the West by a much-read text. Gregory the Great began his life of St Benedict with the words: "Fuit vir vitae venerabilis . . . ab ipso suae pueritiae tempore cor gerens senile" ("he was a man of venerable life . . . even from his boyhood he had the understanding of an old man").[2]

The youthful Balthazar, sagely interpreting the laws—both of God and man—and slowly unravelling their difficulties until, at a stroke, the knot which had confounded the elders is severed, performs a brilliant comic coup de theatre; simultaneously, and with no strain on that comic function, this figure with the young body and the wise old head performs the serious moral work, sanctioned by the best pagan and biblical models, expected of the *puer senex*.

Portia's lesson is intended for each of the principals at the trial—Shylock most directly, but also Antonio and Bassanio. That the lesson will be wasted on Shylock is, by the time of the trial, a foregone conclusion; for just as Portia shows her aptness by confessing her weakness, so Shylock shows his incapacity by his consistently reiterated trust in the sufficiency of the law, the bond, the letter: "My deeds upon my head! I crave the law, / The penalty and forfeit of my bond" (4.1.202–203). It is almost literally the case that Shylock becomes deafer, as well as increasingly speechless, as the play proceeds. From his initial (though deceptive) expansiveness, Shylock's vocabulary becomes more limited and repetitive, as he insists monomaniacally "I'll have no speaking, I will have my bond" (3.3.17). Because he will not hear, he cannot know that the lesson he proudly declares himself proficient in is only the limited, self-defeating lesson of this world, not the truth of the spirit: "The villainy you teach me I will execute, and it shall go hard but I will better the instruction" (3.1.65–66).

Antonio, too, has been hard of hearing in the past. His response to Shylock's "Hath a dog money" speech—his shocking "I am as like to call thee so again, / To spet on thee again, to spurn thee too" (1.3.125–26)—shows how little capable, at that early point at least, Antonio is of hearing Shylock's human voice with its imperative demand for charity. In the complex of learning-teaching relationships, Antonio has indeed been guilty of teaching Shylock the false lesson of "villainy"— a fact which need not, however, lead to an exculpation of the eager pupil, Shylock. At the trial, Portia speaks of mercy to both men, but only one of them is able properly to respond.

Since the mercy Portia urges is not a matter of "compulsion" (4.1.179), Shylock dismisses its possibility entirely: "My deeds upon my head! I crave the law" (202). Refusing Bassanio's well-intentioned but misguided request that she wrest the law to her authority, Portia proceeds at Shylock's demand to fulfill every jot and tittle of the law until it yields the mercy for Antonio that Shylock would not freely grant. As for Shylock, it is consistent with what he himself has repeatedly urged that the language of compulsion is still used with him: "Down, therefore, and beg mercy of the duke" (359).

That Portia's speeches and her dramatic example have been intended for Antonio as well as for Shylock now becomes apparent. The Duke immediately gives up his legal hold over Shylock's life: "That thou shalt see the difference of our spirit / I pardon thee thy life before thou ask it" (364–65). The financial arrangements are more complicated:

> For half thy wealth, it is Antonio's,
> The other half comes to the general state,
> Which humbleness may drive upon a fine. (4.1.366–68)

In light of this official act, which charitably reduces Shylock's liability to the state from half of his wealth to a mere fine, Portia's next brief enigmatic line may at first appear a gratuitous cruelty: "Ay for the state, not for Antonio." No one, after all, has suggested that Antonio follow the Duke's example: why then must Portia appear to put a stop to an action that has not even been considered? With one further line Portia answers this question and allows Antonio—freely, of his own volition and not simply in imitation of the Duke—to show that he has learned the trial's lesson: "What mercy can you render him, Antonio?" (374). Though all the world else may remain deaf, like Gratiano with his stupid response, "A halter gratis, nothing else for Godsake!" (375), Antonio is able to amend his earlier fault. Part of the "mercy" that Antonio is able to render Shylock is unpalatable to modern sensibility, and we will have to consider this huge stumbling block of Shylock's forced conversion in the next chapter. On faith, as it were, let us here assume that Shakespeare intends no coruscating irony, but rather a demonstration of Antonio's increased harmonization, the amending in one gesture both of his own and, perforce, Shylock's spiritual state, in his response to Portia's question. He will simply administer his half of the estate on Shylock's behalf, rendering the principal and any accruing profits to Jessica and Lorenzo at Shylock's death, provided "that for this favour / He presently become a Christian" (4.1.383–83).

Antonio's free decision to administer his half of the estate on Shylock's behalf, with the proviso that at Shylock's death all of it will go to Jessica and Lorenzo, would have seemed more generous to an Elizabethan audience than it does to us, considering the Elizabethan abhorrence of usury. As a moneylender, all Shylock's wealth has supposedly been ill-gained; its total confiscation would not have seemed an unduly severe penalty. It is conceivable, even, that some of Shakespeare's audience were aware of historical precedent for the confiscation of a convert's wealth. For there still existed into the early seventeenth century, although in a state of decline, a curious institution in London called the *Domus Conversorum,* a hostel for Jewish converts that had originally been established in 1232. According to Cecil Roth, the *Domus Conversorum* was set up because, "Legally, converts from Judaism forfeited to the Crown all their property, as having been acquired by the sinful means of usury. Destitute as they were, a hostel was indispensable" (p. 43). The absurdity of the medieval situation—the encouraging (to put it mildly) of conversion, the subsequent reward for which was to be made an impoverished ward of the state—led to a modification of the law in 1280. The king at that time "waived for a seven-year period his legal claim on the property of those who left their faith. From now on they might retain one-half of what they previously owned, though amassed in sin, the remainder (with certain other income from Jewry, including the proceeds of the recently instituted poll tax) being devoted to the upkeep of the *Domus Conversorum* in London."[3]

So there was historical precedent in England both for the confiscation of the convert's property and for the remission of one-half of that penalty. There was historical precedent for enforced conversion as well; but in this matter we must look to biblical salvation-history as well as to the history of nations. I have said that Shylock's unyieldingness suggests, even if in a perverted form, the Old Testament covenant. But the Jew had another claim on the Christian, one which was in fact to contribute to the eventual recall of the Jews to England in 1655. That claim is the Jew's unique and necessary position in the scheme of man's salvation.

In Isaiah it is prophesied that "The remnant shall returne, *euen* the remnant of Iaakob vnto the mighty God" (10:21). And the return of that saving remnant—the conversion of the Jews—must occur before all things can be accomplished and God's kingdom be established. In Romans, St Paul elaborates on Isaiah's prophecy and on the role of the Jews in salvation-history. The question he is addressing for the benefit of his Gentile audience is whether the calling of the Gentiles has entailed the rejection of the Jews; his answer is one of his most elaborate "God forbids!" Paul cites Is 65:2, "And vnto Israel he saith, All the day long haue I stretched forthe mine hand vnto a disobedient, and gainsaying people" (Rom 10:21). God has not rejected the Jews; it is the Jews, rather, who have put their trust in "the workes of the Law" rather than seeking salvation by faith (Rom 9:32): "According as it is written, God hathe giuen them the spirit of slomber: eyes that they shulde not se, & eares that they shulde not heare vnto this day" (Rom 11:8). Because of this deafness, the Law itself has become, as David prophesied, "a snare, & a net, & a stombling block" (11.9)—a verse glossed in the Geneva Bible as follows: "Christ by the mouth of the Prophet wisheth that which came upon the Jews, that is, that as birdes are taken where as they thinke to finde fode, so the Law which the Iewes of a blinde zeale preferred to the Gospel thinking to haue saluation by it, shulde turne to their destruction."

It is not Portia but Shylock himself, in his "blinde zeale" demanding the law, his deeds upon his head, who makes the law "a snare, & a net, & a stombling blocke." Shylock demands it, and Portia gives it: "The Jew shall have all justice" (4.1.317). Bringing destruction upon himself through a vain self-righteousness, and failing to hear the Gospel message of mercy freely granted, Shylock at his trial plays out the role of the Jew as it appears in the New Testament version of salvation-history.

That role has a further dimension, a dimension suggested by Shylock's conversion and by the subsequent comic joys of Act 5. In St Paul's version of Jewish history, the falling off of God's Chosen People is one in a series of "fortunate falls," each preparing the way for a greater joy to come. The "obstinacie"—or as the Authorized Version calls it, the "blindness"—of the Jews has come upon them "vntil the fulnes of the Gentiles be come in" (Rom 11:25). This "secret" Paul imparts to the Gentiles "lest ye shulde be arrogant in your selues," reminding them that "all Israel shal be saued, as it is written, The deliuerer shal come out of Sion, and shal turne away the vngodlines from Iacob" (25–26). Therefore, says Paul, the Jews of the present day have a complex relationship to the newly-chosen Christians: "As concerning the Gospel, they are enemies for your sakes: but as touching the election, they are beloued for the fathers sakes" (Rom 11:28).

And all the more to be beloved for the role Israel plays in God's scheme of "fortunate falls":

> For euen as ye in time past haue not beleued God, yet haue now obteined mercie through their vnbelefe, / Euen so now haue they not beleued by the mercie shewed vnto you, that they may also obteine mercie. / For God hathe shut vp all in vnbelefe, that he might haue mercie on all. (Rom 11:30–32)

Thus salvation was made possible for the believing Gentiles through the unbelief of Israel; and now Israel's unbelief will allow God to show his free mercy to the Jews when in time their unbelief shall pass away. As Adam's disobedience was made the occasion for God's mercy to Adam's descendants, so the Jews, when they have acknowledged the insufficiency of the "blinde zeale" to the law, will discover the mystery of grace. The casting away of the Jews was the reconciling of the rest of the world; and their eventual reception shall be life from the dead for all (Rom 11:15). As the glossator of the Geneva Bible writes: "The Iewes now remaine, as it were, in death for lacke of the Gospel: but when bothe they & the Gentiles shal embrace Christ, the world shal be restored to a new life."

In the medieval cycle plays or a miracle play like *The Croxton Play of the Sacrament*, where present time is regarded *sub specie aeternitatis*, a converted Jew could recognize his glorious culminating place in history and rejoice accordingly. Shakespeare's drama, however, while it affords intimations of the Last Things, accepts stricter limits; it shows mankind, however beautifully arrayed, still wearing its muddy vestures of decay. Thus Shylock's response to the court's merciful extortion of his wealth and his religion is the brief, "I am content"—which may be pronounced bitterly or, as I believe it should be, with a profound weariness, the final stage in that successive weakening we have observed in him since his first bold appearance; followed by his anticlimactic exit lines:

> I pray you give me leave to go from hence,
> I am not well—send the deed after me,
> And I will sign it. (4.1.391–93)

How to react to these proceedings? Gratiano's capering vindictiveness—

> In christ'ning shalt thou have two godfathers,—
> Had I been judge, thou shouldst have ten more,
> To bring thee to the gallows, not to the font (4.1.394–96)

—is certainly *not* intended as the final commentary. Rather, the final commentary is conveyed more lengthily and obliquely, by all that follows in the play. As the nightmarishly bright light of the courtroom recedes and we awaken into the candlelit peace of Belmont, those whose "spirits are attentive" will hear a "concord of sweet sounds" which, entering into the heart, may give a promise beyond all this world's discords of the "harmony . . . in immortal souls."

*Notes*

1  Edgar Wind, *Pagan Mysteries of the Renaissance* (London, rev. ed., 1968), p. 99.
2  *European Literature of the Latin Middle Ages*, Willard Trask (New York, 1953; rpt. 1963), pp. 99–100.
3  Roth, *History of Jews in England* (1941), p. 79.

From *The Harmonies of "The Merchant of Venice"* (Yale University Press, 1978), pp. 119, 121–25, 164–69 abridged. Used by permission.

*Austin Dobbins and Roy Battenhouse (1976)*

## Jessica's Exodus [editor's title]

Capping a century of romantic interpretation of Shylock, Sir Arthur Quiller-Couch in 1926 termed Jessica "bad and disloyal, unfilial, a thief; frivolous, greedy, without any more conscience than a cat." Such an estimate, though it may appeal to readers swayed by Shylock's view of her as "damned," clearly is not that of the play as a whole. The father's moral imagination is comically undercut by his absurd love of gold more than daughter, and Jessica's elopement not only secures Lorenzo's friends as sponsors but also a welcome by Portia at Belmont. Most theatregoers therefore feel no qualms about Jessica's morals; they accept her actions as wholesome and right.

Jessica's sense of values roots in aspects of Hebrew tradition which foreshadow Christian ethics. Her very name, as has been noted by Israel Gollancz and by Barbara Lewalski, is a form of Hebrew *Iscah* (Gn 11:29), which Elizabethan commentators glossed as meaning "she that looketh out"; and this meaning is reflected in her looking "out at window" for Lorenzo's coming. In doing so, Jessica disobeys the repressive decree of Shylock (whose name probably derives from *shalach*, translated "cormorant" in Dt 14:17), but her action may be likened to that of Daniel, who prayed at his window (Dn 6:10) despite a decree forbidding such piety. Jessica's readiness to venture by faith in a "promise" is an attitude characteristic of the Hebrew patriarchs and prophets. Her departure with Lorenzo can therefore be attributed, as Professor Lewalski suggests, to an Israelite righteousness of faith which by obeying spirit over letter anticipates the New Law's superseding of Old Law.

Strictly speaking, Old Law is represented by Shylock only distortedly. When he cries out for "Justice" and interprets Jessica's act of taking treasure as stealing, he is ignoring a paradigm of justice set by Moses which Shakespeare very likely had in mind. In Exodus 3:21–22 (a text which Shylock as a Jew ought to know and respect), God instructed Moses that "when ye go [out of Egypt], ye shall not go empty: but every woman shall borrow of her neighbour, and of her that sojourneth in her house, jewels of silver, and jewels of gold, and raiment: and ye shall put them upon your sons, and upon your daughters; and ye shall spoil the Egyptians." Shylock seems to have forgotten Israel's own practice in leaving Pharaoh's house. For if this charter event in the history of Judaism justified a spoiling of Egyptian wealth, how can Shylock logically object to Jessica's taking ducats and jewels in fleeing his own house, which has become, as Jessica says, a hell? The irony of course is that Shylock has no logic except that of greed since he is, as Lorenzo rightly remarks, a "faithless" Jew. He is no true son of the Jewish worthies he invokes—Jacob, Abraham, and Daniel. On the contrary, when Shylock raises his knife in the trial scene, Shakespeare is emblematizing a parody of Abraham's "sacrifice."

Exodus 3:21–22 (along with 11:2 and 12:35) was a text well known in Christian commentary. Augustine had applied it, in a broad sense, to the general problem of how Christians should treat pagan arts and letters: "When the Christian separates himself in spirit from their miserable society," he should take, hold, and "convert" their treasure to Christian uses (*De Doctrina*, II.40). This interpretation was quoted with approval by Elizabethan moralists such as William Baldwin and Thomas Bowes. The text, moreover, furnished a standard instance for illustrating the difference between seeming theft and real theft. Tertullian, for example, justified the Israelites by explaining that their taking the Egyptian gold and silver was no fraudulent act but rather "compensation for their hire, which they were unable in any other way to exact from their masters."[1] And Aquinas, similarly, declared the Israelite taking of the spoils of the Egyptians to be "no theft," because God ordered it "on account of the ill-treatment accorded [the Israelites] by the Egyptians without any cause" (*S. T.* II-II.66.5). According to Aquinas, "when a man's property is taken from him, if it be due that he should lose it, this is not theft or robbery as forbidden by the decalogue" (*S. T.* II-I.100.8).

Echoing the medieval view, Reformation theologians also commended the action of the Israelites. They tended to make its ethics somewhat more baffling, however, by retaining the word "theft" in their descriptions. Thus the Lutheran Wolfgang Musculus, stretching paradox to the point of apparent contradiction, commented on the spoiling of the Egyptians:

> What was that other than theft? And yet it is not only excused by God's commaundemente, whereof we reade Exod. xi. But it deserueth also comendation of obedience. For they did (sayeth Moyses) as the Lord commaunded, and to do that which the Lord commaundeth, is the praise of true obedience.[2]

A similar view appears in the note added by Tyndale to the conclusion of his translation of the Pentateuch (1530):

> Jacob robbed Laban his uncle: Moses robbed the Egyptians: And Abraham is about to slay and burn his own son: And all are holy works, because they are

wrought in faith at God's commandment. To steal, rob and murder are no holy works before worldly people: but unto them that have their trust in God: they are holy when God commandeth them.

Commentary of this kind tends to reduce the moral issue to the single extenuating circumstance of God's commanding without explaining why God might so command. Commentators who followed Aquinas were more reasonable in that they sought to explain God's command on the grounds of natural law and justice.

Yet the paradigm itself, to any Elizabethan who remembered it, would suggest justification for Jessica's action. Moreover, an anology to Jessica's "theft" may be found in Genesis 31, in the episode of Jacob's spoiling Laban of his sheep and other possessions (an incident which immediately follows the rod-peeling incident with which Shylock was familiar). Did Jacob commit theft? The Anglican Andrew Willet thought not: "Iacob by this meanes doeth recouer but his owne, which was due vnto him in a double right both in respect of his 20 yeares seruice, all which time he serued without wages."[3] This paradigm, as well as the one from Exodus, ought to have given Shylock pause before denouncing Jessica as a thief, for, again ironically, it is he who is behaving like a Laban or a Pharaoh. In this context Shylock's outcry over "my Christian ducats" doubles the irony since in fact the ducats have been wrongfully extorted from Christians (through usury) and now are being rightfully "used" by the Christian Lorenzo and Jessica.

Unlike her father, Jessica remains faithful to the paradigms of historic Judaism. Like the Israelites of old, she seeks to escape from Shylock's all-too-Egyptian house of bondage to a land of promise. Like Jacob, she takes with her property to which she has a natural right.[4] And like Rachel (of whom Ambrose remarked "Happy was Rachel who concealed the false idols"[5]), Jessica carries off, concealed under her clothes, her father's household gods, his barren metal.

But if Jessica is not a thief, can she be guilty of the other charges Quiller-Couch would lay on her—for instance, that of "unfilial" behavior? Jessica eloped because she was "ashamed to be my father's child" and because she had determined to become a Christian. These are extenuating circumstances which even Desdemona in *Othello* does not have; yet in *Othello* the Venetian Senate accepts Desdemona's marriage after hearing her testify that she acted of her own free will. Would Elizabethan moralists have judged more severely?

There is some ground for guessing that the Protestants in Shakespeare's audience may have been more hesitant than Catholics to approve Jessica's elopement. It was customary among the Reformers to interpret the marriage contract as a matter restricted by the commandment to honor one's father and mother. Citing Colossians 3:20 as his proof text, Edwin Sandys calls marriage without parental consent a fault not only "most heinous in the sight of God" but condemned also by "the law of nature, the law civil, the law canon, and the opinion of the best writers."[6] But Aquinas had given the Colossians text a somewhat different interpretation. He explains that when the Apostle says "Children, obey your parents in all things," he is referring to matters within the sphere of a father's or master's authority but not to matters in which a person is subject immediately under God, by whose higher authority each person is taught "either by the natural or by the written law" (*S.T.* II-II.104.5). And on the specific matter of contracting marriage, Aquinas says:

> The maid is in her father's power, not as a female slave without power over her own body, but as a daughter, for the purpose of education. Hence, in so far as she is free, she can give herself into another's power without her father's consent, even as a son or daughter, since they are free, may enter religion without the parents' consent. (*S.T.* Suppl. 45.5)

Aquinas allows a validity even to secret marriage since all that is essentially necessary to a true marriage are "words of the present expressive of consent" by the two contracting parties (*S.T.* Suppl. 45.5). All else, he explains, belongs to the "fittingness" of the sacrament rather than to its essence. The Church's canon law forbids clandestine marriages, he says, but simply as a safeguard because secret marriages are often liable to fraud by one of the parties, or to hasty unions later repented of, and because there is something "disgraceful" about them. Secret marriage is excused from sin, however, when the lovers have a lawful motive.

Jessica's motive in eloping with Lorenzo was the lawful one of becoming a Christian and a true wife. Rightly then she answers Launcelot Gobbo's teasing, in a comic scene, that she is damned by her heredity to Shylock and without hope unless not "got" of her father. "I shall be sav'd by my husband," she replies (cf. Eph 5:23); "he hath made me a Christian." Fleshly fatherhood cannot determine Jessica's moral choice. True, the Fifth Commandment requires children to honor their parents (Dt 5:16). But the New Testament adds a stipulation: "... in the Lord" (Eph 6:1–2). Rightly speaking, then, only by disobeying Shylock could Jessica obey the Lord. The logic of this statement may sound harsh. But it is fundamentally both Christian and Hebraic. Obeying God rather than man, Jessica marries Lorenzo. A seeming disgracefulness is present and acknowledged by Jessica—in her reference, for example, to the shame of her boy's clothing (a matter which Puritan theory judged sinful but which Aquinas would have excused);[7] and a guise of impropriety is acknowledged by Lorenzo likewise, in his saying that he is playing thief. But of real disgracefulness there is none. Jessica's exchange of vows is in fact not wholly secret, since it is spoken in the presence of Lorenzo's friends as witnesses, while Lorenzo calls on "heaven and thy thoughts" as witness. And later there is added to this a church ceremony (see 3.2.303). We can therefore attribute to mere "seeming" whatever aura of scandal the elopement involves; unfilialness and disloyalty are not its moral substance.

But if we can thus clear Jessica of unfilialness as well as thievishness, what shall we say to a third and related charge that she is guilty of deceit and dissimulation?

She does of course dissimulate her sex when she dresses as a boy, an action to which surely no auditor who approves Portia's similar disguising can morally object. But what of Jessica's verbal deception when asked by Shylock regarding what Launcelot Gobbo has been whispering in her ear? Is she telling a lie when she replies: "His words were 'Farewell mistress,' nothing else"? In her defense let us note that there is no lie in her reporting that the substance of their conversation was that she fare well. Also, no lie is involved in simply holding back the amplifying details of what was said.

Both Catholic and Protestant theologians distinguished between lying and dissimulating. Liars, said William Perkins, are guilty of three things: first, of saying what is false indeed; second, of doing so willingly, knowing it to be false; and third, of doing so with a motive of malice.[8] Dissimulation, on the other hand, is of two kinds, according to Peter Martyr: "One, which hath respect onelie to deceiue; the which, seeing it differeth not much from a lie, vndoubtedlie it is sin. . . . But there is an other kind of dissimulation, which tendeth not to the deceiuing of anie man; but serueth onlie to keepe counsell secret, least they should be hindered: and this dissimulation is not to be refused, or condemned as sinne."[9] Dissimulation is commendable, wrote Andrew Willett,

I.   When it is done for deliuerance out of daunger, without the hurt of an other, as Dauid by faining himselfe madde, escaped, . . .

II.   When one dissembleth to profit his brother, as . . . [when] our Sauiour made shewe, as though he would haue gone further [Lk 24:28f], to trie the humanitie of the two disciples. (*Hexapla*, p. 291)

In Shakespeare's play, do we not recognize wicked hypocrisy in Shylock's bargain with Antonio, but permissible deception in Jessica? Jessica dissimulates; that is, she conceals the truth, yet her dissimulation is not evil. Medieval theologians insisted that a pretense be judged by its purpose. Thus, for instance, Jacob's apparent deception of his father Isaac was in Augustine's view not a lie but a "mysterium"; and "if we term that sort of thing a lie, by the same rule we must also account all parables and figures whatsoever" ("Against Lying," ch. 24). Augustine's judgment is followed by Aquinas. Jacob's assertion that he was Esau, says Aquinas (*S. T.* II-II, 110.3), was spoken in a mystical sense, because Esau's birthright was due Jacob by right, and Jacob spoke moved by a spirit of prophecy to signify a mystery, namely, that the younger should supplant the firstborn. Words sometimes, Aquinas insists, contain truth in a figurative or prophetic sense; and sometimes truth may be kept prudently hidden. No lie is involved in such cases.

Jessica's dissimulation, when carefully examined, can be seen as a prophetic prefiguring of later events in the play. Her masking as a page and torchbearer (as Theodore Weiss has observed) foreshadows the later actions of Portia, when as a masked lawyer-page she brings light to bear against Shylock ("So shines a good deed in a naughty world").[10] Shakespeare links Jessica and Portia by involving both in a secret departure from home—in the one case, with resulting dismay by a father; in the other, with resulting bafflement (in Act 5) by a husband. Both of these plotted surprises have as their lesson the theme that a duty-to-save transcends conventional submissiveness. Also, in the play's structure, Jessica's bringing news to Portia of Shylock's villainy provides Portia an impetus for her own decision to undertake a pilgrimage—whose benefits, mysteriously, redound to everyone, including Jessica and Lorenzo. Portia, acting as a Balthazar-Daniel, in a sense completes the exodus from pharaonic Judaism begun by Jessica. Portia's Daniel role, figuratively, effects and fulfills the promise to Abraham that by his "seed" all families of the earth would be blessed.

"If e'er the Jew her father come to Heaven," Lorenzo had remarked in Act 2, "It will be for his gentle daughter's sake." The gentle daughter's sake, in the trial scene in Act 4, is chiefly what inspires Antonio's proposal for Shylock's baptism and his deeding of property to Jessica. Note how this "deed" makes the Lorenzo marriage fully legal by imputing parental consent and also how it opens up a hope of rebinding father to daughter by providing a means. "Art thou contented, Jew?" Portia asks Shylock, and he replies: "I am content." Within the context of the play there is now for him a meaningful future—a future which would not have been possible had he succeeded in his earlier wish to have Jessica married to a Barabbas. Thus Jessica's dissimulation, far from injuring her father, has forwarded his only hope of faring well—in this respect like the benefit which young Jacob bestowed on the dim-sighted Isaac of biblical story. Her action (like Jacob's) has significance as a parabolic "mystery."

Considering all the ways in which traditional theology would sanction Jessica's actions, what flaw in Jessica can critics allege? We have answered Quiller-Couch's catalogue of accusations—except perhaps for the charge of frivolity. Conceivably Sir Arthur might cite as evidence Jessica's honeymoon lark of trading off for a monkey the turquoise ring Shylock was given by Leah, or Jessica's spending fourscore ducats during a night of festivity in Genoa. But is frivolity a sin on festive occasions? If so, we would have to fault equally the frivolity of Portia in Act 5, her monkey-business jesting about her ring. Surely, however, mockery is appropriate to festival. And as for extraordinary spending, this is deemed unthrifty only by a Shylock who never gives dinner parties. Moreover, Shylock's anguish over the Leah-ring is suspect. Why had he ceased wearing the ring if he still valued Leah? If we consider that on the night of his daughter's flight his dreams were not of Leah but of money bags (an ironic contrast to Jacob's dream of a ladder to heaven), we may infer that Shylock's sentiment for Leah was no more than afterthought to justify self-pity and indignation. And if we nevertheless wonder why Jessica could treat the Leah-ring so cavalierly, the answer is perhaps that in Scriptural tradition Leah (the "blear-eyed" wife who symbolizes mere practicality) is less valued than Rachel (symbol of the contemplative life) who represents Israel's and mankind's higher hope. St Ambrose, in the treatise we cited earlier, associates Leah with the letter-of-the-law and Rachel with grace. Such a Rachel is Jessica.

A conjoining of playfulness and insight wraps up the play's action. Act 5 begins and ends on this note. A harmonizing of jest and deeper truth sounds its music from the moment Lorenzo and Jessica come on stage pretending in themselves a likeness to Troilus and Cressida, Pyramus and Thisbe, Aeneas and Dido, or Jason and Medea. The jest depends on the fact that the love story of Lorenzo and Jessica has only a surface likeness to these instances of pagan dotage. Jessica's "stealing" from home has *not* been (like Thisbe's) benightedly rash and accompanied by fear and weeping moans; nor has Lorenzo "stolen" Jessica's soul with Troilus-like sighs. Their love has been neither willowy nor unthrift nor dismayed by shadows. All such comparisons "slander" their love, as Lorenzo wittily concludes. Instead of tragically miscarrying, their venture in love has brought them to Belmont and the safety of its beautiful mountain. And as they await the return of Belmont's pilgrim-mistress, there creeps into their ears, as Lorenzo says, the melody of the music of the spheres:

> Sit, Jessica. Look how the floor of heaven
> Is thick inlaid with patens of bright gold.
> There's not the smallest orb which thou behold'st
> But in his motion like an angel sings,
> Still quiring to the young-ey'd cherubins. (5.1.58–62)

Here the word *patens* suggests, as scholars such as Malone and others long ago noted, an allusion by Shakespeare to the metal plates upon which the bread of the sacrament is placed in Catholic Eucharists. If we follow this suggestion, the orbs are both singing and offering themselves up to God, thus celebrating a cosmic Eucharist. (This is the grandest liturgical image in all of Shakespeare.) Lorenzo pauses over it to regret that our "muddy vesture of decay" hampers our hearing its music.

The observation is apt. For although the lovers have transcended Shylock's dislike of music, they can be granted only a momentary sense of heaven's music before returning to their earthly duty of striking up a Belmont music to welcome Portia's homecoming. She then, as a little candle come home, will reveal through jesting riddle a human and more-than-human mystery of wedlock's ring: it is a double bond in which doctor or physician is the hidden "mystery" meaning behind-and-within that of wife. "By this ring," says Portia, "the Doctor lay with me." This paradox of a love secretly remedial while also wifely is the truth of the play as a whole.

## Notes

1 *Against Marcion*, IV.24. Long before Tertullian, the Jewish philosopher Philo had advanced this interpretation. The action of the Hebrews was right, he

explained, because in the spoil they took "they were but receiving a bare wage for all their time of service," a payment long held back. See *Philo*, tr. F.H. Colson (1961), I.xxv.

2  *Common Places of Christian Religion*, tr. John Man (London, 1578), p. 219.

3  *Hexapla in Genesin* (London, 1608), p. 194. Similarly, Calvin in *Commentaries on . . . Genesis*, tr. John King (Grand Rapids: Eerdmans, 1948), II, 156, says that God "purposed to connect his grace with the labour and diligence of Jacob, that he might openly repay to him those wages of which he had been so long defrauded."

4  See, e.g., Bernard Grebanier, *The Truth About Shylock* (New York: Random House, 1962), pp. 201–202; and Warren Smith, "Shakespeare's Shylock," *Shakespeare Quarterly*, 15 (1964), 197.

5  "Jacob and the Happy Life," tr. M. P. McHugh, *Fathers of the Church* (1972), pp. 160–61.

6  Sandys, *Sermons* (1585), ed. John Ayre (Cambridge, 1842), p. 281.

7  Citing Dt 22:5, Puritan treatises objected to women who "unsex" themselves by wearing men's clothes. Aquinas, on the other hand, judged that a woman's wearing of men's clothes may be done sometimes without sin on account of some necessity, either in order to hide oneself from enemies or for some similar motive (*S. T.* II-II.169–72).

8  *Workes*, 3rd ed. (Cambridge, 1631), III, 266.

9  *The Common Places*, II, 541. Nurses and physicians, Martyr has explained, use good guile and a profitable feigning toward the sick.

10  *The Breath of Clowns and Kings* (New York: Atheneum, 1971), p. 130.

From "Jessica's Morals: A Theological View," *Shakespeare Studies* 9 (1976), 107–120 abridged and slightly revised.

*Mark L. Gnerro (1979)*

# Easter Liturgy and the Love Duet in *MV* 5.1

The love duet between Lorenzo and Jessica that opens the last act of Shakespeare's *The Merchant of Venice* has been praised for its lyrical and allusive beauty, and E. M. W. Tillyard was undoubtedly right in taking H. Granville-Barker to task for slighting the passage as a bit of time-wasting to allow Portia and Nerissa to remove their male disguises. Tillyard was also correct in noting that "this night-piece is the very thing into which the rest of the play issues."[1] Tillyard failed to see, however, that the "earthly paradise" at Belmont was patterned more on celestial and divine love than on recovered natural innocence and harmony. In other words, the play "issues" into the duet even more integrally and religiously than Tillyard himself noticed.

Undoubtedly the play's happy resolution of discord into concord is based primarily on the saving of Antonio from Shylock's clutches, but on a deeper level its happy ending sees Christian marriage (especially that of Lorenzo and Jessica) as a type of the universal harmony introduced into history by the first Easter morn.

The love duet between Lorenzo and Jessica hymns the reconciliation of Ecclesia et Synagoga, of the New and Old Covenants. In short, it celebrates the healing of man's hate and disordered appetites (and not merely those occasioned by money-grubbing materialism). More significant, the love duet points to the resolution of ethical and ethnic conflicts into a higher state of peace and contentment.

Much of the play's action takes place at night with masques and nefarious actions, but with Act 5 comes the dawn and Jessica's reception into the Christian communion by the exchange of nuptial vows. Although Shakespeare casts the love duet (and many of the speeches following it) into the language of classical allusiveness, there is a pervasive strain of imagery drawn from the Easter liturgy, specifically from the vigil for Holy Saturday, suggesting Shakespeare was aiming to show religious grace inspiring natural goodness and reconciliation.

Previous commentators have long been aware of the likely Ovidian and Chaucerian sources for the content of the love duet, but none has noticed its likely formal design in the Preface to the Mass for the Easter Vigil. This vigil (of Holy Saturday) is one of the most beautiful and ancient in the liturgy and it is especially noted for its service of blessing the new fire and the paschal candle, both symbols of the Light which is newly come into the world with the Resurrection of Christ.

The most notable stylistic feature of the duet is its anaphora, the beginning of each brief speech with the same words. There are eight repetitions of the phrase "In such a night as this" in the 24 lines of the duet. The formality of the phrasing elevates the love duet above that of mere private and dallying love into the realm of cosmic love. The exchange between Lorenzo and Jessica becomes a formal anticipation of the later actual exchange of vows, and the anaphora seems to heighten this sense of significant things about to occur.

In the Sarum Missal there are eight uses of the word "nox" and "noctis" in the course of the Preface, with the most common expression "Haec nox est" repeated at the beginning of several sentences. The Preface as a whole begins with a celebration of the escape of the Jews, the Chosen People, from the bondage of Egypt, as a symbol for the escape of the soul from evil. In his translation of the Preface, O. B. Hardison catches something of the anaphora that structures the Latin Preface:

This is the night wherein of old thou didst bring forth our forefathers the children of Israel from Egypt, leading them dry-shod through the Red Sea. This is the night which cleansed away the darkness of sin, by the pillar of fire. This is the night which now delivers, throughout the world, the faithful of Christ from the wickedness of the world and the darkness of sin, restores them to grace, and to the fellowship of sanctity. This is the night in which Christ snapped the chains of death, and rose conquerer from hell. For it availed us nothing to be born, had it not prevailed that we should be redeemed. ...[2]

It would be impossible, of course, to try to determine how Shakespeare came by this phrasing from the liturgy of the Catholic Church, and what prompted him to adapt it to the love duet between Lorenzo and Jessica. In all likelihood, it remained simply as a residue from one of the more impressive moments that had prevailed in English as long as the Old Faith was still normative. In any case, Shakespeare might simply have remembered from childhood the residue of the Easter liturgy as a dramatically appropriate way for Lorenzo and Jessica to celebrate their escape from Shylock.

The imagery of light that is introduced by the love duet is as we might imagine it to be after a play which is so deeply steeped in darkness. In fact, the whole of Act 5 brightens up with starlight, candlelight, and music as the dawn approaches. It is in this sense that the whole play "issues" into the joy and happiness of the exchange of nuptial vows at the end of the play.

### Notes

1    *Shakespeare's Early Comedies* (London, 1966), p. 202.
2    *Christian Rite and Christian Drama in the Middle Ages* (Baltimore, 1965), p. 118.

From *American Notes & Queries* 18 (Oct., 1979), 19–21.

# MUCH ADO ABOUT NOTHING

## Comment and bibliography

The word "Nothing" in this play is punned on for its multiple meanings of "worthless," a "taking note" that is visually superficial, and sighs sung to the notes of "Men were deceivers ever" (2.3.53–62). A big fuss that is hollow characterizes the action. It can come to a happy ending only when a holy friar takes a hand in turning what's hollow into true virtue so that hallowed marriages can occur.

"Nothing" has its equivalent in fashion, or thievish custom, to which gentlemen in Messina are addicted (3.3.117–26). They are unwittingly "deformed," as St Paul would say, by being "conformed to this world" and its fashions which pass away (1 Cor 7:31; cf. 1 Jn 2:17). They need to be transformed by a renewing of the mind. But that can occur only when they have made fools of themselves, then, having had their errors exposed, have made amends in a ritual of penance, and finally prove their good will by an act of faith that transcends fashionable reason but affirms human good sense. In short, we may say, the story is of a "vagrant" love that exhibits its absurd antics until brought to shame and rehabilitated as pilgrim love. Implied is the perennial Christian theme of a fortunate fall that brings woe and confusion but also thereby the possibility of self-knowledge and openness to grace. Dogberry's malapropism sums up the paradox: "O villain! Thou wilt be condemned into everlasting redemption for this" (4.2.56).

Central to the story's design is the Pauline paradox of 1 Cor 1: the "wisdom of the world" is foolishness with God, but God chooses "what is foolish in the world" to shame the wise. In the play's low comedy, Dogberry furnishes a capital instance of a self-important worldling wise in his own eyes but really a fool. His "desartless" watchmen, however, are instances of foolish men in the world's eyes who nevertheless have sound intuition for recognizing a thief when they hear one, even though they fumble the legal terminology for naming his crime.

A knowledge by faith that comes through "hearing" is a major theme in Romans 10 and in Shakespeare's play equally so. In the main plot we see this in Beatrice and Benedick, who begin to have faith in love only after they have overheard a story of their own pride and their wounded neighbor's need. Later, their faith is tested when they face Hero's plight, and here deeds are required of Benedick to prove his love. His challenging of Claudio may seem to have little effect in bringing Claudio to repentance, yet it presents Claudio a model of manliness that sobers him and thus prepares him for the moment when the truth will be revealed by the Watch. After that, the Friar's Christian motto, "Die to live," becomes the recipe for a happy outcome for everyone.

The commentary by Arthur Kirsch perceptively seizes on the biblical allusions to Pharaoh's soldiers and Bel's priests as a key to this play's theme. What is in question is the spiritual and psychological condition of Messina, where persons know each other only by their apparel or looks. This kind of idolatry blinds them until destroyed by a kind of Red Sea purgation, a baptism of self-humiliation. The mystery of hidden selves thus becomes known and genuine marriages can be celebrated.

As supplementary reading, David Ormerod's essay is useful for its firm grasp on the theme of fashion's thievery. Messina's shallow lovers are "creatures of the eye," he notes, but the Friar refuses to be deceived by appearances. Chris Hassel develops the idea that "Man is a giddy thing" who must acknowledge his folly to find true festivity. He describes the drama as enacting an edifying humiliation that is regenerative when aided by penance, the wise "revenge" imposed by Leonato. Roy Battenhouse traces the transformation of Leonato from shallow patriarch to fool and then to true patriarch. Paul Jorgensen cites the Christian theological context of "nothing" and then reviews passages in *Much Ado* and other of Shakespeare's works which associate this word with vacuity, fantasy, and naughtiness.

Barbara Lewalski sees the lovers as undergoing stages of education somewhat similar to the ladder of love outlined in the neoplatonist Bembo's *The Courtier*. Claudio is Bembo's typical "young" lover who judges in terms of sense knowledge; Beatrice attains an intuitive understanding of Hero "in defiance of the testimony of the senses." The concept of redemptive sacrifice at the apex of the ladder of love is imaged in Hero's feigned death. Barbara Parker offers a modification of the views of Lewalski and Hassel. She sees the play as exploring three kinds of defect: lack of self-knowledge, flawed perception, and linguistic abuse.

## *Supplementary bibliography*

Battenhouse, Roy. "Toward Understanding Patriarchy in *Much Ado*," *Shakespeare Yearbook* 2 (1991), 193–200.

Hassel, R. Chris, Jr. *Faith and Folly in Shakespeare's Romantic Comedies* (University of Georgia Press, 1980), Ch. 4.

Hunter, Robert G. *Shakespeare and the Comedy of Forgiveness* (1965), Ch. 4.

Jorgensen, Paul A. "Much Ado About *Nothing*," in his *Redeeming Shakespeare's Words* (University of California Press, 1962), pp. 22–42.

Lewalski, Barbara. "Love, Appearance, and Reality: Much Ado about Something," *Studies in English Literature* 8 (1968), 235–51.

Ormerod, David. "Faith and Fashion in *Much Ado about Nothing*," *Shakespeare Survey* 25 (1972), 93–105.

Parker, Barbara. *A Precious Seeing: Love and Reason in Shakespeare's Plays* (New York University Press, 1987), Ch. 4.

*Arthur C. Kirsch (1981)*

## Impediments and Remedy in *Much Ado* [editor's title]

The action of *Much Ado* is particularly marked by conversations that are wrongly heard or overheard and by sights that are mistakenly perceived. The play implies that such misapprehensions represent a spiritual and psychological, as well as a social, condition; virtually all the characters in the play at one point or another nurse wounds to their self-esteem and are radically self-absorbed. *Much Ado* undoubtedly celebrates the manners of a civilized society, but it also represents, and deeply, the narcissistic "impediments" that make the achievement of such a community at once so difficult and so urgent.

The theological implications of these impediments are adumbrated with unusual emphasis in *Much Ado* in the remarkable dialogue between Borachio and Conrade about the plot against Claudio and Hero—the dialogue that is overheard by the Watch and that eventually leads to Don John's exposure.

| | |
|---|---|
| Borachio | Thou knowest that the fashion of a doublet, or a hat, or a cloak, is nothing to a man. |
| Conrade | Yes, it is apparel. |
| Borachio | I mean the fashion. |
| Conrade | Yes, the fashion is the fashion. |
| Borachio | Tush, I may as well say the fool's the fool. But seest thou not what a deformed thief this fashion is? |
| 2 Watch | [Aside] I know that Deformed; 'a has been a vile thief this seven year; 'a goes up and down like a gentleman; I remember his name. |
| Borachio | Didst thou not hear somebody? |
| Conrade | No; 'twas the vane on the house. |
| Borachio | Seest thou not, I say, what a deformed thief this fashion is, how giddily 'a turns about all the hot bloods between fourteen and five and thirty, sometimes fashioning them like Pharaoh's soldiers in the reechy painting, sometime like god Bel's priests in the old church-window, sometime like the shaven Hercules in the smirch'd worm-eaten tapestry, where his codpiece seems as massy as his club? |
| Conrade | All this I see; and I see that the fashion wears out more apparel than the man. But art not thou thyself giddy with the fashion too, that thou hast shifted out of thy tale into telling me of the fashion? |
| Borachio | Not so neither; but know that I have to-night wooed Margaret, the Lady Hero's gentlewoman, by the name of Hero. . . . (3.3.108) |

Borachio then proceeds to inform Conrade of the details of his deception of Claudio and Don Pedro.

The intrusiveness of Borachio's homily is an indication of the pressure of thought behind it, and we should take him at his word when he insists that he has not shifted out of his tale. His discussion of fashion is a prelude to his revelation of the plot against Claudio and Hero and clearly suggests a spiritual context in which that plot, and consequently the main action of the play, may be understood. Claudio, who is associated with apparel and fashion throughout the play and who has the play's most hot-blooded fantasies, is specifically implicated; but Borachio's references to the Pharaoh's soldiers, god Bel's priests, Hercules, and shortly afterwards to "the devil my master" (3.3.141) extend far beyond Claudio's particular imagination or personality. In Borachio's speech Shakespeare invokes important issues for the audience, and he does so with a deliberation and precision that have not been sufficiently recognized.

The three allusions that Borachio makes in such quick succession all call attention to their iconographic character—a reechy painting, an old church window, a worm-eaten tapestry—and they have considerable significance. The first refers to the episode in Exodus in which Moses and the Israelites passed through the Red Sea and Pharaoh's soldiers were drowned. The episode was commonly understood to be a figure of baptism. The Geneva gloss of Ex 14:27 reads, "So the Lord by the water saved his, and by the water drowned his enemies," and the liturgy of Baptism states the connection explicitly, praising God for leading "the children of Israel thy people through the Red Sea, figuring thereby thy holy Baptism."[1] The episode was also associated with the first commandment and in that context was related to the Redemption itself.[2] In the First Epistle to the Corinthians (10:1–13), St Paul touches upon all these associations and discusses both the Exodus and the meaning of baptism in terms suggesting the ideas that lie behind as well as within Borachio's speech. He asserts that the "nature of man" is lustful and open to temptations, idolatry and fornication foremost among them; that without faith in God and access to his grace, man, like Pharaoh's soldiers, will be destroyed; and that the individual as well as the society of man can be saved only through the sacrament of Baptism and the profession and communion of faith it makes possible and signifies. It is significant, considering the plot that is later engineered by the Friar to redeem the marriage of Claudio and Hero, that this profession and communion, in the words of the liturgy of Baptism, "is to follow the example of our Savior Christ, and to be made like unto him, that as he died and rose again for us, so should we which are baptized die from sin, and rise again unto righteousness, continually mortifying all our evil and corrupt affections, and daily proceeding in all virtues and godliness of living."[3] As we shall see, this is essentially the process that the Friar describes in his hopes, through Hero's feigned death and rebirth, to mortify Claudio's misapprehension.

The second of Borachio's allusions, to "god Bel's priests," also focuses strongly on faithlessness and idolatry. The priests of Bel in the Apocrypha deceive the Babylonian king into believing that "an idole, called Bel" is eating and drinking the offerings that they themselves are consuming with their families in secret; but they are exposed by Daniel, who "may not worship idoles made with hands, but the living God, which hathe created the heaven and the earth, and hathe power upon all flesh."[4] The story may have come to Shakespeare's mind because, like *Much Ado*, it specifically associates the capacity to be deceived by appearances with faithlessness, but even wider connotations of idolatry are germane to the play. The medieval commonplace that the lover who is driven by lustful fantasies makes an idol of his mistress and ultimately is guilty, like Narcissus, of a pathological worship of his own image—the situation of the lover early in the *Roman de la Rose*, for example—had many Elizabethan counterparts, particularly in the sonnet sequences, and has obvious applicability to Claudio, who also, like most lovers in this tradition, has blind faith in what he himself calls the negotiation of the eye. Equally commonplace, and perhaps even more illuminating, is the Elizabethan habit of thinking of idolatry as "spiritual adultery." The metaphor is used frequently in the Scriptures and in the *Homilies*[5] and other Elizabethan commentaries. It is usually related directly both to the institution of marriage and to the second commandment, the commandment that forbids the making of "graven images" and that stresses God's jealousy.

> For no man is so ignorant but that he knoweth how God in the scripture doth, by the parable of wedlock, figuratively set down the assurance and bond wherein by faith we are bound to God. God is our husband and bridegroom: we are his wife and chosen spouse. A chaste and faithful wife giveth ear alone to her husband's voice; him alone she loveth, him alone she doth obey, and, him excepted, she loveth no man at all. Again, on the other side, a shameless, faithless adulteress and whorish strumpet, not worthy to be called a wife, seemeth outwardly to stick and cleave to her husband; but privily she maketh her body common to many men, and loveth other more than her husband, and for the most part burneth on them being cold enough [toward him]. But God is a jealous God, and will be loved and worshipped alone, without any partner to rob him thereof. That is spiritual adultery and whore-hunting, when men do partly love and worship God, and yet notwithstanding, do therewithal give reverence to strange and other gods.[6]

The very assurance with which this sixteenth-century commentator speaks of a common understanding of "the parable of wedlock" should suggest, at the very least, that *Much Ado*'s manifest concern with adultery—in the action involving Claudio and Hero and in the very sensibilities of Benedick and Beatrice—represents something quite different from the dependence of a vulgar comedian on melodrama and obscene jests. Claudio's jealousy is the inversion of God's, and both his misconceived beliefs and Benedick's and Beatrice's fears would, for an

Elizabethan, have been directly related to central tenets of the Christian understanding not only of marriage but of faith itself.[7]

Hercules, the subject of Borachio's third allusion was, of course, one of the
most popular mythological figures in Renaissance art and literature. Borachio's description of him as a blatant adolescent is very unusual, but its import is clear. The
heroic Hercules of the Renaissance was the Hercules at the crossroads who chose
virtue instead of vice, the manly Hercules who through twelve labors rid the world
of monsters. His heroic exploits were routinely interpreted in terms of the Christian psychomachia, and he himself was often regarded as a type of Christ. . . . The
figure whom Borachio describes, a "shaven" Hercules whose "cod-piece is as massy
as his club," is obviously of another type altogether. Shakespeare may be thinking
of Hercules' subjection to Omphale and may also be conflating that with the cut-
ting of Samson's hair by Delilah. Both episodes were understood in the Renaissance as examples of the kind of radical unmanliness, ultimately a denial of God,
that constituted Adam's submission to Eve at the fall and that occurs in all men
when their bodies and souls are not in harmony and when they worship themselves instead of God. In any event, ideas such as these seem to lie behind Borachio's portrait of a young and essentially idolatrous Hercules. I think they also
inform the explicit sexual references to Hercules made elsewhere in the play both
by Benedick, who fears that Beatrice "would have made Hercules have turn'd spit,
yea, and have cleft his club to make the fire too" (2.1.222), and by Beatrice, who
in her turn fears that "manhood is melted into curtsies, valour into compliment,
and men are only turn'd into tongue, and trim ones too. He is now as valiant as
Hercules that only tells a lie and swears it" (4.1.314).

The larger envelope of Borachio's allusions, the whole subject of apparel and
fashion, is one that deeply preoccupied Shakespeare, not only in this play but
throughout his work. It is natural for a dramatist to be interested in the theatrical
possibilities of dress for spectacle and disguise, but coordinate with that interest in
Shakespeare is the pronounced Elizabethan insight, enacted in various ways in
*Much Ado*, that dress and fashion can be manifestations and emblems of man's
deepest sexual vanities. Parolles's spiritual bankruptcy, as we shall see, is virtually
defined by the extravagance of his dress—including, not coincidentally, a massy
codpiece—and so in a different way is Cloten's. In *Cymbeline*, disguises and changes
of clothes have a consistent psychological and spiritual cadence. In both *All's Well*
and *Cymbeline*, moreover, fashion is deeply connected with the virulence of slander and man's susceptibility to it; and in both plays the root of slander is sexual.

The seriousness with which Shakespeare treats the issue of apparel may be in
part an inheritance from the medieval drama, in which Vices and devils were regularly depicted as dandies, but his conception of fashion was ultimately scriptural
and was common in Elizabethan religious thought. In the sermon against excess of
dress, for example, the *Homilies* warned against making "provision for the flesh, to

accomplish the lusts thereof, with costly apparel"; rebuked even wives who sought to please their husbands "with the devil's attire ... in such painted and flourished visages, which common harlots most do use"; and in a reference to 1 Pet 3, the passage also cited in the liturgy of matrimony, advised women to "let the mind and the conscience, which is not seen with the eyes, be pure and lean; that is, saith he [Peter], an acceptable and an excellent thing before God."[8] Such an association of ideas, I think, lies behind many of the images of painted women in Shakespeare's plays including Don John's in *Much Ado*, when he slanders Hero by saying the word "disloyal" "is too good to paint out her wickedness" (3.2.97).

The sermon on apparel in the *Homilies* also cites St Paul, 1 Cor 7:31, "where he teacheth us to use this world as though we used it not...." This allusion is most significant, both because St Paul's advice occurs in the midst of a discussion not of apparel but of marriage and because its phrasing is exceptionally suggestive. The full verse praises those "that use this worlde, as thogh they used it not: for the facion of this worlde goeth away," and it is surely this understanding of "fashion," in its larger scriptural context, that animates Borachio's digression. The whole of the seventh chapter of 1 Cor, as well as part of the sixth chapter, is devoted to a discussion of man's sexual impulses and of the basis and meaning of marriage. Its fundamental premise is a recognition of the combination of energy and infirmity in the flesh that clothes the human spirit. This is the profound biblical note, it seems to me, that Shakespeare strikes in the scene between Borachio and Conrade, holding us still for a few moments as he often does in his comedies, to contemplate the deep mystery of the libidinal instincts, whose vicissitudes can either unite men in love and community or drive them into the isolation of their separate selves.

Considering this theological background it is not surprising that Claudio and his marriage should be redeemed by an action that transparently recollects the death and resurrection of Christ, in the image of whose union with the members of the Church marriage is formed and sanctified, and whose charity is the source and the model for human love. The Friar—whose authority at the end of the play is at once gentle and sure—describes his plan for Hero's feigned death in entirely natural terms, but his speech is in obvious counterpoint to Borachio's and provides the redemptive solution to the spiritual problems that Borachio raises. The Friar speaks of changing "slander to remorse," and continues:

> But not for that dream I on this strange course,
> But on this travail look for greater birth.

He describes how often through loss

>             we find
> The virtue that possession would not show us
> Whiles it was ours. So will it fare with Claudio.
> When he shall hear she died upon his words,
> Th' idea of her life shall sweetly creep

> Into his study of imagination,
> And every lovely organ of her life
> Shall come apparell'd in more precious habit,
> More moving, delicate, and full of life,
> Into the eye and prospect of his soul,
> Than when she liv'd indeed. (4.1.211–20)

The whole weight of the play's preoccupation with fashion is brought to bear on these luminous lines, and it is difficult not to hear in them an allusion to the passage about wives in 1 Peter that is quoted in the marriage liturgy and remarked upon in the *Homilies*. Hero is clearly such a woman as the Epistle describes. Often castigated by critics for her passivity, she is quite literally mild and quiet, and her apparel is never outward even when it seems to be so. Significantly, just prior to the church scene, when Margaret makes a rather conspicuous fuss over the "rare fashion" of Hero's gown, Hero replies only "God give me joy to wear it, for my heart is exceeding heavy" (3.4.13, 22–3), and it is only when her hid heart is figuratively reborn in Claudio, when she comes appareled in more precious habit into the eye and prospect of his soul, that the play approaches its comic conclusion.

| | |
|---|---|
| Claudio | Give me your hand; before this holy friar |
| | I am your husband, if you like of me. |
| Hero | And when I liv'd I was your other wife; [Umasking] |
| | And when you lov'd you were my other husband. |
| Claudio | Another Hero! |
| Hero | Nothing certainer. |
| | One Hero died defil'd; but I do live, |
| | And, surely as I live, I am a maid. |
| Don Pedro | The former Hero! Hero that is dead! |
| Leonato | She died, my lord but whiles her slander liv'd. |
| | (5.4.58) |

### Notes

1  *Book of Common Prayer*, p. 270 (ed. Booty).
2  "Verily, the mystery of our redemption by our Lord Jesus Christ is manifestly contained in the first precept of the ten commandments. For it is evident that the Israelite's free departure out of Egypt was a type or figure of the delivery of the whole compass of the earth, and of all the kingdoms of the world, which should be wrought by Christ our Lord, who hath now already set all the world free from the bondage of sin and hell." Bullinger, *Decades*, I, 218–19.
3  *Book of Common Prayer*, p. 276.
4  The Historie of Bel and of the dragon, 3, 5, and 1–22 passim.
5  See, e.g., "Peril of Idolatry" in *Sermons or Homilies Appointed to be Read in the Time of Queen Elizabeth* (London: Prayer-Book and Homily Society, 1817), pp. 209, 226–9.
6  Bullinger, *Decades*, 1, 233–4.

7   As the liturgy of Matrimony itself suggests, Elizabethans tended to think of adultery and marriage as dialectically opposite states. In his handbook, *The Christen State of Matrimony* (London, 1541) Henry Bullinger devotes much of his discussion to the various positive purposes and duties of conjugal life, but very nearly a third of the treatise constitutes a sermon against the evils of whoredom and adultery.

8   "Excess of Apparel" in *Homilies*, pp. 284, 289, 291.

From *Shakespeare and the Experience of Love* (Cambridge University Press, 1981), 46–54 abridged. Used by permission.

## Comment and bibliography

The favorite metaphor of human life is that of a journey, involving trials through which a hero discovers himself and his world and finds occasion for works of rescue. Athlete of virtue is the term commonly ascribed to Old Testament heroes such as Samson and David, and to Hercules in classical mythology, and to Christians who follow St Paul in fighting the good fight and finishing the course in the hope of a spiritual crown. The Psalter in the Elizabethan *Boke of Common Praier* (1594), John Doebler has noticed, shows a Hercules battling the Hydra. Renaissance poets considered him a type of Christ, and not surprisingly so, since the labors of Hercules in overcoming the Nemean lion and the Hydra fulfil the Davidic injunction of Ps 91:12, "the young lion and the dragon shalt thou trample under foot." And of course the liturgy of baptism binds everyman's soul to fight against "the world, the flesh, and the devil." This duty underlies the allegorical journey of Spenser's Red Crosse Knight and the sequenced trials of Bunyan's pilgrim on his way to the heavenly city.

The story of Orlando begins with his breaking free from the cultural oppression of an elder brother and establishing his own credentials by overcoming a giant, the wrestler Charles. His final labor is a rescuing of the brother from a lioness and a snake, symbols of the violence and envy that have endangered this brother's true potential. Episodes in between include a flight into exile assisted by an Elijah-like servant, a meeting with brother-exiles who introduce him to the "sweet uses of adversity," and an encounter with a friendly shepherd who cures with lively humor his "mad" romanticism for a remembered Rosalind. The friend turns out to be Rosalind in disguise, who in medicining Orlando's passion is wrestling with her own, and who recognizes as the sign of mature love in him the blood he sheds in rescuing his brother. As herself a devotee of Hymen, she then invokes this god of "High wedlock" to preside over an apocalypse of things heavenly and earthly atoning together in a ceremony of eight handclaspings, an icon of the eight souls who found salvation in the ark of Noah.

The concept of adversity as an ugliness that hides a jewel is as ancient as the story of Job or the philosophy of Boethius that misfortune is more beneficial to a human being than good fortune. Its cognates in folklore include the Cinderella story and the riddle of the leaden casket. Its truth is celebrated by Touchstone, the wise fool of *As You Like It*, when he chooses as his bride the plain hard-favored Audrey whose jewel is her honesty, the pearl within the oyster (5.4.61). Audrey lacks all the gifts of an Ovidian lover but she can thank the gods that she is what she is and can pray them to make her honest and give her joy. Touchstone values this, for like Rosalind he is no creditor of the feignings of rhyme, and indeed has provided Rosalind amusement by recalling his capers for Jane Smile and by rhyming a parody of Orlando's verses. Touchstone through his jests is the canny assessor throughout the play not only of courtly pretense and snobbery but also of the ripe-and-rot view of life voiced by the cynical Jaques.

Our anthology provides excerpts of commentary by Alice-Lyle Scoufos, William Watterson, and René Fortin. Scoufos sketches the chief stages in Orlando's moral growth. She notes the excessive violence in his initial dealings with Oliver and Charles, a rudeness corrected by the religious manners of Duke Senior. The final testing she describes as taking place under an Edenic tree, where Oliver is "the ubiquitous wild man" of romance tradition, lost in a dark woods, whose salvation depends on the blood shed for him by an Orlando of Christian charity.

Watterson focuses on the Christian quality of Shakespeare's pastoralism as compared with Lodge's fashionable neoclassicism. He notes that Arden is several times referred to as a "desert" for "eremites," and he sees it as a contemplative place where progress from profane to sacred discourse can occur. Orlando learns here a "sacred pity" and charity and is then awarded the grace of marriage. Arden's running brooks are books like those of the New Testament.

Fortin elaborates on the contrast between the view of mankind set forth by Jaques and that practised by Orlando under a mystic tree. He traces the literary associations of the "ancient oak" in Ovid, Spenser, and the Bible.

For supplementary reading, Barbara Parker's chapter provides an excellent review of the phases in Orlando's spiritual humbling: he must overcome his initial concern for "reputation" and his idolatrous "fancy" of Rosalind. And she must shed her loftiness in correcting Phoebe's, while profiting from Touchstone's electing of substance over facade. Stuart Daley's essays focus on the defects of Jaques and stress the Christian virtues of Corin. John MacQueen points out that whereas Jaques regards Fortune as the supreme power in human life, for Rosalind and Duke Senior the *remedium Fortunae* is Nature. The court in this play, he explains, is a World Upside Down, in which Nature is subordinated to Fortune, but in the forest it is made clear that fortune may control the body but not the soul of human beings. Fortune's domain is the external world but not the "lineaments of nature." Rosalind as an embodiment of the natural and the divine is "all graces" enlarged and nature "distilled" (3.2.138).

Frank McCombie's essay points out parallels of theme between *As You Like It* and *King Lear*. Duke Frederick with his capricious evil foreshadows the unregenerate Lear. The song in *As You Like It* telling us that most friendship is feigning has the theme of man's ingratitude that Lear proclaims in his "Blow winds." Both plays deal with a prince who is cast out and must go through a process of purging. The role of the fool is nearly the same in both, and it takes its inspiration, says

McCombie, from Erasmus's *Praise of Folly*. "Shakespeare was in general much closer in his thinking to the central Christian traditions than are many of us to-day" (p.68).

The play's implausible happenings, Sylvan Barnett remarks, suggest a benevolent providence, as do also the play's biblical allusions and a conversion by Oliver that has the strangeness of St Paul's. Helen Cooper says that Shakespeare's vision of pastoral is that of the poets of the Middle Ages and fulfils their work.

## Supplementary bibliography

Barnett, Sylvan. "'Strange Events': Improbabilities in *As You Like It*," *Shakespeare Studies* 4 (1968), 119–31.

Cooper, Helen. *Pastoral: Medieval into Renaissance* (Totowa, New Jersey: Rowan & L. Littlefield, 1977), pp.176–78.

Daley, A. Stuart. "To Moralize a Spectacle: *As You Like It*, Act 2, Scene 1," *Philological Quarterly* 65 (1986), 147–70.

_____. "Shakespeare's Corin, Almsgiver and Faithful Feeder," *English Language Notes* 27 (1990), 4–21.

Doebler, John. *Shakespeare's Speaking Pictures* (University of New Mexico Press, 1974), pp.21–38.

Knowles, Richard. "Myth and Type in *As You Like It*," *English Literary History* 33 (1966), 1–22.

MacQueen, John. "*As You Like It* and Medieval Literary Tradition," *Forum for Modern Language Studies* 1(1965), 216–29.

McCombie, Frank. "Medium and Message in *As You Like It* and *King Lear*," *Shakespeare Survey* 33 (1980), 67–80.

Parker, Barbara. *A Precious Seeing: Love and Reason in Shakespeare's Plays* (New York University Press, 1987), pp.99–116.

*Alice-Lyle Scoufos (1981)*

## The Testing of Love in *As You Like It*

In Shakespeare's Arden we find an Eden made harsh by post-lapsarian Nature. The wind is cold, and the deer must be slaughtered to provide food for the inhabitants. At times Arden is called "uncouth," and it has within it "a desert inaccessible." But Arden is a place that mirrors truth. It is a place for love's development and fruition, we learn by the end of the comedy. But the success of love comes only after a series of tests in the forest or garden. In *As You Like It* these tests mount to a climax under the ancient tree as Orlando undergoes a severe temptation to let the lioness destroy his brother. The testing scenes in Arden, however, begin much earlier in the comedy.

In Act 2, scene 7, Orlando breaks in upon the banqueting foresters with his sword drawn. He intends to gain by force or violence what he needs for old Adam and himself. He threatens: "Forbeare, I say, / He dies that touches any of this fruite, / Till I, and my affairs are answered." This is the epic Orlando speaking, and we begin to understand why Shakespeare changed the name of Rosader to Orlando. The Herculean hero of both Ariosto's epic and Greene's drama is a man of violence. He frequently uses his great strength destructively. In Greene's play Orlando tears off the leg of a shepherd and enters in Act 2 waving it like the club of Hercules. If we look closely at Shakespeare's Orlando, we find that he too is prone to violent action—even before the interrupted banquet scene. At the beginning of the play he knocks Oliver down and apparently pounds his head in the dirt, an action that sets old Adam hopping in distress. A few scenes later Orlando breaks the neck of Charles the wrestler who is carried off the field unconscious.

In Arden Orlando must learn that violence and physical prowess are not ends in themselves nor are they instruments of revenge. In addition, he must learn that love is more than a passion for a beautiful woman; it includes civility, gratitude, understanding, and charity in its highest meanings. Orlando begins to learn this lesson with Duke Senior's response to his drawn sword: "What would you have? Your gentlenesse shall force, more than your force, Move us to gentlenesse." Orlando's chagrin only increases his embarrassment. His speech reverts to the high civility of liturgical rhythms as his thoughts turn instinctively to the vital conception of nurture:

> If ever you have look'd on better dayes:
> If ever beene where bels have knoll'd to Church:
> If ever sate at any good man's feast:
> If ever from your eye-lids wip'd a teare,
> And know what 'tis to pitie, and be pitied
> Let gentlenesse my strong enforcement be
> In which hope, I blush, and hide my sword. (2.7.119–25)

Shakespeare stresses the message as Duke Senior repeats Orlando's statements. This moral exemplum is intended for Jaques's ears as well as Orlando's, for the moral lesson applies to Jaques's desire to gall and whip the world's follies under the license of the poet's cloak.

The next major testing of Orlando comes in the temptation he faces when he agrees to meet the sprightly Ganymede and court him as though he were the beautiful Rosalind. He says as he accepts Ganymede's challenge, "Now by the faith of my love, I will." This test of the quality of his love is also a test of his capacity for fidelity, for virtuous choice.

The third test comes in that graphic tableau that Oliver describes for the girls at the end of Act 4. The ancient tree, the wild man, the green snake, the hungry lioness, and the sorely tempted Orlando are depicted. Shakespeare has taken a simple scene of adventure from Thomas Lodge's *Rosalynde* and has turned it into the ethical climax of his drama; it contains the formal anagnorisis of the hero. As in the great tragedies where the formal recognition scenes are complex and at times ambiguous because the protagonists are not fully articulate, the images and actions must explicate the mental processes.

In this scene, which happens offstage as do the climactic actions of classical drama, archetypal images pull the pastoral setting suddenly into the mystical realm. Shakespeare intensifies the action with this mysticism that is an important part of the *paradiso terrestre* tradition. Shakespeare's images are dense with allusions, for when a Renaissance poet placed a tree and a snake in the center of a garden or woods, the Edenic reference was automatically created for his reader or audience. In the pastoral tradition stemming from Genesis, the human soul faces original temptation. The doctrine of original sin included not only the idea of mankind as Adam and Eve's progeny inheriting the flawed nature of the first couple, but also the idea that each human soul developing in this life must make a symbolic pilgrimage back to that forbidden tree in Eden and perform once again the fateful act of disobedience. When Orlando approaches the ancient oak that is "moss'd with age" and "bald with drie antiquitie," we note that the tree has been particularized for its setting in Arden, and we note also that Orlando is approaching a severe testing of his moral nature. We know that he is tempted to leave his infamous brother to the lioness, thus gaining his revenge:

> Twice did he turne his backe, and purpos'd so;
> But kindnesse, nobler ever than revenge,
> And Nature stronger than his just occasion,
> Made him give battell to the Lyonnesse. (4.3.127–30)

Orlando's virtuous nature triumphs over the villainous impulse to let the lioness destroy Oliver. Why? The snake and the lioness offer us an answer.

The green and gilded snake is that attractive serpent of Eden, and it has all the sexual overtones that the medieval churchmen associated with Satan in the original temptation. . . . But in Shakespeare's depiction of the Edenic experience, the snake slips into a bush. The snake is used to help identify the Edenic setting, but having done so, it disappears. Sensual temptation is not to be the character of this confrontation. It is no longer necessary because Orlando's love has proved faithful and pure.

Oliver is described as "a wretched ragged man, ore-growne with haire" who lies "sleeping on his back" near the tree. This is an image from emblematic literature. The image is also that of the ubiquitous wild man of the romance tradition who ducks in and out of dozens of medieval and Renaissance stories. He is usually interpreted as the symbol of humanity without divine grace. He is the image of Dante at the beginning of the *Inferno*, lost in the dark woods. The dark woods at the beginning of the *Commedia* is drawn in opposition to the sacred woods that we find at the end of the *Purgatorio*. And Dante, the wild man lost in ignorance and hatred in the dark woods, is the opposite of the regenerated pilgrim who learns his final lesson of love at the foot of the ancient tree.

Just as Adam faced temptation at the tree in Eden, Orlando faces temptation in Arden. Like Adam he has free will to succumb or to resist the impulse to evil, which in this case is self love that blinds man to the nature of true love. The struggle is powerful: "Twice did he turne his backe, and purpos'd so" (to desert Oliver). But Orlando resists the temptation and hurtles with the lioness. We note with satisfaction that our hero, rather than being passive, which is the natural opposite of being violent, uses his prowess to defend his brother. He has channeled his energy into proper action, and in doing so, he is wounded. By spilling his blood for his brother, he resembles the Second Adam whose blood is the premier symbol of sacrifice and love in Christianity.

From "The *Paradiso Terrestre* and the Testing of Love in *As You Like It*," *Shakespeare Studies* 14 (1981), 218–23 abridged.

*William Watterson (1991)*

## *As You Like It* as Christian Pastoral

*As You Like It* is much closer in spirit to the medieval "Tale of Gamelyn" than it is to Thomas Lodge's *Rosalynde* (1590), Shakespeare's principal source and one of the last of the prose romances composed in the euphuistic style. Lodge's self-conscious classicism, characterized by mannered, pseudo-Latinate diction, draws on an equally derivative conception of "Greek" moral philosophy, one which Shakespeare in his turn recast in a Christian vein consistent with the older chivalric material. At the same time, the playwright found inspiration in Lodge's invention of a pastoral subplot, recognizing in it the allegorical possibilities for a comedy both secular and "divine." Original sin, Providence, brotherly love, holy matrimony, and pastoral contentment with the tried estate—these ideas take on fresh life in *As You Like It* without transforming the green world of romance into a barren wasteland of dogma. Like Spenser, who in Book VI of the *Faerie Queene* (1596) represents the quest for courtesy and grace as a single heroic enterprise, Shakespeare conceives of aristocratic education as an apt metaphor for the soul's progress toward salvation. Arden Forest—alternately secular arcadia, allegorical representation of the Fallen World, and typological Eden—is the mystical setting at the heart of the play's spiritual meaning.

Both the hero and the heroine of *As You Like It* must prove their mutual worthiness for marriage by undergoing moral education and spiritual transformation.

Orlando, a hero of nature, not only lacks aristocratic qualities such as articulateness and civility, but worships Rosalind in a way that is idolatrous. Although he invokes a famous biblical parable to complain of his miserable upbringing to his brother in 1.1 ("Shall I keep your hogs, and eat husks with them? What prodigal portion have I spent that I should come to such penury?"), his excess is one of passion rather than purse. He is a muscular youth who easily defeats physical enemies such as Charles the Wrestler, yet falls prey to the subtler temptations of anger and despair. Like Sir Calidore, however, Orlando ultimately overcomes his own sinful nature through a symbolic, and climactic, external action. By slaying the lioness, whose dry udders symbolize lack of charity, he establishes himself as an exemplum of the compassionate and brotherly love of the New Testament. Likewise, his ability to scare away the "green and gilded snake" of envy as recounted by Oliver in 4.3 (the serpent's "unlinking" of itself suggests release from the bondage of the old covenant) makes him out as a hero redeemed in Christ. With the perfection of his spiritual nature manifest in action, Orlando receives for his earthly reward the "heavenly" Rosalind in the usual manner of romance. In fact, he has very little either to do or say in Act 5, his liver "clean as a sound sheep's heart" thanks to the virtuous example and curative counsel of his future wife.

A kind of flesh and blood Beatrice, Rosalind nurtures the rustic Orlando in the courtly virtues of elocution and punctuality. More important, she teaches him the proper moral relationship between wit and will at the heart of Christian discipline. For all of her admirable self-control and aristocratic mien, however, she is not without a trace of the spiritual deficiencies usually attendant on such superiority, namely, pride and love of the world. In a mock-heroic trope she compares herself to the betrayed Christ, observing to Celia that Orlando's hair is "Judas's color" and amplifying her comic blasphemy with the claim that "his kissing is as full of sanctity as the touch of holy bread" (3.4.12–13). No less infatuated than Orlando, she is eager to "cure" him of love-sickness because she craves similar relief for herself. Shakespeare represents her passion—so novel and so unsettling to her—as a kind of necessary penalty (as with Olivia in *Twelfth Night*), the whip and dark room she prescribes serving as a fitting emblem of the humility she herself must learn. What is her castigation of Phebe's pride but a kind of self-exorcism? Ostensibly superior in her masculine disguise as mentor, Rosalind ends up learning as much about herself from the emotional effect that Orlando has on her as he ever learns from her speech lessons. As fellow pupils they exist in equipoise.

The motif of the Fall is central to *As You Like It*, with Arden Forest a pervasive metaphor for post-lapsarian nature. As Helen Gardner pointed out years ago, Charles the Wrestler's equation of Duke Senior's woodland exile with the "golden world" of Antiquity (1.1) is pointedly revised by the Duke himself (2.1), whose version of pastoral is Mantuanesque rather than arcadian. While the idea of the

*felix culpa* will be echoed in the secular lyrics of Amiens in 2.5 and 2.7, the nobleman's tone is unmistakably homiletic:

> Now my co-mates and brothers in exile,
> Hath not old custom made this life more sweet
> Than that of painted pomp? Are not these woods
> More free from peril than the envious court?
> Here feel we not the penalty of Adam,
> The seasons' difference, as the icy fang
> And churlish chiding of the winter's wind,
> Which when it bites and blows upon my body
> Even till I shrink with cold, I smile and say
> This is no flattery; these are counsellors
> That feelingly persuade me what I am.
> Sweet are the uses of adversity,
> Which, like the toad, ugly and venomous,
> Wears yet a precious jewel in his head.
> And this our life, exempt from public haunt,
> Finds tongues in trees, books in the running brooks,
> Sermons in stones, and good in everything. (2.1.1–17)

The spiritual life here is envisioned, paradoxically, as one of active striving in a
pastoral setting of retirement and contemplation. In reality a blessing, the
"penalty" of Adam provides a welcome opportunity to demonstrate the Christian
virtue of patient faith. Devoid of the "aspiring mind" inimical to pastoral, Duke
Senior preaches to his monastic cohorts about the evils of courtly pride and envy.
Like Sir Thomas Browne, he regards nature as the art of God, but he elaborates on
the metaphor by seeing in the forest a hieratic progression from profane to sacred
discourse. Words like "chiding," "say," "flattery," and "persuade" make way finally
for images of holy saying and inscribing. The Mosaic "sermons in stone" permit a
typological identification of the "books in running brooks" as the redemptive
books of the New Testament (in the fourth chapter of *John* Christ equates his gift
of grace with "living waters"), with the Duke's pun on "God" ("good in everything") reinforcing the idea of the fortunate fall. Orlando's Petrarchan scribblings
seem poor by comparison.

In representing Arden Forest as a theatre of sin and, typologically, as an eternal green place, Shakespeare took his inspiration from Book VI of Spenser's great
poem rather than from *Rosalynde*, where pastoral conventions lack religious significance. Just as the land of faery has at its center the paradisal Mount Acidale, so
Arden Forest contains divine mystery at its core (the appearance of Hymen in 5.4
results in Rosalind's antiphonal exchanges with the wedding couples, and I hear in
them the rhetorical equivalent of Spenser's many images of circularity and round-
ness in the vanishing Graces episode). Both allegorists people their landscapes with
hermits, magicians, and "old religious men" to aid those temporarily lost in the
dark wood of spiritual struggle.

More literal than Spenser, Shakespeare gives us a faithful servant named Adam in *As You Like It* whose lifetime of selflessness and loyalty wins him the "new" home of Arden as allegorical equivalent of Eden. This Adam is Elijah-like in his trust in the providential power "that doth the ravens feed," and he likens his old age to "a lusty winter, Frosty but kindly," thus transcending the decadence ascribed to old age by the cynical Jaques. (There is a theatre legend that this Adam was played on stage by Shakespeare himself.) The play also shows us a symbolic "old" Adam, the "wretched ragged man" reclining under a tree (an emblem of original sin in its "dry antiquity" but also of potential new life because the tree's boughs are "moss'd"). An old-Adam Oliver is reborn in grace under this tree. The play places equal emphasis on the virtues of faith and good works. Corin's comment in 2.4 on his master's delinquencies—

> his cote, his flocks, and bounds of feed
> Are now on sale, and at our sheepcote now
> By reason of his absence there is nothing
> That you will feed on

—could apply to both Catholic and Protestant bishops who sell benefices and have more interest in material rewards than in pastoral duty.

Competing temporal schemes in *As You Like It* provide an additional analogical dimension to Shakespeare's allegory. "There's no clock in the forest," says Orlando, in a play in which images of minutes, hours, days, months, years, and even Jaques' seven ages of man adumbrate an idea of time as apocalyptic. If *As You Like It* was first offered during the Twelfth Night season—a likely surmise even in the absence of Amiens' green holly image (2.7)—it played at the jointure of the old and new years. Christmas celebrates the birth of the Messiah and his gift of grace, but to do so must also tragically foreshadow the crucifixion necessary to ensure the Last Judgment. In Rosalind's disturbing image of a thief carted to execution time does indeed "gallop withal," as in Revelation (3:3 and 16:15) where Christ foreshadows the terrible suddenness of his Second Coming.

The theme of conversion—inseparable from that of Providence—is at the heart of Shakespeare's dramaturgy, since it is only the spontaneous changes of heart in Oliver and Duke Frederick that permit the political plot of *As You Like It* to come to happy resolution. In telling of his rescue at the hands of Orlando in 4.3, Oliver renounces his former "unnatural" self as he proclaims how "sweetly tastes" his conversion. Likewise Duke Frederick (called Torismonde in *Rosalynde*, where he is simply killed off in battle) is "converted both from his enterprise and from the world" after meeting with an old religious man. Jaques de Boys, who narrates this account (5.4.150–64), reports how the Duke dispersed a "mighty force" and bequeathed his crown to his banished brother while under the mysterious spell of the Forest. The theme of conversion also extends, although less decisively, to the character of Jaques, a "chartered libertine" and courtly roué wholly of

Shakespeare's invention. His self-appointed task of railing "against the first born of Egypt" seems appropriate for one whose name abbreviates the biblical Jacob and suggests a privy. The Jaques who has sold his lands to see another's may derive his character in some measure from the Wandering Jew of mediaeval legend. Whether he will find at last a rest from his peregrinations is left uncertain at the end of *As You Like It*. He has come at least to recognize a tantalizing mystery: "Out of these convertites / There is much matter to be heard and learn'd."

Charity in its varied forms is one of the principal themes of the play. Corin's famous praise of hospitality ("My master is of churlish disposition / And little reeks to find the way to heaven / By doing deeds of hospitality") invokes Romans 12:13 as well as possibly Matthew 25:35 and 43. Duke Senior's welcoming of Orlando's concern for food for the starving Adam can be seen as an allegory of the eucharist's meaning, since the Duke invites to his table those who have "with holy bell been knoll'd to church / And sat at good men's feasts, and wip'd [their] eyes / Of drops that sacred pity hath engend'red." That "sacred pity" leads Orlando finally to forgive the brother who has wronged him and overcome the lion which, as we have seen, is an emblem of angry righteousness. Like Prospero, he embraces the most difficult lesson in the Sermon on the Mount—to love one's enemy—deciding finally that the rarer action is in virtue, not vengeance.

Although multiple marriages are the stock-in-trade of Shakespearean comedy, *As You Like It* is especially notable for its climactic and supernatural blessing of the "eight that must take hands" (symbolic of the eight who were saved by entering Noah's ark). When Hymen descends to reunite Rosalind with her father in a masque-like atmosphere of music and dance, the stage effect reinforces a sacramental idea in ways perhaps suggestive of the old faith. The God of marriage is represented as an angelic spirit who mediates between mortals and the godhead:

> Then is there mirth in heaven,
> When earthly things made even
> Atone together. (5.4.107–9)

The primary meaning of "atone" in this passage is "are reconciled," a meaning reinforced by Hymen's "Peace ho! I bar confusion / 'Tis I must make conclusion / Of these most strange events." The trope of concord may signify both Christ's atonement for sin and individual atonement in the form of conversion and repentance, the motifs we have seen inscribed in the play's theological allegory. In *As You Like It* earthly love and heavenly love corroborate to bring about marriage as an emblem of grace.

A play which mocks the obsessive nature of human sexual desire and offers its fair share of jokes about cuckoldry, *As You Like It* represents celibacy as a reasonable alternative to wedded love, notwithstanding Rosalind's flippant reference to a "nook merely monastic" (3.2.408). Indeed, the fact that characters refer to Arden as a "desert" six times evokes the idea of the early Egyptian fathers or "eremites."

The chastity of Duke Senior, Duke Frederick, Corin, and the "old religious man" exemplifies monastic virtue in a form associated with the old faith.

Corin as *pastor bonus* exemplifies humility and charity "glad of other men's good, content with my harm" (3.1.93). Here again, Shakespeare departs from Lodge, whose Corydon praises bucolic existence for its freedom from *negotium*: "Satis est quod sufficit." In contrast, Shakespeare's Corin, like Thenot, Piers, and Morrel in *The Shepheardes Calendar*, extols "this shepherd's life" because of its dedication to pastoral care ("seeing [his] lambs suck"). His active virtue ("Sir, I am a true laborer") complements Duke Senior's valuing of the contemplative life. Responding to Touchstone's courtesy-book jargon with the fundamentalism of tautology ("The property of rain is to wet"), Corin holds his own against the vanity inherent in the decadence of "too courtly a wit." In him the playwright seems to hearken back to the Cotswolds of his boyhood, where shepherds watched their flocks with the faithfulness of their counterparts in *Luke*.

The Editor requested this essay from Professor Watterson of Bowdoin College.

*René E. Fortin (1973)*

## "Tongues in Trees" in *As You Like It*

By focusing on a largely unnoticed correlation between two scenes—Act 2, scene 1, which contains Jaques's lamentation over the wounded deer, and Act 4, scene 3, which dramatizes the rescue of Oliver by Orlando—I would like to demonstrate that Shakespeare has subtly transformed his source materials in order to introduce images, drawn from both the classical and Christian worlds, that serve to charge these key scenes with symbolic significance. Jaques indicts man for his cruel and selfish slaughter of animals "in their assigned and native dwelling place" (2.1.63). Taken at face value, his speech seems to propose an unfavorable contrast between men, who are "mere usurpers, tyrants" (2.1.61), and animals, who live in natural innocence. His immediate point, of course, is that men are "fat and greasy citizens," concerned only for their own welfare and indifferent to the sufferings of others.

Act 4, scene 3 presents the other side of the picture; here man, in the person of Oliver, is threatened by hostile animals—the snake and the lion—and it is man who is shown to be capable of true compassion for suffering:

> Under an old oak, whose boughs were mossed with age
> And high top bald with dry antiquity,
> A wretched ragged man, o'ergrown with hair,

Lay sleeping on his back; about his neck
A green and gilded snake had wreathed itself,
Who with her head, nimble in threats, approached
The opening of his mouth; but suddenly,
Seeing Orlando, it unlinked itself
And with indented glides did slip away
Into a bush, under which bush's shade
A lioness, with udders all drawn dry,
Lay couching, head on ground, with catlike watch
When that the sleeping man should stir; for 'tis
The royal disposition of that beast
To prey on nothing that doth seem as dead. (4.3.105–19)

Orlando then rescues his brother, scaring off the snake and twice resisting the temptation to leave Oliver to the lion; his act is one of gratuitous mercy, and its effect upon Oliver, whose intent was to kill Orlando, is to work his instantaneous conversion. We are, on this level, offered a corrective of Jaques's jaundiced view of man, testimony of man's ethical superiority to the animal world.

But the scene offers a great deal more than this corrective; a comparison of it with the cognate scene in Lodge's *Rosalynde*, the proximate source of *As You Like It*, reveals that Shakespeare has adapted it to suit his own purposes. Saladyne-Oliver, located indifferently outside a cave in Lodge, is in Shakespeare lying under an "antique oak," precisely as Jaques had been in moralizing upon the slaughter of the deer. Lodge's Saladyne has repented of his treatment of Orlando and is seeking reconciliation with him before undertaking a pilgrimage to the Holy Land: "I go thus pilgrime like to seeke out my Brother, that I may reconcile my selfe to him in all submission, and afterward wend to the Holy Land, to ende my yeares in as manie vertues, as I have spent my youth in wicked vanities." Oliver, on the other hand, is seeking Orlando in order to kill him and is not converted until after his rescue by Orlando.

The differences are anything but accidental; they seem, in fact, intended to link Act 2, scene 1 and Act 4, scene 3 more closely and to deepen the significance of the issues these scenes explore. The most obvious link between the two passages, and yet the most mysterious, is the imagery of the ancient oak. The oak is indeed, as Coleridge sensed, a remarkable tree in a remarkable forest which contains as well palms and olive trees. The conclusion we should draw, I suggest, is that tree imagery is being used symbolically rather than realistically. On one level, the ancient oak provides an emblem of great age, and especially of the dignity of great age, offering in this capacity a tacit rebuttal of Jaques's sardonic "seven ages of man" speech.

In Ovid's *Metamorphoses* the oak is associated with Jove in the Baucis and Philemon episode (VIII 764–909), and with Ceres in the Erysichthon episode:

He also is reported too have heaven in wicked wyse
The grove of Ceres, and to fell her holy woods which ay

> Had undiminisht and unhackt continewed to that day.
> There stood in it a warrie Oke which was a wood alone.
> Uppon it round hung fillets, crownes, and tables, many one,
> The vowes of such as had obteynd theyr hearts desyre.
> (VIII 927–32)

The oak (or terebinth) has also a place of honor in the Old Testament. Shakespeare would probably have remembered that God appeared to Abraham near the Oak of Moreh (Gn 12:6)—later called the "Diviner's Oak" (Jgs 9:32)—and that Abraham dwelt by the Oak of Mamre, where he built an altar to the Lord (Gn 13:18); that Jacob was commanded to bury his tribe's idols under an oak (Gn 35:4) and that Deborah was ceremonially buried under the Oak of Lamentations (Gn 35:4).

While the oak tree, because of its durability and strength, predictably became an emblem of royalty and stateliness, it also lent itself, particularly because of its association with Bethel (the "House of God"), to more mystical interpretations. There is thus a characteristic conflation of pagan and Christian traditions in the fourteenth-century *Ovide moralisé* in the author's comment on the Erysichthon episode; the oak being destroyed by Erysichthon represents the church and its saints being persecuted by unbelievers (VIII 4269–4276).... We will recall that Rosalind describes the oak under which Orlando sleeps as "Jove's tree" (3.3.225).

The fact that the oak imagery, despite its absence in the sources, has been introduced by Shakespeare strongly suggests that his aim is to exploit the traditional pagan and Christian connotations of the oak. The ancient tree described as "Sacred with many a mystery" in E. K.'s gloss to Spenser's *Shepherd's Calendar* (February eclogue) has become for the moment a primitive hallowed forest, a sacred grove that also contains Biblical palms and olive trees. As a result, the drama of atonement enacted in *As You Like It*, while losing nothing of its worldly zest, assumes cosmic implications.

The addition of the snake to the perils of Oliver (who was threatened only by a lion in Lodge) confirms the symbolic intention of the rescue scene. As Richard Knowles has convincingly argued, the play establishes in the first act a parallel between Orlando and Hercules (1.2.192) and the snake and the lion seem intended to fulfill the allusion, the lion referring to the Nemean lion slain by Hercules and the snake recalling any of his several adventures with serpentine monsters. Medieval allegorists were struck by the many analogies between Hercules and Christ—including their divine origins, the similarity of their labors, their glorious resurrections, and especially their common descent to the Underworld—and saw in the pagan hero a type of Christ. That the canonization of Hercules continued into the Renaissance is attested by Ronsard's "*Hercule Chrétien*" (1555), which recapitulates the medieval tradition, stating as its premise: "*... la pluspart des choses qu'on escrit/D'Hercule est deue à un seul Jesus Christ.*"

There is warrant enough, therefore, within literary tradition for identifying Hercules as a type of Christ, and, in view of this blending of pagan and Christian traditions, for finding yet another compatible source for the snake and lion of the rescue scene, in Psalm 91:

> Thou shalt walke upon the lion and aspe: the young lion
> and the dragon shalt thou tread under fete. (Ps 91:13)

The snake, as the Biblical allusion indicates, is used as a primordial symbol of evil, and this "green and gilded snake" is then fully at home in the quasi-Edenic world of Arden. But what of the lion? The reduplication of evil agents by Shakespeare becomes understandable when one considers how carefully Shakespeare has distinguished between them; for he contrasts the motiveless malignity of the snake, which would wantonly attack a sleeping man, with the nobility and justifiable motive of the lioness, which is attacking in order to feed her young. The distinction being made, apparently, is the traditional Christian distinction between natural evil and moral evil, available in many sources but paralleling closely the comment made by Saint Thomas Aquinas:

> The universe of creatures is all the better and more perfect if some things in it can fail in goodness, and so sometimes fail, God not preventing this. This happens, firstly, because *it belongs to Providence not to destroy, but to save nature*, as Dionysus says (*Div. Nom.* iv); but it belongs to nature that what may fail shall also sometimes fail; secondly, because as Augustine says (*Enchir.*11), *God is so powerful that He can even make good out of evil.* Hence many good things would be taken away if God permitted no evil to exist. (*S. T.* I.48.2)

This seems finally to be the answer to the questions raised by Jaques in Act 2: that there are two kinds of evil, both of them indispensable in the economy of the universe, for it is evil that provides the occasion for the emergence of good. Moreover, the killing of the deer, which evoked Jaques's sentimental response, is a necessary natural evil and morally blameless since it is done out of physical necessity—the motive of the lioness—rather than out of malice—the motive of the snake. The conclusion to which we are directed is that Jaques, whose frustrated craving for an innocent world has embittered him, must reconcile himself with the world as it is; the world, precisely, cannot be "as you like it," the problem of evil allowing for no facile solutions.

In the context of these religious images, which should, I am convinced, be taken seriously, Orlando himself assumes symbolic stature. His action of redeeming Oliver by his own blood is clearly reminiscent of the Christian mystery of man's redemption; like Christ, Orlando has conquered, by the gratuitous expression of love, the moral evil symbolized by the snake. His action is a fulfillment of the statement made earlier by Rosalind in another context: "I see love hath made thee a tame snake" (4.3.70–1) and of the Biblical prophecy quoted above: "Thou shalt walke upon the lion and aspe: the young lion and the dragon shalt thou tread

under fete." As Knowles points out (p. 15), further details add to the symbolic suggestions: "The religious overtones of the events are amplified by several suggestive
details: Oliver receives 'fresh array' from the patriarchal Duke, alters his whole
personality, bears as a token of his savior's sacrifice a napkin dyed with his blood,
and falls immediately in love with a girl named Celia ['heaven']."

Finally, the spontaneity of Oliver's conversion, which has so troubled critics,
now appears to be less the result of Shakespeare's cavalier handling of details than
a deliberate change from the source in order to highlight the mystery of love. The
point of the conversion of Oliver—as well as that of Duke Frederick, who is
turned from his iniquity by an "old religious man" (5.4.154–56)—is precisely its
sheer gratuitousness: the "irrationality" of Orlando's redemption of Oliver, whom
he had no reason to love, brings about Oliver's equally "irrational" conversion. It
is the mystery of grace that is being figured forth in these improbable acts of moral
regeneration. We are, in this consummation of the symbolic pattern, seeing the
drama of atonement being worked out on a theological plane. . . . The symbols are
grounded in the indissoluble literal reality of the play and, while serving to illumi-
nate the central action of the drama, they do not violate its integrity. Shakespearean symbolism, in the comedies as in the tragedies, comes not to destroy but
to fulfill.

From "'Tongues in Trees': Symbolic Patterns in *As You Like It*," *Texas Studies in
Literature and Language* 14 (1973), 569–82 abridged.

# TWELFTH NIGHT

## Comment and bibliography

While the suitability of *As You Like It* to a Christmastide performance is perhaps indicated in the reference by Amiens to the "green holly," the title *Twelfth Night* is a direct reference to the Epiphany of the Christmas season. Does the play's story have actually a typological relationship to Gospel story? In answering this question it may be pertinent to recall the *Second Shepherds' Play* of medieval drama. That play had a double-sided epiphany: centrally, the emergence of an active charity when the shepherds offer their gifts to the "child," and secondly the exposure of the selfish deceptiveness of Mak, who is punished by being tossed in a blanket. Figuratively, does not a blanket-tossing or shameful embarrassment punish the selfish love of Orsino and Olivia, who at the same time are converted to a healthy love by discovering the hidden charity of Viola and Sebastian? Christmas is the season for activating within the life of a contemporary community the well-known hymn to Bethlehem: "Cast out our sin and enter in; / Be born in us today." A purging by which we rediscover the humility of a childlike faith is central to the meaning of Christmas. Ring out the false, ring in the true. Is not this "What you will"?

Barbara Lewalski was the earliest critic to call attention to the Epiphany dimension of *Twelfth Night*. The play's exposing of follies is ministered chiefly by the clown Feste and by his cohort Maria, both representative of witty Good Will and good sense within a household of revelling sots such as Sir Toby and Sir Andrew, and elegant caperers such as Orsino, and dreamers on self-importance such as the veiled Olivia and, more egregiously, the self-loving Malvolio. The drama's ministers of a mysteriously redemptive love, concurrently, are Viola and Sebastian, who witness by their deeds more than by words to a charity that suffers long and is kind and embodies a faithfulness to gracious values. The timely apocalypse of the hidden sacrificial devotion of these visitors in Illyria collapses the delusions of the worldly Olivia and Orsino and begets in them a conversion of heart. Thus is fulfilled figuratively an Epiphany text: "Arise, shine, for thy light is come" (Is 60).

Feste is a holiday Lord of Misrule, a licensed mimicker of the disorders that need to be vented. Orsino is aware that his fancy for Olivia is giddy and skittish; yet he indulges it as a noble longing in which he is ready to die in a show of constancy to the "image" of the creature he loves. A fashionable idolatry such as absorbs this Duke is indeed a "nothing," simply another variety of the shallow love Shakespeare explored in his *Much Ado*. It is a pompous deformation of a man pathetically in need of some deflating. So Feste obligingly sings for him a melancholy song on "Come away, death," in order to help this love to surfeit and be mortified, while at the same time Feste ironically praises Orsino for a "constancy" which is making a "good voyage of nothing." Feste's role is to expose wittily what is motley in the minds and moods of his neighbors while letting us know that there's nothing motley about Feste's own brain—only in the visible "patched" hood he wears as the stalking horse from under which to shoot his barbed wisdom. He correctly describes himself as living "by the church"—a next door neighbor, so to speak. His "ventings" support the church's task (as described in James 1:21 KJV) to cast away all "superfluity of naughtiness," i.e., of nothingness.

A mask or hood similar to Feste's is adopted by Viola. That is, she disguises her charitable love behind the facade of fashionable wooing which she voices in her encounter with Olivia. Her set speech, imitative of the Petrarchan language in which Orsino wishes to present his "suit," serves Viola as a conventional exterior and is in the present situation appropriate, since she is dealing with a lady who herself wears a literal "veil." Olivia's veil, however, is intended to hide not a secret charity but an "inventory" of Petrarchan beauties in her face. Such a veil, though it seems to signal modesty and indeed a kind of monastic retirement, is not really monastic in the religious sense but rather hides under it a proud self that seeks an isolation from responsibility. Olivia retains nevertheless a feminine instinct, and by this she is able to intuit behind Viola's set speech a something "other." It is this mysterious "other" that attracts Olivia and draws her out of her isolation. Olivia is a potential "madonna" (the term Feste four times accords her), but she can be released into that role only by Viola's mediation.

We see the process begin in 1.5, immediately after Viola has spoken cryptically of holding "the olive in my hand" and bearing words "full of peace." Such language glances at the potentiality of meaning in Olivia's own name. It has an import quite other than those flowers of rhetoric which Olivia has felt to be comically rude. "What are you?" she asks. "What would you?" And it is at this point that Viola speaks a language redolent, as Maurice Hunt has recently noted, of an Annunciation like that by the angel in Luke 1:30.

> What I am, and what I would, are as secret as maidenhead—
> to your own ears divinity, to any others, profanation.

To which Olivia replies: "Give us place alone. We will hear *this divinity*" (emphasis added). Viola then speaks of having a "comfortable" doctrine, a phrase that echoes Isaiah 40. "Where lies your text?" Olivia asks; and Viola's reply, "In Orsino's bosom," is paradoxically true, since its *lying* or false version is there, where its true potential or "first chapter" has been suppressed. Equally correct is Olivia's reading its glossed message as "heresy." She asks to hear something "more" than perverse religion. When Viola then asks to see Olivia's face, Olivia responds affirmatively but supposes Viola to be now "out of your text." Viola's text, however, is that the face is excellent only "if God did all" and if its possessor does not bury its graces in a grave. To Olivia's question "What would you?" Viola's reply concludes with "you should pity me"—an answer which awakens Olivia's interest in Viola as a person, especially the "invisible" perfections which Olivia now has an eye for, and to which she hastens to wed herself symbolically with the ring she sends Viola.

This beginning of Olivia's redemption may be said to be like that of a hart that panteth after the waterbrook (Ps 42); the thirst can be allayed only when a companion "heart" is found in 4.1. in the "fair wisdom" of Sebastian, whose name meaning "the venerable" signifies a worthiness to be worshipped. To him Olivia plights her faith before a priest, asking that she may "live at peace" (her name's meaning). The final epiphany comes in the next Act when she discovers she has married, happily so, a husband who is more than Cesario but was signalled through the Caesario personage of Viola.

Viola has signalled to Orsino her true nature as early as the scene in which she speaks of a sister who loved in Patient Silence a man who looked like Orsino. Was not this, she asks, "love indeed"? But he feels for her only a dim attraction until, confronted with a seeming betrayal by this "boy," he swears he will "sacrifice the lamb that I do love"—only to find that this lamb has been a maiden disguising a love for him. His fool-self then collapses and true love emerges.

In the play's final epiphany we hear that even Toby has discovered in Maria a bride for whom he is ready to give up his drinking; apparently he has found "cakes and ale" on a higher plane. Andrew Aguecheek, however, never outgrows his childishness. And Malvolio resists conversion, lost in his "dark house" of self-centeredness. Having lacked perceptivity for the mysterious in Viola, he is doomed to be a time-server of his own shadow. Maria refers to him as "sometimes . . . a kind of puritan," but he has none of the religion of a genuine puritan. Rather, he has the stereotype attitudes of a 'politic' or heathen puritan who worships Fortune as his god, reads letters with an eye for his own "election" to greatness, and piously thanks Jove for his own self-flattering illusions. Chris Hassel has described him as a dramatic contrast to Sebastian.

Our anthology reprints the commentary of Barbara Lewalski and a supplement to it provided by René Fortin. Lewalski, after pointing out the exemplary loves of Viola and Sebastian, suggests that they function as dramatic analogies of the twin human and divine natures of Christ which the Feast of Epiphany celebrates. Alongside this level of theological allegory, Fortin finds the psychological allegory of a society's rites of initiation into adulthood, during which youths come to understand through their tribal wisemen the dual mysteries of femininity and masculinity that co-exist symbolically in human identity and also signal the mystery of sacrificial love.

I have already indicated the value of Maurice Hunt's essay. Other supplementary reading should include the study by J. L. Simmons of aspects of Malvolio's

behavior that reflect features of puritanism conspicuous in Elizabethan controversy. Some of the theological punning by Feste and by Maria has been noted by
Moelwyn Merchant. The "M. O. A. I." riddle has been explained by Inge Leimberg: it is an anagram of "I'm A[lpha] & O[mega]," a motto ironically appropriate
to Malvolio's aspiring to a godlike status. Michael Taylor surmises that Maria's
purpose is to get Malvolio to "pursue inanity to excess" so he may surfeit of it and
die to it. In Sebastian and Viola, Taylor emphasizes their recognition of a dependence on the workings of providence. Marion Bodwell Smith treats well the play's
carnival function of releasing follies that they may surfeit and be purged. The
"clarification" toward which the romance action moves is a "revelation of love" in
tune with Christian Epiphany. Chris Hassel emphasizes the play's dependence on
the Pauline-Erasmian paradoxes of foolish wisdom and wise folly.

## Supplementary bibliography

Hassel, R. Chris, Jr. *Faith and Folly in Shakespeare's Romantic Comedies* (1980), Ch. 6.
Hunt, Maurice. "*Twelfth Night* and the Annunciation," *Papers on Language and Literature*
    25 (1989), 264–71.
Leimberg, Inge. "Trying to Share the Joke in *Twelfth Night* 2.5," *Connotations* 1 (1991),
    78–95; and "Maria's Theology and Other Questions," 1 (1991), 191–96.
Merchant, Moelwyn. "Shakespeare's Theology," *Review of English Literature* 5 (1964),
    72–88, notably pp. 84–85.
Simmons, J. L. "A Source for Shakespeare's Malvolio: The Elizabethan Controversies
    with the Puritans," *The Huntington Library Quarterly* 36 (1973), 181–201.
Smith, Marion B. *Dualities in Shakespeare* (University of Toronto Press, 1966), Ch. 5.
Taylor, Michael. "*Twelfth Night* and *What You Will*," *Critical Quarterly* 16 (1974),
    71–80.

*Barbara K. Lewalski (1965)*

## Thematic Patterns in *Twelfth Night*

Though the point has received little attention, I believe it can be shown that the
central themes and motifs of this play contain something of the religious significance associated with Epiphany and with the spirit of Christmastide. By this
statement I do not imply that the play is an allegory in which characters and incidents are designed to stand for or mean abstract qualities or religious personages.
Nor is Shakespeare's method here much like Plato's mode of allegory, in which a
particular sensible object (here the dramatic fiction) has its own kind of reality but
yet reflects or images forth something in the realm of Forms or Archetypes which
is more real. Rather, Shakespeare's method resembles, and was probably formed
by, that other tradition of allegorical interpretation which was still influential in
the Renaissance, namely the tradition of Christian typology, whereby certain real

historical events and personages from the Old Testament and (more significantly for the present purposes) from certain classical fictions such as the *Metamorphoses* or the *Aeneid* were seen to point to aspects of Christ and of the Gospel story without losing their own historical or fictional reality.[1]

Illyria is one of several idealized locales in Shakespeare's romantic comedies and romances, a "second world" markedly different from and in most respects better than the real world by reason of its pervasive atmosphere of song and poetry, its dominant concern with love and the "good life" (that is, the life of revelry), and its freedom from any malicious villainy. . . . If Malvolio's "Bad Will" (self-love) constitutes the antagonistic force to the life of Illyria we may be directed by this fact to the recognition that the Elysium-like quality of this place emanates from a festival atmosphere of *Good Will* which has banished active malice and radical selfishness and has created a genuine community. These terms invite recall of the Christmas message proclaimed by the angels, rendered in the Geneva Bible as "peace on earth, and towards men good will," and in the Rheims New Testament as "on earth peace to men of good will."

But if Illyria is in some respects related to Elysium as a place of Good Will exhibiting the spirit of the season, it is also a place much in need of the restoration and peace of the Christmastide promises. The name Illyria may be intended to suggest illusion in the sense of distortion, disorder, and faulty perception of self and others; at any rate, as J. R. Brown has pointed out, these are all dominant features of Illyrian life.[2] C. L. Barber notes that "madness" is a key word in this play:[3] almost every character exclaims about the madness and disorder afflicting other people and sometimes himself as well. . . . This pervasive "madness," while it is not malicious or vicious and may even be in some respects restorative, nevertheless leads each person whom it afflicts towards a culpable self-centeredness and a potentially dangerous indulgence of emotional excess. Illyria is badly in need of restoration to order and peace, but such a restoration as will also preserve the merriment, spontaneity, and sense of human community displayed in the "mad" state.

Opposition to the forces of self-love and disorder in Illyria is offered by certain characters who embrace wholeheartedly the human activities of love and merrymaking but who are preserved from "madness" by positive ordering principles within themselves and who project these principles as forces to restore and reorder the community.

Maria embodies one such restorative force within Illyria: sheer wit. Early in the play Feste points to her special quality, terming her "as witty a piece of Eve's flesh as any in Illyria" (1.5.25–26). Maria employs her wit as contriver and executor of the masterful plot against Malvolio: her faked letter is cleverly framed so as to confirm Malvolio's self-delusions about Olivia's regard for him, and the letter's recommendations that Malvolio affect yellow stockings, cross-garters, constant smiles, and surly behavior are brilliantly calculated to insure his self-exposure. The power of Maria's wit is thus addressed to the revelation and punishment of the "madness" involved in self-delusion, self-love, and hypocritic affectation of virtue.

The clown Feste is the second force working from within to reorder and perfect Illyria. In many respects he is Malvolio's opposite, incarnating the spirit of festival Good Will. He frequents Orsino's court as well as Olivia's house, takes part in the midnight revels of Sir Toby, and masquerades as Sir Topas the clergyman coming to exorcise "Malvolio the lunatic". . . . Feste in the guise of Sir Topas the curate (the topaz stone was traditionally thought to cure madness)[4] endeavors to cure Malvolio's "lunacy" by witty mockery designed to point out the true madness of his attitudes. Responding to Malvolio's constant protestations of his sanity, Feste replies, "Madman, thou errest. I say there is no darkness but ignorance, in which thou are more puzzled than the Egyptians in their fog" (4.2.42–44). The exchange about Pythagoras' opinion concerning the transmigration of souls is not merely comic dialogue since it deals with the sources of Malvolio's lunacy: lack of sensitivity to others, lack of concern for any life beyond his own.

The forces of wit and festival—of Good Will—can do much to reorder and restore Illyria but they cannot do everything. They can in large part reclaim Olivia from melancholic surrender to excessive grief, they can control and care for Sir Toby, they can expose the real "lunacy" of Malvolio and cast him forth as comic Satan into the bondage and darkness which was supposedly the fate of Satan himself at the nativity of Christ. But they cannot reform Malvolio, they cannot deal effectively with the love disorders of Orsino and Olivia, and they cannot restore the community as a whole to the "peace" that is the special promise of the season. For this a force must come from outside, presenting a pattern of perfect love and perfect order, and having power to produce these qualities in the community. Such a force enters the Illyrian world in the persons of the twins, Viola and Sebastian.

Though the two are dramatically separate, Viola and Sebastian represent thematically two aspects of the same restorative process. This fact is suggested partly by an identity in their physical appearances so absolute that they themselves recognize no differences. . . . More important, there is a remarkable identity in the events of their lives: both endure a sea tempest, both are saved and aided by good sea captains, both are wooed by and in a manner of speaking woo Olivia, both are forced to a duel with Andrew Aguecheek, both give money to Feste, both are in the end betrothed to their proper lovers. By these parallels the twin motif is made to do much more than to provide occasion for comic misapprehension and misunderstanding, though it does that also in good measure.

Viola, disguised throughout the play as the page Cesario, is the embodiment of selfless love (as Maria is the embodiment of wit and Feste of festival foolery); as such she provides a direct contrast to the self-centered passions of Orsino and Olivia and at length inspires both to a purified love. Herself desperately in love with Orsino from her earliest encounters with him, Viola-Cesario acts with perfect selflessness in her difficult position as his emissary in wooing Olivia. Though she endeavors to talk both Olivia and Orsino out of their hopeless passions, she is above any duplicity to serve her own interest: rather she presses hard her master's case with Olivia, she can pay just tribute to the beauty of her rival, she is moved to pity rather than mockery when she discovers Olivia's unlucky attraction to her disguised self, she never betrays or scorns Olivia's foolish manifestations of affection, and she is even willing to be sacrificed by Orsino in his fit of jealous rage. This pattern of selfless love acts finally to inspire right love in Olivia and Orsino: Olivia's attraction to the "outside" but also to the inner worth of Viola-Cesario brings her to discard completely her self-indulgent grief and readies her for the final transfer of her affection to Sebastian, Viola's alter ego and the right recipient of her love. Orsino is inspired almost at once to love of his "boy" Cesario (Valentine comments on the suddenness and depth of the affection in 1.4.1–3) and is so moved by the story of Viola's constant love and hard service undertaken for him that he loves her at last in her own person.

Because her love is selfless, Viola is able to embrace love fully, freely, and at once, to share in the common human turbulence of feeling attending upon love without ever giving way to the madness and disorder that accompany the selfish passions of Orsino and Olivia; she is thus a pattern of the ordered self as well as of selfless love. In this respect Viola is specifically contrasted with Olivia: both have lost (as they suppose) dearly beloved brothers, but Olivia has disordered herself and disrupted her household by giving way to excessive grief whereas Viola steels herself to act in accordance with the needs and necessities of her situation. Viola is also directly contrasted with Orsino: both are victims of unrequited love, but whereas Orsino gives way to love-sick posturing and giddy behavior, Viola can endure with patience. . . . Because she is ruled by selfless love Viola can wait patiently upon time for the manifestation, the epiphany which must resolve the difficulties. This waiting observes the finest balance between inaction and precipitancy. . . . She never supposes that her own action will in itself resolve all difficulties but commits the event to "time": "O Time, thou must untangle this, not I: / It is too hard a knot for me t'untie" (2.2.39–40). . . . The epiphany must be allowed to come when it will, and she endures in patience until the revelation is given.

Sebastian's role is to bring to determination the issues which Viola begins, and to resolve the difficult situations which she must endure until his manifestation. Whereas Viola must constantly give selfless love and service to others, Sebastian is able at once to inspire selfless, devoted love for himself: his friend Antonio risks danger and imprisonment to minister to Sebastian's needs in the strange town, and later risks life itself for him in undertaking a duel in his supposed defence. The pattern is repeated when Olivia (thinking him Cesario) proclaims her love for him at first sight and proposes a betrothal. His immediate decision to accept that betrothal despite his perception that it is grounded in some error, and his forthright response to the attack of Andrew and Toby in which he gives each a "bloody coxcomb" show a power of firm determination which make possible the restoration of order to the land.

The complementary roles of Viola and Sebastian in Illyria may on the basis of what has been said be seen to reflect the dual nature and role of the incarnate Divine Love Christ, in accordance with the Christmastide theme implied in the play's title. Recognition of such a dimension does not, it should be reemphasized, make the Viola-Sebastian story an allegory of Christ's action in the world, but rather presents this dramatic fiction as a type of that ultimate manifestation of Divine Love—a reflection, an analogue, another incarnation of it.

The dual nature of Christ as human and divine, and the two modes in which his role was executed—his humiliation as suffering servant and his exaltation as divine king—were constantly emphasized in Epiphany sermons and commentaries on the gospel appointed for the Feast of the Epiphany, Mt 2:1–12. Almost all commentators dwelt upon the paradox of the lowly, helpless child receiving testimony to his Kingship and Divinity by the tribute of the Magi and the miracle of the star. A note to Mt 2:1–12 in the Geneva Bible states that "christ a poore child, layd down in a crib, and nothing set by of his owne people, receiveth notwithstanding a noble witnesse of his divinity from heaven [the star], and of his kingly estate of strangers."...Accordingly, an audience would be prepared through the significances commonly associated with the epiphany message to find in a play entitled *Twelfth Night* and presenting twins who embody complementary aspects of the role and power of love, a reflection of the dual manifestation of Christ's action in the world as Divine Love incarnate.

In *Twelfth Night* Viola's role alludes to the human dimension, Christ's role as patient servant, willing sufferer, model of selfless love. Her offer to Orsino, "And I, most jocund, apt, and willingly, / To do you rest a thousand deaths would die" (5.1.126–7) is perhaps the most direct verbal reference to this role. Sebastian reflects the divine dimension, pointed up especially in Antonio's language to and about Sebastian: "I do adore thee so / That danger shall seem sport" (2.1.42–3) and again, "to his image, which methought did promise / Most venerable worth, did I devotion" (3.4.342–3) and then in disillusionment, "But, O, how vile an idol proves this god" (3.4.345). The bloody pates dealt out to Toby and Andrew present Sebastian in the role of judge and punisher, and the final betrothal to Olivia suggests Christ's role as destined "husband" of the perfected soul and of the reordered society, the Church.

In the "epiphany" in the final scene when Sebastian is at length manifested and the double identity is revealed, some of the language points directly to the theological dimension here noted, but at the same time resists simplistic allegorical equations. When the twins are first seen together by the company the Duke's comment suggests and reverses the usual formula for defining Christ as incorporating two natures in one person, observing that there is "One face, one voice, one habit and two persons" (5.1.208). Antonio makes a similar observation, "How have you made division of yourself? / An apple cleft in two is not more twin / Than these two creatures" (5.1.214–16). But the other formulation, a mysterious duality in unity, is suggested throughout the play in Viola's dual masculine-feminine nature,and is restated in the last scene in Sebastian's words to Olivia, "You are betrothed both to a maid and man" (5.1.255). Elsewhere in the final scene Sebastian denies any claim to "divinity" in terms that at the same time relate him to such a role: "I never had a brother; / Nor can there be that deity in my nature / Of here and everywhere" (5.1.218–20).

Sebastian and Viola do indeed bring the "peace" of the season to Illyria through a reordering of its life and its loves. The seven years' peace throughout the Roman world before the traditional date of Christ's birth was commonly seen as a sign of that peace. . . . But the peace pronounced in the Angelic message, "Glory be to God in the high heavens, and peace in earth, and towards men good will" had much more profound and ideal dimensions. . . . In the conclusion of the play Fabian virtually echoes the Isaiah prophecy [of swords turned into ploughshares] in pointing to the wondrous peace established in Illyria: "let no quarrel, nor no brawl to come, / Taint the condition of this present hour, / Which I have wond'red at" (5.1.346–8).

Feste's final song, contrary to much critical opinion, is integrally related to the themes of the play, as developed above. Its opening lines,

> When that I was and a little tiny boy,
> With hey, ho, the wind and the rain,
> A foolish thing was but a toy,
> For the rain it raineth every day.
> But when I came to man's estate,
> With hey, ho, the wind and the rain,
> 'Gainst knaves and thieves men shut their gate,
> For the rain it raineth every day. (5.1.378–85)

seem to allude to 1 Cor 13:11, "when I was a childe, I spake as a childe: I understoode as a childe, I thought as a childe: but when I became a man, I put away childish things." This echo also recalls Paul's classic definition of Christian love which immediately precedes the verse cited and which needs only to be quoted in part for its relevance to the play to be apparent:

> Love suffereth long: it is bountiful: love envieth not: Love doth not boast it selfe: it is not puffed up:
> It doth no uncomely thing: it seeketh not her owne things: it is not provoked to anger: it thinketh no evill:
> It suffereth all things: it beleeveth all things: it hopeth all things: it endureth all things. (1 Cor 13:4–7, Geneva)

And the verse just following the echo mentioned, "For nowe we see thorow a glasse darkely: but then shall wee see face to face. Nowe I know in part: but then shall I knowe even as I am knowen" (1 Cor 13:12), with its graphic symbol for the imperfections of the present life in relation to the ideal fulfillment of love in the future state relates to the tone and burden of Feste's song. His sad and haunting references to the wind and the rain, the thieves and the tosspots, the swaggering and the drunken heads which have been part of life from birth to death since the world began set the play suddenly in a new perspective, that of the real world. Bringing the Twelfth Night celebrations to a close, Feste reminds us that the world we live in is a very great distance from the land of good will that is Illyria, that the restorative forces which had a comparatively easy time there have much more resistant materials to work upon in the real world, and that the golden age foreseen as imminent at the end of the play is in the real world only a far-off apocalyptic vision.

## Notes

1    Erich Auerbach, *Mimesis*, trans. Willard Trask (New York, 1957), p. 171, makes this point most emphatically; "A figural schema permits both its poles—the figure and the fulfillment—to retain the characteristics of concrete historical reality, in contradistinction to what obtains with symbolic or allegorical personification, so that figure and fulfillment—although the one 'signifies' the other—have a significance which is not incompatible with their being real. An event taken as a figure preserves its literal and historical meaning. It remains an event, does not become a mere sign." Roland M. Frye, *Shakespeare and Christian Doctrine* (Princeton, 1963), pp. 63–69, denies that Renaissance writers found religious meaning in classical and secular literature. . . . But in fact there is a widespread Renaissance tradition (carried over from the Middle Ages) of reading classical myths as imperfect types of biblical events, and of taking such analogous episodes as Noah's Flood and Deucalion's Flood, Samson's exploits and Hercules' labors, Orpheus' descent to Hell to rescue his bride Eurydice and Christ's descent to Hell to rescue his bride the Church, as proof that the classical myths in fact derived ultimately from the Bible. . . . Indeed, despite Frye's claim, Golding's verse epistle to his edition of the *Metamorphoses* in *The XV Bookes of P Ovidius Naso* (London, 1587) itself states the rationale for typological reading.
2    John Russell Brown, *Shakespeare and His Comedies* (London, 1957), pp. 160–82.
3    Cesar L. Barber, *Shakespeare's Festive Comedy* (Princeton, 1959), pp. 242–44.
4    See Reginald Scot, *The Discoverie of Witchcraft* (1584), 13.6, p. 294: "A Topase healeth the lunatike person of his passion of lunacie."

From "Thematic Patterns in *Twelfth Night*," *Shakespeare Studies* 1 (1965), 168–81, excerpts abridged.

*René E. Fortin (1972)*

## *Twelfth Night:* Drama of Initiation

We have not, I think, done justice to the richness of the comedies, and particularly of *Twelfth Night*. For, despite its reputation as the most festive of the Shakespearean revels, this drama, without for a moment compromising its proper comic
idiom, embodies on several different levels significant insights into human experience. These insights cannot be fully appreciated until it is recognized that in
*Twelfth Night* Shakespeare is anticipating the dramatic themes and, above all, the
symbolic techniques of his later plays. Drawing upon the symbolic imagination
that he inherited from medieval culture, Shakespeare offers a symbolic drama—
with psychological, anthropological, and theological significances radiating from
the literal action—centering upon Viola and her quest for identity.

The underlying seriousness of comedy has been cogently argued by Northrop
Frye: the comic drive, he holds, is a drive for identity, both social and individual,
the new identity arising from an awakening to self-knowledge. Frye also takes note
of the ritual origins of ancient comedy and argues that the vestiges of primordial
rituals abound in the art of Shakespeare. "When Shakespeare began to study
Plautus and Terrence, his dramatic instinct, stimulated by his predecessors, divined that there was a profounder pattern in the argument of comedy than appears in either of them. At once—for the process is beginning in *The Comedy of
Errors*—he started groping for that profounder pattern, the ritual of death and revival that underlies Aristophanes."[1]

Frye's description of the comic argument is especially relevant to *Twelfth Night*:
Viola, rather than merely going through the motions of the conventional romantic
heroine, can perhaps be better understood as undergoing a symbolic death of sorts
in reaching toward a new identity.

Orsino and Olivia are a matching pair: a young man surrendering to feminine
excesses, especially in the fickleness of his moods, and a young woman who is as
stern and unbending as a man. Viola, the nucleus of this psychological drama,
works out her own search for identity between the errant personalities of Orsino
and Olivia. Her assuming of the masculine disguise symbolizes her sexual ano-
nymity, her own incertitude about her sexual identity. To appreciate her predicament, one must remember that she is placed at a pivotal moment in her psychic
development, being, as Malvolio describes her, "in standing water, between boy
and man" (1.5.152–53). Her sensitivity to the dimension of time provides a further clue to her predicament: on assuming her masculine disguise, she has committed herself to time—"What else may hap, to time I will commit" (1.2.60)—
and has also, in referring to her "being delivered to the world" (1.2.42), used an

image of gestation. Thus when, in groping for proper personal relationships, she confronts situations beyond her powers, she again appeals to time.

> O Time, thou must untangle this, not I.
> It is too hard a knot for me t' untie. (2.2.39–40)

In emphasizing the role of time, Viola is underscoring the fact that she is going through a process of maturation that she cannot force: she is not the mistress of her fate, and she must submit to the mysterious agency of time.

What Shakespeare is implying in this comic version of the "ripeness is all" theme can best be understood in the language of modern depth psychology: The masculine disguise of Viola and the stress upon her age suggest that she is going through an identity crisis, moving from a stage of indeterminate sexuality (or bisexuality) to a mature state of heterosexuality which will be attained when she has found her proper love-object....

Her difficulties are resolved, of course, with the appearance of Sebastian: when he appears, identity problems—dramatic and, by extension, psychological—are resolved and Viola is free to marry Orsino. But even here, in the denouement, one is reminded of the symbolic male disguise and the temporal process which it symbolizes; pointing to her "masculine usurped attire" (5.1.242), Viola warns Sebastian that she is not yet ready to stand forth as Viola.

> Do not embrace me till each circumstance
> Of place, time, fortune do cohere and jump
> That I am Viola; which to confirm,
> I'll bring you to a captain in this town,
> Where lie my maiden weeds. (5.1.243–47)

It is with the donning of her "woman's weeds" (5.1.265) that Viola achieves her proper identity and her proper sexual role.

But the audience is urged to probe further in *Twelfth Night* by an elaborate system of character relationships which invites an identification of Viola and Sebastian as well as Viola and Olivia. As a critic has recently observed, "Cesario is an amalgam of the most attractive traits of both Viola and Sebastian. Genuine love, instinctive but not necessarily directionless, comes about in Olivia and Orsino precisely because of those traits in Cesario most appealing to each, but they are traits shared by Viola and Sebastian as identical twins.... Viola and Sebastian, both of whom are Sebastian, are emblems of a metaphysical possibility."[2]

The temptation to identify Viola and Sebastian is indeed almost irresistible: both are identical in appearance and even in dress: both are near-victims of disaster at sea and are rescued by benevolent sea captains; both are romantically involved with Olivia and drawn into a duel with Aguecheek; and finally, Shakespeare stresses the fact that they are identical twins, "both born in an hour" (2.1.17). They are described as "one face, one voice, one habit, and two persons—/A natural perspective that is and is not" (5.1.208–09).

A similar coalescence between Viola and Olivia is also evident: beyond the hint offered by the similarity in names, both are described as fatherless, both are mourning the death of a brother, and both are groping for their proper sexual roles. Finally there is another coalescence of characters, this time between the two sea captains, that deepens the symbolic significance of the play.

The conclusion to draw from this coalescence of characters is that Shakespeare is alluding to the myth of the androgyne.... This ancient myth, recorded in Plato's *Symposium* and certainly accessible to Shakespeare, persisted into the Middle Ages, when it was made to conform to Christian Revelation: the division of sexes was construed as the result of the sinfulness of the human condition, and only man's redemption from sin would free him from his fragmented state. Accordingly, in various versions of the mythic tradition, prelapsarian Adam and the resurrected Christ are conceived of as androgynous, possessing a sexual completeness symbolic of their fullness of being.[3] Even today, as Mircea Eliade points out, the myth is extant among primitive peoples, finding expression in various forms of ritual androgynization. "If we remember that... non-initiates are considered asexual, and admission to sexuality is one of the consequences of the initiation, the deeper significance of this rite seems to be the following: one cannot become a sexually adult male before knowing the co-existence of the sexes, androgyny; in other words, one cannot attain a particular and well-defined mode of being without knowing the total mode of being."[4]

The coalescence of characters becomes most meaningful against this background. The marriage between Olivia and Sebastian can be seen as a displacement, for obvious reasons, of the Viola-Sebastian marriage, which would symbolize the culmination of the psychic process: the metamorphosis of the "eunuch" (1.2.61) Cesario into the fullness of sexual life. The process may perhaps be better understood in the more familiar terms of the anima-animus relationship elaborated by Carl Jung. In Jungian terms the androgyne is a symbol of the sexual wholeness that is essential for real human love.

But there is more to *Twelfth Night*. What Viola and Sebastian have essentially undergone is a ritual of initiation into a higher form of being; the pattern of death and rebirth symbolizes not only a psychological transformation from adolescence to sexual maturity but also a spiritual transformation, an initiation into the mystery of love. It is evident that the literal level of the play is centrally concerned with love, with the need for all to abandon their respective versions of narcissistic self-love and turn to others in a spirit of giving. It is less evident, however, that the function of the enigmatic Antonio is to deepen this concept of sacrificial love.

The inherence of self-sacrifice in true love is indicated by Antonio's comment on his rescue of Sebastian.

> For his sake
> Did I expose myself (pure for his love)
> Into the danger of this adverse town. (5.1.76–78)

And again, seeing "Sebastian" (really Viola) in difficulty, he declares: "If this young gentleman / Have done offense, I take the fault on me" (3.4.291–92). He, like his namesake in *The Merchant of Venice*, is willing to offer his "pound of flesh" in the cause of friendship and love; the impact of his presence is to remind the audience that, despite the comic atmosphere in which we are enveloped, love may lead to death.

His impact is further deepened by the poetry he speaks.

> This youth that you see here
> I snatched one half out of the jaws of death,
> Relieved him with such sanctity of love,
> And to his image, which methought did promise
> Most venerable worth, did I devotion. (3.4.339–43)

And again:

> That most ingrateful boy there by your side
> From the rude sea's enraged and foamy mouth
> Did I redeem. A wrack past hope he was.
> His life I gave him, and did thereto add
> My love without retention or restraint,
> All in his dedication. (5.1.71–76)

This language is strongly suggestive, first in recalling the pattern of death and re-birth which Viola and Sebastian fulfill and then, most significantly, in charging the Antonio-Sebastian friendship with religious meaning. Antonio, it should be noted, speaks of the "sanctity of love" and describes Sebastian as a person whom he "adores," an image worthy of "veneration" and "devotion." The implication is that, as a result of their experience, Viola and Sebastian have been reborn to a godlike existence, knowing now the sanctity of love. Eliade's analysis of initiation rites is relevant to this near-apotheosis. "Initiatory death is indispensable for the beginning of spiritual life. Its function must be understood in relation to what it prepares: birth to a higher mode of being." "For archaic thought," Eliade explains, "man is made—he does not make himself all by himself. It is the old initiates, the spiritual masters, who make him. But these masters apply what was revealed to them at the beginning of Time by the Supernatural Beings. They are only the rep-resentatives of those Beings; indeed, in many cases they incarnate them."[5] Such a comment effectively delineates Antonio's role: the unexpected intensity of re-sponse that he is able to arouse stems from the religious overtones of his relation-ship with Sebastian. On one level, his role in the play seems to be similar to that of Eliade's "spiritual master," an initiate to a sacred mystery whose mission it is to lead others to a higher spiritual state.[6] The mystery in this case, of course, is the mystery of human love.

On another and more familiar level Antonio—like the sea captain who rescues Viola, serves as her protector, and is also placed in jeopardy by Illyrian society—is a redeemer figure, ready to give his life that another might live. At this point, anthropology touches upon theology, and one is reminded of the religious festival which serves as the background and occasion of the comedy. Although the festive connotations of *Twelfth Night* have dominated critical comment, Twelfth Night is also a religious feast, the Feast of the Epiphany, which commemorates the manifestation of Christ to the gentiles. In the Christian tradition, it is Christ who is the perfect pattern of love into which Antonio is initiating Viola-Sebastian: the incarnation of divine love who has sacrificially redeemed man, otherwise "a wrack past hope." In this incarnation can be found the supreme instance of the love mentioned earlier by Olivia: "Love sought is good, but given unsought is better" (3.1.153). Through Antonio, then, the initiation ritual undergone by Viola-Sebastian is awesomely expanded in meaning: the psychological renewal of the lovers is consummated by a spiritual renewal, and the mystery of human love is shadowed forth in all its splendor.[7] Olivia, one of the new initiates at the conclusion of the play, may well be considered a hypostatization of the mystery of love's epiphany. "Now Heaven walks on earth" (5.1.91).

## Notes

1   Walter N. King, ed., *Twentieth Century Interpretations of Twelfth Night* (Englewood Cliffs, N.J., 1968), p. 11.

2   King, p. 12; see also Barbara K. Lewalski, "Thematic Patterns in *Twelfth Night*," *Shakespeare Studies* 1 (1965) 174–76.

3   Mircea Eliade, *Mephistopholes and the Androgyne,* tr. J. M. Cohen (New York, 1965), p. 104; see also Carl Jung, *Psychology and Religion* (New York, 1958), pp. 29–30.

4   Eliade, p. 112.

5   *Rites and Symbols of Initiation,* tr. Willard Trask (New York, 1958), p. xiv.

6   Joseph Summers has commented in "The Masks of *Twelfth Night*," *U. Kansas City Rev.* 22 (1955): "In this play the responsible older generation has been abolished, and there are no parents at all." I suggest that the natural parents are replaced by the "spiritual fathers" Antonio and the sea-captain.

7   Antonio may be described as a Christ-analogue, a type of the "redeeming lover" which finds its highest expression in Christ. In the same way typologists in the Middle Ages would find Isaac or Jonah to be "types" of Christ.

From "*Twelfth Night*: Drama of Initiation," *Papers on Language & Literature* 8 (1972), 135–46 abridged. Permission by the Board of Trustees, Southern Illinois University, copyright 1972.

# ALL'S WELL THAT ENDS WELL

## Comment and bibliography

Anyone familiar with the Gospels knows that the story has two phases, like a diptych. In the first phase, leading up to his being recognized as the Messiah, Jesus teaches faith and heals the sick. Thereafter comes a ministry of sacrificial love, his going down to Jerusalem to die for the sins of unbelievers and thereby triumph over their rejection of him. These two phases can be found analogously in the story of the heroine of *All's Well*. Growing up in a country whose spiritual condition is represented by a sick king (the maimed Fisher-King of ancient legend), Helena heals him by a miracle of faith and is accorded as a reward the honor of being made the king's heir through a marriage to his son. Significantly, she is of humble circumstances but venerable ancestry, having inherited from a physician father the recipe of faith on which she wagers her life in applying it to her scarcely credulous patient.

But then, embarrassingly, the status she earns by her miracle becomes profitless when she finds that the husband she loves does not love her. He self-centeredly prefers to make a name for himself (somewhat like the disciples of Jesus who concerned themselves about honors), and he evades his bridegroom responsibility. This situation elicits the second phase of Helena's pursuit of Bertram, who is plainly a figure of prodigal mankind in need of being brought to "come home." Helena must seek him out through a religious pilgrimage undertaken as a penance for her own earlier shortcomings. She speaks cryptically of embracing "death . . . to set him free." And appropriately her guardian mentors are St James the apostle of good works, and St Francis the friar of humble holiness. So in travelling to Campostella by way of Florence she visits a Franciscan hostelry, where the widowed proprietress has a chaste daughter named Diana. On learning that Diana is besieged by an untrustworthy suitor recognizable as Bertram, Helena's recipe resembles that of the righteous Tamar of Genesis 38, while at the same time she wins Diana's cooperation and rewards her with a promise of dowry. The bedmate-substitution has its gospel analogue, of course, in the substitutionary atonement enacted by Christ, who "for our sake" God "made to be sin who knew no sin" (2 Cor 5:21). By such a death, mankind was ransomed and released to a reborn life, and so likewise will Bertram be in *All's Well*.

The paradox of "a sinful fact" in which there is no wickedness on the part of the rescuer but only on the part of him who is being rescued (while he blindly supposes himself to be the conqueror) is beautifully summed up in Helena's rhymed explanation at the end of Act 3:

Let us assay our plot, which if it speed
Is wicked meaning in a lawful deed,
And lawful meaning in a lawful act
Where both not sin, and yet a sinful fact.

The deed is lawful because committed by Bertram with a woman who is lawfully his wife, though he does not know this and intends a wicked meaning. Helena's theologically-based explanation is voiced as a kind of riddle to tease reflection by the play's audience. Earlier, a prior riddle was posed in Helena's summing up (in 1.1.166–76) the many roles she would play in her love for Bertram: included were paradoxical ones, such as "friend" and "enemy," "guide" and "sweet disaster." And at the play's end a third riddle is posed by Diana as she points attention to Helena as the fulfiller of the supposedly "impossible" task Bertram had set:

Dead though she be, she feels her young one kick.
So there's my riddle: one that's dead is quick.

It is indeed a resurrection of the quick and the dead—for which Bertram, as soon as he can see clearly, will love her "dearly, ever dearly."

The subplot of the shaming of the boastful and traitorous Parolles provides, as critics have generally noted, a mirroring parallel to Bertram's case. The name Parolles signifies a person of words without any substance of understanding and deed—or as a T. S. Eliot would say, "knowledge of words, and ignorance of the Word" (Chorus, *The Rock*). He is saved at the end nevertheless by confessing his demerits and begging compassion. One of the witty jests of the clown Lavatch is that "O Lord, sir!" is an answer that will serve "all men" on all occasions. That is certainly true in the drama of *All's Well*. Lavatch is a theologically-minded clown. He intuitively associates Helena with grace in his remark that she is "the herb of grace," and earlier he has named her "the tithe-woman," the one-out-of-ten consecrated to God.

Of the many excerpts of commentary on this play that deserve to be reprinted, we have chosen for our anthology a half-dozen. E. M. W. Tillyard appreciates the biblical contexts of Helena's curing of the King. Eric LaGuardia notes that the "scientific" spokesmen surrounding the King doubt the possibility of miracles; evidently the dramatist wishes to make the point that their lazy philosophy of scepticism is a secular malaise which Helena must combat, and that her chief resource for this is an "honest" art she has inherited from a father who belonged to a better and historically prior breed of men. Is Shakespeare here fingering a decadence of his own times? Robert G. Hunter makes the excellent point that Shakespeare's heroine has an adventurous love like that of Helen of Troy, but here combined with a devotion to chastity like that of Constantine's mother, Helena, the legendary discoverer of the true cross. Her sexuality, in other words, is made beautiful by her piety.

Frances Pearce observes that Helena's way of salvation is in tune with the wisdom of Lavatch regarding the difficult way and "narrow" gate of genuine piety, and she notes also that this clown's implication that Helena is driven by the needs of the flesh is coordinate with his belief that she is guided by grace. Her "folly" of youthful passion is thus perfected by a holy folly, an enduring of shameful "death" because of a love that is charity. Pearce calls the play's ending "inherently joyful." John Cox points out pertinently that humility is a distinctly Christian virtue rather than a classical one, and that it requires our understanding of Augustine's critique of pagan virtue, along with a familiarity with medieval religious drama. Peggy Simonds reminds us that Bertram's rebellion runs against matrimony's meaning in Prayerbook liturgy, and that Helena's bedtrick restores the "sacred mystery" of sexuality.

Among the pieces listed for supplementary reading, those by Nevill Coghill and William Toole both tie to biblical typology Shakespeare's use of the motif of bedmate substitution, Toole remarking (p. 157) that "the actions of Christ are re-enacted in another plane" by Helena. Coghill comments that she is more than a clever wench using a bedtrick, since her purpose is a reclamation of Bertram by the help of God and her answer to Bertram's riddle is to become a pilgrim to St Jaques. Carl Dennis explains that the play must present Bertram as vice-ridden in order to make clear the unconditional nature of Helena's love. David Bergeron credits Helena with a "saving grace" that effects a literal healing in the drama's first movement and a metaphorical healing in the second. Maurice Hunt notices that the play's characters "either infuse their words with charity, the essence of the Word itself, or lapse pridefully into corrupted language or even a recreation of Babel." Andrew Turnbull observes that the best expression of the boldness of Helena's virtue is the clown's witty marvelling "That man should be at woman's command, and yet no harm done." Also, Turnbull finds the play's theme well voiced in the subplot, where the first words Parolles utters on being seized are, "O ransom, ransom," and his captors exhort him to "betake thee to thy faith" and "pray, pray, pray."

## Supplementary bibliography

Ashley, Kathleen. "The Guiler Beguiled: Christ and Satan as Theological Tricksters," *Criticism* 24 (1982), 126–37.

Bergeron, David M. "The Structure of Healing in *All's Well That Ends Well*," *South Atlantic Bulletin* 37, 4 (1972), 25–34.

Bradbrook, Muriel. "Virtue is the True Nobility," *Review of English Studies* 1 (1950), 289–301.

Coghill, Nevill. "*All's Well* Revalued," in *Studies in Language and Literature in Honor of Margaret Schlauch*, ed., Mieczyslaw Brahmer *et al.* (Warsaw: Polish Scientific Publishers, 1966), pp. 71–83.

Dennis, Carl. "*All's Well* and the Meaning of *Agape*," *Philological Quarterly* 50 (1971), 75–84.

Hunt, Maurice. "*All's Well That Ends Well* and the Triumph of the Word," *Texas Studies in Literature and Language* 30 (1988), 388–411.

Toole, William B. *Shakespeare's Problem Plays: Studies in Form and Meaning* (New York: Humanities Press, 1966), pp. 135–97.

Turnbull, Andrew. *Motifs of Bedmate Substitution and Their Reconciliatory Functions in Shakespearean and Jacobean Drama* (Ph. D. Dissertation, Indiana University, 1977), Ch. 6, pp. 281–326.

*E. M. W. Tillyard (1951)*

# Theological Tone in *All's Well* [editor's title]

In the conversation between Helena and the King ... what is most evident is her piety and suggestion of a miracle:

> He that of greatest works is finisher
> Oft does them by the weakest minister.
> So holy writ in babes hath judgement shown,
> When judges have been babes; great floods have flown
> From simple sources and great seas have dried,
> When miracles have by the greatest been denied.

The "baby judges" could be Daniel judging Susanna, or the wise "babes and sucklings" of the Gospels. The "flood" is the water struck from the rock by Moses at Horeb and Kadesh; the sea is the Red Sea as described in *Exodus*. In her second speech Helena continues in the same strain in answer to the King's doubts:

> Inspired merit so by breath is barr'd.
> It is not so with Him that all things knows
> As 'tis with us that square our guess by shows.
> But most it is presumption in us when
> The help of heaven we count the act of men.
> Dear sir, to my endeavours give consent;
> Of heaven, not me make an experiment.

Here again there is scriptural reference, in the first line; a general reference to Hebrew kings who denied the truth of the inspired prophets. This accumulation of scriptural reference, this calling in the help of God, and this confidence in a forthcoming miracle combine to give a special character to this portion of the scene. Shakespeare may have got his hint from his original, which runs "The King, hearing these words, said to himself: 'This woman peradventure is sent unto me of God.'"

It is of heaven, not of Helena, that the King makes experiment; and his cure is miraculous, not only as proclaimed by Helena, but, when effected, as reported by Lafeu:

> They say miracles are past; and we have our philosophical persons, to make modern and familiar, things supernatural and causeless. Hence is it that we make trifles of terrors, ensconcing ourselves into seeming knowledge, when we

should submit ourselves to an unknown fear. . . . A showing of a heavenly effect in an earthly actor. . . . The very hand of heaven.

Nor does the conception of Helena as a person specially favoured by heaven cease with her curing the King. The Countess, hearing Bertram has cast her away, says

> What angel shall
> Bless this unworthy husband? He cannot thrive,
> Unless her prayers, whom heaven delights to hear
> And loves to grant, reprieve him from the wrath
> Of greatest justice.

Nor does Shakespeare let the theme of Helena's divine agency drop. In 4.4 she says to Diana's mother

> Doubt not but heaven
> Hath brought me up to be your daughter's dower,
> As it hath fated her to be my motive
> And helper to a husband.

But the most explicitly theological place in the play is the beginning of the culminating scene, 4.3, where the two French Lords comment on Bertram's conduct. Not only the position but the speakers make this comment important. The two French Lords are the choric characters, the *punctum indifferens* of the play, and what they say gives a standard to which the play itself can be referred. After the First Lord has recounted, with strong disapproval, Bertram's seduction of Diana, these words follow:

Second Lord   Now God lay our rebellion! As we are ourselves, what things
                are we.
First Lord       Merely our own traitors. And as in the common course of all
                treasons, we still see them reveal themselves, till they attain to
                their abhorred ends; so he that in this action contrives against
                his own nobility in his proper stream o'erflows himself.
Second Lord   Is it not meant damnable in us to be trumpeters of our unlaw-
                ful intents?

There are two doctrines here: first and most emphatic, the theological doctrine of man's depravity unaided by divine grace; second, the doctrine that great crime will out, and often by the criminal giving himself away, to his ultimate punishment. Bertram, in his acts, has shown himself to be man cut off from grace, and by his indiscreet confidences, his "o'erflowing himself," has prepared his own detection and punishment.

It looks, therefore, as if Shakespeare not only made Helena and Bertram highly realistic figures but made them represent heavenly grace and natural, unredeemed, man respectively.

From *Shakespeare's Problem Plays* (London: Chatto & Windus, 1951), pp. 100–101; 106–108 abridged.

*Eric LaGuardia (1966)*

## Nature Redeemed in *All's Well* [editor's title]

From the very start Helena possesses naturally a purity and healing power which relate her to the content of the divine world. Her qualifications as a purifier or redeemer are eminent, and are revealed to us in the play in a variety of ways. Shakespeare expresses her divinity, of course, in a manner more allusive and circumspect than that used by Spenser or Milton to indicate the same quality in Britomart and the Lady, for the conventions of the romantic mode of *All's Well* will not allow a certain limit of credibility to be exceeded. Helena does not have an enchanted spear, nor can she part a wall of flames; she is not attended by supernatural figures such as the Attendant Spirit or Sabrina. Although she is not surrounded by as much of the poetic marvelous as the other heroines, it is clear that Helena is a figure who represents the proper commerce between the world of spirit and the world of nature.

The first hint of Helena's unusual qualities comes in the form of the striking praise of her physician father spoken by the Countess. He was a man, she remarks, "whose skill was almost as great as his honesty; had it stretch'd so far, would have made nature immortal." We learn that Helena has inherited much of these virtues, and that her own personality contributes a power of goodness: "she derives her honesty and achieves her goodness." The first opportunity for Helena to employ these powers comes with her intention to travel to the court of France in order to cure the King of his fistula and to secure Bertram as a husband. . . . The Countess is not entirely convinced that Helena will be able to cure the invalid King, for "How shall they credit / A poor unlearned virgin, when the schools, / Emboll'd of their doctrine, have left off / The danger to itself?" When Helena arrives in Paris, the King has the same doubts:

> The congregated college have concluded
> That labouring art can never ransom Nature
> From her unaidable estate. (2.1.12–4)

He believes himself past cure because of the failure of scientific knowledge.

Helena asks the King to trust the help of heaven through her and not merely human skill. He begins to feel the power of the young virgin:

> Methinks in thee some blessed spirit doth speak
> His powerful sound within an organ weak;
> And what impossibility would slay
> In common sense, sense saves another way. (2.1.178–81)

With the King's faith in her increasing, Helena makes a bargain with him concerning the choice of husband; the cure is effected, and the court rejoices in astonishment. Helena's first act of purification, the curing of the King, has effects beyond that of simple medical health for one man. We have been led to believe, earlier in the play, that the entire court has its share of corruptions, symbolic of which is the sickness of the King himself. Parolles remarks at one point that the lords of the court "move under the influence of the most receiv'd star; and though the devil lead the measure, such are to be followed." The court is under the influence of a satanic music, a demonic counterpart to the divine music of the spheres.

It is, ironically, Parolles who, together with the faithful old lord, Lafeu, provides us with a characterization of Helena which can leave no doubt about the divine influence she has over the whole society of the play. Lafeu is the first to see that a trust in empirical knowledge has its limitations: "They say miracles are past; and we have our philosophical persons, to make modern and familiar, things supernatural and causeless. Hence it is that we make trifles of terrors, ensconcing ourselves into seeming knowledge, when we should submit ourselves to an unknown fear." He realizes that in Helena there is "A showing of a heavenly effect in an earthly actor." It is Parolles, however, who makes the important conclusion:

| Parolles | Nay, 'tis strange, 'tis very strange, that is the brief and the tedious of it; and he's of a most facinerous spirit that will not acknowledge it to be the— |
| Lafeu | Very hand of Heaven. |
| Parolles | Ay, so I say. |
| Lafeu | In a most weak— |
| Parolles | And debile minister, great power, great transcendence; which should indeed give us further use to be made than alone the recov'ry of the King, as to be— |
| Lafeu | Generally thankful. (2.3.33–43) |

The last words, "generally thankful," may be read as a kind of epigraph for the thematic interests of the play as a whole. It is recognized that Helena's powers could and should be put to further use, and it is her total influence over the world of the play which resolves all conflicts in an atmosphere of general thankfulness. It is an expression suggesting the reintegration of the society, the return of wholeness and purity reflected in the ideal concept of nobility, the solution of Helena's love problem, the restoration of the prodigal Bertram, and the ultimate purgation of the demonic influence of Parolles.

The most important part of Bertram's purification occurs in the ritualized consummation of his marriage with Helena. It is Bertram himself who establishes the conditions of this true marriage in the letter concerning the ring and the child. The irony of this fact, plus the irony of the sexual substitution (Bertram believes he is seducing Diana, not fulfilling the conditions of his letter), indicate to the reader that Bertram was destined to be reconciled with Helena in a chaste love. In other words, the fulfillment of those conditions which were made to seem impossible, and the substitution of Helena for Diana are highly figurative ways of telling the reader that Bertram's fitting and proper place in life is to be married to Helena. His purification, or the purging of those forces which direct him away from Helena, is signified by removing an object of sinful desire (Diana) and replacing it with an object of virtuous desire (Helena). This occurrence is something the reader waits for and expects to happen.

Bertram is purged of Parolles' influence, as is the society as a whole; Parolles himself is cleansed, and then admitted to the court celebration at the end of the play. The reduction or humiliation of Parolles, which strips him of his power and amounts to a purification, takes place through a series of incidents in which he is sent on a foolish mission to recover a lost drum, is captured by his own lords, and made to reveal his villainous and disloyal nature. A curious aspect of the main scene of Parolles' mortification is the consistent use of a number of terms suggesting the Christian purgation of sin. The information given by Parolles which reveals his disloyalty is referred to by one lord as a *confession*. Parolles at one point offers to take the *sacrament*. He pleads for his life and comments, "I would *repent* out the remainder of nature." And, finally, the rarity or monstrousness of his villainy is said to *redeem* him. All, without doubt, comically ludicrous allusions to a religious purgation. Shakespeare's parody of this process not only serves to mitigate the serious or dark overtones of the influence of Parolles in the play, but it also serves as a more earthly counterpart to the spiritual process, consistent with the technique throughout the play of making allusive rather than overt associations between the natural and the divine. Parolles, then, is reduced to ineffectuality as far as Bertram and the society are concerned; in addition, he vows to live in shame as a penance. At the end of the play Lafeu readmits Parolles to the court by saying to him, "though you are a fool and a knave, you shall eat."

In the initiation pattern of action, Parolles attempts to convince Helena of the rightness of his kind of "naturalization," but fails because of the value she attaches to her honor. This amounts to a defeat of the unregenerate level of nature; the victory is reinforced by Helena's success in transforming Bertram's sinful desires toward Diana into the consummation of their marriage. This raising of the level of nature in the direction of an order of virtue is accompanied by an acceptance rather than a rejection of the power of sensual passion. The resulting condition of nature corresponds precisely to Helena's desire to lose her virginity "to her own liking," to move from maidenhood to womanhood without sacrificing the conformity of her life to chastity. It also corresponds to the Countess' observation that both the thorn and the rose are "the show and seal of nature's truth."

The King of France speaks from the perspective of sickness when he remarks that nature can never be ransomed from "her unaidable estate." Helena, whose chastity identifies her with the divine world of order, manages to do just that; she ransoms or redeems nature from its unaidable or fallen estate. The civil restorations and new lives with which *All's Well* concludes are metaphors which, taken together, imitate the ideal of a redeemed nature, a nature which is brought back into alignment with the *lex aeterna*, but which is not totally purged of the sensual forces of life. . . . The image of chaste love figuratively solves the problem of the chaste heroine by reconciling the pure with the passionate; it solves the problem of bi-form man by leading man away from the demonic and toward the divine; and, by extension, it solves the problem of a double nature by making diverse laws a single law.

From *Nature Redeemed* (Mouton & Co., 1966), pp. 160–67 abridged.

*Robert Grams Hunter (1965)*

## Christian Theme in *All's Well* [editor's title]

Miss Jessie L. Weston has made modern readers sufficiently conscious of the antiquity and symbolic force that is contained in the Arthurian motif of the dying king. Something of the same aura surrounds the king of France in *All's Well*. His figure is at the center of the play's sterile, dying world, and Helena's cure of him is an impressive and significant demonstration of her restorative power. That power is of two interrelated kinds. By restoring the king to his natural state of health, she is demonstrating again that she is the darling, the "immediate heir" of Nature. But the play strongly insists that she is more. Her cure of the king is "supernatural and causeless" (to quote Lafew). It is a direct result of the grace of God, whose instrument Helena is. "The greatest grace lending grace" (2.1.164), she will cure the king, and she challenges him to try her ability with the words, "Of heaven, not me, make an experiment" (2.1.157). This duality in Helena's nature is insisted on throughout the play. For Lavatch, the clown, she is at one moment "the sweete Margerom of the sallet, or rather the hearbe of grace" (4.5.16–17), but she has previously been Helen of Troy:

> Was this faire face the cause, quoth she,
> Why the Grecians sacked *Troy* . . . . (1.3.58–59)

Helena is a beautiful and sexually attractive girl who is also a recipient of God's grace and a means by which it is transmitted to others. It is possible that her name has been chosen with both aspects of her nature in mind. She is, on the one hand, Helen, for whose beauty men launched ships and burned towers. On the other hand, she is Helena, who was the daughter of the notoriously merry old Coelus, Earl of Colchester, and one of the first and most famous of British saints. Her major accomplishments were to give birth to Constantine the Great and to discover the True Cross, by means of which she healed the sick and raised the dead.

Though Protestant historians tended to take a jaundiced view of her story, she was by no means forgotten by Shakespeare's contemporaries. One of the London churches and the parish Shakespeare lived in during the 1590s were called after her and her name would presumably have had sacred connotations for the average Londoner.

It is impossible to say which of the two aspects of Helena—the sacred or the profane—is more important. Shakespeare keeps them constantly in balance and to emphasize one at the expense of the other is to throw both character and play out of kilter. The scene in which Helena is introduced to the king is a good example of Shakespeare's strategy in preserving this balance. The scene ends with Helena at her most hieratic and sibylline, declaiming in highly formal rhymed verse her intention of serving as God's instrument in the cure of the king. But the episode begins with suggestions of a quite different kind. The job of convincing the king that he should give Helena an audience is assigned to old Lafew, and he goes about it bawdily—imitating the encomium of a pander, in order to amuse the king and arouse his interest. As with the earlier bawdy of Parolles, the speeches have functions beyond that of getting a laugh. They ensure that in our admiration for Helena's spirituality, we shall not forget her sexual attractiveness.

Compounded of St Helena and Helen of Troy, Helena can fairly be called Shakespeare's most complicated comic heroine. Her complexity is the result of her function in *All's Well*, for the play demands a heroine who combines, in their highest degrees, the attributes of sacred and profane love. On the human, secular level it is necessary that Helena regenerate a dying world in the ordinary human, secular way—sexually and procreatively. But on another level that regeneration must take place in ways other than the physical. The virtue as well as the bodily existence of a dying world must be re-created, and to achieve that, Helena's spiritual forces will be necessary.

The full extent of Helena's task is not apparent until she has cured the king. Before that, we had accepted her assumption that the barrier to the comic ending was, indeed, the disparity in rank between hero and heroine. Now we find out that we have been wrong. The barrier that stands between Helena and Bertram is Bertram. . . . Bertram's rejection of love is simply perverse, and in refusing to make love to Helena, he refuses not only his own pleasure but the means which nature has provided for the defeat of mutability. By doing so, he sets himself against the emotional movement of the play he is appearing in, and leaves his audience baffled, frustrated, and annoyed.

Parolles is a symptom rather than a cause of Bertram's disease—for Bertram's very nature is diseased. Just as the king's natural state of health is corrupted by his illness, so Bertram "corrupts a well-derived nature." To cure him Helena must, in a sense, repeat, on a spiritual and psychological plane, the miracle of the king's restoration to health, and Parolles serves as the fistula, the symptom by which

Bertram's malady can be recognized. Bertram's admiration for this fool and coward is a logical complement to his detestation of Helena. A part of Bertram's corruption is the result of his inability to perceive the true nature of others. He can see neither Parolles nor Helena for what they truly are. This failure of perception is, itself, only an indication of another and, to the Elizabethan, far more dangerous failure—for Bertram is also unable to perceive and to differentiate between the nobility and ignobility within his own character. His admiration for Parolles provides an example of the first of these failures. Parolles' unmasking and subsequent forced assumption of his true role in the world of the play will, as we shall see, provide an action analogous to that in which Bertram is similarly dealt with. It is as symptom and as analogue, rather than as tempter, that Parolles functions most importantly in *All's Well.*

Bertram's intransigence is Shakespeare's donné. He dramatizes it, considers it, comments on it, but he does not explain it. Some of its implications for the play as a whole are clear enough. Man sometimes inexplicably rebels against his own good—against both what is good for him and what is good within him. This is what Bertram does, not only in his treatment of Helena, but consistently throughout the play. The two French lords, Shakespeare's chorus to the third and fourth acts of *All's Well*, comment specifically upon Bertram as his own enemy, and extend their remarks to include us all:

> Cap. E.    Hee hath peruerted a young Gentlewoman heere in *Florence*, of a most chaste renown, & this night he fleshes his will in the spoyle of her honour: hee hath giuen her his monumentall Ring, and thinkes himselfe made in the unchaste composition.
>
> Cap. G.    Now God delay our rebellion as we are our selues, what things are we.
>
> Cap. E.    Meerely our owne traitours. And as in the common course of all treasons, we still see them reueale themselues, till they attaine to their abhorr'd ends: so he that in this action contriues against his owne Nobility in his proper streame, ore-flowes himselfe. (4.3.13–24)

Shakespeare has been at some pains to show us, in the incident of Bertram's attempted seduction of Diana, a man not only contriving against his own nobility, but inspired to do so by an absurdly and ironically misguided sensuality. In order to "flesh his will," Bertram is ready to betray anything. He breaks, first, his marriage vows, then violates his personal honor with a string of lying promises to Diana, and finally, in agreeing to give Diana his "monumental ring," he symbolically betrays the honor of his family. Family honor, the motive upon which he has insisted in refusing to consummate his marriage with Helelna, he is willing to pawn for a few moments of adulterous lust in the pitch dark with Diana. The dark contains, not Diana, but the detested Helena, and Bertram is unaware of the difference.

Helena's substitution of herself for Diana is immediately inspired by Bertram's taunting assertion that he will not sleep with his wife until he has had a child by her. By deceiving him, Helena saves her husband from the violation of his marriage vows and of his honor.... Helena has cured the king and, by obtaining Bertram's ring and becoming pregnant by him, she has fulfilled the tasks which her husband imposed upon her. The dying world of the play's opening scene has been restored to health and fertility. It now remains for Helena to restore Bertram to that state of honor which, we are told, is naturally his. This she can do only by forcing self-knowledge upon him.

The method by which this end is achieved is both predicted and explained by the analogous action of Parolles' unmasking.... In deflating Parolles' pretensions, the French lords are performing a public service, and the way in which they go about it has a strong resemblance to the way in which Helena goes about the cure of Bertram. Like Bertram in his desire for Diana, Parolles, in his desire for life, is ready to promise anything, compromise anything, betray anyone. Like Bertram, the blindfolded Parolles is caught in the dark, and just as Bertram commits adultery with his wife, Parolles betrays his comrades to his comrades. When the blindfold is removed from his eyes, Parolles realizes that he has revealed his true nature beyond hope of concealment or excuse.... When the truth dawns upon Parolles, he has no choice but to become himself and to turn to the charity of his fellow men in the hope that they will accept him as he is. The truth which dawns upon Bertram is more complex. He realizes, first that the girl whom he thinks he has seduced and whom he has had no compunction about slandering, is, in fact, innocent, and has revealed to the king, the countess, and the court of France that Bertram is a lying, promise-breaking seducer. Like Parolles when the blindfold is removed, Bertram must face the fact that the truth about him is irretrievably known, but we have also the sense that for the first time the truth about Bertram has been revealed to Bertram himself.

In Bertram's case, then, the blindfold is removed from the inner eye of conscience, and *humanum genus* is able, as a result, finally to see the evidence of his own corruption. That revelation is no more fortuitous than the unmasking of Parolles. The French lords have played a socially valuable practical joke which results in the return of Parolles to his appropriate station in the world. Like them, Helena has arranged a salutary discomfiture—that of her erring husband. In doing so, she has once again served as the instrument of God's grace.

The Old Countess, reflecting on her son's flight to Italy, asks:

> What Angell shall
> Blesse this vnworthy husband . . . ? (3.4.26–27)

The answer, of course, is Helena, as the countess goes on to explain in the lines that follow:

> he cannot thriue,
> Vnlesse her prayers, whom heauen delights to heare
> And loues to grant, repreeuve him from the wrath
> Of greatest Iustice. (3.4.27–30)

These lines describe Helena, but they do so in terms that inevitably suggest the Virgin Mary. The Arden editor believes that "a straight-forward reference to the Virgin as intercessor is too Popish to be probable"; but a more "Popish" activity than a barefoot pilgrimage to Santiago da Campostella is difficult to imagine, and yet Helena has just left on such an errand when these lines are spoken of her. Shakespeare evokes the Virgin here because Helena's function in the play is similar to that of the Mother of God in the "Popish" scheme of things. Both serve as means through which the grace of God can be communicated to man. Nor is this similarity surprising, for, considered historically, the charitable heroines of the comedy of forgiveness are literary descendants of the Virgin in the medieval narrative and dramatic "Miracles of Our Lady." Ordinarily their function is simply to be sinned against and to forgive, but unlike Hero, Imogen, and Hermione, Helena is called upon to serve as the active agent in the regeneration of the erring hero.

The final scene of *All's Well* draws upon and refers to a belief in the reality of the descent of grace upon a sinning human. The Elizabethan audience believed in such an occurrence not as a theological abstraction, but as an everyday psychological possibility. What happens to Bertram would, I think, have been clear to Shakespeare's contemporaries.

From *Shakespeare and the Comedy of Forgiveness* (Columbia University Press, 1965), pp. 113–31 abridged. Used by permission.

*Frances Pearce (1974)*

## The Way of Redemption in *All's Well* [editor's title]

The way to salvation is the fool's way—the difficult, the humiliating, the absurd way, not the easy, gratifying, paved way—as the Clown tells us in the scene following the "bed trick":

> I am a woodland fellow, sir, that always loved a great fire, and the master I speak of ever keeps a good fire; but sure he is the prince of the world; let his nobility remain in's court, I am for the house with the narrow gate, which I take to be too little for pomp to enter; some that humble themselves may, but the many will be too chill and tender, and they'll be for the flow'ry way that leads to the broad gate and the great fire. (4.5.44–52).

Helena in carrying through the "bed trick" has submitted to hazardous humiliation without being deterred by concern for herself: she has not been "too chill and tender." In accepting the humiliation of submitting to Bertram's lust, she hopes to save him and hopes also to deserve his love, her salvation:

> But with the word the time will bring on summer
> When briars shall have leaves as well as thorns
> And be as sweet as sharp. (4.4.31–33)

With the fulfilling of the word (the conditions Bertram has laid on Helena) she will receive joy and fruitfulness to match the sharpness and barrenness of the suffering she has endured. Although the way to summer is through the hardness of winter, suffering is eclipsed by its end: "the fine's the crown... the end is renown" (4.4.35–36).

We might note that Helena's saving Bertram through the "bed trick" can perhaps validly be seen as an analogue for the divine comedy of man's redemption. That redemption was also achieved through a deception: through the Word becoming flesh, God deceived the devil. The medieval consciousness of the incongruity of God's working to achieve man's salvation through deception—the very means that the devil uses to achieve man's damnation—may be relevant to the felt incongruity in *All's Well* of Helena's using deception to save Bertram. In contriving means by which Bertram can "flesh his will" Helena deceives him (doubly performs the "office of the devil"), yet by this means, however incongruously, heals him of his "sick desires" and opens up the possibility of salvation to him. As Helena conceives his child, Bertram's word is made flesh, given saving meaning both for Bertram and for Helena ("*When thou canst... show me a child begotten of thy body that I am father to, then call me husband*"). As Helena realizes so well herself, not only her hope to save Bertram but also her own hope for salvation depend on her fulfilling of "the word" ("with the word the time will bring on summer"). In submitting to Bertram's lust, Helena accepts the humiliation that may save them both. As the Clown reminds us in Act 4, scene 5, Helena humbles herself so that she may enter by the "narrow gate."

Helena has chosen the hard and narrow way. Bertram in the final scene, like Parolles in Act 4, will try the easy way out of his dilemma and find that it leads to damnation rather than to salvation: like Parolles, the harder he tries to save himself through lies and treachery the more disastrously he betrays himself. Parolles' and Bertram's efforts to save themselves through deception provide an ironic parallel to and inversion of Helena's saving means. Her way is to give saving meaning to Bertram's lying and cruel words, to ransom where he has betrayed. Parolles sums up his own case after his exposure: "Simply the thing I am / Shall make me live ... and Parolles live / Safest in shame; being fool'd, by fool'ry thrive"(4.3.322–23; 326–27). Analogously, Helena's deceit will prove to be the means by which Bertram is saved. Bertram's boast, that not until Helena has the ring from his finger and a child by him will he be husband to her, will be turned against him: when his conditions are met he is made a fool, caught by his own boast, his intended seduction of a maid exposed, recalling with a pun Parolles' words: "Who knows himself a braggart, / Let him fear this; for it will come to pass / That every braggart shall be found an ass" (4.3.323–25).

But while the "bed trick" may be seen as an analogue for redemption, on a more naturalistic level it can simultaneously be seen as an instance of youthful opportunism. Helena's love quest had been mocked at its outset by the Clown's implication that Helena was driven by the needs of the flesh. The Countess saw her passion, more charitably, as "the show and seal of nature's truth" (1.3.127). Helena is inspired and impelled by love: the rashness and folly of her venture are the rashness and folly of a youthful passion. "Love's strong passion" impels Bertram too in his quest for Diana, although Bertram "contrives against his own nobility" (4.3.23). Helena's folly is sanctioned folly: the Countess approves her first venture, the Widow sanctions the folly of her second attempt to deserve Bertram's love. But despite the contrast between Bertram who "solicits" Diana "in the unlawful purpose" (3.5.70) and Helena who seeks "lawful meaning in a lawful act" (3.7.46), the "bed trick" has much of the flavor of youthful opportunism that marks Bertram's passionate quest for Diana's favor. This was not mismanagement on Shakespeare's part. Youthful opportunism has an integral place in the comic harmony he contrived.

Bertram's rebellion illustrates the destructive and self-destructive consequences of proud, blind, self-will. His self-will is contrasted with Helena's humble and clear-sighted courage. Her career illustrates the positive role of will in achieving "destined" happiness, the need for faith and for committed action (folly). Her courage in treading the difficult path of hazardous humiliation is as apparent in the "bed trick" as in her rash venture to cure the King. The need to seize opportunities, clear-sightedly and courageously, when they present themselves is the key to her success. Courage and opportunism both have their place. Helena in the second half of the play is no more a "passive Griselda" than she is in the first. It is the folly of love that gives her power to heal and save Bertram as it had given her power to heal and save the King.

The final scene at Rossillion focuses on Bertram's failure and humiliation and on the anxieties and defenselessness of his "parents" in the face of his dishonor. The play needs a resolution of the darker tones that are heard so strongly in the concluding scene. This resolution is achieved through our perception of the paradox integral to Shakespeare's development of the pattern of failure redeemed by grace: the paradox of the power of love and the powerlessness of love. One who loves has power to bestow life and joy, to heal and save. We are reminded of the power of Bertram's "parents" to rescue and forgive their "prodigal son" at the opening of Act 5, scene three. As Helena returns from "death," she too is seen to have through her love the power to save and heal Bertram. But the power of Bertram's "parents"and the return of Helena itself are subject to the paradox of the powerlessness of love. The dependence of one who loves on the kindness of another is felt with affecting force as Helena returns, not only to bestow life but also to beg life from Bertram. Without his love, Helena is "but the shadow of a wife...The name and not the thing" (5.3.300–01):

> O my good lord, when I was like this maid
> I found you wondrous kind. There is your ring,
> And, look you, here's your letter. This it says,
> *When from my finger you can get this ring*
> *And is by me with child &c.* This is done;
> Will you be mine now you are doubly won? (5.3.303–08)

There is a pathetic and comic (an inherently joyful) relation established between Bertram and Helena at the close of the play; and a pathetic and comic relation established too between the young and old. The recognition that failure may be redeemed by grace, that each one who loves has the power to bestow grace, and that each one who loves is himself dependent on another for grace enabled Shakespeare to contrive a truly comic harmony at the close of *All's Well*.

From "In Quest of Unity," *Shakespeare Quarterly* 25 (1974), 84–87.

*John D. Cox (1989)*

## Helena's Humility [editor's title]

The strongest qualification of class consciousness in *All's Well* is Helena herself, not only because she initiates a cross-class marriage but because she belongs to literary and dramatic traditions whose origin and appeal are popular rather than privileged. What Helena brings with her is not the humanist equation of virtue and nobility enunciated by the king but the medieval conception that true nobleness is humility, an idea whose origin is very different from that of the humanist commonplace. Equating virtue with nobility is a classical idea and probably Platonic in origin; certainly it is epitomized in Plato's memorable image of the philosopher king.

The idea of equating nobleness with Christian humility is patristic in origin.... For Augustine, the death of Christ equates goodness with humility, not with Platonic wisdom.... Augustine makes this point frequently, but perhaps his most forthright statement of it is in *The City of God* X.29, where he chides "the Platonists" for their failure to acknowledge the incarnation and passion of Christ.... The humility of God in becoming human reached its perfection in Christ's identification with the humble in his death. Since Christ was king of kings, it follows that true nobility involves an appropriation of Christ's humility.

Augustine's argument is an important formative factor in the passion sequences of the mystery plays, because they enact the climax of Christ's paradoxical
kingship. The rhetoric of social disdain that appears in Bertram's rejection of Helena is first established in English drama by the likes of Caiaphas, Annas, and Pilate in their rejection of Christ. . . . In socially rejecting Christ, Caiaphas ironically
demonstrates the failure of his own nobility, despite his insistence on established
social hierarchy ("a lord in degre," "min astate," "in diverse degre"), because he
fails to recognize the equation of kingship and humility that Christ represents.
The same irony appears elsewhere in the mystery plays, but particularly in sequences dealing with the torture and execution of Christ. . . . In contrast to the
abuse heaped on Jesus by false noblemen is the language of social elevation used
by those who recognize the transcendent humility he embodies. In the York *Death
and Burial*, Mary, Longinus, and Nicodemus all refer to Jesus as "jente," "jentill,"
or "judged unjente."

The idea that humility is true nobleness appears not only in the mystery plays;
it is pervasive in medieval religious drama. In liturgical drama, it appears as early
as the twelfth century in the Fleury *Slaughter of the Innocents*. Here already is the
ranting worldling, Herod, lacking in emotional self-control and raging against the
white-stoled innocents, who process serenely after the *agnus Dei*, "the hallowed
lamb slain for us / . . . The splendor of the Father, the splendor of the Virgin Birth."

In the *Digby Conversion of St Paul*, Saulus's seventy-line sermon on humility is
the play's climax, where Saulus accounts for his own transformation from boastful
and destructive worldling and admonishes his auditors at the same time:

> *Quanto major es, tanto humilis te in omnibus:*
> The gretter thou art, the lower loke thu be.
> Bere the[e] never the hyer for thy degré.

This variation on the medieval dramaturgy of power helps to explain why *All's
Well* has been understood by many critics as a secular miracle play. Helena describes her social status as "humble" no fewer than three times (1.3.153; 2.1.197;
2.3.83), and she brings with her a power that defies belief—"the rarest argument
of wonder that hath shot out in our latter times" (2.3.7–8). Helena's power, moreover, is benign and restorative, healing the king's disease and eventually winning
Bertram's heart against all social expectation, as the king's coercive power could
never do. In urging the king to make trial of her claim to be able to cure him,
Helena expressly acknowledges that she is a mediatrix of divine power (2.1.149–
54), and in view of Augustine's argument that the Christian reversal of the social
rank is modelled in the incarnation of Christ, it is noteworthy that three allusions
to the incarnation in *All's Well* are all associated with Helena's love for Bertram.
The first is in Helena's apostrophe to her absent husband, after she has received
his letter of rejection: "My being here it is that holds thee hence. / Shall I stay here
to do't? No, no, although / The air of paradise did fan the house / And angels of-

fic'd all" (3.2.122–25). This is one of those luminous comments that ties Helena to the redemptive figures of medieval religious drama. Still another is in Helena's subsequent letter to the countess: "Ambitious love hath so in me offended / That barefoot plod I the cold ground upon" (3.4.5–6). The countess, who consistently thinks like Helena, makes a third such allusion after reading Helena's letter: "What angel shall / Bless this unworthy husband? He cannot thrive, / Unless her prayers, whom heaven delights to hear / And loves to grant, reprieve him from the wrath / Of greatest justice" (3.4.25–29).

The distinctive virtue that Helena represents is recognized by others than the countess. Lavatch, for example, who has a keen eye for courtly foibles, identifies the devil with the court—as the N-Town *Passion Play I* does—and then elliptically states a biblical paradox: "But, sure, he [i.e., the devil] is the prince of the world; let his nobility remain in's court. I am for the house with the narrow gate, which I take to be too little for pomp to enter. Some that humble themselves may, but the many will be too chill and tender, and they'll be for the flow'ry way that leads to the broad gate and the great fire" (4.5.49–55). Lavatch is paraphrasing Mt 7:13–14, one of the many biblical sayings that inspired Augustine's distinction between Christian and Platonic conceptions of virtue.

[Bertram] identifies himself strongly with the kind of privilege that was endorsed in late sixteenth-century courtesy theory. In doing so, he follows a very different social standard from that of his parents. The old count's social attitude is described approvingly by the king in the context where he is not being coercive:

> Who were below him
> He us'd as creatures of another place,
> And bow'd his eminent top to their low ranks,
> Making them proud of his humility,
> In their poor praise he humbl'd. Such a man
> Might be a copy to these younger times,
> Which, follow'd well, would demonstrate them now
> But goers backward. (1.2.41–48)

The king is not describing predatory self deprecation: the old count did not pretend to be humble in order to compel others to assert his true worth. Rather, he treated those who were socially inferior to him without regard to rank, and "he made the humble proud of the fact that he was humbling his own eminence in praising them" [G. K. Hunter's paraphrase].

The old count's behavior is not merely an idealized reminiscence in *All's Well*, because we see it in action in his wife.... The model for her loving response to Helena is her dead husband, as described by the king: she literally uses one below her as a creature of another place, refusing to allow Helena's social inferiority to make any difference. "I say, I am your mother, / And put you in the catalogue of those / That were enwombed mine" (1.3.139–41). In effect, the countess models the social paradox of medieval drama, enacting true nobleness in humbling herself to love one who is hierarchically inferior. The extraordinary empathy between these two women is one of the difficulties that stand in the way of construing *All's Well* as a darkly satirical comedy, for the countess incurs no obligation to Helena (unlike the king) and has nothing to gain by supporting her except an unusually gifted daughter-in-law.

Bertram's mother seems from the outset to be concerned that her son will be a goer backward from his parents' standard, judging by her advice to him as he first takes his leave:

> Be thou blest, Bertram, and succeed thy father
> In manners, as in shape! Thy blood and virtue
> Contend for empire in thee, and thy goodness
> Share with thy birthright. (1.1.61–64)

In the countess's psychomachic conception of Bertram, the kind of virtue that she hopes will contend with his blood is what the countess demonstrates later with Helena, and it is therefore distinct from the king's problematic iteration of the humanist commonplace about virtue and nobility. Bertram does not gain real *virtus* (which encompasses heroic manhood as well as ethical insight and action) until he comes to the end of himself and acknowledges Helena as his wife, both in name and substance (5.3.306).

From *Shakespeare and the Dramaturgy of Power*, pp. 137–44 abridged. Copyright 1989 by Princeton University Press. Used by permission.

*Peggy Muñoz Simonds (1989)*

## Bertram and the Marriage Duty [editor's title]

The marriage liturgy in the 1559 *Book of Common Prayer* is crucial to our understanding of many Shakespearean plays. It is important to remember that in *All's Well* Bertram does actually marry Helena in a formal ceremony offstage. He then runs away from his sacred promise to worship Helena with his body, telling Parolles that "Although before the solemn priest I have sworn, / I will not bed her" (2.3.268–70). We should note that Bertram does not describe his *vow* as "solemn" but the *priest*, thus indicating a disturbing failure to understand the ordinary patterns of language or of religion. In a similar inversion of convention, Bertram— rather than his bride—now becomes the virgin who murders his own posterity (in the sense of Parolles's previous warning to Helena) by refusing to have sexual intercourse with his wife in direct violation of his religious vows: "With this ring I thee wed: with my body I thee worship. . . ." Thus he breaks divine law as well as the social law of the sixteenth century when he withholds his family ring, his body, and his seed from his bride.

The state of matrimony was deemed analogous by Renaissance Christians to the mystical union between Christ and his people or the Church. The Anglican marriage liturgy of the period includes the following prayer: "O God, which hast consecrated the state of matrimony to such an excellent mystery, that in it is signified and represented the spiritual marriage and unity betwixt Christ and his Church, look mercifully upon these thy servants, that this man may love his wife, according to thy Word (as Christ did love thy spouse the Church, who gave himself for it, loving and cherishing it even as his own flesh)." Sexuality within the marriage bond thus becomes a religious "mystery." As Christ died for his people or congregation in order to give them everlasting life, so a husband must be willing to "die" sexually for his wife in order to make her fruitful and to provide new physical life for both the family and the community. For this reason, the king formally exhorts Bertram, "As thou lov'st her. / Thy love's to me religious; else does err" (2.3.182–83).

Secondly, in respect to the significance of the marriage liturgy, the priest reminds the congregation and the couple of Paul's commandment to all married men in Ephesians 5: "Ye husbands love your wives, even as Christ loved the Church, and hath given himself for it, to sanctify it, purging it in the fountain of water, through thy Word, that he might make unto himself a glorious congregation, not having spot or wrinkle, or any such thing, but that it should be holy and blameless." Let us recall once more Parolles's threat that if Helena remains a virgin, she will become "like one of our French wither'd pears." The sacred significance of marriage implies that a husband's love has the important function of keeping his wife beautiful and blameless in the eyes of God. He helps her gain salvation, as she helps him in turn.

Thirdly, according to the Anglican liturgy of Shakespeare's time, the main purpose of marriage was "the procreation of children," although the Church also agreed with the Clown's reasons for marrying as "a remedy against sin, and to avoid fornication," as well as a source of "mutual society, help, and comfort." In denying Helena his bodily worship, Bertram obviously denies her children too. At the same time, Helena is enjoined by her marriage vows to submit to the will of her husband, to think of him as her lord in the sense that Christ is Lord over the Church. Since Bertram wills not to love her, Helena must then find a way to make herself worthy. She therefore sets out on a pilgrimage to atone for her pride in desiring a noble marriage, striving as well to complete the impossible labors her lord has set for her in his letter. While Bertram subsequently magnifies himself in pride by conquering the Sienese army, Helena conquers herself and her natural pride by religious penance. In addition, she accepts the total humiliation of playing the whore for her husband in the dark as the only possible means of consummating their marriage.

I shall not review here the many modern critical objections to the folkloric and "unbelievable" bed-trick which allows Helena to fulfill her tasks and thus her wedding vows. In the play Diana tells us the correct moral response when she observes of her own part in obtaining Bertram's signet ring and his seed for Helena: "I think't no sin / To cozen him that would unjustly win" (4.2.75–76). Moreover, the bed-trick has a very respectable precedent in the Judeo-Christian heritage. The story is told in Genesis 38, a chapter read aloud each January 21 in Elizabethan churches, of how the widowed Tamar tricks Judah into sleeping with her in fulfillment of his neglected patriarchal obligation to provide her with an heir to Israel. Disguising herself as a prostitute, Tamar demands of Judah his cloak, his staff, and his *signet* in pledge for the payment of her fee. The Geneva Bible indicates that Judah's failure to recognize Tamar at this time is an act of providence. The marginal gloss states that "God had wonderfully blinded him that he colde not knowe her by her talke," although Judah finally admits the signet as his and the righteousness of Tamar's deed. She later brings forth twins from this union with the eponymous ancestor of Judah. His first-born son is Pharez or Perez, direct forebear of King David and thus of Christ (Mt 1).

Thomas Malory also relates two important examples of the bed-trick in British legendary history, one perpetrated by a male, Uther Pendragon, and one by a female, the Lady Elaine. The first results in the conception of King Arthur, savior of Britain, and the second results in the conception of Sir Galahad (Gilead), a knightly Christ-figure, who miraculously cures the maimed Fisher King, much as Helena mysteriously cures the King of France in *All's Well*. The bed-trick convention was thus a familiar symbol to the Elizabethans of providence at work in human affairs and was meant to be understood as necessary rather than as immoral.

Both the curing of the King and the bed-trick provide a familiar religio-mythic infrastructure for the plot of *All's Well*. The comedy begins with death and disease, continues with the offer of a cure for present illness in return for a marriage with all its sacred overtones, and ends with the unexpected appearance on stage of a pregnant woman previously believed to be dead. This woman—Helena, or love in all its most luminous aspects—is the physical and spiritual emblem of new life indeed, and her story resonates far beyond the structural confines of the comedy and of the theater itself in the best traditions of dramatic art. The chaste Diana, as "presenter" in Act 5, clearly states in a primitive poetic form the sacred-sexual paradox inherent in both the play and the marriage: "Dead though she be, she feels her young one kick. / So there's my riddle: one that's dead is quick" (5.3.302–303).

From "Sacred and Sexual Motifs in *All's Well*," *Renaissance Quarterly* 62 (1989), 33–59. Excerpts from pp. 50–51, 53–57.

## Comment and bibliography

This play relates "atonement" paradigm to the problem of political reform, an issue that agitated a wide spectrum of parties during Shakespeare's "Reformation" times. It reveals, among other things, that there is little that political action can achieve other than the jailing of Froth and Pompey, unless the task of the moral conversion of individuals is undertaken, an operation that requires the assistance of churchmen and some self-effacing labor on the the part of a ruler genuinely Christian. Shakespeare's most daring innovation when constructing a play around the much-debated topic of an ideal ruler is his depicting of a Duke who knows that he must be more than a judge sitting on a throne and therefore visits his people *incognito* in the guise of Friar. More than that: this Duke asks to be instructed by a friar, seeks to embody the true spirit of a religious vocation, and visits prisons with the wayside explanation that he comes commissioned "from the See / In special business from his Holiness" (3.2.214). This reference to Papal authority was possible, of course, only by Shakespeare's setting his drama outside England in Catholic Vienna; but that choice in itself was conditioned by the fact that the play was being written for a new English monarch whose mother was Catholic, and who during the first year of his reign had made moves toward accommodating both Catholics and Puritans in a "peace" policy.

No other Elizabethan dramatist dared stage friars in as favorable a light as this play does. It may be noted, however, that Shakespeare endows his friars with a genuinely evangelical Christianity, and there is no suggestion in his play that a secular ruler needs the aid of Roman Catholic ecclesiastical courts or of bishops (those prelates which the Puritans disliked but James wished to lean on in an Anglican version). What is needed to achieve meaningful moral reform within society is shown to be not more legislation, or magistrates zealous to punish culprits, but rather an activating of traditional religion's resources of "holiness"—an emphasis with which, we may believe, an Edmund Spenser could sympathize. (A Shakespeare *Concordance* reveals in his plays almost two hundred listings of the word "holy.")

The virtue of justice is emphasized by the play's title. But its biblical phrasing invites multiple meanings. Does it mean "an eye for an eye," or rather a returning of good for evil, whereby one heaps "coals of fire" on a sinner's head? The most enigmatic moment in the play comes when the restored Duke declares to Angelo that the very mercy of the law cries out:

> "An Angelo for Claudio, death for death!"
> Haste still pays haste, and leisure answers leisure;
> Like doth quit like, and measure still for measure.

The first line accords with an equality under law that Angelo himself had hastily said he would live by, before he found the leisure of sinning. But to us of the audience a larger context now surrounds the adage, since we know (as Angelo as yet does not) that Claudio is alive. The Duke has put Claudio's case "on hold," after subjecting him to a figurative death of repentance. May not a "like" justice be accorded Angelo? There is a double meaning certainly in the Duke's threat: "We do condemn thee to the very block / Where Claudio stooped to death, and with like haste." The only block to which Claudio had to stoop was that of humble repentance. His visible release will come at the same time Angelo's comes, namely, when a summoned jailor unmuffles Claudio *as soon as* the Duke has elicited from Isabella a mercy toward Angelo, her wronger.

A repentant Angelo has made amends to Mariana by marrying her, so she begs for him. His double injustice toward Isabella has been his propositioning a nun and also breaking his promise. When for Mariana's sake Isabella excuses both these faults, the former having harmed no one, it turns out that the latter cannot now be called a crime since it was never carried out, thanks to the Duke's secret intervention. The state's charge of judicial murder thus evaporates: Angelo "perceives he's safe" the moment he sees Claudio safe. Each of those two, however, has had the greatly educational benefit of undergoing a "death" followed by a gift of liberation. The law's statutes have served to humble the sinner to prepare him for "grace."

In an age such as Shakespeare's, when not only Catholic missioners but also some Protestant enthusiasts occasionally suffered martyrdom at the hands of the state, the practice of hasty judging can be said to be epitomized by Escalus in Act 5 when he cries against the Friar: "to the rack with him! We'll touse you." Here the usually temperate Escalus, a professional lawyer, has been misled by Lucio's slanders, not merely because Lucio is so clamorous but because the justice of the status quo, of which Escalus is the guardian, is being called in question by the Friar's testimony. Such a situation is an archetypal instance of judicial blindness in high places. Yet the Duke on being "toused" out of his hood pardons Escalus—presumably because the error by the magistrate has providentially benefited everyone by bringing hidden truth to light. Martyrdom has mysteriously this benefit—along with all the irony that in medieval drama attended the "buffetings" of Christ.

A traditional theology undergirds consistently the perspective on life provided by *Measure for Measure*. Offsetting Isabella's momentary cry of indignation, "What corruption in this life, that it will let this man live!" is the Friar-Duke's wise reply: "It is a rupture that you may easily heal." The concept of sin as a rupture accords with the view of Feste in *Twelfth Night* that it is a rent or tear to be patched, and with the Bible's view of it as a "wound" that needs to be bound up by a Good Samaritan. The victim in that parable, although "half dead," was not utterly dead spiritually (as Calvin supposes in *Inst* II.v.19 when describing the "ruin" caused by original sin); for human beings always retain in Catholic theology an ineradicable "image of God" that cannot be destroyed, an ingrained longing for the *Summum Bonum* that makes hearts restless unless they rest in God. Since man is but crippled he can be repaired. Claudio is a biblical lame man who, like the clubfooted Oedipus, is prone to stumble into sin. And Angelo is a self-divided man such as St Paul describes in Romans 7 and Mark pictures as the paralytic who could walk morally only when his inner rift was mended. ("Lord, speak the word only and my soul shall be healed.") Likewise Isabella's love for her brother is paralyzed initially by a division in her between wishing and not wishing his punishment; but healing begins when she responds to the Friar's "one word." From then on she participates with Mariana in a sinless ransom paid as an answer to Angelo's "monstrous ransom" demand. In relation to society a sinner is typically a pirate; that is, he is like one who goes to sea with the Ten Commandments but would scrape one out of the table (1.2.8–10). It is symbolically appropriate, therefore, that Angelo's demand for Claudio's head should be answered by sending him the severed head of a pirate who "died of a fever." Angelo (a thievish pirate) has died morally in a fever of lust during that very night. The Duke-Friar is no "temporary meddler" (5.1.151); he is a wise intervener—as was Moses when intervening to save Israel from Egypt, or as God was when "visiting" his people in Luke 1:68. Christian metaphor is the trademark of Shakespearean dramaturgy.

Four helpful pieces of commentary are reproduced in our anthology. That by Wilson Knight calls attention to the many Gospel parables that echo in the words and actions of the play's Duke. Also, Knight well explains why a stoic lecture on the vanity of mundane life is used by a Christian friar to educate Claudio. The essay by Roy Battenhouse summarizes the analogy between Atonement story and the basic plot of *Measure for Measure*. Then this affiliation is reinforced by a review of the play's Atonement imagery—the motifs of shepherding, fishing, ransoming, and wooing—alongside some exposition of the rationale given these by theologians. The essay by Arthur Kirsch observes that a willful ignoring of these motifs was perpetrated by Dr. Johnson, and has been continued by modern critics who resist the idea that "Shakespeare's Christianity might matter." Kirsch counters this prejudice by explaining how certain fundamental Scriptural texts are integral to the meaning of Shakespeare's text. Only a prudery or cynicism, says Kirsch, can view the bedtrick as obnoxious, and the marvel of the drama is that each of the characters is meted a mercy consistent with justice. Diane McColley defends the providential "physic" that each of these characters undergoes, and she explains how the chastity of Isabella is a necessary instrument of the Duke's cure.

As supplementary comment, Nevill Coghill affirms S. L. Bethell's emphasis on appreciating Shakespeare's "multiconsciousness" of language, and he finds underneath Lucio's naturalistic temper a satanic spirit. Jean Marie Maguin thinks Isabella's white habit of a nun is the most important stage image in the play: she is bound to Christ by a form of *sponsalia per verba futuro*, and it is precisely this that attracts the devil in Angelo. His garden, Maguin observes, has an architecture like that of the "enclosed garden" of the Song of Songs, and here Angelo would turn mystical love into a blasphemous union between Christ's promised bride and the devil. R. W. Chambers has set forth a spirited defense of Isabella's rejection of Angelo's proposition. Dayton Haskin comments that she was right to do so but wrong in the way she goes about it until the Duke aids her. Haskin would emphasize Shakespeare's not-at-all-superficial understanding of how Scripture applies to the problems of practical living. In particular he explains the relevance to the play of St Paul's doctrine of "justification": the trial scene makes clear that persons are not saved by works, yet are accountable for their actions and need to be motivated by a Christlike gratitude. Francis Fergusson defends Act 5 as "composed with the greatest care and in perfect consistency" with the basis of the play. The Duke, he says, is a figure of Shakespeare himself in the role of Grace as theologians have described it. Carole Diffey finds in the play's ending a judgment so accurate and sensitive that it "can genuinely lay claim to mirror the perfect judgment."

Elizabeth Pope, in reviewing various sermons by popular Elizabethan theologians, notices in these a certain failure, not intentional but nevertheless discernible, to reconcile fully the Christian concepts of justice and mercy because of a Renaissance concern for rewards proportionate to "deservings." But Shakespeare, she aptly observes, clarifies the Christian doctrine of his day by "holding it true to its own deepest implications" and thus gives us "a more Christian piece of thinking on this subject than nine out of ten professional Renaissance theologians." G. K. Hunter's notes include commentary on an echo (in 2.4.5) of a Reformation controversy over those who "chew" God in the Eucharist but do not digest his spiritual presence. Louise Schleiner grants that the play's biblical allusions evoke a parallel between the Duke and God, but she thinks the Duke's "quixotic notion" of imitating God involves improvisations only partly successful. Such an assessment can be corrected, however, by reading Victoria Hayne's recent exposition of Elizabethan ecclesiastical law as set forth in Richard Cosin's treatise in 1593. Darryl Gless, oddly, regards the play as an anti-monastic satire.

William Toole's chapter expounds the relevance of biblical typology to the whole structure of the play. Anne Greco's essay describes well Isabella's initial limitations alongside a sincerity that makes possible her spiritual growth. Roy Battenhouse analyzes the agreements and differences between King James's *Basilikon Doron* and Shakespeare's delineation of a truly Christian ruler. The dramatist is offering the king, he argues, a better model of rule than James had been able to envision, thus fulfilling the traditional duty of a King's servant to offer corrective counsel indirectly and inconspicuously.

## Supplementary bibliography

Battenhouse, Roy. "*Measure for Measure* and King James," *CLIO* 7 (1978), 193–216.
_____. A review in *Shakespeare Studies* 12 (1979), 336–42; another in *Connotations* 1 (1991), 197–203.
Bryant, J. A., Jr. *Hippolyta's View* (1961), Ch. 6.
Chambers, R. W. *The Jacobean Shakespeare and Measure for Measure* (1937); rpt. in *Man's Unconquerable Mind* (London: Cape, 1939), 227–310.
Coghill, Nevill. "Comic Form in *Measure for Measure*," *Shakespeare Survey* 8 (1955), 14–27.
Diffey, Carole T. "The Last Judgment in *Measure for Measure*," *Durham University Journal* 66 (1974), 231–37.
Fergusson, Francis. "Philosophy and Theatre in *Measure for Measure*," *The Kenyon Review* 14 (Winter, 1952), 103–20.
Gless, Darryl. *Measure for Measure, The Law, and the Convent* (Princeton University Press, 1979). Rev. by Battenhouse in *CLIO* 10 (1981), 324–28.
Greco, Anne. "A Due Sincerity," *Shakespeare Studies* 6 (1970), 151–74.
Haskin, Dayton, S. J. "Mercy and the Creative Process in *Measure for Measure*," *Texas Studies in Literature and Language* 19 (1977), 348–62.
Hayne, Victoria. "Performing Social Practice: The Example of *Measure for Measure*," *Shakespeare Quarterly* 44 (1993), 1–29.
Hunter, G. K. "Six Notes on *Measure for Measure*," *Shakespeare Quarterly* 15 (1964), 167–72.
Maguin, Jean Marie. "The Anagogy of *Measure for Measure*," *Cahiers Elizabéthains* 16 (1979), 19–26.
Parker, M. D. H. *The Slave of Life* (1955), pp. 110–21.
Pope, Elizabeth M. "The Renaissance Background of *Measure for Measure*," *Shakespeare Survey* 2 (1949), 66–82.
Schleiner, Louise. "Providential Improvisation in *Measure for Measure*," *PMLA* 97 (1982), 227–36.
Toole, William B. *Shakespeare's Problem Plays: Studies in Form and Meaning* (Humanities Press, 1966), Ch. 5.
Turnbull, Andrew. *Motifs of Bedmate Substitution* (Ph. D. Diss., Indiana University, 1977), Ch. 7.
Velz, Sarah. "*Measure for Measure* and Mark iv," *Shakespeare Survey* 25 (1972), 37–44.

*G. Wilson Knight (1930)*

## Measure for Measure and the Gospels

In *Measure for Measure* we have a careful dramatic pattern, a studied explication of a central theme: the moral nature of man in relation to the crudity of man's justice, especially in the matter of sexual vice. There is, too, a clear relation existing between the play and the Gospels, for the play's theme is this:

Judge not, that ye be not judged. For with what judgement ye judge, ye shall be judged: and with what measure ye mete, it shall be measured to you again. (Mt 7:1)

The ethical standards of the Gospels are rooted in the thought of *Measure for Measure*. Therefore, in this analysis, we shall, while fixing attention primarily on the play, yet inevitably find a reference to the New Testament continually helpful, and sometimes essential.

The Duke, lord of this play in the exact sense that Prospero is lord of *The Tempest*, is the prophet of an enlightened ethic. He controls the action from start to finish, he allots, as it were, praise and blame, he is lit at moments with divine suggestion comparable with his almost divine power of fore-knowledge, and control, and wisdom. There is an enigmatic, other-worldly, mystery suffusing his figure and the meaning of his acts: their result, however, in each case justifies their initiation—wherein we see the allegorical nature of the play, since the plot is so arranged that each person receives his deserts in the light of the Duke's—which is really the Gospel—ethic.

Though Christian ethic be the central theme, there is a wider setting of varied ethical thought, voiced by each person in turn, high or low. The Duke, Angelo, and Isabella are clearly obsessed with such ideas and criticize freely in their different fashions. So also Elbow and the officers bring in Froth and Pompey, accusing them. Abhorson is severely critical of Pompey: "A bawd? Fie upon him! He will discredit our mystery" (4.2.29). Lucio traduces the Duke's character, Mistress Overdone informs against Lucio. Barnadine is universally despised. All, that is, react to each other in an essentially ethical mode: which mode is the peculiar and particular vision of this play.... There is thus a pervading atmosphere of orthodoxy and ethical criticism, in which is centred the mysterious holiness, the profound death-philosophy, the enlightened human insight and Christian ethic of the protagonist, the Duke of Vienna.

The satire of the play is directed primarily against self-conscious, self-protected righteousness. The Duke starts the action by resigning his power to Angelo. He addresses Angelo, outspoken in praise of his virtues, thus:

> Thyself and thy belongings
> Are not thine own so proper, as to waste
> Thyself upon thy virtues, they on thee.
> Heaven doth with us as we with torches do;
> Not light them for themselves; for if our virtues
> Did not go forth of us, 'twere all alike
> As if we had them not. Spirits are not finely touch'd,
> But to fine issues, nor Nature never lends
> The smallest scruple of her excellence,
> But, like a thrifty goddess, she determines
> Herself the glory of a creditor,
> Both thanks and use. (1.1.30–41)

The thought is similar to that of The Sermon on the Mount:

> Ye are the light of the world. A city that is set on the hill cannot be hid. Neither do men light a candle, and put it under a bushel, but on a candlestick; and it giveth light unto all that are in the house. (Mt 5:14)

Not only does the Duke's "torch"-metaphor clearly recall this passage, but his development of it is vividly paralleled by other of Jesus' words. The Duke compares "Nature" to "a creditor," lending qualities and demanding both "thanks and use." Compare:

> For the kingdom of heaven is as a man travelling into a far country, who called his own servants, and delivered unto them his goods. And unto one he gave five talents, to another two, and to another one; to every man according to his several ability; and straightway took his journey. (Mt 25:14)

The Duke, disguised as a friar, moves through the play, a dark figure, directing, watching, moralizing on the actions of the other persons. As the play progresses and his plot on Angelo works he assumes an ever-increasing mysterious dignity, his original purpose seems to become more and more profound in human insight, the action marches with measured pace to its appointed and logical end. We have ceased altogether to think of the Duke as merely a studious and unpractical governor, incapable of office. Rather he holds, within the dramatic universe, the dignity and power of a Prospero, to whom he is strangely similar. With both, their plot and plan is the plot and plan of the play: they make and forge the play, and thus are automatically to be equated in a unique sense with the poet himself—since both are symbols of the poet's controlling, purposeful, combined, movement of the chessmen of the drama. Like Prospero, the Duke tends to assume proportions evidently divine. Once he is actually compared to the Supreme Power:

> O my dread lord,
> I should be guiltier than my guiltiness,
> To think I can be undiscernible,
> When I perceive your grace, like power divine,
> Hath look'd upon my passes. (5.1.371–75)

So speaks Angelo at the end. We are prepared for it long before. In the rhymed octosyllable couplet of the Duke's soliloquy in 3.2. there is a distinct note of supernatural authority, forecasting the rhymed mystic utterances of divine beings in The Final Plays.

The Duke, like Jesus, is the prophet of a new order of ethics. This aspect of the Duke as teacher and prophet is also illustrated by his cryptic utterance to Escalus:

| | |
|---|---|
| Escalus | Good even, good father. |
| Duke | Bliss and goodness on you. |
| Escalus | Of whence are you? |
| Duke | Not of this country, though my chance is now |
| | To use it for my time: I am a brother |

|          |                                                                              |
|----------|------------------------------------------------------------------------------|
|          | Of gracious order, late come from the See                                    |
|          | In special business from his Holiness.                                       |
| Escalus  | What news abroad i' the world?                                               |
| Duke     | None, but that there is so great a fever on goodness, that the               |
|          | dissolution of it must cure it: novelty is only in request; and it           |

                   is as dangerous to be aged in any kind of course, as it is virtu-
                   ous to be constant in any undertaking. There is scarce truth
                   enough alive to make societies secure; but security enough to
                   make fellowships accurst: much upon this riddle runs the wis-
                   dom of the world. This news is old enough, yet it is every
                   day's news. (3.2.209–25)

The concluding speech holds the poetry of ethics. Its content, too, is very close to the Gospel teaching: the insistence on the blindness of the world, its habitual disregard of the truth exposed by prophet and teacher:

   And this is the condemnation, that light is come into the world, and men
  loved darkness rather than light, because their deeds were evil. (John 3:19)

The same almost divine suggestion rings in many of the Duke's measured prose utterances. There are his supremely beautiful words to Escalus:

  Look, the unfolding star calls up the shepherd. Put not yourself into amazement how these things should be: all difficulties are but easy when they are
  known. (4.2.219)

The first lovely sentence—a unique beauty of Shakespearian prose, in a style peculiar to this play—derives part of its appeal from New Testament associations: and the second sentence holds the mystic assurance of Matthew 10:26, "there is nothing covered, that shall not be revealed; and hid, that shall not be known." The Duke exercises the authority of a teacher throughout his disguise as a friar. He speaks authoritatively on repentance to Juliet:

|        |                                                              |
|--------|--------------------------------------------------------------|
| Duke   | But lest you do repent,                                      |
|        | As that the sin hath brought you to this shame,              |
|        | Which sorrow is always towards ourselves, not heaven,        |
|        | Showing we would not spare heaven as we love it,             |
|        | But as we stand in fear,—                                    |
| Juliet | I do repent me as it is an evil,                             |
|        | And take the shame with joy.                                 |
| Duke   | There rest. . . . (2.3.30–36)                                |

After rebuking Pompey the bawd very sternly but not unkindly, he concludes: "Go mend, go mend" (3.2.28). His attitude is that of Jesus to the woman taken in adultery: "Neither do I condemn thee: go, and sin no more" (John 8:11). Both are more kindly disposed towards honest impurity than light and frivolous scandalmongers, such as Lucio, or Pharisaic self-righteousness such as Angelo's.

    The play must be read in the light of the Gospel teaching, if its full significance is to be apparent. The Duke, like Jesus, moves among men suffering grief at their sins. We may suggest that he progresses by successive modes—from worldly power, through the prophecy and moralizing of the middle scenes, to the supreme judgement at the end, where he exactly reflects the universal judgement as suggested by many Gospel passages. There is the same apparent injustice, the same tolerance and mercy. The Duke is, in fact, a symbol of the same kind as the Father in the Parable of the Prodigal Son (Lk15) or the Lord in that of the Unmerciful Servant (Mt 18). The simplest way to focus correctly the quality and unity of *Measure for Measure* is to read it on the analogy of Jesus' parables.

Though his ethical philosophy is so closely related to the Gospel teaching, yet the Duke's thoughts on death (in 3.1) are devoid of any explicit belief in immortality. He addresses Claudio, who is to die, and his words at first appear vague, agnostic: but a deeper acquaintance renders their profundity and truth. Claudio fears death. The Duke comforts him by concentrating not on death, but life. In a series of pregnant sentences he asserts the negative nature of any single life-joy. First, life is slave to death and may fail at any chance moment; however much you run from death, yet you cannot but run still towards it; nobility in man is inextricably twined with "baseness" (this is, indeed, the moral of *Measure for Measure*), and courage is ever subject to fear; sleep is man's "best rest," yet he fears death which is but sleep; man is always discontent, striving for what he has not; he is tortured by disease and old age.... Regarded thus, life is unreal, a delusion, a living death. The thought is profound. True, the Duke has concentrated especially on the temporal aspect of life's appearances, regarding only the shell of life and neglecting the inner vital principle of joy and hope; he has left deeper things untouched. He neglects Love and all immediate transcendent intuitions. But since it is only this temporal aspect of decayed appearances which death is known to end, since it is only the closing of this very time-succession which Claudio fears, it is enough to prove this succession valueless. Claudio is thus comforted. The death of such a life is indeed not death, but rather itself a kind of life:

> I humbly thank you.
> To sue to live, I find I seek to die;
> And seeking death, find life: let it come on. (3.1.41–43)

From *The Wheel of Fire* (Oxford University Press, 1930), rpt. 1941, pp. 80–92 abridged. By permission of Methuen & Company.

*Roy Battenhouse (1946)*

## *Measure for Measure* and Atonement Story

The present essay is written in the belief that our latter-day critics have approximated a proper focus on *Measure for Measure*, without as yet achieving it adequately. What Wilson Knight and R. W. Chambers are saying is that the drama is thoroughly and properly ethical, if only we will accept Christian ethics. It would seem to me right to urge at the same time a corollary: that the drama is esthetically acceptable and sound, if we will but measure it by a Christian esthetics. Our critical problem, then, becomes one of discriminating the patterns by which Christian ethics and Christian art declare themselves, and then testing the relevance of such patterns to the actual texture of Shakespeare's drama. Is there manifest in its poetry, let us ask, the imagery, symbol, and myth traditional in Christian story?

Now the one pattern which most finally sets the norm for Christian ethics and Christian art is the story of the Atonement. It is told in Scripture and retold in the liturgies of the Church and the commentaries of her theologians. What is this Atonement story?

Briefly this: a sovereign disguises himself in order to visit his people and reform them. Though he is the Lord of men, he condescends to become their brother. Acting incognito he sows within their history the processes whereby they may be reconciled to him in a just and happy kingdom. By temporarily taking the form of a servant, he is able to mingle intimately in his people's affairs, discover their hearts, prevent and remove sins, intrude wise and far-reaching counsels, and direct all things toward a great Last Judgment when he shall appear with power to establish peace. As setting for this stratagem, Christian story emphasizes certain preconditions: the fact of disorder in the world, resulting from an abuse by men of their free-will; the attitude of the ruler, who desires a non-tyrannical restoration of order; and his benevolent readiness to undertake a remedy for evil. Starting from these premises, the plot is unwound with deliberate care until of a sudden it is discovered to be, miraculously, accomplished. Along the way many subsidiary themes make the story both fascinating and wondrously complex. We see nobility undergoing shame and royalty going "hooded";[1] grace working side by side with law; the wisdom of serpents joined to the harmlessness of doves; the power of petition operating within the realm of providence, the virtue of intercession even within the scheme of predestination.

Bearing in mind these features of the Atonement drama, let us note now the points of resemblance of the action to Shakespeare's play. The opening situation in both stories is that of a people in need of reform. In Shakespeare's Vienna "Liberty plucks justice by the nose"; decorum goes "quite athwart." The Duke, seeing this, wishes to curb license while preserving liberty. His strategy is twofold: he stirs up the arm of the Law by deputizing Angelo, a zealous legalist; and then concurrently "His Grace" undertakes in disguise to prevent the Law from collecting the penalty he has just newly permitted it to claim. From here on the plot is a contest between Law and Grace, both of course having their authority from the "Lord" of the city. Law serves a providential function, yet Grace is ultimately the victor. The disguise chosen by His Grace is that of friar, "spiritual brother" to man. Attired thus, the Duke visits the spirits in prison (Cf. 1 Pet 3:19); brings comfort to the captive Claudio, victim of the just law; shrives the penitent Juliet; watches over the temptation and "fall" of Angelo; enlists Isabella in a remedy for outwitting this "angel"; at the same time aids the needy Mariana; strengthens these disciples of his by his reasoning and authority, and finally commits them to Friar Peter until his coming again. Then, when he comes in judgment, all things undergo apocalypse (cf. 1 Cor 4:5). Isabella initiates the denouement by announcing she has news both "strange" and "true." When later the Duke is unveiled the seeming righteous are convicted of sin, and the seeming sinners are vindicated. Angelo perceives that to his "dread lord" nothing is indiscernible; that His Grace "like power divine" has looked upon Angelo's trespasses. And for Isabella, on the other hand, there are words of welcome: "Come hither, Isabel. Your friar is now your prince." (cf. Mt 25:34. "Come, ye blessed, inherit the kingdom prepared for you.")

From this point on, the Judgment is enriched by still other themes traditionally Christian. The manner in which Justice and Mercy seem to contend in the Duke's court as they work their way to a final reconciliation reminds us of the debate between the daughters of God which brought medieval morality play to its happy conclusion.[2] Medieval teaching regarding the invocation and intercession of saints has its reflection here too; for Isabella responds to Mariana's plea that she intercede for Angelo, and we who watch the action realize that indeed Isabella is hound by charity to do just this, since Mariana has earlier interceded her own body to save Isabella's brother, Claudio.

I have already hinted at the significance of the names which Shakespeare, departing from his literary "sources," has chosen to give his characters. Further attention to this point suggests that the playwright was aware of important overtones in the story he was dramatizing. The name Claudio means, literally, "the lame one"—an old and very apt way of designating sinful man. Isabella declares by her name that she is "devoted to God." And Mariana, without whose gift of herself the ransom could not have been paid and the brother must then have perished, combines in her name (meaning literally "bitter grace") the memory of Mary the virgin and Anna the immaculate mother. Those critics who think Mariana's action in the play is unchaste should be warned against name-calling by noting the name by which Shakespeare has called her. The enemy with whom Mariana has to contend is Angelo, which carries for the reader of Scripture the reminder that Satan, Our Lord's great enemy, was a fallen angel. Against the "devil" Angelo, Mariana fights and plots; but she is willing to marry an Angelo no longer angel but mortal. And for both courses of action she has the Duke's authority. His title, of course, means "leader," particularly in a military sense; and the name Vincentio, meaning victor or conqueror, stresses this connotation (as does his assumed name of Lodowick, meaning "famous warrior"). Any reader of Aquinas may recall that theologian's likening of God to the General of an army, having as his purpose victory over sin. The Duke in undertaking the guise of a friar is able to approve himself to two *bona fide* ecclesiastics—Thomas, whose doubt he dispels; and Peter, to whom he entrusts the tutoring of his protégées.

Further thinking along the lines of Atonement doctrine is unavoidable when we call to mind some of the most celebrated passages of the play. None is better known, perhaps, than the lines of Angelo's lament:

> Alack, when once our grace we have forgot,
> Nothing goes right; we would, and we would not. (4.4.33–34)

Or again, there is the famous speech of Isabella when pleading before the judge for her brother's life:

> Why, all the souls that were, were forfeit once;
> And he that might the vantage best have took
> Found out the remedy. (2.4.106–08)

Both these passages resound with the wisdom of Christian tradition. "We would, and we would not" calls to mind St Paul's discussion (in Romans 7) of the two wills which contended in him before the advent of and in the absence of divine grace. The allusion points at Angelo's lack of grace as the fundamental cause of his frustration, and it lets us know that his present agony is but the old story of the Pharisee Saul—a man self-divided by a law within his members at war with the law of the spirit. Isabella's speech, likewise, revolves about the cardinal facts of sin and grace—this time illumined by memory of the Atonement. "And he . . . found out the remedy" is a clear allusion to the redemption wrought by Christ. Isabella is here reminding Angelo that the most just of all judges, God Himself, *sought out a means for circumventing* his own *just* claim upon man. God could not rest content to see man get his just deserts; he provided a way for man to escape from prison!

But Isabella is addressing a judge who can propose only a "monstrous" means for Claudio's release. It remains for the Duke to correct that. He does it by arranging Mariana's voluntary yet sinless humiliation of her disguised self, then adding a Scripture-like injunction:

> Come, let us go;
> Our corn's to reap, for yet our tithe's to sow.

Mariana's laying down of her body is as the sowing of a tithe. It makes for an atonement in several senses: it fulfils the "promise of satisfaction" exacted by the Adversary; it accomplishes her own physical at-one-ment with her estranged husband; and it makes possible the eventual reconciliation between the Prince and his (spiritually) estranged people. Yet the "suffering" of Isabella-Mariana does not automatically free Claudio; it merely establishes a claim—which the Adversary defies by breaking his contract with Mariana's assistant, Isabella. It is then time for the Duke to return in judgment. But first, his coming is foretold: the Provost is assured by certain secret writings that the Lord of the city will return "within these two days" (cf. the Scriptures quoted by Christ to assure his disciples of his return "on the third day," i.e., two days after his departure).

I have called attention to the finer points of the situation because it is exactly at this moment that the Duke's words rise to an arresting beauty which has made them quoted, by both Knight and Traversi, as one of the most haunting passages in the entire play:

> Look, th'unfolding star calls up the shepherd. Put not yourself into amazement how these things should be; all difficulties are but easy when they are known... Come away; it is almost clear dawn. (cf. Rom 13:12)

Not only the imagery of the star and the shepherd but the very syntax of the language is biblical, and its ring is apocalyptic. The "unfolding star" of the Duke's vision seems to me more symbolic than literal (as is his announcement of daybreak), and it makes best sense when we recall that Christian revelation "unfolds," ushering in "the Day of the Lord." The star—and the shepherd too—have in the Shakespearean context supernatural overtones. The Duke is exercising a pastoral role over his subjects and, even in doing so, understands it as that of a shepherd-of-the-sheep summoned to fulfil a predestined plan.

As reinforcement for this interpretation, it should be recalled that the shepherd analogy—whether in St Luke's parable or in later commentary—is one of the most venerable for describing the work of the Atonement. Thus Irenaeus, for example, speaks of God as a Father who "has in the last times sought us out who were lost, winning back His own, and taking up the lost sheep upon His shoulders, and with joy restoring it to the fold of life."[3]

Shepherding, however, is not the only metaphor in terms of which the drama of the Atonement can find expression. The art of fishing furnished analogy even more fascinating. Christ's promise "Follow me and I will make you fishers of men" had profound implications. Indeed, the imagery of fishing, above all other, appealed to the imagination of disciples in the early centuries. While the favorite art symbol of the catacombs was that of Christ the Shepherd the common password was "Fish"—either drawn in picture on some flat surface, or used in Greek spelling as a rebus of the Christian creed.

In *Measure for Measure* the imagery of fishing obtrudes in Isabella's soliloquy at the end of Act 2:

> O perilous mouths, ...
> Bidding the law make court'sy to their will;
> Hooking both right and wrong to the appetite,
> To follow as it draws! (2.4.172–77)

She is implying that the hungry Angelo is like a fish compelling the law (like a fish-line) to condescend to his appetite. Even more arresting is the use of the fishing metaphor in an earlier speech by Angelo:

> O cunning enemy, that, to catch a saint,
> With saints dost bait thy hook! (2.2.179–80)

Angelo sees Isabella's beauty as a baited hook for catching him in an act of sin. Obscurely he senses, behind Isabella, some "cunning enemy" contriving this temptation of his virtue.

The form of doctrine which Angelo's words point at is commonly known as the "deception of the devil" theory. Presumably because the cross has a shape like a hook, Rufinus quotes Job 41:1, "Can'st thou draw out leviathan with a hook?" as a prophecy of the snaring of the devil by the cross. This idea has its most extended development in Gregory the Great's *Moralia on the Book of Job*;[4] for Gregory was convinced that Job—the wisest and most tenacious of pre-Christian wrestlers with the problem of evil—had here mystically prefigured the problem's solution in the Christian mystery of the Atonement. Gregory says that Our Lord made as it were a kind of hook of himself for the death of the devil, and assumed a body in order that he might bait the Behemoth. This whale, Gregory explains, was rushing hither and thither with open mouth and the hook for his swallowing was suspended in the gloomy waters by a marvelous arrangement; for from Abraham down to Mary the virgin a kind of line was spun for the hook of the Incarnate Lord to be bound to the end of it, to hang in these waters of the human race for the devil's satellites to catch at. Attracted by Our Lord's humanity, the devourer was wounded by his divinity; excited by his open infirmity, the spoiler was pierced through the jaw by his hidden virtue. Other questions which The Almighty addresses to Job enlarge the theme. "Wilt thou put a ring in his nostrils? And bore through his nostrils with stakes?" The ring, says Gregory, signifies the circle of heavenly protection whereby the devourer's cruelty is restrained; it designates the aid of secret judgments by which his cunning is prevented from prevailing. The stakes by which the nostrils are perforated are the sharp counsels and acute senses of the saints.

The drama of Atonement as thus delineated by Gregory has points of at least approximate and teasing similarity with the action in *Measure for Measure.* Angelo when he has succumbed to temptation is a sort of leviathan. But his cunning stratagems are perforated by the sharp counsels of the Friar-Duke. Providentially a fishline is spun: to the corded righteousness of Isabella is joined the sharp love of Mariana; then when Angelo strikes he is "hooked" in a double sense, both deceived and caught. The Duke also forges a ring of heavenly protection which prevents Angelo's cunning from prevailing anywhere, even against Claudio. The beguiler is deservedly beguiled.

Another kind of imagery well known to students of Christian Atonement is that of "ransom." The first suggestion of this is made, ironically, by the saintly Isabella when she proposes, "Hark, how I'll *bribe* you." "How! bribe me!" exclaims Angelo, feeling for the first time a stab of personal interest in the affair. "Ay," responds Isabella, "with such gifts that heaven shall share with you.... Not with fond shekels ... but with true prayers" (2.2.152–6). Angelo, however, sees here a gambit other than Isabella intends, and he warms to the play. He replies at their next meeting with a challenge to Isabella to "redeem" her brother by giving up her body to "sweet uncleanness." With fine discrimination Isabella answers that "Lawful mercy / Is nothing kin to foul redemption" (2.4.112–13). Only a devil's logic would confound Christian charity with mortal sin. Isabella cannot trade her chastity. Yet she strongly desires to save her brother; and when by the Friar's counsel she learns she can seem to comply without endangering her virtue, she adjusts to Angelo's proposition and a bargain is agreed to. But then Angelo, after having received the ransom, breaks his side of the bargain. In this extremity, thanks to the advice of the Friar, Isabella becomes a petitioner like the importunate widow of biblical parable. "Justice, justice, justice, justice!" she cries when the Duke returns as judge. He pretends to brush her off, referring her case to his deputy. "You bid me seek redemption of the devil: Hear me yourself," she replies. For awhile he does not seem to hear. In the end, however, her insistent petitioning—first for justice, and then for mercy—is but the price she pays for a surprising restoration of her brother. She has paid a ransom that consists of self-humbling, which is also the price the Duke has paid in becoming a friar and suffering abuse. It is the "remedy" found out by Christ when "all the souls that were were forfeit." There is irony in the fact that in 2.4 when the young Isabella alluded to this remedy in calling on Angelo to practice it she did not yet recognize that she herself needed to find it out.

The concept of ransom in theological commentary likens God to a good prince who wishes to free souls that have been captured and imprisoned by a rival prince. To bring about their release God assumes a mortal estate which by its beauty attracts the Adversary and allows him to bargain away his power. God does this for three reasons, according to Gregory of Nyssa: first, his goodness, which chooses to free man; second, his justice, which will be exhibited in making redemption a matter of exchange; and third, his wisdom, which is manifested when he "enables the Enemy to apprehend that of which he was before incapable."[5] In Shakespeare's play Angelo figures as a rival magistrate who is enabled by the Duke to apprehend his own moral bankruptcy when he is exposed as a promise-breaker.

But although Angelo's act has been devil-like, he is also a human being who needs to fulfill a marriage contract he has evaded. As human being he is given an unmerited benefit in the bedmate he accepts as payment of his ransom demand, since the disguised Mariana enables him to fulfil his true contract. The arrangement involves a strategy of benevolent deception by a Friar who justifies his use of craft against vice by saying:

> So disguise shall, by the disguised,
> Pay with falsehood false exacting
> And perform an old contracting. (End of Act 3)

Some of us with modern tastes may ask, Is deception ever ethical? Shakespeare's Duke plainly believes it sometimes is. "Virtue is bold," he declares, "and goodness never fearful." Or, again: "The doubleness of the benefit defends the deceit from reproof" (3.1.206, 255).

Here Shakespeare has behind him the teaching of orthodox Catholic ethics. Gregory of Nyssa is authority for the view that deception is like the adulteration of food: sometimes done by an enemy for our poisoning, sometimes done by our physician for our healing. "The one does it to cause death, the other as an antidote"; and "if both drug the food, we must have regard to the motive when we praise the one and blame the other."[6] John Cassian, also, discusses at considerable length the grounds on which a deceit can be justified.[7] It has sometimes been employed by the saints as a cup of hellebore, necessary for the purging of the sick. The patriarch Jacob received greater gains of blessing and righteousness because he was not afraid to acquiesce in his mother's instigation of a lie for this object. And the "pious fraud" with which Hushai tricked Absalom for the salvation of David is not to be blamed; for the Scripture commands us to "Deliver those who are being led to death, and spare not to redeem those who are being killed." Such an ethic is not rationalistic. Rather, as St Paul says in 2 Cor 6:8, Christians approve themselves ministers of God in a paradoxical fashion: "by honor and dishonor, by evil report and good report; as *deceivers* yet *true*." The morality of any action depends on our asking the leading question, "Why did Christ come down from heaven?" and answering it as Irenaeus answered it: "That he might destroy sin, overcome death, and give life to men." Christian action takes its proper "measure" from the story summarized by Irenaeus as follows:

> Man had been created by God that he might have life. If now, having lost life (by sin) . . . he were not to return to life, but were to be wholly abandoned to death, then God would have been defeated . . . But since God is both invincible and magnanimous, he showed his magnanimity in correcting man, and in proving all men . . . but through the Second Man he bound the strong one, and spoiled his goods, and annihilated death.[8]

Gustav Aulén has termed this the "dramatic" view of the Atonement. Its central idea, he points out, is that of a Divine conflict, carried out by *Christus Victor*. The endeavor is "to show that God does not stand, as it were, outside the drama that is being played out, but takes part in it and attains his purpose by internal, not external means; he overcomes evil, not by an almighty *fiat*, but by putting in something of his own."

It should by now be evident how relevant this conceptual framework is to the design of *Measure for Measure*. Shakespeare's Vincentio is presented dramatically in the double role of Duke and Friar. When his Vienna needs reform he introduces two lines of action. He gives a commission to the wielders of law and then himself descends to undertake the directing of forces of mercy. Soon it becomes evident that a legalistic righteousness can not bring salvation. Rather, the law increases sin—both in Angelo who finds opportunity for sin by it, and in Claudio who is driven by it to a second sin, the momentary desiring of his own sister's dishonor. But the Duke's strategy redeems both Angelo and Claudio from the curse of the law. Though it makes forfeit the head of Claudio and then the head of Angelo, the axe never falls. Instead, the "angel" learns he is but a man and the "lame" learn to walk, given "Grace to stand, and virtue [to] go."

Atonement is finally one thing more: a divine romance. This is the most circumambient metaphor, since the whole action of atonement is a work of love. Christian thought insists that the Shepherd-Fisherman-Prince is primarily a King of Love, who puts himself in the role of humble wooer of the human heart, prospective Bridegroom of his "elect." In this role he looks forward to a "marriage"; but first he must win his beloved by courting and serving her. He must persuade her to listen, then to obey, then to suffer for him. His task is to make the bride worthy of him at the same time that he wins her; he must bring out the best in her through a strategic love capable of perfecting the bride. Christian lore leads to a conclusion stated by Claude Chavasse: *Christus Victor* becomes *Christus Sponsus*.[9]

This aspect of the Atonement drama offers, I think, our best guide for understanding the course of the Duke's relations with Isabella. Her character does indeed develop in the play—not exactly "from sanctity to humanity," as Wilson Knight puts it, but rather from the self-divided sanctity and cold humanity of a novice under "law" to the integrated sanctity and warm humanity of a sister to Mariana under "His Grace." Isabella needs an enlargement from her moral isolationism. And how is this accomplished? By a loving stranger's putting in the right word at the right time—or, as the Bible expresses it supernaturally, by a visitation of The Word "in the fulness of time." In the very middle of Shakespeare's play we find Isabella exhibiting a righteousness which would have pained St Clare:

> Die, perish! Might but my bending down
> Reprieve thee from thy fate, it should proceed.
> I'll pray a thousand prayers for thy death,
> No word to save thee. (3.1.143–45)

Five lines later the Friar-Duke interposes his first speech to her:

> Vouchsafe a word young sister, but one word.

To which she replies, "What is your will?" She is now about to be led into an act of grace—as the biblical Eve, conversely, was tempted into sin. The "one word" involves a four-fold remedy.

This virgin is at first cool to her suitor's approach ("I have no superfluous leisure; my stay must be stolen"). But the stranger's fund of gossip regarding Angelo arouses her interest. He offers courtly compliment, couching it in a style of balanced moralizing and entreaty:

> The hand that made you fair hath made you good: the goodness that is cheap
> in beauty makes beauty brief in goodness; but grace, being the soul of your
> complexion, shall keep the body of it ever fair.

The teasing quality of these lines is that their meaning moves at two levels—the natural and the supernatural. The supernatural meaning is that the Creator intends her to be "fair" (i.e., just and magnanimous) to Claudio as well as "good" (i.e., virtuous). A scant measure of the one means a short measure of the other; but grace, animating both, will assure an immortal beauty.

But note that at the "natural" level the wooing constantly suggests the conventions of chivalric romance. The lover presently has a "remedy" for his lady's distress: a scheme whereby she may "do . . . a benefit" without staining her honor. "I have spirit to do" it, she says; "show me how." Then he outlines a plan involving a secret—to which she replies in lover-like fashion, "The image of it gives me content already." The element of surface parallel here to the love-compacts of adulterous chivalry serves but to give dramatic heightening to the interplay of false and true, seems and is, which makes up the enigmatic texture of the play.

When the remedy seems to fail, Isabella's distress is increased: the reward for which she had hoped is treacherously denied her. But the Duke plans for her "heavenly comforts" when she has learned patience; and she can accomplish patience only if she hungers and thirsts for satisfaction, while pacing her wisdom in "that good path that I would wish it go." Isabella must plead shamelessly for justice—and be denied, only to be suddenly rewarded when the Friar unmasks as Duke. Realizing then how much she has "employ'd and pain'd" him, she begs his pardon. This is the beginning of a larger awakening. Mariana now asks her to pardon Angelo, and she does so because she begins to see both a frailty in herself and an indebtedness to Mariana. Experience has taught her how to love. The Duke then proposes in words whose timeworn sound has a timeless meaning:

> Give me your hand, and say you will be mine
> He [the resurrected Claudio] is my brother too. . . .

A moment later he adds another of love's old refrains:

> if you'll a willing ear incline
> What's mine is yours, and what is yours is mine,
> So, bring us to our palace. . . .

Here the bracketing phrases of lines 1 and 3 echo the Christmas-day liturgy of Psalm 45, verses 10 and 15, so that the wondrously "natural" second line is delicately enveloped in an atmosphere of supernatural context. It is the way all true romance, all good comedy, should end.

In Shakespeare's play justice, charity, and wisdom are all present, richly exhibited in the plotted peace which the Friar-Duke effects. The happy ending is one which may be described not inaptly by borrowing words from Isaiah and St Luke: there is release for the captive Claudio, a recovering of sight for the blind Angelo, a setting at liberty the bruised Mariana, and a proclaiming of the acceptable year of the lord Vincentio. The mysterious star mentioned in the play has called up a shepherd who has brought all his sheep safely home, and at the same time the great leviathan has been caught. Vincentio has shown himself as "conqueror" of rebellious wills, not by power of the sword or whip of the magistrate but by *hook* and by *crook!*

## Notes

1 The motif has been well employed by T. S. Eliot in his picture of the Stranger on the road to Emmaus (*The Waste Land*, 362–63):
> There is always another one walking beside you
> Gliding wrapt in a brown mantle, hooded.
2 See, e.g., the conclusion of *The Castle of Perseverance*. The verse *"Misericordia et Veritas obviaverunt sibi; Justitia et Pax osculatae sunt"* is to be found in the first vespers of the office for Christmas Day; hence some of the spectators of *Measure for Measure* on St Stephen's night, 1604, may have remembered it.
3 *Against Heresies*, V.xv.2., tr. in *The Ante-Nicene Fathers* (Buffalo, 1885), I, 543.
4 See *A Library of Fathers* (Oxford, 1850), III, Pt. 2, pp. 569 ff.
5 *The Great Catechism*, ch. xxiii, in *Post-Nicene Fathers*, Second Series, 5, 493.
6 *The Great Catechism*, ch. xxvi.
7 See "On Making Promises," tr. in *Post-Nicene Fathers*, Second Series, 11, 460 ff.
8 *Against Heresies*, III.xxiii, in Aulen, *Christus Victor*, tr. A. G. Hebert (London, 1931), p. 35.
9 *The Bride of Christ* (London, 1939), p. 104.

From "*Measure for Measure* and Christian Doctrine of the Atonement," *PMLA* 61 (1946), 1029–59. This text abridges and revises pp. 1031–55.

*Arthur C. Kirsch (1975)*

# The Integrity of *Measure for Measure*

It is astonishing how many critics are unwilling to take the play's Christian ideas seriously. Alone among Shakespeare's plays, the very title is drawn from the Scriptures—and not from its dark corners, but from the Sermon on the Mount and a passage in Luke which was regularly read in the liturgy of the fourth Sunday after Trinity. The action is dominated by religious images—for most of the play the Duke appears in the habit of a friar, and Isabella appears throughout in the habit of a novice—and the language is suffused with allusions to the Gospels, often to parables, like those of the talents and of the unmerciful servant, which were common currency. At certain points, notably in Isabella's speech on the Atonement, both the language and action are explicitly and deeply concerned with central truths of Christian experience.

To ignore such texts and images and actions, to fail particularly to consider how they might have been understood and have affected Shakespeare's contemporary audience, would seem a wilful if not perverse procedure, and yet this is exactly what many of the play's critics have done, beginning with Dr. Johnson himself. His criticism of the play is instructive. He finds the conclusion deeply offensive:

> The Duke has justly observed that Isabel is "importuned against all sense" to solicit for Angelo, yet here "against all sense" she solicits for him. Her argument is extraordinary.
>
> > A due sincerity govern'd his deeds,
> > 'Till he did look on me; since it is so,
> > Let him not die. (5.1.444–6)
>
> That Angelo has committed all the crimes charged against him, as far as he could commit them, is evident. The only "intent" which "his act did not overtake" was the defilement of Isabel. Of this Angelo was only intentionally guilty.
>
> Angelo's crimes were such, as must sufficiently justify punishment, whether its end be to secure the innocent from wrong, or to deter guilt by example; and I believe every reader feels some indignation, when he finds him spared. From what extenuation of his crime can Isabel, who yet supposes her brother dead, form any plea in his favour. "Since he was good 'till he looked on me, let him not die." I am afraid our Varlet Poet intended to inculcate, that women think ill of nothing that raises the credit of their beauty, and are ready, however virtuous, to pardon any act which they think incited by their charms.[1]

Isabella's reasoning can indeed seem disconcerting, even to the play's so-called Christian critics, and we shall return to it, but what is nonetheless remarkable is how absolutely unforgiving, and specifically un-Christian, Johnson's judgement is. He insists, as so many critics have since, upon an eye for an eye, in contravention of the meaning of the Scriptural sources of the play's title and of Isabella's own earlier, explicit, and eloquent plea for charity:

> Alas, Alas!
> Why, all the souls that were, were forfeit once,
> And He that might the vantage best have took
> Found out the remedy. How would you be
> If He, which is the top of judgement, should
> But judge you as you are? O, think on that,
> And mercy then will breathe within your lips,
> Like man new made. (2.2.72–9)[2]

Johnson, of course, was hardly ignorant of the Bible, and as a man, hardly un-Christian, but he was always distressed by the mixture of profane and sacred material in literature, and throughout his edition of *Measure for Measure* he resolutely refuses to acknowledge Biblical references, even where they are transparent. In one comment he misses an obvious allusion to the Lord's Prayer (2.2.158–60), and in another a reference to Paul's Epistle to the Romans (2.2.31–33); he castigates Warburton for a perfectly sensible reading of Lucio's lines on grace (1.3.24–26);[3] and he even wishes to mute the clear theological import of the speech by Isabella which we have just quoted. The lines, "And mercy then will breathe within your lips, / Like man new made," refer of course to the Redemption, as Warburton at least partly saw when he glossed them as follows in his own edition: "The meaning is that 'mercy will add such grace to your person, that you will appear as amiable as man come fresh out of the hands of his Creator.'" But Johnson will have none of it: "I rather think the meaning is, 'you would then change the severity of your present character.' In familiar speech, 'you would be quite another man.'" What readings like these demonstrate is that Johnson is in fact scandalized by the Scriptural ideas of *Measure for Measure* and prefers, where he can, to remain blind to them. The realms of faith and of experience have simply become too far apart for him to reconcile.

For the generations of critics who have succeeded him, they have often become antithetical. Medieval drama has only recently escaped from the invidious assumptions that its quality increases the farther it gets from the altar, that its real vitality depends upon its comic subversion of doctrine, that its "dramatic," "human" truths are finally different from, if not incompatible with, its "religious" ideas; but these assumptions still persist in Shakespeare criticism. Harriett Hawkins, for example, in attacking moralistic critics of Shakespeare, cites the following verse of Dorothy Parker with evident relish:

> Whose love is given over well,
> Shall gaze on Helen's face in Hell.
> Whilst they whose love is thin and wise
> May view John Knox in Paradise.[4]

Not all critics are so blatant, of course, but a remarkable number are nevertheless resistant to the notion that Shakespeare's Christianity might matter, and they tend to regard any attempt to explore the religious ideas of his plays as necessarily unliterary, necessarily a reduction of creative, human complexity to allegorical abstraction or homiletic piety.

Unfortunately, with *Measure for Measure* such prejudices are fatal, not because the dramatic experience of the play is equivalent to its theological ideas, or should be reduced to them, but because without an understanding of the play's ideas and their connotations for an Elizabethan audience, its dramatic experience is often inaccessible or unintelligible. To Shakespeare the Bible was not simply an eschatological document, but a revelation of human as well as divine truths, and it is precisely the relationship between the two that *Measure for Measure* is about. Once this is appreciated, problems which have vexed scholars can be explained, if not entirely displaced, and the play can assume some coherence of thought and form. Many, if not, as the Duke says, "all difficulties are but easy when they are known" (4.2.204–5), and the beginning of knowledge, in this case, is an apprehension of certain fundamental Scriptural texts.

The most obvious are Matthew 7:1–5, Luke 6:36–42 and Mark 4:21–5. All three were commonly associated by Elizabethan commentators with the parable of the unmerciful servant in Matthew 18:32–45, who, forgiven a debt of 10,000 talents by his king, refused in turn to forgive a debt to himself of 100 pence. Like the passage in Luke, the parable was also a regular part of the Anglican liturgy, the Gospel reading for the twenty-second Sunday after Trinity.

What is apparent about all these texts, even to the modern reader, is that they apply—literally chapter and verse—to the behavior of Angelo, a hypocrite who casts out a mote in his brother Claudio's eye while he has a beam in his, who will not and cannot forgive a small debt even when he comes to know the enormity of his own. What is perhaps less apparent is the implicit stress upon the hypocritical condition of all men who do not perceive their inherent corruption and the infinite mercy of Christ's Redemption. For the obvious hypocrite, like Angelo, is merely a parabolic instance of the hypocritical condition of all Adam's descendants. We are all Angelos, all born with a beam in our eye, with an infected will, with an immeasurable debt of sin from which we can be ransomed only through grace.

Elizabethan commentaries on these Gospels make exactly these points, and in ways which are particularly suggestive for *Measure for Measure*. In his commentary on Luke 6:36–42, for example, Thomas Becon writes:

> For with the same measure, saith he, shall other measure to you, as you have measured with.... I will not rehearse how manifolde waies we have offended hym, through all our life with sinnes. This might worthely be given to us as measure, even death and hell. But what doth God: He putteth awaie that that we have deserved, that is to saie, wrathe, indignation judgement, death, hell. &c. and bringeth to us, heaven, grace, libertie, and a quiete mynde, from the condemnation of the lawe, and of an evill conscience.... This is truely a large and plentifull measure, but whereas thou deniest other the same measure after that, thinke not, but like measure shal be given to thee from God, as thou givest other.[5]

It seems to me that Shakespeare himself shared such beliefs and their implications, but in any event there is no question that in *Measure for Measure* he was interested in dramatizing them. The ultimate burden of the Gospels to which the play refers, as the commentaries universally make clear, is an apprehension, at once theological and moral, both of the possibilities of grace in human life and of the need for it, and it is just this apprehension that it is the Duke's aim to make his subjects learn and Shakespeare's goal to make us experience.

The beam in Angelo's eye is large and its meaning obvious. The beam in Isabella's eye is smaller, and its perception, both by her and by us, more subtle. She is certainly fully committed to the religious ideals she argues before Angelo, but her idealism, not unlike his, is inexperienced and based on an ignorance of her own human composition.

As a number of critics have noticed, there is a strong erotic undercurrent in her characterization. Angelo's lust for her seems to him, and perhaps at first to us, simply perverse and diabolic, but I think we are eventually meant to understand that she herself offers unconscious sexual provocation. There is a hint in Claudio's description of why she might succeed with Angelo:

> For in her youth
> There is a prone and speechless dialect
> Such as move men; beside, she hath prosperous art
> When she will play with reason and discourse,
> And well she can persuade. (1.2.172–6)

But if the equivocation of "prone," "move" and "play" are only suggestive, the erotic drift of at least one of her own speeches is unmistakable. When Angelo asks her, hypothetically, if she would not sacrifice her virginity to save Claudio, she answers:

> As much for my poor brother as myself;
> That is, were I under the terms of death,
> Th' impression of keen whips I'd wear as rubies,
> And strip myself to death as to a bed
> That longing have been sick for, ere I'd yield
> My body up to shame. (2.4.99–104)

What this speech conveys, and her subsequent abuse of her brother (including its hysterical image of incest) confirms, is that Isabella is afraid not only of Angelo's desires, but of her own.

It is in this context that her behavior in the final acts of the play must be understood. After witnessing the scene between her and Claudio in prison, the Duke praises her: "The hand that hath made you fair hath made you good" (3.1.179–80); but he proceeds at the same time to place her in a situation which will enlarge her understanding both of herself and others. He keeps her ignorant that Claudio is alive, but even more important, he involves her intimately with Mariana, a woman whose sexual desires are at once open and legitimate. Nothing is clearer in a stage production than that Mariana wants her man, and far from being a scandal, it is an education for Isabella to help her get him. For when at the end of the play Mariana kneels to ask her to plead for Angelo, and when the Duke, invoking the ghost of Claudio, says "Against all sense you do importune her," it is precisely with a dilated understanding of sense that she is able to respond. She kneels to the Duke, and says,

> Most bounteous sir:
> Look, if it please you, on this man condemn'd
> As if my brother liv'd. I partly think
> A due sincerity govern'd his deeds
> Till he did look on me. Since it is so,
> Let him not die. My brother had but justice,
> In that he did the thing for which he died:
> For Angelo,
> His act did not o'ertake his bad intent,
> And must be buried but as an intent
> That perish'd by the way. Thoughts are no subjects;
> Intents, but merely thoughts. (5.1.441–52)

That Isabella should thus argue her case in terms of law, not Christ, and particularly that she should refer to her own effect upon Angelo, is not a betrayal of religious faith, but an exemplification of it. However legally tenuous it may be, her plea—in behalf of the man who she thinks executed her brother—is surely an extraordinary enactment of the kind of mercy for which she had argued only in theory before; and it is made possible precisely because her recognition of herself as a woman has taught her the human need for mercy. Her sexual awareness is not vanity, it is humility.

The Duke makes his subjects recognize that the corruption which boils and bubbles in Vienna is within themselves, a moral condition, a beam in their own eyes. In the words of the homilist, he makes them turn the eyes of their minds inwards so that they may recognize the principal sins of their own lives and hearts. He also, however, and this is the ultimate purpose of his deceptions and contrivances, enables them to find a redeeming expression of their humanity by bringing them to marriage. Marriage always in Shakespeare has sacramental value, and never more than in *Measure for Measure*, where it is seen as a sanctification of impulses which could otherwise damn us, as the means through procreation by which we can make true coin of the currency of our lives, by which we can—literally—remake ourselves in the image of our Creator. It is thus the most perverse combination of Victorian prudery and modern cynicism to regard the bed-trick as unseemly or to imagine, as one recent director has, that Isabella should recoil from the Duke's proposal at the end of the play. The bed-trick miraculously transforms Angelo's libidinousness, turning it to the consummation of a betrothal he had betrayed, and the Duke's proposal offers the promise that in marriage Isabella can fully express her newborn awareness of herself as a woman. The one action moderates scope, the other restraint—the two poles of sexuality in the play—and both are at once gracious and creative.

Lucio, who becomes the Duke's comic shadow, is also his most serious antagonist. His slanderousness, for Elizabethans, would have marked him as a kin of the Blatant Beast, an enemy both of social and moral order, and would have related him quite directly to the underlying ideas of the play. William Perkins considered slander to be the essential subject of Matthew 7:1–5. The verse, "Judge not, that ye be not judged," he read as a reference to "rash judgment" and as specifically an injunction against slanderers:

> He that gives rash judgment of another, is worse than a theefe that steales away a mans goods: for he robbes him of his *good name*, which (as Saloman saith) *is to be chosen above great riches*, Prov. 22:1.... The backbiter is worse then a murtherer, for he killeth three at once; first, his *owne soule* in thus sinning: secondly, his *neighbour* whose name he hurteth: and thirdly, the hearer who receiveth this rash and injust report: and for this cause the *slaunderer* is numbered among those that shall not inherit the kingdome of God.[6]

Lucio is such a soul as Perkins describes. His licentiousness has the excuse neither of trade, like Pompey's, nor passion, like Angelo's, and his condition is even more desperate than the drunken Barnardine's, because it is consciously faithless. Simply the thing he is shall make him live. Like Mak in *The Second Shepherds' Play*, as well as Parolles in *All's Well That Ends Well*, he constitutes a moral condition, the basic antithesis of the processes by which man becomes new made. Like them also, he is forgiven, though less as a promise of his own regeneration than as a signification of the power of charity.

*Measure for Measure*, like Shakespeare's other tragicomedies, has a generically appropriate overall effect. . . . It remains a marvel, both theatrically and ideologically, that the punishment not only fits but transforms the crime, that mercy can eventually be consistent with justice, and that each of the characters in the play can be meted a measure as good as it is exact. Moreover, both the language and action repeatedly reveal the wonder of regenerated life, not only literally, as character after character is reprieved from death, but more profoundly, as the desire for life is progressively illuminated by the kind of charitable understanding which culminates in Isabella's remarkable plea for the life of Angelo.

This understanding and these paradoxes, of course, are those of Christian experience itself, and in *Measure for Measure*, as in his other tragicomedies, Shakespeare identifies the form of the play with the shape of the life it represents. The Duke speaks explicitly of making "heavenly comforts of despair" (4.3.109), and the idea of *felix culpa* clearly lies at the heart of the play. The action describes an arc which moves dialectically from tragic to comic possibilities: literally from the fear of death to the joy of anticipated marriage, from prison to freedom, from sin to grace. In no other play in the canon is the pattern of *felix culpa* more encompassing or more deep. Tragic experience is not merely the prelude to comic salvation in *Measure for Measure* but the means by which such salvation can be understood and achieved: "For els how can my sinnes be forgiven me, without I felt them and knowledged them."

## Notes

1  *Johnson on Shakespeare*, ed. Arthur Sherbo, *The Yale Edition of the Works of Samuel Johnson*, 8 (New Haven and London, 1968), p. 213.
2  All citations from *Measure for Measure* are from the New Arden edition, ed. J. W. Lever (London and Cambridge, Mass., 1965).
3  See *Johnson on Shakespeare*, pp. 185, 184, and 177–8 respectively.
4  *Likeness of Truth*, p. 5.
5  *A New Postil . . . upon all the Sonday Gospelles*, II (1566), sig. [Ddviii].
6  *Exposition of Christs Sermon in the Mount*, sigs Cc6v–Cc7.

From "The Integrity of *Measure for Measure*," *Shakespeare Survey* 28 (1975), 89–93, 96–97, 100–105 abridged.

*Diane McColley (1980)*

## "Physic Bitter to Sweet End"

Rather than showing men and women as noble but flawed, as in classical tragedy, or as false but exposable, as in classical comedy, the Christian comedy of regeneration shows them worse than they could be and, by a providential process of recognition and reversal, gives them opportunity to become better than they have been. In plays whose plots are in the Aristotelian sense complex, this process works through human beings who, by a willing response to grace, become agents of providence. In *Measure for Measure* Shakespeare provides a range of characters whose fitness or unfitness as instruments of providence stretches from the intransigence of Barnardine and the perversity of Angelo to the patience of Mariana, the chastity of Isabella, and the ministrations of Duke Vincentio, each of whom undergoes "a physic / That's bitter to sweet end" (4.6.5–61).[1]

The moral clarity of *Measure for Measure* is sometimes obscured for modern audiences by two difficulties of interpretation: the quality of Isabella's chastity and the moral implications of Vincentio's use of "pious fraud."[2] Both may be illuminated by attention to the play's central metaphor of "physic."

The theme of physic recurs continually in the play's pathological and medicinal imagery. It begins negatively with the puns on venereal and other maladies in scene two—"thou are always figuring diseases in me," one habitué of the brothels complains as an interpretive signal—and with five uses of the phrase "no remedy"[3] before the Duke tells Isabella "a remedy presents itself" (3.1.201). It appears in frequent use of words like "medicine," "heal," "cure," "mend," and of course "measure," which is a cognate of "remedy." Its thematic core is Isabella's exclamation to Angelo, "Why, all the souls that were were forfeit once; / And he that might the vantage best have took / Found out the remedy" (2.2.74–75).

The Duke's remedy for Angelo's sexual ailment—that of substituting his espoused bride for his intended victim—may seem incompatible with the divine "remedy" Isabella calls attention to because it involves deception. But although for Christians actual falsehood is never justified, there is both classical and Scriptural warrant for the medicinal use of dissimulation when the patient is incapable of reason, as is the case with Angelo, whose blood smothers his other faculties (he tells us in another medical figure) as "foolish throngs" rush to "one that swounds . . . and so stop the air / By which he should revive" (2.4. 20–26). Plato states that "real falsehood" is "an ignorance in the soul which entertains untruth," and "is hateful to gods and men equally"; but "spoken falsehood" may be helpful "as a sort of medicine to avert some fit of folly or madness that might make a friend attempt some mischief."[4] Milton, adducing Scriptural precedent, explains that when "instead of injuring a person by a false statement, we . . . prevent him from inflicting or suffering injury, we are so far from being guilty of deceit towards him . . . that we ought rather to be considered as doing him a service against his will."[5] In *Measure for Measure* the real falsehood is in Angelo's soul, and the dissimulation prevents the mischief he intends. The Duke treats not only the intended mischief but the falsehood in the soul.

Plato adds two pertinent observations. First, "We can make our fiction as good an embodiment of the truth as possible,"[6] a principle that applies to the playwright as well as the Duke. Vincentio's plan replaces Angelo's false plot with one as near as possible to truth: since for Shakespeare's audience the combination of public espousal and cohabitation constituted a *de iure* marriage, the substitution of Mariana for Isabella restores sexual propriety. Second, falsehood is a medicine that "should be handled by no one but a physician"; the only persons licensed to practice deception "either on the country's enemies or on its citizens" are "the Rulers of the commonwealth, acting for its benefit."[7] James I picks up the metaphor in *Basilikon Doron*, a work Shakespeare is thought to have had in mind while composing the play; James advises Charles that a ruler should be "a good Phisitian, who must first knowe what peccant humours his patie[n]t naturally is most subiect vnto." But James' idea of virtue, which Shakespeare mends in Christian terms, is that the King as God's Lieutenant "guards the godly, plaguing the prophane" and should "let the measure of [his] love to euery one, be according to the measure of [each one's] vertue."[8] Vincentio, more redeemingly, guards the godly while healing the prophane, and lets the measure of his love accord with the measure taken by the God who "found out the remedy."

The peculiarly Christian and providential nature of Vincentio's physic is that it is neither merely paliative (as forgiveness with no real cure would be) nor harshly purgative (as exposure and punishment would be) but a homeopathic remedy.

In contemporary medical practice, while conventional treatment supplies a regimen having properties opposite to the excess humour that causes a disease, the homeopathic physician infuses a small dose having the same properties as the excess humour, in order to stimulate the body's natural ability to purge itself. Milton applies the metaphor to drama: it purges us of the very passions it depicts in order "to temper and reduce them to just measure," as "in Physic things of melancholic hue and quality are us'd against melancholy, sowr against sowr, salt to remove salt humours."[9]

Angelo's peccant humour is "false seeming" (2.4.15) erupting in the sexual falseness that is the epidemic disease of the body politic he now heads. The Duke acknowledges the homeopathic nature of his proposed remedy in a rhyme: "Craft against vice I must apply. . . . So disguise shall, by the disguisèd, / Pay with falsehood false exacting, / And perform an old contracting" (3.2.280–85). If this solution seems rather legalistically tit-for-tat, it becomes, with help from Isabella and Mariana, the vehicle of widespread purgation and renewal. Rather than providing an external antidote that would compel Angelo's will (analogously to conventional medicine and authoritarian government) the Duke initiates a purgative reaction in the patient's own conscience (analogously to homeopathic medicine and in conformity with Reformation theology): he uses a small dose of illusion to engage Angelo's God-given ability to cleanse his soul of its enormous falsity and to respond regenerately to grace.

The necessary instrument of the Duke's providential cure is Isabella's chastity. If we are tempted to agree with Angelo that there might be "charity in sin" (2.4.63–64) we need only consult the plot: since Angelo, thinking that Isabella *has* complied, nevertheless orders Claudio's execution lest he avenge his sister, it is clear that if she had done so she would have lost both her chastity and her brother. Angelo's notion is supported, however, in the play's predecessor, Whetstone's *Historye of Promos and Cassandra* (London, 1578), on the thorny grounds of choosing the lesser of two evils. Cassandra, the analogue of Isabella, chooses the "lesser evil" of consenting to sin to save her brother's life, and the king patches up the moral breach by marrying the abused lady to her seducer and condemning him to death, from which she saves him by an instant accession of wifely affection. Emotional credibility aside, Whetstone's play violates Christian sensibilities by applauding a heroine who breaks a divine commandment and whose chief concern is earthly honor. *Measure for Measure* repairs both the emotional and the moral damage. Despite his aberrations into ignorance of soul, Angelo is loved by Mariana, and since he is her "combinate husband" contracted "by oath" (3.1.226–27) she does not scruple to provide the "due benevolence" of the marriage bed that will complete the marriage.

The choice between chastity and charity which Angelo concocts for Isabella is the type of many agonizing choices between purity and compassion faced in a

Christian life or a Christian community; and the play presents it as a false dilemma that those who trust providence must labor to resolve. Chastity is faithfulness to God under the severest trial; charity is ardor for the immortal well-being of each person. Chastity is the preservative of charity; as the sexual chaos that is Vienna's peccant humour shows, it is necessary for a healthy community, founded upon responsibility and trust, in which charity can thrive. Conversely, chastity is impotent without charity, the queen of virtues, whose handmaid it is.

Isabella is concerned not only with earthly honor, as is her prototype Cassandra, but with immortal souls. She begins, as anyone must who wishes to avoid the web of evil and be useful to the powers of goodness, with her own:[10] "I had rather give my body than my soul" (2.4.56); and she persists even when her insistence on obedience sounds harsh: "Better it were a brother died at once / Than that a sister, by redeeming him [that is, ransoming his mortal life], / Should die forever" (2.4.106–08). This response is not wrong in the economy of immortality, but it is rough and inadequate because it participates in the false dilemma Angelo has held up to her. The second soul she is responsible for is her brother's. "I beseech you," she pleads with Angelo, that "he may be so fitted / That his soul sicken not" (2.4.40–41); and even her outraged denunciation of Claudio's desire that she concede to Angelo is concerned for his soul's health: "Mercy to thee would prove itself a bawd"; therefore, lest he ravin down more bane, "'Tis best thou diest quickly" (3.1.150–51). That speech is no remedy, yet compliance would have been worse for Claudio's soul, since to profit from the sins of others is demonic. Later, when she has tasted her own dose of "physic" that's bitter to sweet end—primarily that of thinking her brother dead—Isabella will unite purity to charity and help redeem the third soul in her cure, Angelo's, by pleading for his life. If she had participated in the sin he had intended, she would be in a poorer position to forgive him for it, and his despair would have been the greater. The fourth soul for which she is responsible is that of the child that both recognize might issue from the unholy union he proposes, Angelo in the topical metaphor of counterfeiting (2.4.42–49) and Isabella in declaring "I had rather my brother die by the law than that my son should be unlawfully born" (3.1.192–93).

The vehemence of Isabella's replies is not evidence of coldness but, on the contrary, of ardor. The hardest temptation to resist is that which opposes the apparent good of others to obedience to God. Satan's version of it in *Paradise Lost* is his suggestion to Eve that "petty Trespass" might be "dauntless vertue" on behalf of the whole human race (IX.693–94). But Isabella, unlike Eve, recognizes that no good can come of disobeying God and thus refusing his providence. That is why she must dash the proffered cup with such conviction. Isabella could not have extricated anyone from the web of evil had she become a part of the web. There could be no charity in sin because colluding with sin banishes the powers of goodness and invites invasion by the powers of evil. But there is charity in Isabella's chastity because by its clarity it both discloses and repels evil and empowers her to become a conduit of grace. By means of her obedience, everyone in the play, including Isabella herself, receives opportunity for regeneration and growth. It is for others, as her suffering is for her, a "physic/That's bitter to sweet end."

The theme of physic applies also to another classic false dilemma that the play resolves through interaction of human agency and providential grace: the ancient debate between justice and mercy. Its resolution is not simply the triumph of mercy, but the recognition that, like chastity and charity, each is necessary to the other. Mercy without justice would be a bawd to vice and spread more misery to the innocent; justice without mercy would "bruise to death" (2.1.6) rather than redeem. Redemption is neither vengeance nor simple forgiveness but compassionate cure.

Both Vincentio and Isabella are channels of providence, but each is imperfect without the quality of the other. The Duke is not an allegory of "pow'r divine" (5.1.372) but rather a man laboring through the perplexities of human experience and his own human weakness to imitate God's restorative providence. His charity, at the outset, is incomplete; he had erred on the side of leniency and has learned that "mercy is not itself" (2.1.283) without the justice that restores the sinner and makes amends to his victims. On the other hand, Isabella's purity is also, at the outset, incomplete; it is not yet a "sun-clad Power" but a "fugitive and cloister'd virtue, unexercis'd and unbreath'd"[11] that tries to withdraw from the world and, confronted perforce by evil, turns into rage. Their mutual assistance weds love and truth, by whose cooperation all the characters receive the chance of a new and honest life; and their potential marriage is a prospective source of remedy for the body politic which shows that providence works not only through human beings but also through human bonds.

## Notes

1  Quotations and citations are from the Signet Classic Edition, ed. S. Nagarajan (New York, 1964).

2  On sources for the concept of "pious fraud" and distinctions between lying and dissimulations, see Roy W. Battenhouse, "*Measure for Measure* and the Christian Doctrine of the Atonement," *PMLA* 61 (1946), 1047–48; and (with Austin C. Dobbins), "Jessica's Morals: A Theological View," *Shakespeare Studies* 9 (1976), 114–16.

   Christian consensus on just use of dissimulation in Shakespeare's time, though published after it, may be found in William Perkins, *The Whole Treatise of the Cases of Conscience* (London, 1660), pp. 83–97; John Milton, *De Doctrina Christiana* II, in *The Works of John Milton*, gen. ed. Frank Allen Patterson, 27 (New York, 1934), 297–319.

3  2.1.281 and 285; 2.2.49; 3.1.61–62; 3.2.1.

4  *The Republic of Plato*, tr. F. M. Cornford (Oxford, 1941), pp. 72–73.

5  *Works*, 17: 299–309.

6  *Republic*, p. 73.

7  *Republic*, p. 76.

8  Second edition (London, 1603), pp. 137 and 152.

9  "Of that Sort of Dramatic Poem which is Call'd Tragedy," prefaced to *Samson Agonistes*, in *Works* 12 (1931): 331.

10  Compare, for example, the story of Sir Bors in Malory's *Morte d'Arthur*, in a similar false dilemma between chastity and seeming charity, Bors chooses obedience to God and thus exposes his temptresses as disguised demons (*The Works of Sir Thomas Malory*, ed. Eugene Vinaver, 2 [Oxford, 1967]: 965–66).

11  Milton, *A Maske*, line 792; *Areopagitica*, in *Works* 4:311.

Revised by Professor McColley of Rutgers University from an essay read at an annual meeting of the Modern Language Association in 1980.

# PERICLES

## Comment and bibliography

This comedy is an adaptation of John Gower's medieval version of the story of Apollonius of Tyre. Shakespeare had used one aspect of that story as the outer envelope of his early *Comedy of Errors*, but now in an enlarged version it is the whole story of *Pericles*. This means an omitting of "humorous" comedy associated with carnival festivity. Only a small but lively sample of farcical folly remains, in a brothel scene Shakespeare added to Gower, and the antics there of the bawd and the brothel owner are mere background for the virtues of Marina—much as in *Measure for Measure* the comic Pompey and Froth serve as a naturalistic contrast to the supernaturally-virtued Duke. In neither of these plays are the petty rascals cured, since their evil is of a kind more intentional than that of, let us say, Angelo's lapse from conscience, or Adriana's foolish jealousy in *Errors*, or the blind mistakes of Claudio and Don Pedro in *Much Ado*. The exposing of purgeable disorders was central to the comedies of Shakespeare we refer to as festive. *Pericles* is festive in a special way. Its hero has a right faith (though not matured) to begin with; his story then tells of the perils he must endure and the patience he must learn before arriving at blessedness.

The Bible associates tribulations with the virtue of hope. Auditors of *Pericles* at the Globe may well have been reminded of St Paul's remarks regarding this virtue. Tribulation, he writes to the Romans, "worketh patience, and patience, experience; and experience, hope" (5:3–4); and later he urges them to rejoice in hope and be patient in tribulation, "not slothful in business" of serving the Lord (12:11–12). *Pericles* is a play that abounds in emblematic actions, but certainly its most central emblem is the heraldic "Device" the hero presents to Thaisa when contending for her at Pentapolis: "*In hac spe vivo.*" Her father translates: "He hopes by you his fortunes yet may flourish." The flourishing does indeed begin with the hero's winning of Thaisa in marriage. But soon afterwards misfortune takes this wife away; and the child Marina, the blossom, has to be entrusted to foreign guardians, who later report the child has died. It is in this situation that Pericles is tempted to lose hope. He feels that he has become a plaything of Fortune. Though he "rides out" a tempest he does so apathetically. If we recall St Paul's admonition against being "slothful in business," is not sloth the predicament of Pericles? Until—miraculously—he is visited by a voice from another world, a voice that has a story to tell of successful combat in the midst of misfortune. The voice turns out to be a mediator of family reunion and of discovery of a providential destiny.

A second generation has, so to speak, redeemed the faith and completed the hope of the first generation. *Pericles* accordingly has a plot with two branches. The theological paradigm for this is the Bible's story of how Abraham's faith achieved but then lost its earthly fortune, yet his heirs of hope fulfilled through a child the family's destiny of a Blessing for everyone. Christian hope is associated with the child of promise given to Abraham in old age; and with the Messiah-child proclaimed by Isaiah as the bringer of "comfort" to faithful exiles; and with the child in whom old Simeon of Luke 2 found the "consolation" that permitted him to depart in peace having seen salvation. *Pericles* is a two-phased voyaging in hope: attaining first a happy marriage, but later a family reunion that rewards tribulations suffered with patience. F. D. Hoeniger's wayside comparison of Pericles to Tobit can be expanded: Tobit's eyes had a film of blindness until cured with medicine brought by his child. That is the case figuratively of Pericles.

We have noticed that the metaphor of a journey is often central to a comedy by Shakespeare. In *All's Well* the journey had two phases, a marriage quest and a penitential pilgrimage. In *Measure for Measure* the Duke's journey was described to Friar Thomas as a "visit" to amend a past neglect. In *Pericles* we hear that a "shipman's toil" has been undertaken by a hero who wishes penitently to correct a possible former error. And since this voyage comes after an eye-opening discovery of human depravity, it has analogy to the voyaging of the biblical Noah to escape a world of evil. Further, when the voyaging involves later a disaster at sea that requires a period of reassessment by the hero, the story of Jonah is analogous. Indeed, the overall scope of the drama of Pericles, involving as it does a lifetime of voyaging through tempests to a predestined haven of blessing, suggests mankind's pilgrimaging toward salvation.

The four pieces of commentary which our anthology reprints all call attention to the play's incorporation of Christian symbolism. F. D. Hoeniger describes the play's formal affinity to a saint's life in medieval drama. Howard Felperin enlarges on the purpose stated by Gower, to provide a "restorative" to be sung at Ember eve festivals. The play's characters can be seen to hide personifications from "morality" tradition, Felperin observes, and grace is victorious as in countless miracle plays. In short, the drama is designedly parabolic, "a timeless romantic action with unmistakably Christian relevance." That relevance is made even more evident by Cynthia Marshall, who argues that the drama's seemingly sprawling episodes are actually patterned on the Seven Ages of history discerned in the Bible by Patristic commentators. Thus the symbolic history of the human race is incorporated in one man, Pericles, whose life as a whole illustrates the doctrine of Boethius that Fortune serves the providential order of an omniscient God.

Maurice Hunt elaborates on the thematic import of the play's allusion to Jonah. Jonah's initial shortcoming, his trying to evade testifying against sin, Hunt sees in Pericles and traces as the moral cause of his period of "exile" into melancholy, from which he is rescued by the voice of Marina. This interpretation provides a thread of religious growth within the character of Pericles. Its analogue is Israel's discovery of a missionary purpose during its exile in Babylon, the truth which the book of Jonah was written to convey in parable form. The lesson of *Pericles* is neatly summarized by Patch-breech: keep up "a jangling of the [church] bells." (This lowly fisherman's name Patch-breech allies him with the "patch" Feste, the theologically witty clown of *Twelfth Night*, and he is similarly committed to a mending of faults).

To keep the church bells jangling is a metaphor that aptly summarizes an intention of the present anthology. There will be hope for our understanding of Shakespeare so long as there are readers able to hear church bells. I am listing the books by J. A. Giles and V. A. Kolve because these provide valuable knowledge of traditional Christian lore and its medieval exemplifications.

Other supplementary reading should include Douglas Peterson's treatment of the play as a sequence of "speaking pictures" of occasions in time that try individuals with opportunities for choice. The readiness of Pericles to endure adversity, Peterson notes, makes him a hero of "constancy" able to progress from his discovery of corruption to a resolving of the "discrepancies between truth and seeming" in a Marina of redemptive love. Sara Hanna's essay finds in Pericles a pilgrimage that involves the three stages of vision outlined by St Augustine—corporal, spiritual, and intellectual—in which each stage must combat some form of darkness near to death. The hero's icon of hope, a withered branch that buds with blossoms, is traced by Hanna to one of George Wither's emblems, where it signifies Aaron's rod, a type for the Cross of Christ.

The article by Willem Schrickx is important for its information regarding performances of *Pericles* by traveling players under Catholic sponsorship. Schrickx argues it is likely that the play was on the repertory of the English Jesuit theatre. Why this play was attractive to Catholics is easy to surmise when one considers its contents. Indirectly it can be read as preaching hope to any Christians in England, even papists or puritans, who might feel they were suffering the adversity of cultural exile. And if Maurice Hunt is correct that a theme of the play is the need to open to curative view the faults of monarchs, as Marina does, one can surmise that this call to "mission" was not without some sympathetic auditors at a time when the policies of King James were beginning to dissatisfy considerable segments of public opinion. One wonders whether perhaps a political caution on the part of the editors of Shakespeare's First Folio (1623) precluded the including of *Pericles* in their text.

## Supplementary bibliography

Arthos, John. "*Pericles, Prince of Tyre*: A Study in the Dramatic Use of Romantic Narrative," *Shakespeare Quarterly* 4 (1953), 257–70.

Giles, J. A., tr. "A Chronicle of the Six Ages of the World," *The Historical Works of the Venerable Bede* (London, 1845), II, 219–95.

Hanna, Sara. "Christian Vision and Iconography in *Pericles*," *The Upstart Crow* 11 (1991), 92–116.

Hoeniger, F. D. "Gower and Shakespeare in *Pericles*," *Shakespeare Quarterly* 33 (1982), 462–79.

Kolve, V. A. *The Play Called Corpus Christi* (Stanford University Press, 1966).

Peterson, Douglas. *Time, Tide and Tempest: A Study of Shakespeare's Romances* (San Marino: Huntington Library, 1973), pp. 71–107.

Schrickx, Willem. "*Pericles* in a Book-List of 1619 from the English Jesuit Mission," *Shakespeare Survey* 29 (1976), 21–32.

*F. D. Hoeniger (1963)*

## *Pericles* and the Miracle Play

The play is curiously, and I think significantly, like the vernacular religious drama in its later, more developed, and less rigid forms, especially the Saint's play. One could argue that from plays of this kind, with which Shakespeare was surely acquainted, most of the broad structural features of *Pericles* are derived. They are at any rate paralleled; among them the device of the choric presenter in the person of a poet, the building up of the action out of a large number of loosely related episodes, the treatment of the play as a "pageant" rather than a work of highly concentrated action around a central conflict, the tragi-comic development of the action, the large part taken in it by supernatural powers, and the construction of the whole so as to serve an explicit didactic end.

If this observation is sound, it has far-reaching implications for our understanding of *Pericles*. It would mean that not only its story-material and its presenting chorus are mediaeval, but also its essential dramatic form. And if this is the case, can it perhaps be said to echo the spirit of the bygone age in its underlying thought or purpose also? A look at the play's opening chorus reveals its basic intentions: "The purchase is to make men glorious." It seems no accident that this line also describes adequately the basic aim of the Legends of the Saints and of the miracle plays derived from them.

Of the few surviving English miracle plays, the one which reminds one most closely of *Pericles* is the Digby play of *Mary Magdalene*. Roughly equal to *Pericles* in length, it divides, like *Pericles*, sharply into two parts, though this is probably pure coincidence. The first part is in twenty scenes. The opening five set forth the tyrannous pride and covetousness of Emperor Tiberius, lord of this world. Under him Satan flourishes, Satan's forces beset the Castle of Maudlyn, and Lechery succeeds in tempting Mary Magdalene, one of its inmates and owner. The later scenes present her redemption and the revival of her brother Lazarus, both by Jesus.

Margaret, Martha, and Lazarus return to their castle. The second part is devoted mainly to the rôle played by Mary Magdalene in the conversion of the king of Marcyll (Marseilles). The final six scenes carry her life to its conclusion, showing how she was sustained in the desert by food from heaven and ending in the burial of her body and the ascension of her soul. But it is the section dealing with Marcyll's conversion that has greatest interest for us. In a vision, Magdalene is commanded by Christ to go by ship to Marcyll in order to convert the Mohammedan king. There she persuades the King and the Queen to cast off their allegiance to the heathen gods. As a consequence, the Queen's desire to be with child is miraculously fulfilled. They prepare for a voyage to the Holy Land, but on the way a violent storm overtakes them, and the Queen dies even while giving birth to her child. Similarly as in 3.1 of *Pericles*, the ship's crew demand that both Queen and child be set on a rock. The King himself safely reaches the Holy Land, where he is baptized by Peter. On his return voyage he discovers his babe unharmed on the rock, and his wife suddenly returns to life as if awaking from a trance. They return joyfully, and bless Mary Magdalene, who exhorts them to lead a steadfast Christian life.

It will be seen that in both *Mary Magdalene* and *Pericles* the action is biographical. In both, the protagonist is involved in a series of extraordinary adventures and turns of fortune. Both have a happy ending, largely effected by supernatural intervention.

From the Arden *Pericles*, ed. F. D. Hoeniger (London: Methuen & Company, 1963), pp. lxxxviii-xc abridged. Used by permission.

*Howard Felperin (1972)*

## This Great Miracle

Obviously Shakespeare would not cultivate an archaic medievalism at this stage in his work without sophisticated ulterior motives. Gower's opening speech frankly announces his designs on us:

> To sing a song that old was sung,
> From ashes ancient Gower is come
> Assuming man's infirmities,
> To glad your ear, and please your eyes.
> It hath been sung at festivals,
> On ember-eves and holy ales;
> And lords and ladies in their lives
> Have read it for restoratives:

The purchase is to make men glorious,
*Et bonum quo antiquius eo melius.*
If you born in these latter times
When wit's more ripe, accept my rimes.

The imitation of Gower's jingly rhymes, antiquated diction, and unabashed didacticism is itself skillful, as is Shakespeare's unfolding of the chief motives of the
play—resurrection and restoration—within the first eight lines. The proverbial
Latin tag, the emphatic contrast between "these latter times" and "a song that old
was sung" (a contrast embodied in the resurrected Gower himself) serve to surround the tale with an air of revered antiquity. The "festivals," "ember-eves," and
"holy ales" on which it has been sung are all occasions in the Church calendar.
Shakespeare is telling us though the shorthand of dramatic convention that the
action we are about to witness is a timeless parable for our spiritual recreation.

Antiochus, whose name and eventual fate within the play recall the Macedo-
nian king of the Apocrypha (2 Mc 9:9), could be any number of corrupt and
prideful rulers out of the medieval drama: Herod, Tiberius, Mundus himself.
Cleon, the governor of Tharsus, whose pride and plenty have changed in the
course of worldly affairs to poverty and famine, is right out of the same tradition.
The point is not that Antiochus and Cleon are the "lust-dieted and superfluous
man" of *King Lear* made flesh, but that the morality figures which lurk behind the
flesh-and-blood characterizations of Lear, and which are visible there only in outline, have now been brought out onto the open stage. Antiochus' daughter, nameless and mute for most of the scene, is more a personified abstraction than a character, more like a Nice Wanton or the nameless daughter seduced by her father in
the fragmentary miracle play *Dux Moraud* than like any previous Shakespearean
character. Dionyza, whose real nature will soon be revealed when she tempts Cleon
into having Marina murdered, is not so much the pale shadow cast by Lady Macbeth as the much older figure of Hypocrisy who lies behind Lady Macbeth, one of
the several morality personifications who hides envy behind a mask of gratitude.

*Pericles* not only divides its cast right down the middle into sheep and goats,
the good and the wicked, after the fashion of the earlier religious drama, but like
that drama sets up elaborate moral patterns of contrast and similarity between
them. Antiochus' courtier turned assassin, Thaliard, contrasts with Helicanus,
whom Pericles tests and finds loyal and true. If "Good Helicane" tends to remind
critics of Kent, it is not because he is based on Kent but because Kent is based on
Helicanus, that is, on the good counselors like him in the pre-Shakespearean drama
going all the way back to *Gorboduc* and beyond. Antiochus' incestuous daughter,
whom Pericles disastrously woos, is the moral antitype to Simonides' virtuous
daughter Thaisa, whom he successfully woos and weds, as well as to Marina, who
is not "appareled *like* the spring" (1.1.13) nor looks "*As* heaven had lent her all his
grace" (1 Chorus, 24), but possesses those regenerative powers in earnest. The vicious Antiochus also contrasts in his public role of king (he is repeatedly referred

to as a "tyrant") with the responsible ruler Pericles, as we see him back at Tyre—Gower, as is his wont, moralizes on the opposition between "a mighty king" and "A better prince and benign lord" (2 Prologue 1–3)—and then with "the good Simonides," whose virtues as a prince are remarked on by several of the characters present at his feast.

Virtually everything we learn about Cerimon is there to establish his moral bearings within the design of the play: "Your honor has through Ephesus pour'd forth / Your charity, and hundreds call themselves / Your creatures, who by you have been restor'd" (3.2.43–5). His powers of "restoration" recall the purpose of the tale itself as Gower had stated it in the prologue. His charity aligns him with Pericles, whose gift of corn to Tharsus had brought "them life whom hunger starv'd half dead" (1.4.96), as well as with the good fishermen of Pentapolis, who restored Pericles' sea-rusted armor to him. As a rich man, Cerimon's rejection of wealth and worldly glory contrasts with the antisocial "rich miser" of the fishermen's parable and with the shaky glory of Tharsus and its king and queen. His long monologue has, of course, numerous precedents in the medieval drama, among them the ending of Everyman, where Good-Deeds alone accompanies the protagonist to the grave. When Thaisa's coffin is washed ashore and he applies his restorative art to her "entranced" corpse, the audience would have known exactly what to expect. For the scene also has its medieval precedents; it is analogous to the raising of the Queen of Marcylle, apparently dead after childbirth, and of Lazarus in the Digby *Mary Magdalene*, and Cerimon himself to the Christ of the miracle play. "The heavens through you, increase our wonder," marvels the trusty first gentleman whose choric role in the scene mirrors Gower's in the play as a whole, "And set up your fame forever" (3.2.98–9). It is worth noting that "wonder," the emotion so often appealed to in *Pericles* and the romances, is produced quite differently from "surprise," the more sophisticated effect that plays like those of Beaumont and Fletcher have on us. Surprise depends upon the frustration of our expectation, wonder on the fulfillment of them.

In *Pericles*, nature becomes redeemable, for grace, personified in Marina, abounds even to the worst of sinners, just as it had in countless miracle and morality plays before *Pericles*. Marina culminates a long and popular tradition of incorruptibly virtuous heroines going back to the saint's legend of St Agnes. The pre-Shakespearean drama teemed with such maidens (Susanna, Virginia, Patient Grissil) who seem to have evoked nothing but admiration in contemporary audiences, and whose outlines are still visible in Desdemona and Cordelia. Shakespeare's audience, which retained much of the medieval delight in didacticism, had often "heard the like" and apparently enjoyed hearing it again.

In turning from a relatively naturalistic to a parabolic drama at this point in his career, in exchanging a Pompey for a Boult and a Lucio for a Lysimachus, Shakespeare does not so much repudiate verisimilitude as exchange one kind of verisimilitude for another. T. S. Eliot owlishly remarks that the characters of the last romances are "the work of a writer who has finally seen through the dramatic action of men into a spiritual action which transcends it" and that Shakespeare "makes us feel not so much that his characters are creatures like ourselves, as that we are creatures like his characters, taking part like them in no common action of which we are for the most part unaware." It is not necessary to see *Pericles* as a Catholic drama to realize that it is a catholic one, and that the sense of universality it so powerfully conveys has much to do with its consistent adoption of the methods, if not the dogma, of an older dramatic tradition.

The "patience" that Pericles is said at several points in the play by several characters to lack Gower exhorts us to have, to bear with him as Pericles must learn to bear with misfortune. His impatient outcry upon the loss of Thaisa—"O you gods! / Why do you make us love your goodly gifts, / And snatch them straight away?" (3.1.22–4)—is answered in the final act, as Diana appears to him in a vision, his daughter and wife are restored, and he hears the music of the spheres. He has been "sacred" to the gods in both senses of that primal word, both "cursed" and "blessed," as every man is in the Christian scheme of things, and the extremity of his suffering is recompensed in the sublimity of his exaltation. His recognition scene begins with our apprehension of a purgatorial figure, fasting and virtually dead to the world and ends with a beatific vision, or rather audition, of the music of the spheres. "Come hither," he says to Marina, "Thou that beget'st him that did thee beget" (5.1.194–5), reversing the incest of the first scene into its opposite: the redemptive love of father and child at the center of the Christian mystery and paralleled in this play.

The Christian story is a romance, but not all romances are Christian. Shakespeare takes pains to make clear that we are in a realm of analogy rather than identity. Marina has been "god*like* perfect, the heir of kingdoms, / And another life to Pericles thy father" (5.1.206–7), and as for Cerimon, "The gods can have no mortal officer / More *like* a god than you" (5.3.62–3). Although Shakespeare is straining to its limit the analogy between the action and actors of this "great miracle" and those of the miracle play proper, it remains an analogy. Neptune and Diana, who preside over the action, are the conventional deities of classical romance rather than stand-ins for the high God of Christianity. By employing pagan deities from conventional romance in *Pericles*, and by surrounding them with Christian-providential associations, Shakespeare has the best of both worlds: a timeless romantic action with unmistakably Christian relevance.

From *Shakespearean Romances,* pp. 146–69 abridged. Copyright 1972 by Princeton University Press. Used by permission.

Cynthia Marshall (1991)

## *Pericles* and the Cosmic Overview

Modern readers, accustomed to causal action in drama, have been frustrated by the sparse or unlikely connections between events in *Pericles*. But one of the play's central oddities has been insufficiently noticed: it consists of seven stretches of action demarcated by choric interruptions. The audience's perception of the course of events befalling Pericles and his family—the events generally assumed to be the play's main content—is repeatedly interrupted by the Chorus, Gower. Gower's intrusions compel the audience to dissociate itself from Pericles' adventures, to view the events as might God or an author or Gower himself. The structure of the play, considered from this vantage point, manifests notions of temporality rooted in a medieval metaphysic. The stages of Pericles' life mirror the structure of a symbolic history of the human race. An audience attuned to a figural view of reality, especially an audience retaining memories of the structure of the mystery cycles, might glimpse the skeletal pattern of the medieval notion of the Seven Ages of History that lies beneath the action of *Pericles*.

For Augustine and for those who inherited his metaphysical assumptions, adopting God's eschatological viewpoint presupposed the dual metaphysical order of Boethius, with its parallel divine and mundane planes of reality. According to Boethius, fortune, or the course of earthly affairs, is ordered by an omniscient God, who "sees what is fitting for each individual, and arranges what he knows is fitting." From the earthly viewpoint, the providential order seems to be the random turning of fortune's wheel. If people could achieve the divine perspective, however, they "would judge that there was no evil anywhere" in the work of fortune.

> For whatever lives in time proceeds in the present from the past into the future, and there is nothing established in time which can embrace the whole space of its life equally.... [But God] is permanent in the simplicity of his present, and embracing all the infinite spaces of the future and the past, [God] considers them in his simple act of knowledge as though they were now going on. (*Consolatio* 423, 427, tr. Tester, 1973)

Gower could serve a Jacobean audience appropriately as instructor on Boethian concepts of providence.

The Chorus emphasizes in *Pericles* the provisional nature of fortune. He comments on the limited understanding of the hero:

> Let Pericles believe his daughter's dead,
> And bear his courses to be ordered
> By Lady Fortune.... (4.4.46–48)

Pericles is allowed temporarily to believe a random or even malevolent fortune to be operant in his life, although ultimately this view is corrected. In his epilogue to the play, Gower explicitly notes the relationship between fortune and heaven, observing that Pericles and his family, "although assail'ed with fortune fierce and keen," were "led on by heaven, and crown'd with joy at last" (Epilog 4, 6). The Chorus of Shakespeare's play affirms a central controlling force in the play, beside which "fortune," the apparent randomness of events, is secondary.

Gower ostensibly presents on stage only a portion of the complete life of Pericles, of which he alone has full knowledge, much as God alone, according to Boethianism, can survey human actions in their totality. Gower, then, is an intermediary not just between audience and action, but between temporal and eternal perspectives:

> I do beseech you
> To learn of me, who stand i' th' gaps to teach you
> The stages of our story. (4.4.7–9)

Gower's authorial omniscience and his suggestion of a foreordained action assert a central commissioning intelligence ordering the play's paradigmatic structure.

Everything about Gower would have seemed old-fashioned to a Jacobean audience—the antiquated role of Chorus, his tetrameter couplets and archaic diction, possibly his appearance (Hoeniger, "Gower and Shakespeare," 463–64). So his very presence suggests a medieval response, reinforcing the medieval world view he preaches. The archaeologically produced notion of double time is conveyed through the discrepancy between Pericles' attitude toward his adventures while they are taking place (the attitude largely shared by the audience) and Gower's view of those adventures from his timeless perspective.... The play's structure mimics the discrepancy in human experience between the apparently meaningless sequences of events that compose a lifetime, and the structure of meaning informing that life which would appear from a cosmic perspective.

God's purposes may be mysterious, but the pattern of the Seven Ages posits a discernible divine order shaping history. The popular *Golden Legend* outlines the ages like this:

> The first is from Adam to Noah; the second from Noah to Abraham; the third from Abraham to Moses; the fourth from Moses unto David; the fifth from David to Jesu Christ. The sixth from Jesu Christ unto the end of the world. The seventh of the dying on earth. And the eighth of the general resurrection to heaven.

The different versions which developed were similar enough that each age evolved its hero in the popular mind, a major figure who became the symbol for his entire era. And in each scheme a new age typically begins with a fresh covenant between God and his people, an event that marks a significant manifestation of divine will in the course of human affairs and so alters the previous course of history.

Typology and the theory of the Seven Ages shape history through reference to a timeless realm. The mystery cycles provide one model for representing people as both historical creatures living in linear time and transcendent beings who identify themselves by reference to an eternal realm. The two realms of existence intersect at those moments when the history of Israel is altered by God's intervention, as in the parting of the Red Sea or the birth of Christ, or when humanity defines itself in opposition or obedience to God's command, as when Eve bites the apple or Mary accepts Gabriel's message. The overall sequence becomes a meaningful pattern only though reference to the eternal realm. A concrete pattern is manifested in history; history expresses God's dialogue through time with the human race.

While *Pericles* traces the lifetime of one man, it also seems to outline the history of the human race. The correspondences between the individual and the cosmos that were intrinsic to Renaissance ontology make this structural appropriation natural. A connection between the ages of history and those of humankind was by no means original. Augustine himself had drawn a specific analogy between the growth from infancy of an individual and the developmental history of God's people (*City* 16.43). The Venerable Bede followed Augustine in relating the historical ages to man's "infancy," "childhood," "adolescence," "youth," "senility," and "decrepit old age," leading the faithful to "the seventh age of one endless Sabbath" and expectation of the "eighth age of a happy resurrection" (ed. Giles 220–21). In the visual arts, the two sequences were frequently brought together, as in a twelfth-century stained glass at Canterbury Cathedral that shows the miracle at Cana bordered on one side by the six ages of human life and on the other side by the six ages of the world (Kolve 89–90).

*Pericles* does not follow the seven ages of an individual's lifetime (infant, child, adolescent, etc.). Instead it makes innovative use of a familiar set of traditions by incorporating the symbolic history of the human race into the history of one man. The play explores existence in time by epitomizing cosmic history in a single lifetime. The audience experiences the interplay between Gower's extratemporal vision and the more limited earthly vision of the hero himself. Because the play insists on the interplay between microcosmic and macrocosmic levels, the hero's personal experience merges with or recapitulates biblical history.

The Seven Ages exist as a skeleton beneath the play's action, and recognition of the scheme should be considered a necessary prolegomenon to *Pericles*. The existence of this shaping pattern does not mean that individual scenes are fundamentally different in construction than they would be in a play with a more dynamic plot. Rather, the scheme's influence is felt in the distinctive pattern of theme and image found in the seven sequences. As in the cycle plays, episodes are meaningful for the way they fit into the overall framework. Recognition of the divisions themselves, which demands adoption of the Boethian perspective, is more important than recognizing the peculiar motif of an individual age, even though the two endeavors are clearly interdependent. The pattern of Seven Ages exerts a quiet but distinctive force on the structure of Pericles, similar to that Kolve perceives in the mystery cycles, none of which "openly develops the theme," although "it has undoubtedly caused the Corpus Christi drama to find a distinctive protocycle core" (99).

The relevant parallels in *Pericles* tend to occur near the beginning of each episode, thereby introducing the motif of a particular age. Correspondences with some ages are closer than with others. The first section of *Pericles* carries unmistakable resonances of the myth of the Fall, but the fifth section corresponds only loosely with the Age of David. To an audience familiar with the Seven Ages, the pattern would be established as soon as the first episode with its echoes of the Fall was followed by an action recalling the story of Noah. Why, then, have critics failed to notice the pattern before? For two reasons, I think: first, an unreliable text has discouraged sustained critical attention; and second, modern assumptions of a five-act structure have obscured the play's pattern of seven episodes.

The significant action of the first age is of course the Fall. Pericles' first adventure in Antioch involves the discovery of knowledge (deciphering the riddle) and the concomitant discovery of sin (recognizing Antiochus' incestuous relationship with his daughter). According to the law of the kingdom, the price for Pericles' misdeed—his discovery—is death. The Antioch episode is rich in imagery suggesting the myth of the Fall.... His subsequent flight from the threat of Antiochus' vengeance echoes the wanderings through the world of the fallen Adam. And while Pericles is not actually condemned to labor with sweat on his brow, he undergoes a sort of penance, "punish[ing] that before that [Antiochus] would punish" (1.2.33). Or as Helicanus explains to the Tyrian lords, Pericles,

> doubting lest he had err'd or sinn'd,
> To show his sorrow, he'd correct himself;
> So puts himself unto the shipman's toil,
> With whom each minute threatens life or death. (1.3.21–24)

The hero's shipwreck off the coast of Pentapolis, with the stage direction, *"Enter Pericles, wet"* (2.1.lsd), opens the play's second age, corresponding to the Age of Noah. Pericles, having been "wash'd...from shore to shore" (2.1.6.), has learned the lesson of mortality and he is, like Noah, obedient:

> Wind, rain, and thunder, remember earthly man
> Is but a substance that must yield to you;
> And I (as fits my nature) do obey you. (2.1.2–4)

The presence of the fishermen underlines the special importance of the sea in this age. Fishermen were frequently connected in biblical typology with Christ ("the fisher of men"), so their presence here suggests the motif of redemption so central to the second age, the age of the near-destruction of the human race. Like Noah after the flood, Pericles receives a promise of better fortune after enduring loss and destruction. His fortune turns when the rusty armor drawn up by the fishermen enables him to compete for Thaisa's hand. The armor itself seems symbolic of faith; Pericles' description of it echoes the scriptural "'armor of the Lord'" (Hoeniger, *Pericles* 48–49n). Pericles quotes his father's claim, "It hath been a shield /'Twixt me and death" (2.1.126–27).

The dumb show at the beginning of act 3 shows the court of Simonides receiving news that its "heir-apparent is a king!" (3 Chorus.37). With Antiochus dead, Pericles may set out to reclaim his kingdom, which becomes a kind of promised land for the destitute wanderer. This is the third age, that of Abraham. Pericles boards ship with a pregnant wife; her role is Sarah's, and in her the promise of generation is visually portrayed. Like Abraham, Pericles must be prepared to sacrifice a member of his family. He loses his wife instead of his child, but his words could be Abraham's on the Mount of Vision when Pericles demands of the gods, "Why do you make us love your goodly gifts / And snatch them straight away?" (3.1.23–24). Pericles exhibits a patriarchial faith when, bereft of his wife, he says:

> We cannot but obey
> The powers above us. Could I rage and roar
> As doth the sea she lies in, yet the end
> Must be as 'tis. (3.3.9–12)

The destruction of Antiochus and his daughter—"A fire from heaven came and shrivell'd up /Those bodies, even to loathing" (2.4.9–10)—suggests the burning of Sodom and Gomorrah.

The shift in focus to Marina with the fourth episode of *Pericles* corresponds to the institution of written law in the fourth age, the Age of Moses. Marina herself represents a new code, a different way of dealing with the world. The Age of Moses was represented in the cycle plays by both the presentation of the Decalogue and the dramatization of exile; the latter is particularly relevant to Marina, whose existence in Tharsus and Mytilene amounts to an exodus. (Her first speech in the play concludes, "This world to me is as a lasting storm, / Whirring me from my friends" [4.1.19–20].) Dionyza's plot to kill Marina, who is perceived as a threat to the Tharsian princess, recalls the Pharaoh's slaughter of Hebrew children whom he perceived as a threat. Captive in the brothel in Mytilene (where she is described as "a sojourner" [4.1.136]), Marina is servant to corrupt people, and can rely only on her own faith.

Marina's period of preaching in Mytilene corresponds to the Age of the Prophets. While not exactly a prophet herself, she establishes a reputation for surprising conversions that damages the brothel's business. Marina's powers of speech are emphasized throughout this episode, not only by the Bawd, who says "she would make a puritan of the devil" (4.6.9), but also by the Governor Lysimachus:

> I did not think
> Thou couldst have spoke so well, ne'er dreamt thou couldst.
> Had I brought hither a corrupted mind,
> Thy speech had alter'd it. (4.6.102–5)

Like Daniel in the lions' den, Marina in the brothel suffers a peculiar persecution, but remains steadfast.

The coming of Christ initiates the sixth age, which would, according to most chroniclers, extend over the entire Christian era up to the end of earthly history. The Incarnation marks another important division in history—that between the first dispensation, the time of justice, and the second, the time of mercy. Clearly the course of Pericles' life is altered with the sixth episode; for the first time, grace is apparent in his fortunes. The memorable image of the sixth section of Pericles is the vision of Diana, a manifestation of divinity in the world of the play and "the single symbolic image that expresses the whole play," in the words of John Arthos (265). She directs him to her temple at Ephesus to make sacrifice and recite his story to the people there; clearly she directs him toward reunion with his lost wife. For the first time, the audience can perceive causal order in the events of the play; Pericles' history is being fulfilled, as human history was reaching fulfillment through Christ, according to religious historians.

Hence the end—both goal and conclusion—of earthly history, the seventh age, Augustine's "great sabbath," is represented by the reunion of Pericles, Marina, and Thaisa in the temple of Diana. The scene is set apart from the rest of the play by its hushed tone of mystery. This reunion is more than Pericles could ever have hoped for, and the action is of a different magnitude from the previous adventures. So the seventh age, marking the beginning of eternity, stands against the preceding six ages of earthly time. Although Pericles and Thaisa have not actually died and risen blessed, the motif of death and resurrection pervades the scene at Ephesus:

> Did you not name a tempest,
> A birth, and death? (5.3.33–34)

The audience's understanding of this reunion must include the memories of Thaisa entombed and cast overboard and of Pericles comatose until touched by Marina. Pericles and Thaisa have undergone years of suffering, for no crime but that of being mortal; they now are reborn to a redeemed experience of life that gives as well as takes away. The magnitude of Pericles' and Thaisa's sufferings makes them seem to represent something larger than themselves. The curious sequence of events in their story becomes a significant structure when they are viewed as figures who enact the destiny of the whole human race.

Gower knows, and Pericles learns, that through the consideration of ultimate ends one can achieve self-transcendence. Or as Peterson puts it, "By refusing to surrender to the view that events are random and therefore under the absolute domination of fortune, or that life is merely a matter of ripening and rotting, Pericles [and other characters in the romances] retain their freedom from the deterministic claims of nature" (32). Human existence thus ceases to be a linear sequence of unconnected events and becomes instead a significant conflict leading to redemption.

Complementary to the emblem of patience in *Pericles* is one of hope. In the tournament scene, six knights present their various devices. Sources or analogues have been discovered in contemporary emblem books for each device but that of Pericles:

> His present is
> A withered branch, that's only green at top;
> The motto: *"In Hac spe vivo."* (2.2.42–44)

It has been suggested that Pericles offers an actual withered branch rather than a painted device (Knight 47). The motto "in this hope I live" labels the power of faith at work in the scene: Pericles, "the mean knight," competes in rusty armor salvaged from a wreck, and wins.

The emblems of patience and hope stand in conjunction, indicating two poles of a faithful attitude toward life. In a world where meanings are mysterious, one requires patience to endure the battery of sufferings and hope that misfortunes will not prove finally senseless. The complementarity of patience and hope, peculiarly time-oriented virtues, correspond with Boethian double time: tied to the earthly vision of limits and chronicity, people are promised a glimpse of the saving force of time.

The structure of *Pericles*, obscured by the editorial assumption of five dramatic acts, suggests a reason and purpose for the play's rebuffing of sympathy. The pattern of history's ages and the eternal perspective of Gower both work to pull the audience back from the action, away from sympathetic touch with the characters. The duality of time contemplated in *Pericles* and illustrated in its incorporation of the pattern of the Seven Ages signals an approach to the problem of human suffering that derived largely from a medieval perspective.

From *Last Things and Last Plays: Shakespearean Eschatology*, pp. 61–85 abridged, by permission of the author and the publisher. Copyright 1991 by the Board of Trustees, Southern Illinois University.

*Maurice Hunt (1990)*

## *Pericles* and Jonah [editor's title]

One of the most amusing scenes of the play, the Prince's encounter with three rustic fishermen, burlesques and hence accentuates a motif central to several episodes and speeches that critics, for the most part, have ignored. In fact, Pericles' notorious passivity cannot be truly understood without reference to the motif which concerns a bold verbal protest against evil. The first tempest that Pericles endures washes him ashore in Simonides' Greece, where he overhears Pilch, Patch-breech, and their master describing the evils of their world.

| 3. Fish. | Faith, master, I am thinking of the poor men that were cast away before us even now. |
|---|---|
| 1. Fish. | Alas, poor souls, it griev'd my heart to hear what pitiful cries they made to us to help them, when, well-a-day, we could scarce help ourselves. |
| 3. Fish. | Nay, master, said not I as much when I saw the porpoise, how he bounc'd and tumbled? they say they're half fish, half flesh; a plague on them, they ne'er come but I look to be wash'd! Master, I marvel how the fishes live in the sea. |
| 1. Fish. | Why, as men do a-land: the great ones eat up the little ones. I can compare our rich misers to nothing so fitly as to a whale: a' plays and tumbles, driving the poor fry before him, and at last devours them all at a mouthful. Such whales have I heard on a'th' land, who never leave gaping till they swallow'd the whole parish, church, steeple, bells, and all. (2.1.18–34) |

Such homespun philosophizing possesses a certain appeal. Pericles might realize that the fishermen's little allegory could apply to his own affairs. He has experienced great Antiochus's treachery and the feelings of helplessness attending it. Like great fish, tyrannical men ruled by appetite can and do eat up less powerful mortals, even when the latter are princes. Nonetheless, Patch-breech, not Pericles, completes the allegory and draws a moral:

| 3. Fish. | But, master, if I had been the sexton, I would have been that day in the belfry. |
|---|---|
| 2. Fish. | Why, man? |
| 3. Fish. | Because he should have swallow'd me too; and when I had been in his belly, I would have kept such a jangling of the bells, that he should never have left till he cast bells, steeple, church, and parish up again. (2.1.36–43) |

The fishermen's talk of whales, sin, and the swallowing and disgorging of a man, interwoven with mention of religious restoration, echoes the biblical story of Jonah. Since the moral of the story illuminates the play, a brief summary will be helpful. Jonah found himself in the whale's belly because terrified sailors threw him overboard. Jonah freely became the sacrificial victim when he confessed that he was attempting to flee God's presence. His guilty flight derived from his refusal to obey God's commandment that he publicly proclaim ("cry against") the evil of Nineveh's citizens. Jonah's error involved his failure to believe in Providence; he lacked faith that God would somehow use a public protest, which from a mortal viewpoint appeared dangerous, to bring forth good not only for the sinners but for the proclaimer himself. Resurrected from the beast, Jonah bravely enters the wicked city and, in an act of personal salvation, cries, "Yet forty days, and Nineveh shall be overthrown!" (Jonah 3:1–10). Immediately the Ninevites reform, proclaiming a fast, donning sack-cloth and averting ruin. Jonah's words, faithfully uttered, possess redemptive power.

In *Pericles*, Patch-breech's method for obtaining salvation whimsically recalls the moral of the Jonah story. By jangling the church bells, Patch-breech, if swallowed by leviathan, would work a personal and social resurrection. Despite the comic warping, the thematic connotations of his remark are clear. A vigorous jangling of church bells, a spiritual stirring, defeats a great villain and the evil associated with him. Within the generally serious context of romance, Shakespeare's viewer momentarily enjoys a comic rendering of a familiar truth.

What importance can this truth have for Pericles? Taken by the fishermen's colorful method, Pericles simply exclaims:

> How from the finny subject of the sea
> These fishers tell the infirmities of men;
> And from their wat'ry empire recollect
> All that may men approve or men detect! (2.1.48–51)

At this dramatic moment, Pericles plays the role of the submissive hero. Studied pathos informs his self-portrayal. In his own words, he is

> A man whom both the waters and the wind,
> In that vast tennis-court, hath made the ball
> For them to play upon, entreats you pity him;
> He asks of you, that never us'd to beg. (2.1.59–62)

It is not surprising that Pericles, given his view of himself as acted upon rather than acting, overlooks Patch-breech's message about the redemptive effect of personal stirring. Stirring is generally preferable to passivity, and the Prince at this instant represents the less attractive quality. By making Pericles passive, and by making him the butt of the fishermen's jokes, Shakespeare causes the viewer to value the energetic rustics' insights.

Pericles in Antiochus's court argued at length against the efficacy of a verbal protest against evil. The Prince implied that were he to broadcast Antiochus's incest, the tyrant's "sore" eyes would "see through" his veiled story, discovering a way to silence permanently the narrator. Pericles vows that he will not be like the blind (unperceptive) mole whose protests against evil—its "Copp'd hills"—identify it and bring about its untimely death. He believes that evil "grows worse" when made more known; when sin is declared, not only the teller but innocent people associated with him are also sometimes vengefully struck down.

Pericles remains true to the logic of his tortuous reply; he conceals Antiochus's incest once he has fled to Tyre. Melancholy, however, results from his harboring of the secret. Evil known but closely kept can fester, incapacitating the knower as much as evil contemplated does. As a decreative word, the riddle undoes life as effectively as the Christian Word infuses it. Its perlocutionary force (what it brings about or achieves) devitalizes Pericles, muting him, forcing him to deny the moral promptings of his conscience, eventually draining the life from his cheeks and very being as melancholic stupor predominates.

Still, it would be a mistake to imply that Pericles becomes victimized by decreative words. He chooses to pledge silence. By his commitment to silence, he virtuously desires to protect his subjects from Antiochus's retaliation. Regarded from one viewpoint, Pericles' attempt to convince Antiochus that he will not publish the crime deserves credit. In Act 1, Pericles' situation contrasts with that of Jonah in one important respect: a deity does not order Shakespeare's character to "cry against" vice. Nevertheless, Shakespeare does evoke the tale of Jonah in the subsequent fisherman episode and does suggest that a declaration can defeat evil and restore good.

The ending of Act 1 refutes Pericles' ideas about the relationship between speech and evil. There, Cleon decides to tell the story of Tharsus's "superfluous riots" in order to awaken divine comforters. By introducing his tale with the words, "This Tharsus, o'er which I have the government" (1.4.21), Cleon implies that the ruin of his city partly results from a monarch's fault—his own. His final plea coincides with the arrival of Pericles' fleet of ships. Cleon believes that a savage nation, aware of the vulnerability of Tharsus, expects an easy conquest of starving men. Pericles, admitting that "we have heard your miseries as far as Tyre" (1.4.88), informs him, however, that the ships bring the means for life. Cleon's on stage story resembles a tale reflecting a king's failure, one that appears to produce a comforter—a prince with a saving gift of grain.

In the second act, Shakespeare continues to focus upon the efficacy of protest—in this case a stirring verbal protest. Even though Pericles, his armor recovered, wins the offstage tourney and thus Thaisa's hand in marriage, as a "mean" knight he must demonstrate his worth to Simonides. Unfortunately, Pericles' passivity reaches new extremes in Simonides' hall of state. The Prince claims that his victory comes more by fortune than by merit (2.3.12); he avoids the seat of honor, stating that a lesser place is far more fit for him (2.3.23); he laments time's tyranny and his forlorn life (2.3.37–47); and he denies any skill in dancing (2.3.104). Later, he rejects Simonides' praise of his musical abilities, claiming that he is "the worst of all her scholars" (2.5.29–31). Moreover, when Simonides proposes that the stranger become Thaisa's tutor, Pericles declines: "I am unworthy for her schoolmaster" (2.5.40). Finally, when the King shows him Thaisa's love letter, Pericles fearfully exclaims,

> 'Tis the king's subtlety to have my life.—
> (Kneels.) O, seek not to entrap me, gracious lord,
> A stranger and distressed gentleman,
> That never aim'd so high to love your daughter,
> But bent all offices to honour her. (2.5.44–48)

Such pithless sentiments convince neither the audience nor Simonides that Pericles deserves Thaisa. The hero balks at assuming any role requiring mastery, whether it be one of lover, schoolmaster, or son-in-law to a king. Clearly, Pericles' experience of venturing for Antiochus's daughter, which he finds reflected in a seemingly similar contest for the beautiful Thaisa, has intellectually crippled him. The more courteous that Simonides appears, the more Pericles imagines that he is as inwardly devilish as the earlier fair-speaking giver of a lovely daughter through a trial. However, Pericles strongly reacts to the apparently hostile father's claims that the young man represents a traitor.

> Simonides    Traitor, thou liest.
> Pericles    Traitor?
> Simonides    Ay, traitor.
> Pericles    Even in his throat—unless it be the king—
>     That calls me traitor, I return the lie.
> Simonides (*Aside*) Now, by the gods, I do applaud his courage.
> Pericles    My actions are as noble as my thoughts,
>     That never relish'd of a base descent.
>     I came unto your court for honour's cause,
>     And not to be a rebel to her state;
>     And he that otherwise accounts of me,
>     This sword shall prove he's honour's enemy.
>     (2.5.54–63)

By this vigorous verbal protest, Pericles redeems himself not only in Simonides' eyes but in those of the theater audience also. Dramatically, this speech—not the tourney—wins Thaisa.

In his study of *Pericles*, John Danby distinguishes between Stoic patience, which he equates with apathy, and active Christian patience (patiens), which he describes as a "release of charity." In the play's most famous passage (3.1.56–64), Pericles imagines Thaisa's body, "scarcely coffin'd," plummeting through the sea to the ooze, where "the belching whale" and "humming water" overwhelm her corpse, "lying with simple shells." These images cannot obscure Pericles' mistaken belief that the gods are indifferent to human value. In Danby's analysis of the arresting speech, Pericles "fully realizes death's final 'apathie'—away from the storm, on the sea's floor, 'lying with simple shells': an apathy which is the opposite of patience as death is the opposite of life." [*Poets on Fortune's Hill* (1952), pp. 81–97]. In the Prince's vision, the whale's belching suggests a bestial indifference to human redemption; the image evokes Jonah's experience only to deny its truth.

After Thaisa's sea "burial," Pericles' complaints cease; apparently he grasps the futility of addressing the gods about metaphysical evils. When Dionyza later hypocritically laments Thaisa's loss, Pericles admits that

> We cannot but obey
> The powers above us. Could I rage and roar
> As doth the sea she lies in, yet the end
> Must be as 'tis. (3.3.9–12)

With these words Pericles expresses the proper attitude toward metaphysical evil in the world of the last romances—faithful silence. Yet as happens so often in the play, his triumph is short-lived; Marina's "death" shatters Pericles' spirit and he sinks into the absolute apathy of despair.

Moral evil, on the other hand, warrants verbal rebuke, a point left to Marina to demonstrate during her trials in the Mytilene brothel. Marina complains to the gods; however, she never makes Pericles' mistake of blindly indicting them. More important, Marina knows that moral evil deserves vigorous chastisement. No one, Pericles stated, dares to tell an earthly Jove that he acts wrongly. Marina, on the contrary, courageously risks telling the erring Governor of Mytilene that he dishonors himself by visiting the stews:

> Marina    Do you know this house to be a place of such resort, and will
>             come into't? I hear say you're of honourable parts and are the
>             governor of this place. . . .
>
>             If you were born to honour, show it now;
>             If put upon you, make the judgement good
>             That thought you worthy of it.
> Lysimachus    How's this? how's this? Some more; be sage.
>                                                      (4.6.78–94)

Marina's biting, fearless criticism of a ruler's faults prompts (not retards) good understanding:

> Lysimachus              I did not think
>             Thou couldst have spoke so well; ne'er dreamt thou couldst.
>             Had I brought hither a corrupted mind,
>             Thy speech had alter'd it. (4.6.101–4)

Despite his disclaimer, Lysimachus had brought a degraded mind to the brothel and Marina's sharp words have altered it. Marina's stirring verbal protest proves redemptive for Lysimachus and those patrons subjected to it.

At the beginning of the last act, melancholy Pericles remains concealed behind a curtain on board his ship, withdrawn from the gods who seemingly reclaim their gifts just as mysteriously as they give them. "May we not see him?" Lysimachus asks. Helicanus replies:

>             You may;
>         But bootless is your sight; he will not speak. . . .
>             This was a goodly person,
>         Till the disaster that, one mortal night,
>         Drove him to this. (5.1.32–40)

In this episode, Pericles profoundly dramatizes his original reaction to sin; seeing and hearing no evil was his professed wish after learning of vice. His isolation ironically reflects this desire. Marina confronts it, finally shattering it and introducing her father to the restorative virtues of a story retold. At first, Lysimachus believes that Marina's "sweet harmony" and "other chosen attractions" will "allure, / And make a batt'ry" through Pericles' "deafen'd ports" (5.1.44–46). Marina's song, however, makes no impact by itself; her physic will be her woeful story:

> she speaks,
> My lord, that, may be, hath endur'd a grief
> Might equal yours, if both were justly weigh'd.
> Though wayward fortune did malign my state,
> My derivation was from ancestors
> Who stood equivalent with mighty kings. (5.1.86–91)

Hearing these words, Pericles sees the unknown maiden in a new light.

In Pericles' eyes, Marina's heavenly beauty makes her speech resound truthfully in his ears, and her musical words intensify his rare view. Word and vision wonderfully complement each other, making possible a familiar Platonic coincidence.

> Tell thy story;
> If thine consider'd prove the thousandth part
> Of my endurance, thou art a man, and I
> Have suffer'd like a girl; yet thou dost look
> Like Patience gazing on kings' graves, and smiling
> Extremity out of act. What were thy friends?
> How lost thou them? Thy name, my most kind virgin?
> Recount, I do beseech you. Come, sit by me. (5.1.134–41)

Trusted "by the syllable" (5.1.167), Marina's narration of Cleon's and Dionyza's treachery, bloodthirsty Leonine's attack, and the pirates' mercenary rescue identifies Pericles' lost daughter. Marina opens the book of monarchs' faults. Her words of evils suffered have a homeopathic effect when one grief drives out another and Pericles is fully revived. Marina invites her listeners to remember her trials and imagine her martyr-like faith, comparing these images with personal woes whenever the latter seem extreme.

Marina's invitation extends to the theater audience as well as to Pericles. Pericles' advice that every book of monarchs' acts be kept closed contrasts with Shakespeare's decision to open Gower's and Twine's volumes and stage (publicly proclaim) the chief deeds of Pericles' life. According to Gower, lords and ladies have read the saga of Pericles "for restoratives" (Chorus 1.7–8). Shakespeare's sorrowful play can revitalize its viewer by presenting images of griefs greater than any suffered or imagined possible. Marina's brief tale is such an image. It is the composite—in fact, the miniature—of the play in its cathartic working. Just as her tale of suffering displaces Pericles' grief, promoting his recovery and making possible the formal ending of romance, so the larger tale of Pericles works upon the viewer's woes, placing them in perspective.

Pericles receives from Diana the command to travel to Ephesus, offer sacrifice upon her altar there, and give both his and Marina's trials "repetition to the life" before the assembled worshippers. Pericles obeys a deity's command to tell a story involving evil (the evil of a king) even as his counterpart Jonah finally divulged the wickedness of Nineveh in an act pleasing to God and assuring salvation. Pericles' faithfully told story is restorative; his public narration makes his identity known to the nun Thaisa, who faints upon hearing this revelation. Now, however, no radical conflict in knowing presents itself. The viewer realizes that the problem has been resolved; all the faculties cooperate in revealing husband and wife to each other. Thaisa's eyes and ears record the truth; Pericles is a "Great sir" (5.3.26). Thaisa's vision of her husband opens her ears to his bizarre yet true narrative of the family's preservation. The efficacious working of words has recreated the sanctity of the family as only the theater audience can fully appreciate.

Abridged from *Shakespeare's Romance of the Word* (Bucknell University Press, 1990), Ch. 2. Permission by Associated University Presses.

# CYMBELINE

## Comment and bibliography

The cosmic view of mankind's story in *Pericles* underlies *Cymbeline* also, but now with a focus on the history of the British nation at the time of Christ's nativity. We see a death and rebirth of Britain's ties to Rome, a death and rebirth of the king's hope for royal heirs, and a death and rebirth in the love of the king's son-in-law, Posthumus, for his wife Imogen. As these three strands of the drama's plot interlock they reveal a complex texture of betrayals mended by conversions that turn griefs into joys. The chief agent of redemption is an Imogen who embodies sacrificial love. Disguising herself as a page-boy Fidele when seeking out her erring husband, she undergoes a mock death and resurrection, and then as the servant of a captive Roman nobleman finds opportunity to expose the lies of the Italianate Iachimo who beguiled Posthumus. Her action is analogous to Helena's pilgrimage in *All's Well* and may be regarded as a variant of the same Christian paradigm. Through it is effectuated a liberation that constitutes a new dispensation of grace, such as Christ's nativity originally heralded in the midst of a fallen world of tyrannous politics and warped family life. The story as a whole seems to suggest, further, a figurative re-understanding of the troubled relationship of England and Rome in Shakespeare's own day and the readjustment to be hoped for through a piety such as can emerge amid adversity.

Although *Cymbeline* was listed in the Folio as a tragedy, its ending certainly designates it a comedy of romance. There is potential tragedy, of course, in the foolish wager of Posthumus (so like that of the Roman Collatine in the tragedy of *Lucrece*); but the command of murder that results from his fall into jealousy gets sidetracked by a conscientious servant, and Posthumus himself soon turns remorseful and vows to shed his "Italianate weeds" in order to fight against his fault and "die for thee, O Imogen." His taking on of a "peasant" garb associates him with the exiled Belarius and the royal "sons" who thrive in a rural cave, and who sally forth from it only as salvific defenders of a native justice against foreign interlopers. Their pastoral colony is like Duke Senior's community of political outlaws in *As You Like It* who sing a religious piety. Guiderius and Arviragus have been taught to begin each day with the "holy office" of bowing in adoration of the heavens; and they see in Fidele an "angel" to be welcomed as a primrose flower, whereas Posthumus had mistakenly equated her with a possessed jewel to be boasted of. A spirit of pastoral "brotherhood" in country virtue as opposed to courtly vice is prominent in *Cymbeline*. It perhaps entitles this play to be regarded as participating in the mixed dramatic genre described by Polonius in *Hamlet* as "tragical-comical historical pastoral" poem unlimited.

The drama's recurrent motif of a changing of clothes is no doubt meant to suggest, as Arthur Kirsch has noted, the Pauline doctrine of everyman's need to put off the "old man" and put on the new in righteousness. The arduous penitential process by which Posthumus does this involves stages paralleling those of penance in Catholic theology. The stage which precedes final forgiveness, when as a prisoner Posthumus merrily awaits death by execution, has overtones reminiscent of Thomas More's well-known jesting before his beheading.

In medieval story the myth of an Eagle's transformation by a moulting of feathers was symbolic for Christian readers of spiritual renewal, as has been pointed out recently by Peggy Simonds. In the play, we are told, Posthumus is a worthy man at whose birth in lowly circumstances a heavenly star reigned, and his marriage took place in Jupiter's temple. It is appropriate therefore that he should have his life renewed through a vision of Jupiter himself descending as a "holy Eagle" to place on his breast a tablet granting him a "golden chance." That tablet symbolizes, probably, a promise testified in the Bible through David's "eagle" metaphor in the book of Psalms, and also by the gospel of the Eagle-like apostle, St John. Clearly the vision's symbolism heralds for Posthumus a "second birth" bestowed supernaturally by the heavens.

For Cymbeline at the same time the intervention predicts a regrafting of the lopped branches of his family tree—a metaphor of reconciliation voiced in St Paul's Epistle to the Romans. Significantly, Cymbeline extends reconciliation to include his relation to Rome, shortly after confessing to having learned "our freeness of a son-in-law" through Posthumus. "Pardon's the word for all," he declares. And thus the play as a whole fulfils the paradoxical message voiced by Jupiter: "Whom best I love I cross; to make my gift, / The more delayed, delighted" (5.4.101). Likewise, in the Bible, the gift of Christ's nativity is understood theologically as mankind's second chance, announcing a providence that transforms original sin into a *felix culpa* that elicits saving grace. We know that some neoclassicists in Shakespeare's audience faulted the play *Cymbeline* as being built on "improbabilities." But let us recall that this kind of secular response is recorded in the Bible alongside St Paul's rejoinder that he glories in the "scandal" of the cross.

Shakespeare's associating of the lovely Imogen with "Hark, hark the lark" in 2.3 should remind us of the remembered lark of his Sonnet 29 that "sings hymns at heaven's gate." And perhaps also of his Sonnet 73, which laments "Bare ruin'd choirs where late the sweet birds sang," alluding to places like Tintern Abbey. At least two of Shakespeare's comedies end in an abbey or priory, but here in *Cymbeline* a typological equivalent is the country refuge-sanctuary that harbors Imogen.

Our anthology reprints four pieces of commentary pertinent to any discussion of *Cymbeline*. Homer Swander comments on the mystery of the relationship between free will and predestination in the design of the play, and on the relation of Posthumus's prayer to Jupiter's gift of vision. He traces in Act 5 a "four scene religious drama of atonement" and a two-stage development in the Soothsayer's prophecy. He shows how Shakespeare has altered Holinshed's account of the battle to suggest "something more than natural at work," a marvel in which "the heavens fought" without violating any laws of nature. David Kasten comments that what Dr. Jonson scorned as the "imbecility" of *Cymbeline* is tied to the marvel of the Incarnation. The play's strange truth that "some falls are means the happier to arise" leads to a Soothsayer's vision which echoes Christ's *consummatum est.*

Arthur Kirsch notes the play's suggestions of "atonement" doctrine and of spiritual regeneration through a literalization of the Pauline metaphor of changing clothes. He sees "a sense of Britain's baptism as a nation" at the end of the play in its incorporation into Rome, and he finds the paradox of the fortunate fall in Imogen's thought that "Some griefs doth physic love." He concludes that Shakespeare is telling of a nativity in Britain that "reveals in time a reality outside time." Peggy Simonds relates the transformation of Posthumus to the renewed Eagle of Psalm 103 and Isaiah 40 as emblematized in medieval fable.

For supplementary reading, Robert Hunter's chapter in 1965 on the comedy of forgiveness in this play is still useful. Cynthia Marshall's more recent chapter gives an excellent review of the themes of judgment, forgiveness, and apocalypse central to Advent. She remarks of *Cymbeline* that the Holy Birth changes the world, albeit without the world's knowledge, as though "the tremendous event in Bethlehem" had produced a "moral fallout that settles over the pagan earth" in a surplus of grace. She finds at the play's end overtones of Armageddon in the decisive battle followed by resurrections of the presumed dead. Naseeb Shaheen assembles 43 biblical allusions in the play, including notably the reference to the "swathing" clothes of the exiled babes and the phrase "the heavens fought."

The essay by Peggy Simonds on "Aural Imagery" turns about our need to appreciate the archetypal significance of mankind's being seduced through "hearing" in Genesis but corrected later by a "faith" that comes by "hearing," as Paul testifies in Rom 10:17. In the play a poisoning through the ear is suffered by two major characters, King Cymbeline through his second wife's words, and Posthumus through those of Iachimo, besides also Iachimo's gaining favor with Imogen through false words. As Simonds goes on to note, however, Pisanio mentions as a savior for Imogen an "ear in music," and we see her musical voice bringing her to favor with Cymbeline even before the "senseless speaking" of Jupiter bestows the good news of freedom for Posthumus. Simonds catalogs in the play four redemptive functions "sound" can have—through the music of prayer, through prophetic words, through verbal good news, and through songs of praise such as the concluding "Laud we the gods" (5.5.477) that mends the division between heaven and earth (which began with the first ear-poisoning in Eden). She also provides a source for the Jupiter episode in the play by reproducing an engraving by H. Junius in 1565 that depicts Jupiter, armed with lightning bolts, descending to the natural world on the back of an eagle. And accompanying the Junius emblem is a Latin motto declaring that a "temperate" prince does not "lend a slavish ear" to anyone.

Lila Geller observes that each of the three plots in the play turns about the breaking and renewing of a contract or covenant. She notes further that Elizabethan chroniclers shared the view of Eusebius that the Pax Romana was part of God's preparation for the Incarnation, and they thought of their nation as having a covenantal relation with God.

## Supplementary bibliography

Bryant, J. A., Jr. *Hippolyta's View* (1961), Ch. 12.
Geller, Lila. "*Cymbeline* and the Imagery of Covenant Theology," *Studies in English Literature* 20 (1980), 241–55.
Hunter, Robert G. *Shakespeare and the Comedy of Forgiveness* (1965), Ch. 7.
Marshall, Cynthia. *Last Things and Last Plays: Shakespearean Eschatology* (Southern Illinois University Press, 1991), pp. 12–37.
Moffet, Robin. "*Cymbeline* and the Nativity," *Shakespeare Quarterly* 13 (1962), 207–18.
Shaheen , Naseeb. "The Use of Scripture in *Cymbeline*," *Shakespeare Studies* 4 (1968), 294–315.
Simonds, Peggy M. "Aural Imagery in *Cymbeline*," *Texas Studies in Literature & Language* 24 (1982), 137–54.
_____. "The Marriage Topos in *Cymbeline*," *English Literary Renaissance* 19 (1989), 94–117.

*Homer D. Swander (1966)*

## *Cymbeline*: Religious Idea and Dramatic Design

Shakespeare's consistently developed religious terminology makes Posthumus' crime a sin: in his attempt to murder Imogen, he rejects the "gift of the gods" (1.4.92), the gods' "own" (6.,16), and attacks "divineness" (3.6.44) by means of a "sacrilegious" servant (5.5.220). His remorse is therefore, as one would expect, openly religious, an acceptance not simply of a woman but of grace. When he appears in Act 5 his mind is full of God, and the four scenes that he dominates develop, in their substance and their shape, religious meanings that begin in the earlier acts and conclude only with the last lines of the play.

Most of his soliloquy at the beginning of Act 5 is thus appropriately a prayer in which he begins to see how the gods are working with him—

> You some permit
> To second ills with ills, each elder worse,
> And make them dread it, to the doers' thrift—

and in which he submits himself to the divine will: "make me blest to obey." Furthermore, all of his actions and intentions—the re-evaluation of himself and Imogen, his use of disguise, the plan to strengthen his inner self and to seek death in battle, all those matters in the soliloquy that shape the next scenes—are in the deepest sense religious, for they are framed as prayer. All other meanings, that is, come to serve the religious meaning.

In scene four, Posthumus, now a prisoner of the British, prays again, welcoming his almost certain execution as the "way ... to liberty," the "key / T' unbar" the locks that hold him. But his conscience is still, in spite of all, "fetter'd / More than my shanks and wrists," and he prays the "good gods" to give him "The penitent instrument to pick that bolt; / Then"—*and only then*—"free for ever!" He prays not simply for death but for salvation.

The prayer continues:

> Is't enough I am *sorry*?
> So children temporal fathers do appease;
> Gods are more full of mercy. Must I *repent*,
> I cannot do it better than in gyves,
> Desir'd more than constrain'd; to *satisfy*,
> If of my freedom 'tis the main part, take
> No stricter render of me than my all.
> I know you are more clement than vile men,
> Who of their broken debtors take a third,
> A sixth, a tenth, letting them thrive again
> On their abatement. That's not my desire.
> For Imogen's dear life take mine. (5.4.11–22)

The religious language here is precise, Posthumus carefully moving through the three steps necessary for remission of sins—sorrow, repentance, and satisfaction— and Shakespeare emphasizes the orthodox structure and fullness of the contrition by anchoring those three alternate lines with the operative word (here italicized).

In the very asking for the "pentitent instrument," he has been granted it, as Shakespeare reveals through the divine vision to which the prayer directly leads. In the economy of salvation, God in fact anticipates: the strength to ask for grace is itself a gift of grace, the proof of this in the play coming from the vision in the words of Jupiter himself: "Whom best I love I cross; to make my gift, / The more delay'd, delighted.... Our jovial star reign'd at his birth..." (5.4.101–05). Shakespeare is here evoking the mystery of the relationship between free will and predestination, time and eternity, natural virtue and grace. If natural virtue is all there is, Posthumus—great though his virtues certainly are—cannot escape an essential identification with Cloten; it is only as in two prayers he accepts and in four scenes exercises supernatural virtue that he proves himself worthy of the love that offers such strength. He has, that is, had to earn in time the gift that was freely granted in eternity; though chosen of God, he has nevertheless had freely to choose (after first rejecting) the gift that was always his.

Jupiter's appearance, while it is, as Posthumus knows, a "golden chance" to be embraced by one "steep'd in favours," is also, as he says, a "senseless speaking, or a speaking such / As sense cannot untie" (5.4.131,148). Shakespeare's conception of the relationship between man and god determines the role of Jupiter in the structure of the play. Prevented by this conception from intervening directly (which is not to say that Shakespeare denies the possibility of such intervention; he is simply writing about a more complicated divine mystery), Jupiter can nevertheless miraculously leave behind an accurately prophetic tablet to prove that the consequence of Posthumus' prayer is no mere dream.

In the structure of the four scenes that belong to Posthumus, his prayer provides the last tension—a man reaching toward God—and the result of the vision is the only "comic relief" in the play. When the talkative jailer enters, the agonized images of debt from the prayer become, in one measure of what the vision has accomplished, comic images of payment. Posthumus is "merrier to die" than the jailer is to live; for though he may not understand the vision, he knows where death will take him. His "Death has eyes in's head," a knowledge available through grace to all: "there are none want eyes to direct them the way I am going, but such as wink and will not use them" (5.4.176–194). Thus the four-scene religious drama of atonement resolves itself, by way of goodnatured gallows humor, into a revelation of the tranquillity of the state of grace. And the jailer, meditating on what is for him the mystery of Posthumus, ends the scene with a wish that looks forward to the unity achieved in the next and final scene: "I would we were all of one mind, and one mind good. O, there were desolation of jailers and gallowses!"

The tablet that Jupiter leaves for Posthumus concerns itself largely with Britain's domestic affairs—Imogen's marriage and the preservation of the royal line:

> When as a line's whelp shall, to himself unknown, without seeking find, and
> be embraced by a piece of tender air, and when from a stately cedar shall be
> lopped branches, which, being dead many years, shall after revive, be jointed
> to the old stock, and freshly grow, then shall Posthumus end his miseries,
> Britain be fortunate and flourish in peace and plenty (5.4.138; 5.5.435).

In the last scene, the Soothsayer declares the meaning: Posthumus Leonatus is the lion's whelp, Imogen the tender air, Cymbeline the cedar, and his two sons the branches. The effect of this divination after a second reading of the tablet is to recall the vision at nearly the last moment of the play, climactically emphasizing that it is Jupiter, however restrained he may be as *deus ex machina*, who has designed the reunion of family and kingdom.

At this time Shakespeare also reminds us of the prophetic vision of the Soothsayer himself, which we first hear about in Act 4:

> Last night the very gods show'd me a vision—
> I fast and pray'd for their intelligence—thus:
> I saw Jove's bird, the Roman eagle, wing'd
> From the spongy south to this part of the west,
> There vanish'd in the sunbeams; which portends—
> Unless my sins abuse my divination—
> Success to the Roman host. (4.2.346–52)

For the resolution of Britain's international difficulties—the war with Rome—this vision, with the battle about which it at first appears to have been mistaken but is then proved accurate, functions like the other over the resolution of domestic problems. The British victory is a marvel that occurs before our eyes, and the Soothsayer's vision proves that the marvel is divine.

Shakespeare gives us the battle twice: first, in a brief scene of lengthy stage directions and scanty dialogue; second, in a long narrative description by Posthumus. From any realistic point of view, what happens is at least surprising—four men (Posthumus, Belarius, and Imogen's brothers), apparently peasants, turn the battle against the Roman Army. But in romantic literature we expect such rescues, and the incident in fact comes from Holinshed; it is "history" not romance. The main change Shakespeare makes in taking it over is insistently to suggest that something more than natural is at work.

The insistence begins with Iachimo's belief, after his defeat by the disguised Posthumus, that the British may be gods (5.2.10) and with the awe in Lucius' words: "the disorder's such / As war were hoodwink'd.... / It is a day turn'd strangely" (lines 15–17). In the next scene Posthumus says, "all was lost / But that the heavens fought," and then describes the battle (modestly omitting his own part) in nearly fifty lines of rapid, elliptically vigorous blank verse (5.3.3–51). The scene continues with a comment from an anonymous lord (who had run away from the battle):

> Lord.  This was strange chance:
>        A narrow lane, an old man, and two boys!
> Post.  Nay, do not wonder at it; you are made
>        Rather to wonder at the things you hear
>        Than to work any. Will you rime upon't.
>        And vent it for a mockery? Here is one:
>        "Two boys, an old man twice a boy, a lane,
>        Preserv'd the Britons, was the Romans' bane."
> Lord.  Nay, be not angry, sir.
> Post.        'Lack, to what end?
>        Who dares not stand his foe, I'll be his friend;
>        For if he'll do as he is made to do,
>        I know he'll quickly fly my friendship too.
>        You have put me into rhyme.
> Lord.        Farewell; you're angry.

It is with some complexity that this calls attention to the marvel. The Lord—by avoiding the expected religious (and even the heroic) explanation, attributing everything, instead, to chance, and by cheapening the battle and those fifty vigorous lines into a single flat pentameter—forces Posthumus, until this moment friendly, to turn on him with angry mockery and himself ironically to degrade the heroism into a very bad couplet. We react critically with Posthumus against the lord's verse and recognize with him the badness of his own; but at the same time, Shakespeare manages twice, with these inane one- and two-line summations, to insist that two boys and an old man have defeated the Roman army. The flat verse, even as we react against it, drives home the incredible fact. And through the medium of Posthumus' angry sarcasm, we are led to avoid the lord's simpleminded response. We are apparently to hold fast to the fantastic nature of the event, not to reduce it in any way, and then nevertheless to believe it.

Although no god appears, this marvel that is hard fact calls forth, almost as soon as the Lord leaves the stage, the explanation of which he was incapable: a captain says, "Great Jupiter be praised! Lucius is taken. / 'Tis thought the old man and his sons were angels" (line 84). That they were not literally angels in no way lessens the accuracy of the captain's praise. As with the development of grace in the individual so here with the movement of history: God works from within, violating no laws of nature. Holinshed's historical trio in fact did no less than Shakespeare's, and had nothing but courage and fortunate terrain to explain their victory; it was by God's "appointment" that they happened to be nearby, but the chronicle does not suggest that He helped in the battle. Thus the incident—historical but hard to believe—is right for *Cymbeline*. In his next play, *The Winter's Tale*, Shakespeare will have Paulina make the point explicitly: "It is required / You do awake your faith" (5.3.94).

Divine power verifies itself in more than suggestive remarks, however, doing so most importantly in the prophetic accuracy of the two visions. The outcome of the battle seems at first, of course, to invalidate the Soothsayer's vision; for as he first understands it, it means "Success to the Roman host" (4.2.352). In the next-to-last speech of the play, however—immediately after he interprets the tablet from Jupiter, and Cymbeline voluntarily submits to Caesar—the Soothsayer sees the truth. Much more than a prophecy of victory to either side, his vision promised the transformation of spirit that unites Britain harmoniously with the rest of the world:

> The fingers of the powers above do tune
> The harmony of this peace. The vision
> Which I made known to Lucius, ere the stroke
> Of this yet scarce-cold battle, at this instant
> Is full accomplish'd; for the Roman eagle,
> From south to west on wing soaring aloft,
> Lessen'd herself, and in the beams o' the sun

> So vanish'd; which foreshow'd our princely eagle.
> Th' imperial Caesar, should again unite
> His favour with the radiant Cymbeline,
> Which shines here in the west. (5.5.466–76)

The next speech is the last. Cymbeline says, "Laud we the gods," and both armies go to ratify the peace "in the temple of great Jupiter."

The two visions are, then, parts of one structure, and their similarity functions in Shakespeare's design: Jupiter's eagle appears in both; both involve prophecies that, though at first either misinterpreted or not understood, prove to be accurate, and that, taken together, forecast the entire resolution of an unusually complex plot; both are recalled and their prophecies repeated in full and correctly interpreted in the closing lines of the play; and both constitute proof of that kind of divine control that works through instead of upon man and society.

From *Pacific Coast Studies in Shakespeare*, ed. Waldo McNeir and Thelma Greenfield (University of Oregon Books, 1966), pp. 254–61 abridged. Used by permission.

*David Scott Kastan (1977)*

## The Strange Truth of *Cymbeline* [editor's title]

*Cymbeline* is perhaps the strangest of the final plays, insistently challenging our norms of reality. The ghosts of Posthumus' mother, father, and two brothers appear as he sleeps, and plead with Jupiter to grant him "the graces for his merits due" (5.4.79); Jupiter himself throws thunderbolts and descends riding upon his "holy eagle" (5.4.115); and the plot itself is an intricate and improbable action that leads Dr. Johnson to hoot at "the folly of the fiction, the absurdity of the conduct, the confusion of the names and manners of different times, and the impossibility of the events in any system of life. . . ."

The "unresisting imbecility" that Johnson scorned is, however, the very means by which *Cymbeline* defines the "system of life" informing its unlikely happenings. The bewildering series of reversals and revelations that permit its three plots to come together in a marvelous conclusion leads us beyond the casual notions that settled senses can provide to embrace with awe and wonder the knowledge that "The finger of the pow'rs above do tune / The harmony of this peace" (5.5.465–66). Unquestionably, as Robin Moffet has taught us, the locus of the contrived comic conclusion in the reign of Cymbeline would itself suggest the supernatural perfection of human history, for Cymbeline reigned over

What time th'eternal Lord in fleshly slime
Enwombed was, from wretched *Adams* line
To purge away the guilt of sinful crime:
O ioyous memorie of happy time,
That heauenly grace so plenteously displayed
(*Faerie Queene*, II.x.50)

And although the Incarnation is only allusively present in the play, nowhere better than in its happy end can we see "heauenly grace so plenteously displayed."

The ingenious plot plunges its characters deep into a world of tragic potentiality, and yet in the incredible final scene everything is set right. Bertrand Evans counts no less than twenty-three separate discoveries that are necessary to accomplish this, and "though the strands are many and marvelously interlined, nothing snarls, and no loose end remains at last." Clearly this is no "common passage, but / A strain of rareness" (3.4.92–93). In a single scene, confusion and loss are replaced by clarity and gain. "The time [that] is troublesome" (4.3.21) has become a "gracious season" (5.5.401); everything of value has been restored; families and nations are reunited and at peace. The comic order, as the soothsayer says of his vision, "at this instant / Is full accomplished" (5.5.468–9). And if we hear echoes of Christ's "*consummatum est*," it is because the achievement of harmony in the romance plot provides a secular analogue of "the rarer action" of salvation history.

Joan Hartwig has observed that each of the play's three lines of action partakes of a different set of literary conventions: "the romantic plot of New Comedy revolves about the Posthumus-Imogen relationship; the history play concerns the Britain-Rome controversy; and the pastoral conventions manifest themselves in the situation of Cymbeline's lost sons." Yet this fine perception must be supplemented by the observation that structurally each is the same. Each is a reflection of the essential salvation pattern of innocence/fall/redemption. The individual strands of the plot are initially defined by the same act—Cymbeline's misvaluing of a relationship—which isolates each action literally and structurally. Posthumus and Belarius are exiled from the community of the court, and Cymbeline's Britain from the wider community of the Roman world. Isolated, each action reveals its similar shape as its characters move from error to truth, from skepticism to faith, from hatred to love; and each proves Lucius' observation, "some falls are means the happier to arise" (4.2.403), as each, from the individual regeneration of Posthumus to the familial reunion of the royal family to the international reconciliation of Britain and Rome, provides us an increasingly more inclusive harmony.

From "More Than History Can Pattern," *Cithara* 17 (1977), 39–40.

*Arthur C. Kirsch (1981)*

## Atonement After Fortunate Fall [editor's title]

The spiritual implications of Posthumus's transformation are coordinate with the psychic ones and even more transparent. The whole process by which his marriage with Imogen is reconstituted suggests all the marvelously condensed meanings of the word "atone" in Hymen's description, in *As You Like It*, of the union of husband and wife:

> Then is there mirth in heaven,
> When earthly things made even
> Atone together. (5.4.102)

The Atonement itself is suggested most directly and richly in Imogen's sacrificial death and rebirth, but Posthumus's actions too eventually convey the sense of his reconciliation not only with himself but with God. His discussion and change of clothes, echoing Borachio's meditation on fashion (in *Much Ado*) literalize the Pauline metaphor of spiritual regeneration, the putting off of "the olde man, which is corrupt through the deceivable lustes," and the putting on of "the new man, which after God is created in righteousness, and true holiness" (Eph 4:22–24).

Later, after the British victory, when he pretends to be a Roman and is taken prisoner, he makes a speech of repentance that precisely describes the stages necessary for the remission of sins[1] and that ends with his offering his life for Imogen's as part of the final "audit" of his talents: "For Imogen's dear life take mine; and though /'Tis not so dear, yet 'tis a life; you coin'd it" (5.4.22). Because we know that Imogen has died and been reborn for his sake, we know also, in the words of the Geneva gloss to the parable of the talents, that he will "continue in the knowledge of God, and do good with those graces that God hathe given [him]." Posthumus's speech of repentance is immediately succeeded by the dream reaffirming his name and family, and like his change of clothes both the speech and the dream suggest the pattern of spiritual rebirth that is modelled after and made possible by Christ's sacrifice. I think they also have specific overtones of baptism, a sacrament that explicitly describes a process of death and rebirth and that verifies the identity of the individual by incorporating him into the larger family of God's "holy congregation" (Liturgy of Baptism, *Book of Common Prayer*). There is certainly a sense of Britain's baptism as a nation at the end of the play in its incorporation into Rome and into the peace that ushered in the birth of Christ.[2] A union with Rome is significantly opposed by Cloten, whose jingoism is the political equivalent, and expression, of Posthumus's psychic aggression and narcissism.

Northrop Frye has argued that Shakespeare may have chosen the historical milieu of *Cymbeline* in part because "Cymbeline was king of Britain at the time of

Christ," and he suggests that "the sense of a large change in human fortunes taking place off-stage has to be read into *Cymbeline*," even though, "as a rule reading things into Shakespeare in the light of some external information is a dubious practice."[3] I think Frye is right, though it seems to me that the significance of the contemporaneous life of Christ is sufficiently inherent in the play not to require the kind of extrinsic reading to which he objects. As I have suggested, the play has many Christian images that are precisely defined and have a manifest spiritual referent. Posthumus's penitential transformation is one example, but there are many others, and the entire action, and especially the erotic action, is governed by a redemptive and providential conception of experience. "Some griefs," Imogen says, "doth physic love" (3.2.33), and this idea in particular, the paradox of the fortunate fall, is pronounced in the play.

The paradox is, of course, virtually a generic requirement of a comic action, and as we have seen it is present in abundance in *Much Ado* as well as the problem comedies. Its use in *Cymbeline*, however, is more self-conscious than in the earlier works, even than in *All's Well*, as if Shakespeare wished to call attention to the actual dynamics of the process of change that it signifies. The paradox is repeated in the action and the language of the play over and over again, in the numerous enactments of death and rebirth, and in many speeches. It is insistently linked to the play's preoccupation with the disjunction between outer and inner life and it informs the whole pattern of experience not only of Imogen and Posthumus, but of the entire kingdom of Britain. We are made aware at the start of the play that the potion that the Queen gives Imogen is not only harmless, but beneficent:

> there is
> No danger in what show of death it makes,
> More than the locking up the spirits a time,
> To be more fresh, reviving. (1.5.39)

We ourselves witness the power of the paradox when we see Imogen dying to (and for) her husband to be reborn to a new one, and Lucius makes the experience explicit when he tells her: "Be cheerful; wipe thine eyes./ Some falls are means the happier to arise" (4.2.405). Precisely the same idea is made explicit in the characterization of Posthumus at the end of the play as he himself senses the death of his old self and as Jupiter appears in his dream with the explanation that makes his suffering intelligible.

> Whom best I love I cross; to make my gift,
> The more delay'd, delighted. Be content;
> Your low-laid son our godhead will uplift;
> His comforts thrive, his trials well are spent.
> Our Jovial star reign'd at his birth, and in
> Our temple was he married. Rise, and fade!
> He shall be lord of Lady Imogen,
> And happier much by his affliction made. (5.4.101)

Jupiter's appearance makes manifest the providential power that has been imma-
nent in the play from the start, and as with the comparable scenes in Shakespeare's
other romances it suggests the theophanies of the mystery drama. The birth of
Christ in the Nativity plays is at once the cause and result of the charity that transforms the shepherds' lives, just as the vision of Jupiter is simultaneously the divine
origin and concrete manifestation of the spiritual transformation of Posthumus
and Britain. The sense, therefore, of a transcendent change in human fortune in
*Cymbeline*, though it ultimately has an offstage Christ as its referent, is also inherent in the very structure of the play, for like biblical history in the mystery drama,
Shakespeare's legendary history of the nativity of Britain is essentially a spiritual
fable, the revelation in time of a reality that exists outside of it.

## Notes

1    See Homer Swander, "*Cymbeline*: Religious Idea and Dramatic Design," in
     McNeir and Greenfield, eds., *Pacific Coast Studies in Shakespeare*, (Eugene,
     Oregon: University of Oregon Books, 1966), pp. 255–6.
2    For discussions of the political and historical resonances of *Cymbeline*, see Emrys
     Jones, "Stuart *Cymbeline*," *Essays in Criticism*, 11 (1961), pp. 84–99; and J. P.
     Brockbank, "History and Histrionics in Cymbeline," *Shakespeare Survey* 11
     (1958), 42–9.
3    *A Natural Perspective*, pp. 66–7. Frye's point was anticipated by Robin Moffet,
     "*Cymbeline* and the Nativity," *Shakespeare Quarterly*, 13 (1962), 207–18.

From *Shakespeare and the Experience of Love* (Cambridge University Press, 1981),
pp. 160–63. Used by permission.

*Peggy Muñoz Simonds (1992)*

## The Renewed Eagle [editor's title]

There was a widely known myth about the eagle which Shakespeare and his Renaissance audience knew and which might have allowed the audience to accept
Posthumus as legitimately analogous to the eagle, despite his obvious failings. This
was an early Christian story written down by Physiologus in Greek, possibly as
early as the second century A.D., and regularly included, often with further commentaries, in the bestiaries of the Middle Ages.[1] It reappeared as a commonplace
in Renaissance emblem books and was again recounted in the mythological sec-
tions of early attempts at scientific ornithology, such as the exhaustive 1599 Latin
encyclopedia on birds by Aldrovandi. The myth describes three separate events in
the life of the eagle, all of which were part of an attempt by Physiologus to explain

David's promise in Psalm 103 that "Your youth will be renewed like the eagle's" and to relate the three motifs symbolically to the spiritual fall, reform, and regeneration of humanity. Essentially it is the story of religious conversion, an event which Shakespeare actually dramatizes in Act 5, scene 4, of *Cymbeline*. Moreover, the general pattern of decline into sin, the fall, and the ultimate renewal which this eagle myth describes is roughly analogous to the pattern of Posthumus' life in the play. He betrays Imogen through the sin of pride when he boasts of her chastity in Rome; he falls into the temptation of gaining forbidden knowledge about her chastity which is offered by Iachimo; and he later renews himself through humble penitence and a symbolic change of clothing, or the molting of his fancy Roman feathers.

The first stage of the myth occurs when the eagle has grown old, which Physiologus means us to understand as a spiritual rather than a physical decline. It takes place as the individual becomes increasingly aware of his sinfulness, when he notices that he is wearing the old clothes of Adam and that "the eyes of [his] heart have grown dim." In the second stage of the myth, the bird flies upward and stares directly into the sun, which "burns away his wings and the dimness of his eyes." Physiologus explains this event also in theological terms: "As you fly into the height of the sun of justice [Mal 4:2], who is Christ as the Apostle says, he himself will burn off your old clothing which is the devil's." Thirdly, the eagle falls from the heights. He plunges into a fountain of pure water, understood as another symbol of Christ by Physiologus, and he "bathes himself three times . . . is restored and made new again." This part of the eagle myth is a rather literal image of the sacrament of baptism after conversion, although it may also be interpreted as a reference to the cleansing effect of repentant tears.

Flatteringly termed "the best feather of our wing" (1.7.186) by Iachimo in his conversation with Imogen, Posthumus eventually realizes that he had sinned deeply when he ordered Imogen's death. In Act 5 he initiates the first stage of Physiologus' myth of the eagle when he admits that he had no right to judge his wife:

> You married ones
> If each of you should take this course, how many
> Must murder wives much better than themselves
> For wrying but a little? . . .
> Gods, if you
> Should have ta'en vengeance on my faults, I never
> Had liv'd to put on this: so had you saved
> The noble Imogen to repent, and struck
> Me, wretch, more worth your vengeance. (5.1.2–11)

Understanding at last that judgment belongs to divinity alone, whether Imogen is guilty or not, Posthumus admits the dimness of his eyes or his wrongdoing.

In the second stage of the eagle myth, the bird flies upward to the sun or to divine justice. Posthumus does something similar during his formal repentance, when he submits his own erring will to that of the gods: "And make me blest to obey" (5.1.17). As the sun then burns off the old feathers of the eagle, Posthumus strips off his Roman armor and his courtly clothes, or molts like the eagle: "I'll disrobe me / Of these Italian weeds, and suit myself / As doth a Briton peasant" (5.1.22–24). Changing into the simple garments of a humble peasant, Posthumus continues his reformation with the words "To shame the guise o' th' world, I will begin, / The fashion less without and more within" (5.1.32–33).

The third stage of the eagle myth occurs after the old feathers have been burned off by the sun. "Then at length, taking a header down into the fountain," says the Cambridge *Bestiary*, "he dips himself three times in it, and instantly he is renewed with a great vigour of plumage and splendour of vision." After his descent into poverty and humility and his later formal speech of repentance (5.4.8–23), Posthumus experiences that very night a "splendour of vision" which restores his dead family, the Leonati, to him and actually provides him with what he has desired all along: Jupiter's promise of the restoration of Imogen and of his own eventual salvation.

But much earlier, the author of *The Bestiary*, in his adaptation of Physiologus, had exhorted his readers to imitate the eagle's behavior:

> Do the same thing, O Man, you who are clothed in the old garment and have the eyes of your heart growing foggy. Seek for the spiritual fountain of the Lord and lift up your mind's eyes to God—who is the fount of justice—and then your youth will be renewed like the eagle's.

The eagle motif of repentance and renewal continues with some variations throughout the Renaissance in emblem books. . . . [Behind it] is not only the myth of Physiologus and David's promise of renewed youth but Isaiah 40:31 as well, a verse promising heaven to the faithful: "But they that wait upon the Lord shall renew their strength; they shall mount up with wings as eagles."

In *Cymbeline* Posthumus finally attains such unquestioning faith when he is captured by the British and believes he will die in the morning. In a formal speech of repentance, he asks, "Is't enough I am sorry? / So children temporal fathers do appease; / Gods are more full of mercy" (5.4.11–13). Offering his own life as a sacrificial atonement for the loss of Imogen's life, Posthumus places his soul fully in the hands of a merciful deity. His immediate reward is a dream vision of the descent of Jove's eagle carrying the god on its back, a god who delivers a verbal promise of happiness to come. To seal this promise of salvation for the faithful, Jupiter leaves behind a tablet which very likely symbolizes the New Testament. When Posthumus awakens, he says, "A book? O rare one, / Be not, as is our fangled world, a garment / Nobler than that it covers" (5.4.133–35). After reading its message, he calls it, "Senseless speaking, or a speaking such / As sense cannot untie" (5.4.148–49), or inspired language which can only be understood by an inspired reader.

Emblem 16 in Book III of the *Symbolarum & Emblematum* (1593) by Camerarius[2] examines both individual and church reformation under the suggestive motto, "Vetvstate relicta" (The past shaken off). The woodcut illustrates an eagle standing on a rock by the sea and shaking out its old feathers, or molting. The rock is understood to be Christ, a symbol deriving from 1 Cor 10:4: "And [our fathers] did drink the same spiritual drink: for they drank of that spiritual Rock that followed them; and that Rock was Christ." In fact there seems to be an allusion to this biblical passage in *Cymbeline* when Imogen throws her arms around Posthumus' neck in 5.5 and cries, "Think that you are upon a rock, and now / Throw me again" (262–63). The verse of the emblem tells us that

> *Inveterata tuae jam tandem crimina culpae*
> *Exue, si rediet laeta juventa tibi.*

> (Now at last you must lay aside your deep-rooted faults and vices, if you would have joyful youth returned to you.)

## Notes

1  *Physiologus*, tr. Michael J. Curley (Austin & London: University of Texas Press, 1979), pp. 12–13; *The Bestiary: A Book of Beasts*, tr. and ed., T. H. White (New York: Putnams, 1954), pp. 105–08.

2  Joachim Camerarius, *Symbola et Emblemata*, 2nd ed. (Nuremberg: Voegelinianis, 1605), p. 16.

From *Myth, Emblem, and Music in Shakespeare's "Cymbeline"* (University of Delaware Press, 1992), pp. 320–22; 328–30; 331–32, excerpts abridged. Permission from Associated University Presses.

# The Winter's Tale

## Comment and bibliography

This play, like *Cymbeline*, is the story of a marriage ravaged by jealousy but mended by the sinner's penance and his faithful wife's sacrificial love. And like *Cymbeline*, it concludes with an apocalypse of resurrections of the presumed dead that fulfills a divine oracle. Thus divine providence prevails. As in *Pericles*, however, the story is a branched one of two generations, in which faith and hope on the part of a lost child contributes to the father's regaining of a happiness capped by a family reunion. Moreover, a third and contextual dimension of this complex plot involves the alienation of brother kings, and then the mending of this breach when the second king's jealousy of second generation "gracious" love sends him chasing the lovers to their haven in the other king's country, where an unexpected revelation reconciles the two kings in an apocalypse of joy. The whole story is an "old tale" so improbable, we are told, as to be "hooted at." Yet it leads to the opening of a mysterious "fardel" which dumbs the speech of observers in a passion of wonder over "a world ransomed or one destroyed" by the coming to light of truth, the daughter of time. The network of marvel rests as a whole on biblical paradigm, although of course with an assimilation of motifs from classical myth and Greek romance.

The word "grace" occurs frequently in this play and refers to a social graciousness that is infused with divine grace. Hermione embodies grace when she comes to the aid of her husband Leontes in his desire to persuade Polixenes to extend his visit. The guest then tries to flatter her by naming her a "sacred lady" who arouses in him temptations—to which she replies "Grace to boot," meaning that the gift of grace permeates her ladyship to correct any temptations he may have. Yet her own husband falls into jealousy when her talk succeeds in persuading the guest. Accused unjustly of a lustful motive, she is patient under slanderous condemnation and goes to prison with the comment that this action is "for my better grace." In Act 5 a repentant husband remembers her as being "as tender as infancy and grace." Meanwhile, her exiled child Perdita grows up "in grace" among shepherds, and bestows flowers of grace at a festival she hosts "as I have seen them do in Whitsun pastorals." An aura of Pentecost and divine grace surrounds her troth-plighting to Florizel, in which the lovers liken themselves to turtledoves and thus recall for us the Song of Songs with its overtones of gracious love.

As in the biblical poem, their love is soon tested by adversity and must undertake a voyage in demonstration of the faith expressed in the Song of Songs that "Many waters cannot quench love, neither can the floods drown it," since "Love is as strong as death" (8:6–7). Perdita's miraculous reunion with her father ensues. And here we cannot but note that a Gentleman concludes his report of it with the words: "Every wink of an eye, some new grace will be born." Those words echo St Paul's regarding the grace of resurrection: "In the twinkling of an eye, we shall all be changed" (1 Cor 15:52). In the following chapel scene, such a change is then enacted when an icon of Hermione comes alive as a body of flesh restored.

An important accompanying motif in the play is that of the Good Samaritan. Although not named as such, it occurs in various guises. One example is a subplot episode in 4.3 which G. W. Knight has termed a parody of the Good Samaritan. A shepherd's son traveling to town comes across a man grovelling on the ground who cries, "O, help me, help me!" When the shepherd bends down to show compassion, he has his purse stolen by the fellow who says he has been beaten by robbers. Here the real thief is the fraudulent Autolycus, a scapegrace prodigal whom Shakespeare has brought into his drama to serve as a low-comedy parallel to Leontes in the main plot. That is, just as Leontes called out for help from Hermione, who in stooping to help him got robbed by him of her purse (her good name and her baby), so Autolycus robs the naive shepherd. Autolycus goes on to parallel Leontes in many more ways—for instance, by peddling his trumperies to gullible ears as Leontes peddles to courtiers his trumped up nothings, and by singing of tumbling with doxies like a Leontes fantasizing about a "hobby-horse" wife.

And finally, like the Leontes who shipped off his own child to feed his jealousy, Autolycus decoys the shepherd onto a ship bound for foreign shores, hoping to profit by this roguery. But the ironic result is that providentially the young shepherd has his rank raised to "gentleman" when in the foreign land his "fardel" is opened revealing spiritual riches, whereas Autolycus finds himself left out in the cold and must penitently promise to amend his life if the shepherd will sponsor him with the prince. The shepherd then agrees to befriend Autolycus, thus returning good for evil, just as in the main plot Hermione and Paulina do in forgiving the Leontes who has abused them. These two women, as now wiser Good Samaritans than earlier, work for the recuperation of the self-wounded Leontes. Paulina in particular becomes a spiritual caretaker with pastoral skills such as one can find described, for instance, in St Gregory's *Pastoral Care*. The pastoral element in *The Winter's Tale* is more than the lovely springtime of nature in Bohemia. Whereas Robert Greene had subtitled his romance "The Triumph of Time," Shakespeare has turned this into a triumph of engraced human natures in time.

Paulina's first husband Antigonus perishes because of his faithlessness of cooperating with a tyrant in banishing Hermione's child. We hear Paulina warn: "For ever / Unvenerable be thy hands if thou / Tak'st up the princess" so long as the bastardly charge is on her. Yet Antigonus does so, and even relapses into believing this charge himself. That is why he gets eaten by a bear—the symbolic fate which in the Bible came on the foolish ones who mocked the prophet Elisha (2 Kgs

2:24). But Paulina, who grows spiritually from a prophetic defender of faith by denouncing evil into a pastoral mender of it like the figurative St Paul her name suggests, is at the end of the play given a second husband in the "priestlike" Camillo to provide a third and environing example of "turtledove" romance attuned to the Song of Songs.

Pieces of commentary by S. L. Bethell, Daryll Grantley, John Cox, and François Laroque make up our anthology. Bethell comments on how the dramatic movement of *The Winter's Tale* imitates Christian truth in its pattern of sin, repentance, and restoration, and how the oracle of Apollo becomes poetically a symbol of God's overruling providence. Grantley illuminates the religious import of the play by discussing its allegorical quality and many correspondences to its events that can be found in the Scriptural mystery cycles of English drama. He notes in Hermione's role not only an analogy to Christ under trial but also similarities to the woes of the Virgin Mary and the joys she bestows in legends of redemption. John Cox takes notice of aspects of the characterization of Leontes that have analogy to Herod's tyranny and to Joseph's transition from doubt to faith in medieval drama. Laroque notes Chris Hassel's mention of a performance of the play at Court on an Easter Tuesday and calls our attention to the apposite Scriptural lessons used in the church liturgy at Easter, especially if one supplements these with the lessons assigned for Innocents Day.

As supplementary, the reader will find particularly stimulating J. A. Bryant's exploration of the analogy between the general pattern of *The Winter's Tale* and St Paul's outline of the course of redemption. In Romans 11 the basic metaphor for making nature better is an art of grafting, by which the stock of a good olive tree, from which an original branch has been temporarily cut off, receives and makes fruitful some branches of wild olive, and also thereafter has regrafted into it the broken-off branch. In Shakespeare's play, Bryant would view Hermione and Perdita as "figuring" the good olive tree, and Leontes as the broken-off branch that is later grafted back into this tree, while Florizel and Polixenes are suggestive of the wild olive branches that are meanwhile grafted in to make them bearers of good fruit. That this metaphor enters *The Winter's Tale* as voiced first by Polixenes, who has no understanding of its application to himself, adds to the play's irony, as well as being suitable to the "Gentile" ignorance that Polixenes represents.

Robert Hellenga, in reviewing interpretations of the play that are limited to anthropological lore, finds these inadequate and prefers the "scandal" of Hermione's flesh-and-blood resurrection emphasized by Bryant. Similarly, Brian Cosgrove says that Hermione's resurrection outstrips time as do transcendental meanings in Christian doctrine, and that what the play asks of us is an "imaginative participation" rather than critical speculation. Cynthia Marshall comments that the statue intensifies a concern for the physical and presents Hermione's return as "far more concrete than the 'symbolic theory' would have it" (p. 41). David Kaula observes that the invitation given by Paulina to worship non-superstitiously an icon that "faith" can transform into flesh contrasts with the deceptive "trumpery" hawked by Autolycus, and recommends instead an understanding of Julio Romano's art of naturalistic realism.

The essays by S. R. Maveety and Roy Battenhouse examine the important differences from Greene's romance introduced by Shakespeare's design. One is the sudden madness of jealousy in Leontes, which Maveety says is explicable as a result of original sin and the fallen nature of man. In Christian terms, Leontes' fallen human nature so clouds his reason that he cannot be made to see the truth. Polixenes has a similar handicap, in Maveety's view, and his denial of any hereditary sin is rightly questioned by Hermione. Battenhouse argues that Shakespeare's theme of redemptive grace transforms Greene's story in all its aspects, and he gives particular attention to the developing function of the four "guardian" figures represented in the two shepherds, Camillo, and Paulina. Carolyn Asp suggests that the Lady Philosophy of Boethius can be seen in the curative counseling Paulina offers Leontes. Peter Milward and Derek Traversi both read the drama as a story of foolish sinfulness that is corrected and redeemed by grace.

## Supplementary bibliography

Asp, Carolyn. "Shakespeare's Paulina and the *Consolatio* Tradition," *Shakespeare Studies* 11 (1978), 145–58.

Battenhouse, Roy. "Theme and Structure in *The Winter's Tale*," *Shakespeare Survey* 33 (1980), 123–38.

Bryant, J. A., Jr. *Hippolyta's View* (1961), Ch. 13.

Cosgrove, Brian. "*The Winter's Tale* and the Limits of Criticism," *Studies: An Irish Quarterly Review* 66 (1977), 176–87.

Hellenga, Robert R. "The Scandal of *The Winter's Tale*," *English Studies* 57 (1976), 10–18.

Hoeniger, F. David. "The Meaning of *The Winter's Tale*," *University of Toronto Quarterly* 20 (1950), 11–26.

Iwasaki, Soji. "*Veritas Filia Temporis*," in *Icons in English Renaissance Drama* (Tokyo: The Renaissance Institute, 1992), pp. 1–12.

Kaula, David. "Autolycus' Trumpery," *Studies in English Literature* 16 (1976), 287–303.

Marshall, Cynthia. *Last Things and Last Plays: Shakespearean Eschatology* (1990), pp. 38–60.

Maveety, S. R. "What Shakespeare Did With *Pandosto*: An Interpretation of *The Winter's Tale*," *Pacific Coast Studies*, ed. Waldo NcNeir (1966), pp. 263–79.

Meldrum, Ronald. "Dramatic Intention in *The Winter's Tale*," *Humanities Association Bulletin* 19 (1968), 52–60.

Milward, Peter. "A Theology of Grace in *The Winter's Tale*," in *Shakespeare's Other Dimension* (Tokyo, 1989), pp. 102–24.

Traversi, Derek. *An Approach to Shakespeare*, 3rd edition (London: Hollis & Carter, 1969), II, 289–302.

Velie, Alan R. *Shakespeare's Repentance Plays* (Fairleigh Dickinson University Press, 1972), pp. 91–113.

*S. L. Bethell (1947)*

## Sin, Repentance, and Restoration [editor's title]

Shakespeare does not wholly avoid explicit reference to Christian dogma in *The Winter's Tale* and I hope, by examining the poetic development of the story, to show that it does in fact follow the Christian scheme of redemption. It is not a new mythology that the play presents—not a new interpretation of human experience but the old interpretation newly translated into terms of the romance and all the more faithfully for its synthesis of pagan beauty and Christian truth.

Leontes' sin comes unmotivated, but sin is necessarily without any truly rational foundation. *Quidquid petitur, petitur sub specie boni*: if, therefore, evil is chosen, evil has been seen as a good; everything has been seen in false perspective, so that such a choice must be unmotivated in the sense that it is devoid of adequate motive. Moreover, sinful thoughts such as this unwarranted sexual jealousy, though they may not in reality spring fully grown into the mind, may well emerge with baffling suddenness into the consciousness. We are thus shown Leontes' jealousy (a) metaphysically, as it appears *sub specie aeternitatis*, and (b) as it appears to Leontes himself and presumably to those about him. We are not shown its psychological growth, since its psychological origins are not in question.

The jealousy once asserted, we are given a close metaphysical study of it. The imagery suggests nerves which quiver unhealthily; beginning in imagination directed towards the supposed lovers ("paddling palms and pinching fingers" [1.2.115]), this hypersensitivity goes on to record the irritant effect of jealous thoughts which are to Leontes "goads, thorns, nettles, tails of wasps" (1.2.329). We hear later of sleeplessness—"Nor night nor day no rest" (2.3.1)—which, the physical result of a mental unease, is in Shakespeare the usual accompaniment of sin. Macbeth in murdering Duncan "murdered sleep" (2.2.36) and, as later he sought relief from insomnia in the liquidation of doubtful adherents, so Leontes says that once Hermione is burnt "a moiety of my rest / Might come to me again" (2.3.8).

The most fatal consequence of Leontes' evil opinion is his separation from the rest of the world; he becomes estranged not only from Hermione and Polixenes but from his children and from the whole court. Sin separates the sinner from God and what is God-like; at the same time, like every category of evil, not being of God it has no existence but is a negation or perversion of existence; such is the orthodox Christian opinion as most exactly expressed in St Thomas Aquinas (*S. T.* I.48.1). Leontes' sin is that he mistakes Hermione's graciousness for unlawful love. So long as he harbours this belief it governs his experience and distorts his vision; his sense of order and proportion is gone, so that his universe is no longer the common universe in which the others live but a dream world which he and he alone takes for reality:

> How blest am I
> In my just censure, in my true opinion! (2.1.36)

he says. But to Hermione he is dreaming, though his dream impinges dangerously upon the actual world: "My life stands in the level of your dreams" (3.2.82). Leontes replies with "Your actions are my dreams"—the perfect inversion of reality. Paulina with her reputation for plain speaking calls him "mad" (2.3.71), refers to his "weak-hinged fancy" (2.3.119). To be diseased in judgment so as to take good for ill is to have cast loose from reality; the real gravity of moral failure lies in its metaphysical implications. Practical ill consequences involving others must also follow from inhabiting a distorted world; Leontes piles up his score of sin in ordering the murder of Polixenes, in seeking the death of Hermione and in the exposure of his child; and the effects of his bad dream are felt by his wife and children, by Camillo, who is exiled, by Antigonus and his wife, Paulina, and by the whole nation, since their king is now without an heir.

Hermione's clear vision, firmness and patience contrast strongly with the ill-judged precipitancy of her husband:

> How will this grieve you,
> When you shall come to clearer knowledge, that
> You thus have publish'd me! Gentle my lord,
> You scarce can right me throughly then to say
> You did mistake. (2.1.96)

Here are the Christian virtues. She goes to prison for her "better grace" (2.1.122) and the court, as she goes, spontaneously protest her innocence.

The short scene beginning Act 3 marks a turning point in the play. The oracle of Apollo is poetically built up into a symbol of God's overruling providence. We have (in lines 3–8) a number of epithets evocative of religious awe: "celestial," "grave" and especially "ceremonious, solemn and unearthly." The whole speech with its reference to priestly garments and the offering of a sacrifice, together with the epithets just quoted, sounds almost like a description of the Mass. Power is expressed in

> the ear-deafening voice o' the oracle,
> Kin to Jove's thunder, (3.1.9)

which, Cleomenes says, "so surprised my sense, / That I was nothing"—the familiar mystical annihilation of self in the presence of God. The rest of the scene, in which the oracle is discussed in relation to Hermione, further establishes this religious awe ("rare, pleasant, speedy... Great Apollo Turn all to the best!... Apollo's great divine... gracious be the issue!"). Dion's last words—"And gracious be the issue!" (line 22)—remind us of the repeated references to grace in previous scenes.

At her trial Hermione remains patient and dignified towards men, humble and strong in faith towards God—a pattern of Christian sanctity:

> if powers divine
> Behold our human actions, as they do,
> I doubt not then but innocence shall make
> False accusation blush and tyranny
> Tremble at patience. (3.2.29)

In the second line the last three words are strongly accented and being monosyllabic demand slow enunciation; in the first folio they were printed in brackets for emphasis. Her whole trust is in the oracle of Apollo:

> Your honours all,
> I do refer me to the oracle:
> Apollo be my judge! (3.2.115)

Leontes now adds to his sin a blasphemous disbelief in revelation: "There is no truth at all i' the oracle" (3.2.141). At once he is punished with the death of Mamillius and the apparent death of Hermione. Hermione's sixteen years' separation from her beloved husband is in obedience to the oracle, for the king must live without an heir unless Perdita should be restored to him. It is a voluntary sacrifice, but the divine gifts to humanity are in part contingent upon such self-abnegation in the saints. As for Mamillius, we are made to see how widespread the effect of sin may be, since the death of Mamillius leaves Leontes without an heir and this is an unsatisfactory state of affairs for the whole land; in Act 5 Leontes still thinks of the sin "which was so much, / That heirless it hath made my kingdom" (5.1.9).

Shakespeare has reserved for his last scene the final reconciliation with Hermione. Hermione and Perdita meet and we are to remember that it is the ascetic discipline of Hermione, her obedience to the apparently unreasonable message of the oracle, that has been the instrument, under divine providence, of her daughter's safe return. Florizel and Perdita, whose troth-plight was accomplished by the direction of heaven (5.3.150), have brought new life to Hermione and Leontes and to the whole no longer fatal kingdom of Sicilia; but this new life, this natural vigour, has been supernaturally bestowed and the gracious figure of Hermione, posed on her pedestal, reminds us that the natural is subordinate to and dependent upon spiritual power.

The restoration of Hermione, her coming back as from the dead, is a carefully prepared symbol of spiritual and actual resurrection, in which alone true reconciliation may be attained. Hermione's is not a genuine resurrection; the very staginess of this "statue" scene acknowledges the inadequacy of dramatic means. The poetry itself is quiet and serene in rhythm, simple yet profound in meaning. There is a holy quiet over the scene and Hermione revives to music, so often in Shakespeare a symbol of the heavenly and good, as all stridency suggested evil to him. But the strife of good and evil is not forgotten:

> O royal piece
> There's magic in thy majesty, which has
> My evils conjured to remembrance and
> From thy admiring daughter took the spirits,
> Standing like stone with thee. (5.3.38)

There is an undercurrent here ("evils," "conjured," "spirits") suggestive of the powers of darkness. This tinge of unease in the suggestion of black magic is just enough to point back to the perennial moral and metaphysical struggle in the world. In the resurrection the struggle is past; the spell is lawful and actions shall be holy. This last scene most obviously expresses the future life in terms of the present; its rarified unearthliness is a foretaste of heaven. The themes of redemption and regeneration, now explicit, are related to a poetic suggestion of fulfilment beyond this life.

From *"The Winter's Tale": A Study* (London: Staples Press, 1947), pp. 76–87, 102–104, excerpts abridged. Permission from Harper Collins Ltd.

*Daryll Grantley (1986)*

## *The Winter's Tale* and Early Religious Drama

Even a cursory comparison of the story line of *The Winter's Tale* with that of its source, Greene's *Pandosto*, reveals just how strongly Shakespeare was seeking in the play to underline the idea of redemption. He was prepared to make important changes with respect to the portrayal of the erring king and victim queen, allowing both to survive at the end of the play. In the source story, Pandosto not only had compromised whatever moral ground he had regained through his remorse for his sin by developing a lust for his daughter Fawnia and by his intended cruelty to the girl, her adoptive father, and the servant, but also ultimately had committed suicide. The source story is therefore fairly straightforwardly a tragedy; Shakespeare does not allow this tragedy to occur and also makes the effective climax to Greene's story, the discovery of the lost daughter and the resolution which that brings with it, take place offstage while what takes its climactic place in the play is the "resurrection" of the queen, a scene which both makes powerful use of visual image and is infused with feelings of reverence and blessing. By reducing all the intrigue found in *Pandosto* to the barest minimum in the play, he both makes the didactic point more clearly and elevates the important characters to a plane consistent with their role in the drama of redemption.

The clearly religious and didactic nature of Shakespeare's conception of *The Winter's Tale* appears to have influenced his choice of appropriate form for the play. In dramatizing his theme, Shakespeare emphasizes that he is telling a story not only by the use of strikingly romantic elements but by the title itself, its echo in 2.1.25, and the suggestion in 5.2.28 and 62 that the events of the narrative are like an "old tale." He seems to be presenting us with an illustrative story or *exemplum* much as a preacher would in a sermon. However, his medium is not homily or prose narrative but *drama*, and the closest parallel in this medium is the tradition of religious drama which extended late into the sixteenth century and probably formed a significant part of the dramatic images of Shakespeare's youth. Like *The Winter's Tale*, this drama had as its theme the fall and redemption of man. It was also sufficiently distanced in time to be a source of appropriate forms and images for the dramatization of the "old tale," but was not yet so distant as to be totally unfamiliar to the audiences of the day.

Leontes is given no comprehensible reason for the onset of his jealousy. However, what is important within the scheme of redemption is not the genesis of the jealousy but the fact of the sin and its consequences. Leontes' characterization serves this purpose well; the very name "Leontes" (which Shakespeare did not find in his source) suggests an allegorical type in that it is highly appropriate to the exemplification of kingly wrath in the first part of the play, for it involves connotations of leonine pride and ferocity. However, as in several moral plays and interludes which deal with the progress of a generalized mankind figure through the world, we have also at the opening of *The Winter's Tale* an assertion of innocence. Polixenes' description of his and Leontes' childhood innocence encompasses the ideas of both guiltlessness and unknowingness (1.2.68–70). But unknowingness implies weakness—a common attribute of the innocence of mankind figures at their entries in moral plays and interludes. The assertion of childhood innocence at the beginning of *The Winter's Tale* is therefore in itself a preparation for the fall of Leontes: unknowingness offers no resistance to sin.

Polixenes, of course, shares the initial innocence of Leontes and significantly so since he also must undergo a fall and "redemption" in the course of the play. The "falls" of Leontes and Polixenes are clearly paralleled. In both cases the audience is aware of their states of mind before they are revealed to the other characters, use is made of sudden and dramatic revelation, and they make dire threats of death; both men try to use Camillo to serve their ends, and in each case there is the timely flight of intended victims. The parallel dramatic action supplies, in effect, a second fall and ultimate perception of error. The pattern thus is strongly reminiscent of the repetitive actions of fall and repentance in the interludes and moral plays.

Much of the drama of the change which comes over Leontes derives from the completeness with which he gives in to the feelings with which he becomes prey.

His tone is consistently frenzied, irrational, and anguished. He is in the grip of wrath, a classic victim or *ira* whose effects he exemplifies. Appropriately, his dramatic identity at this point is defined by threats: against Polixenes, to Camillo, to Paulina, to Hermione, and against Perdita. Under these circumstances the revelation by the oracle of Hermione's innocence cannot be expected to have any effect. His point of reference is not the world outside himself but the error which ensnares him, and it is as an exemplification of the effects of this sin that Leontes derives his dramatic force. When the change comes about in him, it happens as suddenly and completely as had his fall, again reminiscent of the sudden switch to complete commitment to repentance.

Polixenes also gives himself over to anger to an extent which, regarded in purely psychological terms, seems excessive: the threats to have a girl's "beauty scratch'd with briars" when he had earlier been expressing unfeigned admiration for her, and to execute an innocent shepherd. What interests us here, however, is not so much the psychology of Polixenes as the contrast and conflict between the older man, prey to the sin of wrath, and the vulnerable innocence of the young lovers: they are figures in a dramatized moral scheme. As in the case of Leontes, it is the suddenness of the move from a state of guiltlessness to one of error which recalls the earlier homiletic drama.

If Leontes and to some extent Polixenes are cast in the roles of the mankind figures of moral interludes, then the female characters are even more clearly constructed in terms of moral forces. Hermione is probably the easiest to see in a symbolic role: this becomes more apparent as she carries an increasing emblematic burden during the progress of the action. We see her first as wife and hostess (1.2) and mother (2.1), but then as Leontes arraigns her, and especially in the trial scene, she accrues moral, even mythic importance by being elevated to a "patient Griselda" figure through her physical and mental sufferings in prison, the calm dignity of her replies, the irrational vehemence of her attacker, and the audience's conviction of her innocence. The revelation by oracle of her innocence, her subsequent "death," and her apparition in a dream to Antigonus help further to transform her from a human character to a saintly symbol of wronged innocence and thus to prepare us for her role in the final scene as a figure of grace and forgiveness. She derives her dramatic power precisely from the allegorical significance she accrues, and thus is the "miracle" at the end of the play made acceptable and meaningful.

Perdita can also be seen in terms of a series of morally charged images. Even when she is a baby Paulina attempts to use her mere presence as "pure innocence" to cure the sin of the king (2.2.39–42). If Hermione grows into an allegorical role, Perdita is thus more or less in one from the start. That she is an important part of the redemptive process is evident first because she, like her mother, is associated with grace. Time refers to her before her entry in Act 4 as "now grown in grace/ Equal with wond'ring" (1.24–25), an allusion to her beauty but clearly with other implications as well. And when she first greets Camillo and Polixenes her words are "Grace and remembrance be to you both" (4.4.76). Second, there is the sense of other-worldliness which sets her apart from others from the time of her birth: in 3.3 the Shepherd sees her as a gift. . . . Third, there is her strong association with Nature, established even before her birth; as Paulina states, "This child was prisoner to the womb, and is / By law and process of great nature, thence / Freed and enfranchis'd" (2.2.59–61). But the connection is more fully developed in 4.4, with all its suggestions of natural virtue and harmony, growth, change, and healing. Fourth, she represents youth and new innocence to redeem maturity from its guilt, but she is also the means by which what is lost to Leontes is replaced.

Paulina is probably the most straightforward moral figure of all in *The Winter's Tale*. If Leontes occupies something of the position of a mankind figure, then she is in the role of his conscience. Not only is she a powerful creation but she is Shakespeare's own and is not found in Greene's story. She is totally fearless in her haranguing of the king in 2.3, and what characterizes her throughout the play is the single-mindedness of her concern that the king should return to and remain on the path of virtue. . . . Leontes puts himself into Paulina's hands. At the end of 3.2 he asks her to "lead me / To these sorrows," and when we next see him, at the beginning of Act 5, she is still guiding him, reminding him of the woman he "kill'd" and advising him not to remarry. . . . It is indicative of Paulina's importance in the story, derived entirely from her key role in the scheme of repentance, that she has the penultimate speech in the play and that Leontes' final words are addressed to her.

Autolycus most resembles the vice in his direct revelations to the audience of his own dishonesty. Echoing the practice in allegorical plays of having moral figures declare their own natures, Autolycus not only associates himself with roguery but also derides virtue. After his successful activities at the fair, he ridicules "Honesty" and "Trust" in a speech (4.4.596–605) which recalls traditional images of the mountebank stretching back to Chaucer's Pardoner. His commentary when he decides to help Florizel is important:

> The prince himself is about a piece of iniquity (stealing away from his father with his clog at his heels): if I thought it were a piece of honesty to acquaint the king withal, I would not do't: I hold it the more knavery to conceal it; and therein am I constant to my profession. (4.4.678–83)

Autolycus, in a manner characteristic of the vice, establishes a rapport with the audience not merely through his regular and extended addresses to them (in 4.3.1–31; 4.4.596–620, 670–83, 832–43; 5.2.113–23), but also through his verbal facility which manifests itself in his deception of the Clown in 4.3, his salesmanship at the fair in 4.4, and in his deception of the Shepherd and the Clown later in the same scene—an act which involves a great deal of gratuitous theatricality on his part.

That the narrative material in *The Winter's Tale* itself suggests the appropriateness of reference to the images of scriptural drama is fairly clear. The story as presented by Shakespeare has many correspondences with the events dramatized in the Cycles: there is a fall from grace at the beginning, the trial and "sacrifice" of an innocent, a birth through which redemption is achieved, a ranting tyrant from whose wrath the infant is saved through exile to another country, and a final "resurrection." While it is pointless to attempt to work out a comprehensive schematic parallel between the events and figures of *The Winter's Tale* and the Christian story of sin and salvation, it is interesting to note Shakespeare's use of images from this drama which are powerful because of the traditional responses they provoke as well as because of their eschatological associations.

Leontes in his rage recalls one of the most dramatically striking of the characters in scriptural drama: Herod.... The fact that Leontes orders the baby Perdita to be thrown into the fire and threatens to dash her brains out with his own hands cannot but have reminded Shakespeare's contemporaries of the figure of Herod with all its diabolic associations. This correspondence is confirmed by Paulina's stress upon the innocence of the baby and by the child's ultimately being taken abroad and thus saved, as in the Flight into Egypt. Mamillius is another innocent who is killed by the actions of Leontes, albeit indirectly, but even this corresponds with the dramatized Herod, since the plays include the murder in error of Herod's own son as well as the king's consequent anguish.

Leontes himself shares another quality with the Herod of the Cycles: a tendency to threaten and bully inferiors. Herod frequently threatens messengers, counsellors, and his soldiers in his rage in much the same way that Leontes coerces Camillo and Antigonus with threats of torture and tries to terrify Paulina. As with Herod, Leontes' wrath is exacerbated by the revelation that his plans have been foiled by the non-cooperation of others.... And Leontes, especially in the encounter with Paulina in 2.2, descends into hurling insults at her ("mankind witch," "dame Partlet," "callat," "gross hag"), at the baby ("bastard," "brat"), and at Antigonus, whose beard he pulls ("dotard," "lozel," "traitor").

For the character and role of Hermione too, the scriptural drama provides many dramatic images. For the trial scene there are several parallels to the representation of the trial of Christ. The situation is similar: on the one hand, there is the innocent accused, and, on the other, the judge whose decision miscarries justice while at the same time he is also concerned to exculpate or at least justify himself.... Christ accepts his death and cannot be intimidated by his accusers, as his reply to them in Towneley XXII shows: "Sich powere has thou nought / To wyrk thi will thus with me/ Bot from my fader that is broght / Oone-fold god in persons thre" (116–17). So Hermione welcomes the punishment with which she is threatened: "Sir, sport your threats: / The bug which you would fright me with, I seek" (3.2.91–92). Further, Christ's prayer to his father for forgiveness for his persecutors is echoed by Hermione's wish that her father were alive to pity her plight without taking vengeance:

> The Emperor of Russia was my father:
> O that he were alive, and here beholding
> His daughter's trial! that he did but see
> The flatness of my misery, yet with eyes
> Of pity, not revenge! (3.2.119–23)

There is, of course, also the resurrection scene at the end of the play. In the Resurrection plays of the Cycles the scene is that of the three Marys' approach to the tomb and Mary Magdalene's encounter with the gardener who reveals himself to be Christ. The scene in *The Winter's Tale* is very similar in terms of the images it presents and the feelings that they generate: first a reverential group approach to the statue, then the focus on the reactions of the single individual, Leontes, whose emotions are most powerfully affected, and finally the revelation. All this involves an emotional build-up akin to that in the Mary Magdalene scenes, and there is even a suggestion of a *noli me tangere* in Paulina's prevention of Leontes' kissing the statue.

If Hermione's scenes recall the dramatic presentation of Christ's life, her role in the story also has correspondences with the life of the Virgin Mary: she too is the bearer of a child in adverse circumstances, through the medium of whom redemption is brought about. Even the accusations of adultery bring to mind Mary's plight in all the extant Cycles in which her account of the Annunciation is doubted by Joseph, who berates her for her alleged unfaithfulness until he is enlightened through a vision. It is likely that the mere presence of the pregnant Hermione on stage would have recalled to Shakespeare's contemporaries the images, which had commonly appeared in both drama and the visual arts, of the most famous pregnant woman of all. Additionally, the constant association of Hermione with grace in *The Winter's Tale* is reminiscent of the salutation of the angel Gabriel to the Virgin in the Gospels: "Ave Maria, gratia plena, Dominus tecum," words which are always included in the Annunciation plays. But perhaps the most telling association of Hermione with the Virgin is her final long speech at her trial:

> The crown and comfort of my life, your favour,
> I do give lost, for I do feel it gone,
> But know not how it went. My second joy,
> And first-fruits of my body, from his presence
> I am barr'd, like one infectious. My third comfort
> (Starr'd most unluckily) is from my breast,
> The innocent milk in its most innocent mouth,
> Hal'd out to murder. (3.2.94–101)

This passage recalls the medieval tradition of listing both the joys and the sorrows of the Virgin. Here Hermione's joys are turned into her sorrows rather as the Virgin's sorrows were derived from the same source as her joys.... The "miracle" of the coming to life of the statue can possibly be seen to echo the legends of the miracles associated with the Virgin and frequently occurring as a result of prayers and offerings to her statue.

Perdita's role in the play clearly has suggestions of the Christ story in it. Enough is made of the new beginning which her birth entails—in the Shepherd's words, "Now bless thyself: thou met'st with things dying, I with things new-born" (3.3.112–13).... The presence of the Shepherd and the baby is sufficient to call to mind images from Nativity plays and through that association to suggest the rebirth of hope on a spiritual level. It is fairly clear to see from this instance why allusions to (or images from) the early religious drama suit Shakespeare's purpose: without the necessity of distortion of the narrative or heavily laden verbal symbolism, they invest the events and characters of *The Winter's Tale* with a spiritual dimension which is important to the theme of redemption in the play.

From "*The Winter's Tale* and Early Religious Drama," *Comparative Drama* 20 (1986), 17–34 abridged.

*John D. Cox (1989)*

## Medieval Precedent in *The Winter's Tale* [editor's title]

Like Herod, Leontes is a slaughterer of innocents, and a stage pattern from Herod's slaughter in the mystery plays in fact appears in *The Winter's Tale* when Paulina enters with the infant Perdita in her arms and boldly confronts the raging Leontes (2.3). In several of the cycles (including the Coventry fragments), the mothers of Herod's intended victims verbally abuse, and sometimes even attack, the soldiers who are trying to destroy the babies in their arms. Critics have noticed the strange mixture of violent farce and horrific inhumanity in Paulina's braving of Leontes. What has gone unremarked is the dramaturgical precedent this effect has in medieval depictions of the slaughter of the innocents.

Leontes' tyranny looks back not only to medieval drama but to Shakespeare's mature tragedies.... Both Leontes and Macbeth achieve the same result in their assault on innocent sufferers: they destroy their own innocence in the process. "What we chang'd / Was innocence for innocence," asserts Polixenes, of his boyhood friendship with Leontes (1.2.68–69). Nothing threatens this friendship until Leontes is seized with the insane jealousy that provokes his abuse of Hermione. Then follows alienation, sleeplessness, and despair, the condition of Macbeth, as well as the condition of a tyrant like Cain in the old plays, when he cuts himself off from the source of life and love, the "great bond" of human community.

Leontes' tyranny and sexual jealousy conflate two traditions of Herod that Shakespeare could have known, one popular and the other elite. The medieval ranter and persecutor of innocents was still widely reputed in the early seventeenth century, and Shakespeare may actually have seen him in Coventry as a child, but another Herod story had been published for the first time in English only ten years before Shakespeare wrote *The Winter's Tale*. Thomas Lodge's translation of Josephus' *Antiquities of the Jews* (1602) includes the story of Herod and his wife Mariamne, which had received numerous dramatic treatments on the continent in the sixteenth century, most of them in the Senecan vein. Two contemporary English plays show the influence of this story, though neither seems to have been staged. The first is Elizabeth Carey's *Tragedy of Miriam* (ca. 1604; published 1613), and the second is *The Second Maiden's Tragedy*, which is almost exactly contemporary with *The Winter's Tale* (i.e., 1610–1611). . . . Mariamne's story is relevant to Hermione's in that it deals with Herod's morbid sexual suspicion of his wife (with no basis in fact), his eventual trial of her and order for her execution, and his profound remorse after her death.

Leontes' tale finally has more than a winter (unlike Herod's, Othello's, or Macbeth's), and Leontes' resemblance to Joseph extends to the transformation of doubt into faith. In both cases, this transformation depends on a child that is rejected *in utero* and unexpectedly restores its father's well-being. The paradox of the child redeeming the father is at the heart of all the plays of Joseph's doubt, and it reappears in another form in *The Winter's Tale* when Perdita's escape to Sicily with Florizel becomes the means of her father's reconciliation with Polixenes and Hermione. The medieval precedent is almost certainly at work here, because the pregnant Hermione is consistent with Shakespeare's stage use of pregnant women as symbols of comic hope. In *Measure for Measure,* Juliet is sullied by Angelo's harsh pursuit of the "old law," though he cannot meet its standards himself. When she appears in the last scene of the play, however, her baby has been transformed by the subsequent action from a symbol of public shame to a symbol of new life and reconciliation. In *All's Well That Ends Well,* Helena's pregnancy has the same kind of ambiguity: from one perspective, it is a product of Bertram's blind lust, which is the play's analogue to Claudio's "too much liberty," Leontes' "bawdy planet," and Joseph's "Frensche gyse." Viewed another way, however, Helena's pregnancy is a miracle that awakens her husband's faith, as Leontes' faith is awakened by a theatrical miracle at the end of *The Winter's Tale*, and Joseph's is awakened by the angel. In *Pericles*, Thaisa appears in dumb show, pregnant with Marina (3 Chorus s.d.), again presaging a father's redemption by a child still enwombed. Both Mary and Hermione courageously endure harsh suspicion, and reconciliation is effected in both cases not only by a once rejected child but by the fathers' repentance and their serene wives' readiness to forgive.

From *Shakespeare and The Dramaturgy of Power,* pp. 210–12 abridged. By permission of Princeton University Press, copyright 1989.

*François Laroque (1982)*

## Christian Liturgy and *The Winter's Tale* [editor's title]

In his book on *Renaissance Drama and the English Church Year* (1979), Chris Hassel establishes a distinction between two main types of correlations between the liturgical tradition and the plays and masques performed on a given festival. The first he calls "genetic" to describe "each work which was clearly named or written for festival performance." The second category, which he calls "affective," simply designates the larger number of plays and masques with no specific or straightforward correlation with the festival day of their performance at Court, but which offered easily perceivable parallels with a biblical or liturgical passage. In the case of what this critic calls an "unusual fitness," the Master of the Revels could put the play on the bill of the ceremonies of the day; and among other examples, Hassel mentions *The Winter's Tale* as "particularly apposite . . . for Easter Tuesday." The source of this correlation is the record of a Court performance on Easter Tuesday 1618 which is listed by G. E. Bentley in *The Jacobean and Caroline Stage*. Indeed one can only agree that the parallel between Christ's resurrection and the coming to life of the statue of Hermione is as apposite as it is inevitable in our Christian culture.

According to *The Book of Common Prayer*, among the lessons prescribed to be read for Tuesday in Easter week one finds Luke 24:1–12 for matins and 1 Cor 15 for evensong. Now fairly close correspondences in words, imagery, and situations may be found between the first ten verses of Luke 24 and the last act of *The Winter's Tale*. The word "stone" is used to designate both Hermione's statue (Leontes addresses it as *dear stone* in 5.3.24) and Christ's sepulchre, while Paulina, a Greek version of Mary Magdalene, indirectly evokes the gaping sepulchre of resurrected Christ when she declares "I'll fill up your grave" (5.3.101). Furthermore, the repetition of the phrase "like an old tale" used by the Second and Third Gentlemen to convey the mixture of surprise and doubt brought about by the unexpected news of the fulfilment of the Oracle does sound like an echo of Luke 24:12, "And their words seemed to them as idle tales and they believed them not," when the holy women reveal to the apostles that the body of the Lord Jesus was not to be found in the sepulchre and that he was risen from the dead.

If we now consider the lesson to be read on the same day for evensong prayer, 1 Cor 15, we will find another interesting parallel between the Gospel and the play, particularly in verses 35–7 which run:

> But some man will say, How are the dead raised up? and with what body do
> they come? *Thou* fool, that which thou sowest is not quickened, except it die:

And that which thou sowest, thou sowest not that body that shall be, but bare
grain, it may chance of wheat, or of some other *grain.* (35–7)

To convey the abstract idea of resurrection, St Paul resorts to images borrowed
from the agricultural and seasonal cycles, which transform the hidden corn seed
into a green stalk rising above the surface of the earth. This short passage seems
quite close to Shakespeare's dramatization of the return of spring to the earth
through the celebration of the shepherds' feast which is presided over by Perdita-
Proserpina, the corn maiden. The conjunction of pagan and Christian symbolism
at the time of the Easter liturgy is even more evident when one reads the following
gloss for Easter Sunday from Robert Nelson's widely used *Companion for the Festivals and Fasts of the Church of England* (1704): "the consideration of things without us, the natural courses of variations in the creatures, raise the probability of
our resurrection. The day dies into night and rises with the next morning; the
summer dies into winter, when the earth becomes a general sepulchre; but when
the spring appears, nature revives and flourishes; the corn lies buried in the
ground, and being corrupted revives and multiplies." This might well be considered as a general description of the essential symbolic motifs developed in *The
Winter's Tale.*

So far, the analogies which have been suggested between the religious symbolism of the play and the liturgy of the Christian year only concern the summer half
of the play and the final reconciliation scene. No correlations have yet been established between the texts of the Christian liturgy and the winter half, in spite of the
similarities which can be pointed out between Christ's and Perdita's life schemes.
Christ's birth in winter is followed by his death and resurrection in the spring,
thirty-three years later, when he is reunited with the Father in Heaven. Perdita,
also born in winter-time, spends sixteen years in another world before she is allowed to recover her true parents in the most miraculous way (an equivalent of
resurrection). In that specific context, Leontes' sudden fit of jealousy and suspi-
cions about a new-born child, leading to the death of the innocents (Mamillius
dies and Perdita is abandoned on a desert shore full of wild beasts), recall Herod's
tyranny and his ordering the slaughter of "all the children that were in Bethlehem." The flight from Israel into Egypt and the navigation from Sicilia to Bohemia are also comparable ordeals for the infant Christ and the newly-born Perdita.
The liturgical source for this is to be found in Matthew 2:13–18, which was the
reading from the Gospel prescribed for the celebration of the Innocents' Day (28
December) according to *The Book of Common Prayer.*

In the words of Chris Hassel, "error seems to have been the traditional hallmark of Innocents' celebrations," as was fit for the period of licence and misrule
which characterized the festivities of the twelve days of Christmas, and the same
author goes on to say that "until the time of the Spectator, Innocents was considered . . . 'the most unlucky day in the calendar.'" In the first half of *The Winter's*

*Tale*, Leontes' jealousy is a form of tragic error just as the confusion that follows its outbreak is a consequence of misrule, that is of his bad government and tyranny. Moreover, the sudden, uncanny fit of sexual insanity on his part is seen by the women as the effect of some evil astronomical conjunction. Paulina speaks of "dangerous, unsafe lunes i' th' king" (2.2.30), while Hermione exclaims:

> There's some ill planet reigns:
> I must be patient till the heavens look
> With an aspect more favourable. (2.1.105–07)

These lines, echoing the unlucky character of the day in popular prognostications, would have seemed particularly relevant for a performance on Holy Innocents' Day. On the other hand, the fact that Childermas, as this festival was also known, was normally associated with folly and rejoicing may be taken as a suggestion to the audience that comedy is not very far behind the furies of the tragic tempest. Indeed tragedy and comedy are very often side by side in this Janus-like play, which does not simply divide into a tragic and a comic half. As in the Miracle plays, laughter lies close to horror and things profane and things sacred sometimes mix to produce a grotesque atmosphere.

Another central motif of this liturgical festival of the Innocents is described by Chris Hassel as that of "the dispersal and reunion of families." One of the lessons prescribed for the day at matins was Jeremiah 31:1–17, which, if present to the minds of those who were watching the play on this festival occasion, could have been applied to Leontes' blighted kingdom as bringing hope of its future regeneration. As it prophesies both the return of the people of Israel "from the North country" and the return of fertility to the earth in a merry dance of shepherds that will put an end to sorrow, it might have been used by whoever was aware of the correspondence, as a foreshadowing of the happy reconciliation of Act 5:

> Behold, I will bring them *from the north country*, and gather them *from the coasts of the earth*, and with them the blind and the lame, the woman with child and her that travaileth with child together; *a great company shall return thither*. . . . Therefore they shall come and sing in the height of Zion, and shall flow together to the goodness of the Lord. . . . (Jer 31:8,12)

From "Pagan Ritual, Christian Liturgy, and Folk Customs in *The Winter's Tale*," *Cahiers Elisabéthains* 22 (Oct. 1982), 25–33; excerpt of pp. 27–29.

## Comment and bibliography

This last of Shakespeare's comedies has as its theme, as do his earlier ones, the workings of divine providence in history. The play's hero Prospero is both a beneficiary of providence and its agent. He tells us at the start that his experience has included paradoxically his being "heaved" into exile but also his having been "blessedly helped" to an island by aid from a charitable Gonzalo and the heaven-inspired smile of Miranda. In order to correct past losses he has developed during his twelve years on the island a project for mediating to his adversaries an experience of storm and miracle similar to his own providential ordeal. He can do this because his studies have given him arts of magic, by which he can cast spells and minister fictive ordeals that test and educate. In this respect Prospero is a dramaturge, like Shakespeare himself, and his project amounts to a justification of a playwright's art, with the "island" serving as his theatre.

By the end of the play Prospero has accomplished the twin goals of his project. He has brought his injurer Alonso to repent and make restitution, and he has brought Alonso's son Ferdinand to a chaste betrothal to Miranda. The denouement is the apocalyptic moment: Alonso finds himself rewarded with the discovery of his supposedly lost son, now alive and royally betrothed, while Ferdinand is rewarded by recovering a father he supposed dead and, more importantly, by discovering the "second life" he has been given in Miranda by "immortal providence," along with a second "father," Prospero. A homecoming of family reunion crowns this epiphany, with Gonzalo offering celebratory praise to the gods for having "chalked the way" to each one's finding of "ourselves." Worship is thus rightly given to Heaven, rather than to Prospero. He has but served as Heaven's agent, and to complete his task he has had to put away his arts of magic and his role of schoolmaster so that each of his protegés may find in redemptive reality itself the basis of inner joy. The limitations of human art are clearly acknowledged by Shakespeare at the same time that art's propaedeutic value is demonstrated.

The story, moreover, has a third level in its low-comedy subplot which concludes with a surprising declaration by Caliban that he will henceforth "seek for grace." The conversion of this natural savage to a desiring of supernatural grace seems a change greater than Prospero himself expected. Here is a creature of bastard parentage and disproportioned manners, whom Antonio holds in contempt as "plain fish" and whose demi-devil nature Prospero had despaired of raising to true humanity through nurture. Incontinent in his passions, Caliban forgets gratitude when moved by greedy appetite and uses for cursing the language taught him by kindly instructors. He is in religion superstitious, ready to worship as a god any man from the moon who feeds him dreams of power. Exploitative "civilized" courtiers can easily turn him into an addict of the bottle who would burn books. Prospero terms him "this thing of darkness," yet acknowledges this darkness as belonging to himself. Indeed, Caliban can be said to embody a disordered nature such as theologians might ascribe to original sin. Prospero's own moments of anger and impatience can be understood by us as his occasional lapsings into the moral weakness of an unregenerate self. He himself needs the sight of Gonzalo in tears and the compassionate words of Ariel to empower his will to accomplish his intention to forgive Alonso. And if in Prospero's case the mending of the gap between good sense and the practice of it is aided by neighboring examples of noble behavior, may not the same be true of Caliban? Experience can teach what books cannot, namely, the emergent reality of a higher good. And this, we may suppose, is happening when Caliban beholds his "fine master" exercising mercy and providing a contrast to the dull fools who led him into a stinking pond. We recall in the earlier Caliban a liking for sweet music and fresh springs, and it is this lurking capacity to transcend his dehumanizing crudeness that flowers when education comes by his recognizing his mistakes. The truth of the play's theme, that providence permits us to fall in order to prepare us for grace, is thus illustrated in Caliban's case no less than in Prospero's own. And Prospero's acknowledgement of a frailty in himself that requires recourse to grace is a benefit brought him through experience.

Voyage literature in general provided Shakespeare precedents for his story of shipwreck and strange adventure. But especially timely were some narratives by English voyagers regarding the wreck of their ship named *Sea-Adventure* on Bermuda in 1609. Miraculously the voyagers were enabled to repair their ship and return home, educated by having experienced "an Egyptian night" that revealed God's providence. God made the hideous place—so one of the published pamphlets declared—"the means of our deliverance." And the writer went on to affirm the Augustinian adage that "What seems a punishment is a medicine."

As an analogue to Prospero's role, Christian auditors at the Globe may well have recalled the story of Joseph. This archetypal dreamer in the book of Genesis, we may remember, was exiled to Egypt by envious brothers who resented his proud aloofness and privileged position. But Egypt educated Joseph, and when circumstances brought his brothers there he hid from them while putting them through ordeals until he brought out remorse in one of them. Then he unmasked and welcomed them to a family reunion with the reconciling words, "Ye thought evil against me, but God meant it unto good" (Gn 50:20). Prospero's attitude is evidently similar, as is also his moral growth from pride to compassionate beneficence.

At the play's beginning Prospero confesses his past neglect of office when rapt in secret studies. Christian playgoers might recall at this point Augustine's dictum:

"No man has a right to lead such a life of contemplation as to forget in his own case the service due his neighbor; nor has any man a right to be so immersed in active life as to neglect the contemplation of God" (*City of God* XIX.18). Prospero's ability to keep in balance the two responsibilities is tested in the fulfilling of his island project. Its contemplative aspect is retained, we note, in the visionary betrothal-masque bestowed on Ferdinand as "some vanity of mine art," but is broken off when Prospero remembers a conspiracy he must deal with. As his basic purpose then "gathers to a head," he acknowledges the limits of his art and puts aside his magician's cloak as preface to the practical action of forgiving Alonso and revealing to him the marriage match that will benefit both houses. He then announces a return to Milan, where his "every third thought" will be the contemplating of his mortality. And his Epilogue asks our prayers. The balance is properly Christian.

Of the five pieces of commentary selected for our anthology, all touch more or less on Shakespeare's dependence on biblical and liturgical paradigms. E. J. Devereux discerns a sacramental quality in the play's imagery. Its language of natural phenomena, he notes, functions as the sign of mysteries—water suggesting a baptism, and the banquet a holy communion. Ariel as a spirit of fire and air mediates a purifying fire and heavenly music, while Caliban's earthiness suggests a nature fallen in original sin. George Slover follows Devereux in reading Shakespeare's language as having a sacramental meaning. The dramatist, he explains, has used his knowledge of nature's processes to construct a "tragical comedy" analogous to that experienced by the Elizabethan voyagers to Virginia. Their interpretation of history in the light of biblical precedents underlies the fictional ordeal Prospero constructs for mediating the work of divine grace. He is a benevolent magus who imitates the "play" of the Magnum Magus in order to awaken faith in redemptive realities.

Robert G. Hunter's essay traces the process of mortification Alonso is made to endure from the guilt Ariel stirs in him and intensifies. Only when Alonso's old self is shattered by heart-sorrow does Prospero lift him out of despair by revealing as alive the persons whose death Alonso supposed he had caused. Patrick Grant finds in Augustine's *Confessions* a parallel to Ferdinand's journey through adversity to charity, and he cites from other Christian literature the association of charity with the "wonderful," as in Miranda. Further, he traces chastity's associations with "castigation" as a preparation for charity's higher love, and thus he accounts for Prospero's chastising of Ferdinand's passions and then rewarding him with a vision of harmony from which "cupiditas" has been banished.

James Walter's commentary draws on Augustine's allegorical interpretation of the creation story in Genesis in order to point up symbolic meanings in Shakespeare's drama. Augustine imagines God's Spirit coming as a storm to disturb the darksome deep and raise its spiritual creature to the light of grace. The "waters," he says, figure a "society of the sea" embittered in infidelity, whereas the "dry land" figures the "society of the virtuous" zealous for life-giving gifts. The conspirators in *The Tempest* represent the first of these, while Gonzalo and Miranda represent the second. Further, Augustine's seeing God's sacraments moving in the waters, and his allegorizing of the "fowls" as figuring prophetic voices of heavenly music, seem to be reflected in Shakespeare's play. When Prospero drowns his book he acknowledges the origins of his poetic art in the flowing waters of natural emotion that issue into signs.

In the list of supplementary reading, Ann Slater's essay is notable for its valuable discussion of Isaiah 29. The name of Ariel is there associated with Jerusalem's altar and holy mountain. The chapter and Shakespeare's play "agree in their shared thematic movement from sin, to punishment involving a trance-like state, to the final coming of understanding, justice and joy" (p. 128). Other themes in this chapter are the futility of subterfuge, the dependence of the natural order on the Creator, and blind eyes coming to see. Slater rebukes those critics who have brushed aside the chapter's "yeast-like impulse to the growth of the play." The essay by Mary Ellen Rickey points out that Prospero assigns rewards and penances "with recognizable precedents in Christian literature." The withdrawn banquet is like Dante's punishment of the gluttonous. The chess game has associations with medieval treatises on chess as an allegory of the game of life. George Herbert's "Providence" alludes to God as a master-player who balances the seasons as in a game of chess.

Lynette Black's essay calls our attention to the number symbolism in Prospero's several references to completing his work by six o'clock. God in Genesis completed his work of creating on the sixth day, and in the sixth age of history (according to Augustine) He became Man to reform us. Prospero's work of recreation proceeds through the mystic's "purgative way" and "illuminative way" to a union in communion at six o'clock. Eugene Wright, after canvassing the attempts of various recent critics to revise the play's meaning, defends Prospero as a colonialist "informed not by selfish political or economic interests, but by what he believes to be the civilized behavior of a rational man" (p. 118).

Barbara Traister observes that in Shakespeare's play the dramatic potential of magic—present but incompletely realized by earlier Renaissance playwrights—is given full development. Shakespeare has dared to present a benevolent magician who displays in theatrical illusions a power to impel auditors to self-examination through fright and delight. But Prospero stops well short of pretensions to deity. Traister sees him, as do such critics as F. D. Hoeniger and Herbert R. Coursen, as planning from the beginning to give up his magic and forgive his enemies but perfecting his self-control within the rhythms of time.

## Supplementary bibliography

Black, Lynette. "Suppertime at Six: Prospero's New Creation," *Publ. of the Arkansas Philological Association* 15 (1989), 59–72.

Coursen, Herbert R. "Prospero's Drama of the Soul," *Shakespeare Studies* 4 (1968), 316–33; enlarged in *Christian Ritual in the World of Shakespeare's Tragedies* (1976), Ch. 6.

Hoeniger, F. D. "Prospero's Storm and Miracle," *Shakespeare Quarterly* 7(1956), 33–38.

Hoyle, James. "*The Tempest*, the Joseph Story, and Cannibals," *Shakespeare Quarterly* 28 (1977), 358–62.

Kermode, Frank. The Arden edition of *The Tempest* (London: Methuen, 1954), pp. xxvi–xl.

Parker, M. D. H. *The Slave of Life* (London, 1955), pp. 176–78; 186–94.

Rickey, Mary Ellen. "Prospero's Living Drolleries," *Renaissance Papers 1964* (1965), 35–42.

Slater, Ann P. "Variations Within a Source: From Isaiah xxix to *The Tempest*," *Shakespeare Survey* 25 (1972), 125–35.

Traister, Barbara. *Heavenly Necromancers: The Magician in English Renaissance Drama* (University of Missouri Press, 1984), pp. 125–49.

Wright, Eugene P. "Christopher Columbus, William Shakespeare and the Brave New World," in Peter Milward, ed., *The Mutual Encounter of East and West, 1492-1992* (Tokyo: Sophia University, Renaissance Institute Monograph, 1992), pp. 111–24.

*E. J. Devereux (1968)*

## Sacramental Imagery in *The Tempest*

Prospero's epilogue to *The Tempest* shows that the play is about the forgiving of sin and the restoration of faith in the bond between men and each other and God, a theme that has been suggested in the play through a pattern of sacramental imagery. There has been death in water leading to new life, or Baptism; there has been sacramental Penance, clearly implied in the terms of repentance and the form through which sins have been forgiven; there has been Communion in the feast so abruptly snatched away from the "three men of sin" by Ariel, fittingly disguised as a harpy, a messenger of divine vengeance; and the play has ended in Matrimony, in which all differences and hatred have been sacramentally purged.

The sacramental imagery seems to be a ramification of a more profound and central pattern of imagery of disintegration and reintegration of elemental nature. Ariel is fire in the ship's rigging; he is air normally; water appears in forms of death, cleansing, and rebirth; and Caliban is earth: the disorder of the elements from which all things are made appears in the chaos of tempest, and their right ordering in the harmony of music, which always accompanies Prospero and Ariel at their work. But air and earth are the elements of spirit and animal in mankind, fire is the element of the Holy Ghost, water is the element of Baptism, and music is divine creation imposing order on chaos. God and man communicate through elements; and so sacramental imagery becomes relevant to Shakespeare's play.

Alonso, Sebastian, and Antonio are guilty of usurpation and the attempted murder of Prospero and his innocent child. Their crime leads to still more sin as Sebastian and Antonio continue plotting even on the island. Caliban has the fallen nature of one still in original sin, and remains inclined to the worst until his "baptism" in the pond enlightens his mind and teaches him to reject his false god Stephano and to "seek for grace" (5.1.294–5). But behind all there is the sin of Prospero. Antonio, whom we meet as a cynical plotter, was once loved by Prospero, and presumably deserved to be loved so; but Prospero's "neglecting worldly ends" tempted him, "Awak'd an evil nature" in him (1.2.89–97), leading to his sin, which in turn led him to tempt Alonso and then Sebastian. So Prospero like Adam brings disorder into the world through his wilfulness and brings punishment on his own flesh and blood, who must suffer to redeem him. But before he can rise above the desire for revenge to the "rarer action" of forgiving, he must undergo a symbolic baptism in the leaky boat with his daughter, who, as he says himself, preserves him. He must repent and moderate his studies and finally set them aside in his great act of faith.

Remission of sin can come only from grace, as Catholic and reformed theologians agreed, and images of grace run though the whole play. At the start of the action there is the obviously pentecostal image of Ariel visiting the ship in the form of St Elmo's fire, the bare idea of which seems to have come to the poet from Strachey's *True Reportory of the Wracke*.

> I flam'd amazement: sometimes I'd divide,
> And burn in many places; on the topmast,
> The yards and boresprit, would I flame distinctly,
> Then meet and join. (1.2.196–201)

It is more clearly figured in the "heavenly music" that fills the island and accompanies Prospero's actions in setting his own life and the lives of his enemies in order.

Mercy for sin and the idea of the happy fall emerge from Prospero's revelations to Miranda: it was "foul play" that put them into the boat, but they were "blessedly holp" to the island (1.2.61–3), which is "full of noises, Sounds and sweet aires, that give delight, and hurt not" (3.2.1334), music that brings everything into order, or grace. Prospero becomes a Lear with a second chance, one who has brought evil into the world through his wilfulness and endangered his innocent child, but is able not only to find forgiveness for himself but to undo his evil. Redeemed or reborn himself, Prospero must apply grace for the salvation of his enemies; he uses his powers properly, directing them to a divine purpose, and arranges a set of circumstances and a liturgy that will restore right order. This is done through figurative Baptism, for in the storm there is "not so much perdition as an hair Betid to any creature in the vesell," and, though "All but mariners Plung'd in the foaming brine," yet they reached shore with their clothing fresher than before (1.2.25ff.), "rather new-dyed than stained with salt water" (2.1.61–2).

Ferdinand is the first affected by the music of grace, which "crept by" him "upon the waters" (1.2.390–7), leading him towards his marriage with Miranda, the final sacramental image of restored order. Ariel's song deceives him into thinking his father dead, but still tells the truth; the old Alonso is dead by water and the new Alonso ready to come to life; everything that fades of him *is* changed "Into something rich and strange" (1.2.399–405), for it is his guilt that fades and he is changing into regenerate man. Ferdinand is unconsciously prophetic when he comments that the song "is no mortal business, nor no sound That the earth owes" (1.2.409–10), for it is not about the death of the body.

But even after "baptism" the court party are denied the banquet that is spread before them with the "Solemn and strange music" that represents the ordering grace of the play. They are instead given a direct reminder of their guilt and a warning of "Ling'ring perdition—worse than any death" that will come to them unless they can avoid it through the only possible means, "heart-sorrow And a clear life ensuing" (3.3.81–2), which are the traditional requirements for sacramental Penance in Catholic theology and repentance in reformed theology. That Prospero continues to hold their guilt over their heads is not at all unreasonable, for imperfectly contrite sinners are more likely to sin again: restored grace is proportionate to the act of free will involved in repentance, and some rise to a higher grace, like Prospero and Alonso, and some to a lesser, like Antonio and Sebastian. The higher characters suffer a spiritual agony, while the court plotters, like the low plotters, are "pinch'd" (5.1.74). Yet all the court party receive Prospero's words: "I do forgive thee" (5.1.78).

Finally there is Matrimony, obviously of great significance in *The Tempest* both as the traditional comic ending and as the instrument of final reconciliation. It is a perfect marriage in the play, for on its perfection depends the happy ending. It would be absurd to suggest that in so carefully constructed a play the constant references to Miranda's virginity are mere fussiness on the part of a doting old father and a priggish young suitor. Ferdinand sees her first as "the goddess" on whom the music of the island attends, as in fact she is: when he asks her whether she is "maid or no," girl or goddess, she ingenuously replies that she is "certainly a maid" (1.2.429–31). Ignoring Prospero's attempts to break in, he cries:

> O, if a virgin,
> And your affection not gone forth, I'll make you
> The Queen of Naples. (1.2.450–2)

Virginity is stressed again after the betrothal in Prospero's warning against "th' fire in th' blood" (4.1.51–4).

> If thou dost break her virgin-knot before
> All sanctimonious ceremonies may
> With full and holy rite be minister'd,
> No sweet aspersion shall the heavens let fall
> To make this contract grow. . . . (4.1.15–19)

Ferdinand hopes to achieve "quiet days, fair issue and long life" (4.1.24). Now Peter Lombard had listed the "goods" of marriage as "faith, offspring, and sacrament." They are, from whatever source Shakespeare may have taken them, the goods to which Miranda and Ferdinand devote their love, and are dramatized in the same order in the masque of Act 4, from which Venus and Cupid (the shamefulness of concupiscence) are excluded. The masque is heralded by Iris, the "heavenly bow," the symbol of the covenant of faith that "the waters shall no more become a flood to destroy all flesh" (Gn 9:9–17). Ceres follows as pure fertility, and Juno gives her blessing.

In its actions the play has run through a few hours; in its theme it has brought about reintegration; in its imagery it has run from Baptism, with which spiritual life begins, through Communion, Penance, and Matrimony, through finally to indulgence and prayers for one who can no longer help himself.

From *Bulletin de L'Association Canadienne des Humanités* 19 (1968), 50–62 abridged.

*George Slover (1978)*

## An Analogical Reading of *The Tempest* [editor's title]

In writing *The Tempest*, Shakespeare went neither to English chronicle nor to Roman biography; rather, he seems to have been engaged by a body of contemporary writings about the Virginia Company's nine-vessel fleet which had left England for the New World on July 25, 1609. In October of 1609, news reached England that the fleet had encountered a terrible storm and that the Admiral ship, the *Sea-Venture*, was lost. In September of 1610, almost a year later, Sir Thomas Gates and others reckoned lost arrived in London to tell the story of wrack and preservation. This chronology is important in savoring the experience behind the Bermuda documents, particularly that issued by the Council of Virginia, *A True Declaration of the Estate of the Colonie in Virginia.*

The *Declaration* is plainly apology: "because the honor and prosperity of this so noble an action [the plantation of Virginia], is eclipsed by the interposition of clamorous & tragicall narrations: the compiler of this relation endevoureth to wash away those spots, which foule mouths . . . have cast upon so fruitfull, so fertile, and so excellent a country" (p. 3). The foul mouths issuing tragical narrations belong to a group of colonists who deserted the colony and found their way back to England. The furious storm which overtook the fleet, the loss of the Admiral ship, the afflictions of the colonists already in Virginia appear to have been read by some as so many signs of God's displeasure with the Virginia enterprise. These critics, moreover, discerned in the calamities a divine punishment due the colonists' unlawful proceeding against the Indians regarding their life and property. The *Declaration*'s defense appears at first reading to be a tightly organized argument under the "three heads of lawfulnesse, possibility, and commoditie" (p. 5). Under the head of possibility, however, one recognizes a mode of persuasion which cuts below appeals to reason to what is plainly an appeal to faith. Capitalizing on the fresh news of the preservation from the raging sea of Sir Thomas and all the *Sea-Venture*'s passengers and crew and their "miraculous" island survival, the Council's controversialist projects a counterconstruction of the events.

> What is there in all this tragicall Comaedie that should discourage us with impossibilitie of the enterprise? when of all the Fleete, one onely Ship, by a secret leake was endangered and yet in the gulfe of Despair, was so graciously preserved. *Quae videtur poena, est medicina,* that which we accompt a punishment of evill, is but a medicine against evill. (p. 11)

Not tragedy but "tragicall Comaedie" is the pattern the *Declaration* writer discerns in the course of events—a movement from the "gulfe of Despair" to gracious preservation.

The *Declaration* author builds credibility for his interpretation of events in the only way the nature of the case allows—by precedent. The maxims he lays down are the rules of providential play, the rules which make God's playing with men in history intelligible and so subject to discourse.[1] They derive from the history of God's dealings with his people as authenticated and hallowed in the Scriptures.

> But that God heard Ionas crying out of the belly of hell, he pittied the distresses of his servants; For behold, in the last period of necessities, *Sir George Summers* descryed land, which was by so much the more joyfull, by how much their danger was despairefull. (p. 10)

> ... as in the great famine of *Israell*, God commanded *Elias* to flie to the brooke *Cedron*, and there fed him by Ravens; so God provided for our disconsolate people in the midst of the sea by foules.... An accident, I take it, that cannot be paralleld by any Hystorie, except when God sent abundance of Quales to feed his Israel in the barren wildernesse. (p. 11)

> *Brachium Domini*, this was the name of the Lord of Hosts, who would have his people to passe the redde Sea and Wildernesse, and then to possesse the land of Canaan.... (p. 19)

Not nature alone but the events of history are sacramental, visible signs of the working of an invisible grace, God's communication of his will to men.

The *Declaration* is an argument about the *meaning* of a certain sequence of actual events.

> Now if *Tertullians* rule be true, *Omnes genus ab origine censendum* that every action is most beautifull in the originall. Can there be a better beginning then from God ... whose footsteps in all succeeding ages have beene followed. (p. 4)

The [Virginia] Company's "so noble an action" unfolds within an unbroken historical sweep which goes back to Babel on the one hand and Troy on the other. The most beautiful original is to be found, however, in "Christs actions." "O all ye worthies," exclaims the *Declaration* in its peroration,

> follow the ever-sounding trumpet of a blessed honour; let Religion be the first aim of your hopes ... and other things shall be cast unto you: your names shall be registered to posterity with a glorious title; *These are the men, whom God raised to augment the State of their countrey, and to propagate the Gospell of Jesus Christ.* (p. 26)

Plainly, the deepest meaning of the Virginia plantation lies in its re-enactment of the apostolic action.

On his part, Prospero's playing implies a new vision of the meaning of his art as magus. His play is conceived as an imitation of, a collaboration in and with, the show of the *Magnum Magus*. In enlisting his magic to serve Providence and its infinitely more powerful art of grace, Prospero fulfills his career as magus, even in discovering the limits of magic art. When the time comes for him to play his personal part in the imitation of the providential action, Prospero finds, I think, that his noble reason is no match for his fury He discovers that, though his magic can bring all his enemies to lie at his mercy, it cannot move his mercy to raise them up to be themselves. He must first abjure his magic (as Alonso later resigns his dukedom) and then stand with the rest in the circle of disenchantment drawn by himself. There, in his true preserver, holy Gonzalo's eyes, listening to the heavenly music of his own ordering and remembering Gonzalo's charity (as he, earlier, had asked the three men to remember their sin)—only there does Prospero find the virtue which makes possible completion of "the rarer action" he intends from the outset. In the circle of disenchantment, Prospero with the rest—"One of their kind that relish all as sharply / Passion as they"—submits to the Magus whose art has power to transmute wills.[2]

... The revels speech in 4.1 effects a leap from the narrowest to the widest horizon of consciousness. Prospero takes the fading of his insubstantial pageant as a figure of the doomsday dissolving of the great globe itself and "all which it inherit." The very syntax of the speech moves inexorably to "dissolve" and "leave not a rack behind." The towers, palaces, temples, the globe itself—in short, the theater and the world, art and nature, human and divine creation—define the realm subject to dissolution, the setting within which "our little life" unfolds. Whether we like it or not, the revels speech raises theological issues, as so many *Tempest* interpretations testify. Typically, speculation focuses on whether Shakespeare would have us understand—or shall I say, would have us believe?—that our little life is rounded not only in a sleep but also in awakening to a reality next to which the life we "know" will appear as dream. Actually, the revels speech raises not merely theological issues: it brings to the surface the play's underlying theology.

For *The Tempest*, two strands in Christian theologizing need to be singled out and related: the understanding of God as play-maker and the conception of sacraments as ways of entering into Christian existence. Hugo Rahner, a historian of religion and patristics scholar, has traced the theology of the playing God and the corresponding anthropology of man the player and the plaything of God—traced it to Heraclitus and Plato, through Greek and Latin Church Fathers (including Tertullian, Jerome, Gregory, Nazianzen, and Augustine), and thence to Christian mystics of the Middle Ages and modern poets. Drawing largely on texts of Medieval and Renaissance mystics, Rahner discusses "the teaching that God's election by grace is a game" in terms most suggestive for reading *The Tempest*.

> The fundamental rule of this divine game is: "He who loses, wins"; and so it was set down by the Spanish mystic and Jesuit lay-brother, Alphonsus Rodriguez in the treatise, both childlike and profound, on "God's play with the soul." What outwardly appears as fate, suffering, or spoken in Christian terms, as a participation in the seemingly senseless annihilation upon the cross, is, for the mystic who sees through all the outer coverings of things, the wonderful calculated playing of an everlasting love, thought out and elaborated with a care for detail of which love alone is capable. (p. 56)

Not only is God's dealing with individual souls spoken of as a playing in the theological tradition Rahner traces, but so is His commerce with the church:

> Now all this applies to the earthly forms of the Church herself, to the sacraments as visible signs of invisible grace, and to the playing which is her liturgy. What occurs in baptism, says Bede, in the mysterious birth from water and the Spirit, is a mystery of which our knowledge is only by faith; seen from the outside it is no more than mere colorful play-acting. (p. 53)

This connection of play and the church's sacramental rituals is of crucial importance to *The Tempest*. Shakespeare's dramatic art engages his audience's desire to make-believe, to take the data of the stage performance *as if* true. At each level, the total performance represents a kind of collaboration. It is only by believing the evidence of the senses that the island sojourners can enter into Prospero's show; only by making believe what unfolds on stage can Shakespeare's audience participate in *The Tempest*. The *Magnum Magus*, whose play is history, likewise possesses an "art" through which He engages His "audience"—who are also actors; more or less consciously, in the play of His fashioning. Like Prospero's magic and Shakespeare's power of make-believe, the "art" of the Magnum Magus is an art of transformation, of creation and recreation. After all, He makes the world and all that is in it appear out of nothing with the words of power "Let there be"; He effects the transformations of time which we call history. It is He who will in time cause "the cloud-capp'd towers, the gorgeous palaces, the solemn temples, the great globe itself" to dissolve and leave not a rack behind. The art of the *Magnum Magus* is intent upon perfecting the play of history. The perfecting of that play, however, consists in the increasing accomplishment of the actors, the perfecting of their desire, making their ill will well, disenchanting the will bound by their giving ear and act to the enchantments of the wicked magician. In the parlance of theology, that divine art is named grace—the divine activity which the tradition Rahner traces conceives as a species of play. As with Prospero's and Shakespeare's plays, so the play of grace engages a certain faculty in those to whom it is addressed—the capacity to believe.

Mysteriously, even the Magnum Magus—wielding the power of the sacraments—is, it would seem, under constraint; subject, so to speak, to the rules of the game, and so, subject to the pathos of losing. The divine playwright creates the will free after the model of his own. His transformations of will are never impositions; they presuppose a yearning for freedom in the will enslaved. As it is possible for Antonio and Sebastian to remain unresponsive to the "solemn music" which gives the rest of the royal party comforting sleep; as it is possible for members of Shakespeare's audience to withhold the childlike make-believe upon which the play's power depends; so it is possible, apparently, to resist even the master magician and will to abide in enchantment, in dreams and images of one's own fashioning, or will to enact scenarios of one's own choosing rather than enter into the history of the one divine play-maker. That is, the play of sacramental grace makes demands not just on the *Magnum Magus* but on the actor-participants of the play. It demands that the participants affirm the scenario which powers the play *as*—not now *as if*—history.

This mode of acting and believing furnishes the Bermuda literature its theological model. For writers of these documents, as for their readers, actual events are replete with the will of God and therefore full of meaning. Unlike sacramental events, the meaning has to be established through a kind of argument. To do this, the event and its underlying action are analogized to a "beautiful original" either in God's or Christ's action. So analogized, the event is incorporated into the sweep of time bounded by Creation and Fall on the one hand and by Judgment on the other, and informed from within by Christ's redemption. Finally, the analogical construction of the event is proposed to and ratified by an act of faith, and so "becomes" history, becomes luminous with the will of God. It is this sacramentalizing mode which Shakespeare, in creating *The Tempest*, seems to have absorbed from the Bermuda literature. And more, it is this mode which seems to have furnished Shakespeare with the means of expressing his own most deeply felt insights into his practice as playwright, into his art as dramatist

Prospero conceives his magicalizing as an interplay between himself, his island subjects, and the *Magnum Magus*. Extrapolating, we suggest that Shakespeare understands his art analogously—as a three-way collaboration involving himself, his audience, and that divine power which alone can make ill wills well. For Shakespeare, poetic art can no more change history than can magic—precisely because it cannot, of itself, change the will. The will, however, can change if it will, but such a change is for Shakespeare a species of miracle. It is possible only with divine assistance, with grace. When it occurs, therefore, such a recreated will is an epiphany of the divine initiative in history. Only in the measure, moreover, that the divine art succeeds in re-creating wills, can it also change history. Human art—poetry and drama in this instance—can do no more and no less than participate in this work. Indeed, only in conforming the ends of human art to those of divine and so allowing the divine art to inform the human can the poet's work become fully effective, fully realized.

The structure of *The Tempest* allows Shakespeare to dramatize analogically an audience's participation in the process of making meaning. In the aftermath of Prospero's double epiphany, Gonzalo exclaims,

> Was Milan thrust from Milan, that his issue
> Should become Kings of Naples? O, rejoice
> Beyond a common joy! and set it down
> With gold on lasting pillars: in one voyage
> Did Claribel her husband find at Tunis,
> And Ferdinand, her brother, found a wife
> Where he himself was lost, Prospero his dukedom
> In a poor isle, and all of us ourselves
> When no man was his own. (5.1.205–13)

In Prospero's epiphanies, Gonzalo catches sight of the true shape of a story—a story which is also, in part, his history, in which he himself has played and is playing a part. He perceives the meaning of his existence transformed by having been caught up all along in a design which mere human wisdom could never conceive—a design capable of drawing community from division, riches from poverty, clarity from confusion. Gonzalo's response to Prospero's epiphanies furnishes a paradigm for that joint creation of meaning to which the poet of analogical bent aspires. Such a poet does something *with*, rather than *to*, his audience. Performers and audience constitute a community not only in the common action of making believe, but also in the common action of believing.

## Notes

1   For the notion of the "playing of God" and its tradition in the West, I owe much to Hugo Rahner, *Man at Play*, trans. B. Battershaw and E. Quinn (New York: Herder and Herder, 1967).

2  Compare Herbert R. Coursen, Jr., "Prospero and the Drama of the Soul," *Shakespeare Studies*, 4 (1968), 325–27.

From "Magic, Mystery, and Make-believe: An Analogical Reading of *The Tempest*," *Shakespeare Studies* 11 (1978), 180–86, 195–205, abridged.

*Robert Grams Hunter (1965)*

## The Regeneration of Alonso [editor's title]

Alonso's corpse, the dirge by Ariel tells us (in 1.2.460–68), lies at the bottom of the sea, where it is undergoing a marvelous transformation. Human flesh and bone fade and change from their mortal substance into the rich permanence of pearl and coral. A different but clearly analogous process does take place in the course of the play. Prospero will afflict his old enemy, Alonso, with a "heart-sorrow" so intense that it will drive him almost to suicide, yet it will result finally not in destruction, but in re-creation. Alonso will endure a psychological death of sorrow and remorse—a kind of sinking into the depths of his own mind. From this he will emerge regenerated, a new man, his psychological and spiritual substance transformed.

The Caliban-Stefano-Trinculo plot to murder Prospero and seize the island is a comic analogue both to Alonso's original crime and to Antonio and Sebastian's frustrated attempt to repeat it. The effect of the analogue is principally a comic reduction of the pretensions of evil through a comparison of them to the deformed and drunken idiocies of the clowns. The most important equation in this analogue is that of Caliban to Antonio. Caliban tempts Stephano to kill the sleeping Prospero just as Antonio had tempted Sebastian to kill the sleeping Alonso:

> Ile yeeld him thee asleepe,
> Where thou maist knocke a naile into his head. (3.2.63–64)

Like Antonio in the original and successful *coup d'état*, Caliban proposes to exchange his subjection to Prospero for a new subjection to a usurper whom he will help to power. Caliban's guilt parodies Antonio's but its source is slightly different. It proceeds from an unsophisticated, "innocent" but inherent corruption (for Caliban's "innocence" is a corrective comment on Miranda's). The source of Antonio's evil is a sophisticated but equally inherent corruption. Caliban in his deformity is a moral portrait (like the one in Dorian Gray's attic) of that "goodly person," Antonio. The Machiavellian cunning and sophisticated amorality of Antonio finally serve impulses which are as stupidly misguided as those of the "debosh'd fish" who takes a drunkard for a god and worships a dull fool. The brutish stupidity of evil, the fact that it is finally absurd—however dangerous—is the point of the parody of the two crimes.

Caliban's proposal to murder Prospero in the comic underplot is followed by the climax of the action which has Alonso at its center. Alonso is a remarkably quiet central figure. He addresses ten words to the boatswain in the opening scene. In Act 2, scene 1, his next appearance, he contributes exactly five words to the first one hundred lines: "Prithee, peace," and, "I prithee, spare." Yet the whole of this long scene revolves around his usually silent or sleeping figure.

For Alonso, the loss of Ferdinand seems to be punishment without a crime, for the memory of his crime against Prospero has sunk to the bottom of his mind. The words of Ariel cause that guilt to rise to the surface—or, more accurately, force Alonso to descend to find it. Act 3, scene 3, opens with Alonso's announcement of his despair:

> Euen here I will put off my hope, and keepe it
> No longer for my Flatterer: he is droun'd
> Whom thus we stray to finde, and the Sea mocks
> Our frustrate search on land: well, let him goe. (3.3.11–14)

This speech demonstrates that the psychological condition of Alonso is now ready to receive with profit the arts which Prospero will practice on it. Alonso is in a state of inward sorrow and grief. By contrast to the wanhope of Alonso, however, Sebastian and Antonio are as far as possible from contrition:

> Antonio      I am right glad, that he's so out of hope:
>              Doe not for one repulse forgoe the purpose
>              That you resolu'd t'effect.
> Sebastian    The next aduantage will we take throughly.
> Antonio      Let it be tonight.... (3.3.15–19)

At this moment Prospero enters, unseen, to witness the discomfiture of his enemies. The "iconography" of the ensuing scene is fascinating in its implications. Strange spirits bring in a table with food upon it, but when the "men of sinne" attempt to "stand to, and feede," Ariel, in the form of a harpy, prevents them and causes the table and its contents to disappear. Shakespeare's contemporaries delighted in such visual or theatrical "metaphors" (perhaps a better term for them would be "emblems"). The "temptation"—if it is that at all—here presented is of "men of sin" by the wise and good Prospero. Furthermore, the one good man in this group of sinners, "the pure Gonzalo," far from resisting the illusion, urges Alonso to trust in it. What occurs when the sinners approach the banquet is not the capitulation of weak men to the blandishments of sensuality, but the prevention of unworthy men from partaking of good things.

Prospero's banquet, I suggest, is a type, not of Satan's temptations, but of the commonest of all symbolic banquets: the Communion table. This is the supper from which notorious and unrepentant sinners are traditionally excluded:

And if any of these [as do intend to be partakers of the Holy Communion] be an open and notorious evil liver, so that the congregation by him is offended, or have done any wrong to his neighbours by word or deed: The Curate having knowledge thereof, shall call him and advertise him, in any wise not to presume to the Lord's Table, until he have openly declared himself to have truly repented and amended his former naughty life, that the Congregation may thereby be satisfied, which afore were offended; and that he have recompensed the parties, whom he hath done wrong unto, or at the least declare himself to be in full purpose so to do, as soon he conveniently may. (*Book of Common Prayer*)

. . . Ariel reveals to Alonso the real cause of his despair at the beginning of the scene. The crime against Prospero has been revenged by the seeming death of Ferdinand. The remainder of Alonso's life will be a torment to him unless he can achieve "heart's sorrow, / And a cleere life ensuing"—in other words, "contrition of the heart" and "an amendment of life," the first and last parts of repentance.

The first effect of Ariel's announcement upon Alonso is to drive him not toward penance and salvation, but toward desperate self-destruction. "The conscience of heinous offenses, and the force of repentance, may be so great, that the mind of man, on each side compassed with fear, may be possessed with despair of salvation" (Nowell *Catechism*). So it is with Alonso:

> O, it is monstrous: monstrous:
> Me thought the billowes spoke, and told me of it,
> The windes did sing it to me: and the Thunder
> (That deepe and dreadfull Organ-Pipe) pronounc'd
> The name of Prosper: it did bass my Trespasse,
> Therefore my Sonne i'th'Ooze is bedded; and
> I'le seeke him deeper than ere plummet sounded,
> And with him there lye mudded. (3.3.120–27)

Shakespeare differentiates Alonso's reaction to Ariel's accusation from that of Antonio and Sebastian. As Gonzalo tells us:

> All three of them are desperate: their great guilt
> (Like poyson giuen to worke a great time after)
> Now gins to bite the spirits. . . . (3.3.131–33)

But the desperation of Alonso is directed at himself. His guilt impels him to attempt suicide. Prospero prevents the desperation from having any physical effect. The miraculous transformation predicted in Ariel's "Dirge" must take place.

The return of reason enables Alonso to complete the process of repentance, which began with his contrition, by confessing his sin and making satisfaction to Prospero:

> Thy Dukedome I resigne, and doe entreat
> Thou pardon me my wrongs. (5.1.133–34)

Prospero rewards the regenerated Alonso with the resurrection of his son:

> My Dukedome since you haue giuen me againe,
> I will requite you with as good a thing,
> At least bring forth a wonder, to content ye
> As much, as me my Dukedome. (5.1.193–96)

The moment of Prospero's "discovery" of Ferdinand and Miranda "playing at Chesse" is the moment of "miracle" that we have seen to be the unvarying climax of the comedy of forgiveness. The resurrections of Hero, Helena, Imogen, Hermione, and Claudio have preceded this, Shakespeare's last "awakening from nightmare." Alonso discovers that the sin of which he has believed himself guilty—the deaths of Prospero and Miranda—has not occurred, and that his punishment—the death of Ferdinand—has been spared him in reality. The love of his son and Prospero's daughter will ratify the reconciliation of their fathers, though Alonso must first request the pardon of Miranda:

> But O, how oddly will it sound, that I
> Must aske my childe forgiuenesse? (5.1.232–33)

Prosper then insists that the time for the torments of conscience is past:

> There Sir stop,
> Let vs not burthen our remembrances, with
> A heauinesse that's gon. (5.1.234–36)

And the good Gonzalo is ready to pronounce his benediction:

> I haue inly wept,
> Or should haue spoke ere this: looke downe you gods
> And on this couple drop a blessed crowne;
> For it is you, that haue chalk'd forth the way
> Which brought vs hither. (5.1.237–41)

According to Gonzalo, the members of Alonso's party have, as a result of their experiences on the island, found themselves.

But what a man finds when he finds himself clearly depends upon the man. For Alonso, the "mortification of the old man" has resulted in the "quickening of the new man," but regeneration is not an automatic process, and there is no evidence that the old Antonio has altered as the result of his mortification. Prospero, before he awakens the sinners from their trance, apostrophizes the unhearing Antonio as follows:

> Flesh, and bloud,
> You, brother mine, that entertaine ambition,
> Expell'd remorse, and nature, whom, with *Sebastian*
> (Whose inward pinches therefore are most strong)
> Would heere haue kill'd your King: I do forgiue thee,
> Vnnaturall though thou art. (5.1.86–91)

"Though thou *art*." Antonio's evil nature has not changed—and Prospero knows it, nor is Sebastian any more trustworthy. Prospero can only control them, as he has controlled Caliban, through the power of his knowledge of their evil:

> Wellcome, my friends all,
> But you my brace of Lords, were I so minded
> I heere could plucke his Highnesse frowne vpon you
> And iustifie you Traitors: at this time
> I will tell no tales. (5.1.143–47)

And yet, he forgives Antonio:

> For you (most wicked Sir) whom to call brother
> Would euen infect my mouth, I do forgiue
> Thy rankest fault; all of them: and require
> My Dukedome of thee, which, perforce I know
> Thou must restore. (5.1.150–54)

Here forgiveness is unjustified by contrition, confession, or satisfaction. If Antonio were to face the Last Judgment of the medieval mystery cycles in the spiritual state in which we find him at the end of *The Tempest*, he would take his place among the damned. To Prospero, however, he is forgivable precisely because Prospero is not the God of Judgment. As a man, Prospero forgives even the unregenerate, for the justice of man should be tempered with as much mercy as man would hope to find upon the Latter Day.

From *Shakespeare and the Comedy of Forgiveness* (Columbia University Press, 1965), pp. 228–240 abridged. Used by permission.

*Patrick Grant (1979)*

## *The Tempest* and the Magic of Charity

Shakespeare first of all gives an important and fairly conspicuous hint about how we can read Miranda-as-emblem by stressing so strongly the theme of her chastity, and Prospero's insistence on his daughter's virginity brings to mind the commonplace Renaissance equation of *castitas* and *caritas*, an association partly invited by the similarity in spelling and partly by the Platonist conviction that to move towards God was to renounce the flesh.[1] The equation is at the centre, for example, of Milton's *Comus*, a work influenced by *The Tempest*, and which cannot be adequately understood apart from the tradition that would read the Lady's chastity as Christian charity.[2] The significance of this familiar combination would certainly not be lost on Shakespeare's audience, for his play underlines it plainly.

Also, the one point in *The Tempest* where Shakespeare seems to allude to the *Confessions* of St Augustine, a seminal work for determining the content of the Christian experience of *caritas* in the Middle Ages, is in Ferdinand's courtship of Miranda. Ferdinand complains "There be some sports are painful, and their labour / Delight in them sets off" (3.1.1–2), recalling Augustine's passage:

> Yea, the very pleasures of human life men acquire by difficulties.... It is also ordered, that the affianced bride should not at once be given, lest as a husband he should hold cheap whom, as betrothed, he sighed not after.[3]

This passage, which describes Ferdinand's situation in *The Tempest* so exactly, occurs in context of a discussion on "what ... takes place in the soul ... on recovering the things it loves," where Augustine alludes to a "storm which tosses the sailor, threatens shipwreck," but which issues eventually in peace and joy. The passage is preceded by a discussion of penitence which leads to the supreme experience of "holy charity." The allusion in Ferdinand's speech and the context in the *Confessions* are both significant: the storm threatening shipwreck and the journey through penitence and hardship (holding back the affianced bride) to charity are strikingly similar in both works. An understanding of this single allusion together with the *caritas-castitas* association may help us to see a further pattern of traditional significances which can be developed under three headings: the association between *caritas* and "wonder"; the association between *caritas*, *castitas*, and "castigate"; and the relation between caritas and Venus.

That Shakespeare puns throughout *The Tempest* on the name "Miranda," which means "wonder," scarcely needs discussion ("O you wonder!" [1.2.427]; "Admired Miranda!" [3.1.37]; "I will ... bring forth a wonder" [5.1.169–70]; and so on). But there is a less generally acknowledged, though commonplace, association between faith, love and the marvelous, for the redeeming, miraculous love of *caritas* is often conceived of as especially "wonderful," and consequently (via the Latin pun) "admired." St Paul, for instance, writing to the Thessalonians, commends the faith and "charity of every one of you all towards each other" (2 Thes 1:3), promising that Christ will "be admired in all them that believe" (2 Thes 1:10). The Douai version renders this "made wonderful," and the Vulgate has "admirabilis." This grouping of words is conventional: in his universally read *Of the Imitation of Christ*, Thomas à Kempis has, for example, a chapter specifically "on the wonderful effect of divine love" (3.5), and he engages in several deliberate plays on the relationship between *caritas* and *mirabilis*. "Behold love's revelation! ... O how admirable (*admirabilis*) is Thy work.... For the charity (*caritas*) of Christ is never diminished" (4.2). He commends the "admirable" grace of the sacrament which "enkindles ... love (*affectum*)" earlier described as "charity (*caritas*)" (4.1).[4] In a similar vein we may recall John Donne's discussion of charity in *Holy Sonnet* XI: "O let me then, his strange love still admire," or again *Holy Sonnet* XII, where he exhorts himself (and his readers) to "wonder at a greater wonder," namely God's redemptive love.[5] Although the association I am suggesting extends to *The Tempest* by inference, it does nonetheless offer grounds for a coherency in the "Miranda-Wonder" wordplay by permitting us to see Shakespeare's pun in context of a fuller meaning consistent with the play's total action.

Returning now to the Augustinian passage on penitence preceding *caritas*, we can suggest another widespread Renaissance tradition which, assuming the association of *caritas* and *castitas*, in turn associates *castitas* with "castigate." The theme of the castigation (rendering chaste) of passion leading to a concord of higher love (*caritas*) has been documented in detail by Edgar Wind.[6] He adduces many examples from the visual arts, though they are also plentiful in literature, perhaps the most obvious literary example being the career of Britomart in *The Faerie Queene*. As an overt representative of chastity, she castigates and chastises with vigour for her entire maidenly career. However, Titian's celebrated painting of "Sacred and Profane Love" provides a more tractable example for the present context. The figures of higher and lower Venus sit on a sarcophagus which is full of water and on which are depicted scenes of violent physical chastisement. Although Wind does not mention it, the sarcophagus may represent the body of death in which we are buried with Christ "by baptism into death" (Rom 6:4), and from which we emerge, chastened, as "new men" dedicated to the admiration of Sacred Love or *caritas* and not to Profane Love or *cupiditas*. In *The Tempest*, certainly, the theme of restoration from death and the ordeal (chastisement) by water is of obvious importance. So also is the ruling of Ferdinand's passions—he is a "patient log-man" (3.1.66) in service of Miranda, "lest too light winning/ Make the prize light" (1.2.452–53), as Prospero says. Prospero himself is dedicated to chastising the other aberrant characters so that they may repent, and in his "nurture" of the higher spiritual love which Miranda represents, the activity of castigation and of repentance and forgiveness is of central importance. As St Augustine concisely puts it (referring to 1 Tm 1:5), "the end of every commandment is charity," and the "greatest of all alms is to forgive our debtors and love our enemies."[7] Specifically, he says that charity is manifest in forgiving those who have done us wrong, and thus, in pronouncing "I do forgive / Thy rankest fault—all of them" (5.1.131–2), Prospero is again acting "in care of thee," as his anger turns to forgiveness and charity.

Finally, the relation of passion (the Profane Love of Titian) to Venus and to the sea storm is a familiar theme, and Shakespeare draws on it. The association of Venus with the sea is of course basic, because the myth attributes her origins to that element. Botticelli's "Birth of Venus" is perhaps the best known explicit example of this story in the visual arts, though during the Renaissance the moist element is continuously associated with venery. So Desdemona's "moist Palm" (*Othello*, 3.4.32), is a sign to Othello (a moor, after all, of "Venus") of her libidinous nature, and in *The Tempest*, which assumes this association, the cupidity and lust which come in various forms from the sea to the enchanted island must be "castigated" and "made new." Here Prospero's masque is again significant, for Venus is banished; "now" (4.1.88) there is no passion as Cupid "Swears he will shoot no more" (4.1.100). Instead there is a "contract of true love" (4.1.133), and the clear opposition at this point of *caritas* and Venus seems deliberate. As the language implies, Ferdinand may *formerly* have been prone to what Prospero calls, before the masque begins, "fire i' th' blood" (4.1.53), but now he appreciates the higher love of *caritas*, the wonder of Miranda. The clarification of Ferdinand's attitude to love during the masque in turn helps to reveal a further pattern of allusions to *caritas* in many of his addresses to Miranda: "the mistress which I serve quickens what's dead" (3.1.6), he claims. Miranda is "worth what's / —Dearest to the world" (39), and he has never loved anyone "with so full soul" (44). "Hear my soul speak" (63), he says, and promises Prospero, "I . . . shall never melt / Mine honour into lust" (4.1.27–8), thus opposing his love to *cupiditas*, the passion of Caliban.

To summarize: first is the Augustinian nexus of sea-storm, labour, penitence, and *caritas*, which the play seems directly to invoke. Second is the traditional Renaissance emphasis on "chastity" and the link between *castitas* and "castigate." Third is the pun on "wonder" and the association of wonder with *caritas*. Fourth is the opposition of sacred and profane love in relation to castigation, along with the opposition of Venus to Miranda in Prospero's masque, which in turn recalls the association of Venus to the sea. Finally is the dedication by Prospero of his every act to the nurture of Miranda and his final emphasis on forgiveness, the consummate art of charity. All this suggests that the intuitions of value imaged forth in Miranda are, not unreasonably summarized by the traditional *caritas*, and that in some masque-like sense they echo through the entire fabric of the play.

## Notes

1 See Sears Jayne, "The Subject of Milton's Ludlow *Mask*," ed John S. Diekhoff, *A Maske at Ludlow* (Cleveland: Case Western Reserve University Press, 1968), p. 168.
2 Ibid., pp. 158ff.
3 *Confessions*, VIII.iii.7, trans. Pusey, pp. 154–5.
4 Trans. Abbot Justin McCann (New York: Mentor Books, 1957), pp. 77, 160, 158.
5 Ed. Helen Gardner (Oxford: Clarendon Press, 1964), pp. 9–10.
6 *Pagan Mysteries of the Renaissance* (London: Peregrine Books, 1967), pp. 146ff.
7 *The Enchiridion on Faith, Hope and Love*, ed. Henry Paolucci (New York: Henry Regnery Co., 1961), p. 86.

From *Images and Ideas in Literature of the English Renaissance* (Amherst: University of Massachusetts Press, 1979), pp. 82–85. Used by permission.

*James Walter (1983)*

## From Tempest to Epilogue

While Shakespeare's tempest reenacts the tempests of the emblem books drawn to figure a primordial chaos near the center of temporal life, the fate of language in the opening scene evokes another traditional emblem, the Tower of Babel. Symbolizing humanity's corrupt striving for self-sufficient power against the heavens, Babel resulted in a confusion of linguistic difference that alienated a unified people from being and from one another. Gonzalo's cry, "We split, we split!" (1.1.59), describes the recurrence of that condition in the time of *The Tempest*, many years after Alonso and Antonio's grab for power. Nevertheless, the aged counselor Gonzalo, the play's exemplary interpreter, trusts in a divine intention working within the changes of the moment and claims, against the Boatswain's avowal of a "chance" universe, to read signs of a destiny in the Boatswain's expressions: "Methinks he hath no drowning mark upon him; his complexion is perfect gallows" (1.1.29–30). Consistently it is Gonzalo, the man of patient faith, who endures trials equably and who discerns through the surface of seeming insignificance the remnant and promise of a just order.

Prospero, also, is a person of faith who once endured a violent sea and subsequent trials, which he describes for Miranda when he recounts their expulsion from Milan:

> There they hoist us,
> To cry to th' sea that roared to us; to sigh
> To th' winds, whose pity, sighing back again,
> Did us but loving wrong. (1.2.148–51)

In retrospect, if not at the time, Prospero can read the displacement of himself and his infant daughter to an almost deserted island as a sign of "providence divine" operating through a sympathetic nature. This initial evidence of his faith suggests that he is not demonic, vengeful, or senilely irascible when he first appears in the play. Although his faith cannot keep him from later experiencing a natural temptation to revenge, his first words to Miranda reveal that his twelve years on the island have tempered his soul to a care, humility, discipline, and clarity of purpose that it previously lacked. Thus his magical control of Ariel and of "all his quality" (1.2.193), symbolic of his broad power to bring forth things, qualities, and persons into more articulate being, is a product and a reward of his patient effort, not the sign of a vice.

*The Tempest* is unusual among Shakespeare's plays in that its title calls first attention, not to a great personage or to some human mood or effect, but to a natural phenomenon. This phenomenon, moreover, is placed in conjunction with several others of tremendous metaphorical resonance: the sea, human exile, human conspiracy, an island, a ship, and a society rejuvenated. If *The Tempest* has few metaphors in which "something abstract (e.g. an intellectual quality or attitude) is interpreted by an image,"[1] the reason is that metaphor has become more structural in this play and is less obvious as a rhetorical embellishment. Chosen for their powerful natural appeal to the imagination and their authority in the tradition of allegory, the figures that establish the setting, oppositions of characters, and progression of plot in *The Tempest* make visible certain archetypal desires, states, and actions common to the experience of Christian pilgrims.

Particularly in *The Tempest*, Shakespeare exploits the suggestive potential of a *paysage moralisé*, a physical scene that allegorically figures forth the spiritual substance of its inhabitants. Not only does this insular landscape figure their inward spirits, it induces them into self-revealing and self-summarizing action in the world, so that, like Dante's damned and redeemed souls, they experience their spiritual conditions in a physical way.

This special world gains some of its poetic resonance and philosophic depth from the tradition of allegorizing scriptural motifs that Augustine skillfully practices in books 11–13 of *The Confessions*, where he attempts a complete figurative reading of the story of Creation in the first verses of Genesis. Shakespeare must have been familiar with at least some of Augustine's works, and there is good evidence that *The Tempest* self-consciously addresses some of the autobiography's concerns, but in the poet's way of concrete realization. In this sense, Shakespeare's play revises Augustine's more abstract reflections on the work of Providence in human life. Whereas in the final books of the autobiography Augustine allegorically interprets an ancient text, disembodying its spiritual truths from their physical images in the light of a fuller revelation, Shakespeare reincarnates the same allegorical figures by incorporating them into a mimetic image of life.

In a passage that seems to foreshadow *The Tempest*, Augustine imagines God's Spirit coming as a storm to disturb the darksome deep and raise its spiritual creature to the enlightenment of grace. As Augustine discourses on the deep, he characterizes its flaw more particularly as forgetfulness; although God's waterspouts call out to it, "it is sad, because it relapseth, and becomes a deep, or rather perceives itself still to be a deep."[2] Thus the figure is expanded from a metaphysical principle to a psychological one: it subsists as a dimension of the creature's soul. The embittered souls of Alonso, Antonio, and Sebastian fit the psychological archetype in *The Tempest*.

According to Genesis, God gathered the "waters" into one place and let the "dry land" appear—figures, Augustine says, of two societies, one embittered in infidelity and the other righteous in continence (238). Since both live under the firmament, each is restrained by Law; but the effect of the Law on "the society of the sea" is only to increase conflict by the bounds it imposes on their impatient and wicked desires, causing "their waves [to] break one against another" (238). This figure functions to make carnal, selfish human beings see and feel the quality of natural antagonism among them. In contrast, "the dry land" is the society of the virtuous, who are zealous for life-giving gifts of God; their works of mercy, firstfruits of the Spirit, are a "sweet spring" irrigating the land and bringing a rich harvest. In *The Tempest* Prospero, Miranda, and Gonzalo, who "would fain die a dry death" (1.1.66), fit this archetype.

To protect the dry land from its potential barrenness, God has "Let the waters bring forth ... the moving creature having life, and the fowls that fly above the earth" (241). In perhaps his boldest allegoresis, Augustine interprets the moving creature as God's sacraments, which "have moved amid the waves of temptations of the world [the 'sea society'], to hallow the Gentiles" in baptism; and he interprets the fowls as God's prophets, who also derive from the waters. ... It is the "tempestuously swelling" human race flowing like a brackish sea out of Adam that requires the sacraments, as well as "dispensers to work in many waters, after a corporeal and sensible manner, mysterious doings and sayings" (242). The sacraments issuing from the waters below the firmament are signs of the same Spirit that is figured by the sea in *The Tempest*, and the voices of God's prophets resounding in the open firmament of God's Book are a type of the "heavenly music" that will aid Prospero in working on the senses of the conspirators to renew their minds and bring out of their earth a "living soul."

I have summarized parts of Augustine's allegory in detail because I think it compares significantly with Shakespeare's profound look in *The Tempest* at the poet's ability to redeem a world degenerated in the imaginations of the degenerate. Moreover, Augustine's implied ranking of interpretive and poetic productions can help explain the disparagement of poetic drama in the play, expressed puzzlingly in Prospero's occasional guilt, his allusion to "Some vanity of mine art," his promised abjuration of his "rough magic," and his Epilogue. Shakespeare seems to agree with Augustine about the dangerous vanity of shows, yet the poet finds a perspective that can transform spectacle into a potentially restorative activity.

Antonio's plot is only one of several attempts by characters in *The Tempest* to make a new society based on a "new man." This project, in fact, is the central theme of the play, uniting by counterpoint episodes quite unrelated by cause and effect. While Antonio plots on one part of the island, Caliban plots on another; and, more innocently, so does Ferdinand after he discovers Miranda, only to have his eros subsumed within Prospero's more inclusive "project." All the lesser plots are marked by degrees of impatience and forgetfulness, whereas Prospero's depends specifically on his attained powers of patience, verbal precision, and memory working under the rigor of a narrow time limit. Prospero finally enjoys a measure of success in his creative endeavor, but in each of the other plots the "new man" in view only too readily discloses an unavoidable legacy from the old Adam, from whom pours "the brackishness of the sea ... the human race so profoundly curious, and tempestuously swelling, and restlessly tumbling up and down" (Augustine 242).

The suggestive device Stephano uses in trying to entice Caliban into his service illustrates the plot of the three low characters in the play and its elaboration of themes I have discussed: holding up a bottle of wine rescued from the shipwreck, Stephano commands, "Here, kiss the book.... Come, swear to that; kiss the book" (2.2.130,142). He uses the bottle as an ersatz scripture, a new basis of authority in his regime. Of course at the moment he is merely acting out the comic antics of a drunken butler; but his gesture, following his remark that the wine will "give language" to Caliban, is a reminder of humankind's problematic relation to language. Stephano's solution is the simple one of drink; instead of the laborious approach to meaning through signs, he chooses the quick ecstasy of liquor applied directly to the pain of living.

Some commentators on *The Tempest* believe that Prospero waxes dangerously heartless until the last part of the play, when Ariel moves him to pity and mercy for the usurpers. As the still legitimate ruler of Milan, Prospero is, rather, being wisely merciful as he rightfully attempts not simply to punish the criminals but to restore them to good faith and conscience. His early success is evident when the court party reappear after having stumbled for a time "Through forthrights and meanders." Their resultant "madness"—"even with suchlike valor men hang and drown / Their proper selves" (3.3.58–59)—is a type of Augustine's sea society, in which souls, like waves, "break one against another" (238) and sink toward the gates of death. In the words of Ariel, however, "destiny ... the never-surfeited sea / Hath caused to belch up you" (3.3.53–56).

Prospero's chief work regarding these sinners is to use the island's intrinsic power to bring hidden motives into the open and to restore memory, for to have their lives made whole, the conspirators must imaginatively reexperience crucial moments when their natural feelings and consciences were insensible. Only thus can moments lost in the "dark backward and abysm of time" (1.2.50) be redeemed and the coherence of the story line be restored in hope. Thus, Prospero directs Ariel to put before the court party a banquet that tantalizes their hunger and greed; when Ariel in the guise of a Harpy retrieves the banquet, they are forced to experience the illusoriness of the things they have desired and consequently to feel what they themselves are. The device is directly effective, for Alonso exclaims:

> O, it is monstrous, monstrous!
> Methought the billows spoke and told me of it;
> The winds did sing it to me; and the thunder,
> That deep and dreadful organ pipe, pronounced
> The name of Prosper; it did bass my trespass. (3.3.95–99)

As Alonso suddenly remembers not only his trespass but also the justice of the universal order, he makes an appalling connection: "Therefore my son i' th' ooze is bedded." His consequent impulse to "seek him deeper than e'er plummet sounded / And with him there lie mudded" (3.3.100–102) expresses the paralyzing remorse pulling him downward and figures the spiritual state to which his greed and treachery have brought him.

Clearly, Prospero, though once at fault for his idolatry of the liberal arts and of theoretical wisdom, has learned to justify his private study of books by turning it to a human and public purpose. Further proof of his achievement is the masque he has Ariel enact for Miranda and Ferdinand. A figural embodiment of his attained wisdom and art, this lovely vision displays in content and form the temper of Prospero's maturity. It presents Iris, goddess of the rainbow—properly played by Ariel[3]—mediating to bring together Ceres, who haunts the sea marge, and Juno, who inhabits the sky, in a "donation" of dance and song for the "blessed lovers." Prospero remarks that they are "Spirits, which by mine art / I have from their confines called to enact / My present fancies" (4.1.120–22). In the allegory, their "confines" are simply the natural phenomena in which they dwell and Prospero is a poet-magician whose personifying art calls them forth to make them more articulate for their audience. Through language, gesture, music, and theme, the masque speaks of a providential regularity in nature as the source of our daily bread and reminds us of God's continuing creation.

The poetic images of Prospero's masque enhance nature by ceremoniously revealing its essences and, in the process, unveiling a wonderful variety in a single harmony. This vision, requiring silence and stillness in the viewers, approaches through imagination Augustine's "intellectual vision," a pure apprehension of the eternal forms sustaining material substances; according to Patrick Grant, the tenor of this vision is God's providence for his human creature.[4]

For literary criticism, one of the most controversial parts of *The Tempest* has been the abrupt anger that makes Prospero cut short the masque, sending the confused revelers back to their confines. Obviously upset, he exclaims, "I had forgot that foul conspiracy / Of the beast Caliban and his confederates" (4.1.139–40). Prospero's outburst has at least two causes: the villainy of Caliban and his troop, which thwarts the temporal realization of the poet-magician's lovely vision and provokes a just anger, and Prospero's disappointment with himself for almost repeating the mistake that lost Milan its sovereignty. At that earlier time Prospero had yielded to the temptation of beautiful ideas, now he momentarily allows the beautiful masque to seduce him from reality.

Like Prospero, the lovers are enthralled by the masque, as they must be if it is to draw their imaginations to a full sense of its meaning. But his interruption initiates their transition from the exalted vision of art to temporal responsibilities:

> Our revels now are ended. These our actors,
> As I foretold you, were all spirits and
> Are melted into air, into thin air;
> And, like the baseless fabric of this vision,

> The cloud-capped towers, the gorgeous palaces,
> The solemn temples, the great globe itself,
> Yea, all which it inherit, shall dissolve,
> And, like this insubstantial pageant faded,
> Leave not a rack behind. (4.1.148–56)

As Prospero once again cautions his audience about the insubstantiality of the masque, he broadens the compass of his larger plot to include speculation on human destiny. In a vast sweep, he foresees a conclusion for all temporal being—specifically, for all symbolic vessels of political power, religious worship, and artistic creation ("the great globe" puns on Shakespeare's own stage, where no "racks," or theatrical scaffolds, will remain). Viewed in the light of eternity, for which human life is created, all mortal being is essentially spectacle: "We are such stuff / As dreams are made on, and our little life / Is rounded with a sleep" (4.1.156–58)—not annihilated, but "rounded" according to the cyclic progressions of nature "with a sleep" that anticipates, the general tone and outlook of the play's conclusion imply, a consequent awakening.

It is natural for Prospero, as he sees his project ending, to experience flashes of revenge against those who made it necessary; but he does not lose sight of the just purpose he framed from the beginning and for which he has continued to study his books. Therefore he can confidently tell Ariel that "Time / Goes upright with his carriage" (5.1.2–3), implying his own attunement with a providential march of time. Near success, he reviews the agents who have performed the acts he has directed:

> Ye elves of hills, brooks, standing lakes, and groves,
> And ye that on the sands with printless foot
> Do chase the ebbing Neptune, and do fly him
> When he comes back; you demi-puppets that
> By moonshine do the green sour ringlets make,
> Whereof the ewe not bites; and you whose pastime
> Is to make midnight mushrumps, that rejoice
> To hear the solemn curfew. (5.1.33–40)

These spirits of nature are all "Weak masters," subordinate to Prospero's power to direct them. When Prospero wishes to wake "sleepers" from their graves, he may use these spirits as assistants; but their effect is limited, for they enact the directives of a "rough magic" proportioned to carnal mortals and tempestuous seas. Prospero's "potent art" thus works in an element that is entirely natural.

Therefore when Prospero confronts the conspirators and *requires* "Some heavenly music. . . . To work mine end upon their senses" (5.1.52–53), he must turn to more radical means. Paradoxically, he must "abjure" the very power that has brought him near the end of his project. His new aid of "heavenly music"—whether it corresponds to the prophets Augustine saw figured as "fowls of the sky" or to angels figured as "waters above the firmament" or simply to divinely granted grace—is a force explicitly beyond the direct control of Prospero's magic. Still,

Shakespeare's verse implies, Prospero can summon it by his humble gesture of emptying himself of his instruments and arts of earthly control.

The "staff" and "book" that he intends to sacrifice are, of course, the ordinary trapping of a magician; but his peculiar art of transformation in *The Tempest*, wrought through Ariel, whom he controls by language "To th' syllable" (1.2.505) and by thoughts the dainty spirit "cleave[s] to" (4.1.164), has continually linked Prospero with poetry. Thus, in making him declare,

> I'll break my staff,
> Bury it certain fathoms in the earth,
> And deeper than did ever plummet sound
> I'll drown my book (5.1.54–57),

Shakespeare is acknowledging not only the limits of poetic art but its origins in the ebbing and flowing waters of natural emotion and passion that issue into signs. "Staff" perhaps conveys writing instrument as well as king's scepter and magician's wand, while "book" suggests both Prospero's own book and the tradition of literature from which Prospero has learned.

Only by his humility, faith, and charity, moving him from self-reliance to prayerful petition for others, does Prospero assist the essential harmony of the watery voices with the earth's power of generation in the souls of the conspirators:

> Their understanding
> Begins to swell, and the approaching tide
> Will shortly fill the reasonable shore,
> That now lies foul and muddy. (5.1.79–82)

This passage brings forth positive connotations of the tempest figure that have for the most part been hidden. After erupting into violence in the first scene, the sea remains a haunting power, lying just under the play's language, imagery, and action, at times swelling into visibility to remind us of change. Its waves correspond especially to Prospero's "beating mind," where a tempestuousness continues in his life; and the masque, in which that beating rhythm finds the form of visionary poetry through the magician-poet's craft, is a temporary meeting of his own sea's tide with its reasonable shore.

As a coda to the multiple meanings in *The Tempest*, Prospero's Epilogue fits a definition of the form by Hugh of St Victor:

> The things we have analyzed in the course of learning and we must commit to memory we ought, therefore, to gather. Now "gathering" is reducing to a brief and compendious outline which has been written or discussed at some length. The ancients called such an outline an "epilogue," that is, a short restatement, by headings, of things already said.... The fountainhead is one, but its derivative streams are many: Why follow the windings of the latter? Lay hold upon the source and you have the whole thing.... the memory of man is dull and likes brevity, and, if it is dissipated in many things, it has less to bestow upon each of them. We ought, therefore, in all that we learn gather brief and

dependable abstracts to be stored in the little chest of memory, so that later on, when need arises, we can derive everything else from them.[5]

Prospero's final words are an epilogue in this sense, although the perspective is somewhat complicated by the speaker's having stepped out of a concluded fiction to address an actual audience. In this movement outward, foreshadowed in earlier parts of the play, the Prospero of the Epilogue is caught with one foot in fiction and one in history. Having finished his fictional "project," he initiates a more direct project that assumes a diminished distance between art and reality and a specific effect in his audience.

Specifically, he asks his audience to act by assisting his voyage to Naples, where in his public roles as father and as Duke of Milan he will approve his daughter's marriage and thereby dispose the political future of his dukedom. His future, however, awaits the will of his audience consciously to return, renewed by his art, to *their* "Naples," the places of their private and public actions. Their transformation will be manifest in "the help of [their] good hands" and their "Gentle breath."

Prospero's request, of course, imitates the actor's conventional appeal for face-saving applause from the audience; but in view of Shakespeare's inclination to transform conventions while using them by the polysemy of words and the emergent qualities in things and events, it would be wrong to rest in the common interpretation of these phrases. Throughout *The Tempest*, "hands" are prominently instrumental in gestures and deeds of both treachery and friendship, as a look at a Shakespeare glossary can confirm. "Breath," of course, is the sign of life and spirit and the means of speech. Prospero, then, is petitioning his audience not merely for applause that will help rupture the illusion but also for better deeds and gentler speech as they make their transition from spectators to citizens.

Strangely, he asks them as well for prayer, whose very effort can move Mercy, much as he earlier assumes divine assistance merely as the result of his desire for it. Sins requiring forgiveness, the play has shown, are his past inordinate attraction to human wisdom and created beauty and his tendencies to revenge and presumption, perhaps typical occupational hazards for the poet. That a fictional character should ask a real audience for prayer is most strange, unless one remembers that Prospero is still Prospero, that despite his breach of his world's boundaries he still holds the audience in the domain of poetry. He is asking them, then, not immediately to pray but to *imagine* prayer and openness to grace as a possible means to human freedom from guilt and sin. Making this plea is as close as he can come to the stance of a prophet and still remain a poet.

In the eschatological perspective that joins the aesthetic one in the Epilogue, all human words, deeds, and creations depend for their final meaning and their only substantiality on their subordination to the work of Mercy. Hence the poet-prophet must release the audience from the confines of the play's beauty in itself and move them to use their freedom to realize all the meanings of what they have witnessed. By interpreting the play in their consequent thought and through their deeds of love, the audience win a freedom that is identical with Prospero's freedom to renew every traveler to his isle.

## Notes

1 Wolfgang Clemen, *The Development of Shakespeare's Imagery* (Harvard University Press, 1951), p. 192.
2 Augustine, *Confessions*, tr. Pusey (New York: Collier, 1961), pp. 235–36.
3 Irwin Smith, "Ariel and the Masque in *The Tempest*," *Shakespeare Quarterly* 21 (1970), 213–16.
4 *Images and Ideas in Literature of the English Renaissance* (University of Massachusetts Press, 1979), p. 8.
5 Hugh of St Victor, *The Didascalion of Hugh of St Victor*, tr. Jerome Taylor (Columbia University Press, 1968), pp. 93–94.

From *PMLA* 98 (1983), 60–73 abridged. Permission of MLA.

## The Rising of the Dead

Chancel arch, St. Peter's, Wenhaston, Suffolk, c. 1500
By permission of University Presses of Florida

# Part III

# On Shakespeare's Histories

## Fame (Rumor) Leading Mars

From Vincenzo Cartari, *Imagines Deorum*,
tr. Antonio Verderius (Lyons, 1581).
Permission from *Shakespeare Studies*

# ON SHAKESPEARE'S HISTORIES

## Introduction

A belief that all history is governed by a divine providence was inherited by the Elizabethans from classical authors and from Christian tradition. Therefore alongside the history recorded in the Bible they read stories of other peoples, ancient and modern, not only for the pleasure of hearing about colorful personalities, but also with a concern to observe the consequences of good and bad ways of life. Histories were considered to be mirrors of universal truths useful for guiding the reader in his daily life. Shakespeare's histories are mirrors of this kind.

The section of English history most studied in Shakespeare's day was that stretching from the times of Richard II, the last of the Plantagenet rulers, to the accession of Tudor rule under Henry VII. Edward Hall, an admirer of Henry VIII, had surveyed this period in a chronicle that glorified the accomplishments of Henry V and Henry VII in contrast to the disorders suffered by England under Henry IV, Henry VI, and Richard III; and when intepreting this contrast Hall saw it as evidence of God's favoring of political virtue and punishing of political vice. Traditional theologians have usually been wary of equating political success with moral merit, since, as Augustine noted, the wicked are often successful in regard to the goods of fortune. Hall tended to blur a distinction between eternal goods and temporal benefits; yet his estimates were followed more or less by the compilers of Holinshed's chronicle and by the poet Daniel in his epic on England's civil wars. For these authors, civil dissension was the worst of all evils and its remedy was a national unity through obedience to the king.

Shakespeare, however, seems to have had a more complex view of this whole matter. We sense this if we ponder the various biblical allusions he adds as a context when dramatizing the historical materials furnished by the chronicles. By making central to his *Richard II*, for instance, a gardener's tracing of England's calamity to Richard's Adam-like neglect to care for his garden, Shakespeare provides a prior and more comprehensive moral than the one later voiced by the Bishop of Carlisle when preaching against Bolingbroke's rebellion, the fault which Hall made central to his moralized chronicle. In Shakespeare's view, we infer, Hall's emphasis on political obedience is a half-truth that scants the more ultimate matter of everyone's duty to God. Elsewhere, too, we can infer that Hall's ideal of a "politicke" government seemed to Shakespeare to scant something more important, namely, that a governor have in his heart God's grace—a matter which is called to our attention, for instance, by Hastings in *Richard III* when he laments his folly of having neglected the grace of God by trusting instead the grace of mortal man. All merely political approaches to virtue, so Shakespeare seems to imply, are shortsighted. The horizons of history are larger than that—as his own dramas will show.

Important to Shakespeare was the difference between the virtue by which Richmond became Henry VII and the virtue of Henry V. If we look closely at the earlier Henry, we find him lacking in divine grace despite his boasts of having it. Tillyard was much distressed by a coarseness in this Henry's manners and intellect; yet it did not occur to Tillyard to consider whether the crudity might be a punishment by God—for this king's sin of worshipping earthly crowns. The wrath of God, says Paul in Romans 1, is revealed against idolaters by giving them over to the impurities of their own hearts, allowing them to substitute an animal-like glory for the glory of God. Such a characterization fits Shakespeare's Henry V, who can be said to have dehumanized himself and made bloody robbery his nation's occupation. The punishment assigned by Dante to Alexander the Great, that of wading in blood in hell's circle of the violent against neighbor, would seem to apply to Henry.

Moreover, any reader of Shakespeare familiar with Augustine's overview of history could have placed Henry V's type of virtue as being more Roman than Christian. What characterized the heroes of pagan Rome, Augustine explained in Book V of his *City of God*, was an obsessive love of human honor through the arts of subjugating and vanquishing nations, which is no true virtue for Christians. Augustine was a major authority also, however, for the doctrine that God lets tyrants and hypocrites reign because of the sins of the people, and that he gives earthly power both to the impious and to the pious as he sees fit (V, 19, 21). So any spectators of Shakespeare's drama informed by Augustine's orthodoxy would expect to find included under providence a tyrant such as Richard III as well as a pious Henry Richmond, besides any illustrious but guileful coveter of honor such as Henry V.

Do the eight histories of Shakespeare's two tetralogies have a unified story to tell? Modern critics who are skeptical of any doctrine of providence find no chain of meaning. Some think the playwright was using his dramatic personages simply as spokesmen for the conflicting ideologies he found in his chronicle sources or in the political currents of his own day. But such an approach ignores the importance of a drama's plot, through which is revealed what happens as a consequence of the quality of thinking of various personages. Can we not see in each of Shakespeare's histories the outcome of some phase in the movement of the nation's life? And do not the successive phases have a continuity that constitutes a meaningful pattern? Edward Berry in a careful review of the four plays that culminate with *Richard III* titled his study *Patterns of Decay* (1975), because he discerned a central theme of "political disintegration" underlying each play and binding together the series as a whole. Indeed, he named the successive stages of this disintegration: first a breakdown of ceremony, then of legal system, and then of family loyalty, thus progressively dissolving all "communal" ties until human love has nothing to turn about except Richard's monstrous self. Richard's blaspheming of charity yet claiming title as "the Lord's anointed," says Berry, makes him the Anti-Christ dragon of

Revelation 12, thus tying him to Old Testament and New Testament orthodoxies of providence. Paradoxically he unwittingly serves God by inflicting punishments that purge sinners and arouse consciences to pray for a deliverer, divinely provided in Richmond.

Now if we may regard this pattern as the unifying thread of the one tetralogy, how can we connect with it the development within England that is dramatized in the sequence from *Richard II* to *Henry V*? This prior span, surely, is not lacking in signals of a decline in the nation's moral fibre and cultural health. The decline in *Richard II* may be said to begin with a lapsing from an "other Eden" that made England renowned for "Christian service and true chivalry." This Eden continues to be revered by Mowbray, but not by Richard nor by John of Gaunt's son. Only a counterfeit of Christian service remains in Henry V. Under Henry IV the ideal was implied in this king's vow to make a pilgrimage to the Holy Land in penance for sin. But political advantage moved Henry IV to postpone keeping this promise, and when he died remorseful but unrepentant he bequeathed to his son only the self-serving duty of busying "giddy minds with foreign quarrels," rather than any duty to fulfill the father's unpaid vow. (Unpaid debt, and the evading of paying it, is a major topic of Falstaff's jesting.) The reign of Shakespeare's Henry V presents a hollow (not truly hallowed) version of chivalry, decorated nevertheless with ceremonies of ostensible piety adroitly managed through deceitful diplomacy. The subsurface significance of such kingship is revealed in the irony of Henry's confession that he is serving "idol ceremony" and receiving in reward only vain titles and loss of heartsease. The cultural result, we later learn, is the gaining of a garden "grown to wildness" and a human savagery "unnatural" in everything (5.2.84). Is this not a worse state than the unpruned garden of Richard II? The logical next stage of England's decline is the breakdown of patriotic ceremony with which *Henry VI* begins.

What Shakespeare's eight histories are evidently mirroring is a chain of phases of England's lapsing from a chivalry dedicated to a Christian-Eden ideal. The stages consist of the progressively defective versions of chivalry we encounter from one reign to the next, and the progressive impoverishment of community life that accompanies this. When a nadir is reached in the moral nihilism of Richard III, Henry Richmond provides a reassociating of chivalry with divine grace and a serving of Christian goals. Mention of taking "the sacrament" occurs, significantly, near the beginning of *Richard II* and at the end of *Richard III*. The Eucharist is, by implication, at the hub of public welfare.

Regarding Shakespeare's independent histories of two English kings, John in the twelfth and thirteenth centuries and Henry VIII in the sixteenth, our anthology's limitations of space permit only a brief word of comment. These plays, although sometimes termed the Prologue and the Epilogue to the other eight, have rarely been studied with a focus on manifestations of providence. In *King John* the monarch's conflict with the papacy and with his nobles when they rebel has been viewed chiefly with an interest in the role of the Bastard son of Richard the Lion-hearted as a supporter of English nationalism. More thought needs to be given to the significance of John's death by a fever, the concurrent washout by tide and tempest of his troops and of enemy armadas and of all bastard-like ambitions, while a restorative patriotism is mediated by the knight Hubert after his conversion by the child Arthur. (See, e.g., my analysis of "Religion in *King John*," *Connotations* 1 [1991] and continued in 2 [1992].)

*King Henry VIII* presents us a spectacle that has buffeted audiences—between wonderment at this king's cloth-of-gold paradings, pity for the genuine virtue he scuttles in divorcing Katharine, and puzzlement over Cranmer's prophecy of a Phoenix-like Elizabeth. Readers of this play need to examine more fully the thematic significance of Wolsey's discovery of the "vain pomp" of worldly glory and the wretchedness of anyone who "hangs on princes' favors." Shakespeare is not blind to deceitfulness in princes. And he has a Boethian sense of a divine providence that overrules the turnings of Fortune's wheel.

### Fortune's Wheel

From Barclay's
The *Shyp of Folys of the Worlde* (1509)

## Comment and bibliography

The opening question in *Richard II* regarding who is the traitor is given its basic answer, an ironic one, when Richard himself betrays traditional rites of justice. On St Lambert's day he interrupts a ritual dedicated to the honor of God and substitutes rulings calculated to advantage himself. He thereby usurps God's judgment. Holinshed had not seen the story in that light. He had faulted Richard only for his dissolute life "given to the pleasure of the body." But in Shakespeare's play, as Hermann Ulrici noted as early as 1839, the "first rebel" is Richard himself, who with his own hand sows the seed of revolution. The moral Ulrici drew was that "the highest earthly power is not exempt from the eternal laws of the universe" and that any majesty claiming to be of God "loses its title as soon as it abandons its only foundation in the grace of God." As a reinforcement of this interpretation, I would add Augustine's concept that disobedience punishes disobedience (*City of God* XIV.15): thus Bolingbroke's rebellion, although wicked, can be seen as a providential punishment of Richard.

In Act 4 when Richard hands over his crown to Bolingbroke he speaks bitterly of being compelled by Judases to "deny my sacred state." But at this point he is shedding only the outward insignia of an office whose inward and spiritual grace he has forfeited long before. Kingship's sacramental function he has continuously been replacing with ceremonial caprice. Richard's notion of himself as a glorious sun is pretentious, and his pose of Christlikeness reveals actually a desire like old Adam's to be like God. Queen Elizabeth had good reason to feel uncomfortable about the analogy she reportedly recognized between Richard and herself.

Several major aspects of the drama have been linked together in the commentary by Herbert Coursen which our anthology abridges. Important is the initial contrast between a Richard who is hiding a past crime and an honest Mowbray whose repenting of a former sin has been sealed by his taking the sacrament. Mowbray sought pardon for having planned an ambush; but in the present situation Bolingbroke may be setting an ambush for Richard. Richard dodges repentance by responding with a counter-ambush. But an innocent Mowbray is thereby victimized and Bolingbroke is handed a grievance. Richard's hidden sin has led him to betray the rites of community justice he was expected to mediate as head of the kingdom's mystical body. His further distortions of caretaking open the door to a rebellion by Bolingbroke, which Richard both denounces and fatalistically aids. We notice his breakdown of integrity into a willy-nilly doubleness of will which sets "the word against the word." Coursen cites an Elizabethan *Homilie* on "falling from God," which tells of Adam's incurring as punishment an unfruitful land. Figuratively that is the punishment evident in Richard and the realm he governs. Richard's tragedy essentially is that he destroys the "spiritual premises" of kingship, a point Coursen elaborates more fully in his *The Leasing Out of England* (1982).

Among the essays for supplementary reading, Stanley Maveety's offers a tight argument for the influence of Genesis 2–4 on Shakespeare's structuring of England's calamity. The texture of the tragic action, Maveety contends, likens Richard to Adam's and Cain's sin against sanctity, with Bolingbroke's crime then signaling a worsening relationship between God and man that foreshadows a quarrelsome community of depravity. Imagery of exile, banishment, and wandering accompanies the "second fall of cursed man," and the play closes with Bolingbroke's finding himself bloodied with Cain's guilt. Berninghausen's essay also touches on these points.

Tillyard's idea that Richard's conduct of the tournament is indicative of medieval ideals has been disputed by several essayists. It indicates rather, says Peter Phialas, Richard's deficiency in medieval chivalry. John Elliot, who thinks so too, traces Richard's tragedy to his "misunderstanding of the nature of kingship" and notes that he comes to recognize eventually his having wasted time and being wasted by time. Wilbur Sanders calls Richard's view of kingship a "sadly gelded version" of the medieval concept of the sacredness of kings, a mere husk of the traditional view, which emphasized a king's function as shepherd, father, and physician. Shakespeare was mirroring in Richard, Sanders suggests, an analogy to the Elizabethan administration's so-called orthodoxy and its tragic consequences.

The essay by Battenhouse calls attention to blind spots in the reading of Scripture by the Elizabethan *Homily Against Disobedience*. Then he surveys the plights of ironic self-contradiction which in Shakespeare's play beset all the characters who try to follow the kind of nonresistance advocated in that homily. Palsy becomes endemic, and of notable significance is the impotent isolation into which the Bishop of Carlisle gets himself by failing to give the king any pastoral counsel to repent and amend his life. This bishop has abrogated the duty of a Nathan or an Elijah.

Clayton MacKenzie, after citing Elizabethan authors who likened England to Eden, elaborates on the significance of Richard's abandonment of Christian chivalry. It constitutes a "second fall of cursed man" and begins a cultural slide into spiritual hollowness that portends dead men's skulls and general woe.

## Supplementary bibliography

Battenhouse, Roy. "Tudor Doctrine and the Tragedy of *Richard II*," *Rice University Studies* 60 (1974), 31–53; rpt. in part in Mark Scott, ed., *Shakespearean Criticism* (Detroit: Gale Research) VI, 402–09.

Berninghausen, Thomas. "Banishing Cain: The Gardening Metaphor in *Richard II* and the Genesis Myth," *Essays in Literature* 14 (1987), 3–14.

Bryant, J. A., Jr. *Hippolyta's View*, Ch. 2.

Coursen, H. R. *The Leasing Out of England: Shakespeare's Second Henriad* (University Press of America, 1982), Ch. 2.

Elliot, John R., Jr. "*Richard II* and the Medieval," *Renaissance Papers 1965* (1966), 25–34.

_____. "History and Tragedy in *Richard II*," *Studies in English Literature* 8 (1968), 253–71.

Fergusson, Francis. *Trope and Allegory* (1977), pp. 91–99.

MacKenzie, Clayton. "Paradise and Paradise Lost in *Richard II*," *Shakespeare Quarterly* 37 (1986), 318–39.

Maveety, Stanley. "A Second Fall of Cursed Man: The Bold Metaphor of *Richard II*," *Journal of English and Germanic Philology* 72 (1973), 175–93.

Phialas, Peter C. "The Medieval in *Richard II*," *Shakespeare Quarterly* 12 (1961), 305–10.

Sanders, Wilbur. *The Dramatist and the Received Idea* (Cambridge University Press, 1968), pp. 143–93.

*Herbert R. Coursen, Jr. (1976)*

## Hollow Ritual in *Richard II* [editor's title]

Comedy imitates the deeper rhythms of the Communion Service and moves toward Communion, specifically the intersection of the lines of comedy and the Communion of the marriages at the play's end. But a tragic hero tends to move away from the creative and healing power of supernature and pulls his world with him, so that the world itself plunges away from the possibilities of Communion, further and further away from the positive potentiality of social and religious ritual.

Shakespeare employs medieval heritage as he received it from the Elizabethan Communion Service, not as proven fact but as *potential* truth to be perceived by his tragic hero and, invariably, as the truth against which the fall of that hero must be measured. Whether he perceives the truth or not, he invariably denies it, to discover in his own way "the paradox of Christian doctrine, that nature without grace is unnatural."[1] The tragic pattern is neatly defined by Battenhouse:

> The Shakespearean hero's defective action shadows Christian paradigm in the same sense that falsehood inevitably depends upon truth, or the corruption of anything depends upon the good it corrupts.[2]

The inevitable contrast between potential comedy and actual tragedy that Shakespeare structures into his tragedies creates the response Auden defines: "At the end of a Greek tragedy we say, 'What a pity it had to be this way'; at the end of a Christian tragedy, 'What a pity it had to be this way when it might have been otherwise.'"[3]

Richard's hand in Gloucester's murder denies him the support to his kingship that ritual should provide. He cannot reconcile Bolingbroke and Mowbray. Richard is disqualified from the priestly role and can only preside over the anti-rituals the play will present. Bolingbroke's indictment associates Mowbray with a crime having universal implications:

> That he . . . like a traitor coward,
> Sluic'd out [Gloucester's] innocent soul through streams of blood;
> Which blood, like sacrificing Abel's, cries
> Even from the tongueless caverns of the earth,
> To me for justice and rough chastisement. (1.1.100–06)

If Richard *is* responsible for it (and we can't be sure until John of Gaunt tells us he is), he has committed an archetypal crime which, like the murder of King Hamlet, must have deep negative reverberations within his kingdom.

Richard cannot allow either Bolingbroke or Mowbray to win the trial by combat. Bolingbroke's accusation aims at Richard. Bolingbroke can pose as defender of the right, but his resolution has a more specific pitch, as Richard knows and Mowbray reiterates:

> What thou art, God, thou, and I do know;
> And all too soon, I fear, the King shall rue. (1.3.204–05)

Bolingbroke's victory would vindicate him as the kingdom's prime exponent of justice (the king's role), enhance his already obvious popularity with the people, and greatly increase his strength as Richard's rival. Richard must intercede. But Richard's interrupting speech is self-refuting; his hidden participation in a crime undermines his role as impartial magistrate and indeed, ultimately, permits Bolingbroke to assume the role of justicer for the kingdom. Richard cannot permit "the rites of knighthood" (1.1.75) to fulfill themselves because he, "God's substitute / His deputy anointed in His sight, / Hath caused [Gloucester's] death" (1.2.37–39).

Richard's untenable position is emphasized both by the aspiring Bolingbroke and by Mowbray, who responds convincingly to the accusations dealing with the funds Richard sent him, and who apologizes again to Gaunt. He dismisses the main charge, however, with less than three ambiguous lines:

> For Gloucester's death,
> I slew him not; but to my own disgrace
> Neglected my sworn duty in that case. (1.1.132–34)

Does he mean that he ignored the order to protect Gloucester or to slay him? In Holinshed, Mowbray claims to have saved Gloucester's life "contrarie to the will of the king." Shakespeare makes him intentionally brief and vague. He is looking at the guilty man, and hoping perhaps that Richard will resolve the debate. Further, Mowbray defends himself against Bolingbroke's charges by citing his religious observances:

> But for you, my noble Lord of Lancaster,
> The honourable father to my foe,
> Once did I lay an ambush for your life,
> A trespass that doth vex my grieved soul;
> But ere I last receiv'd the sacrament
> I did confess it, and exactly begg'd
> Your Grace's pardon; and I hope I had it. (1.1.135–41)

Mowbray describes here the comic pattern embodied in Communion—repentence and pardon. The irony, however, is that Richard himself is unwilling to fulfill the external forms for regaining inward spiritual health. Instead, Mowbray is banished, a banishment dictated by political considerations which emerge from the king's abandonment of the religious premises Mowbray had embraced.

One of the operative words for the condition Richard has engendered is "hollow." Ritual is without its spiritual core. Aumerle's parting from Bolingbroke must be "hollow" (1.4.9); Northumberland must see in the face of England "the hollow eyes of death" (2.1.270); Gaunt must find a "grave, / Whose hollow womb inherits naught but bones" (2.1.82–83); and Bushy and Green, followers of Richard, must be "grav'd in the hollow ground" (3.2.140). The only unhollow element in a world where positive value has no substance must be "grief," which "boundeth where it falls, / Not with empty hollowness, but weight" (1.2.59).

If the king is hollow, so must his kingdom be. "Landlord of England art thou now, not King" (2.1.95–113). His imitation of "fashions in proud Italy" (2.1.8) draws his attention from the deeper English heritage that Gaunt celebrates:

> This other Eden, demi-paradise,
> This fortress built by Nature for herself
> Against infection and the hand of war,
> This happy breed of men. . .
> Renowned for their deeds as far from home,
> For Christian service and true chivalry,
> As is the sepulchre in stubborn Jewry,
> Of the world's ransom, blessed Mary's Son. . . (2.1.42–56)

Later we discover that the only character in the play able to translate this conception of England's heritage into reality is Mowbray, who does it not in England but in some corner of a foreign field:

> Many a time hath banish'd Norfolk fought
> For Jesu Christ in glorious Christian field,
> Streaming the ensign of the Christian cross
> Against black pagans, Turks, and Saracens;
> And, toil'd with works of war, retir'd himself
> To Italy; and there at Venice gave
> His body to that pleasant country's earth,
> And his pure soul unto his captain Christ,
> Under whose colours he had fought so long. (4.1.92–100)

Mowbray has exported the English virtues described by Gaunt, has, it would seem, taken with him the country's chivalric quality, leaving England devoid of medieval glory and ready for the myriad skulls Carlisle envisions as the island's future.

It is impossible to overemphasize the significance of Richard's defection from true kingship. Since, as Kantorowicz points out, Richard represents "the mystic body of his subjects and the nation,"[4] his sacramental function is profound. His body politic is like the elements of the Communion Service at the moment they become functional, that is, at the moment of transmission. The king "was 'liturgical' as a king because, and in so far as, he represented and 'imitated' the image of the living Christ."[5] He was "human by nature, divine by grace,"[6] thus imitating the dual nature of the elements—Christ and bread, body politic and body natural, the latter, like the bread and wine, the medium within which incarnation occurs (and it is an occurrence, *not* a residence). The king imitates as well, of course, the dual nature of Christ (divine and human, body politic and body natural). The "doctrine of theology and canon law," says Kantorowicz, "that the Church and Christian society in general was a '*corpus mysticum* the head of which is Christ' has been transferred by the jurists from the theological sphere to that of the state, the head of which is the king."[7]

The king is the medium through which his subjects and his nation participate in the larger spiritual mysteries of the cosmos. The king imitates Christ: his subjects imitate Christ's disciples within the kingdom as within the Communion. But like the individual communicant, the king must understand his role and understand that its efficacy depends upon the choices he makes, choices that either confirm or undermine it. As with the elements, the sacramental fusion must occur within the king. It does not merely *reside* there, as Richard tries to insist.

Richard has separated himself from the role as king, and thus has removed his realm from the sources of health. He has "leased out" his realm (2.2.59), has put the realm "in farm," has "grown bankrupt like a broken man" (2.1.256–7). His "commercial exploitation of a sacred trust"[8] creates the condition whereby traitors wound the living earth, "march . . . upon her peaceful bosom, / Frighting her pale-fac'd villages with war" (2.3.92–4) because, as Reese suggests, when the ruler is a guilty man, rebellion is one of the manifestations of his guilt.[9]

In the simplest terms, England and Richard have fallen from God. "He that hath suffer'd this disordered spring," says the Gardener, "Hath now himself met with the fall of leaf" (3.4.48–9). "O, what pity is it," the Gardener continues,

> That he had not so trimmm'd and dress'd his land
> As we his garden! We at time of year
> Do wound the bark. . . . Superfluous branches
> We lop away, that bearing boughs may live;
> Had he done so, himself had borne the crown,
> Which waste of idle hours hath quite thrown down. (3.4.55–66)

While the *Homilies* abound, as does the Bible, in garden imagery that almost inevitably conveys an allegorical sense of Eden, it is perhaps not accidental that the Homily "of falling from God" should employ garden imagery more abundantly than any other, dealing as it does, and as *Richard II* does, with "a second fall of cursed man" (3.4.76). The Homily illuminates the garden imagery of the play by suggesting that what happens to the individual who falls from God must extend automatically to the kingdom of the king who falls from God. "As long as a man doeth prune his vines, doeth dig at the rootes, and doeth lay fresh earth to them, hee hath a mind to them, he perceiveth some token of fruitfulness that may be re-covered in them. But once he falls from God, as by pride and sinne we goe from God, so shall God and all goodnesse with him goe from us.... he will let us lie waste, he will give us over...." The Homily talks of "a goodly vineyard" made by God for his beloved children:

> And when he looked that it would bring him foorth good grapes, it brought forth wild graps: and after it followeth, Now shall I shew you (saith God) what I wil doe with my vineyard: I will plucke downe the hedges, that it may perish:... God at length doeth so forsake his unfruitful vineyard, that hee will not onely suffer it to bring foorth weeds, bryers, and thornes, but also further to punish the unfruitfulness of it. Hee saith he will not cut it, hee will not delve it, and hee will commaund the cloudes that they shall not raine upon it.

Richard, clearly, is responsible for the transition from the garden Gaunt celebrated to an England where only "blood.... shall manure the ground" (4.1.137), where "blood" will be the only medium of growth (5.6.46).

While Richard's deposition of himself is the logical consequence and indeed the inevitable destiny of his decisions, he *states* the truth only once: "I wasted time, and now doth time waste me" (5.5.49) .... Richard's creation of "the absent time" (2.3.79) leads to his own complicated metaphor of time:

> now hath Time made me his numb'ring clock.
> ... So sighs and tears and groans
> Show minutes, times, and hours; but my time
> Runs posting on in Bolingbroke's proud joy,
> While I stand fooling here, his Jack o'th' clock. (5.5.50–60)

Richard plays with his fate in what Traversi has termed "an academic exercise in poetic pessimism."[10] Richard tries to translate word into flesh:

> My brain I'll prove the female to my soul,
> My soul the father; and these two beget
> A generation of still-breeding thoughts,
> And these same thoughts people this little world,
> In humours like the people of this world.
> For no thought is contented. The better sort,
> As thoughts of things divine, are intermix'd
> With scruples and do set the word itself

Against the word:
As thus, "Come little ones," and then again,
"It is as hard to come as for a camel
To thread the postern of a small needle's eye." (5.5.6–17)

Richard neglects the crucial qualification that Christ makes: it is a "riche man" (in Matthew, Mark, and Luke [Geneva Version]) who cannot "enter the Kingdome of God." Christ explains this in the tenth chapter of Mark, a passage that was very familiar to Elizabethans by dint of its incorporation into the Sacrament of Baptism: "whosoever doeth not receive the kyngdome of God, as a lytle chylde: he shall not entre therin." For Richard to penetrate the paradox he would have to see the impiety that brought him down and recognize that he must *become* a little one, must be born again, to achieve spiritual health. By penetrating the paradox, he could have seen why he, "the proud king," is excluded from his own kingdom, a paradigm of God's Kingdom.

York's plight is similar when he finds he can be loyal to the new king only by betraying his son. He too "set'st the word itself against the word" (5.3.116–19). According to his duchess, a wife divided against her husband, York engages in false prayers:

He prays but faintly and would be deni'd;
We pray with heart and soul and all beside...
His prayers are full of false hypocrisy;
Ours of true zeal and deep integrity.
Our prayers do out-pray his; then let them have
That mercy which true prayer ought to have. (5.3.103–10)

The Duchess of York praying for pardon suggests to us a disjunctive analogue to the Duchess of Gloucester begging for revenge, but both imply that the choices made by Gaunt and York have been *unnatural*:

and though thou liv'st and breath'st,
Yet art thou slain in him. (1.2.24–25)

Is he not like thee? Is he not thine own?...
He is as like thee as any man may be. (5.2.94–108)

Gaunt has supposed that to be loyal to his king he must ignore a brother's murder; York supposes that to be loyal to the other king he must demand a son's death. The word *against* the flesh—into such dilemmas are the characters thrust who inhabit the world Richard has divided.

The "word against the word" is but a prelude to the internecine struggle Carlisle predicts for what was "a Christian climate" (4.1.130):

O, if you raise this house against this house,
It will the woefullest division prove
That ever fell upon this cursed earth. (145–47)

A fallen world can only fall further, however, when the sacrament that Mowbray took as a medium toward the pardon of John of Gaunt is used as a sanction for regicide:

> Before I freely speak my mind herein,
> You shall not only take the Sacrament
> To bury mine intents, but also to effect
> Whatever I shall happen to devise. . . . (3.26–34)

> A dozen of them here have ta'en the Sacrament,
> And interchangeably set down their hands,
> To kill the King at Oxford. (5.2.97–99)

Such an oath is, according to the Homily against Swearing and Perjury, "unlawfull and ungodly," but it represents the setting of one word against another—precisely the "woeful division" Richard engenders and Carlisle describes.

On his return from Ireland, Richard alternates between wildly unrealistic hopes and a self-dramatizing despair. He seeks an army in the sky:

> God for his Richard hath in heavenly pay
> A glorious angel; then, if angels fight,
> Weak men must fall, for Heaven still guards the right. (3.2.60–62)

But because Richard assumes that his role confers privilege but no concomitant responsibility, he throws away "respect, / Tradition, form, and ceremonious duty" and pursues "that sweet way . . . into despair" (3.2.205). His impulse to play the martyr encourages the development of despair and the inevitable movement of Bolingbroke into the vacuum of rule: "A king, woe's slave, shall kingly woe obey" (3.2.210). Here, Richard makes his body natural, his woe, ruler over his body politic.

The Deposition Scene rings with religious references—Judas, Pilate—part of Richard's pageant of betrayal. But the allusions to Judas can only be ironic. Not only was Richard wrong when he flailed his executed cronies, Wiltshire, Bushy, and Green, as "each one thrice worse than Judas!" (3.2.132), but since Judas was possibly the only disciple to be of Christ's kindred, Richard's allusion points as much at his own betrayal of Gloucester ("Abel") as at his supposed betrayers. A double-sidedness appears, indeed, in Richard's suggestion that *he* is responsible for his deposition while at the same time he blames those around him for his downfall.

Since only "the hand of God / . . . [can dismiss] us from our stewardship" (3.3.77–78), only Richard can perform the offices of prayer and response in the anti-"service" of his deposition. The actual deposition speech is the anti-ritualistic center of the play, the inevitable result of Richard's defiance of the premises of his kingship.

Richard's parting from his queen illustrates the inevitable anti-rituals that must continue in the world after his deposition. Richard had prevented Bolingbroke's marriage, Bolingbroke had accused Bushy and Green of making "a divorce betwixt [Richard's] queen and him" (3.1.12). The separation of Richard and his queen is more than a divorce, it is an anti-marriage, an analogue to Richard of his "unkinging":

> Doubly divorc'd! Bad men, you violate
> A twofold marriage, 'twixt my crown and me,
> And then betwixt me and my married wife;
> Let me unkiss the oath 'twixt thee and me . . . (5.1.71–74)

Their parting represents a ritual separation of what was fused in marriage:

> Queen       And must we be divided? Must we part?
> K. Richard   Ay, hand from hand, my love, and heart from heart. (81–82)

Instead of becoming one flesh, they, "two together weeping, make one woe." Again, grief becomes ultimate reality. They marry sorrow and self-destruction, appropriately, since Richard has engendered the inevitable division between king and man, king and kingdom, king and queen. The ceremony that joined them hoped that they might "abide in thy love unto their lives ende." The anti-ritual that parts them ends with the queen's thoughts of death and Richard's words "the rest let sorrow say."

Richard's defection as sacramental king has denied sacrament to his kingdom, has led inevitably to the ritual stripping of his body politic by his body natural and from thence to the sacrilege of Exton's deed:

> Exton, thy fierce hand
> Hath with the King's blood stained the King's own hand. (5.5.111)

The original murder—"all the precious liquor spilt" (1.2.19)—culminates in the final murder:

> As full of valor as of royal blood!
> Both have I spilled; O would the deed were good!
> For now the devil, that told me I did well,
> Says that the deed is chronicled in hell. (5.5.114–17)

In Henry IV's world, the dead Richard represents the resolution of one dilemma through the introduction of another. Now the very guilt of Abel's blood which he tried to pin on Mowbray at the beginning has been incurred under Bolingbroke's own aegis by Exton. The blood that has stained the land now tinges the land's new king.

> Lords, I protest, my soul is full of woe
> That blood should sprinkle me to make me grow. (5.6.45–46)

Although Bolingbroke projects a crusade "To wash this blood from off my guilty hand," his plight is clearly that which he assigned Exton: to wander with Cain through "shades of night."

The projected crusade never occurs, and later we find that even *it* was politically motivated. Piety in the history plays that follow is subordinate to politics;

ritual belongs to the world destroyed by the strange cooperation of Richard and his rival. Ceremony becomes empty or worse. Henry V will evaluate it as "poison'd flattery" (4.1.268).

## Notes

1  M. D. H. Parker, *The Slave of Life* (London, 1955), p. 132.
2  *Shakespearean Tragedy* (Bloomington, Ind., 1969), p. 264.
3  W. H. Auden, "The Christian Tragic Hero," *New York Times Book Review*, 16 December 1945.
4  Ernst H. Kantorowicz, *The King's Two Bodies* (Princeton, N.J., 1957) p. 39.
5  Ibid., p. 43.
6  Ibid., p. 46.
7  Ibid., p. 52.
8  R. J. Dorius, "A Little More than a Little," *Shakespeare Quarterly* 11 (1960), 19.
9  M. M. Reese, *The Cease of Majesty* (New York, 1961), p. 244.
10  D. Traversi, *Shakespeare: From Richard II to Henry V* (Palo Alto, California, 1957), p. 47.

From *Christian Ritual and the World of Shakespeare's Tragedies* (Bucknell University Press, 1976), pp. 25–74, abridged and revised with the author's assistance.

## Comment and bibliography

Richard when going to prison had predicted a future enmity between the "mounting" Bolingbroke and his "ladder," Northumberland. The love of wicked men, he explained, converts to fear and hate, which turns them to danger and death. We hear this prophecy recalled in *2 Henry IV* 3.1 by a sin-sick and melancholy Henry, who in bewilderment excuses his past actions as compelled by necessity and attributes their foul outcome to the mockeries of chance. The play's action, however, has shown us that Henry's troubles with the Northumberland clan began when his fear prompted him to refuse to ransom Mortimer and also to refuse brave Percy the customary right of a knight to retain some of the prisoners he captured when fighting on the king's behalf. Fearing that Mortimer and the prisoners could be used to challenge Henry's shaky title, the king acts to protect self-interest above all else and thus arouses hatred from the Percies, who now accuse him of breaking his oath to them, not only in the present situation but also in the past by making himself king in violation of his oath at Doncaster.

Thus, ironically, the very participants in the earlier oath-breaking turn against Henry and berate him as a "vile politician" lacking in gratitude. A graceless hypocrite he indeed is—but so equally are they. And since neither side can trust the other a showdown inevitably occurs—first at Shrewsbury, where the lunatic "honor" of Hotspur expends itself on the counterfeits of kingship Henry employs to survive, and then later at Gaultree forest, where an Archbishop's party counterfeiting religion gets mowed down by the treacherous "honor" of Henry's representatives. A political "success" that is morally bankrupt is evident when in Henry's name John of Lancaster butchers those to whom he had pledged health and friendship a moment earlier. Are we not witnessing a fulfillment of Northumberland's Cain-like prayer, "Let order die"? King Henry concurrently dies in a fit of apoplexy, accompanied by a sense of guilt that prompts him to propose a foreign war to wipe from public "memory" the father's crooked ways. Knighthood in these plays is the knight err-antry of "gentlemen of the shade" under Cain's curse of "shades of night."

Besides the Cain theme, which readers of Augustine will recall is prototypal of an Earthly city built on strife in contrast to a city of faith represented by Abel and Abraham, two other biblical contexts are important to *Henry IV*. One is the elaborate initial reference to "the blessed feet ... nailed / For our advantage." This is a clear allusion to Christ's ransoming of mankind, to which Henry's proposed crusade is implicitly dedicated. But significantly, Henry's evading of this ransoming project is accompanied by a refusal to ransom Mortimer, a comparable duty in feudal custom. The two decisions signal a politics of selfish advantaging that disregards heaven's means of grace. A second important biblical context is Isaiah's description of unholy Israel at the time King Uzziah died. The well-known first chapter of Isaiah cries out against a sinful nation of rebellious children, as witnessed by a sick head, a faint heart, a body with no soundness in it, a city that has become a harlot, and princes who have become "companions of thieves." These symptoms, including a Mistress Quickly invented by Shakespeare (to follow up *Richard II* 5.3.16) as a symbol of the harlot-chivalry now central to England, are all evident in the two-part panorama of *Henry IV.*

Imagery of broken promises, madcapery, freebooting, and counterfeiting characterize in *Henry IV* a body politic which opposing parties refer to as "diseased," yet try to profit from—as if to "turn diseases to commodity." That phrase by Falstaff sums up the vicious cleverness he wittily parodies in his role as licensed fool. Some critics have viewed Falstaff as simply a ludicrous Satan-figure. But others, such as Traversi in the commentary reprinted in our anthology, see in Falstaff's jests a canny mirroring of his political superiors and the whole cultural scene, which he peppers with tantalizing biblical allusions that testify a Christian intelligence in Falstaff. Thus a critical question arises: Is Falstaff really misleading Prince Hal, or, rather, is he making it his occupation to humorously mimic vice for the moral enlightenment of the Prince—in this potentially healthful way turning diseases into profit?

My essay on "Falstaff as Parodist" attempts to spell out in considerable detail the argument for regarding Falstaff as a charitable dramatizer of vices, which he enacts fictionally as the foolish absurdities latent in Old Adam. These absurdities characterize England's leaders as assessed by a Falstaff who is a candle amid the spiritual darkness of his times. Many readers may find difficult this hypothesis regarding the enigma of Falstaff, but it should appeal to all who feel that he is more than a mere buffoon and that his antics relate significantly to the political history in the drama's main plot. When he names himself Prince Hal's good angel and calls himself an old "young" man, let it be recalled that this is the *puer senex* paradox noted in Portia by Lawrence Danson, and traced to Isaiah 40 by Peggy Simonds when commenting on *Cymbeline* (see *infra*).

Ronald Berman's account of the play's motifs of disease and counterfeiting is pertinent supplementary reading. The imagery of disease includes, he points out, fevered imaginations, droopings of spirit, and fits of rage (Berman should have mentioned also "the malady of not marking," a spiritual deafness). The counterfeiting includes lies and masquerade: Henry's pride in having "dressed" in humility, his use of mock-selves at Shrewsbury (a virtual apotheosis of counterfeiting), and the "smooth comforts false" of Rumor. A deformation toward bestiality accompanies guilt, says Berman: "Men are no longer images of God but of the beasts whose practices they imitate" (p. 23).

L. C. Knights, citing the parable in Luke 14 of builders who lacked resources for their project, notes in *2 Henry IV* a recurrent mood of disappointed hopes. A feeling of being time-bound and doomed is the consequence of aspirations tied to Fortune's wheel.

H. R. Coursen views Henry's reign as but a step in the decline of English kingship "from sacrament to ceremony." Henry's platitudes about God and justice "have nothing to do with God and little to do with any concept of intrinsic justice." He can chastise Worcester for not bearing himself "like a Christian," but neither side has any Christian premise in its purpose.

H. M. Richmond's chapters contain apt comments on King Henry, Prince Hal, and Falstaff. Henry's calculations are "utterly divorced from the springs of humane values." Prince Hal's eye for political advantage is "in harmony with the universal decay of English society under Henry," and his "will to supplant" is indicated in his premature seizing of the pillowed crown, which he excuses with such ingenious self-exculpation as to persuade the father of his political finesse and potential. Falstaff's role approximates that of the Vice in a morality play, but he is "nearer Christian salvation" in that he recognizes his own defects (p. 153). The play as a whole repudiates Hotspur's view of bravery but "validates something very like Falstaff's."

Willard Farnham, interestingly, traces the symbolic lineage of Falstaff to St Bernard's reference to his cloister's sculptures of the grotesque as "a marvelous kind of deformed beauty and beautiful deformity." Medieval religious art delighted in figuring an ape placed in indecent likeness to man, and in bordering manuscripts of David and Moses with slouching men of animal horns and ears. The "monstrous" as part of the mystery of human comedy Farnham sees Falstaff as representing.

## Supplementary bibliography

Berman, Ronald. "The Nature of Guilt in the *Henry IV* Plays," *Shakespeare Studies* 1 (1965), 18–28.

Bryant, J. A., Jr. "Prince Hal and the Ephesians," in *Hippolyta's View*, pp. 52–67.

Coursen, H. R. *The Leasing Out of England: Shakespeare's Second Henriad* (University Press of America, 1982), Ch 7 (pp. 151–77).

Farnham, Willard. *The Shakespearean Grotesque* (Oxford at the Clarendon Press, 1971), pp. 1–68.

Knights, L. C. "Time's Subjects," in *Some Shakespearean Themes* (Stanford University Press, 1960; 1966), pp. 42–54. Compare R. Chapman, "The Wheel of Fortune in Shakespeare's Historical Plays," *Review of English Studies* 1 (1950), 1–7.

Richmond, H. M. *Shakespeare's Political Plays* (New York: Random House, 1969), pp. 141–74.

*D. A. Traversi (1962)*

## Falstaff's Functions [editor's title]

The description Falstaff gives of the Prince, using his father's supposed words, is in itself a criticism, realistic and sardonic, of the whole family: "That thou art my son, I have partly thy mother's word, partly my own opinion, but chiefly a villanous trick of thine eye, and a foolish hanging of thy nether lip, that doth warrant me." It is not thus that Henry does actually speak to his son, nor is it true to say that the relationship between them is of this kind. That relationship is on the contrary truly tragic, and becomes more so as the father grows older and more conscious of the weariness that besets him through life; but the disillusioned clarity, even the coarseness, of Falstaff's description corresponds to something really present, that makes itself felt time and again in the Prince's attitude towards his life in the taverns and is a symptom of the detached inhumanity which is one ingredient of his political sense. This is not the Prince as he is, but it is one true aspect of him as seen by an eye clear and unfailing in its realism in the world in which this aspect is most in evidence. To bring out that aspect in those who surround him is the first of Falstaff's functions in the play.

The second is to provide on the basis of this clarity of vision a criticism of the whole political action, on both the loyalist and the rebel side, which leads up to the dubious battle in which it concludes. In this action, and especially in its warlike phases, Falstaff is involved without being of it or subdued to the spirit, now cynical, now wordily "honourable," in which it is habitually conceived. His comments on the motives of the rebels are characteristically clearheaded; his reaction to Worcester's disclaimer of responsibility for the rising is summed up in the phrase "Rebellion lay in his way, and he found it" (5.1). More revealing still, because based on sentiments more deeply human beneath the comic vision, is his attitude towards the pressed troops placed under his command to lead into battle. He has, as always, no particular illusion about the nature and the origins of this human material, "the cankers of a calm world and a long peace" (4.2); but his very account of them in the same speech as "discarded unjust serving-men, younger sons to younger brothers, revolted tapsters, and ostlers tradefallen," together with many other references, implies an awareness of social issues possessed by no other character in the play. This awareness is based in its turn upon Falstaff's outstanding quality, the capacity for human sympathy which marks him out in a world of calculation and inspires the respect for human life implied in his magnificent ironic reply to the Prince when the latter sums up his contingent as so many "pitiful rascals"—"Tut, tut; good enough to toss; food for powder, food for powder; they'll fill a pit as well as better; tush, man, mortal men, mortal men" (4.2). For the

Prince as for all his world, soldiers are mere pawns, the wretched instruments of political calculation to be considered from the point of view of their possible efficiency in the tasks imposed upon them by their leaders; for Falstaff alone they are human victims, individuals exposed to the manipulations of discreditable interest, "mortal men" and as such to be respected after detached and unsentimental scrutiny in the very sordidness of their tragedy. He is keenly aware that " honour" in the mouths of politicians who have been brought to battle by a combination of past selfishness and present refusal to face their responsiblities is an empty word and a delusion. "I like not such grinning honour as Sir Walter hath" (5.3) is his final comment, at once human and dispassionate, on the waste implied in a battle based on causes so suspect.

These observations bring us to a third characteristic of Falstaff, the one which is perhaps the ultimate source of his strength and the key to Shakespeare's deepest conception in this play. There is in Falstaff a true and rare combination of the warm, alert humanity we have already noted with a background, continually present, of inherited Christian tradition. It is reasonable to suppose that the latter element makes itself felt in a spontaneous acceptance of the inheritance, still not so distant from Shakespeare, of the mediaeval religious theatre. We may sense the presence of this inheritance in the readiness with which Falstaff in his phrasing draws upon images and ideas which derive their force from their relation to crucial moments in the familiar Christian drama. When he calls upon his tavern companions to "watch to-night, pray to-morrow" (2.4), the effect of the phrase depends largely upon its relation to the originally Christian ethic. He shares with his audience a whole world of imagery, drawn upon in such phrases as that in which his troops are described as "slaves as ragged as Lazarus in the painted cloth, where the glutton's dogs licked his sores" (4.2).The ease with which the theatrical passes into the religious reference is clearly seen in his comment on Bardolph's nose (3.3), to which he refers as "a Death's head or a *memento mori*"—"I never see thy face but I think upon hell-fire and Dives that lived in purple." In such phrases we feel what the strength of a still-living popular tradition could offer to the dramatist. Assimilated into his utterances it enables Falstaff to bring to his criticism of the political action around him a realism that, in its profounder moments, is neither self-regarding nor cynical, but that derives from a balanced view of man's destiny. At his best Falstaff, recognizing his own faults, gives them a taste of tragic significance: "Thou knowest in the state of innocency Adam fell; and what should poor Jack Falstaff do in the days of villainy? Thou seest I have more flesh than another man, and therefore more frailty" (3.3). Falstaff's tone is in part ironical, mocking as usual; but the reference to the physical flesh here is subsidiary to the spiritual meaning of the word sanctioned by Christian theology.

From the Norton Critical Edition of *Henry the Fourth, Part 1*, ed. James L. Sanderson (New York, 1962), pp. 328–30 abridged.

*Roy Battenhouse (1975)*

## Falstaff as Parodist

It was suggested by Lord Fitz Roy Raglan in 1936 in his *The Hero* that "Shakespeare had in the back of his mind the idea that Falstaff was a holy man." And W. H. Auden, more recently, has argued in cryptic fashion that Falstaff, while overtly a Lord of Misrule, is nevertheless at heart "a comic symbol for the supernatural order of charity."[1] By other scholars there has been an understandable reluctance to pick up or probe this possibility. And no doubt few of today's playgoers think of imputing charity to a Falstaff whose prankish chicanery and braggadocio seem to make him the very image of traditional vice, garnished at one time or other with all the Seven Deadlies. Yet may not the fulsome display of reprobation be more mask than inner man? One of Auden's tantalizing comments is to remind us that the Sermon on the Mount enjoins Christians to show charity through a *secret* almsgiving. Could this be a clue to the enigma of Falstaff's behavior? Perhaps so, I think, provided we put beside it Lord Raglan's intuition that Falstaff's vocation in the public world is that of court fool and soothsayer. Such a double hypothesis, in any case, seems to me to warrant a trying out and testing. For it could mean that while as "allowed fool" Falstaff is shamming vices and enacting parodies, his inner intent is a charitable almsgiving of brotherly self-humiliation and fatherly truth-telling.

A clown, if and while Christian at heart, must mask his piety under absurd posturings. His office is to offer spectacle of himself in the lineaments of folly, as a mirror to the great of their own imperfections. But this occupation runs the risk of banishment at the hands of princes whose morals are those of worldly self-advantage and political expediency. To such the Fool's mirror can seem mere nonsense, even when it reflects marginally the Christian premise that "God hath chosen the foolish things of the world to confound the wise." (1 Cor 1:27) Consider, for instance, Lavatch in *All's Well.* On the one hand this clown says he's a knave who can serve "A prince of darkness, alias the devil," yet at the same time he warns this prince-of-the-world to "remain in's court (because) I am for the house with the narrow gate" (4.5). How can such a paradox be grasped unless we recall the Christian "mystery" that everyman is both a player and a pilgrim? The double-sidedness of human destiny is set forth in *As You Like It*, where Jaques views the world as a stage for players while Orlando writes the verses that speak of "pilgrimage" (3.2.128). May not Falstaff be a Christian pilgrim underneath his role of profane fool? Compare Anatole France's *Our Lady's Juggler.*

Let it be said at the start that my thesis, novel though it largely is, is not without wayside support from the observations of other scholars. Alfred Harbage has remarked acutely that

> Falstaff is the least effective wrongdoer that ever lived. He is a thief whose
> booty is taken from him, a liar who is never believed, a drunkard who is never
> befuddled, a bully who is not feared.... Even his lechery is a doubtful item.[2]

The real Falstaff is in full control of his wits at all times, despite his praise of sack and despite those wine bills which he has, as clown, no doubt planted in his pocket (as Hazlitt suggested) for the sake of the comedy they will produce when his pockets are picked. And as for a lechery which Harbage terms doubtful, how can we believe it at all of the fat sixty-year-old whom we see in Mistress Quickly's tavern? The pose of fornicator, says W. H. Auden, is jolly pretense, while all that we actually see Falstaff doing in this scene is defending Nell from a bully, Pistol, then setting Doll on his knee and making her cry out of affection and pity for him.

Falstaff differs in one very important respect from a vice character such as Ambidexter in Thomas Preston's *Cambises*: Ambidexter goes about planting suspicion, tempting Cambises to hatred and fratricide, and constantly glorying in his skill as a beguiler. By contrast there is in Falstaff, as various scholars have observed, no vicious guile. His lack of malice was noted by Maurice Morgann as long ago as 1777. Falstaff through his role as fall guy and buffoon is a comic butt of laughter and by his wit a cause of wit in others. Is this not so indeed in the later *The Merry Wives of Windsor?*

Critics who have seen in Falstaff a Lord of misrule may be correct, except for their own inadequate understanding of the role's implications. It developed historically, we need to be reminded, as a Christian holiday exercise. Its licensed mimicking of inverted moral order served two concurrent purposes: (1) that of releasing mimetically, and thus confessing, the disorders of Old Adam behavior which Everyman has in him; and (2) that of indicating indirectly the mystery of the New Adam to which Everyman is properly called and obligated. The medieval Feast of Fools was underpinned by this large sense of the landscape of history, in which the sacred encompasses the profane.

Do we doubt that Falstaff belongs within this tradition? Let us recall that Poins terms him "the martlemas," that is, a St Martin's Day summer (*2 H4* 2.2). Or let us recall that Doll affectionately calls him a Bartholomew boar-pig (*2 H4* 2.4). Bartholomew was the disciple, elsewhere in the Gospels named Nathaniel, whom Jesus described as a man "in whom there is no guile" (Jn 1:47); and from the twelfth century on into the nineteenth his Saint's Day was the occasion of a great public Fair including sideshows and rowdy entertainment. This fair owes its origin, moreover, to a monk who had been a court jester under King Henry I. Having decided to become a monk, he built first a monastery near the shrine of St Bartholomew and soon afterward an annual fair in the saint's honor.... We know that in medieval custom the Feast of Fools was engaged in by choir clerks, chaplains, and vicars. They understood their horseplay paradoxically, as both a "venting of the natural lout beneath the cassock" and at the same time an affirmation of Christian faith. Vested in pontificals, E. K. Chambers tells us, they sang the *Magnificat* to the embellishment of a hooting of sacrilegious ditties.[3]

Falstaff may be alluding to an occasion of this kind when he speaks of having lost his voice with "halooing and singing of anthems" (*2 H4* 1.2). In this same scene he rejects the stuffy Chief Justice's notion that he can be writ down as a wasted candle, the better part burned out. No, he replies; rather, a wassail candle, that is, a festival one. And he adds that although of tallow, he has capacities of wax—a reference, I think, to the wax candles used on church altars. Like a choir clerk on holiday, he is here playing to his social superior, a Lord Chief Justice. And throughout the pose of deafness in this episode it should be evident that Falstaff is slyly commenting on a deafness in his superiors, a disease in *them*. He has heard, he says, that the king has fallen into a discomfort—an apoplexy, a lethargy, a whoreson sleepiness, a kind of deafness. Falstaff implies that it is *this* he is troubled about, whereas the Chief Justice lacks the patience to digest its significance. The sleepiness Falstaff talks of has its proper gloss, very likely, in the Scripture passage used by the Church to begin Advent, St Paul's summons, "Now is the time to awake out of sleep"; and in the Advent collect that prays "Almighty God, give us grace that we may caste awaie the woorkes of darkenesse and put upon us the armor of light." This kind of armor (I think Falstaff knows) has been neglected, its meaning not marked, by a King Henry and a Lord Chief Justice who are spiritually too sleepy to desire it.

The times, Falstaff goes on to say, are coster-monger times—that is, times when everything is measured by its cash value. Because of "the malice of this age," the gifts most "appertinent to man" are disvalued, and valor is reduced to a taming of bears—which implies, I would say, that the function of bearherd has replaced that of Shepherd. And the times are also those of no true repentance, even on Prince Hal's part. Rather, merely a comic substitute, a repenting "not in ashes and sackcloth, but in new silk and old sack." In other words, old wine in new bottles—the reverse of New Testament injunction. Or, a secondary meaning of Falstaff's phrase could be: "old ransacking in new silken rhetoric," the old destructiveness clothed now in sleek diplomacy. These facts of his times, it seems to me, Falstaff knows and is teasingly making jest of while insisting, with equal truth, that *he* is no ill angel, nor in any way a misleader of the Prince. Rather, the Prince is misleading *him*: "God send the companion a better Prince."

The mock-trial in 2.4 gives Falstaff opportunity for putting on record (as if making a legal "deposition") his answer to the charge that he is a white-bearded Satan. Not so, he replies, unless you regard it a sin to be old and merry. To banish Falstaff would be as perverse a mistake, he warns, as to hate Pharaoh's fat kine while cherishing lean kine. There are fascinating implications in this biblical allusion. Through it Falstaff is intimating, I would say, that England under King Henry is comparable to an Egypt of spiritual darkness under a troubled Pharaoh, and that Falstaff embodies within his English-Egypt a God-given plenty that could save England from the famine figured in lean Prince Hal. The implications hidden under Shakespeare's biblical echoes have been sadly neglected by commentators. Study of them can vastly repay our attention. When they appear in the talk of so canny a fellow as Falstaff, they can be something like the tip of an iceberg signalizing a subsurface context which is relevant by analogy to the events taking place in Shakespeare's story.

Falstaff when comically impersonating King Henry includes some pompous sermonizing as follows:

> There is a thing, Harry, which thou hast often heard of, and it is known to many in our land by the name of pitch. This pitch, as ancient writers do report, doth defile; so doth the company thou keepest. (*1 H4* 2.4.410)

As editors note, the allusion is to Ecclesiasticus 13:1. But why does Falstaff's Henry ascribe it vaguely to "ancient authors"? Very likely because Henry, here being impersonated as a Euphuist, is being credited with a pretentiously shallow knowledge like that of John Lyly's Euphues. The neo-Greek Euphues was a showy moralist who pirated scraps of authority from sources he knew only superficially, using their adages in utilitarian fashion to give himself a reputation as wiseman, while he lived a wanton life and betrayed friends. Falstaff is analogizing Euphues to King Henry: England's king of politics is about as trustworthy as Lyly's king of rhetoricians in Shakespeare's own day, each being (if rightly assessed) an absurd moralist. Readers who remember Henry's practices during his rise to power ought to realize how little right he has to lecture against thievery. Indeed, Henry's chief concern, as portrayed by Falstaff, is not so much to upbraid Hal's thievery as to mend Hal's reputation for respectability. Hence in the interview scene we will hear Henry object to Hal's associating with "rude society" and "shallow jesters" and recommend instead a courtesy "stolen" from heaven and dressed in robes pontifical. Falstaff's prior parody of this attitude contains a very accurate characterization of King Henry's courtliness or courtesy.

But to return to our biblical allusion: Was "rude society" what the author of Ecclesiasticus had in mind when warning against pitch? Only in a very different sense from King Henry's. Henry understands pitch as referring to social inferiors, "vulgar company" (3.2.41). But what the Bible writer Ben Sira means by pitch is high and mighty persons who are morally rude in offering a friendship that is false and beguiling. It is evident that what *pitch* signifies for Ben Sira is the high-stationed manipulator who uses a hollow courtesy to hoodwink the unwary, offering an unmerciful companionship which turns out to be false friendship. Compared with Ben Sira, King Henry warrants Falstaff's impersonation of him as comic in his preaching, in that when invoking an ancient author's text whose true meaning he does not know he distorts it and overlooks its application to himself. (This is much like the Wife of Bath's sermonizing as portrayed by Chaucer: she alludes to texts from St Paul which, did she but know it, condemn her out of her own mouth.)

If only Prince Hal were less shallow he would perceive that here, in moral fact, is the truth about his father Henry; and he would guess at Falstaff's hidden warning to expect in Henry a conscience eager to entangle Hal in its own pitch. Falstaff goes on to imply that if Hal, like Cambises' queen, risks a liaison with this King, he can expect a bedfellow who will cherish him only so long as he condones the King's bloody policy and supports it. But alas, throughout this scene, what Hal appreciates is solely the absurdity of Falstaff's supposedly madcap language and foolery, not the insight into England's cultural situation and its headmaster which Falstaff's swiftly moving vignettes have capsulized as babble and oracle rolled into one.

When, for his playing of the King, Falstaff chooses, as if haphazardly, the three stage props of chair, dagger, and pillow, Prince Hal's response is merely to make fun of Falstaff:

> Thy state is taken for a join'd stool, thy golden sceptre for a leaden dagger,
> and thy precious rich crown for a pitiful bald crown. (*1 H4* 2.4.376–78)

But the regalia of royalty selected by Falstaff constitute, though Hal does not realize this, a parable of the pitiable baldness of Henry's kingship. The point has been recognized by at least one modern commentator, James Winny:

> these [three] comic properties have a satirical point as sharp as the dagger which this alehouse King clutches as his badge of authority. The usurper whose crimes have debased the dignity of his royal office enjoys as much right to crown and throne as Falstaff's makeshift properties suggest.[4]

In other words, Falstaff is enacting a figure of King Henry's makeshift royalty. What such royalty amounts to, morally and ontologically, is a reduction of office from throne to mere stool. And now with a dagger his only scepter of power, a cushion must substitute for the round of golden duty which a crown properly signifies and which Henry lacks.

Simply by consulting a Bible concordance, one can discover that Ezekiel used a pillow image to describe the false peace that lying prophets devise. Lying prophets, says Ezekiel (13:18), are like women "that sowe pillows under all arme holes and make vailes upon the head" to hunt souls and pollute them. With Ezekiel's meaning in mind, I came across it again when reading the *Policraticus* of John of Salisbury. Here it occurs at a point where John is discoursing on false or hireling shepherds. In these knaves, he says, there is

> no valor to protect the truth in time of danger, in all things it is payment that they seek. . . . So long as they prosper in their own concerns, so long as they realize the objects of their ambition and avarice, they hold in small account the loss of the things of Jesus Christ.

> These are the men that sew *cushions* and place pillows beneath the head of a whole generation to snare souls [Ez 13:18], and consume the milk and clothe

themselves with the wool of the sheep which they have as it were led into the sleep of negligence or rashness. But a thief is proved by his works.[5]

Can anyone find a better commentary than this, I wonder, on the works of Henry Bolingbroke? The only thing better I can think of is to hide all this commentary under a lightning flash of emblem, as Falstaff the artist does.

The farce at Gad's Hill enacts a political parody. Its moral is stated in Falstaff's comic cry, "A plague upon it when thieves cannot be true one to another." King Henry has been thieving from the Percies, while all they can do is fulminate and concoct a retaliation which turns out to be politically about as farcical as Falstaff's concocted story of how he peppered and paid home two men in buckram suits. We can easily infer that Falstaff is here playing a mock-Hotspur role in the whole jest, even to the point of magnifying valiancy as Hotspur is later satirized for do-ing—taking on "some fourteen" in an hour. The difference between main plot and subplot is merely that whereas Hotspur undertook a real rebellion and a genuine thievery when prompted by the devious King Henry, Falstaff undertook only a mock thievery and a storybook retaliation against his treacherous setter-on, Prince Hal. That is the difference between history and art. Yet art has its own truth, a figurative truth, which refutes Prince Hal's notion that Falstaff's story is a mere pack of lies. "Art thou mad?" replies Falstaff; "Is not the truth the truth?" It is not Falstaff who is here clay-brained. "By the Lord," he concludes, "I knew ye as well as he that made ye." When Falstaff swears by the Lord, we had better believe him.

The truth about England's times and cultural situation has meanwhile been figured quite bluntly by low-class knaves in an innyard scene. "This house is turned upside down since Robin Ostler died," remarks a carrier of the party that will soon be robbed. And Prince Hal's proxy, Gadshill, after pumping this carrier for secret information, boasts that his own party is made up of maltworm noble-men who ride up and down on the commonwealth to make her their booty, after first liquoring her with their brand of justice. Through such language, the com-monwealth is being likened to a whore and her customers. Hence when we en-counter Mistress Quickly, a scene later, we are prepared to understand her inn, also, as a kind of emblem of England in miniature. It is a hangout for Corinthian lads, whom the Hostess appropriately calls "harlotry players." And when a sheriff knocks on the door to interrupt their games, this figure seems reminiscent of the fell Sergeant Death in the old play *Everyman*, who entered to announce a day of reckoning. The sleeping Falstaff, with pockets full of testimony to wastrel living, symbolizes foxily the state of the household.

It is to this tavern that Falstaff returns, after a scene in which we see Prince Hal offering repentance not to God but to King Henry, and vowing to serve him by putting on a "bloody mask." Such an unchristian version of repentance is the object of some parody mumblings by Falstaff as he enters the tavern. Then, sum-moning Bardolph (who had betrayed Falstaff), Falstaff declares that Bardolph's nose is as red as the fires of hell; indeed, it suggests Dives, the biblical glutton, who robed himself in purple but burned in hell. Bardolph's face, says Falstaff, needs amending, for at present its only usefulness is to serve as a comic lantern on the ship of state. The reference to Bardolph as "our admiral" suggests to me that Falstaff is indirectly commenting on Prince Hal. That is, he is saying that ship's-officer Hal, by indulging a nose for political advantage and forgetting "what the inside of a church is made of," has become a Dives of purple robes ("garment all of blood") and fiery face (its "stain" a "bloody mask"), now serving as a lantern on King Henry's ship of state, yes, but a comically hell-bound instance of knighthood.

The Dives allusion is one Falstaff cannot let alone. He turns to it again in Part 2 of the play, when talking about the refusal of a certain "Master Dumbledon" to provide him clothes:

> Let him be damned, like the glutton! Pray God his tongue be hotter! A whoreson Achitophel! (*2 H4* 1.2.34–35)

Here the Dives of hot tongue is being compared to Achitophel, the traitor who for a hoped-for worldly advantage deserted the good King David to serve instead a vain and self-righteous Absalom. Whom could Falstaff be glancing at? If we look about for a politician who is supporting a usurper, we can scarcely miss the secret object of Falstaff's comment since the supporter of Henry IV who has deserted Falstaff is Prince Hal.

Why does Falstaff prompt dialogue about disease and tailoring on his first entrance into Part 2 of the play? Because these two motifs now characterize the drift of England's history and will do so throughout the play's subsequent action. Various other characters tell us that the commonwealth is sick; Falstaff's talk is about the nature of this sickness. But, as we have already noted, he finds the land's Chief Justice deaf to any true understanding. This Justice, like his superiors, is interested only in tailoring a new military expedition for his own security. To Falstaff, such a prescription for the land's disease is mere waste (or waist); it ignores the *heart* of the matter. "I can get no remedy," he laments, "against this consumption of the purse." His chief meaning is that bankruptcy is the ironic result of the public seeking for "security." Exhaustion of the spiritual exchequer is the looming fate of Bolingbroke and his opponents alike, after a lifetime of extended credit and unpaid debts.

Readers of the scenes in Gloucestershire ought to suspect that Justice Shallow is in some way figurative of the state of England. For one thing, the names of the recruits Shallow offers Falstaff are obviously metaphoric of a general impoverishment, which Falstaff highlights when examining Shadow, Feeble, Wart, Mouldy, and Bullcalf.[6] Then there is also Justice Shallow's giddy justice in "countenancing" William Visor, a knave, and his nostalgia for Nightwork and a *bona roba*; and (as James Winny has noted) his "lip-service to death by uttering sententious platitudes while eagerly watching the market":

> Death, as the psalmist saith, is certain to all, all shall die.
> How a good yoke of bullocks at Stamford fair? (3.2.38–39)

Though as country squire this Justice has now outgrown the cheeseparing look of his famined youth, and has "a goodly dwelling and rich," he himself speaks the truth of his attainments when in his cups: "Barren, barren, barren, beggars all" (5.3.8). Such a confession, I suggest, might equally be King Henry's.

And why this barren outcome? In Shallow's case, we can relate it to his fractional memory of what the "psalmist saith." Shallow (like a Dr. Faustus reading Scripture) has picked up only the first half of a text, Psalm 90:3, "Thou turnest man to destruction." Ignoring the other half, the biblical call to "Return," Shallow sees man as simply fated to die. He has ignored also the Psalmist's explanation that toil and trouble are signs of God's wrath on man's secret sins, for which the remedy is as follows:

> 12. Teach us so to nomber our dayes, that we may applie our hearts unto wisdome.
> 14. Fil us with thy mercy in the morning; so shal we rejoice and be glad all our dayes.
> 17. And let the beautie of the Lord our God be upon us, and direct thou the worke of our hands upon us, even direct the worke of our hands.

Wisdom, mercy, joy, and God's beauty are notably absent from Shallow's life. And it can scarcely be happenstance that Shallow's melancholy follows, by less than a hundred lines, a similar melancholy in King Henry (3.1.45–56). Neither Henry nor his mirror likeness, Shallow, has had an ear tuned to the Good Book.

Falstaff's death as reported in *Henry V* gives us our final clue to his character. Here Nym's lament that the King "hath run bad humors on the knight" and Mistress Quickly's that the King "has killed his heart" set the tone. But more important is Mistress Quickly's faith that Falstaff is "not in Hell." He is "in Arthur's bosom," she says, and his going was finer than a "christom" child's. This tribute, in its comic muddling of religious language, indicates to us a Mistress Quickly whose intuition of Falstaff's goodness outstrips her understanding of it. Her limits of comprehension we can see in her report of how she comforted Falstaff when on three or four occasions he cried out "God, God, God." She hastened to counsel that there was no need yet for him to trouble himself with such thoughts. Her horizons are foggy, yet they do not blot out her belief in Falstaff's honesty and trueheartedness (stated at the end of *2 H4* 2.4). Through her very babblings and misplacings, we can guess at facts which her assessment shortchanges. The dying man may have been crying out to God not in desperation, but as commending his soul to God. And if his countenance resembled what her fuddled language glances at, a "chrism" child (one anointed with holy oil), the heaven he went to must have been Abraham's bosom, not Arthur's, or at least not merely Arthur's.

And of what "table of green fields" was Falstaff thinking? Several scholars have suggested an allusion to the "green pastures" of the Twenty-Third Psalm. There is added support for this conjecture, I think, if we consider also the psalm's "table" image and the one of anointing with oil. All three images cluster around Falstaff. So it is very possible that he who in *1 H4* 2.4 had said, "I would I were a weaver, I could sing psalms" was at his death mumbling to himself ("reciting," says Hardin Craig) the Psalmist's confession of faith.

Falstaff has been practicing Ephesians 5: redeeming time through making manifest "unfruteful workes of darkenes" in "dayes [that] are evil," while secretly "speaking *unto your selves in psalmes* and hymnes, and spiritual songs, singing and making melodie to the Lord *in your hearts*" (Geneva; emphasis mine). Compared with this, Prince Hal's purpose has been but a counterfeit redeeming, reductively political. Falstaff has been unable to redeem Hal, but he has wittily re-deemed in the sense of re-estimated the worth of Hal's purpose. This has been the ironic base of the playfulness between Falstaff and his world.

Falstaff's entire role has shown how wise he is about the ways of Caesar, Cambises, Euphues, gay Corinthians, and Ephesians of the *old* church (i.e., worshipers of Diana, servitors of illusion, in a comedy-of-errors world of enticingly silver but actually coppersmith values). And his insight for understanding this world of fog and moonshine, I have argued, derived from St Paul, the Gospels, Psalms and Proverbs, the Apocalypse, and the piety of an urbane Ben Sira, that ancient contender against the Hellenists who outdid them with his Ecclesiasticus. Out of a perspective grounded in this heritage, Falstaff was able to devise his double-sided mirrors of comic nonsense and authentic truth, while combining in his own person a pilgrim vocation with the earthly occupation of playing Fool.

By repeated references to the parable of Dives and Lazarus, Falstaff has figured his times as those of the rich fool Dives, and himself as the age's Lazarus, fated to enjoy only crumbs from the table of its rulers, but with an inner faith in the table of Psalm 23. The Lazarus parable, in my reading of the play, is more central than that of the Prodigal Son, at least for interpreting Falstaff. For although Falstaff may have been a once-upon-a-time prodigal, he is at heart now a Lazarus, mirroring in his merrily accepted "sores" the wounded relationships of the Dives world, "the injuries of a wanton time" (*1 H4* 5.1.50). As jester he can offer, for the taking away of grief, a delightful mockery of the "honor" catechism of present Diveses, and simultaneously can covertly witness to his own inner Holy Land pilgrimage, while glancing at the aborted one of King Henry and Prince Hal. Their plight is indeed humorous—and as old as that of Goodman Adam fallen among thieves (through traveling, as Augustine would say, to Jericho's city-of-the-moon and leaving man's mystical Jerusalem). For what is history if not the existential manifestations of some latent paradigm; and what is art if not the simultaneous hiding and disclosing of the present's radical significance through *figura*?

Since Dover Wilson turned to parable for his well-known interpretation of the *Henry IV* plays, may not I be pardoned for doing so, too? Wilson invoked the Prodigal Son story, interpreting Shakespeare's Hal as a prodigal who repents by returning to his father's house: to Chivalry in Part 1, and to Good Government in Part 2. Yet as a parallel to the biblical hero something is askew. Critics of Wilson's analogy have objected that Hal is a much more businesslike traveler into a far country than his anonymous predecessor; he assures us he is going to enjoy *just enough* riotous living to make his father glad to see him home again, and this purpose makes his action chiefly political. More significantly, is not the father to whom Prince Hal returns a counterfeit of the Bible's father? While King Henry may *seem* like the biblical father in proposing for his son a royal "robe," that robe (ironically) is Hal's own blood which, as calf, he is being asked to risk; and the "ring" (or crown) which Hal is given in Part 2 establishes on him nothing but the "giddy" justice of a tennis-game war. The whole transaction is thus secularized man's ironic substitute for true chivalry and good government. What Hal has come home to, spiritually, is a Dives table.

This ambiguous "placing" of Hal's success—Respectability achieved by a diminished Humaneness—is the measure of Shakespeare's sense of history in *Henry IV.* The "new" Harry will be a "mirror of all Christian Kings," but alas in a rather Turkish way (if we consider substance more than surface) which merely counterfeits Christian values. His reign will be as colorful as his justice is shallow, and with barren consequences. Falstaff rightly divined and forecast "a good shallow" young fellow. He saw in him a Majesty lacking in "grace." (*2 H4* 2.4.235; *1 H4* 1.2.17–18)

Falstaff is inevitably downgraded as compared to Hal by critics insensitive to tonalities of rhythm and allusion. Some, seeking to schematize the drama within a formula of Aristotelian ethics, credit to Hal a golden mean between the extremes of moral excess they see in Falstaff and Hotspur. Others prefer a Hegelian formula, by which they can see Hal as outwitting Falstaff and outfighting Hotspur, thus transcending them both. And still others, trying for a "balanced" view, read both Falstaff and Hotspur as irresponsible and childlike, while Hal is said to mature into the responsible king England needs, although sacrificing inevitably a child's attractive spontaneity. But none of these interpretations can explain the drama's sandwich-style placing of main plot and comic-plot scenes. And in supposing that maturity and childlikeness must be qualities exclusive of each other, a medieval *topos* is being ignored, that of the *puer senex* (the old young man, more charming than in youth), inspired by Bible texts which value a spiritualized childlikeness. According to Ernst R. Curtius, one extrabiblical instance of this topos is the *Passio SS. Perpetuae et Felicitatis*, where the martyrs are vouchsafed a vision of God "as a hoary old man with snow-white hair and a youthful countenance."[7]

We need to have this topos in mind when we read Falstaff's dialogue with the Lord Chief Justice. Falstaff poses a riddle by saying: "You that are old consider not the capacities of us that are young" (*2 H4* 1.2.173–74). The Justice then expresses incredulity that Falstaff should call himself young, in view of his white beard, among other things. To which Falstaff replies:

> My Lord, I was born about three of the clock in the afternoon, with a white head and something a round belly. . . . The truth is, I am only old in judgment and understanding. (187–92)

Here, wittily stated, is the *puer senex* paradox. Moreover, it is accompanied by a biographical statement that can be understood, I think, only as a figurative "born again" such as Nicodemus, in John 3, was given. And the time reference to three o'clock in the afternoon reflects probably Mark 15:39, the hour when a Roman centurion cried out his discovery, "Truly this man was a Son of God."

An eye-opening experience *analogous* to the centurion's (proportionately similar, not identical) could very possibly have been Falstaff's. When? On an afternoon at Coventry, I suggest, when Thomas Mowbray was banished, unjustly sacrificed to Richard's self-protectionist policy. Accepting the unjust sentence, Mowbray went to Venice, where we are told he gave "his pure soul unto his captain Christ, / Under whose colors he had fought so long" (*R2* 4.1.99–100). In such circumstances, what choice of vocation might Mowbray's page (whom Shallow tells us Falstaff was) decide on? A page's training was often that of wit-cracking along with apprenticeship in knighthood; and a Falstaff "born" by his experience at Coventry may well have decided that, like a disciple separated from his lord, he could witness for him through a role of jester-knight. But such a choice involved for Falstaff, as we know, an ultimate fate like that of his master, Mowbray: death amid exile. "Sweet peace conduct his sweet soul to the bosom / Of good old Abraham."

A groundling who after attending a performance of *Henry IV* goes away with the haunting feeling that he has seen a jolly old St Nick or a Robin Hood cannot be altogether wrong. For the play not only shows Falstaff outwitting "St Nicholas' clerks," but, much later, in backwoods Gloucestershire, offering "a health" to Justice Silence and thus loosing the tongue of this dumb man to sing—of Shrovetide, and of "Robin Hood, Scarlet, and John." That is miracle enough. Let skeptics try to evaporate it if they can. But if they suppose preferable the counterfeit miracle of Hal's "conversion," or the sanctimony with which Hal's brother John hails Falstaff's banishment as a "fair proceeding," generations of Falstaff lovers must and will demur. Unless, of course, one means by *fair* a Vanity Fair's ironic comedy.

## Notes

1 *The Dyer's Hand* (New York: Random, 1962), p. 198. Auden adds, p. 206, that Falstaff radiates happiness without apparent cause, and "this untiring devotion to making others laugh becomes a comic image for a love which is absolutely self-giving."
2 *As They Liked It* (New York: Macmillan, 1947), pp. 75–76.
3 *The Medieval Stage* (Oxford University Press, 1903), I, 268 and 325.
4 *The Player King* (London: Chatto & Windus, 1968), pp. 106–07.
5 John Dickinson, tr., *The Statesman's Book* (New York: Knopf, 1927), pp. 242–43.
6 Further, I sense an analogy between these five recruits and the five principals of the Gaultree episode. Mouldy and Bullcalf, who are allowed to buy themselves off, are in this respect like Westmoreland and John of Lancaster; whereas Shadow, Feeble, and Wart are mirror equivalents of Mowbray junior, the Archbishop, and Hastings, the three who are "pricked down" for execution. Individual characterizations support each of these analogies.
7 *European Literature and the Latin Middle Ages*, tr. Willard Trask (New York: Pantheon, 1953), pp. 98–101.

From "Falstaff As Parodist and Perhaps Holy Fool," *PMLA* 90 (1975), 32–52, abridged and revised by the author.

### Lazarus Borne To Heaven

### Dives Cast Into Hell
Lincoln Cathedral, West Front

# King Henry V

## Comment and bibliography

Whereas Henry IV conspicuously lacked gratitude and grace, his son presents himself as a "Christian" king who relies on God's grace. He is careful to submit to the judgment of an Archbishop the question of his "right" to the French throne, and only when his cause has been "well-hallowed" does he boldly proclaim his determination to pursue it in God's name and with the aid of God's grace. Phrasings of piety abound. When he executes conspirators who oppose his policy he thanks God for bringing their treason to light. And when he wins the battle at Agincourt he immediately gives God all the glory. On these facts Shakespeare follows Holinshed's portrait. But Holinshed evidently regarded Henry V's claim to France as valid, and his piety as admirable, whereas Shakespeare provides contexts that very much call in question both those assumptions.

According to Holinshed, the Archbishop told Henry "his war was just, his cause good, and his claim true." But Shakespeare has the Archbishop say equivocally: "The sin upon my head, . . . unwind your bloody flag!" In Holinshed, Henry repeatedly refers to his "just cause" and makes this the central theme of his oration before the Agincourt battle. But Shakespeare's Henry dares only a single glancing reference (and then from under disguise) to "his cause being just." At once the statement is questioned by a soldier named Williams, whose reply is that the king will have to answer to God for the injuries his soldiers are led into when "blood is their argument." Henry dodges that point. Moreoever, Henry's pre-battle oration as presented by Shakespeare omits all mention of the justice of the war (although Holinshed's account mentioned it three times) and instead makes central the "honor" Henry's followers will win, an incentive supported by Henry's equivocal plea: "If it be a sin to covet honor, I am the most offending soul alive."

The focus here on coveting honor might recall for readers of Augustine the unChristian obsession with honor he ascribed to Rome's heroes who sought honor by subjugating their neighbors. It was in this connection that Augustine asked his most celebrated political question, namely: "Without justice what are kingdoms but great piracies?" He illustrated by citing the "excellent reply" made to the great Alexander by a pirate he accused of molesting the seas: "Because I do it with a little ship only, I am called a thief; thou doing it with a great navy art called an Emperor" (*City of God* IV.4). Can it be mere happenstance that Shakespeare brings into his drama a comparison of King Henry to Alexander? The spokesman is Fluellen, comic not only because he so amateurishly attempts Plutarch's method of Parallel Lives, but also because he bungles the point that Henry's turning away of Falstaff was just as unmagnanimous as Alexander's killing of Cleitus, since a betrayal of friendship characterized both actions (Falstaff's heart being "killed," as Quickly reports).

When Henry is termed a "conquering Caesar" by the play's Chorus, we may pertinently recall Falstaff's parody of the brevity of Caesar's capacity for friendship (*2 H4* 2.2.120): "I commend me to thee, I commend thee, and I leave thee." That is an absurd magnanimity. But Rome's Julius Caesar, the "hook nos'd fellow" (*2 H4* 4.3.40), is a typological equivalent of Alexander; and Alexander's tawdry great-ness-of-heart is significant for our evaluating of Henry—especially because the comparing him with Henry is introduced just after we've seen a "killing" analogous to Alexander's but more spectacular in scope.

Henry's order to kill prisoners receives (in the Quarto text) an immediate echo in Pistol's cry "Couple gorge"—the slogan we have heard Pistol voice two scenes earlier. Gower's approval of Henry's order to cut throats, "O 'tis a galant king!" echoes the view of Holinshed, who wrote, "A right wise and valiant challenge" alongside his account of Henry's sending a herald to threaten the French that not only the prisoners already taken but any others taken if the French renewed the battle "should die the death without redemption" (Bullough, *Sources*, IV.398). Shakespeare, earlier, has made throat-cutting the slogan of Henry's admirers—as is evident at Harfleur, where Macmorris tells us: "There is throats to be cut, and works to be done," invoking in support of this Christ's name and his own hope of salvation. Indeed, the dramatist lets Henry proclaim his real creed in the final words he utters during his disguise-visit with his troops on the night before Agin-court: "It is no English treason to cut French crowns, and tomorrow the King himself will be a clipper." Here the connotations of "clipper" are three-fold: purse-cutting (thievery), head-cutting (manslaughter), and coin-cutting (counterfeiting). To an English conscience, he is saying, there's nothing treasonable in any of these. That sums up well Shakespeare's perception of Henry's England. At the same time, the dramatist uses the play's Chorus to voice a ceremonial patriotism that has the earmarks of an Erasmian praise of folly.

What may we suppose, then, has been God's role in the "miracle" of Agincourt? That miracle has been as much a human contrivance as is later, in *2 Henry VI*, the pretended miracle of Simpcox which this Henry thanks God for; superstition is a theological vice the son inherits from his father. The theological truth, as Au-gustine's *City of God* tells us, is that earthly benefits are given to both wicked and good rulers, but true happiness is reserved for genuine lovers of God. Or, Chris-tians knowledgeable in Catholic tradition might recall the answer Aquinas gives to the plaint of the Psalmist (in Ps 72:2) that the "wicked are not scourged like other men." Aquinas replied: "The very fact that they receive temporal goods is detri-mental to their spiritual good," for the Psalmist goes on to speak of them as held fast in their pride (*S.T.* I-II. 87.8). In other words, their own vice punishes them.

An essay by Gerald Gould in 1919 is the earliest instance I can find of an ironic reading of King Henry. Gould called attention to the evidence of Henry's hypocrisy and unscrupulous brutality and his false friendship toward Falstaff. H. C. Goddard was the first critic to declare bluntly that Shakespeare's Henry confuses Mars with the Christian God and practices a Machiavellian ethic (pp. 255, 267). Our anthology reprints abridged excerpts from Goddard's trenchant perceptions. His earlier study of irony in Chaucer equipped him for observing such matters as Henry's adroitness in shifting responsibility onto others, the illogic of the Archbishop's legal brief, his misleading fable of the bees, Henry's skill in manipulating an appearance of righteousness, the obtuseness of Henry's adulators, and the distinction that must be drawn between the Chorus and the poet. Shakespeare's irony lets us know that Henry's reference to "Another fall of man" (2.2.142) applies actually to the speaker himself (p. 231).

For supplementary reading, C. H. Hobday's cursory observations are pertinent, as are also the comments by Honor Matthews on the "machiavel" in Henry and her judgment that only the later misanthrope Timon of Athens is as desperately careless of the ravages of war. Ralph Berry accepts as incontrovertible an ironic reading of the play, and in illustration of Henry's fraud gives us a catalogue of his uses of "therefore" followed by illogical conclusions. Andrew Gurr demonstrates that the Archbishop and Henry hold a "commodity" view of the commonweal, such as Erasmus criticized. David Kastan, citing Goddard, agrees that Henry's piety is held up for criticism. My own several articles support Goddard's view with much additional evidence from the play. For instance, the Archbishop ignores Numbers 36:3 and thus distorts with a half-text; Henry's rhetoric allies him not only with Herod but with "Assyrian slings"; and Katharine's language lesson reveals England's values to be those of bilbow, nick, and sin.

## Supplementary bibliography

Battenhouse, Roy. "*Henry V* as Heroic Comedy," in R. Hosley, ed., *Essays on Shakespeare and Elizabethan Drama* (University of Missouri Press, 1962), pp. 163–82.

_____. "The Relation of *Henry V* to *Tamburlaine*," *Shakespeare Survey* 27 (1974), 71–79.

_____. "*Henry V* in the Light of Erasmus," *Shakespeare Studies* 17 (1985), 77–88.

Berry, Ralph. *The Shakespearean Metaphor* (London: Macmillan , 1978), pp. 48–60.

Gurr, Andrew. "*Henry V* and the Bees Commonwealth," *Shakespeare Survey* 30 (1977), 61–72.

Gould, Gerald. "A New Reading of *Henry V*," *The English Review* 29 (July 1919), 42–55. Rpt in Michael Quinn, ed., Casebook Shakespeare's *Henry V* (1969), pp. 81–94.

Hobday, C. H. "Imagery and Irony in *Henry V*," *Shakespeare Survey* 30 (1977), 107–13.

Kastan, David S. *Shakespeare and the Shapes of Time* (Hanover, N.H., 1982), Ch. 3.

Matthews, Honor. *Character and Symbol in Shakespeare's Plays* (1962), pp. 51–66.

Merrix, Robert P. "The Alexandrian Allusion in Shakespeare's *Henry V*," *English Literary Renaissance* 2 (1972), 321–33.

*Harold C. Goddard (1951)*

## Henry V

Can anyone believe that Shakespeare in his own person would have called Henry "the mirror of all Christian kings" and then let him threaten to allow his soldiers to impale French babies on their pikes and dash the heads of old men against the walls; or called him "this grace of kings" and then let him declare of the prisoners,

> we'll cut the throats of those we have,
> And not a man of them that we shall take
> Shall taste our mercy;

that he would have pronounced Henry "free from vainness and self-glorious pride," after dedicating a good part of two plays to showing how he wanted to imitate the sun and astound the world by emerging suddenly from behind clouds—and not only wanted to, but did?

As poet, [Shakespeare] must tell the truth. But to tell the truth about a great national hero at a time when patriotism is running high calls for courage. To tell it and to keep the piece in which you tell it popular calls for more than courage. Shakespeare did as life does. Life places both its facts and its intoxicants before us and bids us make out of the resulting clash what we can and will. So does the author of *Henry V.* Through the Choruses, the playwright gives us the popular idea of his hero. In the play, the poet tells the truth about him.

The previous play ended with these words from John of Lancaster:

> I will lay odds, that, ere this year expire,
> We bear our civil swords and native fire
> As far as France. I heard a bird so sing,
> Whose music, to my thinking, pleas'd the king.
> Come, will you hence?

The present play, after a Chorus that forecasts the coming conflict, opens with a conversation between the Archbishop of Canterbury and the Bishop of Ely that takes war for granted, though Canterbury does not refer to it in so blunt a term but, more tactfully, as "causes now in hand ... as touching France." What the King's brother, a little bird, a Chorus, and two Bishops agree in foreseeing is certainly coming. Henry has obviously made up his mind to follow his father's advice to busy giddy minds with foreign quarrels.

War being deemed desirable, the next thing is to find a reason for it. The opening of the play is dedicated to a search for sound moral ground for the attack on France. Fortunately for Henry, the Archbishop of Canterbury not only has such a sanction at hand but has a motive for bringing it forward. By a happy chance, he has discovered that what is good for the Church coincides with what the King has decided is good for his kingdom. In Henry IV's reign a bill had been introduced to confiscate the better half of the church's wealth. Because of the troubled times it had never come to passage. But now it has been revived:

| | |
|---|---|
| Canterbury | Thus runs the bill. |
| Ely | This would drink deep. |
| Canterbury | 'Twould drink the cup and all. |
| Ely | But what prevention? |
| Canterbury | The king is full of grace and fair regard. |
| Ely | And a true lover of the holy church. |
| Canterbury | The courses of his youth promis'd it not . . . |

and the two men digress from the subject in hand to comment on the miraculous change that has come over Henry. "But, my good lord," says Ely, returning to the main point,

> How now for mitigation of this bill
> Urg'd by the commons? Doth his majesty
> Incline to it, or no?

Canterbury           He seems indifferent,
> Or rather swaying more upon our part
> Than cherishing the exhibiters against us;
> For I have made an offer to his majesty . . .

This offer, he goes on to explain, is that the clergy shall make the greatest contribution ever recorded to the war chest of the sovereign. It will obviously be better for the church to make a large gift and so forestall confiscation than to give little or nothing and have its wealth expropriated.

> Ely         How did this offer seem receiv'd, my lord?

(There is another word, also of five letters, that would define the nature of the proposed transaction more precisely than "offer." But it would be too much to expect either of these churchmen to employ it.)

> With good acceptance of his majesty,

says Canterbury, answering Ely's question,

> Save that there was not time enough to hear,—
> As I perceiv'd his Grace would fain have done

and the Archbishop proceeds to tell of another trump card he had up his sleeve which an interruption prevented him from putting on the table before the King:

> The severals and unhidden passages
> Of his true titles to some certain dukedoms,
> And generally to the crown and seat of France
> Deriv'd from Edward, his great-grandfather.

In a word, the Church will supply not only treasure for the war chest but a justification for making the war. What more could Henry ask? This is far more than his spiritual and political "father," the Lord Chief Justice of the previous play, would have had to offer in the circumstances. That may seem a cynical way of putting it, and Henry's words, when he resumes the interrupted conversation in the next scene, seem to make it utterly unwarranted. The King begins by warning the Archbishop not to incite him to war on specious grounds. Think of the blood that will be spilt, he reminds him, every drop of which will be a just complaint against whoever begins an unrighteous conflict.

> We charge you in the name of God, take heed. . . .
> Under this conjuration speak, my lord,
> And we will hear, note, and believe in heart,
> That what you speak is in your conscience wash'd
> As pure as sin with baptism.

Nothing could sound more moral and humane (though a suspicious mind might find a Chaucerian ambiguity in that last phrase). But we must judge Henry by his acts, not by his words.

The King must have an irreproachable reason for making war. The one thing that his claim to the French throne must be is *clear*. But when the Archbishop goes on to expound that claim, clear is the one thing it does not seem to be. The sixty-odd lines Canterbury devotes to it make one of the most complicated passages of pure exposition in Shakespeare and one of the most difficult to assimilate without an opportunity to study it minutely. No one could possibly take it in in the theater. Any stage director would be certain to cut it drastically. Yet attention to it in detail is indispensable to an understanding of the scene.

The gist of Henry's claim rests on the fact that his great-great-grandmother was the daughter of Philip IV of France, the only bar to its legitimacy being the Salic law under which succession through the female line is illegal. Even if the title had been a technically good one, time had had the same effect on it as a statute of limitations. But its very age seems to recommend it all the more to the learned Archbishop. His speech consists of an elaborate discrediting of the Salic law. Under analysis it turns out to be (as it is even in Holinshed, whom Shakespeare follows closely here) a colossal piece of ecclesiastical casuistry with a highly ironical application to the situation in which Henry finds himself.

That situation itself, without any historical assistance, is ironical enough. Henry's father had seized the English throne—with disillusioning consequences. His son now proposes to seize the French throne in the hope—shall we say, of wiping out his father's sin? The Archbishop's speech rubs in the irony, for all the genealogical details he cites fit with damning neatness the situation in which Henry finds himself, and tend to undermine the very claim they are brought forward to substantiate. How far the learned Archbishop is intentionally obscuring the issue, and how far it is obscuring him, is difficult at times to make out. But if the style is the man we are entitled to believe the worst.

To prove that Henry will not be a usurper if he seizes the crown of France in defiance of the Salic law he cites the cases of three French kings who themselves inherited through the female. The first one deposed another king (*as Henry IV did Richard II*). The second "usurped the crown" by pressing his title

> with some shows of truth,
> Though in pure truth it was corrupt and naught,

(*just as the Archbishop is urging Henry to press a similar title at the moment*). The third, who was sole heir to this usurper (*as Henry V was to Henry IV*), was so uneasy in his mind about his title (*as the first Henry was*) that he could not keep quiet in his conscience (*as the second Henry is now, by his present enterprise, proving that he cannot*). The allusiveness of all this to the pending question makes cynical in the extreme the citation of titles "corrupt and naught" as precedents in support of a claim supposed to be pure and substantial. It is like pointing to a dog's mongrel ancestors to prove it a thoroughbred. But the effrontery of the Archbishop's reasoning exceeds even this. The kings of France unto this day, he says to Henry in conclusion, want to bar your title to their throne because you inherit it through the female line, when, all the while, their own titles are crooked and were usurped from you and your progenitors because they were inherited in precisely the same way. The very thing that proves the title of a French king crooked—namely, inheritance through the female—serves, by some twist of ecclesiastical logic, to prove the title of an English king good. Heads you lose, tails I win.

The Archbishop (soon afterwards) likens human polity in a well-ordered state to that of the bees. The bees, it turns out, have nearly everything in their community that men have except archbishops and armies. No high churchmen of the hive are mentioned. And as for fighters, this is the way the Archbishop tries to squeeze them in:

> Others, like soldiers, armed in their stings,
> Make boot upon the summer's velvet buds,
> Which pillage they with merry march bring home
> To the tent-royal of their emperor.

As if bees hovering above flowers, or the fruitful communion of the two, could be compared to the clash of enemies on the battlefield, or honey to the spoils of war! The Archbishop is as deficient in his science as in his symbolism.... What fun Shakespeare must have had making such a fool of his Archbishop, knowing all the while that his audience would swallow his utterances as grave political wisdom.

. . . .

Agincourt! "It was a famous victory." Five scenes are dedicated to the battle. The third scene shows Henry receiving word of the deaths of the Duke of York, who led the van, and the Earl of Suffolk. Exeter, who brings the report, draws a pathetic picture of their final moments, and declares that on the field he wept at the sight. "I blame you not," says Henry,

> For hearing this, I must perforce compound
> With mistful eyes, or they will issue too.

Why should Shakespeare give nearly a whole scene to the deaths of two men who have played practically no part in the story? For the sake of the battle atmosphere, it will be said. But Shakespeare generally subordinates his picturesque effects to drama. And so he does here. The last four lines of the scene reveal why the first thirty-four were written. An alarum sounds, and the King cries:

> But hark! what new alarum is this same?
> The French have reinforc'd their scatter'd men:
> Then every soldier kill his prisoners!
> Give the word through.

From tears to orders for the death of the prisoners—all in a second. The complete presence of mind of a great field commander! So it might seem. But we recall the King's directions to his troops, just after he sent Bardolph to his death, which ended: "when lenity and cruelty play for a kingdom, the gentler gamester is the soonest winner." Then he followed a cruel act by gentle words. Now he follows tearful words by a cruel act. These sudden polar reversals are too characteristic of Henry to be attributed at bottom to anything but his own nature. But perhaps in this case the killing of the prisoners was "necessary," it may be suggested. Shakespeare does not make us wait long for more evidence on that point.

The fourth battle scene seems to digress even further. Yet it is one of the best illustrations in all the author's works of the rule that the more casual and incidental one of this scenes appears to be, the more significant and central it often is. What this one appears to be is just a bit of conversation between Fluellen and Gower, two of the King's officers, precipitated by the killing of the prisoners. What it is, if I am not mistaken, is nothing less than Shakespeare's last judgment on the rejection of Falstaff.

Gower and Fluellen, the Welsh officer who is forever quoting the military precedents of the Greeks and Romans, imply that the killing of the prisoners is an act of retaliation because French stragglers killed the English boys guarding the luggage. But the previous scene proves that this is not the case. Gower suggests the additional motive of personal revenge: "besides, they have burned and carried away all that was in the king's tent; wherefore the king, most worthily, hath caused every soldier to cut his prisoner's throat. O, 'tis a gallant king!" Do not suppose for a moment that Gower is ironical, however sarcastic those last words sound.

"Ay," says Fluellen, taking up the reference to the King's gallantry, "he was porn at Monmouth, Captain Gower. What call you the town's name where Alexander the Pig was born?" "Alexander the Great," Gower returns, not relishing Fluellen's Welsh English. But Fluellen will not accept the correction: "Why, I pray you, is not pig great? The pig, or the great, or the mighty, or the huge, or the magnanimous, are all one reckonings, save the phrase is a little variations." "I think Alexander the Great was born in Macedon," says Gower, coming back to Fluellen's inquiry.

Whereupon Fluellen, taking up the alliteration of Monmouth and Macedon, proceeds to draw a parallel—how deadly, not Fluellen but only the attentive reader realizes—between Harry of Monmouth and Alexander the Pig of Macedon. That "Pig," of course, must have delighted the groundlings. But there is more in it than that. For consider: Alexander the Great has become the symbol for all time of insatiable lust for blood and conquest. "No more lands to conquer." The allusion in itself, in a play whose theme is imperialism, would be suspicious. Henry is bent on the subjection of France by force. Once upon a time he had admonished Falstaff to "leave gormandizing." But that was long ago. The parallel between Henry and Alexander, Shakespeare more than hints (and now we see the reason for Court's first name), goes considerably beyond the fact that the places where they were born both begin with the same letter. Even Fluellen sees that much, innocent as he is of the deeper import of what he is saying:

> There is a river in Macedon; and there is also moreover a river at Monmouth. It is called Wye at Monmouth; but it is out of my prains what is the name of the other river; but 'tis all one, 'tis alike as my fingers is to my fingers, and there is salmons in both. If you mark Alexander's life well, Harry of Monmouth's life is come after it indifferent well; for there is figures in all things.

and he goes on to draw a parallel between Alexander's killing, when drunk, of his best friend Cleitus, and Henry's rejection of Falstaff. (Like the soul of Banquo, Falstaff will not down.)

| | |
|---|---|
| Fluellen | Alexander, God knows, and you know, in his rages, and his furies, and his wraths, and his cholers, and his moods, and his displeasures and his indignations, and also being a little intoxicates in his prains, did, in his ales and his angers, look you, kill his best friend, Cleitus. |
| Gower | Our king is not like him in that: he never killed any of his friends. |
| Fluellen | It is not well done, mark you now, to take the tales out of my mouth, ere it is made and finished. I speak but in the figures and comparisons of it: as Alexander killed his friend Cleitus, being in his ales and his cups; so also Harry Monmouth, being in his right wits and his good judgments, turned away the fat knight with the great belly-doublet: he was full of jests, and gipes, and knaveries, and mocks; I have forgot his name. |
| Gower | Sir John Falstaff. |
| Fluellen | That is he: I'll tell you there is goot men porn at Monmouth. |
| Gower | Here comes his majesty. |

And King Henry enters. "'There's no art to find the mind's construction in the face.' *Enter Macbeth.*" Henry's entrance is like that, casting back a reversed significance over the scene that has gone before.

Fluellen, in comparing Henry and Alexander, has pointed out one incidental contrast: that whereas Alexander "in his ales and his angers" murdered Cleitus, Harry "in his right wits and his good judgments" turned away Falstaff. But *was* the King, whether angry or not, in his right wits and good judgments at that fatal moment? That is the debated point. And now, as if in living answer to the question, Henry enters with the words:

> I was not angry since I came to France
> Until this instant.

And he commands a herald to ride up to certain horsemen on the hill that "offend" his sight and order them either to come down and fight, or to quit the battle, under the threat of being hurled to death. And he adds:

> Besides, we'll cut the throats of those we have,
> And not a man of them that we shall take
> Shall taste our mercy. Go and tell them so.

Fluellen's parallel is more pitiless than he realized. Alexander the Pig himself could hardly have been more magnificently angry than Henry is at this moment. It is one thing to kill prisoners in an emergency, or through "necessity." It is another to kill them on principle—and to promise to kill those not yet taken. Henry is drunk with wrath. How venial Fallstaff's addiction to sack compared with this intoxication! Henry's father had warned us of this weakness of his son:

> give him line and scope,
> Till that his passions, like a whale on ground,
> Confound themselves with working

and we remember Henry's reproach against the three traitors who seemed, but were not, "Free from gross passion or of mirth or anger."

Thus, unobtrusively, near the end of another play, does Shakespeare slip quietly in his own comment on the rejection of Falstaff. For what else can it be? What other purpose has the scene? And how it confirms what went before!—the rehearsal of the rejection in the tavern; the rejection itself on the street; and now this reversion to it on the battlefield, when we see it in true perspective. Shakespeare "manifests no disapproval," says George Brandes, "where the King sinks far below the ideal, as when he orders the frightful massacre of all the French prisoners taken at Agincourt. Shakespeare tries to pass the deed off as a measure of necessity." Brandes has just remarked in the previous paragraph: "Shakespeare was evidently unconscious of the naïveté of the lecture on the Salic law." But possibly the poet is less guilty of casuistry in the one case, and naïveté in the other, than Brandes thinks.

A herald enters and the King inquires: "Are the dead number'd?" "Here is the number of the slaughter'd French," the herald replies, and delivers papers showing that ten thousand French have been slain and twenty-nine English. No, not twenty-nine thousand, nor twenty-nine hundred. Twenty-nine! A battle? Call it rather, according to your point of view, a massacre or a miracle. And the disparity is even more startling in another respect. Henry takes particular satisfaction in the fact that most of the French dead are of high estate:

> in these ten thousand they have lost,
> There are but sixteen hundred mercenaries;
> The rest are princes, barons, lords, knights, squires,
> And gentlemen of blood and quality

and he reads the names of the noblest of them. (Shakespeare can make even a list of proper nouns significant.) But for the English it turns out that they have lost one duke, one earl, one baronet, and one esquire. Among those of "blood and quality," then, the proportion is somewhat more than eighty-four hundred French to four English! The inference seems inescapable that it must have been the English commoners who accounted for a large number of the French knights and nobles. Henry should have been grateful surely to the rank and file. Was he? This is the way he announces it:

> Where is the number of our English dead?
> Edward the Duke of York, the Earl of Suffolk,
> Sir Richard Ketly, Davy Gam, esquire:
> None else of name; and of all other men
> But five and twenty.

"Be he ne'er so vile, this day shall gentle his condition." "None else of name." Again, it makes a difference whether it is before or after the battle. And instead of expressing gratitude to the Bateses and Courts and Williamses of his army of yeomen, Henry characteristically attributes his triumph wholly to God and within the space of a little more than a dozen lines declares:

> Oh God! thy arm was here.
>     Take it, God,
> For it is none but thine!
> And be it death proclaimed through our host
> To boast of this or take the praise from God
> Which is his only.
> God fought for us.

And he orders that *Non nobis* and *Te Deum* be sung.

We have no quarrel with Henry's gratitude to heaven for a victory that must indeed have seemed to him like a miracle, but his reiteration of it becomes psychologically suspicious in the highest degree. It ends by looking less like giving thanks to God for the victory than like putting the responsibility on God. We recall those two chantries and those five hundred poor. Like his father with his crusade to Jerusalem, Henry is haunted by the specter of Richard II. For him, too, the wheel is coming full circle, and in license in bringing God into military matters he comes perilously close to talking like the Richard who placed his faith in celestial armies. "So Chrish save me, I will cut off your head." Anybody can get the irony of that. Henry's confusion of Mars with the Christian God is of the same order. Any one of his references to the God of Battles with which this play is filled is a trifle. In the aggregate they become an avalanche.

The Chorus of the fifth act likens the celebration after Agincourt to an imperial triumph in ancient Rome and to an imaginary welcome in London of the Earl of Essex after a hypothetical suppression of the Irish rebellion. These dubious references to imperialism, Roman and Elizabethan, stress once more the distinction that must be drawn between the Chorus and the poet. In the light of the consistently disparaging allusions to Caesar throughout Shakespeare's works, the implied comparison of Essex to a "conquering Caesar" defines plainly enough what Shakespeare conceived to be the relation of his play to the events of his own day.

But, even without this, the cumulative testimony to what Shakespeare thought of Henry V's French conquest is utterly crushing. The irony of his rejecting Falstaff with his petty robberies only to embrace the shade of his father with his stolen crown and his advice to commit mightier thefts; the shaky character of his title to the throne of France, his unwillingness to understand that title, and his insistence that it be underwritten by the church; the passion into which he was sent by those innocent symbols of his youth, the tennis balls; his acceptance of church property to carry on his war, coupled with his swift dispatch of Bardolph to death for stealing from a church; his democratic protestations before the battle along with his quick consignment of them to oblivion after the victory; the continual juxtaposition of his boastfulness and Pistol's; his confession the night before Agincourt that even his own throne was not his own; the little loot of the underworld and the huge conquest of the King: all these things, and others, confirm the fact that he had turned his back on the wildness of his youth only to confirm it on a grand scale in the anarchy of war. No one but a person very ignorant of the mathematics of chance could attribute to coincidence the agreement of so many details. "Who, I rob? I a thief? Not I, by my faith," cries Hal when the Gadshill escapade is first proposed. To which Falstaff replies that the Prince comes "not of blood royal" if he cannot steal. "Well, then," Hal relents, "once in my days I'll be a madcap." Did cap ever fit better than this madcap fitted the future? What wonder that the future put it on! What it all adds up to is that the Battle of Agincourt was the royal equivalent of the Gadshill robbery. If Shakespeare did not mean it, it means itself.

From *The Meaning of Shakespeare* (The University of Chicago Press), pp. 217–24, 248–51, 254–55, 259–60. Copyright 1951 by The University of Chicago. Used by permission.

# KING HENRY VI, PARTS 1, 2, 3

## Comment and bibliography

Part 1 begins with the funeral of Henry V being interrupted by the news of French towns lost and the dauphin's being crowned. Thus even before the coronation of young Henry, his father's gains are disappearing. Soon strife breaks out between the boy's proud Protector and a Cardinal who represents a churchmanship now fully politicized and trafficking in a licensing of sin. Before long, old rivalries are revived between the Yorkists and the Lancastrians. In France, meanwhile, the spirit of Henry V survives as embodied in Lord Talbot, "scourge" of the French, who skirmishes back and forth against the "scourge" of the English, an Amazonian Joan of Arc. She is a fiend who has enchanted the French to believe she has been sent by the Holy Ghost, while Talbot, who takes his inspiration from an all-consuming love of fame, name, and titles, is termed "a fiend of hell" by Frenchmen, to whom he boasts he will stamp out their hearts with his horse's heels and make "a quagmire" of their mingled brains. These two models of patriotism, on opposite sides yet both of them morally defective, seem to have magical resources until the one dies deserted by his allies and the other is burnt as a sorceress. By the end of Part 1, however, there arises from Joan's ashes, so to speak, a Circe-like Margaret of Anjou who is likened to Helen of Troy, and whom young Henry impulsively marries at the cost of breaking his contract to another lady. Thus England begins to be victimized by a domineering female as France had been, signaling a new phase of moral decline.

Part 2 records England's further cultural erosion brought on by a rigged court trial of the kingdom's Duke Humphrey, in which Henry plays a Pilate's role. Jack Cade then leads briefly an anarchic revolt by the peasants.

Part 3 depicts a developing civil war that is climaxed emblematically by a battle in which sons and fathers slay each other while Henry retires to a molehill to lament the bloody times. Henry all along has been a spokesman of peaceful sentiments unaccompanied by practical intelligence. He himself has contributed to the strife by unnaturally disinheriting his son. Vacillating like the earlier Richard II, he has first declared himself ready to "unpeople this my realm" rather than "leave my kingly crown," but then weakly has consigned it to the Duke of York as heir on condition that Henry be allowed to remain king during his lifetime. Occupancy of office rather than using it to achieve the good of the commonwealth characterizes his feckless career. But York, whose ambition soon drives him to oath-breaking and a premature grab for the crown, encounters Margaret-led enemies who mock him with a paper crown in a bloody ceremony on a molehill that has an ironic likeness to the mocking of Christ. Here is a case, not infrequent in Shakespearean drama, in which a salvation-paradigm is grotesquely echoed in the midst of a society tied to revenge and Fortune's wheel, as if to remind us of a good potential that is being perverted by lovers of vanity. Evil actions, after all, must manifest a deprivation of the good, on which residually they depend in a Christian metaphysic.

For our anthology, four short pieces of commentary have been selected as an aid to appreciating the religious dimension of these plays. Both Jonathan Smith and William Watterson take note of the perversions of shepherding that characterize the French and English leaders. Watterson focuses in particular on King Henry's empty piety. Emrys Jones reviews Shakespeare's use of patterns of dramatic action which some of his auditors would have encountered in the once popular mystery pageants. John Elliott comments on the "parody of the Crucifixion" in *Henry VI, Part 3.*

For supplementary reading, Edward Berry's book is of primary importance, charting as it does the three-part pattern of decay represented by the three parts of *Henry VI.* Faye Kelly reviews the theme of "broken oaths, deceit, and treachery" in this trilogy as a whole. The commentary by John Cox focuses on "the contrast between sacred paradigms and human action" in the *Henry VI* plays, in this way adding to the evidence that Jones presented regarding the influence of the medieval mystery plays on Shakespeare's art. Cox argues also that Augustine's view of Roman history prior to Constantine as a tawdry struggle for domination is echoed in Shakespeare's patterning of *Henry VI.*

## Supplementary bibliography

Berry, Edward. *Patterns of Decay: Shakespeare's Early Histories* (University Press of Virginia, 1975), pp. 1–74.

Bevington, David. "The Domineering Female in 1 *Henry VI*," *Shakespeare Studies* 2 (1966), 51–58.

Cairncross, Andrew. Arden ed. *King Henry VI, Part 1* (London: Methuen, 1960), pp. xl-xlii; *Part 2* (1962), pp. l-lii; *Part 3* (1964), pp. liii-lxi.

Cox, John D. *Shakespeare and the Dramaturgy of Power* (Princeton University Press, 1989), pp. 89–96.

Kelly, Faye L. "Oaths in Shakespeare's *Henry VI* Plays," *Shakespeare Quarterly* 24 (1973), 357–71.

Shirley, Frances. *Swearing and Perjury in Shakespeare's Plays* (London: Allen & Unwin, 1979).

*Jonathan Clark Smith (1974)*

## The Denial of the Shepherd

Joan's valedictory in *Henry VI, Part 1* is a curiously combined claim to nobility and sainthood at the same time. It begins:

> First let me tell you whom you have condemn'd:
> Not one begotten of a shepherd swain,
> But issued from the progeny of kings;
> Virtuous and holy, chosen from above,
> By inspiration of celestial grace,
> To work exceeding miracles on earth.
> I never had to do with wicked spirits. (5.4.36–42)

The speech is a series of lies, but it is only the first one—the denial of the shepherd father—that clearly indicates the "wrong" conception of the saintly role, apart from the matter of Joan's false performance. It is the denial of the humility and self-sacrifice of the archetypal "good shepherd," and the replacement of those qualities with the over-reaching ambition to exalt the self, even at the expense of the immediate family. The thematic significance of the scene is that Joan's act of denial symbolizes and foreshadows a universal tendency in these plays to set self-advancement ahead of all ethical considerations, forgetting, in particular, one's proper relationships with others. As that tendency gains in strength, individuals' spheres of loyalty shrink. When King Henry faces assassination in *3 Henry VI* 5.6 he mentions that the shepherd (referring on the direct level to his guard) has fled, leaving the "sheep" to the "wolf," a conclusion whose validity on a general level is supported by the escalated use of imagery of beasts of prey in *Part 3*.

The "point of no return" on the descent into this chaos is the murder of Humphrey of Gloucester in *Part 2*, an event clearly marked by the imagery as a betrayal of a "shepherd." York speaks, in fact, of snaring "the shepherd of the flock" (2.2.72), referring to Humphrey. Gloucester's resignation is called for in a scene (invented by Shakespeare) that focuses symbolically on giving up the "staff" of office (2.3.22–38). There is a reminder that staff and shepherd are related images (as in the Twenty-Third Psalm) in Humphrey's final speech:

> Ah! thus King Henry throws away his crutch
> Before his legs be firm to bear his body.
> Thus is the shepherd beaten from thy side,
> And wolves are gnarling who shall gnaw thee first. (3.1.189–92)

The importance of Gloucester's downfall is marked on the stage by the sudden emergence of a rioting mob.

The shepherd, of course, is in Biblical tradition a commonplace image for Abel, Abraham, David and Christ, and by extension, for clergymen and religious leaders in general. The hireling, says Jesus in John's gospel, "seeth the wolf coming, and leaveth the sheep. . .because he is a hireling, and careth not for the sheep" (Jn 10:12). The appropriateness of this symbolic rank for Henry is clear in his abandonment of Gloucester and then his son; and it is reinforced at the time of the speech by his physical position outside the battle. As Robert Pierce has noted in his *Shakespeare's History Plays* (1971), Henry's longing to be a shepherd is ironic because "it undermines what the symbol in this sense represents, the guiding role of the king" (p. 70). His people scattered to an extreme, Henry wants to abdicate not only the responsibilities of the kingship, but even personal responsibility for the minutes of one's own life.

Joan's powers come to an end in *1 Henry VI* 5.3, a scene that generally parallels the pathetic encounter of Saul and the witch of Endor in 1 Samuel 28. Joan appeals to the "substitutes / Under the lordly monarch of the north" (i.e. agents of Satan) and speaks to them as "familiar spirits," a frequently used term in the Old Testament condemnations of sorcery. The marginal note in the Geneva Bible reads: "He seketh not to God in his miserie, but is led by Satan to unlawful meanes, which in his conscience he condemneth." Both Joan and Saul seek assistance in a coming battle, and both are disappointed. Joan says "they forsake me" and concludes that France will fall with her:

> My ancient incantations are too weak,
> And hell too strong for me to buckle with:
> Now, France, thy glory droopeth to the dust. (27–29)

The last line, in its context, is an ironically appropriate echo of Isaiah 19:3, "Thy voice shall be, as of one that hath a familiar spirit, out of the ground, and thy speech shall whisper out of the dust."

The tenor of false religion or even blasphemy runs beneath the surface of the trilogy, and surfaces in trivial as well as significant ways. Margery Jourdain conjures fiends "By the eternal God" (*2 H6* 1.4.24), and the Duchess of Gloucester threatens with her "ten commandments" to assault the Queen (1.3.142). The dying Bedford unconsciously twists the Nunc Dimittis (Lk 2:29): "Lord, now lettest thou thy servant depart in peace, For mine eyes have seen thy salvation" becomes "Now, quiet, soul, depart when heaven please, / For I have seen our enemies' overthrow" (*1 H6* 3.2.110–11). Similarly, Joan echoes one of David's Psalms, but distortedly. David, praying for the faithful in Jerusalem, declared: "They shall prosper that love thee, / Peace be within thy walls, and prosperity within thy palaces" (Ps 122:6–7). Joan, referring to the Parisians, says, "Peace be amongst them, if they turn to us: / Else ruin comes within their palaces" (*1 H6* 5.2.6–7). The most basic premise of a "good shepherd" is that he should be self-giving in service to his people. The Duke of York's reversal of this role is so extreme that he regards the entire nation as merely functional to his personal ambition (*2 H6* 3.1.349–52). He becomes, however, a mock-savior who suffers death (*3 H6* 1.4.94ff.) under circumstances that parallel Christ's ironically.

From *Destiny Reversed: A Study of Allusion Patterns in Shakespeare's "Henry VI"* (Indiana University Dissertation, 1974), excerpts from Chapter 2.

*William Watterson (1991)*

## Parodic Shepherding in *Henry VI*

Shakespeare's "theology" in the Henry VI trilogy owes much to the techniques of characterization in the old morality plays, allegories in which virtues and vices are personified. His schematic use of pastoral imagery, with its biblically sanctioned emphasis on watchfulness, humility, and faith (*vide* Psalm 23, Ezekiel 34:1–34, Isaiah 39:11, and the New Testament *passim,* especially John 10), is likewise traditional, and consistently frames a spiritual ideal against which to measure "fallen" characters from the Three Estates—noblemen, clerics, and commoners—as they fashion postlapsarian history in their sinfulness. Although Poggioli has denigrated this kind of Christian pastoral in *The Oaten Flute* (1975) on the grounds that it serves merely as "allegorical travesty and satirical mask" (p. 122), it derives from the well-established canon of complaint and eclogue known to Shakespeare through a medieval tradition culminating in the Latin poems of Baptista Spagnolo. Spagnolo's *Eclogues* were standard school texts in England until the eighteenth century. Shakespeare draws on *topoi* of good and bad shepherds along with images of lambs and wolves to excoriate pride and worldly ambition and to valorize duty and contentment with the tried estate.

La Pucelle is a negative *exempla* of the original *pastor bonus*, Jesus Christ. Fashioning herself as extraordinary agent of God's will, she disguises her prideful will to power by emphasizing her rustic origins. Her vain preoccupation with skin hues implies an all too worldly comparison of her own complexion to that of the Virgin Mary, signaling petty envy:

> Dolphin, I am by birth a shepherd's daughter.
> My wit untrained in any kind of art.
> Heaven and our Lady gracious hath it pleased
> To shine on my contemptible estate.
> Lo, whilst I waited on my tender lambs,
> And to sun's parching heat displayed my cheeks,
> God's mother deigned to appear to me.
> And in a vision full of majesty

> Willed me to leave my base vocation
> And free my country from calamity. (*2 H6*.1.1.72–80)

The blessed shepherd motif is particularly strong in the nativity story in *Luke*, but Joan's magnetic attraction is to earthly kingship. In the wake of her dramatic rise to power, she claims royal blood for herself in Act 5, wholly suppressing her origins and condemning her shepherd father as a "base ignoble wretch."

A man of "mildness, peace and prayer," Henry VI for all his piety fails in the active duties of kingship, relinquishing power to the wicked Queen Margaret and her paramour Suffolk. She despises her husband precisely because of his supposed holiness (*2 H6*, 1.3.55–60), but this holiness is more ceremonious than substantial. His action is reminiscent of weak Pilate's when he hands over Duke Humphrey to his enemies though he knows him to be innocent and says so. *The Mirror for Magistrates* represents Henry as morally duplicitous, for there he insists his fall is caused by "destiny and fate" rather than any fault that would deserve "due punishment of vice." Yet even as he protests his innocence he also laments his "unlawful" marriage to Margaret and sees his violation in previous contract as an example of "the payneful playing of those that breake their lawful bandes." At best inconsistent, he is at the worst totally ignorant of himself.

Ineffectual as king, Henry in his famous pastoral soliloquy at Towton further reveals a man of specious virtue. It is as sinful for a monarch to wish for a shepherd's estate as it is for a shepherd to wish for a crown, and Henry's rejection of the active life of virtue which is Christian kingship constitutes a culpable fantasy:

> O God! Methinks it were a happy life,
> To be no better than a homely swain,
> To sit upon a hill as I do now,
> To carve out dials quaintly, point by point,
> Thereby to see the minutes how they run—
> How many makes the hour full complete,
> How many hours bring about the day
> How many days will finish up the year,
> How many years a mortal man may live.
> When this is known, then to divide the times—
> So many hours, must I tend my flock,
> So many hours, must I take my rest,
> So many hours must I contemplate,
> So many hours must I sport myself,
> So many days, my ewes have been with young,
> So many weeks, ere the poor fools will ean,
> So many years, ere I shall shear the fleece...
> So minutes, hours, days, months, and years,
> Passed over to the end they were created,
> Would bring white hairs unto a quiet grave.
> Ah, what a life were this! How sweet! How lovely! (*3 H6*.2.5.21–41)

Henry reduces Christian pastoral to empty convention. Essentially sentimental, his bucolic fantasy, like Marie Antoinette's at Le Hameau, is grounded in ease and convenience rather than the appeal of duty and good works. Fugitive from the responsibility of pastoral care, he can only envision the shepherd's life as a kind of *negotium* in which minutes, hours, days, weeks, months, and years are tallied up (there is something joyless in all those "musts"). Mistaking the spiritual life for a set of physical routines, he still manages to see himself as a paschal victim at the hands of Gloucester in one last bravura conceit:

> So flies the reakless shepherd from the wolf;
> So first the harmless sheep doth yield his fleece,
> And next his throat unto the butcher's knife. (*3 H6*.5.6.7–9)

Submitted at the Editor's request by Professor Watterson of Bowdoin College.

*Emrys Jones (1977)*

## Passion Play Echoes in *Henry VI* [editor's title]

When in his twenties Shakespeare came to write plays of a historical or tragic kind, he would have had the Passion plays of his boyhood as a dramatic paradigm, carried lightly, perhaps half-consciously, at the back of his mind; it would have seemed a well-tried way of making a powerful tragic effect on an audience. Indeed if he saw the mystery cycles—and saw them on a number of occasions—before he became aware of more neo-classical ways of writing tragedy, those Passion plays may well have taken a position of absolute priority in his mind, seeming to him more moving, more natural, more fundamental, forms of tragic drama. And in any case the narrative of Christ's ministry and death was the supreme narrative, the prototype of all suffering and all tragic action. It was one of Shakespeare's distinctions as a tragic dramatist to remain imaginatively faithful to this tradition of his childhood.

In describing Shakespeare's early "tragedy" of Duke Humphrey and the typical mystery play treatment of the Passion I have tried to bring out, without forcing the evidence, a marked general resemblance in conception and structure. In making such a comparison we must, as far as possible, ignore the differences in status and morality between the persons concerned (Christ, Duke Humphrey), and consider simply the forms traced by the dramatic action. The four features I have distinguished in the typical Passion plot seem to recur in the action devised by Shakespeare to dramatize the chronicle account of Humphrey's fall: the stress on the enemies of the victim-protagonist, and on their virulent malice; the conspiratorial method of their undertaking against him; the legalistic procedure they find it expedient to adopt, with a consequential wide range of hypocritical speech-tones; and the progressive isolation of the hero, whose friends are powerless to help him. There seems to be no other dramatic source for an action shaped in this way than the mysteries: classical tragedy, for example, offers nothing as close. There is too a confidence in Shakespeare's handling of Humphrey's tragedy which perhaps suggests that he felt he was doing it in an approved, well-attested way—a way approved by audiences already accustomed to that kind of dramatic action.

This general resemblance is borne out by the choice of character types in *2 Henry VI*. Among the court faction it is Margaret and Cardinal Beaufort, the most implacable of Humphrey's enemies, who most pointedly recall Caiaphas and Annas. Their affinities with the two priests are largely a matter of the way they are conceived as vocal personalities, speaking parts: the voices of all four are at times abrasively harsh, at others almost primly sanctimonious, but always in fact unrelentingly hard. The note is always one of pure hate unsatisfied until it destroys its object. Beaufort of course has a further likeness to Caiaphas and Annas: he too wears clerical vestments and is as little troubled by reminders of his holy office as they are. Henry VI, on the other hand, seems to combine in himself two roles. He recalls Pilate, the head of state, sympathetic to the hero-victim, yet powerless or without the will to help him. But he also has at least some of the qualities of the Virgin Mary. Henry swoons on hearing of Humphrey's death; in paintings of the Crucifixion, though not in the four extant play cycles, Mary too is often shown swooning. And, as we have seen, Henry compares Humphrey to a "calf," himself to the "dam," the wailing mother robbed of her "darling"; in this extended simile (3.1.210–220) the relative ages of Henry and Humphrey are quite ignored so as to bring out the maternal relationship felt by the King at this moment of loss. And, in the same speech, his line

> Thou never didst them wrong, nor no man wrong

can be matched by a characteristic one of Mary's (in the York *Mortificacio Christi*, 143):

> Allas! he did never trespasse.

In *2 Henry VI* the salient structural devices were the two scenes of baiting, the first exploding briefly, the second more extended and elaborated into a climax. Their dramatic antecedents seem to be those obligatory scenes in which Jesus is interrogated and ill treated by his assembled enemies. The number and duration of these scenes vary according to the cycle, although they always receive strong emphasis. With his rhetorically trained sense of economy and climax, Shakespeare reduced them to the minimum of two. We have therefore in the two baiting scenes an impression of a repeated series, in which we progress from the smaller to the greater; but there is no excess, no waste. Such scenes are planned with precision; their brevity increases their impact.

I remarked of the final scene of Humphrey's tragedy—the discovery of his body and the prolonged clamour that ensues—that there seemed to be something in the crime that was felt to be almost preternatural: it was not only a murder of an individual but a cataclysm in the entire order of nature. This is no doubt partly explained by the real importance of Humphrey's death in the setting of the incipient Civil Wars. But there may also be another dimension in Shakespeare's treatment, which can be accounted for by referring back to the Passion sequences. It is as if something of the uniquely heightened atmosphere of the Passion plays, their awe and horror, their unqualified seriousness, found an echo in this scene of violent death—as if the suggestion of ultimate climax, proper to depictions of the Crucifixion, had been carried over into the smaller-scaled secular tragedy of the fall and death (the "passion") of the "good" Duke....

Probably the outstanding tragic scene of *3 Henry VI* is that (1.4) in which York is taken alive at the battle of Wakefield and is taunted by Margaret and Clifford before they stab him to death. Shakespeare's mention of a "molehill"— "Come make him stand upon this molehill here," says Margaret—makes it clear that he was following Holinshed's, and not Hall's, account:

> Some write that the duke of Yorke was taken aliue, and in derision caused to stand vpon a molehill; on whose head they put a garland in steed of a crowne, which they had fashioned and made of sedges and balrushes; and, hauing so crowned him with that garland, they kneeled down afore him (as the Iewes did vnto Christ) in scorne, saieng to him: "Haile king without rule! haile king without heritage!" And at length, hauing thus scorned him with these and diuerse other despitefull words, they stroke off his head, which (as you haue heard) they presented to the queene.

Perhaps it was Holinshed's parenthesis that gave Shakespeare his cue, for the scene of York's death recalls more than one of the violent torture scenes in the mysteries (although, again, Shakespeare need not have known any of those extant).

The last of the trial scenes in the York Plays ("The second *Trial before Pilate* continued; the *Judgement of Jesus*") shows Jesus whipped by the soldiers before being clothed in purple and pall, set on a seat, crowned with thorns and made to hold a reed for a sceptre. The soldiers then jeer at him:

> i Mil.   Aue! riall roy and rex judeorum!
> Hayle! comely kyng, that no kyngdom has kende,
> Hayll! vndughty duke, thi dedis ere dom,
> Hayll! man, vnmyghty thi menye to mende. (33.409–12)

and the other soldiers join in the "hail" chorus. This anticipates in a general way Margaret's long taunting speech to York, set on the molehill, in the course of which she sets a paper crown on his head. But another mystery play comes closer to the tone and substance of what she says. This is *The Buffeting (Coliphizacio)* in the Townley Plays. In this, Caiaphas indulges himself in a long diatribe against Jesus, who keeps silent. Although in Shakespeare's scene York is eventually given a chance, which he seizes, of making a full reply to Margaret, during her long speech he too keeps silent—thus making an effect, while it lasts, comparable to that of the silent Christ. The whole of Caiaphas's speech (127–80) is relevant, and the jeering is on the same topic: how dare you call yourself a king! It is no doubt possible that Shakespeare was merely recalling the Gospel narratives, without having the mystery plays in mind here. But in view of the prominence given in the mysteries to the malice of Christ's accusers—their long insulting diatribes and the various ways in which Christ's physical sufferings and humiliations were protracted on the stage—it seems likely that something of this ritual of torment was carried over into Margaret's role in this scene.

From *The Origins of Shakespeare* (Oxford University Press, 1977), pp. 51–55 abridged. Used by permission.

*John R. Elliott, Jr. (1968)*

## The History Play as Drama

Relevant to what I have been saying about the Christian origins of historical drama is the ritual quality that Shakespeare gives to particular scenes in order to broaden their meaning and to make clear their relation to the larger historical pattern of the whole. One very striking instance of this occurs in the scene depicitng the torture of York by Clifford and Queen Margaret in *3 Henry VI*. The details of this scene—the molehill, the paper crown, the mock comfort of the bloody handkerchief, the scoffs and taunts of the captor, even the unexpected dignity and resignation of York himself—all force us to see the murder of York as analogous to the sacrifice of Christ. The scene is, in fact, a parody of the Crucifixion. The most interesting thing about the parody is that it is conveyed entirely by the stage action—there is no hint in the dialogue that any of the characters involved perceive it or intend it. Yet it is unmistakable to the audience, and Shakespeare was certainly aware of what he was doing, for he was following a passage in Holinshed which had explicitly drawn the comparison between the mocking of York and the scourging of Christ. In the play, however, only the audience is made aware of the full significance of the event that takes place before them. What for the characters, in their immediate apprehension of the event, is simply one of the bloody accidents of life is, for the audience, a part of the recurrent historical pattern of suffering and redemption.

　　I cannot prove that Shakespeare actually saw one of the performances of the Corpus Christi Play that were still being given during his lifetime, but the intensity of this scene, its cruelty and grotesqueness, and especially the elaboration of the motives and emotions of the torturers, seem to me to go far beyond either the Biblical account or Holinshed and to suggest a debt to those terrifying Crucifixion episodes in the Corpus Christi Play. And it seems that I am not alone in my suspicion. Ernest Talbert in *Elizabethan Drama and Shakespeare's Early Plays* (1963) has argued, on the basis of records from Coventry, that a direct transition took place in English popular drama during the 1580's from Biblical cycle to historical cycle, a transition that he finds reflected in the structure of Shakespeare's first tetralogy (pp. 175–6). Whether or not this is so, the scourging of York is by no means the only scene in these plays that seems to be modeled upon an episode from the Corpus Christi Play. The scene in *Richard III* in which the three Queens join in mutual lamentation for the murder of their sons strongly calls to mind the episode of the Massacre of the Innocents in the Biblical cycles, with its mandatory scene of the lamentation of Rachel, and it does so, I think, for important structural and thematic reasons. Dramatically, it is in this scene, rather than in the announcement of Richard's marriage at the end of the play, that the real union of the Houses of Lancaster and York takes place. Through the parallel with the Massacre of the Innocents Shakespeare shows that it is a union made possible only by suffering and sacrifice, a union that gives meaning to the seemingly gratuitous violence of history. Only when they have first been united in suffering can the rival houses at last be united in joy. Biblical allusion thus serves much the same function in Shakespeare's histories as the typological correspondence between episodes in the Corpus Christi Play: it enables the audience to see at any given moment the relation of that moment to the historical pattern of the whole. It is one of the ways found—or inherited—by Shakespeare to combine the immediacy of drama with the perspective of history.

From *Research Opportunities in Renaissance Drama* 11 (1968), 26–27. By permission of Northwestern University Press.

# KING RICHARD III

## Comment and bibliography

I n the middle of *3 Henry VI* the Duke of York's son Richard tells us in soliloquy his intention to get the kingly crown for himself by using the Protean arts of a Machiavellian dissembler to serve hell and please the shadow of his solitary self. By the time *Richard III* opens, this self-confessed villain has become the slayer of both King Henry and his son, has saluted with a Judas kiss his own brother Edward, the new king, and is planning the removal of another brother, the Duke of Clarence. All this accords with his stated creed that he has "no brother" and intends to celebrate his own deformity by showing he can excel in being bad. We may see here an apostle of the spirit of Cain, motivated like Cain by an envy of the divine grace he lacks. Replacing that grace is a counterfeited "Christian" love that proves its seductive power in the midst of the funeral of King Henry by wooing and winning the heart of Anne, that king's daughter-in-law and the widow of the young prince whom Richard has slain. In the scenes that follow, he manages nine further murders and successfully usurps the kingship. He is able to enjoy it, however, only for a brief day (4.1.6) before night comes on with ghosts from the past that foretell his Doomsday, a downfall mediated by a Richmond who invokes aid from "the prayers of holy saints and wounded souls" (5.3.241).

The apex of Richard's power is achieved and its crackup begun through his massacre of two innocent young princes, an act which rouses against him all the mothers of the "babes," both young and adult, whom he has victimized in his tyrant's version of anointed deputy of God. The choral *ubi sunt* of these formerly contending women marks their recognition of the vanity of goods devoid of justice, and prompts their risking a commitment to an intervener from outside. It also grounds Elizabeth's subsequent ability to parry Richard's tempting her with "fortune" and "this earth's glory." One's destiny, she tells Richard, depends on whether or not one avoids grace. A decision similar to Elizabeth's we hear the Bishop of Ely has made, perhaps as the result of his reflecting on the folly of his earlier obedience to Richard's request for strawberries, or on the disgraceful sycophancy of the two bishops who lent their presence to Richard's London show of slanderous piety, or on the betrayal of "sanctuary" by an Archbishop too easily taken in by Richard's cajolery. Crisis situations require a person to choose whether he will serve God or Mammon. Even Buckingham, Richard's ladder to the crown, begins to recover some native conscience when asked to murder children but finds payment uncertain. He, however, can only flee in despair while recognizing ironically how his own words have been turned on himself by a divine All-Seer who turns the swords of wicked men to their own bosoms. On this score he foreshadows the fate of Richard, who ultimately discovers in himself last-minute flickerings of conscience he can put down only with a desperate bravado that exhausts itself in futile cries offering his kingdom for a horse.

A mysterious providence embraces the drama as a whole. Richard both capsulizes in his own person the sins of England's past and scourges purgatively the sins of his neighbors. A sinful England in effect punishes itself through its bondage to a corrupt Richard who ministers chastisements unwittingly providential. He becomes, as commentators have noted, an embodiment of the Anti-Christ "beast" of the Book of Revelation, who brings a tribulation that serves to test souls and elicit self-knowledge through an Armageddon experience that prefaces a new world order. For those capable of faith and prayer, providence turns their past evil into good. Even the hardened Richard is brought to cry out "Have mercy, Jesu" and to flirt with the truth about himself; for in Shakespeare's story he suffers torments of conscience—whereas in Hall's chronicle he was depicted as visited only by devils plaguing him. Shakespeare's sense of providence differs substantially from Hall's.

Recent commentary by Emrys Jones has called the attention of critics to the Christian lore underlying Shakespeare's differences from Hall's vision. Our anthology reprints an abridgment of Jones's remarks on the significance of Shakespeare's bringing into his dramatization an "All Souls" motif and the encouragement of Richmond by a visitation comparable to Constantine's. All Souls was the medieval holiday on which, in popular belief, souls from Purgatory could appear to persons who had wronged them and could offer prayers for persons of faith. Shakespeare's play is congruent with a belief in Purgatory. Buckingham's historical death by execution on All Souls' Day, 1483, has been elided with the battle of Bosworth Field in 1485 as furnishing its cultural atmosphere. At the same time Constantine's vision, familiar to English audiences from Catholic wall paintings commemorating his piety and that of his saintly English mother Helena, is analogized in the experience of Richmond in a drama that would have been regarded by Shakespeare's contemporaries as complimenting their Queen Elizabeth, who had been likened to Constantine by John Foxe, the revered Protestant historian.

Alongside Jones's essay, Tom Driver's deserves presentation because of its tracing in *Richard III* a biblical pattern of a "conflict of times" leading up to an apocalyptic Doomsday. Scott Colley's essay warrants attention because of its learned summary of the many similarities between Richard and the biblical Herod. And Phyllis Rackin's recognition of providential design in *Richard III* is notable, particularly since she is an advocate of today's New Historicism and chooses to suppose (in a paragraph following those here reprinted) that Shakespeare was momentarily experimenting with a theory of design which he soon found unsatisfactory.

For supplementary reading, the essays by John Harcourt and Alistair Fox trace the upside-down relationship between Richard's creed and St Paul's. Also they offer an analysis of ironic parallel between Richard the mocker of Christianity and the biblical Saul of Tarsus who persecuted Christians until his deeper conscience witnessed against him. Scraps of Scripture permitted each a very temporary triumph. Clifford Huffman expounds the significance of Clarence's dream as a parallel to and foreshadowing of Richard's on Bosworth Eve. Both show a concern with divine punishment. Both have the perspective of one whose lost "gems" mock the man who has so misvalued life as to risk it for earthly jewels. Both end by bypassing conscience, as Pilate did. The play's phrase "worm of conscience" has been traced to medieval drama by Irving Matus. William Toole has noted that the mutiny of Richard's real conscience in a conflict of "self against self" is foreshadowed by the division between the two murderers earlier in the play, and also by the separation of the crowned Richard from his "other self," Buckingham.

Chris Hassel's essays explore fully the play's themes of prophetic fulfillment and apocalypse in history. He finds an overarching providence in accord with the Bible. He traces the patterns that gradually emerge to clarify for the audience how providence works. Edward Berry takes issue with those critics who would fault the play's design as incoherent. Bettie Anne Doebler cites *ars moriendi* tradition as a standard for measuring Richard's last moments. Roy Battenhouse examines Richard's psychology of villainy and how his tragedy can arouse our pity and fear.

## Supplementary bibliography

Battenhouse, Roy. *Shakespearean Tragedy* (1969), pp. 187–92.

Berry, Edward. *Patterns of Decay* (1975), pp. 80–103.

Doebler, Bettie Anne. "'Dispaire and Dye': The Ultimate Temptation of Richard III," *Shakespeare Studies* 6 (1974), 75–86.

Fox, Alistair. "*Richard III*'s Pauline Oath," *Moreana* 57 (1978), 13–23.

Harcourt, John B. "'Odde Old Ends, Stolne . . .': King Richard and St Paul," *Shakespeare Studies* 6 (1974), 87–100.

Hassel, R. Chris, Jr. "Last Words, Last Things: St John, Apocalypse, and Eschatology in *Richard III*," *Shakespeare Studies* 18 (1986), 25–40.

———. "Perceptions of Providence in *Richard III*," in *Songs of Death: Performance, Interpretation, and the Text of "Richard III"* (University of Nebraska Press, 1987), pp. 89–121.

Huffman, Clifford. "'Unvalued Jewels': The Religious Perspective in *Richard III*," *Bucknell Review* 26 (1982), 58–73.

Matus, Irving L. "An Early Reference to the Coventry Mystery Plays in Shakespeare?" *Shakespeare Quarterly* 40 (1989), 196–97.

Toole, William B. "The Motif of Psychic Division in *Richard III*," *Shakespeare Survey* 27 (1974), 21–32.

*Emrys Jones (1977)*

## Bosworth, All Souls, and Constantine [editor's title]

In dramatic terms what 'Bosworth' means is not so much the battle itself—of that we are given only a brief token show—as the eve of battle, the occasion richest in imaginative potential and significance: the long sequence of evening, night, and early morning during which Richard and Richmond sleep and dream and in dream are visited by ghosts. In stage terms the procession of ghosts *is* the battle of Bosworth. When the ghosts have gone, Richard is defeated, as his long soliloquy shows.

But the irruption of ghosts into the stage action is by no means sudden and unheralded: at two earlier points, in 4.4 and 5.1, the audience are alerted to what is to come through references to spirits who are felt to be watching the action and waiting for the final judgement. So the ghosts of the newly murdered Princes (they are called "souls") are twice appealed to, first by their mother Elizabeth (4.4.13) and then, more emphatically, by the Duchess of York in her final curse on Richard, when she looks ahead to the day of battle:

> My prayers on the adverse party fight;
> And there the little souls of Edward's children
> Whisper the spirits of thine enemies
> And promise them success and victory. (4.4.190–3)

Finally, and most weightily of all, when Buckingham is led to execution (5.1) he apostrophizes the invisible souls of the dead who are watching him in his last hour:

> Hastings, and Edward's children, Grey, and Rivers,
> Holy King Henry, and thy fair son Edward,
> Vaughan, and all that have miscarried,
> By underhanded corrupted foul injustice,
> If that your moody discontented souls
> Do through the clouds behold this present hour,
> Even for revenge mock my destruction!

He then goes on immediately to say: "This is All-Souls' day, fellow, is it not?" And twice more in this short scene he refers to All Souls' day, his "body's doomsday." But in the last reference he converts the term into a metaphor: he is dying not on any feast-day but specifically on that day which had a special bearing on the state of his soul:

> This, this All-Souls' day to my fearful soul
> Is the determin'd respite of my wrongs;
> That high All-Seer which I dallied with

> Hath turn'd my feigned prayer on my head
> And given in earnest what I begg'd in jest.

Although this is an appropriately weighty speech to mark Buckingham's last moments (he is the last of Richard's victims), Shakespeare is still preparing for the culmination of this second movement in Bosworth eve. On that night, a very special night in the national calendar, ghosts are to walk in procession—or as Richard puts it when he wakes from his dream:

> Methought the souls of all that I had murder'd
> Came to my tent . . .

So from Buckingham's death on All Souls' day we pass almost at once to the night when "the souls of all" Richard's victims return to curse him.

This ghost scene is often disparaged by critics who approach it more as a passage in a literary text than as part of a dramatic performance; but it is surely a remarkable invention. That Shakespeare invented it must be stressed. The historical sources gave Richard "a dreadful & a terrible dreame" (in Hall's words) in which he was tormented by devils; Shakespeare transferred this to Clarence, and while he kept the fact of Richard's dream he gave the dream itself an entirely new content. Otherwise there is no known source for this visitation of ghosts on the eve of battle, one of the great images of the play.

In the first place, Shakespeare must have taken a hint from the fact, provided by history, that Buckingham was executed on All Souls' day (2 November 1483). In the chronicles, this event was separated by a considerable space from the battle of Bosworth (22 August 1485): only Shakespeare brings the two events so close together. To Elizabethans, All Souls' day was a relic of pre-Reformation England. The three days of All Saints' eve (31 October), All Saints and All Souls' eve (1 November), and All Souls (2 November) had traditionally been a time of remembrance of the faithful dead. Early in Elizabeth's reign, bell-ringing during these three days was prohibited as a papist superstition.[1] But though the observance of All Souls was suppressed, some of the traditional associations lingered for a considerable time. What Shakespeare was free to do was to make figurative use of the festival in a play: being suppressed, it perhaps became all the more readily available for imaginative adaptation. This, then, is the reason why Buckingham so pointedly draws our attention to All Souls: it prepares us for the procession of souls that is to appear on Bosworth eve.[2] The actual date of Bosworth is quite immaterial as far as Shakespeare's use of All Souls' is concerned. What matters is that a close link between the two occasions is established in terms of the stage performance, so that the fifth act becomes in effect a kind of All Souls sequence.

All Souls was a festival of the dead. The faithful living commemorated the faithful dead and, through prayer and almsgiving, tried to alleviate their sufferings in purgatory. But it was also popularly believed to be a time when the dead might return to the living; indeed folklorists have collected a mass of evidence to show that throughout western Europe All Souls has been associated with the appearance of ghosts. On All Souls' eve the dead might return home, or else the procession of the dead (the *cours des morts*) might be witnessed. "Throughout the Middle Ages it was popular belief that the souls in purgatory could appear on this day ... to persons who had wronged them during their life."[3] This last belief is the one with the most obvious bearing on *Richard III*: the ghosts of Richard's victims return to plague him. In the procession of the eleven ghosts the play even offers its own version of the *cours des morts*.

All Souls probably displaced an older pagan festival which was also held in November and which also involved the return of the dead; and like Guy Fawkes' day, which came to displace Hallowmas and All Souls in post-Elizabethan England, these early November festivals were celebrated with bonfires. A folklorist has written of Guy Fawkes' day in terms which are relevant to the significance of All Souls: "It superseded the older festival of Hallowmas taking over the bonfires, the bell-ringing, and the general liberty which characterized the older festival." She goes on to suggest that these fire-festivals "mark the end of the old year or the end of a particular season.... The bonfire is a destruction of the bad luck and rubbish of the past, so that it shall never return to vex the future."[4] This theme of the ending of a phase of experience—of a season or a year—and the ritual destruction of the dead past is another belief which clarifies the imaginative conception of *Richard III*. The play is also concerned with the casting-off of an old order, fatigued and guilt-ridden, to make way for a new. England under Richard is like the Patriarchs in limbo waiting for deliverance (this feeling of not quite hopeless waiting is particularly acute in the scene in 4.4 of the exhausted women). It is an end-of-the-year, end-of-the-cycle play, in the course of which England is to negotiate its critical dynastic change.

The associations clustering around All Souls throw light on the conception of Bosworth eve, but without explaining it entirely. That conception is a strange and powerful one; indeed it has an imaginative grandeur which familiarity with the play may cause us to overlook. The occasion, the eve of a great battle, is to mark the inauguration of a new dynasty. The scene is the two military camps, with the chief antagonists plunged in sleep, while around them in the dead of night move supernatural visitants. No source for this nocturnal camp scene is known. There is, however, one famous event which offers some striking likenesses to it. This is the occasion of the dream of Constantine which, seen in its full setting in the history of Christianity, was a turning-point of unparalleled momentousness. The Roman empire had been invaded by the infidel Maxentius. The details of the story vary in different versions; but the one most relevant is as follows (from Caxton's translation of *The Golden Legend*):

> And whan constantyn had assembled his hoost he went and sette them ageynst that other partye, but assoone as he began to passe the ryver he was moche aferde, bycause he shold on the morne have batayle, and in the nyght

as he slepte in his bedde an aungel awoke hym, and shewed to hym the sygne
of the crosse in heven . . . "In this sygne thou shalt overcome the bataylle."[5]

Next day Constantine carried a cross into battle, routed the enemy, and himself
embraced Christianity.

The story of Constantine's dream became attached to the Legend of the True
Cross (as told, for example, in *The Golden Legend*), and in the Middle Ages became a popular subject in art, the best known and the best instance being the fres-
coes at Arezzo by Piero della Francesca. Indeed someone coming from *Richard III*
to these paintings could hardly fail to be reminded of it by Piero's treatment of the
Dream of Constantine. The sleeping king is shown in his tent, with other tents
visible in the background; poised above the tent is an angel holding a cross and
pointing to Constantine's face. The subject was well known in England, in part
because St Helena, mother of Constantine and discoverer of the True Cross, was
traditionally held to be English-born.[6] Shakespeare's own birthplace proves this as
well as any: Stratford-upon-Avon had its Guild of the Holy Cross, whose chapel
had wall-paintings showing the Legend of the True Cross. (They have since dis-
appeared, but were visible until the early nineteenth century: according to the
sketches of Thomas Fisher, there was a small inset in one of the paintings showing
Constantine's vision.)[7]

The Constantine of this tradition was of course a medieval and Catholic one.
But after the Reformation he continued to occupy the minds of at least some
Englishmen, though now in a different role. The first dedication to Queen Elizabeth of John Foxe's enormously influential *Acts and Monuments* (the "Book of
Martyrs") opens with the name "Constantine" and develops an elaborate comparison between Constantine and Elizabeth—for Foxe, both were supreme benefac-
tors to the Church. According to Foxe, Elizabeth was in fact a second Constantine, not inferior to him and perhaps even greater.

For the Bosworth sequence, then, two motifs came together: All Souls gave the
ghosts, returning to wound the conscience of the man who had wronged them,
while Constantine's dream gave the occasion of the eve of battle and the saluta-
tions which the ghosts bestow on Richmond.

Although Shakespeare does not name Queen Elizabeth in the play's concluding speech, there can be little doubt that she is shadowed in the person of Richmond her grandfather (and in any case shares her name with his Queen). Richmond is the play's Constantine, while for her people Elizabeth was the second
Constantine, Empress and Head of the Church. So at its first performances, and
whenever it was performed within her reign, *Richard III* brought the events of the
previous century right up to the present moment as it was experienced by the audience. Shakespeare offers more than a theatrical entertainment: he creates an occasion for national thanksgiving and communal prayer:

Now civil wounds are stopp'd, peace lives again—
That she may long live here, God say amen!

## Notes

1  J. Brand, *Popular Antiquities of Great Britain*, ed. W. Carew Hazlitt, (1870), I.218–19.
2  In his edition of the play E. A. J. Honigmann comments: "I think it possible that the Buckingham scenes were slightly changed before the play was finished: prophecy and fulfilment dovetail so meticulously elsewhere that it is odd that Buckingham has not foretold his death on All Souls' day, as he asserts several times in 5.1" (p. 19). The comment is perceptive, but it is unnecessary to postulate any change of plan. The three references to All Souls are used to point forward rather than back. To have introduced the references earlier (e.g. in 2.i) would only have muffled the effect.
3  *New Catholic Encyclopedia*, (Washington, D. C., 1967), I.319.
4  Charlotte S. Burne, "Guy Fawkes' Day," *Folklore* 23, (1912), 409–26.
5  *The Golden Legend* (The Invention of the Cross), tr. Caxton, ed. F. H. Ellis (1892), II.483.
6  The Legend of the True Cross, including Constantine's Dream, is depicted on a fine twelfth-century cross at Kelloe, outside Durham. The cross is well reproduced in Fritz Saxl's *English Sculptors of the Twelfth Century* (1954).
7  *Ancient allegorical, historical and legendary paintings . . . at Stratford-upon-Avon*, ed. J. G. Nichols, (1838).

From *The Origins of Shakespeare* (Oxford University Press, 1977), pp. 226–32 abridged. By permission of Oxford University Press.

*Tom F. Driver (1960)*

## Nemesis and Judgment in *Richard III*

The irony of the story of Richard, as dramatized by Shakespeare, lies in the fact that he operates on a different schedule of time from the ultimately victorious forces. That is, Richard's desires and ambitions are, in the course of the play, to be proved vain. As "minister of hell" (1.2.46) he cannot win against the "captain" of God (5.3.108). Shakespeare, true to the religio-national character of his theme, has expressed the conflict of good and evil wills in something like the biblical understanding of a conflict of times.

Like many of the heroes in Shakespearean tragedy, Richard moves too quickly. He is intemperate and hasty in fixing the day of the Prince's coronation. "Tomorrow, in my judgment, is too sudden," says Derby; "For I myself am not so well provided / As else I would be were the day prolong'd" (3.4.45–47). The short scene of fourteen lines wherein the Scrivener marks "how well the sequence hangs together" in the intemperate execution of Hastings is inserted solely for the purpose of showing how much ahead of any proper order Richard and Buckingham are acting (3.6).

In Act 4, scene 4, Margaret reminds Elizabeth that Richard's outrageous acts have unnaturally changed her "infant morn to aged night." In fact, Richard's whole campaign has so upset the natural order of time that when the climax is reached on the day of the battle the sun refuses to shine (5.3.275–87). According to clock and calendar, which Richard consults, the sun "should have brav'd the east an hour ago," but as it is, it will be "a black day."

It is possible for Richard (or any man) to get so out of harmony with time because time in this play is not merely a quantity to be measured by the movement of stars or the flowing of sand in the glass. Time is laden with purpose, and therefore it tends to gather itself together, as it were, into certain particular moments when long-prepared actions are completed and great issues are decided.

The action of *Richard III* gathers toward two predominant "times"—the coronation of Richard and the Battle of Bosworth Field. Shakespeare has accentuated these "times" by building the rhythm of the play about them. Before each of them the pace accelerates. Before the coronation, the haste expresses, as we have seen, Richard's intemperateness. It does the same before Bosworth, but there it is even more important that the sense of acceleration expresses also the culmination of a decisive, judgmental action which has long been in preparation.

Near the end of Act 2, the pace begins to quicken. Only the two young princes stand between Richard and the throne, and they are virtually no obstacle at all. The excitement first appears among the citizens (2.3). Shakespeare wishes to show that events are stirring which involve the whole society. Thus the citizens, moving about exceedingly fast, for what reason they scarcely know themselves, pause only long enough to remark on the news of the king's death and to lament a land governed by a child who has not yet come to "his full and ripened years" (14), or else one governed by the Duke of Gloucester. They remark on the "untimely storms" (35) of the day's news and then hie themselves away. The next scene opens with the Archbishop's announcement that the crown prince and his escort will arrive in London "tomorrow, or next day." A messenger comes with news which sends the women and the young Duke into sanctuary.

References to speed and haste now appear more and more frequently, and according to Shakespeare's usual technique when the action is accelerating, there are increasing references to the hour and the day. Rivers, Grey, and Vaughan are dispatched in a short scene of twenty-five lines (3.3), and Hastings falls out of favor and loses his life before dinner of the same day (3.4.97). Meantime, the nobles have assembled to decide "when is the royal day?" Buckingham wants to know if all is "ready for the royal time." Ely suggests "tomorrow" as a "happy day" (4.3–6), which Derby believes is too sudden (45).

A slight lull now ensues as Buckingham and Richard unsuccessfully try to prepare the citizens to agree to the coronation (3.5), but at the end of the scene things speed up again. The scrivener scene follows, devoted to the importunity of Hastings' death. The citizens are won in the scene with Richard "between two Bishops," and Buckingham gets his "consent" to be crowned "tomorrow" (3.7.242, 244). In the following scene (4.1), in which Lady Anne with unwitting irony bids her friends "a happy and a joyful time of day," Stanley brings news of the coronation "one hour hence" (29) and bids Dorset flee to Richmond with "all swift advantage of the hours" (49).

The impetuous movement is now interrupted, although not halted. The appearance of the women and their speeches of lamentation (in this scene and especially two scenes later in 4.4) serve to slow down the movement, to give it perspective. In this post-coronation lull, the second "special time" of the play begins to receive its preparation. Richmond's name is mentioned for the first time (4.1.43) at the summit of Richard's success—less than an hour before the coronation. From that point forward, all acceleration of the action will be, although Richard does not know it, toward the Earl of Richmond's victory.

The precarious—that is to say, the temporary—nature of Richard's reign is emphasized by Shakespeare upon the very moment when we see the tyrant wearing the crown. The scene of his pomp (4.2) opens in this manner:

> K. Rich.  Stand all apart. Cousin of Buckingham!
> Buck.     My gracious soverign?
> K. Rich.  Give me thy hand.
>           (*Here he ascendeth the throne. Sound.*)
>           Thus high, by thy advice
>           And thy assistance, is King Richard seated;
>           But shall we wear these glories for a day;
>           Or shall they last, and we rejoice in them? (1–6)

The movement in the next forty lines is from long range hope that "these glories" may last forever to recognition that the future may be secured only by immediate, drastic action. The contrast between Richard's "Or shall they last, and we rejoice in them?" (6) and his brutal "Speak suddenly; be brief" (19) could not be more telling.

The fundamental irony of Richard's position is that, having reached the crown by a succession of "untimely" acts, he wishes to hold his crown forever, and does not know that time is already preparing for him to be quickly dispatched from the world he had thought himself free "to bustle in" (1.1.152).

With Margaret's speech at the beginning of Act 4, scene 4, the tide clearly turns. Her first two lines are calculated to put one in mind of the first two lines of the play.

So, now prosperity begins to mellow
And drop into the rotten mouth of death.

The first speech was cast in the imagery of warmth, sun, and ripening. This one twists that imagery into a picture of decay, a growth past its time and therefore certain of destruction. The meaning of this present time is that Richard's time is over. The "now" of providence replaces the momentary "now" of the "usurping boar." Rapid developments are followed by a scene of twenty lines in which Derby, dispatching Sir Christopher Urswick to Richmond, bids him "hie thee to thy lord" (19).

The next scene (5.1, only twenty-nine lines) is remarkable. Its sole purpose is to establish the fact that the crucial time of judgment is at hand. With artful restraint, Shakespeare articulates this theme most explicitly in the mouth of Buckingham, leaving the application to Richard to be inferred by the audience. "Holy King Henry," Edward, Vaughan, "and all that have miscarried"are thought to "behold this present hour" (4–8). The day is none other than All-Souls' day, which Buckingham perceives to be his "body's doomsday" (10–12). The following lines play repeatedly upon the theme of "this day":

This is the day which, in King Edward's time,
I wish'd might fall on me.... (13–14)

This is the day wherein I wished to fall. ... (16)

This, this All-Souls' day to my fearful soul
Is the determin'd respite of my wrongs. (18–19)

When time is as laden with fulfillment as this, we are in the same kind of temporal understanding as the Fourth Gospel's "The hour cometh and now is" (John 4:23).

The ensuing scene (5.2) brings Henry, Earl of Richmond, to the stage, arriving in England at the height of the power of the homicidal king, when "this foul swine / Is now even in the centre of this isle" (10–11). The episodic Act 5, scene 3, alternating between the camps, is full of references to time, especially to the morrow. On Richard's side, these references sound heavy, for he has "no alacrity of spirit" (73); but on Richmond's side they are light and beneficent, since "True hope is swift and flies with swallow's wings" (5.2.22–23). The action draws itself to a climactic close according to a time schedule with which Richmond is in essential harmony and Richard at cross-purposes.

While Richard's condition is hopeless, England's in fact is not. That is because England is to receive one who will redeem the time. The news of his approach arrives immediately after the queen withdraws. By the eve of the battle, which follows after only 182 lines, time has begun to be viewed as promising a redeeming hour to separate a glorious future from a darkened past. Richmond has urged his soldiers "to reap the harvest of perpetual peace / By this one bloody trial of sharp war" (5.2.15–16).

The past enters the night preceding the battle in the person of the ghosts of the murdered, who "sit heavy" on Richard's soul, but who bring Richmond encouragements and prophecies of victory. Much has been made of these visions as characterization of Richard in his troubled conscience. One should, however, beware of pressing the internalization too far. The scene puts Richard and Richmond side by side on the stage and shows that the same past which destroys Richard is the basis of his conqueror's victory, through the help of "God and good angels" (175).

The battle is the shortest in Shakespeare. The overarching pattern is now so clear that there is no point in delaying the outcome. Richard's choices were made earlier. Here he has none.

The short scene which follows the battle (5.5) is, however, extremely important, for it summarizes the temporal pattern upon which the play has been based. The day has been won by God and the soldiers' arms—a providential act in which the exertion of men is necessary. The "bloody dog is dead." The past is remembered in its infamy. The "royalties" have been "long-usurped" but now are restored to proper brows (4–6). Heaven has "long-frown'd" upon the country's factional strife. "England hath long been mad and scarr'd herself" (23), brother against brother, father against son, house against house (21–28).

All that is past. For the present, Richmond looks after the immediate needs: whether George Stanley lives, proper burial for those slain in battle, pardon for the soldiers "That in submission will return to us" (17), and, most important, taking the sacrament.

The word sacrament has deep poetic meaning here because it is symbolic of all which Richmond accomplishes, raised to a divine plane. By partaking of the sacrament, he becomes the priestly representative of England atoning for the past sins of the realm. The sacramental act recalls the shedding of blood. Thus it stands in sharp relief against the crimes of

> The wretched, bloody, and usurping boar,
> That spoil'd your summer fields and fruitful vines,
> Swills your warm blood like wash. . . . (5.2.7–9)

The sacrament also recalls deliverance—from bondage in Egypt, and from the power of sin and death at Calvary.

Most important, however, is the fact that the sacrament means union and peace, and this theme Richmond proceeds to elaborate. He will "unite the white rose and the red," asking heaven to smile "upon this fair conjunction" (19–20). Past strife has torn the land asunder, but

> Now civil wounds are stopp'd, Peace lives again;
> That she may long live here, God say amen! (33–41)

The entire speech which ends the play falls into a schematic design of past woe, present amnesty, royal marriage, and future peace stretching to the end of time.

This pattern is apocalyptic. To find its roots, one must go to the Book of Revelation. The parallel is clear. Richard is a beast, entrenched in power at the center of the realm (5.2.7–11), who must be overthrown in decisive battle (14–16). Bosworth is Armageddon. From its "one bloody trial of sharp war" will be reaped "the harvest of perpetual peace" (15–16), reminiscent of the angel's command in Revelation 14:16: "Put in your sickle, and reap, for the hour to reap has come, for the harvest of the earth is fully ripe."

It becomes clear that *Richard III* is cast according to the pattern of the traditional Christian conception of history in which, at the proper time, decisive and redemptive action is taken. The structure and the language of the play (elements which belong to the manner of imitation of the action) are in harmony with and calculated to express the redemptive-historical nature of the action.

From *The Sense of History in Greek and Shakespearean Drama* (Columbia University Press, 1960), pp. 87–103 abridged. Used by permission.

*Scott Colley (1986)*

# Richard III and Herod

I would argue that one figure in Richard's complex background is the Biblical Herod, hardly an obvious model for the tyrant, but one whose presence haunts the shadows of Shakespeare's play.

The literary Herod sprang to life from brief references in the second chapter of Matthew in which the Magi trick the monarch who fears the child born to be King of the Jews. Herod orders the slaughter of all male infants under two years, but misses his prey when an angel warns Joseph and Mary to flee. The historian Josephus recounts at some length the story of King Herod, who then enters the European literary tradition through the writings of the Church Fathers and continental mystery plays of the Feast of the Epiphany. Josephus writes that for his execution of Jewish patriots Herod was punished by a series of disgusting diseases, including fevers, itches, and running sores. The vivid clinical description affected later portrayals of the literary Herod, whose physical ailments were considered punishments for his slaughter of the innocents, and fit emblems of his violent personality and behavior.

In medieval tradition, Herod is crafty and double-dealing. The *glossa ordinaria* relates that "Herod promises devotion, but sharpens his sword; covering up the malice of his heart with the colour of humility. He feigns in words and means to worship Him Whom he secretly intends to kill. His person is represented by the hypocrites who pretend to seek God and never desire to find Him."

General parallels to Richard III are clear enough: promising friendship and loyalty, Richard sharpens his sword; he covers the malice of his heart with false humility, and he merely pretends to honor those he secretly intends to kill. Richard's relationships to his brother Clarence, to the family of Queen Elizabeth, and to the heirs of Edward IV are marked by an apparent loyalty and piety that mask treachery. There are more than general parallels, however, that link Shakespeare's Richard to the Biblical and literary Herod.

Shakespeare refers more than a dozen times in Richard III to the murder of babes and children as well as to the slaughter of innocents. These references are manipulated in complex ways by Shakespeare and do not constitute a simple pattern of equivalence between Richard as child-murderer and Herod as child-murderer. Indeed, the initial reference to the slaughter of an innocent is directed toward Queen Margaret, who is reminded by Richard that she had earlier murdered his brother Rutland:

> Richard    And God, not we, hath plagu'd thy bloody deed.
> Elizabeth  So just is God, to right the innocent.
> Hastings   O, 'twas the foulest deed to slay that babe,
>            And the most merciless, that e'er was heard of.
>            (1.3.181–84)

Rutland was no babe; in fact he was older than Richard himself, but both Shakespeare and his chronicle sources refer to Rutland and other adult male victims as "babes" in order to heighten the pathos of their deaths. George Stanley, a married man, is described (5.3.96) as if he were a child in Richard's clutches.

Clarence seems to compare himself to certain Biblical victims when he says to his assassins: "Are you drawn forth among a world of men / To slay the innocent?" (1.4.170–71). After the murder of Clarence, the second murderer remarks, "How fain, like Pilate, would I wash my hands / Of this most grievous murder" (1.4.262–63). The reference to Pilate naturally brings to mind the execution of Christ, as well as other episodes of tyranny and bloodshed in the story of Christ's infancy and manhood. Clarence is hardly an innocent, as he recognizes in his famous dream, but he is a victim nevertheless. So too are his children, termed "Incapable and shallow innocents" (2.2.18) by their grandmother.

The true innocents of this tragedy, of course, are the young sons of Edward IV, the Prince of Wales and his younger brother, the Duke of York. Of the several dozen significant characters in Shakespeare's sprawling play, these boys are among the few who do not carry the burdening guilt of past violence and crimes. Indeed, it is Richard's insistence upon the slaughter of such innocents that drives Buckingham into rebellion and marks the beginning of Richard's downward slide. These boys are characterized as "tender babes" for whom the prison walls become a "rough cradle for such little pretty ones" (4.1.98–100). The ruthless Tyrrel, in reporting their deaths, says,

> The tyrannous and bloodie act is done;
> The most arch deed of piteous massacre
> That ever yet this land was guilty of. (4.3.1–3)

This is no ordinary murder. Richard's first assault upon a family member moves a killer to recall Pilate; this next assault moves Tyrrel and his accomplices to imagine the butchery of two archetypes of innocence. (See 4.3.10–20 for elaboration.)

Parallels between episodes in various Corpus Christi "Slaughter of the Innocents" plays and Shakespeare's tragedy demonstrate the persistence of the Herod narrative in the English literary and dramatic traditions. As in *Richard III*, the Towneley version juxtaposes three murderers and three mothers who speak in words that parallel the sad laments of Shakespeare's wailing ladies of Act 4:

> Alas, my bab, myn innocent, my fleshly get! For sorrow
> That God me derly sent, of bales who may me borow?
> Thy body is all to-rent! I cry both euen and morrow,
> Veniance for thi blod thus spent. . . .

And yet in Shakespeare's play as in the story of Herod, the tyrant's true rival is already in the safety of another country. Richmond remains in France, and others slip out of England to join him. Early in Act 4, Elizabeth tells Dorset to join those in exile:

> Thy mother's name is ominous to children.
> If thou wilt outstrip death, go, cross the seas
> And live with Richmond, from the reach of hell,
> Go: hie thee, hie thee from this slaughter-house. . . . (4.1.40–43)

Herod is alerted to the birth of his rival by the sudden appearance of the Magi and the confirming Biblical prophecies which his court scholars reveal to him. A high-comic scene in most of the cycle versions of the story shows Herod dumbfounded at the revelations of the ancient texts. The raging king vows to turn such prophecies back upon themselves. Richard is also troubled by a prophecy:

> I do remember me, Henry the Sixth
> Did prophesy that Richmond should be King,
> When Richmond was a little peevish boy.
> A king... perhaps.... (4.2.94–97)

The Quarto text expands upon Richard's musings: "How chance the prophet could not, at that time, / Have told me—I being by—that I should kill him?" (4.2.98–99). It is only moments after Richard's introspection upon prophecies that Tyrrel enters to report the deaths of the two princes. Here, juxtaposed, are two instances of Richard as the murderer of children: once in his thoughts and once in actuality.

When Herod hears news about the insecurity of his reign, he rants and raves, threatens to beat his messengers, and nervously calls for wine:

> This boye doth mee soe greatly annoye
> That I waxe dull and pure drye.

> Have done and fill the wyne in hye;
> I dye but I have drinke!
> Fill fast and lett the cuppes flye..... [Chester, "Magi"]

Richard similarly strikes a messenger in 4.4, and later says "give me a bowl of wine. / I have not that alacrity of spirit / Nor cheer of mind that I was wont to have" (5.3.73–75). In the N-Town Herod play, the king is amazed that he is challenged by an innocent:

> How should a bairn wax so bold
> By beastes if he born be?
> He is young and I am old,
> An hardy King of high degree.

Richard in a similar mood bellows, "In the chair empty? Is the sword unsway'd? / Is the King dead?.../What heir of York is there alive but we?" (4.4.469–71). And like the Herods of the cycles, Richard is amazed that a "Paltry fellow," "a milksop" (5.3.324; 326) would dare challenge so experienced and seasoned a commander as himself.

A crippled Herod appears in a number of manuscript illuminations, stained glass windows, and roof bosses that show the tyrant in twisted, contorted postures. In a description of a thirteenth-century English psalter, Meyer Schapiro notes this odd, cross-legged pose of Herod that he thinks is characteristic of tyrants generally in such illustrations [*JWCI* 23 (1960), 18]. In *Drama and Imagery in English Medieval Churches* [1963], M. D. Anderson reproduces photographs of as many as four of the Norwich transept roof bosses in which Herod appears in a contorted or twisted posture. While the posture may be a stylized depiction of a raging tyrant, it is remarkable how closely the morally and physically twisted Herod suggests the crippled, withered tyrant Richard III.

Also in Norwich is a stained glass window at St Peter Mancroft which shows the massacre of innocents in which Herod is seen skewering his young victims on the end of his short curved sword or falchion. In the Coventry Smiths' accounts of 1490, there is mention of funds expended for the repair of "a fawchon [and] sceptur for Herod," clearly for a Corpus Christi performance. Herod was thus imagined both in Corpus Christi plays and in some religious art as an Eastern potentate with falchion in hand.[1] Lady Anne, in speaking of the death of her "husband" at Richard's hands, links Richard to the same weapon:

> Queen Margaret saw
> Thy murd'rous falchion smoking in his blood,
> The which thou once didst bend against her breast,
> But that thy brothers beat aside the point. (1.2.95–98)

One of Richard's most notorious deceptions recalls another of the Herod stories. This is his surprising arrest and execution of the innocent Hastings. Richard blithely requests a gift of strawberries from the Bishop of Ely before suddenly claiming he has been bewitched and crippled by Queen Elizabeth and Hastings's Mistress Shore:

> Thou art a traitor:
> Off with his head! Now by Saint Paul I swear
> I will not dine until I see the same. (3.4.75–77)

When Hastings delays a moment, the impatient Ratcliffe insists, "Come, come, dispatch: the Duke would be at dinner; / Make a short shrift: he longs to see your head" (3.4.94–95).

Several scholars have surmised that Richard's oath by Saint Paul to see the head before dinner recalls a similar oath recounted in Acts 23:12–15 in which a group of Jews swear they will neither eat nor drink until they have killed St Paul.[2] Shakespeare's possible recollection of the threat against St Paul may have been reinforced by his simultaneous memory of the feast at which Herodias's daughter Salome dances before Herod Antipas, so pleasing him that she can demand the head of John the Baptist. This second Herod had determined to marry Herodias, his brother's wife, and thus had brought on the wrath of John the Baptist. The story is well known: Herod grants Salome's wish and the head is brought to the banquet table on a platter. Shakespeare probably conflated the several Biblical stories of murder and a severed head when he wrote the Hastings scene. Richard himself is a character who pursues a forbidden marriage (the incestuous nature of which is brought to his attention by his intended bride's mother). The figure of Herod Antipas might well have stimulated Shakespeare's imagination when he composed the scene in which the incestuous Richard demands the head of his enemy before he dines.

In Richard III, Shakespeare demonstrably had in mind Pilate and the death of Christ, the slaughter of innocents, the grief of their mothers, and the reign of a crippled, incestuous tyrant whose twisted physical appearance mirrors his diseased moral sensibility. Outwardly contemptuous of his adversary, but inwardly fearful of certain prophecies about him, Richard embarks upon the slaughter of all "infants" and "babes" who stand in his path to the throne. He slays one rival with a falchion, and sends assassins to murder the others. An amalgam of historical figure, Roman despot, tragic villain, and Biblical archetype, Richard of Gloucester is a character who illustrates many dimensions of his crowded family tree.

## Notes

1  Anderson, p. 156.
2  John B. Harcourt, "King Richard and Saint Paul," *Shakespeare Studies* 7 (1974), 90; Alistair Fox, "Richard III's Pauline Oath," *Moreana* 15 (1978), 14.

From "Richard III and Herod," *Shakespeare Quarterly* 37 (1986), 451–58 abridged.

*Phyllis Rackin (1990)*

## Providential Design in *Richard III* [editor's title]

Richard believes (as well he might, given his background in the *Henry VI* plays) that the world runs on Machiavellian principles, but almost from the first the audience is given reason to believe that he may be mistaken. Prophecies, prophetic dreams, curses that take effect—all suggest that supernatural forces are involved in the events that Richard believes and claims are completely under his control. For instance, we have Richard's clever manipulations and self-congratulatory soliloquies as he arranges his brother Clarence's death, but we also have Clarence's prophetic dream and death's-door recognition that his impending doom is, in fact, a recompense for the crimes he committed in the time of Henry VI.

Richard thinks he is living in a world governed by Machiavellian *Realpolitic*, but Shakespeare places him in a world governed by providence, a dissonance that produces heavy dramatic irony in the scenes when Richard gloats happily about the success of his machinations while the audience, informed not only by their foreknowledge of Richard's historically appointed doom but also by the intimations of a providential agenda provided by the women's prophecies, know better. At the end of the play, Richmond, the agent of providence, heralded by prophetic dreams and heavenly imagery, kills the tyrant and takes over, but not before Richard has been forced to suffer the horrified recognition that he does indeed live in a providential universe, one where he will be punished now and forever for the crimes he committed in the past.

*Richard III* offers a neat, conventional resolution to the problem of historical causation. All the cards have been stacked in advance, and the entire play reads like a lesson in providential history. In the first English treatise on historiography, *The true order and Methode of wryting and reading Hystories* ... (1574), Thomas Blundeville advised.

> As touching the providence of God.... though things many times doe succeede according to the discourse of man's reason: yet mans wisedome is oftentymes greatlye deceyved. And with those accidents which mans wisedome reiecteth and little regardeth: God by his providence useth, when he thinketh good, to worke marveylous effects. And though he suffreth the wicked for the most part to live in prosperitie, and the good in adversitie: yet we may see by many notable examples, declaring as well his wrath, and revenge towardes the wicked, as also his pittie and clemencie towardes the good, that nothing is done by chaunce, but all things by his foresight, counsell, and divine providence. (F3)

A "notable example" of providential justice, the entire action of *Richard III* is subsumed in the ideological scheme that Blundeville recites. Richard "greatlye deceyves" himself and the other characters, but Shakespeare's audience knows from the beginning that this is a providential universe and that Richard will fall. The audience came into the theater knowing Richard's history and they came to see a play called "The Tragedy of Richard III." That knowledge offers the audience a privileged vantage point, removing them from the flux of human temporality and placing them in the omniscient position of providence itself.

The only threat to that position is Richard himself, who reaches out to seduce the audience by the sheer energy and dramatic force of his characterization. By the end, however, even Richard has been subsumed in the providential scheme, . . . like the devil himself, as an unwitting instrument for the fulfillment of a providential plan. Killing off all the characters stained by the lingering guilt of the Wars of the Roses, Richard purges the kingdom to make it ready for Richmond's accession. Richard is a "factor" (4.4.72), a purchasing agent acting for a superior power, even though he denies the authority of that power and supposes he acts on his own behalf.

In *Richard III* Shakespeare reconstructs the history he has already written, retroactively imposing a providential order that makes sense of the Machiavellian chaos he depicted in the Henry VI plays. The women's litanies of old wrongs and the repeated pattern of Richard's victims recalling just before they die the past crimes for which they are now about to pay subsumes the events they recall into a teleological providential plot.

From *Stages of History: Shakespeare's English Chronicles* (Cornell University Press), pp. 63–65. Copyright 1990 by Cornell University. Used by permission.

# Part IV

# On Shakespeare's Tragedies

ADAM AND EVE ENTER THE WORLD OF SUFFERING AND DEATH
From *Boccace des Nobles Malheureux* [1506?]
By permission of The British Library

# ON SHAKESPEARE'S TRAGEDIES

## Introduction

Understanding of tragedy was confused at the beginning of the twentieth century by a heritage of Romantic assumptions. One of these was a notion that poetry is chiefly self-expression rather than the imitation of an action. Shakespeare was supposed to be experiencing a turmoil of mental anguish and metaphysical doubt when he wrote his tragedies. According to Edward Dowden's widely accepted formulation, he was at this time "in the depths," the third of the four phases of spiritual biography Dowden posited for him. First came a phase as entertainer when Shakespeare wrote his early comedies; this was labeled "in the workshop" by Dowden. Then as Shakespeare's curiosity developed he wrote histories, which Dowden called a period "in the world." But some crisis in the poet's personal life, occasioned in part perhaps by the death of his son Hamnet, turned him to write tragedies to voice his suffering. Beyond this there emerged, however, a period "on the heights," a serenity he achieved in the romances that crown his career. Dowden's explanation lasted until 1934, when C. J. Sisson's lecture to the British Academy on *The Mythical Sorrows of Shakespeare* effectively demolished prevailing theories of the biographical genesis of Shakespeare's art.

A second and concurrent Romantic assumption was that tragedy is the story of mankind's striving against circumstances that oppress the noble individual. This concept leans on, and in part perhaps derives from, Shelley's idealistic aspiration to create a dignity for the human soul through a Promethian heroism. In this view, tragedy could be interpreted as simply the misery that accompanies a progress in man's evolving idealism. An admiration for man's sublime potential was the emotion chiefly evoked. There was no mention of a human being's rival resources of grace and rude will, such as Shakespeare's Friar Laurence asserts; rather, a "triumph" was attributed to the hero who suffers in a devotion to his heart's imagination. Thus the suppositions of a secular idealism replaced those of traditional Christianity. And since in the late nineteenth century Hegel came to be regarded as the chief expounder of this idealism, it should not surprise us that A. C. Bradley's book on *Shakespearean Tragedy* (1904) was imbued with premises notably Hegelian.

Shakespeare's tragic heroes, Bradley explained, are the products of a universal moral order developing toward its own self-perfection. Each personage is a bundle of conflicting interests and ideas determined by this moral order, which "produces Iago as well as Desdemona, [and] Iago's cruelty as well as Iago's courage." Bradley's language in sketching this is very abstruse. The moral order, he tells us, becomes untrue to its own soul of goodness when it produces evil in persons; falling into conflict with itself it makes them suffer and waste themselves to save itself. Yet the tragic hero in perishing escapes from evil into freedom. Thus Antony, for instance, "touches the infinite" in the passion that ruins him; and Othello's death reveals "the power of man's unconquerable mind." Bradley supposed these readings of his were impartial. He also said they proved Shakespeare's ability to view the world without regard to anyone's religious beliefs. But Bradley was imposing on Shakespeare the crypto-religion of Hegel, whose quasi-gnostic view of history lets necessitating laws take over the function of human free will and removes any need for divine grace.

A rescuing of Shakespeare from Bradleyanism began with the studies of Willard Farnham and Lily B. Campbell in the mid-1930s. Farnham's survey of tragic tales from Boccaccio to Shakespeare found hardly any that conclude with a hero ultimately triumphing. Rather, they were stories of persons who fell from prosperity to misery, often as a punishment for a misdeed, but in any case as a warning against putting one's trust in mutable goods to the neglect of eternal goods. Whereas a person of goodwill can benefit from misfortune by having his virtue refined, a person of self-pleasing will brings on himself a tragic loss of his own welfare. This lesson of the vanity of Fortune's goods and the destructive result of human vices was found by Lily Campbell to be characteristic of Elizabethan commentary on tragedy. She therefore did not hesitate (in her 1959 edition) to call Bradley's concepts loosely impressionistic and bewildering.

In *Shakespeare's Tragic Heroes: Slaves of Passion* Campbell attempted to explain four of the tragedies in terms of the suffering each of the protagonists brings on himself by his passion. Her approach, however, was handicapped by a limitation she was unaware of. She supposed that she could better Lydgate's focus on tragic "action" by concerning herself rather with "passion." For was not passion the cause of sin and vice? Here she overlooked the role of erring reason in guiding passion into vice. Instead, she accepted as Shakespeare's own view the theory voiced by Hamlet, that tragedy is caused by an overgrowth of "some complexion" that breaks down "the forts of reason." This view, however, is a Stoic one which regards reason as merely the restrainer of passion; it can explain vice only as a lapse into "madness," the explanation we hear Polonius give while unable to account for the "method" in this madness. Plutarch, however, had quoted the view of Socrates (in a passage Campbell reproduced) that reason when muddled by passion can misdirect action. And Aristotle had explained vice as a misjudgment by man's rational faculty when yielding to passion's pressures. That is why Christian moralists in Shakespeare's era persistently emphasized "right reason," being aware that a defective reasoning causes vicious acts. Augustine had held that reason needs to be subservient to God or divine light in order to rule the passions rightly. And Lily Campbell herself, in quoting from John Reynold's *Tragicall Histories* (1621), includes his statement that God contemns affections that exceed "the bounds of charity"—here implying that charity is the needed ultimate ruler of the passions. So Campbell could have had a better than Stoic view if she had weighed the larger context of passion in these other source materials. By neglecting to carefully do so, her book produces conclusions unnecessarily simplistic—for instance, that *Hamlet* is a study of the passion of grief. More important, surely, are the *errors* of judgment that misguide passion.

Most Elizabethans would have said that drama as the imitation of an action requires a representation of the movement of human beings in the process of relating themselves to realities outside themselves, namely, God and angels, neighbor human beings, and the natural order, each of which should be given its proper due. Mistakes in doing so were sins, which injured both the health of the agent and the welfare of others. Tragedy involved a "big mistake" (*hamartia megale*) when assessing the real good, a mischoosing of vice under the semblance of virtue. *The Sinners Guide* (1598) described man's situation as that of being beset by tempters who

> endeavor to color evill with good, and to sell vice under the show and semblance of vertue, and so to hide the temptation, that it seemeth not temptation, but reason. For if they assault any man by ambition, by covetousness, by wrath, or desire of revenge, they persuade him that it is altogether agreeable unto reason to desire this, that this or that affection desireth; and that it is against reason not to lust after that, that it lusteth after. After this manner they pretend reason, that they may so much the more easily deceive them, who are ruled by reason. Wherefore it is very necessary that we should have sharpe-sighted eyes, that we may see the hook lurking within the baite, least we be deceaved with the shadow and likelihood of goodness. (pp. 374–75)

*The Sinners Guide* is a treatise by Luis de Granada, a Spanish divine, translated into English by Francis Meres. And Francis Meres was an Anglican clergyman, who in his *Palladis Tamia* (1598) was the earliest literary critic to provide us a judicious evaluation of Shakespeare's works. Meres called Shakespeare England's best poet of tragedies. To understand the basis of Meres's appreciation one needs to read as context his *Sinners Guide*, along with the Church Fathers to whom he refers when giving us the framework of his intellectual and spiritual horizons.

From the passage we have quoted from Meres it seems evident that he must have regarded Shakespeare's tragic heroes as the victims of their own mistaking of "shows" of goodness for the real thing. He no doubt regarded as tragic Richard II's ambition for glory, and assessed as delusory Richard's final effort, "Mount, mount my soul! Thy seat is up on high." *Hamlet* would have been read by Meres as the story of a gifted prince who mistakenly pursued revenge as a supposed good. And *Macbeth* would have been seen as this hero's mistaking as virtue his wife's version of "courage." Meres would have agreed, certainly, with the truth voiced by Queen Elizabeth in *Richard III*, that "avoided grace" brings a destiny of doom.

A clarification of human self-understanding was the dramatist's aim. From Aristotle and medieval artists Shakespeare inherited the view that a poet imitates action in order to bring about a psychic cleansing or catharsis in his auditors. Specifically, a purging of their emotions of pity and fear was the formal goal desired when staging a poetic tragedy. Auditors were expected to engage these emotions in their response to the action presented. And if their initial response is a pitying and fearing identical with that of the story's protagonist, they are sharing an impure or self-indulgent form of these emotions that needs cleansing. The observable consequences of the tragic hero's action, however, invite the audience to see that a wrong-headedness is causing his kind of pity and fear. Accordingly, spectator-readers can detach from approving the actions of this hero and begin to pity his moral disorder or blindness and to fear a similar fate in oneself. Thus pity and fear in the audience get refined toward what truly ought to be pitied and what truly ought to be feared.

Our anthology's essay on *Romeo and Juliet* by John Andrews includes some helpful discussion of catharsis. Further comment on the Christian theory operative in Shakespeare's tragic art is provided by various other items in the anthology.

### Wisdom is free from Fortune

From Theodor de Bry, *Emblematum Liber*, 1593
By permission of Princeton University Press

# ROMEO AND JULIET

## Comment and bibliography

There never was a story of "more woe," this tragedy concludes, than that of Juliet and her Romeo. Who or what, we ask, was responsible for the woe? In the opinion of Romantic critics from Coleridge onwards the action's catastrophe is due to mischances and malignant stars, while the young lovers are innocent and blameless. Various of the drama's details, however, do not support this assessment—for instance, the lovers' hiding of their marriage from community knowledge, Romeo's fire-eyed slaying of Juliet's kinsman, Juliet's use of pretenses to mislead her parents, her drug-taking to escape a dilemma, Romeo's buying poison to escape his grief, his killing of Paris for attempting to deter "unhallowed toil," and finally the choice of each of the lovers to commit suicide. Such actions imply, certainly, errors of judgment and a misuse of free will. Yet the story ends with the parents promising to erect statues in pure gold to honor the "true and faithful" lovers. Can we explain this anomaly? Perhaps we are expected to take the ending ironically, by recalling from the *Merchant of Venice* Shakespeare's adage that "All that glisters is not gold." Lack of insight can characterize the persons in a tragedy.

For guidance, let us investigate how the matter is handled in Arthur Brooke's *Tragicall Historye of Romeus and Juliet* (1562), Shakespeare's immediate source. Brooke's ending is similar to Shakespeare's: the Montagues and Capulets, he tells us, raised a stately tomb of marble in memory of their children's "so perfect, sound, and so approved love." We can be sure, however, that Brooke is being ironic. One indication is his letting Juliet say that her self-stabbing will witness to "the most perfect league betwixt a paire of lovers"—although, only a few pages earlier, the narrator had termed Juliet a wily wench "who did not stick to lie," and he has discoursed very early in his story on the theme of "Oh how we can perswade ourself to what we like!" (line 428). Another indication of irony is Brooke's depicting Romeo's swallowing of poison right after a long prayer to "Lord Christ." Brooke's narrator empathizes fulsomely with every feeling and fantasy the lovers have; yet that he is doing so with tongue in cheek is made fully evident in Brooke's preface "To the Reader." Here the story is said to be about a couple of unfortunate lovers who "yielded their libertie thrall to fowle desires," and we are exhorted to be warned thereby against "wicked lust."

Although Shakespeare does not similarly presummarize, he provides an abundance of clues for our discovering his play's point. He shows Romeo addicted to a love described as "doting"; Juliet finds in herself a "too much cherishing" such as one gives to a wanton bird. Cupid's arrow, we are told, causes this kind of love, and it is resisted by the chaste Rosaline because she is too wise to spare the "huge waste" it makes. (We may recall that in Shakespeare's *The Tempest* Cupid is banished from Prospero's wedding masque, and that in *Twelfth Night* Orsino's indulgence in Petrarchan sentiments is adjudged a "heresy.") Act 2's Prologue tells us that Romeo and Juliet swallow a "sweet bait" with a sharp hook. Benvolio calls Romeo's love a poisonous "infection" of the eye, and later he names it a "blind" love that best befits the dark. From the very begining it impels Romeo to lock out "fair daylight" and make an artificial night—foreshadowing thus his finding his rest with worms in a tomb at the drama's end. We are being shown, in effect, a love that parodies divine love.

In no other play of Shakespeare's (except *Macbeth*) is there so persistent a contrasting of light and darkness in the imagery employed, along with attention to the bewitching substitute for light offered by earthly beauty. Juliet's beauty is Romeo's substitute "sun," regarded by him as the one source of light in an otherwise dark world. His "religion of the eye" worships face, and regards her lips as a holy shrine. Identifying Juliet with heaven, he declares his life a hell when banished from Verona. The absurdity of this religion is evident when we hear him lament in 3.3 that "carrion flies" may steal "immortal blessing from her lips" while he is condemned to "fly" away. His phrase regarding immortal blessing is intended by Shakespeare to remind us of the erroneous aim of Dr. Faustus to find immortality in the lips of Helen of Troy in Marlowe's well-known tragedy. Romeo is by implication a sensualist like Paris. Juliet on her part makes Romeo "the god of my idolatry" (2.2.114), and on her wedding night she begs the sun to gallop away so that "cloudy night" may cover from sight her amorous rites. This Epithalamium is a most unconventional one, not only because it is sung in solitude by the bride, but because in her repeated invokings of "night" she is looking forward not to a fruitful life with her husband but to his death and stellification:

> Take him and cut him out in little stars,
> And he will make the face of heaven so fine
> That all the world will be in love with night
> And pay no worship to the garish sun. (3.2.22–25)

Are we to suppose it healthy to "be in love with night"? (One of the ironies of history in our day was Robert Kennedy's quoting of those lines in the eulogy he gave at his brother Jack's funeral; Robert was quite unaware of the deadly import of the wish he was voicing.) Sunlight can be labeled "garish" only by someone with an erroneous view of life.

Occasional critics have commented that this drama is a *liebestod* like that of Tristan and Isolde, inasmuch as a subconscious love of death impels Romeo and Juliet. When the opening Chorus speaks of "the fearful passage of their death-marked love," one meaning of that phrase can be that they have made death the sea-mark of their sailing. Lady Capulet's exasperated "I would the fool were married to her grave" (3.5.140) forecasts ironically the marriage to death that Juliet chooses in committing suicide. A predisposing influence may be the feud between Verona's houses, but it can scarcely be a compelling one if we notice that Old Capulet protects Romeo at the masked ball, and earlier has said he thinks it "not hard" to keep the peace. The feud is merely an inherited proclivity for self-display—as in the servant Samson's boast that "I am a pretty piece of flesh" (1.1.29). Theologians would call it a manifestation of "original sin," an impaired health that permits but does not compel actual sin. But of course if one is unwilling to forgo vanity, a paradoxical "loving hate" can erupt—as we see happening at the beginning, the middle, and the end of the play. That this happens may be traced to a religion of the "I" (a glorifying of the ego), which is closely akin to a religion of the "eye." It leads to strife with neighbors and within oneself, and the result is a confused self-divisiveness that seeks its rest in death. What a pity it had to be thus. "There but for the grace of God go I."

Our anthology of commentary on this play begins with W. H. Auden's perceptive observation that everyone in Verona contributes to the tragedy by desiring to "cut a figure" and be important. In other pages of Auden's essay, not here included, he lists the mischoices of various personages and alongside each instance states what ought to have been done and could have forestalled the tragedy. The commentary by Francis Fergusson focuses on the lurking dangers of self-indulgent romance, citing as a comparable case the tragedy of Paolo and Francesca as told by Dante. The essay by John Andrews uses categories from Augustine and Boethius to explain the defective choices by which the lovers make themselves Fortune's fool. Also he discusses how the drama's action effects in us a catharsis.

In the supplementary bibliography, Roy Battenhouse provides a discussion of the dramatic details by which Shakespeare creates irony. He gives particular attention to the shortcomings depicted in Friar Laurence and Prince Escalus, and to an ironic affinity between the apothecary in Mantua and Laurence's drug-dealing. Also he takes note of the play's number symbolism and the ironic use of Christian names. Barbara Parker builds on the view of Battenhouse and emphasizes the spiritual darkness of Romeo's "religion of the eye," the unbridled passion of the "galloping" steeds invoked by Juliet, and Friar Laurence's notable failure to abide by his own moral axioms. Following Augustine, she describes "courtly love" as a parody of Christianity and comments on Ovid's irony in describing the "disease" of love. Douglas Peterson and Stanley Stewart both discuss medieval ideas of necessity and free will in order to point up Romeo's culpability for his tragedy. Joan Holmer notes that the runaway eyes in Juliet's Epithalamium mark her as a fugitive from daylight who yields to a vagabond love. Franklin Dickey places Romeo and Juliet alongside Antony and Cleopatra as examples of "unwise" lovers who misuse reason.

## Supplementary bibliography

Auden, W. H. *Romeo and Juliet*, ed. Francis Fergusson (Dell, 1958), pp. 21–39.

Battenhouse, Roy. *Shakespearean Tragedy* (1969), pp. 102–30.

Dickey, Franklin M. *Not Wisely But Too Well* (The Huntington Library, 1957), pp. 102–17.

Holmer, Joan Ozark. "'Runaways Eyes': A Fugitive Meaning," *Shakespeare Quarterly* 33 (1982), 97–99.

Parker, Barbara. *A Precious Seeing: Love and Reason in Shakespeare's Plays* (New York University Press, 1987), Ch. 8; also Ch. 2 (Ovidian *vis à vis* Christian love).

Peterson, Douglas. "*Romeo and Juliet* and the Art of Moral Navigation," *Pacific Coast Studies in Shakespeare*, ed. Waldo McNeir (University of Oregon, 1966), pp. 33–46.

Stewart, Stanley. "Romeo and Necessity," in *Pacific Coast Studies*, ed. McNeir (1966), pp. 47–67.

Whitaker, Virgil K. *The Mirror up to Nature* (The Huntington Library, 1965), pp. 113–18.

*W. H. Auden (1958)*

## The Tragedy of *Romeo and Juliet* [editor's title]

The tragedy of *Romeo and Juliet* is not simply a tragedy of two individuals, but the tragedy of a city. Everybody in the city is in one way or another involved in and responsible for what happens.

Further, it is a play about sympathetic, basically well-meaning people—the only character who could be called bad is Tybalt—who come to disaster because each insists on having his own way irrespective of the common good. Much of the evil in the world is caused by the refusal of human beings to accept themselves and the world as it is in favor of some false picture more flattering to their self-esteem. Further, this tendency to illusion is fostered by idleness; he who works soon learns that he cannot succeed unless he accepts reality. The tragedy of *Romeo and Juliet* is the tragedy of a social group which has nothing to do but feud with their neighbors, give parties, cultivate elegance of manner and speech, and indulge their emotions. The fatal weakness which affects them all, even the lovers, is a wish to show off. Instead of asking, "What ought I to do?" or even "What would I really like to do?" they ask "If I do this, what sort of a figure shall I cut in the eyes of others?"

The tragedy of Romeo and Juliet is one that could only occur to two people who loved each other very much. Yet the fact that they kill themselves is, in the profoundest sense, a failure to love, a proof of selfishness.

That most people will never become guilty of this particular failure is to their discredit; they do not care enough about another person to be tempted. When circumstances prevent their love being gratified, they have a good cry and take up with someone else. Romeo and Juliet are tragic figures because both are absolutely committed and can truthfully say "Either you or no one," but when fate answers "no one," the love they bear each other is not perfect enough to support them and they destroy themselves.

To kill oneself for love is, perhaps, the noblest act of vanity, but vanity it is, death for the sake of making *una bella figura*.

From "Commentary by W. H. Auden," in the Laurel *Romeo and Juliet*, ed. Francis Fergusson (New York: Dell, 1958), pp. 22–23, 38–39 abridged.

*Francis Fergusson (1977)*

## Romantic Love as Lost

Anyone who reads *Inferno* 5 (the canto which recounts the story of Paolo and Francesca) and *Romeo and Juliet* must feel that the two works present very similar visions of youthful love when it leads to death. This love is in both cases strictly romantic: a passion of the *gentili* which demands total commitment, mysterious though it is to the lovers. In both cases it is obeyed literally, before its meanings can be realized, and that is one sufficient reason why it leads to death. Shakespeare presents it in a populous full-length play, Dante in a few lines in one canto; and their methods are therefore necessarily different. But at the same time the principles of their plot-making, their characterization, and their symbolism or metaphorical structure are closely analogous, for both poets are imitating the same action: literal obedience to romantic love.

The young are the most capable of "hazarding all," and the least able to wait patiently until their love reveals its meanings. When he first sees Paolo and Francesca, Dante separates them from the older victims of lust: "Poet, willingly would I speak with those two that go together and seem so light upon the wind." He then plots the narrative in order to give the impression of great speed. This is partly achieved by recounting his relation to Francesca at the same time she tells us of hers to Paolo. Dante, as he listens, is overcome almost at once, and we see that Francesca from the first could not resist Paolo. Francesca's final narrative, in answer to Dante's question how love permitted them "to know the dubious desires," is only twenty-one lines long, but every bit of it embodies that movement of spirit which consists in being moved, immediately and irresistibly. The two swift sequences end when Francesca says, "*quel glorno più non vileggemmo avanti*" ("that day we read in it no further"), and Dante faints with pity.

Shakespeare also took care to make his plot give the effect of speed. The action is all concentrated between Sunday and Thursday night, and it is like a race between Romeo and Juliet and Tybalt, and between the young and the older Veronese. While Romeo is meeting Juliet, marrying her, and spending his one night with her, Tybalt kills Mercutio and Romeo kills Tybalt, thereby incurring his banishment to Padua. The racing effect is repeated when Juliet's funeral overtakes her wedding to Paris, and again when Romeo, Paris, and the friar all rush to Juliet's tomb at the end of the play. Both poets use the plot to show how their lovers lacked the time to learn anything about the love they were so desperately obeying.

The wedding that turns into a funeral is a plot device mirroring the course of this love into darkness, much as the wedding-funeral confusion in *Much Ado About Nothing* mirrors a love moving the other way, toward life and light. Dante has room only for the dark air on which his lovers ride, but Shakespeare can present the love "whose view is muffled still," the love that without eyes can see "pathways to his will," with a rich interplay of light and dark throughout the play. Thus the imageries of the two poets are differently developed, but they are similar in principle, for they imitate the same vision of romantic love.

One may be tempted to see the "death-marked" love of Paolo and Francesca and of Romeo and Juliet as the love of death. Denis de Rougemont has traced the love of death in the romantic tradition from the Provençal poets to its culmination in Wagner's *Tristan und Isolde*. He shows how Wagner makes his romantic love into a mystique signifying infinitely desirable death. This passion is the only reality here on earth; in the Tristan story, as Wagner tells it, it determines not only the characters but the whole world in which they exist, pointing always to the mystic void of death. But Dante and Shakespeare do not see passion as the one reality; they see it as one condition suffered by their young people, and their young people as inhabiting a world created not by passion but by God. Paolo and Francesca and Romeo and Juliet may often see their world as passion paints it for them—and so may the reader. But Dante and Shakespeare do not: they see the world, with their "medieval realism," as real; and their lovers' passion as only one mode of human love. And they are both careful to indicate where it fits in the scale of human loves, even as they seduce their readers with it.

Dante of course places the love of Paolo and Francesca in the huge context of the whole *Commedia*; but when we first meet it, in hell where "the good of the intellect is lost," he makes it feel to us, as it does to them, like the sole reality. Dante is told by Virgil that Paolo and Francesca sinned through lust, but that bit of knowledge does not reach him intimately enough to render him immune: he *actually* knows only their literal state, and he can beg Francesca "by the love that leads them" to explain that love to him. Francesca, who feels the love in Dante's voice, obeys. The language of love is the only means of communication in this circle, and by sticking to it Dante gives the reader only a literal—and therefore irresistible—knowledge; and the proper end of the sequence is Dante's fainting.

Shakespeare uses the friar to place Romeo's and Juliet's relentless infatuation where it belongs in God's universe. We first meet the friar early in the morning after the Capulet party, collecting herbs in his garden, and rejoicing in the wonderful and perilous order of the natural world:

> The earth that's nature's mother is her tomb;
> What is her burying grave that is her womb.
> And from her womb children of divers kind
> We sucking on her natural bosom find;
> Many for many virtues excellent;
> None but for some, and yet all different.
> O mickle is the powerful grace that lies
> In plants, herbs, stones, and their true qualities.
> For naught so vile that on the earth doth live,
> But to the earth some special good doth give;
> For naught so good, but strained from that fair use,
> Revolts from true birth, stumbling on abuse. (2.3)

The friar's vision is like Virgil's, as he explains it in Purgatorio 17 and 18: the love that moves all creatures, animate and inanimate, plant, animal, and human, may produce either good or evil, depending on the "use" made of it.

Infatuated Romeo appears toward the end of the friar's discourse, and we are ready to see his love deviating from the divine order. The friar at once tries to explain this to him:

> Is Rosaline, that thou didst love so dear,
> So soon forsaken? Young men's love then lies
> Not truly in their hearts but in their eyes. (2.3)

And when Romeo tells him that Rosaline did not, like Juliet, "grace for grace and love for love allow," the friar answers: "O, she knew well / Thy love did read by rote that could not spell." He means that Romeo's love sees only literally, like a child who pronounces words without getting their meaning. It is Romeo's purely literal understanding of his love that determines its fate throughout the play.... The friar's vision serves to make us understand the death-marked love, but not to cure it.

It would be gratifying to know exactly what Shakespeare read to enable him to transform his source (Bandello's story), lift it to poetry, and see its action in the light of the romance tradition as understood by classical Christianity. That one can never know; but one may recognize the close kinship between Romeo and Juliet and Paolo and Francesca, and see that the two great poets saw the action of romantic love in the same way.

From *Trope and Allegory* (1977), pp. 11, 15–22, abridged. Copyright 1977 by the University of Georgia Press.

*John F. Andrews (1974, revised 1992)*

# Falling in Love: The Tragedy of *Romeo and Juliet*

What happens in *Romeo and Juliet*? What did a dramatist of the 1590s want the "judicious" members of his contemporary audiences to see and hear, and how did he expect them to feel, as they attended the play a later age would laud as the most lyrical of all love tragedies? Before I hazard a response to what is admittedly an unanswerable question, I should make it clear that what I'm really posing is a query about the "action"[1] of Shakespeare's drama, and more specifically about the effect such an action might have been intended to have on a receptive Elizabethan playgoer.

As the late O. B. Hardison emphasizes in the commentary that accompanies Leon Golden's 1968 translation of Aristotle's *Poetics*,[2] there is much to be said for interpreting the earliest technical term for tragic effect, *catharsis*, as a word that means "clarification," and for conceiving of the experience it describes as one that takes place, not in the characters of a dramatic work, but in the audience that participates vicariously in those characters' thoughts, emotions, and interchanges. Hardison reminds us that Aristotle defines tragedy as that category of imitation (*mimesis*) which produces pleasure through a cogent representation of fearful and pitiable incidents. He and Golden stress the passage in which the great philosopher observes that realistic renderings of even the most displeasing subject delight the viewer by assisting perception and eliciting insight. And they infer that when the father of dramatic theory speaks of the purgation that results from a tragedy, he is focusing primarily on the learning any coherently constructed work of art fosters: the sorting out, the clearing away of confusion or temporary misapprehension, that occurs as a responsive spectator notices, and appreciates, an aesthetically satisfying pattern of logical connections. When Aristotle refers to the catharsis that derives from a well-devised imitation of fearful and pitiable incidents, then, Hardison and Golden deduce that he is probably thinking of the enlightenment— the sense of mental relief and psychic release—that a member of the audience enjoys when he or she is able to make sense of a sequence of happenings that initially strike an onlooker as disparate and disorderly.

When we bring this concept of catharsis to bear upon the various species of tragedy, we discover that in some instances the intellectual, emotional, and ethical clarification attained by an attentive theatergoer parallels the hard-earned wisdom of a character who has arrived at self-knowledge through a siege of suffering. In tragic actions which feature this kind of recognition (*anagnorisis*) the central figure is divested of any impurities of mind or heart that impede "Clearer Reason" (*The*

*Tempest*, 5.1.68), and he or she acquires a degree of awareness that approximates the comprehension a perceptive member of the audience obtains by tracing and assessing the character's fortunes.[3]

In some instances the clarity a tragic figure realizes is a judgment that amounts to self-condemnation, as happens in *Richard III* and *Macbeth*. In these dramatic sequences the protagonists acknowledge their own guilt and wretchedness in ways an audience can endorse. In other instances the down-cast hero goes beyond an accurate mental evaluation of himself to a remorse that penetrates the conscience, as with the title characters of *Othello* and *King Lear*. Here the protagonists feel sorrow for what they perceive themselves to have done, and in the second case if not the first the audience may be led to conclude that the hero has gone a step further—from remorse to repentance, to a resolve to do whatever is required to make amends for the pain he has inflicted on others and cleanse his own soul.

In rare instances a tragic protagonist proceeds all the way to a complete reconciliation with himself, with those he has injured, and with the Heavens. In these sequences the protagonist arrives at a sense of "at-one-ment" that signifies redemption. In dramatic actions in which this kind of conversion occurs the central figure wins deliverance through an epiphany that transports him or her past the point where even the most sage of witnesses can hope to follow. In Sophocles' *Oedipus at Colonus*, for example, or in Milton's *Samson Agonistes*, the central character is granted a culminating vision in which death is swallowed up in a kind of victory. The hero completes his mission nobly, and as he expires he crosses the threshold to a mysterious but presumably more exalted realm on the unseen side of this world's veil of tears. Here the clarification that takes place in the protagonist surpasses the apprehension of the viewer, and the catharsis that issues in the well-tuned playgoer is akin to ecstatic rapture: a "calm of mind"[4] that accompanies the wonder evoked by powers that move as to awe.

In most tragic actions the audience's catharsis is something that can be more aptly described as a sense of "woe" or "pity"[5] for a character whose grasp on reality is shown to be in some way defective. As we watch a misguided protagonist come to grief under the lamentable circumstances that tragedies usually depict, we feel a wrenching disparity between our own observations and those of the focal figure. If we receive the kind of catharsis the usual tragedy is designed to provide, in other words, we emerge with an understanding that is both broader and more lucid than the impaired perception of the lost hero or heroine.

So what do we find when we turn our attention to *Romeo and Juliet*? As we watch this play do we sense that the protagonists share our view of what undoes them? Do we feel that in the end they transcend our vantage to claim a better world elsewhere? Or do we finally conclude that they fail in some manner, and lack the insight to assess their failure with the acuity an alert audience acquires by contemplating their "misadventur'd piteous overthrows" (Prologue. 7)?

Adherents can be found for all of these interpretations and more. There are many who accept the title characters at their own estimate, perceiving them as helpless pawns of conditions they have no means of countering. There are some who react to them with admiration, even reverence, canonizing them as pure "Sacrifices" of their families' "Enmity" (5.3.304). And there are a few who blame them for intemperance and hold them responsible not only for their own tragedies but for the untimely deaths of several other characters.

Perhaps the best way to enter the world of the play is to take note of its cosmic imagery, its all-pervasive references to Fortune, Fate, and the Stars. If we hope to recapture something of the experience *Romeo and Juliet* provided its original audience, we need to come away from the tragedy with a conception of what it would have meant in Shakespeare's time to be a victim of "fatal Loins," to feel like "Fortune's Fool," and to seize upon the extremest of measures to "shake the Yoke of inauspicious Stars" (Prologue. 5; 3.1.144; 5.3.111).

The most important locus for medieval and Renaissance thinking about Fortune and Fate was Boethius' *Consolation of Philosophy*, a Latin dialogue that had probably been written in A. D. 524. Chaucer had used the *Consolation* extensively in the fourteenth century, and it remained so popular in the late sixteenth century that it was translated into Elizabethan English by no less a personage than the Queen herself. When Shakespeare alluded to the *Consolation*, then, he would no doubt have assumed that any literate member of his audience would be nearly as familiar with this masterwork as with the Bible and the Book of Common Prayer.[6]

Any playgoer who had read Boethius would have known that the *Consolation* involves a conversation between Lady Philosophy and a statesman who has fallen into disfavor and now awaits death. The imprisoned political leader is the author himself, and he calls upon a personification of Wisdom to explain why Fortune has treated him so cruelly. During the exchanges that ensue, Lady Philosophy points out that "Fortune" is properly to be regarded as a fictional abstraction, a symbolic embodiment of the role of mutability in human affairs. To those who view her aright, Dame Fortune is nothing more than a convenient name for the fickle and seemingly irrational "Goddess" who bestows and withdraws such worldly gifts as riches, honors, political office, fame, and pleasure. Lady Philosophy acknowledges that many people mistakenly believe that happiness is to be found in the possession of goods that are subject to Fortune's caprices. But she insists that those who examine their lives carefully will eventually realize that the only felicity which lasts and is free from anxiety is that which is fixed on a supreme Good higher than, and unaffected by, the vicissitudes of Fortune. Lady Philosophy doesn't deny that Misfortune is painful, but she insists that if we take it in the right spirit it provides a salutary reminder that everything in this life is fleeting. In the process it encourages us to focus our sights on Heaven, where, according to an even more authoritative spiritual guide, "neither moth nor rust doth corrupt, and where thieves do not break through nor steal" (Mt 6:20).[7]

Many writers used the terms "Fortune" and "Fate" interchangeably, but Boethius drew a subtle distinction between them. For him "Fortune" was a name for Mutability itself, for what we now refer to as blind Chance. "Fate," on the other hand, was his term for a higher authority that presided over Fortune's seeming arbitrariness. For Boethius, and for subsequent Christian philosophers, Fate (or Destiny, as it was often called) was actually a pagan disguise for Providence, and the author of the *Consolation* saw it as a cosmic principle that was ultimately benign, though forever shrouded in obscurity.

Boethius was valued in Renaissance England for the way he had adapted Christianity to a quasi-Stoic frame of reference. In similar fashion, St Augustine was revered for the way he'd made Christianity fit a quasi-Platonic framework two centuries earlier. Augustine's treatise *On Christian Doctrine*[8] and his monumental discourse on the *City of God* were both familiar to educated Elizabethans, and Shakespeare's contemporaries would have seen the author of these two works as a theologian whose writings were fully compatible with Boethius' philosophy. Boethius' dichotomy between those pursuits directed to the Supreme Good (which is immutable) and those directed to all lesser goods (which are mutable) would have been accepted, then, as merely another means of expressing Augustine's distinction between those pursuits that lead to the supreme felicity of the City of God (Jerusalem) and those that leave one mired in the confusion and frustration of the City of Man (Babylon).

According to Augustine, all movement of the soul is prompted by the Will, and that which moves the Will is Love. Love, then, is the basic motivating force in human behavior, and it falls into two categories: (a) Sacred Love, or *caritas* (charity), which urges the Will in the direction of eternal life, and (b) Profane Love, or *cupiditas* (cupidity), which pulls the Will in the direction of temporal life. From Augustine's viewpoint, the sole purpose of religion and ethics is to teach believers what things are to be loved and enjoyed in and of themselves and what things are to be employed in the service of true Love. In his system the proper relation to things (loving and enjoying only the things of God, and using the things of this world solely in obedience to God) is *caritas*; the improper relation to things (loving and enjoying the things of this world, and abusing the things of God for the sake of temporal things) is *cupiditas*.

The cohesion between Augustine's theology and Boethius' philosophy becomes evident as soon we note that only those things which are temporal are subject to Fortune. To be under the sway of Fortune, then—to seek happiness by setting one's heart on those goods that are subject to Fortune's bestowal and removal—is to be guilty of *cupiditas* (misplaced or inordinate love). On the other hand, to rise above Fortune's sphere by aspiring to the immutable Supreme Good—to seek happiness through union with that which lies beyond the realms of Fortune—is to live in accordance with *caritas* (well-placed and duly ordered love).

But what about the Stars? How did they relate to Boethian and Augustinian thought? According to most medieval and Renaissance thinkers, "the Stars" (the Sun, the Moon, the Planets, and the constellations of the Zodiac) exercised a degree of influence on Earth, and this influence conditioned the general and particular destinies of human beings. But it was commonly believed that the Stars could directly affect only the material and corporeal levels of existence. Since Will and Reason were regarded as spiritual rather than physical (material or corporeal) in nature, it followed that these faculties of the human soul could not be influenced directly by the Stars. Will and Reason could be affected by the lower parts of the soul (the Senses and the Passions), however, if they did not maintain proper control over these earth-bound dominions; and the lower nature (since it was corporeal in composition) could, in turn, be influenced by the Stars. If the Will or the Reason allowed themselves to be usurped by the Senses or the Passions, then, they became subject to indirect astrological influence and thus to Fortune.[9]

Let us sum up. As we've observed, Fortune, Fate, and the Stars were perceived in Shakespeare's time as interwoven concepts, and all three were integral to a system of ethics that drew heavily on the writings of Boethius and Augustine. Through these concepts, errant behavior could be depicted by any of several interchangeable means of expression: as unfortunate behavior caused by the influence of the Stars, as irrational behavior caused by the whims of Fortune, as improper and intemperate behavior caused by Reason or Will's subjection to the senses or the Passions, or as disobedient, sinful behavior caused by misplaced or inordinate Love. For an alert Elizabethan, the name one applied to wrongheaded behavior was of little moment; the only thing that mattered was that sooner or later a person recognize it as a course that would result in disaster if it continued unchecked.

We should now be in a position to return to the questions posed at the outset. What "happens" in *Romeo and Juliet*? Do the lovers succumb to forces beyond their control? Do they somehow triumph over the circumstances arrayed against them and emerge as martyrs, as unblemished agents of redemption? Or do they "fall in love" in some ethical and theological sense that would have been meaningful to an audience familiar with Augustine and Boethius?

Suppose we begin our scrutiny of the action by reviewing some of the perspectives the play offers on the protagonists' romantic attachment. The Chorus who speaks the Prologue to Act 2 describes Romeo's sudden infatuation with Juliet as "Young Affection" gaping to be the "Heir" of "Old Desire" (lines 1–2); he goes on to suggest that the only reason Juliet has replaced Rosaline in Romeo's heart is that this time Romeo's feelings are requited (line 5). From the Chorus' point of view, then, what draws Romeo to Juliet is no different in kind from what attracted him to Rosaline. The young hero is simply shifting his attention to a more receptive subject as he responds to the erotic spurring implicit in his name.[10]

Friar Lawrence's initial response to Romeo's news about "the fair Daughter of rich Capulet" (2.3.58, 66–68) echoes the Chorus' sentiments:

> Is Rosaline, that thou didst love so dear,
> So soon forsaken? Young Men's Love then lies
> Not truly in their Hearts but in their Eyes.

In a way that recalls Mercutio, who refers to his friend as "Humours! Madman! Passion! Lover!" (2.1.7), and Benvolio, who comments that "Blind is his Love, and best befits the Dark" (2.1.32), Friar Lawrence appears to feel that, notwithstanding its intensity, Romeo's zeal for Juliet is as likely to be a manifestation of "Rude Will" as of "Grace" (2.3.28). Hence the old man's admonition to "love moderately" (2.4.14).

Despite his solemn advice, however, the Friar does nothing to impede the "wanton Blood" (2.5.71) that he and Juliet's Nurse both see in their eager charges. Before he even speaks with Romeo's betrothed, Friar Lawrence agrees to channel the youths' ardor into a clandestine marriage. With the Church's sanction, then, they consummate their vows within twenty-four hours of their initial encounter. So much for moving "wisely and slow" (2.3.94).

There can be no question that what draws Romeo and Juliet to each other at the outset is physical attraction. But would it be just to assert that their union is based on nothing more elevated than erotic desire? I think not. The poetry with which they declare their feelings makes it well nigh impossible for us to conceive of any situation in which the protagonists could ever again be severed, let alone drift apart. After all, to preserve herself for the husband to whom she had plighted troth, Juliet defies and deceives her parents, evades a match that would advance both her own fortunes and her family's, dismisses the Nurse when the old retainer's pragmatism becomes the voice of "Ancient Damnation" (3.5.235), and drinks a potion she fears may be lethal. Meanwhile, for his part, Romeo proves more than willing to "give and hazard all" (*The Merchant of Venice*, 2.7.16) to uphold his pledge to Juliet. As we see the lovers increasingly isolated by events and, more importantly, by the folly of their elders and the insensitivity of even their closest confidants, we cannot help responding with sympathy for their predicament and admiration for the courage their consecration to each other inspires.

But if the tie that binds Romeo and Juliet is the most precious thing the setting of Shakespeare's tragedy affords, does it follow that we are meant to regard the lovers' "extreme Sweet" (2.Chorus.14) as a delicacy that supersedes all other treasures? Are we to join our hearts and minds with the protagonists' fathers and erect statues of "pure Gold" (5.3.299) to honor the title characters' fidelity to each other and to Love?

Perhaps so, but I find it difficult to locate a lot to celebrate in the events with which the play concludes. Old Capulet and Old Mountague clasp hands at long last, and if only by default a feud that has wrought untold devastation appears to be history. But at what cost? According to the city's sovereign, the only thing that remains when all is said and done is "A glooming Peace"—that and the Prince's haunting pronouncement that "All are punish'd" (5.3.305, 295).

So what are we to make of the mood with which the final scene draws to a close? Is it possible that Shakespeare expected his audience to include the lovers themselves in the Prince's stern accounting of Verona's "Woe" (5.3.309)? Can it be that a relationship so rare that it has become proverbial, a bond that appears indissoluble, was meant to be viewed as in some way wrong? The answer, I submit, is yes. I think it more than likely that the playwright intended to have his earliest theatergoers see Romeo and Juliet as protagonists whose tragic flaw derives from the same source as their strength and beauty: the very fact that their devotion to each other is so all-consuming that it eliminates everything else from consideration.

At their first greeting Romeo bows before Juliet as if she were a "holy Shrine" and he a "Pilgrim"; Juliet accepts this description of their venue and grants Romeo's "Pray'r" "lest Faith turn to Despair" (1.5.96, 99, 104, 106). In the Balcony Scene, the next time the protagonists meet, Romeo describes Juliet successively as "the Sun," as "bright Angel," and as "dear Saint," and he tells her "Call me but Love, and I'll be new baptiz'd" (2.2.3, 26, 56, 50). Juliet responds in kind and declares Romeo's "gracious Self" to be "the God of my Idolatry" (2.2.114, 115). What this imagery implies is that Romeo and Juliet are forswearing an old creed in favor of a new. In Act 3, having just learned of his banishment, Romeo says "Heav'n is here / Where Juliet lives" (3.3.29–30). To be exiled from Juliet's presence is, for Romeo, to be condemned to outer darkness. A few hours later, as the lovers are saying farewell on the morning that ends their one night together, their aubade suggests that their lives are now fundamentally "out of Tune" (3.5.27) with the lark, the daylight, and other manifestations of harmonious natural order.

From these and numerous other passages it is demonstrable that the relationship between Romeo and Juliet is a species, however refined, of *cupiditas*—a form of pseudo-worship in which one's deity is a creature rather than the Creator. Each lover views the other as the Supreme Good. Each accords the other a degree of adoration that Augustine (and innumerable later theologians) had defined as properly directed only to God. Their love becomes a universe unto itself, and when they are deprived of it each of the protagonists concludes that there is nothing left to live for.

But of course if Romeo and Juliet fall victim to idolatry, it is because they also succumb to passion. By indulging the senses and emotions, they allow first the concupiscible (pleasure-driven) and later the irascible (wrath-driven) divisions of the lower, sensible soul to gain hegemony over the rational soul (the Reason).

At the beginning Romeo is subject to the melancholy of a frustrated suitor. He keeps to himself, and when he is sighted by even his closest friend he slips into a "Grove of Sycamour" (1.1.125). Romeo is himself a "sick-amour," a youth afflicted with love-sickness, and his father observes that

> Black and portendous must this Humour prove
> Unless Good Counsel may the Cause remove.

Romeo's Reason emits warnings, both in the dream to which he several times refers in 1.4 and in the misgivings he expresses at the end of that scene, but he allows Mercutio's set-piece about Queen Mab to convince him, against his better judgment, to put his fear of "Consequence" out of mind. As Romeo consents to attend the Capulet ball, however, his pivotal comment makes it obvious that what his intellect tells him is being suppressed by an act of will: "he that hath the Stirrage of my Course / Direct my Suit" (1.4.112–13).[11]

From this point on, the hero plunges headlong into action. At his first glimpse of Juliet his senses are so entranced that he is oblivious to the threat posed by Tybalt. Later, in the Balcony Scene, it is Juliet, not Romeo, who expresses apprehensions; he declares "thy Kinsmen are no stop to me" (2.2.70) and defines himself as a bold mariner (2.2.83–85). Disregarding her instinctive caution, Juliet allows herself to be seduced by such bravado and agrees, against *her* better judgment, to become the partner of her suitor's rash ventures.

Up to this juncture the concupiscible passions have dominated the behavior of both lovers. Following Romeo and Juliet's hasty marriage, however, the irascible passions begin asserting themselves. Almost as soon as he departs from his wedding Romeo comes upon an incipient quarrel between Mercutio and Tybalt. The fresh bridegroom is not yet ready to reveal his new kinship with the Capulets, and as a result his conciliatory reply to a challenge Tybalt thrust at him is misinterpreted by Mercutio as an expression of "calm, dishonorable, vile Submission" (3.1.76). Romeo's hotheaded friend steps in to defend the honor he assumes a lethargic and cowardly Mountague is incapable of maintaining for himself. In an urgent attempt to prevent needless conflict, Romeo lunges between the two duelers. Unfortunately the protagonist's efforts at peacemaking prove fatal to Mercutio, and Romeo's ally dies cursing the house of Mountague as vehemently as he had earlier scorned the Capulets.

To this moment in the scene Romeo has "thought all for the best." For the first time in the play, he has acted with judgment, restraint, and genuine valor. But now he finds himself in an unaccustomed position. By turning the other cheek and trying to comport himself as an honorable gentleman, he has unwittingly made himself appear dishonorable and contributed to a calamity. After a too-brief pause for reflection, he reacts to the "Plague" in his ears by accepting

Mercutio's erroneous judgment on measured behavior that the audience will have recognized as anything *but* "Effeminate" (3.1.112, 114, 122). Casting aside his momentary self-control and rationality and yielding to an idolatrous concern for the kind of male "Reputation" that demands vengeance, Romeo spurns "respective Lenity" to make room for "Fire-ey'd Fury (3.1.119, 131–32). He disregards the Prince's prohibition against further bloodshed and takes the enactment of "Justice" into his own hands (3.1.189–91).

The slaying of Tybalt functions as the turning-point in the action. Before this development there has been at least a possibility of success for Romeo and Juliet. Capulet and Mountague have both shown a willingness to end the feud, and there has thus been some basis for the Friar's optimism that the marriage of a Capulet to a Mountague might bridge the way to a more harmonious future. With the deaths of Mercutio and Tybalt, however, the hostility between the two factions is rekindled, and the Prince can see only one way to prevent further carnage: by removing Romeo from "fair Verona" before more "Civil Blood" makes more "Civil Hands unclean" (Prologue.2–4).

By the time Romeo arrives at the Friar's cell in 3.3 he is practically beside himself. Upon learning that he has been banished, he falls to the ground, his abject posture symbolizing the topsy-turvy state of a soul no longer led by Reason. In this condition he draws a dagger, and only the Friar's intervention forestalls an instant suicide:

> Hold thy desperate Hand!
> Art thou a Man? Thy Form cries out thou art!
> Thy Tears are Womanish; thy wild Acts
> Denote th' unreasonable Fury of a Beast!
>           . . .
> Hast thou slain Tybalt? Wilt thou slay thy self?
> And slay thy Lady that in thy Life lives
> By doing damned Hate upon thy Self?   (3.3.107–17)

The answer to the Friar's last two questions will turn out to be affirmative. And the questions and answers that precede them explain why.

In 4.1 Juliet comes to the Friar's cell, like Romeo with a knife, and like Romeo determined to take her own life. Seeing in her "the strength of will to slay [her] self" (line 72), the Friar suggests a less desperate remedy for her difficulties. He then gives her a potion that will suspend her bodily functions for enough time to allow her to be mourned and buried. Meanwhile he sends a message to Juliet's husband. Due to unforeseen difficulties Romeo fails to receive it, and a day later he has no way of knowing that there is literal truth in his servingman's euphemistic report that the heroine is "well" and "sleeps in Capel's Monument" (5.1.17–18).

Now the protagonist descends into an even deeper depression. Purchasing poison from an Apothecary whose appearance resembles that of Despair in Spenser's

*Faerie Queene*,[12] he makes his way to Juliet's tomb. Upon his arrival, as he dismisses his man Balthasar, Romeo depicts himself in language that summons up memories of the Friar's rebuke in 3.3.107–17:

> The Time and my Intents are savage wild,
> More fierce and more inexorable far
> Than empty Tigers, or the roaring Sea. (5.3.37–39)

The pertinence of these words is almost immediately borne out when the desperate title character is provoked by an uncomprehending Paris and kills him. Moments later Romeo's portrayal of his "Intents " is illustrated yet again when he downs the liquid he has brought with him to the cemetery:

> Come, bitter Conduct; come, unsavory Guide.
> Thou desp'rate Pilot, now at once run on
> The dashing Rocks thy seasick, weary Bark. (lines 116–18)

Within seconds Juliet awakens to find her dead husband, and his example inspires her to plunge his dagger into her own breast. Thus does Romeo "slay" his "Lady" by "doing damned Hate" upon himself (3.1. 116–17). And thus does Shakespeare emblematize the fatal consummation of a union forged in unregimented idealism.

We should now be in a position to comment on the roles of Fortune, Fate, and the Stars in *Romeo and Juliet*. As we have observed, the protagonists are prompted by their concupiscible passions into an idolatrous relationship that makes them vulnerable to forces beyond their ken. As chance would have it, these forces combine to unleash the irascible passions that destroy Mercutio, Tybalt, Paris, and eventually Romeo and Juliet themselves. To put it another way, by forfeiting rational governance over their own behavior, the lovers subject themselves to the waywardness of happenstance. They become Fortune's fools (3.1.144). In a sense that they don't recognize, they become "fated."

In the process, by reducing themselves to menial servants of emotional and astral influences that would have had no power to manipulate them if they had kept their souls under the guidance of Reason, they become "Star-cross'd" (Prologue.6). Ironically and sadly, at no point in the action are the "Stars" more securely in command than at the moment when a tragically misled Romeo commits a mortal sin in a futile effort to "shake" their "Yoke" from his "World-wearied Flesh" (5.3.111–12).

It should not escape our notice, of course, that most of the play's other characters are also culpable victims of Fortune, Fate, and the Stars. The Capulets have sought to rise in worldly status, using their daughter as an unwilling instrument to that end, and that is one of the reasons we cannot bring ourselves to place much blame on Juliet for disobeying her unfeeling parents. It seems altogether apt that the Capulets' "ordained Festival" turns to "black Funeral"; they learn by bitter trial that on the Wheel of Fortune "all things change them to the contrary"

(4.5.84–85, 90). Meanwhile Mercutio, Tybalt, and Paris all submit in their own ways to Fortune's turns and suffer the consequences.

Even the sententious Friar can be seen as Fortune's plaything. For a man of the cloth he seems inordinately preoccupied with his worldly standing (hence his well-intended but ill-advised efforts to use unauthorized means to end the city's feuding, and hence his frantic scurrying about to cover his traces and avoid being caught at the graveyard in Act 5), and many of his error-prone judgments and makeshift expedients presuppose an improvident reliance on Fortune's notoriously unreliable cooperation.

In many respects the play's society as a whole is shown to be at the mercy of Fortune, Fate, and the Stars. The setting for Shakespeare's tragedy is, after all, a microcosm of postlapsarian humanity. And in this context the fates of Romeo and Juliet turn out to be a "Scourge" (5.3.292), a divine judgment, in senses that exceed the meaning intended by the Prince.

But how should all of this affect an audience experiencing the drama? Ultimately, like most of Shakespeare's tragedies, *Romeo and Juliet* appears designed to leave us with an enhanced appreciation of what it means, in Christian terms, to be human. If we've profited as we ought to from the action, we will know the protagonists better than they know themselves. And we will understand—alas, in a way they do not—what brought their story to its grievous denouement.

And how will we appraise the "Death-mark'd Love" (Prologue.9) of these beautiful and pitiable youths? If we have attended to what we have seen and heard, our sentiments will echo the humility and compassion implicit in a sixteenth-century cleric's prayer of thanksgiving. As he witnessed a small company of wrongdoers being carted off to their dooms, he said "But for the grace of God, there goes John Bradford."

## Notes

1   For Shakespeare's own use of the terms "judicious" and "action," see Hamlet, 3.2.1–52. All quotations from the plays are referenced to *The Guild Shakespeare*, a 19–volume set I've recently edited for the Doubleday Book & Music Clubs (New York: Guild America Books, 1989–92).

2   See *Aristotle's Poetics: A Translation and Commentary for Students of Literature* (Englewood Cliffs, NJ: Prentice Hall, 1968), particularly pages 115–20. My thinking on catharsis in Shakespeare has also been richly informed by the late Virgil K. Whitaker, especially in *The Mirror Up to Nature* (San Marino: The Huntington Library, 1965), and by Roy Battenhouse, above all in *Shakespearean Tragedy: Its Christian Premises* (Bloomington: Indiana University Press, 1969).

3   The situation I describe here is the norm for Shakespearean comedy and romance, where catharsis ("dis-illusionment") must occur in the central characters in order to bring about the unification that constitutes a happy ending.

4   *Samson Agonistes*, line 1758.

5   See *Hamlet*, 5.2.375, and *King Lear*, 5.3.231–32.

6   The edition of *The Consolation of Philosophy* that I have used is the translation
and commentary by Richard Green (Indianapolis: Bobbs Merrill, 1962).

7   Friar Lawrence invokes "Philosophy" in 3.3.55–56 of *Romeo and Juliet* when he
explains to a desperate Romeo that he should welcome "Adversity's sweet Milk."
Both here and later in the play (see 5.5.65–83), the Friar calls attention to Lady
Philosophy's teaching that "bad" fortune is actually better for us than what we
incorrectly think of as good fortune.

8   I am indebted to the translation and commentary by D. W. Robertson, Jr. (New
York: Liberal Arts Press, 1958). Robertson also discusses *On Christian Doctrine*
extensively in *A Preface to Chaucer* (Princeton University Press, 1962).

9   For a more detailed exposition of the relationship between astrology and
medieval and Renaissance psychology, see Walter Clyde Curry's "Destiny in
*Troilus and Criseyde*" in *Chaucer and the Medieval Sciences* (New York: Oxford
University Press, 1926).

10  Romeo's surname in all the original texts is spelled "Mountague." Given
Shakespeare's wordplay on "ague" (fever) in "Sir Andrew Ague-cheek" (as the
name of the foolish suitor is rendered in First Folio text of *Twelfth Night*), it
seems reasonable to assume that the playwright was fully aware of the symbolic
potential in "Mountague." See *Love's Labor's Lost*, 4.1.1–4, for related play on
"Mounting."

11  Here I retain the Second Quarto spelling Stirrage, which plays on stir (compare
1.1.9, where Gregory observes that "To move is to stir") and reminds us that
Romeo's "Steerage" will prove that "Love" can be considerably more "rough"
(1.4.27) than the jesting Mercutio suspects.

12  *F. Q.* 1.9.17–54. I owe this observation to Professor Joan Hartwig of the
University of Kentucky, who called it to my notice in 1971.

Revised from "The Catharsis of *Romeo and Juliet*," in *Contributi Dell'Istituto di Filologia Moderna*, Serie inglese I, ed. Sergio Rossi (Milan: Catholic University, 1974), pp. 142–75. Republished in John F. Andrews, ed., *"Romeo and Juliet": Critical Essays* (Garland: New York, 1993), pp. 403–22.

# HAMLET

## Comment and bibliography

When Hamlet confesses to having "shot my arrow o'er the house" and hurt Laertes, his metaphor of a misdirected arrow is that of *hamartia*, the term used by Aristotle to describe tragic error and used in the New Testament to designate sin. Hamlet comes to acknowledge that he has done a "wrong" to Laertes. But he fails to see this act as Shakespeare invites us to do as a wronging also of himself, a self created by God with a potential for true goodness. That failure is what makes Hamlet's life ultimately tragic, a pitiful wasting of his great talents by a misusing of them. He has brought about the destruction of the whole house of Denmark when he dies at the end "ill about my heart" yet self-satisfied.

As is usual in a tragic hero, Hamlet experiences remorse but no genuine repentance. His wronging of Laertes he ascribes to a madness, as if his own willing had no part in the madness—as if it were not he himself who resolved to put on an "antic disposition" and then delighted in the thought of doing "bitter business," and after doing it proceeded to shuffle off on "heaven" his scourging of other people. By ascribing to Heaven or to madness his *hamartia*, Hamlet supposes that he can free himself from having "purposed" evil. Yet he himself has made revenge his purpose and has relied on this to justify a knavery toward and contempt for his friends, Rosencrantz and Guildenstern. Dr. Johnson declared Hamlet's apology to Laertes a falsehood. So must we, unless our eyes are as closed as Hamlet's against the truth.

The drama makes a prominent allusion to the biblical Cain. We hear Claudius at prayer condemn himself for the "primal eldest" crime of a brother's murder. If we ask what caused this crime, the answer of Genesis 4:9 is that it stemmed from Cain's question, "Am I my brother's keeper?" whereby he shuffled off responsibility for any caretaking. One reason for the many soliloquies in *Hamlet* is Shakespeare's intention to let us see this prince in the process of moving from troubling thoughts to criminal action. An act has "three branches," the play's clown tells us in alluding to the distinction between acts of thought, word, and deed. And we may recall that in Matthew 5 Jesus traces the crime of murder to its prior manifestations in angry thoughts and verbal insults. Scholastic psychology likewise distinguished three stages in the willing of an act: first, the thought, then the delectation, and then consent. Shakespeare by dramatizing these stages in Hamlet's willing of the killing of Claudius enables us to see Hamlet's purpose growing into an act that becomes as murderous as that of Claudius, his brother in crime.

The Prince who asks Laertes to pardon his *hamartia* has begun that same scene with a soliloquy in praise of rashness. Indeed, we have seen him prone to rashness ever since he broke away from the restraints of Horatio and Marcellus to follow the beckoning of his father's ghost. He would "haste" to know what may sweep him to revenge, is eager to wipe from his brain "all saws of books," and to swear a compact with a spirit that speaks from the cellarage where hell was conventionally located. Worse still, Hamlet accepts without question the Ghost's portrait of himself as a "radiant angel," and of Gertrude as motivated by "lust" for a Claudius as worthless as "garbage." In adopting his father's perspective, Hamlet becomes a calumniator of his neighbors. When he names Claudius a paddock, a bat, and a tomcat he is being unfair to Claudius, who despite his sin is a human being who longs to repent but gets no help from Hamlet the angel in black. Likewise the castigation of Gertrude by Hamlet, in which her love for Claudius is denounced as hellish and swinish, goes far beyond any evidence we have to justify the cruel harangue. And equally intemperate is Hamlet's naming Ophelia a bawd and her father a fishmonger, and Rosencrantz and Guildenstern "adders fanged." Such language is like arrows shot wildly over the house, causing wrong and injury. Thus there is *hamartia* in Hamlet's acts of speech and not merely in his careless swordsmanship. When he dismisses Polonius as a "rash, intruding fool," the irony is that those words unwittingly describe the speaker himself. True, Polonius has behaved like a silly ass. But Hamlet's crowing over him with contempt is more than assinine; it is devilish proud and wantonly destructive. And it drives Claudius, simply as the commonwealth's protector, to seek a way to get rid of Hamlet.

When at the end Horatio sums up the cost of "purposes mistook"—unnatural acts, casual slaughters, and deaths put on by forced cause—we wonder at Shakespeare's skill in maintaining our sympathy for a hero so deeply implicated in crime. How has the dramatist managed this? Giving him in Horatio a confidant who can still call him "sweet prince" is one means. Another is the details that support Ophelia's estimate of him as a "noble mind" which, even when blasted with madness, sounds like "sweet bells" out of tune. His great gifts of nature and art are evident even when greatly disturbed. Moreover his idealism is intense, and takes as its object of admiration a father in whom "every god did seem to set his seal, / To give the world assurance of a man" (3.4.62–63). Theatre auditors of an idealistic bent can easily identify with Hamlet's enthusiasm for such manhood—although from a Christian point of view it can be recognized as the idolizing of a dignity whose aspects are all pagan. The natural inclination of most auditors is not to pause over that defect. When a father has become a national hero in a wagered combat against a foreigner, his success seems to sanction a filial piety toward him. And such a piety is intensified when a suspicion that the father's subsequent death was by foul play is corroborated by secret revelation. That discovery challenges in Hamlet a "calling" to revenge—which romantic critics such as Coleridge and

Bradley have considered a sacred duty. With their perspective the ethical issue gets reduced to the problem of why Hamlet delays to fatten the region's kites with the offal of Claudius. Bradley was quite ready to call "healthy" Hamlet's revenge feelings and his "loathing" of his uncle, and Hamlet's melancholy was explained as "forced" upon him by the shock of discovering his mother's infidelity.

That Gertrude may be really innocent of marital infidelity is simply not considered by readers predisposed to pity any sensitive intellectual who feels betrayed by a wicked world. But Shakespeare is relying on the story's pattern of events to correct and refine this drossy pity in readers by redirecting it toward the victims of Hamlet's antipathy, and eventually to lead us then to Ophelia's insight that unless "God be at your table" none of us knows "what we may be" through grace and prayer and penitence. True pity should be for our failures in charity. The theological clown in the play elaborates on this truth by saying that we but dig our own graves unless we perceive that the Church builds stronger than the gallows—a secret that makes possible a cheerfulness and song. Revenge without mercy is only a wild justice devoid of salvation—as Shakespeare has been letting us discover ever since his *Merchant of Venice*.

Five pieces of commentary have been chosen for our anthology. The first is Eleanor Prosser's well documented argument that the Ghost cannot be a spirit of health and cannot be from Purgatory, since his behavior and language violate Christian norms. Secondly, Cherrell Guilfoyle discusses the significance of the play's opening scene: its winter setting is like that of Christmas story, but the action being launched is in opposition to the message of Christmas. A contrast between the visitation of angels in Luke and that of the armor-clad apparition in *Hamlet* is very evidently designed by the dramatist. Thirdly, Roy Battenhouse describes the lapsing from Christian norms that characterizes Hamlet as he chooses not only a perversion of divine law but also a negligence of the rule of reason and of warnings from conscience. By a progressive callousness, this hero takes on the role of Isaiah's "scourge" and ends his career as a co-celebrant with Claudius in what amounts to a Black Mass that parodies holy communion. His tragedy exhibits thus an upside-down salvationism, a lamed mimicking of the "mousetrap" strategy of Atonement story.

James Black contrasts Hamlet's vows with the Sermon on the Mount's instruction against swearing. Further, he likens Hamlet's vowing to that of Jepthah's, called "rash" in the Geneva Bible. When Hamlet terms Polonius a Jepthah, implying that this father is sacrificing his daughter for his own glory, Black thinks Hamlet is touching also, perhaps unconsciously, on his own rash vow which has caused him to foreswear his "holy vows" to Ophelia. D. W. Robertson sees Hamlet as a moral weakling. The Prince manifests a vice of sloth, and with a will "incorrect to heaven" he abuses his mother by slandering her innocence. Against all evidence, says Robertson, Hamlet assures Horatio that the Ghost is "honest," and uses a playlet to attack maliciously Gertrude and Claudius. For no good cause he murders his best friends, and his "readiness" in the face of Providence involves no penitential cross-bearing but only a fatalistic commitment to smiting fellow human beings. His tragedy is that of a befuddled agent of destruction.

Among items listed for supplementary reading, Norman Austin's essay summarizes well the moral quality of the Ghost, the prime mover of the play's action. The portrait this father gives of himself as a model husband is dubious, says Austin, since he has lived by violence and is indifferent to anyone's honor but his own. Exhibiting the bitterness of an ego deprived of its pleasures and seeking revenge, he can not be from Purgatory but rather from a doom in Hell's fires. Battenhouse, in writing on Hamlet's apostrophe to man, analyzes this prince's Renaissance humanism as one of dividedness between idealism and nihilism because he has forfeited the unifying Christian virtues of faith, hope, and charity. On Hamlet's Advice speech, Battenhouse observes that its injunctions against "mouthing" are violated by Hamlet himself because revenge feelings require rant to express them. Elsewhere, Battenhouse expounds the "baptized Aristotelianism" of Shakespeare's artistry in *Hamlet*.

Victor Strandberg makes the point that Hamlet's unChristian subordinating of love to revenge dehumanizes him and sets in motion destructive activities. Geoffrey Hughes argues that Hamlet's willingness to damn Rosencrantz and Guildenstern puts him among the lost, despite the stoic Horatio's generous invoking of flights of angels. Eleanor Prosser's learned study reviews well the whole tragedy, except for her judgment at the end regarding Hamlet's redemption. Various other critics (of whom Gideon Rappaport can serve as an example) have similarly argued that the play ends with a saved Hamlet; but they neglect to distinguish between the "permissive" will and the "elective" will of God. In Christian doctrine, God permits the death of all men but elects to salvation only those who die "in the Lord." As Donald Stump perceives correctly if somewhat shakily, Hamlet progresses into becoming like Cain. John Andrews argues carefully that Shakespeare expected "judicious" members of his audience to achieve a detached view of Hamlet and to see that this protagonist "does not experience catharsis." Arthur McGee concludes that Elizabethan auditors would have seen Hamlet as ending with a fatalism that heads him toward hell.

Alan Sinfield has argued plausibly that Hamlet's sense of a "special providence" resembles Calvin's and prompts an acquiescent fatalism in the prince. Sinfield thinks Shakespeare is using the drama to exploit "the embarrassments in Calvinism" and present a dissatisfaction with "orthodox theology" felt by humane Elizabethans such as Launcelot Andrewes. Unfortunately, Sinfield neglects to say that Shakespeare (like Andrewes) did not regard Calvinistic predestinarianism as "orthodox" Christianity. For Shakespeare, actually, may not Hamlet's deathbed Calvinistic fatalism signal a tragic loss of orthodoxy in the prince?

## Supplementary bibliography

Andrews, John. "Catharsis in *Hamlet*," in Koshi Nakanori, ed., *Poetry and Drama in the English Renaissance* (Tokyo: Kinokuniya Co., 1980), pp. 1–20.

Austin, Norman. "Hamlet's Hungry Ghost," *Shenandoah* 37 (1987), 78–105.

Battenhouse, Roy. "Hamlet's Apostrophe to Man," *PMLA* 66 (1951), 1073–1113.

_____. "The Significance of Hamlet's Advice to the Players," in Elmer Blistein, ed., *The Drama of the Renaissance* (Brown University Press, 1970), pp. 3–26.

_____. *Shakespearean Tragedy* (1969), pp. 152–58; 215–66 (on *Hamartia* in Aristotle, Christian Doctrine, and *Hamlet*); 377–80 (on Claudius at Prayer).

Bedell, George C. "The Prayer Scene in *Hamlet*," *Anglican Theological Review* 51 (1969), 114–24.

Doebler, John. "The Play Within the Play: the *Muscipula Diaboli* in *Hamlet*," *Shakespeare Quarterly* 23 (1972), 164–69; rpt. in *Shakespeare's Speaking Pictures* (University of New Mexico Press, 1974), pp. 95–105.

Guilfoyle, Cherrell. "The Role of Ophelia in *Hamlet*," *Shakespeare's Play within Play* (1990), pp. 7–19.

Hankins, John. "Religion in Hamlet: The Bible," and "Religion in Hamlet: Repentance," in *The Character of Hamlet and Other Essays* (University of North Carolina Press, 1941), pp. 172–221.

Hughes, Geoffrey. "The Tragedy of a Revenger's Loss of Conscience: A Study of *Hamlet*," *English Studies* 57 (1976), 395–409.

McGee, Arthur. *The Elizabethan "Hamlet"* (Yale University Press, 1987).

Prosser, Eleanor. *Hamlet and Revenge* (Stanford University Press, 1967; 2nd ed. 1971), esp. Chapters 3–7.

Rappaport, Gideon. "Hamlet: Revenge and Madness," *The Upstart Crow* 7 (1987), 80–95.

Sinfield, Alan. "Hamlet's Special Providence," *Shakespeare Survey* 33 (1980), 89–98.

Strandberg, Victor H. "The Revenger's Tragedy: Hamlet's Costly Code," *South Atlantic Quarterly* 65 (1966), 95–103.

Stump, Donald V. "Hamlet, Cain and Abel, and the Pattern of Divine Providence," *Renaissance Papers* (1985), 27–38.

*Eleanor Prosser (1967; 1971)*

## Spirit of Health or Goblin Damned?

There can be little doubt that Shakespeare's audience understood the symbolic meaning of the cock. An ancient belief—found in traditional Jewish writings and in Horace, and made specifically Christian by such writers as Prudentius and St Ambrose—held that roving demons scattered in fear at cockcrow, and Le Loyer specially related the belief to his discussion of demons appearing as dead souls.[1] The Witches' Sabbath customarily began at midnight and lasted until cockcrow, at which time Satan fled terrified. As the herald of the day, the cock is the voice of light and thus of grace; in banishing night, he banishes darkness and sin. Thus Christian tradition held that cocks crowed all night at the Nativity and again at the Resurrection. More specifically, the cock symbolized the voice of Christ when it called Peter to repent, a belief reflected in the familiar weathervane cock on church steeples.[2]

To be doubly sure that his audience understood the significance of the Ghost's response to the cock, Shakespeare added explanatory speeches by Horatio and Marcellus. The Ghost "started like a guilty thing / Upon a fearful summons," and Horatio is reminded that only "extravagant and erring spirits" are banished by the herald of the sun. Good spirits, as we noted earlier, can appear at any time. Marcellus agrees and notes that evil spirits are dispelled during Advent by the night-long crowing of the cock. Modern producers make a serious mistake when they cut Marcellus's speech, for it does much more than merely "give a religious background to the supernatural happenings."[3] As H. D. F. Kitto notes, it gives "the logical and dynamic centre of the whole play. We are in the presence of evil."[4]

If we read without preconceptions the Ghost's long speech in scene 5, we should be struck by its almost exclusive reliance on sensual imagery. Like Iago, it paints a series of obscene pictures and then insistently highlights the very images that Hamlet had tried to blot out in his early soliloquy: "that incestuous, that adulterate beast... shameful lust ... lewdness ... sate itself in a celestial bed ... prey on garbage." Hamlet had known that for his own sanity he must not visualize that bed, but the Ghost rivets his eyes upon it. The culminating exhortation is not to purge the "royal throne of Denmark." It forces Hamlet again to peer into the horror that sickens him:

> Let not the royal bed of Denmark be
> A couch for luxury and damned incest.

Can this be a divine agent on a mission of health and consolation?

This Ghost cannot be a penitent soul from Purgatory. It says it is, but are we intended to believe it? It does, to be sure, speak of its agony at dying without the sacraments, but the reference serves as one more detail to intensify Hamlet's pain. Moreover, a subtle hint has been planted that is to bear terrible fruit in the Prayer Scene. The Ghost's attitude toward its suffering is also telling. Does it humbly confess its sins, acknowledging the justice of its punishment? On the contrary, it "groans" and "complains" of the agony resulting from its being unfairly deprived of final sacraments. For centuries editors have tried to give "O, horrible! O, horrible! most horrible!" to Hamlet on the grounds that the reaction ill befits a spirit of grace. So it does. A Purgatorial penitent would be a loving figure of consolation, but the Ghost that Shakespeare created dwells on the horror of its pains. The exclamation is a logical climax to the extended assault on Hamlet's emotions.

At that cry of horror, when Hamlet's agony is at a peak, the Ghost gives him the tragic burden: "If thou hast nature in thee.... Revenge...." Nothing in the scene suggests that a divine minister is appealing to Hamlet's "nature" as a creature made in God's image whose role is to fulfill His commandments. Throughout the speech it has been appealing to Hamlet's "nature" as an instinctive creature of passions and appetites—"fallen nature," the theologian would say. Thus its challenge to Hamlet to prove his "nature" by committing murder is the same type of challenge heard in Lady Macbeth's "Are you a man?" That this is the issue as Hamlet himself is later to understand it will become clear in "To be or not to be." The Ghost, then, fails the test that every member of Shakespeare's audience undoubtedly would have recognized as the crucial one, a failure that scholars have been trying to rationalize for two centuries: its command violates Christian teaching.

Does the Ghost, in fact, pass any of the religious tests? Well, it appears as a man, not a hop-toad, and no one mentions that it smells of sulphur. On every other test, it fails. Is it humble? How is it conceivable, it asks, that Gertrude could "decline? Upon a wretch whose natural gifts were poor / To those of mine." (Characteristically, it draws our attention to the physical.) Is it in a charitable state? It is thoroughly vindictive, seething in its own hatred and aggravating Hamlet's loathing. Is its voice sweet, soft, musical, and soothing, or "terrible and full of reproach"? The actor who intones these lines with melodious grace is deaf to the meanings of words. Does it carefully refrain from charging others with sin? Its mission is to condemn Claudius. Does it beg Hamlet's prayers? It says "remember *me.*"

Some critics have tried to explain these unsettling facts as further proof that the Ghost is from Purgatory on the grounds that his anger, vindictiveness, and sensuality merely indicate that he has not yet been sufficiently purged. This argument will not do. The purpose of Purgatory is not to reform a sinner but to erase the debt of punishment incurred by past sins that were repented before death. As Thomas More emphasizes, in Purgatory no soul can be angry, for all are in a state of grace.

But, it will be objected, the Ghost urges Christian forbearance for Gertrude. Admitted. But that is what we are warned the Devil will do: in order to disguise himself as an angel of light, he will, like Richard III, "clothe [his] naked villany" "with a piece of scripture" (1.3.334–38). Catholics and Protestants both agreed that the mere repetition of Christian doctrine proved nothing. Both warned that we must be alert to the speaker's ultimate purpose. Let us note the context:

> If thou has nature in thee, bear it not;
> Let not the royal bed of Denmark be
> A couch for luxury and damned incest.
> But, howsoever thou pursuest this act,
> Taint not thy mind, nor let thy soul contrive
> Against thy mother aught: leave her to heaven. . . .

The lines are brutally ironic. "Taint not thy mind"? For over fifty lines, the Ghost has done everything possible to taint Hamlet's mind with lacerating grief, sexual nausea, hatred, and fury.

Even though we have been caught up in the emotions of the scene, Hamlet's reaction when the Ghost vanishes should jolt us:

> O all you host of heaven! O earth! what else?
> And shall I couple hell?

He is not merely adding a third power to his invocation of Heaven and earth. The sexual image ("couple"), reflecting the success of the Ghost's insidious method, is plain: shall Hamlet join himself to Hell? Even in his distraction, he again raises the dreadful possibility. But the moment of perspective is fleeting as the rush of emotion leads him to embrace the image of his father:

> Remember thee!
> Yea, from the table of my memory
> I'll wipe away all trivial fond records,
> All saws of books, all forms, all pressures past,
> That youth and observation copied there;
> And thy commandment all alone shall live
> Within the book and volume of my brain.

"Taint not thy mind"? He will wipe away all precepts, all codes, all that he has learned from books and experience. He does not say that he will erase all petty ideas in order to concentrate on his duty to his father. "Thy commandment *all alone* shall live / Within the book and volume of my brain." And that commandment is to exact revenge. So committed, he fixes his mind on his victim, furiously focusing on the image of the "smiling, damned villain."[5]

I can find no warrant in the play for believing that the Ghost is on a divine mission. Not once does the Ghost suggest that its command to revenge is the will of God. Not once does it suggest that its command—"Revenge his foul and most unnatural murder"—means anything other than what Hamlet takes it to mean: brutal, unqualified murder in direct retaliation. Any doubt is eliminated when Hamlet is told to pursue revenge in any way he chooses so long as he leaves Gertrude to Heaven. By implication, Claudius is not to be punished by Heaven. The Ghost treats Hamlet as if he were a private agent who is to act out of purely personal motives. "Remember me," says the Ghost, not "Cleanse Denmark in the name of God." Of course Hamlet may, in later scenes, qualify the command in his own mind. But in the first act, the Ghost is presented as malign.

The curious cellarage scene enforces this impression. We can probably never know exactly how Shakespeare's audience responded to the scene, much less exactly what Shakespeare intended. The repeated shifting of ground in order to swear suggests a specific convention,[6] but a study of stage tradition helps little. As Nevill Coghill has noted, however, three of Hamlet's lines, together with his actions and those of the Ghost, provide several clues.[7] The significant sequence is as follows:

> (The Ghost cries from under the stage.)
> Ah, ha, boy! say'st thou so? art thou there, truepenny?
> (Hamlet shifts ground; the Ghost shifts and cries again.)
> Hic et ubique? then we'll shift our ground.
> (Hamlet shifts; the Ghost shifts and cries again.)
> Well said, old mole! canst work i'the earth so fast?
> A worthy pioner! Once more remove, good friends.
> (Hamlet shifts.)

The clearest clue lies in the third line. We have noted that demons were believed to frequent mines, and Hamlet echoes this belief when he hails the "old mole" as a "worthy pioner" that works in the earth. That Hamlet is mockingly addressing an assumed demon seems likely when we find Toby Belch referring to the Devil as a "foul collier" (*Twelfth Night*, 3.4.130).

The Ghost is, of course, speaking from beneath the stage, the familiar abode in Elizabethan drama of demons, furies, and damned souls. Only a "goblin damn'd" speaks from the abyss of Hell. In *The Malcontent*, Malevole greets Mendoza with "Illo, ho ho ho, arte thou there old true penny?" (3.3). It is significant that the line is a deliberate echo: Malevole is addressing a devilish villain. Hamlet's mocking tone, his almost taunting familiarity, could not be directed toward a spirit of health from Purgatory.

Scholars have been driven to fantastic lengths to explain this unavoidable fact. We read that Shakespeare is tricking his audience by stopping for a playful parody; the printer is tricking the reader by including a scene from the old "Ur-Hamlet"; the Ghost is tricking Hamlet; Hamlet is tricking the Ghost; Hamlet and the Ghost together are tricking the two amazed observers. The most popular explanation is the last: that Hamlet and the Ghost both pretend the voice is a devil to mislead Horatio and Marcellus. How could the audience be expected to know this? It is just as misled. And what motive could both Hamlet and a good Purgatorial spirit have for making Horatio and Marcellus think their Prince is in league with the Devil? "To terrify them into silence" is an inadequate answer. There is one logical explanation. Shakespeare made the Ghost act like a devil because he wanted his audience to notice that it acts like a devil.

## Notes

1  Pierre LeLoyer, *IIII Livres des Spectres* (1586), II. 489.
2  Roy Battenhouse, "The Ghost in Hamlet," *Studies in Philology* 48 (1951), pp. 180–81. Christopher Devlin, *Hamlet's Divinity and Other Essays* (Carbondale, Ill., 1963), p. 31. Catholic scholars believe that the cock-crow Hymn of St Ambrose in the Liturgy for Sunday Lauds finds clear echo in the play: "The herald of the morning sounds, and calls out the sun ray. Wakened by him the day-star frees the sky from darkness: at his note the troops of prowling

outlaws (*Hoc omnis erronum cohors*) forsake their baleful course." Father Devlin suggests that "extravagant and erring" looks like an etymological rendering of the Latin words *erro, erronis,* meaning "a lawless vagabond."

3    J. Dover Wilson, *What Happens in Hamlet,* 3 ed. (Cambridge, 1961), p. 67.

4    H. D. F. Kitto, *Form and Meaning in Drama* (London, 1959), p. 255.

5    Hamlet has said he will clear the "table of [his] memory" and put the Ghost's command in "the book and volume of [his] brain." The imagery indicates that the "tables" are not in his pocket but in his mind.

6    Joseph Quincy Adams suggests that a clue may be found in the Chester *Processus Prophetarum.* Balaam, prevented by God from cursing the children of Israel, three times shifts his ground at the suggestion of Balak in an attempt to defy God's commandment. "Some Notes on Hamlet," *Modern Language Notes,* 28 (1913), 40.

7    *Shakespeare's Professional Skills* (Cambridge, Eng., 1964), pp. 9–16.

From *Hamlet and Revenge,* 2nd ed. (1971), pp. 121–22, 134–41, excerpts abridged. Used with permission of the publishers, Stanford University Press.

*Cherrell Guilfoyle (1980)*

## The Beginning of *Hamlet*

Emrys Jones, in his studies of "scenic form," has described how many of the actions of the mysteries were used by Shakespeare, principally in his histories. "These [medieval] patterns," Jones has written, "are in fact the means whereby the action of the play is carried deep into the audience's mind."[1] The subjects of the mystery plays, which were highly selective, were those Bible stories of which the "immemorial authenticity" (again Jones' phrase) can only ring truer with each fresh representation, narrative sequences which develop into myth, and produce an imaginative impression beyond that of language.

I am not suggesting that Shakespeare used a particular scene from one or more plays to inform the structure of the opening scene in *Hamlet,* but rather that he used a myth built up by slow accretion which to himself and to his audience carried the full charge of the manifestation of Christ to the people. The story of the shepherds on Christmas night, as recounted in Chester, in York, and in Coventry would be the story told to children and passed down from mother to child—that story, and not the canon version which, before the publication of the Authorized Version of the Bible, was not so widely known.

Many critics have written of the power and impact of Shakespeare's opening scenes, and in particular of the opening scene of *Hamlet.* Coleridge, Bradley, Adams, Kitto, Wilson Knight have variously described the extraordinary atmosphere evoked on the platform of Elsinore. "At the start of each of his tragedies," wrote L. C. Knights, "Shakespeare establishes the 'atmosphere'—something that is not just a vaguely effective background but an integral part of the play's structure of meanings." For Dover Wilson, the ghost is "the instrument for setting the plot in motion."[2] I should like to suggest that it is, rather, the whole of the first scene that does this, by means which may now seem obscure but were not so at the time when the use of the scenic forms of the old plays would at least stir subconscious memories and feelings in the audience.

In *Hamlet's* opening scene there are three men—"witnesses," as they are called by Dover Wilson—who are on guard. In the English mystery plays the shepherds are also three, an extrapolation from the three Magi, who in turn derived their trinitarian number from the three gifts which they carried. In *Hamlet*, it is Marcellus, Bernardo, and Horatio who are to witness the apparition. The men are not participants in the main action; they are onlookers, representatives perhaps of ordinary people, to whom something supernatural is shown.... It is a night guard, and the night is very cold. The second Towneley shepherds' play opens with "Lord, what these weders ar cold!" In the lyrical Coventry play, "Thys nyght yt ys soo colde" is used three times, like a refrain.[3] St Luke gives no indication of the weather; but by the fourth century Christmas had been fixed near midwinter, to coincide with the old winter solstice feasts, and the tradition of the cold night in the field was carried into the stable in Bethlehem, where the Christ child shivered with cold until warmed by the breath of the animals.[4] In *Hamlet* there is an echo of Francisco's "'tis bitter cold" (1.1.8) in 1.4.1, with Hamlet's "The air bites shrewdly; it is very cold."

The mystery play shepherds are not together in a group to begin with, but enter severally, calling to one another. In York and Coventry the sheep are lost as well as the fellow-shepherds. There is much hallooing to one another across the heights. The calling and questioning is used in *Hamlet* for both Bernardo's entrance and, later, Marcellus and Horatio's; and in 1.5.14 there is an echo of the Coventry play ("illo, ho, ho") as Marcellus calls to Hamlet.[5]

The contrast in movement to the tranquil Christmas scene is carried further by the shepherds' words. Both in soliloquy and in conversation they grumble and fret—about sheep rot and bad weather, discomfort and poverty.[6] Similarly it is clear in the first scene of Hamlet that "something is rotten"; Francisco's few lines have no other function but to convey anxiety, uncertainty, and an unexplained sickness at heart.

The first sign of something strange afoot for the shepherds is the appearance of a brilliant star. This apocryphal event, borrowed from the story of the Magi, is in all the mystery plays. In *Hamlet*, the star is pointed out by Bernardo (1.1.39). Immediately afterwards, the apparition is there.... [It] gives no message to the witnesses on the platform. The men, as "sore afrayd" as the shepherds were at first, can express only bewilderment. Their uncertainty has a strange analogy with the mystery plays, for at first the shepherds also do not understand what is happening. In Chester there is a long colloquy about the meaning of the *Gloria*; and a similar passage appears in *Ludus Coventriae*.[7]

Finally, at the end of the scene, the dawn rises: "But look, the morn in russet mantle clad / Walks o'er the dew of yon high eastward hill" (1.1.166-67). The dawn was the accepted symbol of the birth of the Son of God, as celebrated in the famous hymn *A solis ortus cardine* and elsewhere. Shakespeare's scene, like the shepherds' scene, opens just after midnight and ends at dawn.... Just before Horatio sees the dawn in *Hamlet*, Marcellus gives his beautiful speech (according to Kitto, Shakespeare at his most dangerous)[8] about the calm and hallowed nights of Christmas.

The Coventry Shearmen and Taylors' play begins with the messianic prophecies of Isaiah, giving "the initial emphasis on expectation" which Hardison noted in the Mass.[9] The initial emphasis in *Hamlet* is the opposite—"'tis bitter cold, / And I am sick at heart" (1.1.8–9). Towards the end of the play Hamlet echoes this foreboding line with "but thou wouldst not think how ill all's here about my heart" (5.2.210). When the first scene gets under way, the antitheses are more precise. The men are guarding not sheep, the symbols of peace, but an armed castle. There is a description of the preparations for war, which contravene the fourth commandment in not dividing "the Sunday from the week" (1.1.76). The star which Bernardo sees is not in the east, but in the west (1.1.36). The apparition does not come down from above, or in from stage right, as did the angel in the mystery plays, but up through the trap or in from stage left—the traditional place for the "sulph'rous and tormenting flames" (1.5.4) to which the apparition must return.[10]

Unlike the angel, clothed in radiance (cf. the "armour of light" in the reading for the first Sunday in Advent, *Romans* 13:12), the apparition is in full armor of a different kind—"cap-a-pe," "from top to toe," "from head to foot," "in complete steel" (1.2.200, 228; 1.4.52); such insistence that he is fully armed cannot be without significance.... The warlike nature of the apparition in 1.1 is borne out by his "martial stalk" and also, it seems, by his martial temper, for he frowns as once he did "in an angry parle" (1.1.66, 62).

A further antithesis is in the silence of the *Hamlet* apparition before the three witnesses, something which, as Jones points out, is clearer in performance than in reading of the text. It contrasts with the angel's message to the shepherds and with the singing of the *Gloria* by the "multitude of heauenly souldiers." The sinister nature of the silence is echoed in 1.5 when the ghost, from below, insists that the witnesses must remain silent; the shepherds on the other hand "published abroade the thing, which was tolde them of that childe." (Luke 2:17)

Lastly Marcellus and Horatio speak of the contrasting effects of the crowing of the cock. The night-long singing during Advent welcomes the birth of the Savior;

the same song sends "th'extravagant and erring spirit ... To his confine," and Marcellus immediately remarks, "It [the apparition] faded on the crowing of the cock" (1.1.154–55, 157).

So much for formal, structural, and atmospheric antithesis. The fundamental antithesis seems to lie in the import of the angel's message in contrast to the message in *Hamlet* from the apparition "confined to fast in fires" (1.5.11). As noted above, the message in the mystery plays is expounded by the shepherds as well as by the angel, and in the Coventry play the prophets re-enter to describe and elucidate the scene after it is over. However it is presented, the message is basically always the same: a Son is born of a virgin mother, and he will bring redemption to man through forgiveness. In *Hamlet*, there are two obvious antitheses; the angel speaks of the birth of the Son, the apparition of the death of the father (the "common theme" referred to by Claudius in rebuking Hamlet [1.2.103–4]).

Both in the mystery plays and in *Hamlet*, the messages relate to sins which are to be expunged. The keynote of the antithesis is the manner in which this is to be achieved. For the shepherds, it is by the heavenly way of forgiveness; for Hamlet, it is by revenge. L. C. Knights wrote of the "accepted Christianity" (of Marcellus's speech) ". . . which, it seems in place to remark, is directly opposed to the code of revenge."[11] In terms of the supernatural messages from the angel to the shepherds and from the apparition to Hamlet, the antithesis is even more precise.

The revenge / forgiveness antithesis brings us back to Marcellus' speech. This has often been taken as no more than a pious and very beautiful digression. Bradley comments on the "bewitching music" of the lines, Dover Wilson on the "beautiful lines . . . on the peace of Christmas-tide, lines that perhaps do more than any other speech in the scene to give a religious background to its supernatural happenings." L. C. Knights introduced the remark quoted above with "Now I cannot believe that these lines were put in for the sake of an incidental bit of 'poetry'." Kitto goes much further; for him, Marcellus' speech gives "the logical and dynamic centre of the whole play. We are in the presence of evil." Night speeches traditionally evoke evil; three times in *Hamlet*, in and around the central play scene, there are traditional allusions to night and evil—first rugged Pyrrhus "whose sable arms, / Black as his purpose, did the night resemble"; then "Lucianus" with his "midnight weeds," and Hamlet's own reflections on "the very witching time of night," which according to Kitto, "can hardly fail to bring back to our minds what was said on the battlements about nights that are wholesome and nights made hideous because of unnatural sin."[12]

Marcellus' is therefore an antithetical night speech; it evokes the calm and grace of the nights of Christmas, the scenic form of which has just been enacted, only to contrast the nights that the Danes are then living through. . . . Significant is the use in this speech of the word "Savior," the word used in Luke 2, and used nowhere else by Shakespeare. The special grace of Christmas is that man is to be saved by forgiveness of his sins; the inference is that whatever is to happen in the play to come will be the opposite.

## Notes

1 Emrys Jones, *Scenic Form in Shakespeare* (Oxford, 1971), p. 8.
2 L. C. Knights, *An Approach to Hamlet* (London, 1960), p. 38; J. Dover Wilson, *What Happens in Hamlet* (Cambridge, 1935), p. 74.
3 *Coventry*, ed. Hardin Craig, 207, 225, 435 ("This othur nyght soo cold").
4 E. Hennecke and W. Schneemelcher, eds., *New Testament Apocrypha* (London, 1963), p. 363; cf. *Coventry*, 287ff.
5 *York*, ed. Smith 34–35, 37–39; *Coventry*, 206, 217.
6 Cf. *Chester*, ed. Deimling, 13–16; *Towneley* (I), 24ff, ed. A. C. Cawley.
7 *Chester*, 372ff; *York*, 58; *Ludus Coventriae*, 81, ed. K. S. Block.
8 H. D. F. Kitto, *Form and Meaning in Drama* (London, 1956), p. 254.
9 Hardison, *Christian Rite and Christian Drama in the Middle Ages* (Baltimore, 1965), p. 46.
10 Dover Wilson points out in his note on 1.5.151 that the "cellarage" was commonly called "hell," a derivation from the mystery plays.
11 *An Approach to Hamlet*, p. 45.
12 Kitto, p. 313. *Hamlet* 2.2.456–57; 3.2.257, 391.

From *Comparative Drama* 14 (1980), 137–58 abridged, and Cherrell Guilfoyle, *Shakespeare's Play Within Play* (Medieval Institute Publications, 1990), pp. 21–39.

*Roy Battenhouse (1969)*

## Hamlet's Evasions and Inversions

The moral flaw evident in the Ghost, his lapsing from Christian norms which are residual in his language but neglected in his judgments, is the same flaw we are shown more at large in Prince Hamlet. Repeatedly, Shakespeare allows Hamlet some Christian phrase which is in ironic contradiction to Hamlet's un-Christian attitude accompanying it. Thus there is indicated the fact that Hamlet might have avoided his downfall, had he but paused to think on the gospel truths vestigially present in his own vocabulary. Dramatically, Hamlet's bits of Christian language are important as evidence of canons he is bypassing in his yielding to self-pleasing imagination. Since he is not utterly without knowledge of the Christian rule, but impetuously overlooks it, his persistence in revenge is a fault of his own making. His ignorance is voluntary—and all the more ironic because Shakespeare lets Hamlet cry: "let me not burst in ignorance." Deftly, Shakespeare is presenting an ignorance due to what Aquinas would call "sins of omission."

This point can be illustrated with numerous examples. In Hamlet's first scene on stage, we hear him say of his mother's remarriage:

> Would I had met my dearest foe in Heaven
> Or ever I had seen that day, Horatio.

Here the phrase about meeting one's foe in heaven reminds us of a wish which Christians ought to have (the salvation of self and enemy alike); but Hamlet is using the idea to express something abhorrent. A moment later we hear his oath, "For God's love"—thus heightening the irony. What he wishes, in the name of God's love, is a knowledge not of saving mysteries but of his father's Ghost, and (as we presently see) of the "foul play" which he suspects this day-avoiding visitor can reveal. A scene later, when he resolves to remember this Ghost's revenge commandment all alone in his brain, he does so (by Shakespearean irony) with the vow "Yes, by Heaven." Here he is taking Heaven's name in vain, violating the third of the Decalogue's commandments, having earlier violated its first and second ones. Then, after making an antic compact with the Ghost, he demands an oath of secrecy from his friends. This time he invokes as sanction: "So grace and mercy at your most need help you." What relation can grace and mercy have, actually, to the purpose Hamlet is treasuring in his heart? Ironically they signalize for us the values Hamlet is bypassing. And the same is true of Hamlet's later random oaths—for instance, his "'Sblood" and "by'r Lady" when he is indignant that his father is no longer idolized; and his oath "'Swounds" as he grabs Laertes by the throat. These oaths point to paradigms of Christian love which Hamlet might have appreciated, had he but taken the trouble. Auditors of the play may overlook this fact while the drama is being staged; yet it is embedded in the fabric of the action for our potential apprehension. Shakespeare, while engaging our imagination and emotions in a sympathy for Hamlet, is also at the same time defining the tragedy of an ignorance due to neglect.

Shakespeare's story differs notably from its versions in Saxo and Belleforest. These earlier chroniclers had set their tale in pre-Christian times, and thus had been able to define the hero's motives simply in terms of a pagan vengeance efficiently carried out—in Belleforest, in order to comfort the "shade" of an indignant Horwendil in Hades.[1] On this level they were writing a success story. Amleth, through using a madness wholly feigned, outwits the publicly known slayer of his father and succeeds in destroying this usurper and his court in a planned holocaust, after which he is elected king by a grateful populace. This version avoids the deeper question Shakespeare raises, that of an unintended ignorance in the hero's moral purposing. Shakespeare turns into genuine tragedy a tale which in Saxo and Belleforest had been largely epic in character and tone.

Occasionally I have been asked by students what other course of action Hamlet might have taken. What other ethical option was possible? I answer that if one poses this question as an ethical one purely, and without regard to the kind of action Shakespeare needs for his tragedy, then at least three other choices are conceivable for a man in Hamlet's shoes. He might, if he could but acquire the charity to desire a wholesome remedy for Denmark's ills, offer himself for training in a Christian friars' Order. For obviously Denmark's lethargic church needs at least one holy man of God to reawaken it; and the creative value of such a vocation for a prince is made plain by Shakespeare in *Measure for Measure*. Or, alternatively, Hamlet might have chosen a political role, such as Malcolm chooses in *Macbeth*, by fleeing suspected tyranny and then in exile awaiting such evidence of misgovernment as might justify a military invasion to take away the tyrant's power. Or, thirdly, he might have charged Claudius publicly with treachery and challenged him to a trial by combat—the procedure of Edgar in *King Lear*. In the Christian Middle Ages, this was the approved way of appealing for justice in doubtful cases. The vocation either of knight or of friar could have become a salvific one. But thus to turn the community's plight into a happy ending would be wholly unsuitable to the needs of tragedy, namely, a *tragic* hero. Hence, from the outset, Shakespeare so characterizes the disposition of Hamlet as to make improbable any of these ethical "might have done's." It is improbable that a Hamlet who has been accustomed to being the cynosure of all eyes would, on a sudden, humble himself to a role of patient rescue. (It is hard for a "rich" man, says Scripture, to enter "the kingdom of heaven.") So Shakespeare shows Hamlet choosing, instead, a private and "antic" form of priesthood, in melancholy suits of solemn black, and a mischievous version of statesmanship, in which the sword is used only for profitless dueling. Thus Hamlet's blind choices parody unintentionally the theoretical "might have done's" of an enlightened ethic. For tragedy requires exactly such irony.

The Hamlet of Shakespeare, therefore, is a hero who comes to grief through his mistakes. And each of his mistakes stems from what Aquinas would have called a double carelessness: at the highest level, neglect of Divine Law (through Hamlet's idolatry of his father's dignity and "commandment");[2] at a secondary level, neglect of the "proximate" rule of human reason (through his yielding to inordinate imaginations and unruly passions). Both levels of mistake are dramatized in Hamlet's reaction after hearing the Ghost's message. For here, in an episode which climaxes Act 1 and defines the basic quality of Hamlet's madness, we see him abandoning himself to conjuring, and lapsing into what Hamlet's friends call "wild and whirling words." A precedent in Elizabethan drama for this conjuring scene has been pointed out by Nevill Coghill.[3] In *Jack Juggler* (1570), Jack vows in proof of his name to play at juggling: "I will coniure the mole and God before" (line 110). This reference makes clear that the "mole" was a traditional devil figure, and that to conjure with him was conventional for a Vice character.

Antic behavior is not in accord with Hamlet's own ideal in saner moments— with his ideal of "blood and judgment ... well commingled"; of using all gently and not ranting; of being immune to fortune and to passion's slavery. But it accords with a fault Aquinas had described: "A man who is in a state of passion fails to consider in particular what he knows in general... [for] the reason is somehow fettered so as not to exercise its act freely, even as in sleep or drunkenness" (*S. T.* I–II.77.2). The fact that Hamlet is, on this occasion, drunk with rapture would diminish the vice of his capering, in the view of Aquinas, by making it accidental rather than directly intended. But that does not, when we consider its prior causes, excuse it of voluntariness. It but makes it the more pitiful, and tragically human.

If closely looked into, all Hamlet's particular mistakes in the play give evidence of a culpable carelessness. His accepting of Osric's invitation to a duel is but a final instance. Here the circumstantial facts suggesting the likelihood of a trap are numerous: the King's known aptitude for underhanded murder; his obvious need to silence Hamlet; a desperate Laertes, whom Hamlet has given cause for revenge and then further has offended by mad attack at Ophelia's grave; and Osric's conspicuous willingness to let Hamlet make a fool of him, if thereby Osric can humor Hamlet into consenting to the duel.[4] If only Hamlet had used his reason to weigh these circumstances, surely he could have surmised what was in store for him. He has, moreover, a kind of misgiving in his own heart, which Horatio suggests he listen to. But this also Hamlet shoves aside, through a fatalistic urge to "Let be." His subconscious will, evidently, is courting an opportunity to let himself go—to let rashness be praised. Basically this same explanation, I think, can be made as to why, earlier, Hamlet makes the mistake of putting on a playlet which gives away, unintentionally, his own secret; why he then misjudges the King's departure from it as the frighted flight of a "pajock," although circumstances could have told him that Claudius was here making an exit much to his credit in the public eye; why Hamlet makes no effort, in the closet scene, to find out what is behind the arras before stabbing through it; and why, afterwards, he makes no effort to avoid being sent to England, although he has forewarning of the plan. He prefers to tempt fate by neglecting reasonable considerations.

Robert Heilman has analyzed acutely the "quest for ignorance" in several of Shakespeare's tragic heroes.[5] He has commented on Lear's "stubborn clinging to blinders," and on Macbeth's "rejection of perceiving" by a narcoticizing of what he knows—through slipping into violence as both "a surrogate for knowing" and a barrier against it. Hamlet's case, I have been showing, corroborates this pattern for tragedy. Hamlet's subconscious quest is to evade his own knowledge of Heaven's canon against self-slaughter. He does this by counting his life "at a pin's fee"—and other people's lives too. True, he can feel enough compunction to "repent" for having slain Polonius, yet even here he evades genuine repentance by excusing his act as something Heaven has "pleased" to do through him, who is Heaven's scourge and minister. Here Heilman has noted Hamlet's impulse "to hedge repentance around with implicit self-justification," and has noted further that Hamlet's plea to Gertrude, "Forgive me this my virtue," is spoken to justify a claim to being "kind," rather than in self-criticism. In neither apology, we may add, is Hamlet repenting of his spirit of contempt. Nor does he resolve to be more humane in the future toward human fools like Polonius. On the contrary, he turns almost immediately to new imaginations of ecstatic slaughter: his "two schoolfellows" are but "adders fanged," whom it will be most sweet "sport" to blow to the moon! "They must sweep my way / And marshall me to knavery. Let it work."

Hamlet's notion of himself as Heaven's scourge should recall for us the biblical concept elaborated most clearly in Isaiah 10.[6] There the Assyrian is called the "rod" of God's anger, used providentially for punishing the sins of backsliding Israel. But Assyria's intentions are not truly righteous, only speciously so. Assyria has no desire to honor God, but rather its own glory. Hence Isaiah declares that when the day comes that Assyria begins to vaunt itself before God, attributing its victories to its own arm, God will cast this scourge into the fire and destroy his glory. In the case of Hamlet, have we not perhaps reached this point of boasting, either at the end of the play scene when Hamlet boasts to Horatio the success of his mousetrap, or more finally at the end of the closet scene when he flaunts in imagination the glory of his "craft"? If so, perhaps we may add that at these moments Hamlet is being cast, without realizing it, into the fire that will destroy him—the fire of the aroused anger of Claudius.

By the time Hamlet calls himself Heaven's "scourge and minister," he seems aware that such an office is a punishing one which also punishes its representative. Yet he continues to glory in violence. Rightly to be great, we find him saying a scene later, is to "find quarrel in a straw" when honor is at stake; hence let "My thoughts be bloody or be nothing worth!" Then, in a scene with Horatio, he boasts of his statecraft in sending Rosencrantz and Guildenstern to sudden death, "Not shriving time allowed." Here, as in his killing of Polonius, he is afterwards evading his own need for shrift. Yet, superstitiously, he can believe in shrift enough to let the thought of its being denied to his fellows enhance his sense of triumph, his implicit boast of dooming these men eternally.

Some interpreters of the play would like to regard Hamlet as a converted soul after his sea voyage—a man who is no longer a scourge but now a "saved" minister.[7] But the facts of the play, it seems to me, allow us no such conclusion. It is true that Hamlet acknowledges, fatalistically, a "divinity that shapes our ends"; but in doing so, he is praising not God ("in whose service is perfect freedom": Prayer Book), but rather "rashness" (in whose service Hamlet has found himself free to revenge). The "perfect conscience" he is longing to attain is one that will sanction a slaying of Claudius by viewing him as "this canker of our nature"—not as a *man* with a canker *in* him, but a mere evil substance. At the play's beginning, Hamlet had shown enough vestigial Christianity to cry out "Angels and ministers of grace defend us." But in subsequent moments of elation, including that at the play's ending, he forgets any such considerations. He becomes himself the minister, rather, of a poisoned chalice, and in that sense a fellow celebrant with Claudius in a Black Mass. Here the ritualizing of revenge has served to make it acceptable to the maimed consciences of Claudius and Hamlet alike as a kind of impersonal duty. It is the play's final instance of maimed rites.

For the gaming role of Black Priest, Hamlet has become ready by a progressive callousness—figuratively like the crab going backward, to which he had alluded in 2.2. The "readiness" proclaimed by him in his "augury" speech of 5.2.230 has nothing in common with that enjoined in Scripture (Mt. 24:44): "Be ye therefore ready, for in such hour as ye think not the Son of Man cometh." The Scripture means being ready, through responsible behavior, for the coming of Christ as judge. Hamlet means being ready for rashness and the opportunity it can bring to play judge. A biblical echo, the sparrow reference, when found in this upside-down context, alerts us to the tragic parody in Hamlet's version of readiness.

When calm returns to him on his deathbed, Hamlet regains enough residual humanity to respond to Laertes' request for exchange of forgiveness with a gallant reply: "Heaven make thee free of it" (that is, of fault). Yet it is noteworthy that he does not confess to any guilt of his own, as Laertes has done in his cry: "I am justly killed with my own treachery." Hamlet admits to no treachery, only to a wounded "name," which he enjoins Horatio to salve with a "tale." He is not contrite, as Laertes here is, or indeed as Claudius at least tried to be in the prayer scene of Act 3. It is paradoxical that Claudius and Laertes are in one sense more intellectually Christian than Hamlet, in that they clearly know they have offended against both "conscience and grace" (4.5.134, e.g.), whereas Hamlet has so identified revenge with conscience (i.e., with the conscience of a Greek Pyrrhus, which Hamlet has chosen to make-believe) that he can judge his killing of friends to be "not near my conscience," can feel no regret over slaying "brother" Laertes, and can poison Claudius with a "perfect conscience." Hamlet's callousing of natural conscience is thus displayed alongside Laertes' lapse of having given "to negligence" his conscience. Shakespeare is mirroring polar versions of moral evil, foils to each other.

In Horatio's summary speech on the tragedy, there are mysteries of cause which even he does not penetrate, though they are latent in the play's design as shaped by Shakespeare. One of these mysteries, as I have indicated, is that the "unnatural acts" have been caused by human negligence of Divine Law. Involved in Hamlet's case is the moral flaw of an evasion of those norms which are Denmark's and Hamlet's own baptismal heritage, and an idolizing, instead, of the man-centered canons of an "antique" world of pagan chivalry, through which man is betrayed into "antic" behavior. Through mistaking revenge for a filial duty, Hamlet (and, in a different way, Claudius and Laertes too) has allowed more than a little of the spirit of Nero to enter the human bosom—even though there is not, as in Nero's case, the extreme of a literal slaying of mother and a literal suicide.[8] There has been, however, a figurative slaying of mother in the disaster indirectly brought upon family and country, which are everyman's mother. Eight lives are sacrificed by Hamlet in a "purge" which parodies the purging action of Christian regeneration (for which, incidentally, the number eight is a traditional symbol).[9] "Whosoever slayeth Cain," says Genesis 4:15, "vengeance shall be taken on him seven fold." If Claudius is symbolically Cain (3.3.37), then his slayer, Hamlet (in legend, Lamech), suffers as God's vengeance on his revenge action the guilt for, and loss of, seven further family lives.

This tragic denouement manifests the mystery of divine judgment. True it is that in the corrupted currents of "this world," offense's gilded hand may shove by justice and preempt law, as Claudius has said.

> But 'tis not so above.
> There is no shuffling, there the action lies
> In his true nature, and we ourselves compelled
> Even to the teeth and forehead of our faults
> To give in evidence.

Hamlet has given us testimony that his own action has been that of Heaven's minister as merciless scourge. Further, the evidence of the play is that Hamlet, in using his father's signet to seal a sentence on his "friends," has usurped an authority to which he has not been publicly elected, and that in his whole role as scourge his justice has been of a tyrannical kind. Yet even a tyrant's deeds can subserve the justice of Heaven's wrath on the "something rotten" in Denmark, namely, all Denmark's neglect of brotherly love. According to Aquinas,[10] God permits scourges as his ministers because of the sins of the people. This fact does not excuse the wickedness of the scourge, but testifies rather to God's use even of the wicked to serve His providential purposes. The scourge in turn, Aquinas adds, suffers a divine vengeance, even in this world, in the fate of his self-made isolation from his fellow men and in the likelihood of his death by human retaliation. Is this not, indeed, Hamlet's fate? Meanwhile, however, a scourge's wild and cruel justice provides sinners an occasion to pray for Heaven's mercy—as Ophelia does before her death. And although we must say that Hamlet's final slaying of Claudius is an act of treason—as the bystanders rightly call it—yet it is also justice in a bleak mode, such as scourges are permitted to minister.

God's providence, although mysterious, is not as inscrutable as it seems to Hamlet. Boethius and Augustine understood it as a harmonious ordering of the disorder in nature introduced by man's cupidity. "A man's heart deviseth his way: but the Lord directeth his steps" (Prv 16:9). For Aquinas likewise, "all human affairs are subject to eternal law"—the affairs of good persons, by their acting in accord with it; but the affairs of wicked persons by their being imperfectly subject as to their actions, yet this imperfection on the part of action being "supplied on the part of passion, insofar as they suffer what the eternal law decrees concerning them, according as they fail to act in harmony with that law" (*S. T.* I–II.93.6). And Nicholas Trivet could say of the sinner: "Although he recedes, with reference to the end, from the order of the divine will in one way, he nevertheless falls into the order of the divine will in another; for in leaving the order of mercy, he falls into the order of justice."[11]

Shakespeare himself offers for our pondering, in this connection, a comment by the witty First Clown in the graveyard scene:

> The gallows does well, but how does it well? It does well to those that do ill.
> Now thou dost ill to say that the gallows is built stronger than the church;
> Argal, the gallows may do well to thee.

In other words, the man who prefers the justice of the gallows to the justice of the church may find the gallows doing well to him by punishing him for this ill judgment. But furthermore, as this Clown elsewhere remarks: 'Tis a pity that, in this world, "great folks" should have more countenance than their Christian fellows to drown or hang themselves. The whole world of the court, including the great Hamlet, is here being assessed through apt metaphor.

### Atonement's tragic parody

If we are willing to entertain a theological perspective there is finally one other, more comprehensive way of viewing the tragedy of Hamlet. I find it suggested by St Augustine's tracing of his boyish theft of forbidden pears (a general archetype of all sin or *hamartia*) to a "rottenness" in his own moral life. This involved, he says, his mimicking of a "maimed liberty," in perverse imitation of God:

> Wherein did I even corruptly and pervertedly imitate my Lord? Did I wish even by stealth to do contrary to Thy Law, because by power I could not, so that being a prisoner I might mimic a maimed liberty ... a darkened likeness of Thy Omnipotency? Behold, Thy servant, fleeing from his Lord and obtaining a shadow. O rottenness. . . .[12]

Here is an ultimate key to the logic of Hamlet's personal tragedy. For Hamlet, without realizing it, does pervertedly imitate his Lord. That is, he apes by his welcoming of rashness man's true liberty of obedience to charity. As a "scourge" Hamlet imitates inversely Christ's role as suffering servant. His flight from reality pervertedly imitates Christian pilgrimage; his being visited by a ghost is a reverse analogy to a baptism or a Pentecost; his longing for "the witching time of night" inverts the Christian hope; his gnostic wish that his flesh may melt and free him parodies a Christian desire for transcendence; and his Manichaean melodrama of "mighty opposites" counterfeits the Christian concept of a warfare between God and Satan. To sum it all up: Hamlet's strategy for setting the world right is a perverse imitation of the method of Atonement in Christian story.

Consider, in this last connection, St Augustine's metaphorical description of Christian atonement:

> The Redeemer came and the seducer was overcome. And what did our Redeemer to him who held us captive? For our ransom he held out *His cross as a trap*; he placed in it as a bait His blood.[13]

Or, again, this passage from Peter Lombard:

> Our Redeemer held up *His Cross like a mouse-trap* to our captor, and baited it with his Blood . . . God therefore became a man and died to overcome the devil.[14]

Yes, in a shadow-way, Hamlet does the same. With his celebrated "mousetrap" (the staging of a murder play) he plays God, as it were. He imitates Christ's work in a fascinating upside-down way. Whereas God in Christ put on flesh, that is humanity, in order that through this Man the world might be saved, Hamlet (substituting a reverse kind of incarnation) relinquishes his humanity to put on a mask of madness and thus visit a wicked world with his condemnation. Biblical echoes are here, but all of them in a transvalued version, a counterfeit version, an unwitting parody of atonement.

"The decision to return to Elsinore," so Roy Walker has written, "is to Hamlet in his degree what the decision to go to Jerusalem was to Jesus."[15] Perhaps so, but what a difference in degree! In lauding the mysticism of Hamlet's "obedience to divinity within," Walker fails to see that this obedience is but a tragic perversion of Christian mysticism. Or, again, there is G. Wilson Knight's comment: "In his own Renaissance terms, he [Hamlet] has attained to his Kingdom of Heaven."[16] This may be true; but we must not be misled, as Knight seems to be, into a confusing of the true biblical kingdom with its demonic analogue. Nietzsche's gospel is not Christ's nor, as Knight seems to think, an approximation to Christ's. It is in fact its rival version. Hamlet's delight in playing the antic is a reverse parallel to St Paul's willingness to be a fool for Christ; just as Hamlet's acceptance of fits of melancholy as a mode of mission is the tragic counterfeit of Paul's "When I am weak, then I am powerful" (2 Cor 12:10).

"Souls in their very sins," says St Augustine, "seek but a sort of likeness to God, in a proud and perverted, and so to say, slavish freedom."[17] A playwright who understands this has a basic clue for the structuring of Christian tragedy. He will recognize that tragedy can be a dark analogue of Christian redemption, a blind version of Atonement. Recall, for example, besides Hamlet's priestlike behavior, Macbeth's taking of a cup at the striking of a bell and celebrating pale Hecate's rites; or the elaborate language of sacrificial offering with which both Brutus and Othello envelop their crimes; or Romeo's drinking the cup at "Saint" Juliet's tomb-altar; or Richard II's imagined humiliation as a Christ betrayed by Judases. In each case, the tragic hero has taken as his god some imagination of his own heart, to which he then offers his life in an unintended mimicking of divine action.

The Shakespearean hero's defective action shadows Christian paradigm, in the same sense that falsehood inevitably depends upon truth, or the corruption of anything depends upon the good it corrupts. By ineradicable implication, a perverse nobility implies nobility, a defiled humanity implies something great that can be defiled. Waywardness is nothing but an ironic righteousness; just as evil is nothing but a deficient good. Thus tragedy, paradoxically, points us to the high calling man might have achieved, by showing us the empty shadow of it which he has chosen as his fate. In this respect, tragedy may be likened to an experience in Plato's cave, through which we are invited to discover that our backs are to the light. Or, it may be likened (as by T. S. Eliot) to a "wasteland" quest, whose apocalypse comes in a "decayed hole in the mountains" where there are towers "upside down in air... Tolling reminiscent bells." Reminiscent bells, deep-down inklings of the higher order betrayed, haunt the career of tragic heroes and heroines.

Understanding this, the Christian artist can perfect the logic of tragedy. He can give to any tragic downfall its proper shape as a "mistaken" version of religious self-abandonment, a topsy-turvy salvationism. Then, when the total action is rehearsed before an audience, some spectators will afterwards say, "How sad it had to be thus"; whereas others, who see the deeper meaning, will say, "How sad it had to be thus when it might have been otherwise." These two responses are the ones W. H. Auden has phrased in attempting to distinguish between the effect of Greek tragedy as compared with Christian. But I think this distinction can apply equally as well to two levels of our response to Shakespearean tragedy. For the levels are not necessarily mutually exclusive: the second can be added to the first as the fuller dimension of a progressive experience on the part of a spectator. The first is but an initial surface level of response to which all of us incline in our moods of half-enlightened paganism, whereas the second is a deeper level of response to which we may subsequently attain by drawing on the insight any man can have as a soul *naturaliter christiana*. Shakespeare himself dramatizes these two moods in a significant passage in *Richard III*. Commenting on the death of the two young princes, Richard remarks fatalistically: "All unavoided is the doom of destiny"—to which Elizabeth replies, "True, when *avoided grace* makes destiny" (4.4.218).

## Notes

1   See A. P. Stabler, "King Hamlet's Ghost in Belleforest?" *PMLA* 76 (1962), 18–20.

2   The dispositive cause of Idolatry, Aquinas explains (*S. T.* II–II.94), is a defect of nature on the part of man, either through ignorance in his intellect or disorder in his affections, both of which involve guilt. Further, idolatry (which is a

species of superstition) is the gravest of sins, since it lessens the divine sovereignty by setting up another God in the world, and "there is no kind of sin that idolatry does not produce at some time, either through leading expressly to that sin by causing it, or through being an occasion thereof."

3 *Shakespeare's Professional Skills* (Cambridge University Press, 1964), p. 11.

4 Because Hamlet rates Osric as a "waterfly," many producers of the play have thought Osric wholly effeminate and have played him as merely laughable. But I find convincing Nevill Coghill's contention that Osric is "a man who knows that his task is to bring Hamlet at all costs to fight the proposed duel. Therefore Osric puts up his smokescreen of affected language. Every time Hamlet starts aside from the wager into some digression, Osric brings him back to it with a short turn. In the end the fish is landed, and even the watchful Horatio has been deceived by the angling Osric." See *Talking of Shakespeare*, ed. John Garrett (London, 1954), pp. 46–47.

5 See Heilman, "'Twere Best Not Know Myself': Othello, Lear, Macbeth," in *Shakespeare 400* (1964), ed. McManaway, pp. 88–98; and Heilman's "To Know Himself: An Aspect of Tragic Structure," *Review of English Literature* 5 (1964), esp. pp. 48–49.

6 For Elizabethan commentary on this concept in Isaiah, see my "Tambulaine, the 'Scourge of God'," *PMLA* 56 (1941), 337–48.

7 E.g., Fredson Bowers, "Hamlet as Minister and Scourge," *PMLA* 70 (1955), 740–49.

8 Regarding parallels between Nero and Hamlet, see William Montgomerie, "More an Antique Roman than a Dane," *The Hibbert Journal* 59 (1960), 67–77.

9 The number eight can signify either renewal (as do the eight souls saved in Noah's ark), or conversely it can signify a false renewal (as do the eight bushels of florins in Chaucer's *Pardoner's Tale*).

10 *On Kingship*, tr. Phelan and Eschmann (Toronto, 1949), Chs. 6–8.

11 Trivet, as cited by D. W. Robertson, *Preface to Chaucer* (Princeton University Press, 1962), p. 26. See also Augustine, *City of God*, XXII. 2.

12 Augustine, *Confessions* II.[vi.]14 (Everyman ed., p. 29).

13 Sermon 130, *Post-Nicene Fathers*, First Series, VI, 499.

14 *Sentences* III.19, as quoted by C. Lattey, *The Atonement* (Cambridge, 1928), p. 164.

15 Walker, *The Time is Out of Joint* (London, 1948), pp. 143–44.

16 Knight, *Wheel of Fire*, 5th ed. (New York, 1957), p. 323.

17 Augustine, *On the Trinity* I.2.5.

From *Shakespearean Tragedy* (Indiana University Press, 1969), pp. 244–51, 260–65, abridged and revised.

*James Black (1978)*

## Hamlet's Vows

The lines in which Hamlet dedicates himself to the mission which the Ghost has set him ring with an echo which so far as I can tell has not reached the ears of any commentator upon the play. "I have sworn't," he says at the conclusion of his speech (1.5.92–112) which immediately follows the Ghost's departure. The speech begins,

> O all you host of heaven! O earth! What else?
> And shall I couple hell?

As a "swearing-in" Hamlet's asseveration and vow both echo and contravene an article of the Sermon on the Mount:

> Sweare not at all, neither by heaven, for it is the throne of God:
> Nor yet by the earth: for it is his foote stoole. (Mt 5:34–5)

As we shall see, the echo is more than fortuitous: the injunction against heedless swearing is not the only principle in the Sermon which bears upon Hamlet's situation.

Not only has Hamlet disregarded or broken away from the Sermon's directions against swearing: he also has sworn to exact an eye for an eye. He will ask Horatio, "Is't not perfect conscience to quit [Claudius] with this arm?" (5.2.67–8), but will receive no answer; and he desperately tries to justify striking back in his soliloquy "O what a rogue and peasant slave...":

> Am I a coward?
> Who calls me villain, breaks my pate across,
> Plucks off my beard and blows it in my face,
> Tweaks me by the nose, gives me the lie i' th' throat
> As deep as to the lungs—who does me this,
> Ha, 'swounds, I should take it: for it cannot be
> But I am pigeon-livered and lack gall
> To make oppression bitter. (2.2.574–81)

But his bitter rationalizing of retaliation seems hollow if set beside the words which in its anatomical details it seems to echo, "Whosoever shall smite thee on thy right cheke, turn to him the other also." And Hamlet's catalogue of his own personal wrongs in this soliloquy (significantly, not the wrongs done old Hamlet) sits uneasily with the Geneva's marginal gloss on this part of the Sermon: "Rather receive double wrong, than revenge thine own griefs" ("I knew you must be edified by the margent" is a remark Horatio will direct at Hamlet later in the play: 5.2.157).

A. C. Bradley says that Hamlet "habitually assumes, without any questioning, that he *ought* to avenge his father," and "Whatever we in the twentieth century may think about Hamlet's duty, we are meant in the play to assume that he *ought* to have obeyed the Ghost."[1] To agree with this conclusion we would have to accept that the play itself is the thing, a mere Senecan artifact embalmed and hermetically sealed in its own atmosphere; and, so far as *Hamlet* is concerned, Samuel Johnson would have been right in his judgement that Shakespeare sometimes "carries his persons indifferently through right and wrong, and . . . leaves their examples to operate by chance. This fault the barbarity of his age cannot extenuate."[2]

It also can be argued, of course, that when he has vowed in the first act Hamlet does not thereafter consistently assume that he ought to obey the Ghost: he at least speculates upon the possibility that it may have been a damned ghost that he has seen, or that the Ghost might have been a devil in a pleasing shape (2.2.602–7; 3.2.78–82). His appalling doubts about the task he has undertaken are voiced chiefly in the soliloquies. But what also appears to surface in at least one of Hamlet's speeches is an uneasiness in his mind concerning swearing itself. In 2.2 he abruptly changes subjects on Polonius. Polonius is listing the accomplishments of the players when Hamlet interjects, "O Jephthah, judge of Israel, what a treasure hadst thou!" and sings a snatch of what he calls a "pious chanson" to remind the nonplussed courtier that Jephthah's treasure was "One fair daughter, and no more, / The which he loved passing well" (2.2.408–13).

In Shakespeare's time, Jephthah, for what the Geneva margin calls "his rashe vowe and wicked performance of the same," was a famous pattern of reprehensible swearing. In *Henry VI Part III* Clarence says, "To keep that vow were more impiety / Than Jephthah's when he sacrificed his daughter" (5.1.93–4); and the Homily Against Swearing and Perjury uses him as a cautionary example:

> As well they use the name of God in vaine, that by an oathe make unlawfull promises of good and honest things, and performe them not; as they which doe promise evill and unlawfull things, and doe performe the same. . . . Of them that make wicked promises by an oathe, and will performe the same, we have example in the Scriptures, chiefly of Herod, the wicked Jewes, and of Jephthah. . . . The promise which [Jephthah] made (most foolishly) to God, against God's everlasting will and the law of nature most cruelly he performed, so committing against God a double offence.[3]

After Hamlet has given him the snatch of song, Polonius' response is:

|          | Still on my daughter. |
|----------|------------------------|
| Hamlet   | Am I not i' th' right, old Jephthah? |
| Polonius | If you call me Jephthah, my lord, I have a daughter that I love passing well |
| Hamlet   | Nay, that follows not. (2.2.414–18) |

Either Polonius does not quite catch Hamlet's drift or else he is resisting the implication that as a Jephthah he will sacrifice even his only daughter for a political advantage. He may feel that Hamlet has hit uncomfortably close to his plan of "loosing" Ophelia to Hamlet for the purpose of extracting information (2.2.158–66): Ophelia is a "Jephthah's daughter" in this sense.

But if we accept this exchange only as Hamlet "harping on daughter" (2.2.187) and baiting Polonius, we get no more from the business than Polonius himself understands. Polonius is talking about playing when Hamlet interrupts him. The purpose of playing, as Polonius understands it, is the recital of a standard repertoire—tragedy, comedy, history, pastoral, and so on. As Hamlet understands it, the purpose is to hold the mirror up to nature, "to show virtue her own feature, scorn her own image, and the very age and body of the time his form and pressure" (3.2.20–4). Is it merely an accident that as Hamlet talks to the players about the purpose of playing he should seem to echo in "the very age and body of the time his form and pressure" those words in his speech of dedication, "I'll wipe away . . . all forms, all pressures past"? The form and pressure of this present time of his is the substance of his vow—that matter which is now engraved upon the table of his memory. And as Polonius talks about playing and Hamlet thinks of it, perhaps Polonius momentarily becomes for Hamlet the nearest convenient mirror, a glass in which Hamlet sees not just Polonius the prating fool and ruthless intriguer, but also himself, a Jephthah. In "O Jephthah, judge of Israel" Hamlet may be harping not just upon Polonius and his daughter, but upon his own rash vow. For in terms of that vow Hamlet is a Jephthah too. Strikingly, while on the subject of playing-mirroring Hamlet also mentions Aeneas (2.2.451) and out-heroding Herod (3.2.14). Aeneas was famous for having sworn love to Dido and then being forsworn; Herod was not only "represented in the mystery plays as blustering and grandiose,"[4] he also is used in the Homily as a type of wicked swearer.

The vow that Hamlet has sworn is of the Jephthah-kind delineated in the Homily: a wicked promise sealed by an oath, with intention of performance. As swearing in the *manner* by which Hamlet has vowed is condemned in the Sermon on the Mount, so swearing to the *matter* of his vow is condemned in both the Sermon and the Homily. Obviously, the ethics of Hamlet's vow are very doubtful, and Hamlet's Jephthah allusion may arise, as I have suggested, out of his meditation upon this fact.

During their first exchange of words in the play Ophelia tries to remind Hamlet of his former addresses to her:

| Hamlet | I never gave you aught. |
| Ophelia | My honoured lord, you know right well you did, |
| | And with them words of so sweet breath composed |
| | As made the things more rich. (3.1.96–9) |

These addresses were "the holy vows of heaven" so roughly disvalued by Polonius, the "music vows" lamented by Ophelia (3.2.159). Hamlet here repudiates the memory of them because the word he has given to the Ghost has come after, and between. To break his promise to the Ghost would be to bear out what the Player King in *The Murder of Gonzago* observes: "What to ourselves in passion we propose, / The passion ending, doth the purpose lose" (3.2.192–3). The former vows to Ophelia (who just might be in the enemy camp) are at tragic cross-purposes with the fatal promise; and so Hamlet, a Jephthah who has vowed, must put away from him the daughter of Jephthah-Polonius.

The tragic situation of Ophelia, so deeply committed to both her father and the man she loves and breaking between the "mighty opposites" (5.2.61–2) in the Danish court, reflects the dilemma of Hamlet himself. And of course her plight emphasizes the link between Jephthah-Polonius and Jephthah-Hamlet. Little wonder that at times it is impossible to be certain whether it is the dead parent or the exiled lover who is the theme of her mad singing: "How should I your true love know? . . . He is dead and gone, lady" (4.5.23–32). She sings as well a curious Valentine song about love and commitment, about idle swearing and broken vows:

> Ophelia   Indeed, la, without an oath, I'll make an end on't—
> [sings]    By Gis and by Saint Charity,
>           Alack and fie for shame!
>           Young men will do't, if they come to't,
>           By Cock, they are to blame.
>           Quoth she, Before you tumbled me,
>           You promised me to wed. (4.5.57–62)

She is singing of the tradition whereby the first girl seen by a young man on St Valentine's day was to be his true-love—a customary obligation which doubtless, if Ophelia had her way, would be more honoured in the observance than in the breach. Hamlet is or has been her true love, but unknown to her he has made another commitment.

Hamlet's vows precipitate his and Ophelia's tragic plight in a Denmark whose king knows at what time to promise, when to pay—and who in fact recognizes the falseness of his "most painted word" (3.1.54). We may follow through the play a trail of broken promises with the hero—"promise-crammed," as he ironically describes himself (3.2.92), and with examples gross as earth of faithless vows all around him—clinging loyally to an oath, however irreligious, to perform a task which is both wrong and impossible.

## Notes

1  *Shakespearean Tragedy* (London, 1960), pp. 76–79.
2  "Preface to Shakespeare," in *Johnson on Shakespeare*, ed. Raleigh (Oxford, 1959), p. 21.

3   *Certaine Sermons or Homilies, Appointed to be Read in Churches* (1640), II, 48–49.
4   Dover Wilson, New Cambridge *Hamlet*, p. 274.

From *Renaissance and Reformation*, New Series 2, No. 1 (1978), 33–34, 38–45, abridged.

*D. W. Robertson (1980)*

# A Medievalist Looks at *Hamlet*

My own views are more extreme than Eleanor Prosser's, and differ in detail, although I should like to commend her highly for her careful research in primary sources and for her willingness to take seriously what she found there. The attitude adopted here was first formed many years ago and is in part a reaction against popular views of *Hamlet* that seek to make the protagonist admirable, in spite of the fact that he is an obvious moral weakling and an unrepentant felon, or to make him sympathetically "understandable" as an innocent adolescent in search of "identity." Shakespeare would have been completely unable to understand the latter view, since it reflects a peculiarly modern problem; the former would have been grossly repugnant to his sensibilities and inconsistent with attitudes toward tragedy current in his time. It is unfortunate that the morality of Shakespeare's tragedies has often been misunderstood since the shortsighted and historically inaccurate observations of Dr. Johnson, and today we suffer also from a reaction against nineteenth-century literalism and hypocrisy that makes it difficult for us to understand, much less to sympathize with, the moral principles embraced, often with surprising enthusiasm, by our medieval and Renaissance ancestors in Western Europe. These were frequently classical in origin, although transformed by attitudes that were then thought to be distinctively Christian. Above all, we should be aware of the fact that such principles were then practical, not merely theoretical, and necessary to the preservation of a reasonably livable social environment, however they may differ from views about human nature and society fashionable today.

I think that no one familiar with commonplace Christian ideas can fail to recognize in Hamlet obvious symptoms of what was called Sloth, the first of the vices to follow Pride in her procession in Spenser's *Faerie Queene*, and the "nurse" of all the rest (1.4.18–20). Sloth was not mere laziness, although it could be that, but a vice with spiritual as well as physical manifestations. Chaucer's Parson, who will do as a reasonably conventional authority, defines sloth as "angwish of troubled herte," which sounds like melancholy, and it is indeed true that melancholy was an attribute of sloth. The slothful man, the Parson tells us, does not wish to do any good thing but falls into despair, an aspect of the irremissible sin against the Holy Spirit, or God's love, which was conventionally exemplified in the person of the suicidal Judas.

Is Hamlet slothful? When we first meet him, he is dressed strikingly in black, a little like Spenser's monkish vice, wishing he were dead. The world, he thinks, is an "unweeded garden," because his mother has married Claudius after mourning the death of the elder Hamlet for only a month. Claudius is justified in saying that extended mourning "shows a will most incorrect to heaven." But Hamlet is obviously much more concerned about his mother's marriage than he is either about his father's death or the welfare of the state of Denmark. In fact, he accuses her of lust, certainly a villainous thought that the Parson might well have characterized as "bilge," since it is consistent neither with the Commandment "Honor thy Father and Mother," with the reflection of that Commandment in the Elizabethan catechism, nor with the character of Gertrude as we see it in the play. She has acted with obvious innocence, but with questionable judgment, on the advice of her Council; and her chief weakness seems to be an unshakable affection for her son. As for Hamlet, the idea that he should die to escape the unweeded garden of the world, instead of getting busy with his hoe, hardly demonstrates any fortitude. Moreover, by traditional standards, those who think the garden of the world to be hopelessly unweeded probably need a little weeding themselves. Our "hero" is not a very attractive character at the outset, and there is no reason to think that Shakespeare wished to make him so.

Hamlet rashly proceeds to confront the Ghost, even if it be a "goblin damned," denying that it can influence his soul, not because his soul is rational, but on the dubious ground that it is immortal, as if there were no immortal souls in Hell. Horatio's warning that he might lose his "sovereignty of reason" is futile, probably because not much of this sovereignty exists in Hamlet. "Desperate with imagination," or without rational control, Hamlet approaches the apparition, which immediately calls for revenge. Hamlet takes the bait at once, but soon displays those symptoms of sloth that will make him a lackluster avenger as well as a lackluster Prince. Responding to the Ghost's "Remember me," he vows to forget all trivial records and "saws of books," and then, almost in the same breath, proceeds to draw forth his notebook to record the saw, "one may smile and smile and be a villain." And when we meet him again in the second scene of the second act he is reading a book. Although the Ghost demands a vicious course, revenge, Hamlet blithely and foolishly assures Horatio that it is "honest."

Hamlet, having heard (as Shakespeare may have heard in the story of Alexander Phereus in Plutarch) that tragedies "make mad the guilty and appal the free" so that tyrants proclaim their guilt, cries, "O Vengeance!" and prepares the play *The Murder of Gonzago*. The reaction of the King to this bit of indirection does not, of course, prove his guilt to the court, for in the play the nephew of the player king murders him, not his brother, and the audience generally, if they thought of it at all, had every right to conclude that the play was a veiled threat on Hamlet's part to murder his uncle. It is clear that Hamlet should have used open means to restore order in his kingdom. The playlet is thus a merely malicious form of trifling, and is directed as much against the Queen as it is against Claudius. But she hardly reacts as a guilty person, for her first words to Hamlet afterward are "Hamlet, thou hast thy father much offended."

We should not forget that in Shakespeare's time Christianity was still a religion of love, not of righteousness, except perhaps among some extreme Puritans or other grim Old Testament literalists. Love reasonably directed is charity; love directed toward oneself or self-satisfaction through a creature is cupidity. Shakespeare's comedies for the most part cheerfully demonstrate the triumph of reasonable love, a theme consistent with what Jonson calls his "open and free nature"; his tragedies exhibit the destructive powers of malice, which is inverted love, the worst part of any vice.

Can a man be deliberately cruel to his mother and not unnatural? I hardly think so. When he so affrights her that she calls for help, Polonius reveals his presence behind the arras, and Hamlet (with princely courage, shall we say?) draws his sword and thrusts it through a man who cannot see him and whose identity is unknown to him. Our courageous and noble prince proceeds at once to go to work on his mother, maligning the father of his beloved Ophelia and seeking to demonstrate with the aid of a picture that his natural father was a better-looking man than Claudius and hence a more worthy object of her cupidity. He should be concerned about the state, not about his mother's taste in male flesh, which is not only irrelevant but not, in Gertrude, a great sin. Sexual pleasure with a husband is ordinarily a venial, not a deadly sin, and Gertrude is clearly no lusty young wench. But he succeeds in confusing her, denies emphatically that he is mad, and proceeds at once with obvious relish to plot against the lives of his best friends, Rosencrantz and Guildenstern.

He sends them off to England to be killed, "not shriving time allowed." Thus he thinks to damn them. With his usual false heroics, he boasts to Horatio,

> Why, man, they did make love to this employment.
> They are not near my conscience; their defeat
> Does by their own insinuation grow.
> 'Tis dangerous when the baser nature comes
> Between the fell and incensed points
> Of mighty opposites.

Horatio, who, if he had been entirely honest, should have objected to this piece of obdurate malice, simply says, "Why, what a king is this!" What a king, indeed! A man who murders his best friends for no good cause, hoping to slay their souls as well, and then denies any repentance for his deed, certainly deserves something.

Perhaps it is relevant to point out that impenitence is an attribute of sloth, and that it constitutes the worst sin of all, the irremissible sin against the Holy Spirit, or God's love.

As the end approaches we are reminded of Providential justice in a speech that has won for Hamlet more sympathy than he deserves. "There is," he says, "a special providence in the fall of a sparrow." He continues, "If it be now, 'tis not to come; if it be not to come, it is now; if it be not now, yet will it come. The readiness is all." The echo of Matthew 10:29—"Are not two sparrowes solde for a farthing, and one of them shal not fall on the ground without your Father?"—implies, because of the Scriptural context that would not have been lost to most members of the audience, that men are more important than sparrows, so that they have an obligation, in spite of the enmity of father, mother, or other relatives, to take up their crosses. Has Hamlet taken up his cross with patience and fortitude, or has he sought to outwit fortune with lies and "assays of bias"? The banal remarks about the time of departure reflect mere fatalism, an aspect of slothful "rechelessness." A man is "ready" when he has been a faithful servant, not a servant who begins to "smite his fellows" (Matthew 24:42ff.; Luke 12:42ff.). A part of man's "cross," and, as everyone knew, an essential feature of his "readiness," is penance, but Hamlet has just announced proudly that the murder of his schoolfellows is not on his conscience, and he is about to excuse himself to Laertes for the murder of Polonius. He was not to blame; his "madness" did it. This shows no contrition whatsoever, and Hamlet demonstrates no "readiness," either in word or in deed.

Hamlet's only real concern is for his own worldly reputation. It is for this that he stays Horatio's suicidal impulse, hoping, with persistent "wisdom for himself" that he can save it. There are no signs that his "godlike reason" does not still "fust unused" within him. He shows no realization of the kind exhibited by Laertes, no contrition for his abuse of his mother and Ophelia, much less for his murders. He has forgotten that "Foul deeds will rise / Though all the earth o'erwhelm them, to men's eyes."

Horatio sums up the play very well:

> So shall you hear
> Of carnal, bloody, and unnatural acts,
> Of accidental judgments, casual slaughters,
> Of deaths put on by cunning and forced cause.
> And, in the upshot, purposes mistook
> Fall'n on the inventors' heads.

Thus has Heaven directed the state of Denmark, not by intervening, but simply by allowing those "wise in themselves" to bring about their own destruction. Elizabethans did not regard befuddlement as a virtue, either personal, intellectual, "aesthetic," or moral. Hamlet faces no real "ethical dilemma," and there is no evidence whatsoever that he redeems himself. Malice, whether it proceeds from greed, ambition, sloth, jealousy, or frustrated appetite, spreads like a disease and can destroy a family or a kingdom as well as a man. This is what Shakespeare wished to demonstrate in his tragedies, and indeed demonstrated very well in this one.

# OTHELLO

## Comment and bibliography

Jealousy is a self-centered love that feeds on self-glorifying imaginations. How did Othello, a Venetian hero and noble Moor, fall into this mistaken passion? Romantic critics such as A. C. Bradley read him as simply flawless until his virtue gets turned against him by a devilish Iago. But more realistic observers have noticed in Othello, long before Iago's temptings begin, a flair for self-dramatizing and an intense interest in himself. "My parts, my title, and my perfect soul / Shall manifest me rightly," he tells us on his first appearance in the play. He relies for his sense of worth on "my services which I have done the signiory." Public esteem for earned merit is evidently what he treasures most. His love for Desdemona has arisen, he explains, because she admired his exploits and pitied his hardships. He values her, it would seem, as the most devoted "fan" of his own star performance. Critics such as F. R. Leavis (in 1937) and Leo Kirschbaum (in 1944) called attention to this "pride" in Othello and its accompanying shallow knowledge both of the real Desdemona and of himself. Bradley's mistake was to adopt Othello's view of himself. Alert subsequent critics have recognized that Othello's proneness to narcissism is what makes him vulnerable to Iago's creed as voiced typically in the boast to Roderigo, "I follow but myself" (1.1.59). Ironically, it is by directing Othello to look within that Iago destroys him, for inside himself Othello finds his jealous fear of being disgraced in public esteem. A shallow self, dependent on externals for its identity, lacks knowledge of an intrinsic self and of the virtue of humility that is man's best resource.

It is not surprising therefore that Iago can seduce Othello by urging him to regard "good name" as the immediate jewel of his soul. Bible proverb, it is true, rates good name as more to be valued than silver or gold—but far less than good deeds of love and mercy. To make good name one's *summum bonum* is spiritually disastrous. In the Bible it is the flaw that condemns the "scribes and pharisees" who would cleanse the outside of the cup but not the inside, and who "strain at a gnat and swallow a camel"—as Othello does when scrutinizing surface appearances but never penetrating to the heart. "Trifles light as air / Are to the jealous confirmation strong / As proofs of holy writ" (3.3.327). A lost handkerchief—lost in fact during Desdemona's act of compassion for Othello's headache—outweighs in importance to him the evidence of goodheartedness in her act. Othello's obsession with protecting his imagined sense of honor may remind us also of the jealousy of the tyrant Herod in the Bible, and we may recall that Judas leagued himself with the Herodians and the pharisees when he betrayed Jesus to them. The spiritual kinfolk of Othello are the Bible's self-righteous pharisees and Herodians and (we may add) a stoic mentality that cultivates an "apathy" of indifference toward the needs and feelings of others while yet indulging a passion for name and fame. (Othello's judgmental self-righteousness toward Desdemona is comparable to that of the stoic Brutus toward his friend Cassius in *Julius Caesar*.) A secular idealist can become madly stony-hearted, but always of course in the name of public order. The flaw of stoic virtue in Christian eyes was that it made its adherents into statues of stone. It relied on a reasoning devoid of grace, and therefore inclined Christians of a stoical bent toward Pelagianism.

Desdemona's virtue is of a different stamp from Othello's. When at their reunion in Cyprus he dotes in his "own comforts," she speaks in plural pronouns of their future together. When rebuffed by her husband she makes excuses for him and tells Iago "we must not think men are gods." When struck by him and called "Devil," she weeps; when told by him she is false, she but asks him to explain and offers simple denial, "As I am a Christian." She goes to bed asking God to send her uses "Not to pick bad from bad but by bad mend." Cassio has hailed her sincerely as "divine Desdemona" and turns to her as his intercessor when dismissed by Othello. Supposing that her husband will want to be reconciled to the friend who aided his courtship, she cannot imagine his misinterpreting her advocacy. On suffering his unexplained accusations she tells us that "unkindness may defeat my life, / But never taint my love." Every theatre audience has wanted to come to her assistance. Othello remains blind to the mercy she continues to voice after her strangulation. He dies in stoic fashion, as T. S. Eliot observed, trying to cheer himself up.

Our anthology reprints first of all the explanation of Othello's tragedy offered by David Jeffrey and Patrick Grant, who emphasize the hero's obsession with "reputation" and evaluate it by the moral norms of the Bible, St Augustine, Boethius, and Erasmus. Jeffrey and Grant also make evident that the malignity of Iago is not "motiveless" (as Coleridge supposed) but rather is motivated by envy. Second, some comments by Roy Battenhouse develop in detail the play's suggested analogy of Othello to Judas; also he notices imagery which contrasts Othello with holy Job and with St Veronica. Thirdly, the Folio's reading of "base Judean" is supported with multiple evidence by Joan Holmer.

Several items in the supplementary bibliography give testimony to the correctness of the phrase "base Judean." Nasseeb Shaheen notes that Geoffrey Fenton, on whose *Tragical Discourses* (1567) Shakespeare could have relied for his plot, likens the Moor to Judas the betrayer of Christ. Cherrell Guilfoyle thinks that Shakespeare's imagery suggests not only a Judas-Othello but also the biblical Herod, whose jealousy led him to slaughter innocents. S. L. Bethell's careful review of the "diabolic" in the play's imagery (none of it derived from Cinthio) sees this as signaling the damnation not only of Iago but of his pupil Othello also. Bettie Doebler argues that Shakespeare invites in the spectator a recalling of the *ars moriendi* tradition that evaluates suicide as damnable. Paul Siegel and Paul Ramsey, disagreeing with critics who credit Othello with a deathbed repentance, find instead conclusive evidence of his damnation.

Othello's concern for the Egyptian handkerchief signals for Herbert Coursen the hero's lapsing from his baptismal heritage into a preference for pagan mysteries. Coursen also contrasts Othello's view of marriage with Christian teachings in the Bible and in the Elizabethan *Homilie on Matrimonie*, and notes how a parody-marriage with Iago replaces Othello's marriage to Desdemona. Ruth Levitsky points out that Protestant and Catholic theologians alike faulted the stoic ethic for its emphasis on self-sufficiency. Othello's noble greatness serves a selfish goal.

Othello's claim to value Desdemona more than "perfect chrysolite" has a hidden irony, as Lawrence Ross shows by tracing the chrysolite image to Rv 21:20, and as Lynda Boose shows by tracing it to Song of Songs 5:14. The gem's biblical associations with a holy love provide a contrast to Othello's idolatrous love. John Wall observes that the "monstrous birth" Othello conceives by giving an open ear to Iago has an implied contrast to the holy birth conceived by the Virgin Mary's kind of listening in gospel story.

## Supplementary bibliography

Battenhouse, Roy. "Iago's Pelagianism," in *Shakespearean Tragedy* (1969), pp. 380–84.

Bethell, S. L. "Shakespeare's Imagery: The Diabolical Images in *Othello*," *Shakespeare Survey* 5 (1952), 62–80.

Boose, Lynda E. "Othello's 'Chrysolite' and the Song of Songs Tradition," *Philological Quarterly* 60 (1981), 427–37.

Coursen, Herbert R. *Christian Ritual and the World of Shakespeare's Tragedies* (1976), pp. 204–34.

Doebler, Bettie A. "Othello's Angels: The *Ars Moriendi*," *English Literary History* 34 (1967), 156–72.

Guilfoyle, Cherrell. "Medieval Scenic Form in the Last Scene of *Othello*," *Comparative Drama* 19 (1985), 305–20.

Heilman, Robert. *Magic in the Web: Action and Language in 'Othello'* (University of Kentucky Press, 1956), pp. 41–43; 96–98; 154–68; 603–18.

Kirschbaum, Leo. "The Modern Othello," *English Literary History* 11 (1944), 283–96.

Leavis, F. R. "Diabolic Intellect and the Noble Hero," *Scrutiny* 6 (1937), 259–83; and *The Common Pursuit* (New York, 1952), pp. 135–59.

Levitsky, Ruth. "All-in-All Sufficiency in *Othello*," *Shakespeare Studies* 6 (1970), 209–21.

Milward, Peter. "More on 'the base Judean'" *N&Q* 36 (1989), 329–31.

Ramsey, Paul. "Othello: The Logic of Damnation," *The Upstart Crow* 1 (1978), 24–35.

Ross, Lawrence J. "World and Chrysolite in *Othello*," *Modern Language Notes* 76 (1961), 683–92.

_____. Edition of *Othello* (Indianapolis: Bobbs Merrill, 1974).

Shaheen, Nasseeb. "Like the Base Judean," *Shakespeare Quarterly* 31 (1980), 93–95.

Siegel, Paul. "The Damnation of Othello," *PMLA* 68 (1953), 1063–78, and *PMLA* 71 (1956), 279–80.
Wall, John N. "Shakespeare's Aural Art: The Metaphor of the Ear in *Othello*," *Shakespeare Quarterly* 30 (1979), 356–66.

*David L Jeffrey and Patrick Grant (1970)*

# Reputation in *Othello*

Othello dies in Cyprus because he cannot endure the ill-esteem of his peers in Venice, and their denigration of his good name. Granted, he suffers to realize he has been made to murder his wife as Iago's dupe, but he does not stab himself in a blind frenzy of grief for this reason, rather as one realizing that his power and command are taken off (5.2.332) and his reputation destroyed. It is possible, pursuing this line of thought, to interpret the main action of the play as basically concerned with good and bad fame. For it is an initial faulty attitude to fame that tinctures Othello's love for his wife and provides the opportunity for Iago to initiate the plot that destroys his master.

We must distinguish between earthly fame and heavenly fame, a contrast based on Scripture. A distinction between earthly vanity and heavenly glory is often made, for instance in Galatians 1:10: "For do I now persuade men or God? Or do I seek to please men? For if I yet pleased men, I should not be the servant of Christ." . . . In Augustine, the classic definition of the two loves, *caritas* and *cupiditas*, one based on "the enjoyment of God for His own sake, and the enjoyment of one's self and one's neighbour in subordination to God," the other aiming at "enjoying one's self and one's neighbor, and other corporeal things, without reference to God,"[1] is central to the contrast which underlies the important discussion of fame in *De Civitate Dei* (V, 12–20). There Augustine distinguishes true glory based on the "love of righteousness" and the "love of God," from the false glory of the pagans based only on renown among men and "desire of human praise."[2]

Distinctions, therefore, between such concepts as charity and the law, the New and Old Testaments, the glory of God and glory of men, are of the essence of the contrast between fame or reputation which is good (based on the referral of personal glory to God) and fame which is bad (based on glorification of the self). As late in the seventeenth century as Milton's *Paradise Regained*, this is the import of Christ's reply to Satan, where Job is described as famous "in Heaven, on earth less known; / Where glory is false glory, attributed / To things not glorious, men not worthy of fame."[3]

An important corollary to the Augustinian synthesis is the further connection of good and bad fame to the philosophic tradition that descends through

Boethius. It is clear that in the *Consolation of Philosophy* there is a link between the idea of fame and the figure of Lady Fortune. In the Middle Ages, indeed, fame is traditionally the sister of Fortune, as Chaucer reminds us when talking of fame and "her suster, Dame Fortune."[4] Certainly in the *Consolation of Philosophy* Boethius must discover not only the error of his attachment to Lady Fortune, but also the wrong-headedness of his anxiety about loss of good reputation among men. He must come to see the folly of his complaints against Providence in Book I. These include the long catalogue of his services to the state, adduced as evidence of the good name which he sees as unjustly destroyed.... He must learn that proper fame is not based on human acclaim, as eventually he does, under the guidance of Philosophy.

It is helpful to establish this link between fame and fortune for no other reason than the obvious one that a fall from high place on the Boethian wheel of fortune is a commonplace model for Elizabethan tragic dramatists. It is thus easy to see how Shakespeare could readily accommodate Othello's interest in fame to the conventional framework of tragedy. Thomas Sackville demonstrates this relationship in the first stanza of *The Complaint of Henry Duke of Buckingham* from that celebrated repository of tragic predicaments *The Mirror for Magistrates*, where are combined both concepts, honour and fortune:

> Who trusts too much in honour's highest throne
> And warely watch not sly dame Fortune's snares:
>
> . . . .
> Behold he me, and by my death beware.

Nor is there any doubt that the distinction between good and bad fame was itself commonplace. Considering merely two of the most popular school textbooks of the day we find the distinction made ubiquitously and with clarity. Erasmus' *Enchiridion Militis Christiani* (the title itself suggests affinities with the theme of *Othello*) and Vives' *Introductio ad Sapientiam* were read by Elizabethan schoolboys, and there are strong arguments that Shakespeare knew them. In the *Enchiridion* Erasmus claims "the only true honour proceeds from true virtue," and "even this reputation it is sometimes necessary to avoid," for "the sole honour that a Christian must look for is to be approved by God, not by men."[5] Vives distinguishes good and bad reputation in terms of a similar contrast between the approval of God and the approval of men. "Let every man descend into himself," he advises, and "there he shall discover how little attaches to him from fame, from reputation, from veneration, and from the honour bestowed by the people from which he would take glory."[6]

Othello's love is conditioned from the beginning by his attitude to fame, and this, essentially, is what proves fatal to him. In language that reminds us of Boethius, Othello is confident even before he meets the senate that the many times he has risked his personal safety for the welfare of the state will stand in his favour before his accusers. He assures Iago that reputation will protect him:

> Let him do his spite;
> My services, which I have done the signiory,
> Shall out-tongue his complaints; 'tis yet to know—
> Which, when I know that boasting is an honour,
> I shall promulgate—I fetch my life and being
> From men of royal siege, and my demerits
> May speak unbonneted to as proud a fortune
> As this that I have reach'd. (1.2.17–24)

Although this attitude must appear to approach a view of reputation that errs by relying too heavily on earthly fame, it is nevertheless true that Othello is not without justification at least for his confidence. He has not broken the letter of the law. He has married Desdemona legally, by her own consent and within the auspices of the church. The senate, therefore, he knows must protect him, and he maintains a noble and imposing righteousness, all the more impressive when those around him are in turmoil. Yet, to wish to be judged, as he does, in terms of the law alone is also surely to tempt providence with self-righteousness. The total attitude which we see in Othello, insisting however confidently on justice and the law, and relying for vindication on a good reputation among men, certainly courts the condition we have described.

The influence which Othello allows the acclaim of men to exert upon him is of course not confined to this single instance. It can be traced throughout the play as a motif which is of singular importance for the interpretation of the career of Othello as tragic hero. Even in the account of the courtship in the first act we find Othello winning Desdemona by accounts of his military prowess, by stories of "battles, sieges, fortunes" (1.3.130), of "moving accidents by flood and field" (1.3.135). Two lines near the end of this famous courtship speech encapsulate its real significance:

> She lov'd me for the dangers I had pass'd,
> And I lov'd her that she did pity them. (1.3.167–68)

Judging from these lines, Othello's love for his wife would seem to be based on her acclaim of his military reputation, and there is no attempt by Othello to offset this by referring his love, on the model of good fame, to God.

This argument does not at all imply, however, that Shakespeare makes of Othello a simple cardboard representation of the wrong kind of fame. Hardly. The speech we are discussing is one of the most compelling and beautiful in the play, and even the Duke remarks on hearing it, "I think this tale would win my daughter, too" (1.3.171). But while critics are often content to suggest that the naive, splendid, and magniloquent Othello has married idealistically for love despite convention, and that we should feel sympathetic to such affirmation of romanticism, we might suggest a modification, rather than a cancellation of this view. Othello's poetry is of course admirable, as is his composure in face of the abuse he endures. We do indeed find ourselves hoping that things will work out well for him. But there is already, if we have eyes to see it, too much evidence that they will not. Even from the beginning we can detect in Othello a foolishness as well as merely a naivete, and what is more disconcerting, there is a certain blindness to this foolishness. Othello not only flaunts convention; he does so for the wrong reasons. His self-esteem as a man of reputation invites him to a love relationship that can only be described as uncarefully meditated. But for the moment fortune and her sister fame are conspiring in his favour.

Other places where Othello invokes reputation may now come to mind. In his explanation of why he desires Desdemona to accompany him to Cyprus, the overwhelming insistence of Othello's argument is that his reputation as a soldier will not be impaired by her presence, and the Duke should therefore give his assent:

> And heaven defend your good souls that you think
> I will your serious and great business scant,
> For she is with me; . . . no, when light-wing'd toys,
> And feather'd Cupid, foils with wanton dullness
> My speculative and active instruments,
> That my disports corrupt and taint my business,
> Let housewives make a skillet of my helm,
> And all indign and base adversities
> Make head against my reputation! (1.3.266–74)

From the beginning Othello sees love and marriage as readily imbued with implications for fame and reputation.

Again, when Cassio is cashiered we learn from Emilia that Othello will not hear a suit because:

> the Moor replies,
> That he you hurt is of great fame in Cyprus,
> And great affinity, and that in wholesome wisdom
> He might not but refuse you. (3.1.45–48)

Othello will not hear Cassio, it appears, because the injured Montano is a man of reputation of "great fame," and no doubt for Othello to commiserate with Cassio in such circumstances would be to jeopardize the integrity of his own reputation. Not only do we suspect Othello of some expediency here, but there can be no clearer example of the dangers of bad fame. For had Othello refused to let this expediency overrule mercy, and concern for reputation overrule charity, had he given Cassio a hearing, he would have protected himself against the plot which destroyed him.

Reputation once more becomes a central issue when Othello becomes convinced that he has lost Desdemona:

> O now for ever
> Farewell the tranquil mind, farewell content:
> Farewell the plumed troop, and the big wars,
> That makes ambition virtue: O farewell,

> Farewell the neighing steed, and the shrill trump,
> The spirit-stirring drum, the ear-piercing fife;
> The royal banner, and all quality,
> Pride, pomp, and circumstance of glorious war!
> . . . .
> Farewell, Othello's occupation's gone! (3.3.353–63)

Why Othello's occupation should be so irrevocably destroyed by his wife's supposed adultery is hard to see, except in terms of the fact that his love of his wife is bound up in an unfortunate manner with his self-esteem as a man of reputation. It is worth noting here that Iago detects this too. As he drives Othello towards the outburst we have just cited, he is careful to torment the Moor with suggestions of the painful consequences of the loss of good name among men:

> Good name in man and woman, dear my lord;
> Is the immediate jewel of our souls:
> Who steals my purse, steals trash, 'tis something, nothing,
> 'Twas mine, 'tis his, and has been slave to thousands:
> But he that filches from me my good name
> Robs me of that which not enriches him,
> And makes me poor indeed. (3.3.159–65)

Finally, as we have seen, even as he dies Othello's mind returns to reputation. Perhaps we may say in consequence he does not ever recognize the whole truth about the error of his ways, and in the last folly of his suicide, when he cannot see any hope for himself of the mercy he denied both Cassio and Desdemona, we discover the real tragedy of the story.

Duped into believing his wife a whore, agonized by the thought of his fame destroyed in the eyes of men, Othello the "old man" so rigorous in his application of the law, is led by his "ancient" to insist on justice. But it is a perverted justice he seeks, neither informed by wisdom (*sapientia*) nor tempered by mercy, but based on the abuse of passion and supported by specious evidence interpreted by the logic of reason (*scientia*). From this pursuit only chaos can ensue. So Othello's heart is hardened. He shuts himself off from wisdom, love, good fame, and murders his wife. He becomes fortune's fool, prey to circumstance, and to the tyranny of his own passions. His human nature is perverted, and he is reduced to incoherency as his noble poetry is debased by gross and bestial language, until finally he cuts himself off from salvation by the crime of self-murder.

As the play ends, Othello comes to recognize himself as fortune's fool (5.2.324) but his recognition serves only to emphasize the enormity of his final crime. He takes his own life, not overwrought and deprived of the use of his faculties, but calmly, and with knowledge of the circumstances of his act. To the end he maintains his crucial and mistaken allegiance to bad fame. He sees himself, ironically, as one who loved "not wisely, but too well," never appreciating that one cannot love well without wisdom. So his last request involves the future of a reputation which he will not live to see traduced. His death is moving, perhaps even noble. But these emotions we must temper with pity, that such a potentially great soul should be led to such foolishness, dying, as it were, by his own knife.

## Notes

1  *On Christian Doctrine*, 3, 10, ed. Philip Schaff, *A Select Library of the Nicene and Post-Nicene Fathers of the Christian Church* (Buffalo, 1887), II, 561.
2  *The City of God*, V, 14, ed. Schaff, II, 96–97.
3  *Paradise Regained*, III, 68–70, ed. Merrit Y. Hughes, *John Milton, Complete Poems and Major Prose* (New York, 1957).
4  G. Chaucer, *The House of Fame*, 1. 1547, ed. F. N. Robinson, *The Works of Geoffrey Chaucer* (Cambridge, Mass., 1933).
5  *The Enchiridion*, tr. and ed. Raymond Himelick (Bloomington, Ind., 1963), p. 188.
6  *Introduction to Wisdom. A Renaissance Text Book*, ed. Marion Tobringer (New York, 1968), p. 92.

From *Shakespeare Studies* 6 (1970), 197–203, 206–07, abridged.

*Roy Battenhouse (1969)*

# Othello as a Judas

The analogy closest to the completed circuit of Othello's career is the one touched on by Paul Siegel's observation that this hero's act of self-murder follows the example of Judas. In Othello's own last speeches there are signals of this analogy in his likening himself to "the base Judean" who threw away a pearl "Richer than all his tribe" and in his final comment:

> I kissed thee ere I killed thee. No way but this,
> Killing myself, to die upon a kiss.

Although some editors have preferred to read "Indian" (Quarto, 1622), the twin images of priceless pearl and deadly kiss evoke the Judas who betrayed with a kiss, and whose bargaining away of Christ-the-pearl inverted tragically the parable of the merchant of Matthew 13:45. Othello all too obviously has become "egregiously an ass," as Iago predicted (2.1.318), and in this respect is the Judas of Elizabethan proverb (see *Love's Labor's Lost* 5.2.631). Furthermore, the fact that Judas was Christ's only disciple from his own tribe of Judah, and thus was a traitor to family in betraying Christ, must have made him in Shakespeare's eyes a particularly apt archetype for the domestic tragedy of Othello.

In what more specific ways could the story of Judas be parallel to the tragedy of Othello? Let us recall some aspects of the biblical account. In Matthew 26 (see also John 12), Judas is concerned for the worldly value of a certain "alabaster" cruse, and not for the mystery which this vessel is devoted to celebrating. When the ointment from the alabaster is poured out on the feet of Jesus by Mary (in Western tradition usually identified with Mary Magdalene), it signifies her understanding of his mission of sacrifice in the work of atonement. Judas does not understand the mystery of atoning sacrifice. He upbraids Mary's act, by the norm of his own narrower kind of righteousness. He thinks her alabaster vessel should have been committed solely to his treasury, so that he could use it for conventional works. Need I expound the analogy of this attitude to that of Othello in his valuing of the "monumental alabaster" (5.2.5) of Desdemona's body? Throughout the drama he has supposed that her body should be devoted solely to himself and his ideals of nobility—and not at all to that "reconciliation" in the name of "grace" for which Desdemona pleads (in 3.3.47) because she wishes to "atone" Othello and Cassio (4.1.244).

Judas so resented Mary's act that he decided to turn to Christ's enviers to make a covenant for Christ's betrayal. Othello similarly, because he resents Desdemona's Christlike hope for atonement, makes a covenant with her envious adversary, Iago. At a Last Supper during which Christ speaks of his body as a memorial unto the "forgiveness of sins," Judas prefers to go out into the night to keep a bargain of betrayal. Likewise Othello, when offered a bedroom communion with Desdemona, has no mind for forgiveness but instead, in loyalty to his own blind sense of justice, mocks the reality of communion with a perverse kiss of death. Judas discovered afterwards, to his shame, that he had betrayed "innocent blood"; and as recompense he hanged himself. Even in his remorse he had not come to understand the meaning of forgiveness. The same is true of Othello, even though he too has seen forgiveness exampled before his very eyes in the spirit of the righteous one he has victimized. Thus Othello's tragedy involves not merely the "mistake" of having slain an innocent person but the deeper sin of rejecting grace—by neglecting the "mercy" to which Desdemona was dedicating her alabaster body while also preserving this "vessel" (4.2.83) for Othello.

We need not infer that Shakespeare was equating Desdemona with Christ. She quite sufficiently identifies herself by her oath "As I am a Christian" (4.2.82), and in the bedroom scene by her cry "Heaven have mercy on me!" (5.2.33). This does not mean that her life has been without fault. Indeed, earlier in the play, out of her pity for human suffering, she has committed a number of indiscretions. One of them is glanced at by the clown in Act 3, scene 4, when he jests: "I will catechize the world for him; that is, make questions and by them answer." The clown is here wittily suggesting that Desdemona is better at catechizing than at understanding her pupil—which is certainly the case in her manner of approaching Othello on Cassio's behalf. In this sense, there is some truth in her ultimate testimony, after Othello has strangled her, that "Nobody, I myself" is responsible for her death—although it is also true that she dies "guiltless" of Othello's specific charge and yet is forgiving this fault in her "kind lord." These three utterances, spoken almost surrealistically as if from a world beyond death, carry the paradox of a humble confession of fault on the part of a Christian who fulfills charity in her death.

This mystery a Judas-like Othello has profaned by backsliding into the noble "barbarian" he was before his baptism. His tragedy can be traced to a majestic loyalty to blind ideals. A self-centered mode of virtue has caused him to fall victim to Iago's tempting, and later, when the facts are set right, to pursue a vain glory one more step to a brutally honorific suicide.

Once we ponder Othello's overall likeness to Judas, it makes fully coherent his underlying psychology. I do not mean that we see him as deliberately cuing his attitude by reference to Judas; indeed, the final allusion in his mouth is probably more of Shakespeare's making than comprehended by its speaker. To us, however, it becomes a clue for understanding this hero as a man whose love of name has made him blind to charity; and thus his jealousy can be seen as something more than a sexual jealousy. We can be aware, in retrospect, of a jealousy for personal honor which both preceded and continues after his disbelief in Desdemona's chastity. And this explains why, in the midst of his sexual jealousy, Othello could exclaim:

> I had been happy if the general camp,
> Pioners and all, had tasted her sweet body,
> So I had nothing known. Oh, now forever
> Farewell the tranquil mind! Farewell content!

His peace of mind is dearer to him than Desdemona. Hence, ironically, he would rather have her defiled and himself ignorant of it, if thereby he may retain an undisturbed confidence in himself. Such a narcissistic love of self-image accords with his attitude at the beginning of the play: "My parts, my title, and my perfect soul / Shall manifest me rightly" has been his boast. He has felt no compassion for Brabantio, or later for Cassio. Having developed none for Desdemona either, he is consistent in denying compassion ultimately to himself, his own flesh and blood.

Othello's stance in his first scene, when Brabantio with officers comes to seize him, is emblematic and constitutes a parody of Christ's attitude when arrested at Gethsemane. Othello says chidingly to his accusers: "Keep up your bright swords, for the dew will rust them." Christ had said to Peter: "Put up your sword into the sheath; the cup which the Father hath given me, shall I not drink it?" The situations have a strange affinity. But Christ's gentle rebuke was to an over-eager defender, not to his arresters; and it was said out of a willingness to suffer humiliation, not with Othello's intention to "out-tongue" complaints against him. In the drama, it is an instance of inverted analogy. And it is possible, perhaps, to see another such upside-down analogy to Christ at a midpoint in the play, when Othello is offered a handkerchief by Desdemona to soothe his anguished head but impatiently brushes aside this napkin. Any playgoer familiar with the Veronica legend (one of the Stations of the Cross in churches) might see here a parody of Christ's suffering brow and a contrast to Christ's acceptance of Veronica's napkin. Whether Shakespeare had in mind these analogies some readers may doubt. But one can say that in the two episodes I have mentiond, both of them at important points in the drama, their artistic shape conveys an added meaning if referred to the paradigms I have cited, and we know Shakespeare to have invented both scenes without any hint from Cinthio.

He has invented also a later scene in which Othello, after rejecting Desdemona's testimony that "Heaven" knows her honesty, retreats into the self-pity of an ironic Job. Here, in the verbal references to "affliction," "sores" and "patience," all scholars have recognized allusions to Job. But by implication Shakespeare is portraying a grotesque aping of holy Job. Job when tested called on Heaven to resolve his perplexities. Othello is taking his whole vision of life from a Satan-like Iago. And after saluting patience only conditionally, Othello soon calls on the "cherubin" Patience to "look grim as Hell!" Thus he would make the cherubin's office, traditionally that of charity, sanction his own demand for revenge. Ever since his vow by "yond marble heaven" (3.3.460), his justice has reflected a heart turned to stone. As a would-be priest of this heaven, Othello can weep only over Desdemona's supposed apostasy from his own ideal, and over his own supposed obligation to offer her up in sacrifice to it. He begins Act 5, scene 2, by communing self-centeredly with his own soul and its sense of "cause"; and then, as if aping a celebrant at a service of Tenebrae, he ritualizes his task to "Put out the light, and then put out the light." He is thus like Judas who gave himself to the "night" of a Pharisaic self-righteousness. The accumulative analogies touched on cohere with the Judas one, which resonates finally in Othello's speech of suicide.

When made aware of his crime against Desdemona, Othello partly shuffles off responsibility for it onto fate, the stars, and his merely "unlucky" deeds. Instead of being contrite for his vengefulness, he blames only his folly and ignorance. He blames his ignorance of Desdemona's innocence—but not his own ignoring of Christian duty in having sworn a "sacred vow" to serve revenge, nor his now continuing to ignore Christian duty by turning to self-slaughter. On Othello's last speech, Gratiano comments: "All that's spoke is marred." And Gratiano is a commentator who has earlier told us what a "desperate" turn involves: it involves a "fall to reprobation" (5.2.209). Othello is clearly among the reprobate by Shakespeare's implication. We may say of his suicide that it is related to Christian sacrifice by disjunctive analogy—just as Dante's bleeding wood-of-the-suicides is inversely analogous to the holy wood of Calvary. It is we, however, and not Othello, who can undersand it thus. His vision must be from within a narrower frame than that which is implied in the play's total design.

From *Shakespearean Tragedy* (Indiana University Press, 1969), pp. 95–102 abridged.

*Joan Ozark Holmer (1980)*

## The "Base Judean" [editor's title]

Let us consider anew the case for "the base Judean" reading. The arguments that have been marshalled for the "Judean" reading are: (1) Judas was the only one of the twelve disciples who was a Judean; (2) the *Geneva-Tomson Bible* explains "Iscariot" with a significant juxtaposition of words, for Judas' home is "in the *tribe* of *Judah*" (italics mine), and Judas was seen as representative of the Judeans, the only "tribe of the world" to fall from Christ, although analogically any sinful man could be a Judas and Judean crucifying Christ anew through sin (see Heb 6:6); (3) Shakespeare never uses "tribe" elsewhere to indicate Indians; (4) the shared identity of the first syllable of *Juda*s and *Jude*an invites the suggestion of Judas; (5) Judas, like Othello, betrayed innocent blood; (6) Judas' token of betrayal was a kiss not unlike Othello's "I kiss'd thee ere I kill'd thee" (5.2.359); (7) "pearl" conveys familiar Biblical connotations that support the "Judean" reading; and (8) the crucial modifiers, "the" and "base," raise more problems for "Indian" than for "Judean."[1] We might also note that Judas' kiss was popular as a proverb which Shakespeare used (see Tilley, J92), and the very gesture of "throwing away" with one's own hand (5.2.347–48) may perhaps relate to Judas' gesture of throwing away the silver for which he had exchanged Christ: "And when he had cast downe the silver pieces in the Temple, he departed and went, and hanged him self" (Mt 27:5).

The issue of Othello's foolishness as opposed to "ignorance" tends to complement the "Judean" reading because Judas was not ignorant that what he threw away was valuable, and his action was not only foolish but "base" and therefore greatly lamented later. The "Jewishness" of Othello's and Judas' gesture would have been strikingly clear to an Elizabethan audience who, as G. K. Hunter has demonstrated, understood "Jewishness" as a moral condition of spiritual blindness to true value, applicable to Christians as well as infidels—the "Jewish choice" being to throw away Christ; Judas, the first of Christ's chosen few to betray Him, typified this choice, as in George Herbert's poem "Self-condemnation" where the "Judas-Jew" is one who "doth love, and love amisse,"[2] or as Othello puts it, "one that lov'd not wisely, but too well" (5.2.345).

Othello's tears shed before he kills Desdemona clarify through parallelism the significance of his tears shed before killing himself. In both situations Othello's emotion is heartfelt but misguided. That Othello believes his "cruel tears" and sorrow are of a "heavenly" nature (5.2.21) indicates his blindness to the nature of true heavenly sorrow which is redemptive and not destructive, which seeks first to save through loving forgiveness and not kill through vengeful judgment. If we are moved then by Othello's tears, we are also moved to hoping that sorrow will stay his hand. So also we are moved by his final tears, but then we do not know that his hand stays—only for a moment—upon his sword. If we feel his first weeping was misspent because it afforded Desdemona no mercy, must we not also view his final weeping in a similar light?

Lawrence Ross explains the important theological context for understanding the difference between mere sorrow and true repentance. On the basis of extensive evidence from homiletic literature, he demonstrates that Shakespeare's audience would have clearly understood the difference between true confession and repentance as opposed to its signs without its spirit or "Judas repentance":

> Some thinke all weeping and lamenting for sinne is repentaunce: so should Esau, Judas and Caine repent.

> ... howsoever *temporaries* [i.e., temporary believers] and unregenerate men may make an outward confession as *Saul, Judas, Pharaoh*, and others did, yet the truth is there is much guile in their confessions.... Confession must come from an honest heart, purposing not to sinne....

Ross contends that although Othello is not "hypocritical," he is "self-deceived" because his sorrow is not that which prompts true repentance but rather "worldly sorrow which, as St Paul writeth, 'causeth death.'" Since Christian literature traditionally images repentance as spiritual medicine, Ross finds that Othello's comparison of his tears to "med'cinable gum" is not merely decorative fancy: The point of the image is that Othello believes his tears are "med'cinable" as the tears of repentance are supposed to be. But the outcome of his repentance proves him mistaken; for "that weeping is not good, which blindes the eye of our faith, but only that which quickens it" and his failure to effect "a change, or departure from sinne" marks his grief the "unreformed sorrow" of the desperate man whose eye of faith can see no hope of genuine cure.[3] Tragically Othello's "subdued eyes" subdue him quite.

In only Matthew's gospel are Peter's denial of Christ and his consequent remorse immediately juxtaposed with Judas' remorseful confession and suicide (26:75, 27:3–5). Clearly Matthew's juxtaposition of these two sinners' different responses educates the reader about how to repent truly. The *Geneva Bible* states that Peter "was lively touched with repentance by the motion of Gods Spirit," for men fall so that they might "fele their owne weaknes and acknolege his great mercie" (26:75, gloss). Peter, although weeping bitterly, does not hastily embrace suicide because he does not despair of God's mercy.... Built into Othello's final speech are juxtaposed and contrasting exemplars of repentance, Myrrha and Judas, by whom we can evaluate the nature of Othello's repentance as a moral or only an emotional change. Othello compares his tears to Myrrha's, but the superficiality of that comparison is revealed when he chooses to follow not Myrrha's but Judas' response to woe.

Erasmus' *Enchiridion*, an extremely popular work and a "grammar school text" which Shakespeare could have been expected to know well, contains a passage that cogently explains why Othello's and Judas' suicides are so morally mistaken. "The charite of a christen man [Erasmus writes] knoweth no properte: let hym love good men in Chryst / evyll men for Chrystes sake ... he shall hate no man at all / no more veryly than a faithful physicyan hateth a sycke man: let hym be an enemy onely unto vices: let hym despyse the commytter of sacrilege / not the man: *let hym kyll the turke / not the man: let hym fynde the meanes that the evyll man perysshe suche as he hathe made hym selfe to be / but let the man be saved whom god made...*" (italics mine).[4] Erasmus' passage clearly indicates that Othello acts in an un-Christian manner, killing not the Turk or evil man within him whom he had made but rather his very self whom God made.

## Notes

1 See Richmond Noble, *Shakespeare's Biblical Knowledge* (1935; rpt New York: Octagon, 1970), pp. 90–92; 272–73; Roman B. Halas, *Judas Iscariot* (Washington: Catholic University Press, 1946), p. 40; Lawrence J. Ross, ed., *Othello*, pp. 246–47, 261.

2 Hunter, "The Theology of Marlowe's *The Jew of Malta*," *Journal of the Warburg and Courtauld Institute* 17 (1967), 214.

3 Lawrence J. Ross, *The Shakespearean "Othello": A Critical Exposition on Historical Evidence*, (Diss. Princeton 1956), pp. 1021–23; Ross, ed., *Othello*, p. 248.

4 Erasmus, *Enchiridion* (London, 1533), ch. xv, sigs. N2–N3.

From "Othello's Threnos: 'Arabian Trees' and 'Judean,'" *Shakespeare Studies* 13 (1980), 150–53, 157–61, excerpts abridged.

# TROILUS AND CRESSIDA

## Comment and bibliography

The editors of the 1623 Folio intended to place this play immediately after *Romeo and Juliet*, but withdrew it from that position on encountering a legal snag over rights to the text. Belatedly able to print it, they tucked it in between the histories and the tragedies although without a listing in the volume's table of contents. The story is clearly a tragedy. It is based chiefly on Chaucer's *Troilus and Criseyde*, and it turns about Chaucer's theme of the brevity and brittleness of earthly glory. Its love story tells of the self-defeat that followers of Cupid bring on themselves, while its interlocking story of Troy's war tells of a city destroyed by a cupidity for reputation.

The passion of Troilus for Cressida is like Romeo's for Juliet in being engendered by the physical beauties his eye seizes on. He mentions these in the play's opening scene when telling Pandarus he is "mad In Cressid's love." By the middle of the play he can describe himself as a "strange soul" longing for "waftage" to the fabled Elysian fields "Where I may wallow in the lily beds / Proposed for the deserver." With the help of Pandarus, who is an accommodating friend not unlike (although not as naive as) the Friar in *Romeo and Juliet*, Troilus comes to enjoy those fields in the bed of Cressida, who like Juliet is equally love-stricken but modestly withholds her consent until his labors of courtship have demonstrated his deserving. Cressida, however, is more sophisticated than Juliet and warns Troilus that along with a "kind of self" that resides with him she has "an unkind self" that will "leave" to be the fool of another, since only the "gods above" have a wise love. "I will presume in you," replies Troilus, a constancy that outlives beauty's "outward" aspect and thus be "uplifted." Her response is, "Prophet may you be!" To that hope she swears and goes on to declare that to swerve from it would deservedly label her false. Momentarily, she is pledging a lifting above cupidinous love to a kernel of constant love.

But the next morning brings a crisis in the news that Cressida's father wants her returned to him. She meets it by telling Pandarus, "I will not go." Her expressed readiness to "forget my father" approximates the norm of Genesis 2:24. Troilus, however, does not support this resolve; he tells her she must be handed over. Four times she questions this decision, but receives the reply, "No remedy." He blames "the blest gods" for taking her away, and says that "Injurious Time" is robbing him of her. "Be *thou* true," he insists, unaware of the irony of his own falsity. With a Troilus thus unwilling to be "constant" to anything other than a sentiment for her, Cressida relapses into accepting from the Greeks whatever protection Diomedes may temporarily provide. She settles for the melancholy truth that "The error of the eye directs our mind" (5.2.113) and acknowledges her own turpitude. But Troilus, made desolate by what he regards simply as *her* revolt against the bonds of heaven, concludes by turning to a "Hope of revenge" to hide his inward woe. We recognize in both lovers a betrayal of the prophetic hope they swore to.

The self-centered "constancy" of Troilus in the love story is paralleled by the self-centered "perseverance" of Achilles in the war story. In the middle of the play and while Troilus is bedding with Cressida, we hear in the Greek camp a lecturing of Achilles by Ulysses, who is telling him that the only remedy against losing "reputation" as a warrior is to persevere in deeds required by the public's liking for "new-born gawds." He must forgo a serving of Cupid, he is told, and instead fight Hector as a service to the fashions of the present time, or else his public will give their worship to Ajax. He takes this advice in order to outdo Ajax for public honor—thus illogically overlooking the fact that the only honor Ajax is actually getting is a reputation for prideful and stupid self-display. Surely, this kind of perseverance is intended by the dramatist to nudge us into recalling the very different norms of, let us say, *The Castle of Perseverance* in medieval drama—just as, similarly, the so-called "constancy" of Troilus is a challenge to us to remember Shakespeare's Sonnet 116, where true love does *not* bend with the remover to remove.

In the Trojan camp, meanwhile, the war over Helen has been debated and defended in a Council scene of contradictory arguments. Troilus has argued for the keeping of Helen because it would be dishonorable to avoid the wife one has chosen—a reasoning he will later forget in Cressida's case. Paris has argued that giving up Helen would impute a blame for his theft and would disgrace his compatriots who approved it. Hector's reply is that pleasure and revenge have "ears more deaf than adders" to the voice of true decision, and he appeals to Aristotle's moral philosophy of the laws of "nature and nations" to support the conclusion that Helen should be returned. But having arrived at this truth, Hector nevertheless resolves to set it aside because "our joint and several dignities" depend on keeping her. Thus Hector ends by agreeing with Troilus that their own future canonization by fame depends on their fighting against her return. In short, a reputation for glory is more important to them than obeying moral laws.

But, ironically, it is this very concern for reputation that causes Hector to spare in the name of courtesy the life of a downed Achilles, who after retiring returns with a gang that slays an unarmed Hector to assure Achilles the reputation of victory. After all, unfair play is the quicker way for gaining renown and for overthrowing the enemy's city to boot. Cassandra's warnings to Hector, dismissed as foolish by Troilus, come true.

The ironic futility of Hector's bravery is highlighted by a scene that immediately follows his sparing of Achilles. Seeing an anonymous Greek in "goodly armor," Hector vows to "hunt thee for thy hide," and then counts his "day's work done" when he has got the armor, only to find within it a "most putrified core." Considered naturalistically, the victim's body cannot have putrified so immediately, as S. L. Bethell was the first critic to point out, and hence Shakespeare's language here is metaphorical or figurative—like the language of "whited sepulchre" used in the Bible to describe hypocrites whose fair "outside" covers over an inner life that is morally rotten. Moreover, as Bethell adds, this truth applies to everyone in the play except Cassandra and Andromache. It states thematically the import of the play as a whole.

Supporting it is another biblical echo, the one voiced by Pandarus when he asks, "Is love a generation of vipers?" He is responding to Paris's description of love as hot deeds, and to the comment of Helen, "This love will undo us all. O Cupid, Cupid, Cupid!" The associating of such love with a generation of vipers can bring to mind for Christian auditors the use of this phrase three times by Christ in Matthew's gospel (3:7; 12:34; 23:33), where it describes the Pharisees who speak fair words from an evil heart and will be adjudged to hell for their lack of good fruit. It is by echoes such as these that the dramatist's Christian framework for understanding the tragedy of ancient Troy becomes fully evident.

Our anthology includes two pieces of recent commentary. One is David Kaula's expounding of the significance of the Trojan-Greek "mad idolatry." The play's contexts that refer to Helen, Kaula points out, call to mind the whore of the book of Revelation and Elizabethan commentaries on this archetypal captivator of foggy minds. Moreover, in the play as in the Bible, idolatry is punished with a "botch." Secondly, a short essay by Maurice Hunt brings out the irony theatre-goers could perceive in several speeches of the play where a Christian implication is touched on but abandoned by speakers who prefer a diminished meaning of their own language. They unwittingly illustrate St Paul's contention that the Gentiles are responsible for their tragedy when, while capable of knowing the Supreme Good, they prefer an idolatrous worship of the creaturely.

For supplementary reading, very useful is Barbara Parker's commentary on the warped perceptions in both the Trojan and the Greek camps. The Trojan apotheosis of Helen, she notes, is paralleled by Aeneas's apotheosis of Agamemnon, who fails to see the indictment of himself in the contention by Ulysses that the sun's "medicinable eye" corrects ills. Furthermore, while time is blamed as the devourer, it actually winnows away illusion's husk. Stephen Lynch details the delusions of Troilus, including Hector's profane hope of sainthood through Helen's canonizing him and Cressida's sanctifying him. Regarding Hector, Lynch remarks that the warrior he kills resembles his own parading of a goodly appearance lacking in intrinsic virtue, and in this respect may remind us of the Prince of Morocco in *The Merchant of Venice*. V. M. K. Kelleher regards the moral failure of Hector as "the single most important event in the play," since it relates ironically to the better man he might have been.

John Cox points out that already in *Lucrece* 1476 the woe of Troy was traced to a "trespass of thine eye" in Paris, and that in the play when Cressida chooses trespass she does so (like Adam in Genesis) against her better knowledge. Roger Owens observes that the Prologue's allusion to Deadly Sins outlines the moral failings that will be the concern of the remainder of the play. Cassandra's reference to "polluted offerings" emphasizes the cultural sin.

J.A. Bryant adds to Bethell's observations the contextual pertinence of Matthew 23 as a whole in its denunciation of those who preach but do not practice, who do their deeds "to be seen by man," and who reject prophets and wise men. Shakespeare may well have meant to associate Elizabethan England in some sense, Bryant thinks, with the Greek and Trojan world of misty motives and misdirected loves.

## Supplementary bibliography

Bethell, S. L. *Shakespeare and the Popular Dramatic Tradition* (London, 1948), pp. 122–28; rpt. New York, 1970.

Bryant, J. A., Jr. *Hippolyta's View* (1961), Ch. 5.

Cox, John D. "The Error of Our Eye in *Troilus and Cressida*," *Comparative Drama* 10 (1976), 147–71.

Kelleher, V. M. K. "*Troilus and Cressida*: Shakespeare's Vision of Fallen Man," *Unisa English Studies* 11 (1973), 8–14.

Lynch, Stephen. "The Idealism of Shakespeare's Troilus," *South Atlantic Review* 51 (1986), 19–29.

_____. "Hector and the Theme of Honor in *Troilus and Cressida*," *The Upstart Crow* 7 (1987), 68–79.

Owens, Roger. "The Seven Deadly Sins in the Prologue of *Troilus and Cressida*," *Shakespeare Jahrbuch* 116 (1980), 85–92.

Parker, Barbara. *A Precious Seeing: Love and Reason in Shakespeare's Plays* (New York University Press, 1987), Ch. 7.

Parker, M. D. H. *The Slave of Life* (1955), pp. 76–87.

*David Kaula (1973)*

## "Mad Idolatry" in *Troilus and Cressida*

*Troilus and Cressida* is one play that has almost escaped the "theologizing" kind of analysis Roland M. Frye repudiates in *Shakespeare and Christian Doctrine*. True, several biblical allusions in the play have been identified, but so far only J. A. Bryant, Jr. has tried to discover a thematic significance in any of them. Typical of the general trend of *Troilus* criticism in this respect is the most recent book-length study of the play, which, even though it seeks to examine it in relation to its cultural context, finds nothing in it that needs to be explained with reference to the Bible or specifically Christian ideas.[1]

This neglect may seem justified in view of the play's pagan setting and concentration on the secular activities of love and war. Yet it does offer several indications that it is concerned in some way with religious matters. The central situation of the play, the war over Helen, is defined by Hector as an act of false worship or "mad idolatry," a making of the "service greater than the god" (2.2.56–57). Troilus bears this out when he exalts Helen to the point of comparing her to the pearl of great price (2.2.81–83), and when he claims that by fighting for her the Trojans will gain a kind of sainthood or "canonization," a "promised glory" worth more than the "wide world's revenue" (2.2.202–06). While the Greeks for obvious reasons show little inclination to idolize Helen, they have certain idolatrous practices of their own. They display a rather strained reverence for Agamemnon's "godlike seat" (1.3.31), they manipulate Achilles and Ajax as if they were rival deities competing for their "worship" (2.3.177–183), and Ulysses deifies the state when he equates it with "providence" and describes the "mystery" in its soul

> Which hath an operation more divine
> Than breath or pen can give expressure to. (3.3.203–04)

These attitudes are augmented by a great many references in the play to religious objects and ceremonies—to gods, altars, sacrifices, oaths, prayers, prophecies, adorations, maledictions, and the like.

It might be argued that Shakespeare is using religious language here primarily for decorative purposes, merely to add rhetorical or imagistic embellishment to activities he still intends to be judged in secular terms. Whenever Shakespeare repeatedly resorts to a certain terminology, however, it is well to consider whether he might be presenting it as an implicit commentary on the attitudes he is dramatizing. If he shows the Greeks and Trojans as variously engaged in "idolatrous" forms of worship, then presumably he has in mind a contrary mode of worship, a legitimate way of serving both gods and lesser beings. It is this implied perspective that might be illuminated by the biblical allusions in the play, not only those identified by Richmond Noble, but also a number of others that have not been noticed before.

In one sense the most important character in *Troilus* is Helen, for even though she appears in only one scene, through her conduct she directly or indirectly motivates everything that happens in the play. In their several discussions of Helen, the other characters see her from sharply contrasting viewpoints, sometimes as a creature of "inestimable" beauty and value, sometimes as a "whore" and "contaminated carrion." If all her attributes are considered together, she seems to have much in common with a biblical figure often mentioned in contemporary religious polemics and one that indeed seems to have had an influence on Shakespeare's portrayal of Cleopatra. This is the Whore of Babylon, both as she is depicted in Revelation 17 and 18 and as her image is elaborated in the several Elizabethan commentaries on Revelation. Both she and Helen are objects of intense

idolatry, including kings and merchants among their worshippers; both are outwardly gorgeous and inwardly corrupt; both are identified with great wealth, with
bloodshed and death, and with intoxication, madness, and disease.

The parallel is first suggested in Troilus' outcry against the sounds of battle in
the opening scene:

> Fools on both sides! Helen must needs be fair,
> When with your blood you daily paint her thus. (1.1.86–87)

Troilus intimates not only that Helen is a "painted" woman but that the color she
is painted is red. The Whore of Babylon is "araied in purple and skarlat" (Rv 17:4,
Geneva) and is the cause of massive bloodshed: "And in her was founde the blood
of the Prophetes, and of the Saintes, and of al that were slaine upon the earth" (Rv
18:24). Although the word "painted" is not applied to the Whore of Babylon in
either the Geneva Bible or the other sixteenth-century translations, it often occurs
in the Protestant commentaries on Revelation. "Shee hath painted her face,"
writes Gifford, "and hath set forth her selfe in such worldly pompe, bewtie, glory
and riches, as the like hath not been seene";[2] and Junius produces an analogy to
Troilus' image of blood-painted Helen when he writes: "She is red with blood,
and sheddeth it most licentiously, and therefore is coulored with the blood of the
Saints."[3]

At the beginning of the second scene Helen is described as accompanying
Hecuba

> Up to the eastern tower,
> Whose height commands as subject all the vale,
> To see the battle. (1.2.2–4)

Geographically the eastern tower would not seem to be the most suitable one for
viewing a battle on the Trojan plains, but there is a biblical precedent for both its
location and its height in the tower that was built by men who came from the
"East" and said: "Goe to, let us build a citie and a tower, whose top may reach
unto heaven" (Gn 11:4). Babylon's eastern location is emphasized by Fulke when
he compares it to Rome: " For that which Babylon in the East was to the Jews, the
same is Rome, whiche is, Babylon, the west to the Christians."[4] Gifford also identifies "Babell in the East" with "Rome the Westerne Babell" (p. 343). Situated on a
tower "Whose height commands as subject all the vale," Helen rules over all the
kings and princes who are fighting for her, as the Whore of Babylon is said to be
the "great citie, whiche reigneth over the Kings of the earth" (Rv 17:18).

In the Trojan debate a few scenes later, Troilus expresses a very different attitude towards Helen when he replies to Hector's charge that "she is not worth
what she doth cost / The keeping":

> Is she worth keeping? Why, she is a pearl
> Whose price hath launched above a thousand ships
> And turned crowned kings to merchants. (2.2.81–83)

As Noble points out, the lines seem to contain not only a Marlovian echo but also an allusion to Matthew 13:45–46: "Againe the kingdome of heaven is lyke unto a marchant man, that seketh good perles. Who having founde a perle of great price, went and solde all that he had, and boght it." In applying this image to Helen, Troilus is implicitly identifying her with the heavenly kingdom or New Jerusalem, the city that, personified as the bride of Christ, opposes the Whore of Babylon in Revelation.

Before Troilus delivers his defense of Helen, Hector has already presented the counterargument in what are among the most important thematic lines in the play:

> 'Tis mad idolatry
> To make the service greater than the god;
> And the will dotes that is attributive
> To what infectiously itself affects,
> Without some image of th' affected merit. (2.2.56–60)

More succinctly, when Paris argues for keeping Helen, Priam rebukes him with the words: "Paris, you speak / Like one besotted on your sweet delights" (2.2.142–43). Such terms as "mad idolatry," "dotes," and "besotted" are repeatedly used by the commentators in describing the intoxicating effect the Whore of Babylon has on her devotees. Bullinger writes that "beying infected with errours, yea rather asotted, and cleane out of their wittes, they have ben madde in Idolatrie";[5] Fulke that "they are in mad dotage" (f.110); Gifford that they are "blinded and besotted with the love of the whore" (p. 128); and Junius that the Whore is "in deed most pernitious, besotting miserable men with her cuppe, and bringing upon them a deadly giddinesse" (p. 65). Later, in the one scene where Helen herself appears, Paris shows just how besotted he is when he unintentionally describes her as exercising a lethal enchantment: "Sweet Helen, I must woo you / To help unarm our Hector" (3.1.138). As Helen has already disarmed the vacillating Hector in one sense, so she will be the cause of his disarming in another when Achilles finally catches him with his armor off.

In direct contrast to Troilus' glorification of Helen, Thersites several times bluntly labels her a "whore," and it is this view of Helen that is elaborated in the final discussion of her in the play. When Paris asks who deserves Helen best, himself or Menelaus, Diomedes replies, "Both alike":

> He, like a puling cuckold, would drink up
> The lees and dregs of a flat tamed piece. (4.1.61–62)

The metaphorical connection between wine-drinking and sexual corruption also appears in the portrait of the Whore: "the inhabitants of the earth are drunken with the wine of her fornication" (Rv 17:2); her cup is "ful of abominations, and filthines of her fornication" (Rv 17:4).

Although Shakespeare in his portrayal of Helen nowhere directly paraphrases Revelation, there seem to be enough similarities between Helen and the Whore of

Babylon to indicate that he was thinking of a connection between the two. Such a connection would not be as implausible as it may seem at first, for since Troy from the Virgilian standpoint was considered the forerunner of Rome, and since in Revelation Babylon is likewise identified with Rome, their two female representatives could easily be interpreted as analogous. Also as Troy was traditionally regarded as justly punished for its presumption and its sensual excesses,[6] so Babylon is one of the main biblical emblems of godless pride and luxury. In a play Shakespeare was certainly familiar with, Marlowe's *Dr. Faustus*, Helen had already been presented, if not as a counterpart to the Whore of Babylon, then as the object of a dangerously misguided devotion. In Faustus' eyes she is not merely the "peerless dame of Greece" but "heavenly Helen." In kissing her he finds heaven in her lips, an illusory promise of immortality that for the moment enables him to forget the imminence of his damnation (5.1.90–105).

Shakespeare for no obvious reason chose to set the action of the play in the seventh year of the war, as Agamemnon indicates: "after seven years' siege yet Troy walls stand" (1.3.12).[7] The number seven assumes an obvious importance in Revelation, with much of the apocalypse unfolding through sequences of seven seals, trumpets, and plagues. The sevenfold process culminates in the downfall of Babylon, when the city will be visited with "plagues" and "burnt with fire" (Rv 18:8).

Of the seven plagues described in Revelation the most significant one in this connection is the first, called a "noysome, and a grievous sore" in the Geneva Bible but a "noysome and a sore botch" in the Great Bible and the Bishops' Bible (Rv 16:2). According to Bullinger, this botch "signifieth a canker, a fistula, and swelling sores or boyles, but chiefly the pockes of Inde, which others call the disease of Naples, some the French pockes, and some the Spanish" (p. 482). The botch is mentioned in *Troilus* when Thersites at his first appearance attributes running "boils" to the "General" and calls him a "botchy core" (2.1.2–6), a curse that equally applies to the whole camp both because of the double meaning of "General" and because Agamemnon is supposed to represent the "nerves and bones of Greece, / Heart of our numbers, soul, and only spirit" (1.3.55–56). The botch is also among the diseases mentioned in the series of frightful curses with which Moses threatens the idolatrous Israelites in Deuteronomy:

> The Lord shall smite thee in the knees, and in the thighes, with a sore botch, that thou canst not be healed: even from the sole of the foot unto the top of thine head. . . . He will bringe upon thee all the diseases of Egypt. (Deut. 28:35, 60)

The itch, the scab, and the phrase "from the sole of the foot unto the top of thine head" are matched in Thersites' line to Ajax: "I would thou didst itch from head to foot."

In the comments on the botch, Gifford, referrring to St Paul's attack on idolaters in the first chapter of Romans, claims that it is the direct result of idolatry or "spiritual whoredome" (p. 307). As Thersites' curses suggest, there seems to be a similar connection between the metaphorical diseases of the Greeks and their various idolatrous practices, including not only their "warring for a placket" but also their "worshipping" of Achilles and Ajax. In Revelation we find analogies to the latter activity, in the image of the beast with seven heads and ten horns (Rev 13:2–4). Cressida's servant describes Ajax as a similar composite beast: "This man . . . hath robbed many beasts of their particular additions" (1.2.19). In a later scene the Greek commanders, prompted by Ulysses, pretend to "worship" Ajax and treat him as an "idol" (2.3.182). Another idolized beast-figure in the Greek camp is "god Achilles" (1.3.169), who is called by Thersites an "idol of idiot-worshippers" (5.1.6).

An episode near the end of *Troilus* that symbolically recapitulates the theme of idolatry and its consequences is the death of Hector at the hands of Achilles and his Myrmidons. This event appears to be an act of retribution, for Hector's final act before his death is to pursue and kill the knight whose glamorous armor he covets even though he recognizes the corruption it conceals:

> Most putrefied core, so fair without,
> Thy goodly armor thus hath cost thy life. (5.8.1–2)

Satisfied with this prize, Hector then "*Puts off his helmet, and hangs his shield behind him*" (5.8.4, s.d., Folio), thus rendering himself defenseless against Achilles. Although he has amply demonstrated himself to be the most rational and magnanimous character among the Trojans, in his covetous pursuit of the knight in goodly armor he repeats the same error he committed in deciding to fight for Helen even though he clearly recognized the "mad idolatry" of doing so. In Ulysses' terms, he lets himself be seduced by another gilded "gawd," another "present object" that appeals to the "present eye."[8]

If this emphasis on the religious elements in *Troilus* seems to result in an unwarranted "theologizing" of a play obviously pagan in its setting, the answer is that Shakespeare would hardly have been the first Renaissance writer to interpret a classical fable from a Christian viewpoint. The Tale of Troy had already been moralized by Petrarch and such commentators on the *Aeneid* as Landino and Fabrini,[9] and Chaucer and Marlowe had dealt with Troilus and Helen in similar terms.

## Notes

1  Robert Kimbrough, Shakespeare's *Troilus and Cressida and Its Setting* (Cambridge, Mass., 1964) briefly refers to an undefined "Christian humanism" (pp. 151, 167–68) but does not contain a single reference to the Bible.
2  George Gifford, *Sermons upon the whole Booke of the Revelation* (1596), p. 326.
3  Francis Junius, *A Briefe and Learned Commentarie upon the Revelation of S. John* (1592), p. 65.

4  William Fulke, *Praelections upon the Sacred and Holy Revelation of S. John*, tr. George Gifford (1573), f. 93v.

5  Henry Bullinger, *A hundred sermons upon the Apocalipse* (1561), p. 507.

6  See Don Cameron Allen, "Some Observations on *The Rape of Lucrece*," *Shakespeare Survey* 15 (1962), 95–96.

7  For this location of the action in the seventh year there is no precedent in any of the English versions of the Troy legend available to Shakespeare.

8  S. L. Bethell points out the symbolic function of the episode as it relates to the play as a whole: "The 'sumptuous armour' with its 'putrefied core' . . . becomes a symbol of all the play presents to us, an allegorical enactment of the theme of 'fair without, foul within,' which is applicable almost everywhere in the Troy and Troilus stories as Shakespeare re-writes them" (*Shakespeare and the Popular Dramatic Tradition* [London, 1948], p. 104).

9  See Allen, pp. 95–96.

From *Texas Studies in Literature and Language* 15 (1973), 25–38 abridged, by permission of the University of Texas Press.

Maurice Hunt (1991)

## *Troilus and Cressida* and Christian Irony [editor's title]

Almost twenty years ago, J. L. Simmons demonstrated, in what has remained the most comprehensive reading of its kind to date, that Shakespeare's Roman plays contain a multitude of allusions to Christian motifs and ideas that encourage playgoers to interpret the ancient world ironically. When Shakespeare's pagan heroes and societies fail in a chosen enterprise, the unavailability, or absence, of one or more redemptive values, identified as Christian by dramatic allusion, usually ensures their lack of success or downfall.[1] Simmons does not apply his thesis to Shakespeare's Greek and Trojan play, *Troilus and Cressida*. Nevertheless, the many Christian allusions that David Kaula and J. A. Bryant, Jr., among others, have found in *Troilus and Cressida* suggest that this classical play of Shakespeare's most likely would respond to Simmons' method of analysis.

Near the midpoint of *Troilus and Cressida* appears an apparently trivial episode whose Christian overtones have not been described by critics. Pandarus and a Servant begin Act 3 with the following dialogue:

| Pandarus | Friend, you! Pray you a word. Do you not follow the young Lord Paris? |
| Servant | Ay, sir, when he goes before me. |
| Pandarus | You depend upon him, I mean. |
| Servant | Sir, I do depend upon the Lord. |
| Pandarus | You depend upon a notable gentleman; I must needs praise him. |

| Servant | The Lord be prais'd! |
|---|---|
| Pandarus | You know me, do you not? |
| Servant | Faith, sir, superficially. |
| Pandarus | Friend, know me better, I am the Lord Pandarus. |
| Servant | I hope I shall know your honor better! |
| Pandarus | I do desire it. |
| Servant | You are in the state of grace. |
| Pandarus | Grace? Not so, friend, honor and lordship are my titles. What music is this? |
| Servant | I do but partly know, sir, it is music in parts. |
| Pandarus | Know you the musicians? |
| Servant | Wholly, sir. (3.1.1–20) |

Initially, the talk between Pandarus and the Servant concentrates upon two different ideas of dependence. When the Servant remarks that he physically follows his master whenever Lord Paris walks ahead of him, Pandarus rephrases his question, "You depend upon him, I mean." The statement becomes Pandarus' rather conceited way of saying "You are his servant." A kind of comedy involving linguistic misapprehension distinguishes the beginning of the dialogue. The Servant, however, appears to have ended the confusion by replying, "Sir, I do depend upon the Lord." When Pandarus, his exasperation momentarily relieved, asserts, "You depend upon a notable gentleman; I must needs praise him," the Servant dutifully exclaims, "The Lord be prais'd!" Elizabethans were accustomed to hear this utterance apply primarily to the Christian deity. So automatic is the conditioned response of Shakespeare's audience, both in the past and present, to this formulaic utterance that the immediately prior dialogue is colored by it. The Servant's utterance "Sir, I do depend upon the Lord" becomes ambiguous. On the one hand, he simply could be repeating himself; he literally follows behind Lord Paris, a dependent servant. On the other, the conditioned auditor revalues the fading words into a negative answer; he does not depend upon Paris but upon God—an anachronistic possibility that makes Pandarus' reply ("You depend upon a notable gentleman; I must needs praise him") ironically comic.

In the setting of a classical play, minor characters allude to Christian values that could save major personages if they had a truly miraculous Lord upon whom they could depend.[2] Analysis of the latter part of the dialogue between Pandarus and the Servant suggests that only a being like the Christian deity can provide the essential referent and means for truly gauging and knowing the humanity in which one seeks redress or comfort. When Pandarus asks the Servant, "You know me, do you not," the latter character answers, "Faith, sir, superficially." After Pandarus identifies himself as an aristocrat ("I am the Lord Pandarus"), the Servant exclaims, "You are in the state of grace." Like his utterance "The Lord be prais'd," the Servant's statement "You are in the state of grace," which was used by Elizabethans to describe either election by God or a divine blessing, evokes a redemp-

tive power. Glossing the Servant's judgment as referring to a "spiritual state necessary to salvation," a recent editor of the play writes: "Pandarus takes it as referring
to social rank and replies that he is not entitled to be addressed as 'your Grace'
(used to one of the royal blood) but only as 'your honor' and 'your lordship.'"[3]
"Grace? Not so, friend, honor and lordship are my titles," Pandarus replies.

The humor here is multi-level. In the first place, the joke is on Pandarus for
confusing a socially elitist meaning of grace with a condition of spiritual salvation.
One could say that he, like Greeks and Trojans in general, in the absence of any
authoritative, spiritually redemptive values, inflates the importance of aristocratic
rank. By his smug correction of the Servant, Pandarus proves he is not in that
state of grace which Elizabethan Christians placed above social ranks. The Servant's mild oath, "Faith, sir, superficially," spoken when Pandarus asks him if he
knows him, acquires an ironic charge.

Shakespeare alludes to an epistemology capable of potentially better knowledge in a passage of *Troilus and Cressida* which begins with a reference by Ulysses
to a book he appears to be reading:

> A strange fellow here
> Writes me that man, how dearly ever parted,
> How much in having, or without or in,
> Cannot make boast to have that which he hath,
> Nor feels not what he owes, but by reflection;
> As when his virtues, aiming upon others,
> Heat them, and they retort that heat again
> To the first giver. (3.3.95–102)

A century ago, critics seemed to have established that the "strange fellow" to
whom Ulysses refers is Socrates and the book Plato's *First Alcibiades*. But an Elizabethan playgoer trying to imagine the book in Ulysses' hand might guess it to
be—anachronistically—a volume concerned with Christian theology, because of
the lesson Ulysses is drawing:

> I do not strain at the position—
> It is familiar—but at the author's drift,
> Who in his circumstance expressly proves
> That no man is the lord of any thing,
> Though in and of him there be much consisting,
> Till he communicate his parts to others. (3.3.112–17)

T. W. Baldwin spoke for a number of critics when he detected an allusion in
Ulysses' resumed speech to the Christian teaching of spending charitably for others those talents held in stewardship, an idea memorably presented in *Measure for
Measure* I.1.29–40.[4] This allusion crystallizes other Christian overtones in the passage. Coming relatively soon after its appearance in Pandarus' and the Servant's
dialogue (3.1.1–20), the word "lord" in the utterance "no man is the lord of any
thing" resonates with the spiritual significance it acquired there.

Shakespeare thus employs diction encouraging the recognition of an ideally reliable value giver upon whom humankind might depend. On the windy plains of Troy, however, no man is the lord of anything because the Lord who would charge daily life with a final meaning has not been born. It was when Christ entered the world to extend mercifully his figure and the heat of his love that a true understanding could replace the process of evaluation that Ulysses and other Greeks and Trojans perform so tragically.

If read with Christian eyes, the clue to a right knowledge was in the observation by Ulysses that humankind

> Cannot make boast to have that which he hath,
> Nor feels not what he owes, but by reflection;
> As when his virtues, aiming upon others,
> Heat them, and they retort that heat again
> To the first giver.

This passage, if it does not equal the Parable of the Talents, resembles it, suggesting at least the dynamics of Neoplatonic Christianity. Joseph Mazzeo has described how Pseudo-Dionysius the Areopagite established and St Bonaventura developed an immensely influential theology of light that is also love—a religious model that English Renaissance poets invoke in their works.[5] In this hierarchical theology, all of creation, including humankind, is thought of as so many *specula*, or mirrors, catching the rays of divine light / love as it streams from godhead and reflecting it.[6] In this respect, the "first giver" of Ulysses' speech is not a charitable mortal but the First Giver, who enjoys a "retorting" to him of the heat of his own divine virtue reflected in his creatures.

In commenting on the doctrine in *Troilus and Cressida*, Kenneth Muir has asserted that Ulysses' dynamics of reflected light derives from the scriptural "Let your light so shine before men that they may see your good works."[7] The good works of Christians, however, are not the only bearers of God's light. To a lesser extent, the whole world of creatures and their doings reflects it. Old Testament wisdom literature emphasized this truth, as did also Christian Neoplatonists. "Indeed, the whole of the created universe is nothing but a system of mirrors reflecting their Cause," Bonaventura claimed, "and they imitate a process by which we enter into the internal mirror of our mind where the divine lights shine in the form of the light of the intellect."[8] A light of love continuously reflects through creation to bind all creatures to God in a single whole. Bound so together, men and women can know themselves as well as others, at least partially.

"You know me, do you not?" Pandarus asked the Servant. "Faith, sir, superficially," was his reply. Perhaps the tragedy of these Trojans is that they know one another (and themselves) only superficially. The light of God in his works does illumine their minds superficially. This is the case when Hector recognizes and affirms the "moral laws / Of nature" (2.2.183–89). Hector's insight represents

Shakespeare's demonstration of the truth of Romans 1:18–23—that God partially revealed to all men and women "his eternal power and deity . . . in the things that have been made." But unrighteous men, says Paul, do not obey this truth; instead of seeking after God, they "become fools" by exchanging His glory for an image "made after corruptible man." Hector does this in Shakespeare's drama. After nobly arguing that morality dictates Helen's return to her husband Menelaus, Hector abruptly insists that Trojan face-saving requires keeping her and continuing the savage war (2.2.189–93). Hector thus suppresses a knowledge he has. He does so because a returning of Helen would not serve to "canonize" him with worldly fame. Here is a dramatic irony that could be perceived by playgoers, notably by Christian readers with a perspective such as John Donne brought to his poem "The Canonization." Canonization, for Shakespeare's Greeks and Trojans, means an idolatrous version of sainthood. It means a glorifying of some human image in preference to God. It means a denying of laws as perceived in nature, simply because some image of the self is more flattering to the human will. Certainly the debate over "canonization" in *Troilus and Cressida* would have challenged Shakespeare's audience no less than this topic challenges readers today.

## Notes

1   *Shakespeare's Pagan World: The Roman Tragedies* (University Press of Virginia, 1973).
2   Maurice Hunt, "Compelling Art in *Titus Andronicus,*" *SEL: 1500–1900* 28 (1988), 197–218, esp. 204–6.
3   *The Riverside Shakespeare*, p. 467.
4   Baldwin, in *A New Variorum Edition of Shakespeare, "Troilus and Cressida,"* ed. Harold N. Hillebrand (Philadelphia: Lippincott, 1953), p. 412.
5   *Medieval Cultural Tradition in Dante's "Comedy"* (1960; rpt. New York: Greenwood Press, 1968), pp. 1–90.
6   Mazzeo, pp. 15–16, 20–21.
7   *Shakespeare's Comic Sequence* (New York: Barnes & Noble, 1979), pp. 119–20. Muir cites Mark 4:21 and Matthew 5:15.
8   Mazzeo, p. 36.

Abridged from "Shakespeare's *Troilus and Cressida* and Christian Epistemology," forthcoming in *Christianity and Literature* 42 (1993), Number 2.

# KING LEAR

## Comment and bibliography

In the medieval *Castle of Perseverance* covetousness is a vice resurgent in old age. *King Lear* is the tragedy of an old man who coveted love, the most precious of all gifts, and preferred mouth-honor to the good heart hiding in his child Cordelia. The test posed by Lear, "Which of you shall we say doth love us most?" can be found in Luke 7:42, where the correct answer is: the one who "forgave" the most. Lear has no notion of the virtue of forgiveness when the play opens, but by the time the play ends he will have learned it from Cordelia, from her silent actions more than by words. Her dying for him has analogy to Christ's death by hanging, and it causes Lear to cry out, "Look there!" He is fulfilling thereby the "See better, Lear" which had been urged on him in Act 1 by a loyal physician.

The tragedy as a whole is shaped by a Christian sense of history. Lear's pagan quest for love's meaning develops through exploring the realities of Nature, Law, and Grace. His initial error of pride is allied implicitly to Adam's and Eve's when a choral speaker in the play refers to Cordelia as one who "redeems nature from the general curse which twain have brought." And a large network of allusions places Lear as an instance of Prodigal mankind, the "old man" of Pauline theology, misled into a course of spiritual self-destruction until sought out and re-clothed by a rescuer who takes him "out of the grave." Lear must be providentially changed, as the Bible's King Nebuchadnezzar was, by undergoing a period of madness. He must become an outcast (cf. Dan. 4:25) so that he may discover the "no good divinity" of the notion that "I" was everything. Only by suffering can he come to look for insight to the Suffering Servant sacrificed for him. Through anguish, however, Lear comes to glimpse a hopeful mystery, nature's "blest secret." Played out on a landscape of primeval suggestiveness, this drama has the earmarks of universal fable and is considered by many to be Shakespeare's greatest masterpiece.

A subplot enriches and reinforces the central theme. Whereas Lear begins as a lover of "I," the Earl of Gloucester's "eyes" are his measure of value, and so he is easily beguiled into mistaking letters and surface appearance for truth. Only when physically blinded as a consequence of this folly does he acquire the insight to confess, "I stumbled when I saw." He adds that he would say he "had eyes again" if he could but see with his "touch" the good Edgar he shamefully abused. When saying this he is being led by anonymous Edgar, who as a fugitive from this father's wrath has now met him in need. What response can best minister a reconcilement? One that speaks incognito to the despair that is impelling the old man toward suicide. By allowing him to enact an imagined leap into nihilism, Edgar can arrange for him the unexpected discovery of a good earth under him at the bottom of his fall and the voice of a cheerful neighbor telling him his life is a miracle. This therapeutic exorcism is the subplot's chief marvel—or "improbability," as neoclassical critics would say. It effectively converts Gloucester to a faith in "ever gentle" gods, preparing him thus for the later blessing of a reunion with Edgar that enables him to die in an ecstasy of joyous grief. His finding love's meaning through tribulation and pilgrimage parallels and interlocks with Lear's experience.

Unlike the tragic heroes of Shakespeare's earlier plays, Lear begins to repent his error before the end of Act 1, so that the bulk of the drama becomes a purging of his initial mistake. "I did her wrong," he says remorsefully of Cordelia when he discovers the selfishness of the sister he foolishly preferred. His first corrective impulse is to denounce "Monster ingratitude"; but on encountering more of this in his second daughter he invokes thunderbolts from heaven and bares his own head to these, although considering himself "more sinned against than sinning." Presently his wits begin to turn, simultaneously toward madness and toward compassion for outcasts such as his poor Fool and homeless wretches. And when Poor Tom, "whom the foul fiend vexes," preaches to Lear a morality learned from a court-inflicted beggary, Lear values this "unaccommodated" wiseman. He proceeds to mock his own "cut to the brains" by crowning himself with weeds and naming the world "a great stage of fools." Then Cordelia's search-party brings him to her tent for a healing sleep, from which he awakens to spiritual Daylight. His later grief when she is taken from him may be likened to that of Christ's disciples on Good Friday, a deep anguish, but not without hope. The story thus ends as close to the gates of comedy as is possible for a tragedy.

The Pauline paradoxes of the folly of worldly wisdom and the wisdom of worldly folly run through the play. An instance of the first is Lear's initial desire to assess "deservings." Cordelia's uncalculated sacrifice represents the second. Both of these paradoxes are presented in a riddling way by Lear's loyal Fool. He jests, on the one hand, that Lear had "little wit in thy bald crown" when he gave his golden one away, and that he has pared his wit on both sides and left nothing in the middle (1.4.160–85). On the other hand, after counseling Kent to "Let go thy hold when a great wheel runs down a hill, lest it break thy neck with following," he announces that he as fool will stay and "let the wise man fly" because he is no knave but a loyal servitor (2.4.70–83). Lear's violations of common sense are thus noted but are balanced by a faithfulness to him that transcends mere reason. Since Cordelia replaces the Fool as Lear's steadfast companion after Act 3, an affinity between those two is implied, and indeed is indicated when Lear cries out at Cordelia's death, "My poor fool is hanged." A single actor can take both the parts on stage. The critic Enid Welsford remarked as early as 1935 that it seemed to her "quite certain" that this play was "dedicated to the reiteration of the wilder paradoxes of the Gospels and of St Paul" (*The Fool*, p. 268).

Various aspects of the play's patterning are touched on in the pieces of commentary excerpted for our anthology. Peter Milward brings into focus the major biblical themes involved. Roger Cox reviews the drama's thoroughgoing dependence on St Paul's message in the Corinthian letters. Maynard Mack takes notice of an archetypal quality of parable and homily. Joseph Summers would rehabilitate A. C. Bradley's reading of Lear's final words. Walter Stein, perhaps remembering G. M. Hopkins's allusion to the "cliffs of fall" in *King Lear*, values the play's probing of the extreme verge of human experience where mystery lies. John Cunningham sees Lear's stages of spiritual pilgrimage as analogous to those celebrated liturgically in the office for Christian catechumens on Holy Saturday. Joseph Wittreich comments on the appropriateness of the play's having been performed on a St Stephen's night.

The supplementary bibliography contains valuable auxiliary commentary. The avowedly Christian interpretation of R. W. Chambers in 1940 has been widely influential. It probes the significance of Shakespeare's departure from the story's ending in Geoffrey of Monmouth, where Cordelia dies by suicide. Shakespeare refers to this as a false story invented by Edmund, and shows her instead as a murdered victim on whom "the gods throw incense"—a pious death that is reinforced by a subplot drawn from Sidney's *Arcadia*. George Kernodle's essay of 1945 observes that the structure of *King Lear* derives from the medieval artistic principles of parallelism and prefiguration. John Danby contends that the play "is our profoundest expression of an essentially Christian comment on life." J. C. Maxwell's thesis that it is "a Christian play about a pagan world" is repeated with approval by Kenneth Muir in his Arden edition of the play (1952). Virgil Whitaker, likewise, reads *King Lear* as "a profoundly Christian tragedy about a pre-Christian world, undeniable proof that it is possible to write Christian tragedy" (p. 240). Of course, there have been various rejoinders by anti-Christian critics, but as René Fortin points out they rely on dogmas of their own that presuppose a "poetic justice" not in accord with the New Testament doctrine reflected in the play.

The significance of the differences between the *Leir* play and Shakespeare's drama is explored by James Jones and Stephen Lynch. They observe that the anonymous playwright uses biblical references in a heavily didactic manner and with a melodramatic sense of divine justice, whereas Shakespeare employs a medieval method of figural realism that echoes biblical truths. Lynch finds this "more deeply Christian than its predecessor." Margaret Hotine finds echoes in *King Lear* of the church's St Stephen's Day readings in Proverbs and Ecclesiastes. David Kaula finds biblical sources for the play's imagery describing the cliff at Dover. Russell Peck mentions some analogies in the Bible to Edgar's exorcism of

Gloucester and notes further that Edgar is both a literal and a figurative godson to Lear. John Murphy delves into Harsnett's polemic against exorcism and describes *King Lear* as "in part an answer" to Harsnett, but fails to clarify in what respect this is so.

Richard Matthews answers critics who question the sincerity of Edmund's conversion; he sees in Edmund's yearning to "do some good" a parallel to Lear's final grasping for a goodness. Roy Battenhouse traces in Cordelia and Edgar a spiritual progress from an initial small defect to a rich maturity, and he comments on the imagery of apocalypse in Act 5. Peter Milward annotates with biblical references various of the play's meditative passages, and would summarize the whole drama as an enacted sermon on the theme of man's discovering his nothingness and with it the miracle of being created anew out of nothing. David Ormerod finds significance in Gloucester's being brought to rest under the shadow of a "Tree," which in Christian iconography has filiations with the Cross. Duncan Harris argues that the ending of *King Lear* "depends for its astonishing effect on those ideas usually associated with the Christian conception of man's place in the world." The titles of still other essays indicate their respective emphases.

## Supplementary bibliography

Battenhouse, Roy. "Moral Experience and Its Typology in *King Lear*," *Shakespearean Tragedy* (1969), pp. 269–302.

Chambers, R. W. *King Lear* (Jackson, Son & Co., 1940), excerpted in *Shakespearean Criticism*, ed. Laurie Harris and Mark Scott (Detroit: Gale Research Co.), vol 2 (1985), 170–74.

Danby, John. "*King Lear* and Christian Patience," *The Cambridge Journal* 1 (1947–8), 305–20; rpt. in *Poets on Fortune's Hill* (London: Faber and Faber, 1952), pp. 108–27. Also his "Correspondence on *King Lear*," *Critical Quarterly* 3 (1961), 69–71.

Davidson, Clifford. "The Iconography of Wisdom and Folly in *King Lear*," in Tibor Fabiny, ed., *Shakespeare and the Emblem* (Szeged, 1984), pp. 189–214.

England, Eugene. "Cordelia and Paulina: Shakespeare's Healing Dramatists," *Literature and Belief* 2 (1982), 69–82.

Fortin, René E. "Hermeneutical Circularity and Christian Interpretations of *King Lear*," *Shakespeare Studies* 12 (1979), 113–25.

French, Carolyn. "Shakespeare's 'Folly': *King Lear*," *Shakespeare Quarterly* 10 (1959), 523–29.

Greer, David. "Sleepest or wakest thou iolly shepheard," *Shakespeare Quarterly* 43 (1992), 224–26.

Guilfoyle, Cherrell. "The Redemption of King Lear," in *Shakespeare's Play Within Play* (1990), pp. 111–27.

Harris, Duncan S. "The End of *Lear* and a Shape for Shakespearean Tragedy," *Shakespeare Studies* 9 (1976), 253–68.

Hennedy, Hugh L. "*King Lear*: Recognizing the Ending," *Studies in Philology* 71 (1974), 371–84.

Hotine, Margaret. "Two Plays for St Stephen's Day," *Notes and Queries*, n.s. 29 (1982), 119–21.

Jones, James H. "*Leir* and *Lear*: Matthew 5:33–37, The Turning Point," *Comparative Drama* 4 (1970), 125–31.

Jorgensen, Paul. *Lear's Self-Discovery* (University of California Press, 1967), pp. 9–20; 30–31.

Kaula, David. "Edgar on Dover Cliff: An Emblematic Reading," *English Studies in Canada* 5 (1979), 377–87.

Kernodle, George. "The Symphonic Form in *King Lear*, in *Elizabethan Studies . . . in Honor of George F. Reynolds* (University of Colorado, 1945), pp. 185–91.

Lynch, Stephen. "Sin, Suffering, and Redemption in *Leir* and *Lear*," *Shakespeare Studies* 18 (1986), 161–74.

Matthews, Richard. "Edmund's Redemption in *King Lear*," *Shakespeare Quarterly* 26 (1975), 25–29.

Maxwell, J. C. "The Technique of Invocation in *King Lear*," *Modern Language Review* 45 (1950), 142–47.

Milward, Peter. "Notes on the Religious Dimension of King Lear," *English Literature and Language* (Tokyo) 23 (1986), 5–27; and "On the Frontiers of Criticism: Lear's Sermon," 28 (1991), 3–15.

Murphy, John. *Darkness and Devils: Exorcism and King Lear* (Ohio University Press, 1984), pp. 198–217.

Myrick, Kenneth. "Christian Pessimism in *King Lear*," *Shakespeare 1564–1964*, ed. Edward Bloom (Brown University Press, 1964), pp. 56–70.

Ormerod, David. "'The Shadow of This Tree': Fall and Redemption in *King Lear*," Deutsche Shakespeare-Gesellschaft West *Jahrbuch* 1977, pp. 98–108.

Peck, Russell A. "Edgar's Pilgrimage: High Comedy in *King Lear*," *Studies in English Literature* 7 (1967), 219–37.

Siegel, Paul. "Shakespeare's Kneeling-Resurrection Pattern and the Meaning of *King Lear*," in *Shakespeare in His Time and Ours* (University of Notre Dame Press, 1968), pp. 108–21.

Snyder, Susan. "King Lear and the Prodigal Son," *Shakespeare Quarterly* 17 (1966), 361–70.

Whitaker, Virgil K. *The Mirror up to Nature* (Huntington Library, 1965), pp. 211–40.

*Peter Milward (1969)*

# The Religious Dimension of *King Lear*

How, it may be asked, can a Christian view emerge from a play whose background is entirely pagan, and from which the Christian language of the source-play has been sedulously removed? In the first place, it may be pointed out that, while the background is ostensibly pagan, the language of King Lear—that is to say, the language of Shakespeare himself—is far from being entirely pagan. It is charged with more or less recognizable echoes of the Bible and of Christian homiletic material; and when they are all taken together, they constitute an important thematic undercurrent of thought and imagery in the play.

With regard to Cordelia, she is evidently, in terms of the play's ostensible background, a good pagan following the natural light of reason and conscience. But in terms of the language of the play, she evokes so many Biblical and Christian parallels that many scholars and critics have found in her a figure of Christ himself. In the opening scene the very words in which she states her inability to speak, "I cannot heave my heart into my mouth" (1.1), echo the words of Ecclesiasticus 21:26: "The heart of fools is in their mouth; but the mouth of the wise is in his heart." It is later, however, when she has been cast off by her father, that her likeness to Christ is first signalized in the words addressed to her by the King of France:—

> Fairest Cordelia, that art most rich, being poor;
> Most choice, forsaken; and most lov'd, despis'd.

His words echo St Paul's description of Christ in 2 Corinthians 8:9: "He, being rich, for your sakes became poor, that ye through his poverty might be made rich"—and possibly also his depiction of the Christians in the same epistle, 6:10: "As poor, and yet making many rich."

Subsequently, on her return to England, she declares her true motive: "O dear father! It is thy business that I go about" (4.4)—in words that contain a precise echo of Christ's reply to his parents in the temple: "Knew ye not that I must go about my father's business?" (Lk 2:49) The tears she sheds on that occasion, moreover, are described by the Gentleman to Kent as the "holy water from her heavenly eyes" (4.3). The strife she shows in her face between "smiles and tears" recalls the foreboding of Proverbs 14:13: "Laughter shall be mingled with sorrow, and mourning taketh hold of the end of joy," and so points to the sad ending of the play; but at the same time the comparison used by the Gentleman, "Her smiles and tears were like a better way," suggests the "more excellent way" proposed by St Paul in his famous hymn to charity in 1 Corinthians 13. Finally, when she is reunited with her "child-changed father," she exclaims: "And wast thou fain, poor father, to hovel thee with swine and rogues forlorn?" (4.7)—echoing the words of Christ's parable of the Prodigal Son, in such a way as to imply that Lear is himself the prodigal returned home after his riotous life and clothed anew in the garment of grace.

The fore-going echoes and implications are all, as it were, crowned by the cryptic declaration of the Gentleman to Lear:—

> Thou hast one daughter,
> Who redeems nature from the general curse
> Which twain have brought her to. (4.6)

No doubt, these words have a precise literal meaning in the immediate context of the play: the "twain" are Goneril and Regan, the "nature" is that of Lear, and the "curse" is the madness to which he has been brought by their ingratitude. But in the wider context of the play and its audience, it is surely pig-headed not to recognize in the words deeper implications of Christian theology—where the "twain" are Adam and Eve, the first parents of mankind, "nature" is human nature, "the general curse" is that of original sin which has infected the whole *genus humanum*, while "redeems" is the work of a redeemer who is here identified with "a daughter," whether Mary as the Second Eve or Christ himself as the Second Adam.

As for Edgar, the language he uses is at least as much Christian as Stoic. Once he assumes the disguise of a mad beggar, Edgar almost immediately adopts the language of Scripture—as though Shakespeare felt there was no further need to observe the restrictions of his pagan background in the words of a madman.

> Obey thy parents; keep thy word justly; swear not; commit not with man's sworn spouse; set not thy sweet heart on proud array.

His mad exhortations to the odd company in the hovel are a tissue of commands from the Old and the New Testament:—

> "Children, obey your parents" (Eph 6:1); "That which is once gone out of thy lips, thou must keep and do" (Dt 23:23); "Swear not at all" (Mt 5:34); "Thou shalt not commit adultery" (Ex 20:14); "Likewise also the women, that they array themselves in comely apparel, with shamefastness and discreet behaviour, not in braided hair, either gold or pearls or costly apparel" (1 Tm 2:9).

In his disguise as a madman, moreover, Edgar elicits from Lear the reflection on man's fallen condition, "Is man no more than this?"—with its echo of Ps 8:4: "What is man, that thou art mindful of him?" To his own father, Edgar seems not so much a man as a worm—like the Messiah in Ps 22:6: "But I am a worm and no man."

The climax of Edgar's function in the play comes when he rescues his father from suicide. In particular, he exhorts his father to "think that the clearest gods, who make them honours of men's impossibilities, have preserved thee" (4.6)— words which find a closer parallel in the New Testament (cf. Lk 1:37: "No word shall be impossible with God," and Mt 19:26: "With men this is impossible, but with God all things are possible") than in any Stoic source. His description of himself as "a most poor man, made tame to Fortune's blows" is, likewise, inspired at least as much by the Christian beatitudes of poverty and meekness (Mt 5:3,5) as by the moral ideal of Stoicism.

As for the last scene of his combat with Edmund, he proposes an exchange of charity in terms that Dr. Johnson could not help regarding as a Christian anachronism. Even his remark about his father's fate—"The gods are just, and of our pleasant vices make instruments to plague us" (5.3), where W. R. Elton oddly discovers the *lex talionis* of Moses—is uttered in no vindictive spirit, but as a statement of a law in nature which is given twice in the *Book of Wisdom*: 11:21: "Wherewithal a man sinneth, by the same also shall he be punished"; and 13:23:

"Whereas men have lived dissolutely and unrighteously, thou hast punished them sore with their own abominations."

Thirdly, it is interesting to notice how many allusions to the Book of Job are scattered through the play. When the Fool notes that the old king is now no more than "Lear's shadow" (1.4), a veritable "nothing," there is an echo from Job 8:9: "for we are but of yesterday, and know nothing, because our days upon earth are a shadow." Then, Lear's repeated prayers for patience, "You heavens, give me that patience" (2.4), besides their echo of Ps 39, strongly resemble the mood of Job, whose patience, proverbial though it may be, is by no means a model of silent endurance. No doubt, the tempest or whirlwind out of which God spoke to Job in the climax of the Book is at the back of Shakespeare's mind in his presentation of the storm in which Lear at once loses his old wits and acquires new knowledge of himself. Kent's general reflection, "Nothing almost sees miracles but misery" (2.2), echoes Job 36:15: "It is the friendless he rescues in their need, speaks home to them through the afflictions they endure." Finally, in the tragic conclusion of the play, Lear's lament over Cordelia, "Thou'lt come no more" (5.3), recalls the words of Job 7:9–10: "He that goeth down to the grave, shall come up no more. He shall return no more."

In spite of all these parallels, however, between *King Lear* and the Book of Job, there remains one glaring difference: that, whereas Job has his possessions restored to him at the end in greater abundance (according to the moral ideas of the Old Testament), Lear's sorrows have their culmination in his death over the dead body of Cordelia. In such an ending W. R. Elton in *King Lear and the Gods* (1966) sees an affront to religious orthodoxy, and "a *Hamlet*-like confusion of values in terms of a chiasma of ethical and religious ideas and consequences" (p. 337). But this interpretation seems to assume an Old Testament view of morality and retribution; whereas it seems to me that Shakespeare is moving in *King Lear* from such a view, which is satisfied in the reconciliation-scene, to the view of the New Testament, which expects the reward of goodness not in this life, but after death.

If the character of Lear is aptly illustrated in his time of distress with reference to the Book of Job it is further illustrated in his time of recovery and return to Cordelia with reference—as we have seen—to Christ's Parable of the Prodigal Son. It is not only in *King Lear*, but in a surprisingly large number of his other plays, that Shakespeare draws on the imagery and ideas of this parable—though it is here perhaps that his use of it reaches a climax and extends to the whole meaning of the play. From the very beginning, when Lear banishes Cordelia from his court, it is paradoxically not Cordelia, but Lear himself who goes wandering "into a far country," away from the true knowledge of himself. With his knights he lives, according to Goneril, in "riotous" fashion—with a more than verbal reminiscence of the Prodigal Son who is said to have "wasted his goods with riotous living." The outcome is that his "substance" is converted into "shadow"—"Lear's shadow," as the Fool points out in answer to his master's indignant question: "Who is it that can tell me who I am?" (1.4). Driven out, therefore, into the storm, without sustenance for his belly, he is forced to take shelter in a rude hovel—"fain," as Cordelia later says, "to hovel him with swine and rogues forlorn" (4.7). In the hovel, there are indeed "rogues" of a sort—the mad beggar and the Fool; but there is no mention of "swine," which come from the parable, where the Prodigal Son "would fain have filled his belly with the husks that the swine ate." Then, when he is finally reunited with his daughter, Lear is significantly welcomed by her as "this child-changed father"—with the implication that the father and the child of Christ's parable have changed places in Shakespeare's play. She also sympathizes with him, in this scene, as "poor perdu"—the poor one who has been lost, but now is found—even as the father in the parable rejoices that "this my son was dead, and is alive again, was lost, and is found."

Of these two, however, Lear and Cordelia, it is rather the latter who may be called a figure of Christ; and her unjust death by hanging further recalls the manner of Christ's death on the Cross. This fate is foreshadowed in the words of Lear: "Upon such sacrifices, my Cordelia, the gods themselves throw incense" (5.3), which clearly echo St Paul's words in Heb 13:16: "With such sacrifices God is well pleased." If, then, Cordelia is a figure of Christ in her death, of whom would Lear have reminded his Christian audience, when he comes on the stage with her dead body in his arms, but the mother of Christ—in the position made famous by the *pieta* of Michelangelo? This parallelism is further underlined by the more explicit echo of Christ's Passion contained in Kent's exclamation: "Is this the promised end?" with Edgar's rejoinder: "Or image of that horror?" Here we have a clear evocation of "the great Doom's image," as in *Macbeth* (2.3), or the general "compt," as in *Othello* (5.2), whereby Shakespeare customarily imparts a universal resonance to his tragedies. So, too, for Lear it is a heavy hour now that he has lost Cordelia; and if his feeling is analogous to that of Mary, the "mother of sorrows," the feeling of Kent and Edgar may be compared to the hopelessness of the disciples of Christ after his death on the Cross and before his resurrection. The "weight of this sad time" (5.3) expressed by Albany in his concluding words exactly conveys the feelings of the Christian liturgy after the Good Friday service, before the celebration of the resurrection in the Easter vigil.

From "The Religious Dimension of *King Lear*," *Shakespeare Studies* (Japan), 8 (1969–70), 48–73; the present essay abridges pp. 61–72.

*Roger L. Cox (1969)*

## *King Lear* and the Corinthian Letters

First Corinthians 1 through 4 comprehensively treats the paradoxical relation of wisdom and foolishness, just as First Corinthians 13 is the definitive statement on Christian love. To cite only one passage among many, "If any one among you thinks that he is wise in this age, let him become a fool that he may become wise. For the wisdom of this world is folly with God" (1 Cor 3:18–19). Robert Heilman has demonstrated in *This Great Stage* the extent to which Shakespeare exploits this theme in *King Lear*.[1] My purpose is to point out that the treatment of the play's major theme (love) and that of a secondary theme (wisdom and foolishness) apparently have a single source—the book of First Corinthians. One further point remains to be made in this connection, however; and that is the manner in which Shakespeare binds the two themes together. A single example will suffice. On different occasions Lear, in all his natural wisdom, tells both the Fool and Cordelia (whom he finally calls "my poor fool") that "Nothing will come of nothing" (1.1.90) and that "Nothing can be made out of nothing" (1.4.126). Yet Lear, though he begins as "nothing" (1.4.185) because he "has not love," turns himself, through suffering, into "something"; by "becoming a fool" he makes himself capable of love. Thus paradoxically, in *King Lear* Shakespeare, by converting wisdom into foolishness, produces "something" (a man capable of love) out of "nothing" (one who "has not love").

On what grounds in the Corinthian letters may we assert that Lear "has not love"? The demonstration is simple. We merely take three of the key words used to describe love in First Corinthians 13, *patient*, *kind*, and *endure*, and examine Shakespeare's use of them in *King Lear*. A. C. Bradley concluded his famous discussion of the play by saying that it "seems to preach to us from end to end, 'Thou must be patient,' 'Bear free and patient thoughts.'"[2] The word *kind* is particularly useful, since in Shakespeare *unkind* frequently involves the meaning of *unnatural* and thus becomes connected with another element of the play's meaning. Perhaps the most famous lines in the entire play are those spoken by Edgar in the last act, "Men must endure/Their going hence, even as their coming hither; / Ripeness is all." An examination of how Lear uses these three words and how the other characters apply them to him may yield some insight into the structure and meaning of the play.[3]

When Lear curses Goneril, Albany interrupts the eloquent tirade by saying, "Pray, sir, be patient." But Lear continues, "Detested kite, thou liest. . ." (1.4.252–253). Later, when Goneril tries to reduce his retinue, Lear says, "I can be patient, I can stay with Regan, / I and my hundred knights" (2.4.225–226). Then in the speech which begins "O reason not the need!" he prays, "You heavens, give me that patience, patience I need!" (2.4.266). During the storm, in words that echo Cordelia's at the beginning of the play, he says, "No, I will be the pattern of all patience;/I will say nothing" (3.2.37–38). At the mock trial, Kent asks Lear in a way that points up the irony of the play, "O pity! Sir, where is the patience now / That you so oft have boasted to retain?" (3.6.57–58). Even Gloucester learns the necessity of patience before Lear does. Just before he "leaps" upon the heath, he prays, "O you mighty gods! / This world I do renounce, and in your sights, / Shake patiently my great affliction off" (4.6.34–36); and after the "leap" he vows, "Henceforth I'll bear / Affliction till it do cry out itself / 'Enough, enough,' and die," to which Edgar responds, "Bear free and patient thoughts" (4.6.75–80). Ironically, it is after this that Lear, who still must learn the meaning of patience fully, tells Gloucester, "Thou must be patient. We came crying hither…." (4.6.175).

When Gloucester does what he can to comfort the raging Lear, Kent comments upon Lear's "impatience" and associates the idea of kindness with the gods: "All the power of his wits have given way to his impatience. The gods reward your kindness" (3.6.4–5). And late in the play, Kent once more puts his finger on the irony of Lear's position:

> A sovereign shame so elbows him; *his own unkindness*,
> That stripped her from his benediction, turned her
> To foreign casualties, gave her dear rights
> To his dog-hearted daughters--these things sting
> His mind so venomously that burning shame
> Detains him from Cordelia. (4.3.42–47)

When Kent had first invited Lear to enter the hovel, Lear hesitated, saying, "This tempest will not give me leave to ponder / On things would hurt me more, but I'll go in" (3.4.24–25); and one cannot help thinking that he rants about "his unkind daughters" in order to escape what "would hurt him more"—the thought of "his own unkindness" to Cordelia.

The third defining term is *endure*. Appropriately, it is first used (negatively, of course) by Goneril. Irritated by the behavior of Lear and his followers, she cries, "I'll not endure it. / His knights grow riotous, and himself upbraids us / On every trifle" (1.3.5–7). Kent describes the storm as "too rough / For nature to endure" (3.4.2–3), but moments later when Lear characterizes himself as an "old kind father," the king insists, "I will endure" (3.4.18). Regan, competing with her sister for Edmund's "love," tells him, "I never shall endure her" (5.1.15). Edgar gives the word its broadest application in the lines "Men must endure / Their going hence, even as their coming hither" (5.2.9–10); and at the end of the play Kent says of Lear, "The wonder is, he hath endured so long" (5.2.317). Thus ironically Lear, who has "ever but slenderly known himself" (1.1.292–293), calls himself a "kind father," and insists "I will be the pattern of all patience" and "I will endure." But Kent, who sees the king more clearly than Lear sees himself, always lays bare the real difficulty. At the crucial moment he asks, "where is the patience now / That you so oft have boasted to retain?" He understands that "a sovereign shame," the memory of "his own unkindness, / ... Detains him from Cordelia." And after Lear is dead, Kent observes that "the wonder is, he hath endured so long."

Some critics have objected, on the basis of realism, to the fact that Lear and Gloucester remain blind so long to the virtues of Cordelia and Edgar. But if we use the Corinthian letters as the frame of reference for interpreting the play, the explanation is simple. We have indicated that both Gloucester and Lear are "natural" men, more interested in the counterfeit of love than in love itself; and according to St Paul, "The natural man receiveth not the things of the Spirit of God: for they are foolishness unto him: neither can he know them, because they are spiritually discerned" (1 Cor 2:14 KJV; the RSV uses the words *unspiritual* and *natural* interchangeably. Incidently, this passage immediately follows the one which Bottom comically misquotes in *A Midsummer Night's Dream*, 4.1.218–221). As for Lear's progress through the action of the play, another of St Paul's comments seems applicable: "That was not first which is spiritual, but that which is natural; and afterward that which is spiritual" (1 Cor 15:46 KJV). Being a natural man, Lear is long unable to perceive Cordelia's love, which is one of "the things of the Spirit of God." Her behavior seems mere foolishness to him; and only after he has been refined and made spiritual by suffering can he recognize those things which are "spiritually discerned."...

Cordelia's death has presented a problem for some critics. But the objections to her death are purely moral ones; most of them may be reduced to the contention that she does not deserve to die. Kenneth Muir answers these objections intelligently: "Of those critics who complain that she died guiltless we can only enquire if they would rather she had died guilty."[4] They would probably respond in words like these: "By no means; but she ought not to die at all in the play." This, however, is tantamount to saying the play should imply that she "lives happily ever after"; and this contention is surely as far removed from both tragedy and Pauline Christianity as it could possibly be. We are told that Cordelia "redeems nature from the general curse / Which twain have brought her to" (4.6.202–203), and such redemption is not achieved without sacrifice. According to St Paul, a human being is like a kernel of wheat in that it "does not come to life unless it dies" (1 Cor 15:36). ...

The symbolic action in the play which has been singled out for perhaps more discussion than any other is Lear's "unbuttoning," his disrobing. Robert Heilman devotes a whole chapter of *The Great Stage* to what he calls "The Clothes Pattern," which he regards as being (among other things) an index of Lear's spiritual progress: "If we see the movement of Lear from well-accoutered king to half-clad fugitive, from putting off of cares to giving up of life, we also observe his progress from eyeless rage to seeing beneath the surfaces that deceived him."[5] The evidence that Heilman presents is certainly enough to convince almost anyone that the imagery of clothing is a highly important vehicle for meaning in the play and that there is a fundamental ambiguity about that meaning. Again St Paul provides the key to understanding the work:

> For we know that if the earthly tent we live in is destroyed, we have a building from God, a house not made with hands, eternal in the heavens. Here indeed we groan, and long to put on our heavenly dwelling, so that by putting it on we may not be found *naked.* For while we are still in this tent, we sigh with anxiety; *not that we would be unclothed, but that we would be further clothed, so that what is mortal may be swallowed up by life.* (1 Cor 5:1–4)

Ultimately, even in *King Lear,* it is not merely clothes but "the flesh" which deceives us by concealing the reality beneath the surface of things. When Gloucester desires to kiss Lear's hand, the king replies, "Let me wipe it first; it smells of mortality" (4.6.132).

The imagery of sight and blindness, to which Heilman devotes another long chapter, likewise has its counterpart in the Corinthian letters. The passage just quoted continues in this fashion: "So we are always of good courage; we know that while we are at home in the body we are away from the Lord, for *we walk by faith, not by sight*" (2 Cor 5:6–7). Paul, like Shakespeare after him, uses the imagery of cloth to illustrate the relationship between sight and blindness, between faith and the lack of it. With the unbelievers, "a veil lies over their minds; but when a man turns to the Lord the veil is removed" (2 Cor 3:15–16). Moreover, Paul anticipates the speeches of Cordelia, Kent, and Edgar in which they urge sincerity and directness as the only way of confronting blindness:

> We have renounced disgraceful, underhanded ways; we refuse to practice cunning or to tamper with God's word, but *by the open statement of the truth we would commend ourselves to every man's conscience in the sight of God.* And even if our gospel is *veiled,* it is veiled only to those who are perishing. In their case *the god of this world has blinded the minds of the unbelievers.* (2 Cor 4:2–4)

The sight-blindness paradox receives nearly as full a treatment in 2 Corinthians as the foolishness-wisdom paradox does in 1 Corinthians; and together they elaborate the love theme, which is fully stated in 1 Corinthians 13.

### Notes

1   "Reason in Madness" and "Madness in Reason" are the titles of Chapters 8 and 9 of *This Great Stage* (Seattle, 1963).

2   Bradley, *Shakespearean Tragedy,* p. 330.

3   The word *endure* (1 Cor 13:7) is used in both the Geneva Bible (1560) and the Bishops' Bible (1568); *patient* (1 Cor 13:4) first appears in the Rheims translation (1582; 2nd ed., 1600). The King James Version (1611) is the first to

make use of the word *kind* (1 Cor 13:4); before that, *courteous* (Bishops' Bible) or *benigne* (Rheims translation) was preferred. It is significant, however, that the authors of the King James Version, who were men of Shakespeare's own generation, regarded *kind* as a more appropriate word in this context than either *courteous* or *benigne*.

4   Introduction to the Arden *King Lear*, p. lviii.
5   Heilman, p. 83.

From *Between Earth and Heaven* (New York: Holt Rinehart, 1969), pp. 82–83, 85, 87, 89–90. The essay originally appeared in *Thought* 44 (1969), 4–28, copyright by Fordham University Press.

*Maynard Mack (1965)*

## Archetype and Parable in *King Lear*

Perhaps the clearest route to the aspect of *Lear* that belongs to parable is by way of its sources. In general, I think, discussions of Shakespeare's sources, in this play and others, have erred by defining the term too narrowly, paying almost exclusive attention to specific books—in the case of Lear, to Sidney's *Arcadia*, the old play, and two or three other works that may have contributed some details—while virtually ignoring larger, admittedly vaguer, but equally cogent influences, which frequently determine the way in which the specific source is used. It is difficult, for instance, to account for what Shakespeare made of the old play apart from the influence of some such governing archetypal theme as that embodied in folk and medieval renderings of the Abasement of the proud king.[1] In one common form of this archetype, the king comes from swimming or his bath to find his clothes and retainers gone. His role has been usurped by an angel sent from heaven to teach him, in the words of the Magnificat, that God humbles the proud and exalts the humble. In his nakedness, he finds that the evidence of his kingliness, indeed his whole identity, is gone. Assertions that he is in fact the king and efforts to regain his throne lead those around him to mock him as a madman. Standing at last among the beggars outside his own palace, wind torn, tormented by hunger and thirst, he acknowledges his true position, repents his former arrogance, and is then enlightened by the angel and restored to power. As in *King Lear*, there is humbling of pride here, nakedness and beggary and madness, loss of "identity," suffering in the cold; there is also, in the story's point, the theme which Professor Muir rightly emphasizes in his edition of *King Lear* as the governing conception of the scene where Goneril and Regan are tried by a "mad beggar, a dying Fool, and a serving man"—*He hath put down the mighty from their seat, and hath exalted the humble and meek.*

In the finest of all the retellings of this archetype, the repudiated king is not driven out but made the court Fool and compelled to take his food with the palace dogs.[2] This is a detail that may (or may not) have something to do with Lear's hallucination in the farmhouse that "the little dogs and all, Tray, Blanche, and Sweetheart, see, they bark at me." In this version, the king's repentance comes when he has gone in the usurping angel's retinue to Rome, where to his dismay his former fellow-rulers, the Emperor and Pope, do not recognize him at all, and suppose him to be a mad fool. In a moment of insight the king sees a likeness between himself and the great Nebuchadnezzar who was also brought low and lived in a desert for many years on roots and grass.[3] He is moved to repentance and in his humble prayer acknowledges himself to be only "thy fool, Lord." In the past when asked who he is, he has "euere . . . seide he was lord." Now the angel asks the question again, and the reply comes: "A fool." On this, the angel reveals himself, and the king is restored.

In some aspects of its structure, *Lear* was also influenced by procedures its author had found useful in the comedies. Curiously teasing, but too tenuous to pursue, is the apparent recollection of Launcelot Gobbo, with the "fiend" at his elbow and meeting his blind father, in Edgar; and, again, of the words of Bassanio, as he justifies choosing the leaden casket, in France's speech valuing Cordelia as "most rich, being poor." We come on firmer ground with the scuffle of Edgar and Oswald. Edgar at this point plays the role of a poor countryman, speaks in a rural dialect, wields a cudgel; Oswald, who has been presented throughout the play as courtly, insinuating, servile, commands a sword. Yet Edgar kills him, and the event is usually taken to signify some sort of ascendancy of soundhearted "nature" over corrupt "nurture," such as is exemplified in the resistance of Cornwall's servant to the blinding of Gloucester and repeated at a higher level in Edgar's conquest of Edmund. Precisely such an "exemplary" combat Shakespeare had used before in *As You Like It*. There, Orlando, the unschooled country youth, meets Charles, the Court's professional wrestler, epitomizing in his easy victory the superiority of all those in the play who are blessed with Nature's goods over those who possess Fortune's, while at the same time foreshadowing the further successes of "Nature" and her followers in the forest of Arden.

Kent in the stocks brings us back to that distinctive feature of *King Lear* with which we began: its combination of parable and parable situations with acute realism. . . . All could see and sympathize with Kent's visible *persona*, the loyal servant and ambassador of an imperious old man whose reaction to this insult to his majesty and parenthood would be apprehensively anticipated as matter for the coming scenes. But here onstage, at the same time, was an emblem, an archetype, a situation timeless and recurrent, catching in a mirror the world's way with virtue when separated from power. To some—those who knew their Bible best—it might bring reminiscences of the story of Paul and Silas, when by the magistrates of Phillippi they were thrown into prison and the stocks, only to be miraculously released at midnight by an earthquake as they sat singing psalms; and doubtless these members of Shakespeare's audience would suppose they knew precisely what he meant (as no one else ever has) by Kent's reference to miracles when he says in soliloquy, "Nothing almost sees miracles But misery."

*King Lear*, as everybody knows, is a treasury of such patterns and a tissue of such incidents. Lear himself, as Professor Harbage among others has pointed out—flanked in that opening scene by "vices or flatterers on the one hand, virtues or truth-speakers on the other"[4]—stirs memories of a far more ancient dramatic hero, variously called Mankind, Everyman, Genus Humanum, Rex Vivus, Rex Humanitas, Magnificence, etc. He is about to endure an *agon* that, while infinitely more poignant and complex than theirs, has its roots in the same medieval conception of psychomachia, interpreting man's life as "the arena of a Holy War between the contending forces of his own nature."[5] Somewhere in the deep background of the causes that call him to this trial may still lurk the notion of the Summons of Death, which sometimes precipitates the psychomachia in the early Morality plays—now lingering on only in the hint Lear gives that he has divided his kingdom, in order that he may "unburden'd crawl toward death." The persons surrounding him are in some sense (again as in the Morality plays) extensions of himself, who will struggle to assist or defeat him.

Though the complexity of the play as a whole sets it worlds apart from this tradition, one cannot but be struck by the number of details in *King Lear* that seem to derive from it. The opening scene, as noted, partly parallels an episode in most of the Moralities wherein one or more vices cloaked as virtues drive a wedge between the gullible hero and the virtues that support him. Lear's blind self-confidence on this occasion, though a trait of character, is also, one feels, the exemplary self-confidence of the Morality hero—proud man, "drest in a little brief authority," performing his tricks before a heaven in which it is not clear there are any angels left to weep. The road Lear soon must travel, like the road which Eugenio is advised to travel in the interlude *John the Evangelist* and which others will travel as far forward in time as Bunyan's pilgrim, includes psychological landmarks like the "mede of mekenesse," the "path of pacyence," the "lande of largenes;"[6] and though the places in Lear's pilgrimage are no longer, like these, known stages in a certified spiritual progress, and the heavenly destination is no longer clear, the sense of journey to some form of consummation remains.

## Notes

1  For a discussion of the main forms of this story see Lillian H. Hornstein, "King Robert of Sicily: Analogues and Origins," *PMLA* 79 (1964), 13–21.

2  King Robert of Sicily: see *Middle English Metrical Romances*, ed. W. H. French and C. B. Hale (New York, 1930), pp. 937 ff.

3  One cannot but wonder whether the stories told in Scripture of the punishment of Nebuchadnezzar, who for his pride was driven mad and made to live on grass as a beast among the beasts, may not lie somewhere in the background of Lear's madness.

4  In his Introduction to the Pelican *King Lear* (1958), p. 22.

5  Bernard Spivack, *Shakespeare and the Allegory of Evil* (1958), p. 73.

6  Lines 95–97.

From *"King Lear" in Our Time* (University of California Press, 1965), pp. 49–50, 53–54, 56–59, abridged. By permission of the author.

*Joseph H. Summers (1984)*

## The Ending of *King Lear*

Lear's "Ha!" marks the moment of a new "discovery," when he thinks that Cordelia is speaking to him. He has learned that he can no longer trust his senses for a full or accurate account of external reality. At the beginning of the play he had heard and believed the words of Goneril and Regan and he had heard and failed to understand those of Cordelia. These and later "crosses" have provided Lear with an experiential basis for profound scepticism concerning his perceptions. So now he believes that she *is* speaking to him and that it is only her "soft, / Gentle and low" voice that prevents him from hearing precisely words, the emotional import of which he is sure—since they come from Cordelia. The question, "What is't thou say'st?" is addressed directly to Cordelia; the description of her voice, to those surrounding figures who were just before dismissed (with all the world) as murderers and traitors. With the last sentence, "I kill'd the slave that was a-hanging thee," he addresses Cordelia once again, telling her of the one recent event she may not have known.[1]

When the Officer confirms his statement, Lear for the first time truly notices those around him. He hesitantly recognizes Kent, but he cannot follow the news that Kent and his "servant Caius" were the same man, and he agrees without interest or knowledge that his eldest daughters "have fordone themselves, / And desperately are dead" (291–2). From line 274, he seems distracted from the reality of Cordelia's body, but he cannot be much interested in those other persons and events. It is during Albany's speech (295–304) that Lear must again become conscious of the dead Cordelia, and with some sort of paroxysm that elicits Albany's "O! see, see!" Lear is once again sure of her death:

> And my poor fool is hang'd! No, no, no life!
> Why should a dog, a horse, a rat, have life,

And thou no breath at all? Thou'lt come no more,
Never, never, never, never, never! (305–08)

Lear's former convictions that "she lives" and that she spoke to him are rejected either as illusions or as possibilities now past. With that conviction, "Pray you, undo this button" seems to indicate that, once again, "this mother" swells up toward his heart and that he is almost suffocated by his emotion and the attendant rush of blood.

But after the touchingly ceremonial "thank you, Sir" to the character who has helped him undo the button, Lear turns back to Cordelia with, once again, a new and opposite conviction, this time an overwhelming and final one:

Do you see this? Look on her, look, her lips,
Look there, look there! (310–11)

If one insists, hard-headedly, that it is sheer delusion, one may still consider it a consummation devoutly to be wished: to die in the conviction that one's dearest loved one is not, as one had thought, dead, but alive. But beyond this, Lear's final convictions that Cordelia is alive and that her lips move are overwhelming recognition of the reality that he has come to know: that the things he has learned from Cordelia about the nature of love (what he has come to perceive as Cordelia's astonishing essence) are more truly alive than anything else in his world. Cordelia's lips speak at this moment more than any other human lips he could ever imagine.[2] Lear had earlier asked Cordelia, "Have I caught thee?" His last lines indicate that he has indeed, in a sense he had hardly anticipated, by the depth of his unbearably joyful knowledge of a reality and truth that triumph over death and fate and time.

## Notes

1   In his effort to demonstrate that Lear learned nothing and that there is no consolation of any kind at the end of the play, W. R. Elton argues that Lear not only fails in the *ars moriendi* but also ends with "defiance of the heavens, commission of a confirmed murder . . . and a final heroic vaunt" (*"King Lear" and the Gods*, p. 259). I know of no generally accepted usage of the word "murder," legal or moral, past or present, that would justify its application to Lear's killing of the "slave that was a-hanging" Cordelia. It is difficult to imagine an ethical standard (except a totally pacifist one hardly envisaged in the play) by which the action could be censured.

2   Sigurd Burckhardt wrote, "He ends, it might seem, where Gloster, with his 'Let's see,' began. But he dies believing that he has seen living breath, not letters—words, not signs" (*Shakespearean Meanings*, Princeton, 1968, p. 258).

From "The Ending of *King Lear*," in *Dreams of Love and Power: On Shakespeare's Plays* (Oxford: Clarendon Press, 1984), pp. 111–13. Used by permission.

*Walter Stein (1969)*

## The Extreme Verge in *King Lear*

The symbolic immediacy of the cliff that isn't there—"How fearful / And dizzy 'tis to cast one's eyes so low"—embraces much more than Gloucester's personal experience. In its context, it also stands proxy for Lear's—who has been physically absent since the Fool's liquidation, and is presently to reappear at his most lunatic and most profound; and indeed it distils the entire tragic rhythm of the play.

For this scene not merely compresses the movement from sheer despair—"you are now within a foot / Of the extreme verge"—to acceptance (through Gloucester) of Edgar's unconditional commitment to "free and patient thoughts":

> henceforth I'll bear
> Affliction till it do cry out itself
> "Enough, enough," and die.

It obliquely interprets this movement, in terms of Gloucester's "blindness." Gloucester, deceived and betrayed by Edmund—as he had once been deceived by the "sport at his making"—is now once more suffering deception:

| | |
|---|---|
| Gloucester | Methinks the ground is even. |
| Edgar | Horrible steep: |
| | Hark! do you hear the sea? |
| Gloucester | No, truly. |
| Edgar | Why then, your other senses grow imperfect |
| | By your eyes' anguish. |
| Gloucester | So may it be indeed. |
| | Methinks thy voice is altered, and thou speakst |
| | In better phrase and manner than thou didst. |
| Edgar | You're much deceiv'd; in nothing am I chang'd |
| | But in my garments. |

Even in saying this, Edgar is deceiving him; and yet he is merely telling the truth. For indeed Gloucester is "much deceived"—much, much deceived: more than ever in his present despair—and there *are* cliffs of fall before his feet. Edgar's "deceptions" are thus themselves deceptive: in reality they are not deceptions at all—he remains the thing itself throughout his transformations—but the truth.

The complexity of this situation exactly corresponds to the complex revelatory rhythm of the play as a whole (just as its compound of absurdity and tragic force reflects its general tone). Under Edgar's supervision, Gloucester's blindness is turning into a sort of seeing: "Thy life's a miracle," Edgar assures him; and surely it is?

> Look up a-height; the shrill-gorg'd lark so far
> Cannot be seen or heard: *do but look up.*

Of course, he knows very well that Gloucester will have to reply: "Alack! I have no eyes." But there is nothing cruel or unnecessary about his exhortation. Gloucester is ready, at last, to assent:

> Think that the clearest gods, who make them honours
> Of men's impossibilities, have preserved thee.

And, in his blindness—"I see it feelingly," as he later tells Lear—he *sees*:

> henceforth I'll bear
> Affliction till it do cry out itself
> "Enough, enough," and die.

What Edgar thus points to, and Gloucester painfully grasps, is among the play's central "reasons of the heart"; while at the same time, it defines the very nature of such "reasons." The very "cruelty" of the scene—whose apparent gratuitousness has so often been taken as its essential meaning—is in fact the tragic surpassing of cruelty: tragedy pushed beyond mere tragic outrage. If it is "cruel," it is cruel only as Job is cruel (since the facts of tragic experience are cruel). If affliction *must* be borne—and the play makes us see that it must—the world ceases to be bottomlessly absurd.

*Lear* descends deeply into the heart's mind; and it is the depth of its penetration of "patience" that releases the play's tragic joy. For "patience," here, is not simply a moral achievement: essentially, it is an insight into existence. It is the practical acknowledgment—partly the seed, partly the fruit—of a cosmic apprehension, an incipient apprehension of the cause of thunder. "Ripeness is all" thus implies a whole order of things—that ultimate order that has been put to the test by the play, an order in which there is *meaning*—even (perhaps even especially) in affliction and heartbreak and death, and in which it makes sense to say: "Upon such sacrifices, my Cordelia, / The gods themselves throw incense."

From *Criticism as Dialogue* (Cambridge University Press, 1969), pp. 107–11 abridged. Used by permission.

*John Cunningham (1984)*

## *King Lear*, the Storm, and the Liturgy

In 1960 Barbara Everett wrote that A. C. Bradley's interpretation of Lear's death "is now accepted almost universally." Bradley held that the king dies "by an agony ... not of pain but of ecstasy" that Cordelia is alive, and he thought that we might properly call the play "*The Redemption of King Lear*." Everett, however, demurred and held that Lear dies in "supreme tragic horror at the corpse" of Cordelia. In the same year, J. K. Walton could find evidence only of the old man's grief, and in 1974 Thomas Van Laan concluded that the king had "completely lost contact with external reality." Nicholas Brooke went even further, suggesting that Lear's "final retreat to madness" makes "it impossible to retain any concept of an ordered universe." John D. Rosenburg saw Lear's "deluded hope" as "the last and the cruelest of the play's mockeries."

Yet twenty years after Everett began the series of attacks on the almost universally accepted interpretation, Joseph Summers returned to argue Bradley's thesis— but with a difference: the joy that overcomes Lear is not that Cordelia lives here below but rather that the things which he learned from her about the nature of love "are more truly alive than anything else in his world," for Cordelia's "astonishing essence" is love. Earlier, in 1975, Richard Matthews had recognized Cordelia as a symbol of the love that embraces the whole world of the play. In this essay I hope to support the position of Summers and Matthews by drawing attention to a metaphor that other critics of the play have not discussed.

Those critics who have observed that the old king suffers a process of regeneration have not remarked how much of the ancient rite of baptism Shakespeare may have drawn upon in describing the renewal of the king. The principal source for study of this sacrament is, of course, the Bible as interpreted by the early fathers. Of course, there was no catechumenate in Shakespeare's day; but the Lenten preparation and the ancient rites of baptism at Easter remained the norm by which the sacrament was understood in the sixteenth and seventeenth centuries.

The catechumens' progress through the renunciations of Lent, into the baptismal pool, and out of it is said to effect sacramentally a new life in them; in an analogous way, the journey of Lear and Gloucester away from the court, into the storm, and out of it leaves them morally and spiritually reborn. In both cases the old is put off and the new is put on. My point is that baptism is a metaphor of the reformation that they experience; or, to put the matter another way, Shakespeare recognizes in the contours of the two men's moral and spiritual change a type of the mystic destruction and recreation thought to be effected sacramentally by baptism.

### In the Wilderness

The church teaches that disobedience separated Adam from God and exiled him from Eden. His Fall brought enmity among men, between men and animals, and among the animals; it brought thorns and thistles in the cursed earth. Disorder invaded the cosmos, and sickness entered man's body. Sin enslaved man to the darkness of error. In the night of his exile, Nicodemus came to Jesus and learned that by baptism one is born again. The catechumens begin their progress when they move away from the exiled, sinful and dying "old Adam," who will be crucified and put off during their baptism on Easter Even.

*King Lear*, being a play and not a rite, does not provide exact parallels with the liturgy; yet the world of Lear, like that of the exiled Adam, is fallen and plagued by disease, enmity, darkness, physical and spiritual death. It is like the cold world of Lent; it offers catechists who teach renunciation and who lead into the wilderness those who would put off the old man.

The nature seemingly regnant in the play is unprofitable and fierce; it is Adam's unredeemed world of sin and death. The cursed ground produces "fumiter, . . . hardocks, hemlock, nettles." This nature is also bestial, plenteous with the enmity of the "detested kite," the "wolvish visage," the sharp "serpent's tooth." Moreover, the animals but figure the bestiality of fallen human nature. Goneril is "sharp-tooth'd . . . like a vulture"; she and Regan are tigers, not daughters. This nature is infected with the sickness of the Fall: with ague and cold, with "the indispos'd and sickly fit." Goneril speaks better than she knows when she sends Oswald to say, "I am sick." The bastard Edmund worships this deadly nature as a "goddess," to her his services are bound. Lear, too, prays to "Nature," this same "Goddess" of barrenness and death, to "dry up" Goneril's organs of increase.

In this fallen world stand forth Lear and Gloucester, two aged fools, types of all the progeny of the banished old Adam. Lear's "hideous rashness" in disowning Cordelia, Kent sees as the act of a "mad . . . old man." Goneril calls Lear an "old man" among "old fools." Both Goneril and the Fool tax Lear with being old before he is wise. In several ways Gloucester has "follow'd the old man" and has an "old heart."

When Lear "divide[s] / In three [his] Kingdom," he, like Adam, exiles everyone. Without intending to do so, Lear effects a fortunate exile upon Kent. He looses him from the moral and spiritual night of "our Kingdom"; thereby, he frees Kent to shape his "old course in a country new" where "freedom lives." Likewise, Lear does Cordelia "a blessing against his will," exiling her to the "dear shelter" of "the Gods," to a "better where." Edgar, of whom Goucester says "I never got him," is also cast out of the corruption of the court. Finally, without intending to do so, Lear, in giving the old kingdom to Goneril and Regan, imposes upon them the moral "banishment" that Kent proclaims that realm to be.

In exiling himself, Lear, like Adam, looses upon his kingdom the darkness of night. He begins by announcing his "darker purpose"; and he proceeds to act blindly without the light of Apollo. The Fool defines the state that Lear has brought upon himself, saying, "Out went the candle, and we [are] left darkling." The kingdom becomes a place of "darkness and devils"; and the stormy night is, as Gloucester says, "hell-black." Lear calls himself "the Dragon," an emblem throughout Revelation of Satan.

The Fool is the first of Lear's "schoolmasters," of the king's catechists; and he teaches Lear that his pretended renunciation has indeed been enforced upon him. When Lear can "take the Fool with" him, he can learn of the genuine casting off that has come upon him; he can learn that he is "nothing," "an O without a fig-ure." From this nothing which renunciation brings, creation may eventually rise. Like Lear, Gloucester early offers to renounce the world—he says, "I would un-state myself"—and the action of the play brings enforced renunciation upon him, too. Like Adam, Lear and Gloucester are thrust out of the "opulent" land ample with shadowy forest and wide-skirted meads and made to join Tom in the country of "low farms," of "penury . . . near to beast." With Tom they must "outface / The winds" of a winter world, where "for many miles about / There's scarce a bush." Unlike the catechumens who gladly enter the desert of Lent, Lear has been driven into the "wild field," the wilderness where the storm occurs.

### Into the Baptistry

In the dark church of Easter Even the Chistians, by liturgy, think to re-enact the mystery of death and resurrection; by this rite, the catechumens are said to be sacramentally "grafted . . . [into] the similitude of [Christ's] death" (Rom 6:3). They now put off the old man; and, facing west, the region of visible darkness, they "forsake the devil and all his works, [and] the vain pomp, and glory of the world." Christ hanging naked on the cross regained for humanity the primitive innocence lost in the Fall. Therefore, the catechumens put off their clothes which represent the garments of skin covering the old fallen Adam, emblems of vanity and corruption; and they enter the baptismal poot naked.[1]

Descending into the waters, the catechumens leave behind both the captivity to Satan and the forty days—or forty years—in the wilderness, Christ having "sanctified the . . . Jordan and all other waters to the mystical washing away of sin." Noah's Flood, where sin was judged and destroyed, is a type of the baptismal rite which "utterly abolish[es] the whole body of sin." Likewise, the apocalyptic judg-ment and fiery destruction of sin at the end of time is a type of baptism.[2] Accord-ing to St Paul, the old Adam in the catechumens is conformed to the death of Christ—"buried . . . with him by baptism"—in the font which is their grave.[3]

In the darkness of the storm, Lear and Gloucester confront devils and, like the catechumens, renounce them. Lear comes to recognize his own mortality and sin, and he puts off his clothes and figuratively goes into the waters, asking judgment of sin and calling down destruction upon it. The storm occurs on a "hell-black night," during which Tom sounds repeated warnings to Lear about devils that are all around: about the Prince of Darkness, about the "foul Flibbertigibbet," about Nero, "an angler in the Lake of Darkness," about Swithold and Modo and Mahu. Tom's vision is a mad one with which Lear instantly identifies—What! "Has his daughters brought him to this pass?" But the mad vision is true: for in the mock trial, Lear sees his infernal daughters where Tom sees fiends. Having encountered the devils, Lear renounces "hell, . . . darkness, . . . the sulphurous pit," saying, "Fie, fie, fie! / Pah, pah!" Gloucester also endures exorcism, and Edgar is present then, too, when "some fiend" with "horns whelk'd" parts from him. Both Gloucester and Lear, in order to put off the old man must, like the catechumens, be freed of the "foul fiend."

Salvation for Kent and Edgar has depended on putting off their clothes; and Lear learns from Edgar to cast off his own. In Tom, Edgar has become the kind of nothing requisite for new creation. Lear comes upon Tom, "a poor, bare, forked animal"; and he is moved to put off his own commodities, saying, "Off, off, you lendings! Come; unbutton here." Renouncing the "vain pomp, and glory of the world," he figuratively enters the waters of the grave, going into the storm accompanied by Edgar, his godson, at whose baptism Lear stood as sponsor.

The cataclysmic waters of the storm destroy the old man in Lear as the baptismal waters are said to destroy the old Adam in the catechumens. At the beginning of the storm, Kent and a gentleman observe its continuity in the cosmos (the "fretful elements") and in the little world of man. Lear associates the contentious storm with the "tempest in [his] mind"; therefore, in calling for "things [to] change or cease," in bidding "the wind [to] blow the earth into the sea" or "the curled waters" to "swell...'bove the main," he implicitly asks for the destruction of the old man in him as well as of the old world.

Noah's Flood and the apocalyptic fire are types, as we saw, of the annihilation effected sacramentally in baptism. Lear asks for a second deluge to spout until it has "drench'd our steeples, drown'd the cocks" on them. He calls upon "cataracts and hurricanoes," thereby alluding to "the flood-gates of heaven" in Genesis 7:11 and 8:2 which describe Noah's Flood. The judgment and destruction of sin effected in the Great Flood and to be made final at the Apocalypse Lear calls for now (3.2.49–60).

"When the rain [comes] to wet" him, Lear, with his lendings off, figuratively enters the water, like a grave, fathom and half; and it "invades [him] to the skin." After the storm, the Quarto allows Tom one line from a song—"*Come o'er the bourn, Bessy, to me*"—in which Muir says that "a lover calls upon his sweetheart to come to him across a stream." The text of the song throws light on the action of the play. The lover is "Christ [who] ... clepys" to "Besse [who] ys mankynd" in "this world blynde'; he calls to her, "Cum over the burne, Besse, to me." Surely the stream is a type of Jordan.[4]

### Out of the Baptistry

When the catechumens emerge from the baptistry, they have come to new life. Having renounced Satan, facing west, they turn and say the Creed, facing east which represents the region of light, the Second Coming, and Christ himself.[5] Like Christ rising from the grave on Easter morning, they are said to rise from the womb of the baptistry born "anew of water and the Holy Ghost." They have put on the "new man," Christ, the second Adam. The healing of the leprous Naaman in the Jordan is one Old Testament type of baptism. Likewise, in the rite, the catechumens have figuratively crossed Jordan; they have entered the paradise of the church, the new Eden.

The transformation which the storm effects in Lear and Gloucester is not so tidy as that brought about sacramentally by the liturgy. As late as 4.6, Lear still wants to "kill, kill, kill, kill, kill, kill." Yet the changes have their commencement in the storm. During it Lear's understanding of love begins the process of being purged of selfishness, and he joins the communion of those who suffer. Thereby, he emerges from hellish isolation. Imagery of darkness gives way to that of light. Lear moves east toward light and toward the saving and restorative medicines that Cordelia has for him. She sees to it that he has new clothes, proper for the new kingdom to which he has made his hard way.

In Cordelia, light will be restored to the play; and, through her, Lear will come to new life and will enter the new kingdom of forgiving love. Even in the dark night of the storm, light begins to replace darkness: Gloucester comes to Lear, "a walking fire," "a little fire in a wild field." He directs the king eastward to Dover, toward light. At Dover is Cordelia, whose face is "sunshine and rain at once," with whom is " fair daylight."

She asks if her poor father "hovel[ed]," like the Prodigal Son, "with swine . . . / In short and musty straw"; she asks if he "is . . . array'd." When the Prodigal returned from the far country, his father gave him a robe appropriate for his restoration. A gentleman assures Cordelia that Lear has fresh garments proper for his "country new." She asks after Kent's clothing also, beseeching him to "be better suited"; and Edgar, too, is "chang'd . . . in [his] garments."

With Cordelia by, Lear "wakes" to a new life, as "out o' th' grave"; he is healed of the old infirmities; and he is brought out of madness to a kingdom new. Cordelia asks restoration to "hang / [Its] medicine on [her] lips" that her kiss of charity may "repair" Lear's "violent harms." Edgar, too, uses imagery of medicine; he "trifle[s] . . . with [Gloucester's] despair . . . to cure it." Cordelia's ministry restores Lear; or, rather, out of the "ruin'd piece of Nature," it brings new life.

### At the Gate of Death

St Cyril of Jerusalem instructed the catechumens that baptism into Christ's death is an emblem of the death that comes to every man and that death is a second baptism.[6] The purpose of baptism, according to the church's teachings, is to bring the catechumens "finally . . . to the land of everlasting life." Therefore, the Church has anciently commemorated her saints on the day of their death when they are born into eternity.

To argue, as several critics after 1960 have, that Lear dies in despair or deluded while Gloucester and even Edmund go to good deaths makes nonsense of the patterns of the play and renders it incoherent; but for Lear to die well, he must have enforced upon him a final renunciation. Having been reunited with Edgar, Gloucester is ready to die; having been reunited with Cordelia, Lear is not. Lear begins the play seeking love in the wrong way, and seeking a perversion of love. This corrupt affection is purged in the storm. When he is awakened at Dover by Cordelia's kiss, he mistakes the bearer of love for Love itself; and he falls into idolatry. For him to know the Reality, the emblem of it must be taken from him. The life in prison with Cordelia that Lear vainly imagines as heavenly would indeed immure him. To "take upon [one's self] the mystery of things" on this side of the grave, to presume to be as "Gods spies" here below is indeed delusion; and Cordelia must die in order for Lear to be released from his delusion.

By her death, the final renunciation is enforced upon Lear. Earlier he imperatively says, "Off, off, you lendings! Come; unbutton here"; in death he puts off the garment of flesh, humbly asking aid, courteously giving thanks for it: "Pray you, undo this button; thank you." In the Quarto, he joins Cordelia in death at this point and enters mystery with her. The Folio gives him the further words, "Do you see this? Look on her, look, her lips, / Look there, look there!" For Joseph Summers, the lines suggest that Lear experiences, with more than his earthly "eyes [which] are not o' th' best," a vision through the grave, beyond the grave, of the Reality he is even then coming to see face to face. In both versions he is "delivered from the burden of the flesh," from "the miseries of this sinful world," from "the rack of this tough world."

The apostle who saw that the rock from which the Israelites drank in the wilderness was Christ and who understood them to be "baptized under Moses in the cloud" instructed a civilization in how to read Christ's name on each page of the Old Testament. That civilization learned of its own how to moralize classical mythology and literature and to recognize there divine analogies. We need not be surprised, therefore, that in an old story from Pagan Britain Shakespeare discerned hieroglyphics of the pattern of redemption and of the rite that his civilization thought effected it.

## Notes

1 Jean Daniélou, *The Bible and the Liturgy* (Notre Dame: University of Notre Dame Press, 1956), pp. 37–39.
2 Daniélou, pp. 41–42, 75–79, 102–03; baptismal office, *BCP*, pp. 270–75.
3 The Epistle (Rom 6) for the Sixth Sunday after Trinity, *BCP*, p. 185.
4 Kenneth Muir, Arden *King Lear*, p. 132n. For the song, see John Stevens, *Music and Poetry in the Early Tudor Court* (Cambridge University Press, 1979), p. 348.
5 Daniélou, pp. 31–32.
6 Daniélou, p. 44.

From "*King Lear*, the Storm, and the Liturgy," *Christianity & Literature* 34 (1984), 9–30 abridged.

*Joseph Wittreich (1984)*

## "As it was played . . . St Stephans night"

Whether or not Shakespeare's play is properly described as Christian, its title page, together with its Fool, aligns it with a formal occasion, designated by the liturgical calendar, for contemplating man's inhumanity to man and, in its reference to St Stephen, advances the notion, developed by John Foxe, that persecutions and martydoms are but the harbingers of notable conversions. Roy Battenhouse hints at such a connection—and at such a conception—when he remarks, with reference to *King Lear*, that "St Stephen's death did not waste his goodness, since through it he offered a haunting and lasting witness to the life of charity he embodied: What was wasted was the persecutor's evil will. Providential order permits sinful men to waste their energies. It permits also, on the part of innocent persons, miseries which can be endured as sacrifices, through which higher goods are testified to and become efficacious."[1]

The collocation of play and feast day is in many ways apt; for quite apart from Battenhouse's suggestion, Stephen was also associated with a philosophy wherein history, gathering around certain nodal points, crystallized around outstanding figures as well. Preoccupied with the question of how, and in what ways, God's will manifests itself in history, Stephen is credited with discovering a pattern in history—a rhythm of debasement followed by exaltation. . . .Stephen's conception of history is emphatically prophetic rather than legalistic; and, important for our purposes, his last sermon recalls past history in order to unravel current history.

Bernard McGinn reminds us that the day of St Stephen held special importance within the liturgical calendar; for on that day "justice was born," and this was also the day of emperors and kings, for the name of Stephen means "crowned."[2] We should remember, too, that John Foxe stimulated extraordinary interest in the lives of the martyrs whom he represented as principal actors in a drama out of which unfolded the tragedy of history and that, by now, among the martyrs Stephen was the foremost example of Christian charity, was said to mark the movement of man's emergence out of the darkness into light and of his deliverance from the law into love. An inexplicable, pointless tragedy, Stephen's death was nonetheless cited as evidence of the exalting effects of such tragedy.

One begins to wonder if the highly elusive liturgical structure of medieval drama may not have some bearing on *King Lear*, especially when one recalls the long tradition of Christmas plays together with the fact that the Last Judgment was an especially prominent subject during the Advent season: the First and Second Comings harmonized in a liturgical chord, an epistle of Incarnation sounded with a gospel of Judgment. Here, we should also remember the timetable of the theatrical season: the habitual opening on December 26; the tendency of the times to correlate drama with the liturgical calendar; and the fact that the liturgy was established by the Book of Common Prayer.

The readings for St Stephen's Day are Psalms 116–119, Ecclesiastes 4 and Proverbs 28, Isaiah 56 and 57, and Acts 6 and 7. Ecclesiastes 4 and Proverbs 28 provide the proper lessons; the Epistle comes from Acts 7, and the Gospel from Matthew 23. As the Apocalypse is said to do, *King Lear* itself seems to "carry the melody of the church's liturgy," at least its more somber tones, and, again like the Apocalypse, is "oriented around the Incarnation."[3]

No specified reading argues more forcibly for a connection between liturgy and play than the following passage from Ecclesiastes: "Better is a poore and wise childe, then an olde and foolish King, who will no more be admonished" (4.13)—a passage that reverberates throughout *King Lear*. Goneril tells Lear: "you are old ..., should be wise" (1.4.247; cf. 2.4.147–51); his Fool, a boy, tells him: "Thou should'st not have been old till thou hadst been wise" (1.5.45–46), and later: "here's a night pities neither wise men nor Fools" (3.2.12–13); and Lear tells Cordelia: "I am a very foolish ... old man" (4.7.60). In Ecclesiastes 4.14, we learn that "out of prison he cometh forthe to reigne, when as he that is borne in his kingdome, is made poore." Born to his kingship, Lear surrenders it and becomes poor, but leaving the prison at the end of the play, with his "poor fool ... hang'd" (5.3.305), the kingdom is restored to Lear: "we will resign, / During the life of this old Majesty, / To him our absolute power" (5.3.298–300). Compassed round by dead bodies, Lear sees that his foes, the real fools of this play, have all tasted the cup of their deserving, that evil has been destroyed or has destroyed itself, as if to affirm the wisdom of Ecclesiastes 4.5: "The fool foldeth his hand, and eateth vp his owne flesh."

Other readings contribute reinforcement to this hypothetical connection between liturgy and play, especially those passages from Proverbs, which counsel that "wicked men vnderstand not iudgement" (28.5), "a prince destitute of vnderstanding, is ... a great oppressour" (28.16), "a man that doeth violence against the blood of a persone, shal flee vnto the grave" (28.17), "He that robbeth his father ... & saith, it is no transgression, is the companion of a man that destroieth" (28.24), and finally that "when the wicked rise vp, men hide the[m]selues: but when thei perish, the righteous increase" (28.28). The dialectics of Shakespeare's play involving a youthful and wise fool and an old and foolish king, an even distribution of good and wicked characters (the latter divesting their fathers of their belongings), the annihilation of the evil and survival of the good, even the dialectical relationship of the play with its sources, can be accounted for by the premises and concerns set forth in the Book of Proverbs.

Other readings for the day, Acts 6 and 7, represent Stephen as Shakespeare depicts Cordelia—as an idealized embodiment of virtue; and as Lear imagines himself—as "the pattern of all patience" (3.2.37). And in their reference to Saul, struck blind that he might see, these same readings suggest the paradox of blindness and vision, as well as the prophetic themes of conversion and redemption, sleeping and waking. The Gospel for the day, Matthew 23, addressing blind men and fools, speaks of prophets and wise men who have been senselessly killed, of all the blood spilled going back to Abel, and, though this is a "generation of vipers" (23.33), offers the assurance first that the exalted shall be abased and the humble exalted, and second that in time the persecutors themselves will perish as happens in *King Lear* but not in Lear's story as reported in the chronicle histories. Psalms 116–119 cry out for righteousness in a world marked by injustice—and for deliverance from a world compassed round by death. The usual readings for the day, Isaiah 56 and 57, besides reminding us that Geoffrey of Monmouth had placed Lear's story near the time of Isaiah's prophesying, proclaim the existence of justice, even in a world where men are beasts and devourers, blind and without knowledge, and where the righteous continue to perish although there is no peace for the wicked.

Out of the liturgical readings for, and around, St Stephen's Day emerge the apocalyptic themes and concerns of Shakespeare's play. This is the time, we are reminded by the Advent texts, for casting off darkness and putting on the armor of light so that in the last days we may rise into life immortal; this is the time for waking out of sleep, for preparing for the prophets by tuning our ears and sharpening our vision. Even if people are everywhere surrounded by darkness and afflicted by despair, the light will break, we are assured, and man's redemption is drawing near. Not only was the Last Judgment an especially prominent subject during the Advent season, but December was the month to which were confined most of the few assigned readings from the Book of Revelation. Chapters 1 and 22 were assigned to St John's Day, December 27, and Chapter 14 was assigned as an epistle for Holy Innocents' Day, December 28. Apocalyptic texts are thus designated for the days immediately following the Feast of St Stephen and have the effect of bringing out from the concealment of the Advent epistles and gospels themes that will have a special, albeit ironic, bearing on *King Lear*.

## Notes

1    *Shakespearean Tragedy* (Indiana University Press, 1969), p. 194.
2    *Visions of the End: Apocalyptic Traditions in the Middle Ages* (Columbia University Press, 1979), p. 173.
3    See Jaroslav Pelikan, *The Emergence of the Catholic Tradition: 100–600* (University of Chicago Press, 1971), p. 133, and Jacques Ellul, *Apocalypse*, tr. George Schreiner (Seabury Press, 1977), p. 47.

From *"Image of That Horror": History, Prophecy and Apocalypse in "King Lear"* (The Huntington Library, 1984), pp. 114–19 abridged. Used by permission.

# MACBETH

## Comment and bibliography

Macbeth's tragic career develops in accord with the stages of moral deterioration enumerated by Augustine: "Of a froward will was a lust made, and a lust served became custom, and custom not resisted became necessity" (*Conf.* VIII.10). A froward will is indicated by the extravagant ferocity of the swordsmanship reported of Macbeth in scene 2, a kind of courage more concerned with its own excellence than with subduing the enemy (the concern of Macduff in the play's closing scene, where even a "monster" is offered the option of life for surrender). It is this frowardness that makes Macbeth vulnerable to the suggestion of murder that knocks at his ribs on hearing confirmed a part of the witches' prediction, and it becomes a lust of ambition when his wife offers to arrange a "sovereign sway and masterdom" if he will but "beguile" the time. When a residual conscience warns him of the this-world consequences of violating heaven-sanctioned duties, Macbeth is persuaded to put aside his fears by his wife's plan for avoiding earthly retribution and by her challenge to him to be "a man" by courageously willing what he desires. But once Macbeth consents to this lust, a serving it becomes his custom as sin plucks on sin and he adds a plan to murder Banquo. In the subsequent situation, a sliding into mass murders seems a necessity for his security. Thus progressively he dehumanizes himself and comes at last to liken himself to a bear tied to a stake.

There are many ironies in this sad story of self-betrayal. One is that Macbeth's manhood gets "proved" by letting his wife teach him a serpent-version of good and evil, as in the Genesis tragedy in which normal roles of gender were inverted. A further irony is that her plan to transfer the guilt to grooms deprived of reason in a "swinish sleep" gets contradicted by their ability to cry "God bless us," whereas the real swinishness is the deprivation of reason into which she leads Macbeth by getting *him* drunk with incitements to vainglory. ("As drunkennesse obscureth reason, so vaineglory corrupteth discretion" is a maxim of St Chrysostom quoted by Francis Meres in his *Palladis Tamia* [1598], our earliest book of literary criticism that praises Shakespeare.) A major irony is that Lady Macbeth by her display of a dare-devil resoluteness enables in her husband merely a quasi-ignorant act. His own reason has warned him only a moment earlier that heaven's cherubin will "blow the horrid deed in every eye"; yet her flimsy reasoning permits him to believe that the deed's horror can be escaped. So for the moment he overlooks the eye of his own conscience, which will begin causing him trouble immediately after his deed. Conscience can be suppressed but it revives to torment its abuser.

The play delineates with precision the psychology of ignorance. "Let not light see my black and deep desires," says Macbeth when his ambition is to have done the unnamed deed his eye fears to see. And Lady Macbeth, when abnegating her milk-giving nature, invokes "thick night" so that "heaven" may not peep through this blanket to cry "Hold" to her serving of spirits of darkness. But this instinct of a murderous will to put out the light induces a blindness that causes "imperfection" in the crime—as we learn in 3.3 from the bewildered assassin who asks "Was't not the way?" after his obeying of Macbeth's injunction to "mask the business from the common eye" permitted the escape of Fleance. A desire for ignorance, ironically, cooperates with the "equivocation of the fiends" which Macbeth later blames for his tragedy. Ignorance is indeed like a drink that "provokes the desire but takes away the performance."

Criminal ambition can be awesome, however, in the wounds it inflicts on "The Lord's anointed temple" and on the commonwealth of Scotland. It unties winds of violence that almost strangle the traveling lamp of Day. It causes daily new widows to howl. It infiltrates households with government spies (a practice not unknown in Shakespeare's England). It can drive the tyrant to pray for a confounding of nature's *germens*, or creative seeds, in a desperate hope of quieting his "restless ecstasy." But once "renown and grace are dead," his life is reduced to a treadmill of "sound and fury," signifying nothing. A desecrating of the hallowed results in hollowness.

Scotland is given a rescuer in Malcolm, a prince who intuits that the "face" of things is not to be trusted. In fact, he masks his own virtues in order to test the sincerity of Macduff, which he knows will be revealed only by the tone of voice of Macduff when put in a crisis of choice. Malcolm's concern is to distinguish "grace" from the mere "brows" of it. So the moment Macduff pleads in anguish the sanction of Malcolm's sainted parents, he can be prudently embraced. For Malcolm's aim is a medicining of Scotland with support from heaven. His taking the boughs of trees as his army's aegis signals a redress like that of the "branch" symbolism in Bible prophecy. To "dew" the flower and drown the weeds is Lennox's metaphor for stating this purpose. (In Shakespeare, as in the Bible, dew is a symbol of divine grace—like the "gentle rain" of *MV*.) In victory, Malcolm's healing role is attested by his promise to call home exiled friends and perform "by the grace of Grace" all else needful. The Christian virtue of Malcolm is a saving donnée of the story.

Selected for our anthology are pieces of commentary which indicate the play's dependence on patterns in Christian lore. Roland Frye makes evident that the punishments suffered by Macbeth accord with predictions in Isaiah, Job, and Psalms. Paul Jorgensen notes that Macbeth's crime is like that of Judas and of Cain, and that it brings him pains of sense and pains of loss, the two kinds of punishment that characterize hell in Scholastic theology. Glynne Wickham comments on the "Harrowing of Hell" episode in the English cycle plays as a subtext for Shakespeare's scene of Macduff's knocking at the gate, and he notes as a subtext for Macbeth's duplicity and slaughtering of innocents the biblical Herod of the Mystery cycles. Roy Walker finds significant the associating of Duncan and Macduff with the island of Iona and with St Columba. Harry Morris sees reflected in *Macbeth* the concept of Dante that souls can suffer in hell before their bodies die, and further he finds the medieval iconography of Judgment Day reflected in the disorders in nature that accompany Macbeth's act of sacrilege.

In the supplementary bibliography, several of the items canvass various biblical influences on the play, and several others discuss correlations with Dante's *Inferno*. W. H. Toppen in reviewing Shakespeare's depiction of conscience in the play finds it accords with a Christian understanding. Walter Clyde Curry's book of 1937 surprised its readers by arguing that *Macbeth* is integrated by doctrines inherited from the medieval scholastics—for instance, Augustine's concept of nature's *germens*, and the theory of demonic spirits elaborated by Aquinas, and the doctrine in both these theologians that a residual dignity remains in a sinner's deteriorating character since there is a good in human nature that can be diminished but never quite destroyed. The early essay by L. C. Knights was notable for its challenging of A. C. Bradley's vaguely impressionistic account of evil, noticing instead Shakespeare's imagery of a holy supernatural that surrounds Duncan and provides a "temple-haunting martlet" outside Macbeth's castle. This emphasis was given support in 1958 by G. R. Elliott, who stressed the play's motif of "grace," read the "husbandry of heaven" as symbolically putting out its candles to call Macbeth back from his ambition, and attributed to Christian faith the resoluteness of Malcolm. Francis Fergusson has analyzed carefully the downward and the upward phases in the play's action. Roland Frye has delineated the stages of "consent" by Macbeth in Act 1.

Herbert Coursen associates Macbeth with a fall from grace like that of Adam and Lucifer, while elements of Eve and Lillith are reflected in Lady Macbeth. Lady Macbeth's "feint" in 2.3 suggests the scheming plotter of the early scenes, and her "faint" predicts the sin-haunted woman of Act 5. Arthur Kirsch finds "explicit and emphatic" Augustinian reverberations in the play; particularly germane is Augustine's comment that Adam in abandoning God "grew toward nothing" and suffered the misery of futility. Dolora Cunningham traces Macbeth's self-induced hardening of heart and finds this in accord with sermon literature that says "long custom of sinne" takes away the feeling of sin. Yet since, according to St Bernard, the ills the soul suffers are "superinduced" on a goodness which is the gift of the Creator, they "deform" an order they cannot destroy. So Macbeth remains conscious of loss, even when he has brought on himself a darkened understanding and frozen affections. Cunningham concludes with an important generalization: "Macbeth makes his spirit inaccessible to the light of grace, as do practically all of

Shakespeare's tragic heroes. If they had not done so, they would not finally be tragic" (p. 46).

## Supplementary bibliography

Battenhouse, Roy. *Shakespearean Tragedy* (1969), pp. 195–99.

Bernad, Miguel. "The Five Tragedies in *Macbeth*," *Shakespeare Quarterly* 13 (1962), 49–61.

Coursen, Herbert R. "In Deepest Consequence: *Macbeth*," *Shakespeare Quarterly* 18 (1967), 375–88.

Cunningham, Dolora. "*Macbeth:* The Tragedy of the Hardened Heart," *Shakespeare Quarterly* 14 (1963), 39–47.

Curry, Walter Clyde. *Shakespeare's Philosophical Patterns* (Louisiana State University Press, 1937; 2nd ed. Peter Smith, 1959), Chs. 3–4.

Davidson, Clifford. *The Primrose Way* (Conesville, Iowa: John Westburg & Associates, 1970), esp. pp. 5–32; 86–90.

Elliott, G. R. *Dramatic Providence in "Macbeth"* (Princeton University Press, 1958).

Fergusson, Francis. "*Macbeth* as the Imitation of an Action," in *English Institute Essays* 1951; rpt. in *The Human Image in Dramatic Literature* (Doubleday, 1957), pp. 115–25.

———. "Killing the Bond of Love," in *Trope and Allegory* (University of Georgia Press, 1980), Ch. 3.

Frye, Roland M. "Launching the Tragedy of Macbeth: Temptation, Deliberation, and Consent in Act 1," *Huntington Library Quarterly* 45 (1982), 1–19.

Jack, Jane H. "Macbeth, King James, and the Bible," *English Literary History* 22 (1955), 173–93.

Kirsch, Arthur. "Macbeth's Suicide," *English Literary History* 51 (1984), 269–96.

Knights, L. C. "How Many Children Had Lady Macbeth?" in *Explorations* (London, 1946).

Laroque, François. "Magic in *Macbeth*," *Cahiers Elizabéthains* 35 (1989), 59–84.

Milward, Peter. *Biblical Influences in Shakespeare's Great Tragedies* (Indiana University Press, 1987), pp. 112–55.

Morris, Harry. "*Macbeth*, Dante and the Greatest Evil," *Tennessee Studies in Literature* 12 (1967), 23–38.

Muir, Kenneth. Arden edition of *Macbeth* (Methuen, 1951), pp. lxi–lxxii.

Toppen, W. H. *Conscience in Shakespeare's "Macbeth"* (Groningen, 1962).

Tyson, Edith S. "Shakespeare's *Macbeth* and Dante's *Inferno*," *Iowa State Journal of Research* 54 (May, 1980), 461–68.

Walker, Roy C. *The Time is Free: A Study of Macbeth* (London: Dakers, 1949), pp. 154–72 ("Did Heaven Look On?").

Whitaker, Virgil. *The Mirror up to Nature* (Huntington Library, 1965), pp. 265–75.

*Roland Mushat Frye (1952)*

## Macbeth and the Powers of Darkness

Encompassed as he is with the demonic enticements of the Weird Sisters, and with the relentless incitements of his wife, Macbeth succumbs to temptation and murders his king and kinsman. The result, of course, is his own succession to the throne of Scotland. In exchange for the crown he has sold his immortal soul to the devil, or, in his own words, has given his "eternal jewel ... to the common enemy of man." What does it gain him? What is his reward? Scotland, to be sure, is his. He has put himself into a position to enjoy the swelling acts of that "imperial theme" which had earlier been so seductive to his imagination, and yet he learns that what

> should accompany old age,
> As honor, love, obedience, troops of friends,
> I must not look to have; but, in their stead,
> Curses, not loud but deep, mouth-honor, breath
> Which the poor heart would fain deny and dare not.

His fears, he says, stick deep, for him there is no sleep without "terrible dreams," and he concludes he had

> better be with the dead,
> Whom we, to gain our peace, have sent to peace,
> Than on the torture of the mind to lie
> In restless ecstasy.

Macbeth's experience, his inner torments, and the utter lack of peace, recall the words of Isaiah, "There is no peace, saith the Lord, unto the wicked," and those of Job, "The wicked man travaileth with pain all his days ... A dreadful sound is in his ears: in prosperity the destroyer shall come upon him ... Trouble and anguish shall make him afraid; they shall prevail against him." Just as with Isaiah's wicked man, there is no peace for Macbeth, for he has, as he admits, put rancors in the vessel of his peace. Just as the book of Job puts a dreadful sound in the ears of the wicked, so with Macbeth "every noise appals," and just as Job declares that trouble and anguish make the wicked man afraid, so Macbeth confesses to being "cabined, cribbed, confined, bound in To saucy doubts and fears."

Fearful for the precariousness of his own power and for the restlessness of his subjects, beset with enemies within and without, Macbeth returns to the Weird Sisters for guidance:

> for now I am bent to know,
> By the worst means, the worst. For mine own good
> All causes shall give way; I am in blood

> Stepped in so far that, should I wade no more,
> Returning were as tedious as go o'er.

When he speaks these words, Macbeth stands near the point of no return, but he has not yet passed it. He can still return, though "that were as tedious as go o'er," and yet returning would mean repentance and restitution. This alternative Macbeth never explicitly considers, as he operates upon the premise that "Things bad begun make strong themselves by ill." Thus he eventually determines to know the worst by the worst, and to seek his security at the hands of the demonic.

Macbeth's second meeting with the Weird Sisters takes place at the "pit of Acheron," and as Acheron was thought to be a river in hell, this assignation may be seen as occurring, symbolically, at the very gates of hell. Like King Saul with the Witch of Endor, Macbeth unquestionably breaks what Shakespeare's age regarded as the laws of God and man when he purposely seeks out the hags. He himself suggests as much when he declares:

> Infected be the air whereon they ride,
> And damned all those that trust them!

And yet he does freely trust them, and relies entirely upon their faithfulness when they promise him security in his tyrannical power and in his earthly life.

This security evidently brings Macbeth relief from the uncertainties and the plagues of fear and of conscience. At Acheron he resolves to act so that he may

> tell pale-hearted fear it lies,
> And sleep in spite of thunder.

From this point onwards, Macbeth says no more of all the feverish conflicts within himself, of the tortures of a mind filled with scorpions, and of all the other torments which had been so acutely suffered and so vividly expressed. He has reached that stage which Shakespeare's age would have recognized as the hardening of the heart, when the sinner becomes so deeply involved in evil that his conscience seems to die and his whole security is rested upon the diabolic. Thus, with no further thought for the damnation of his deeds, Macbeth avidly accepts the diabolic counsel to be "bloody, bold, and resolute," and at once sends his henchmen to murder the defenseless family of Macduff, "Wife, children, servants, all That could be found." From this moment on, the king declares, the very firstlings of his heart shall be the firstlings of his hand, and he continues to sup "full with horrors" until he finds that

> Direness, familiar to my slaughterous thoughts,
> Cannot once start me.

As a result of this ruthless tyranny, Scotland is so filled with death and horror that "sighs and groans and shrieks that rend the air" are too common to command notice, while

each new morn
New widows howl, new orphans cry, new sorrows
Strike heaven on the face.

The effect of all this brutality upon the leaders of Scotland is galvanic. Macduff, already suspect of Macbeth, seeks out Prince Malcolm where he has sought refuge in England. There Ross joins them, and others prepare to attend upon the standard of the rightful king of Scotland. The saintly king of England supplies soldiers under Siward, and to this nucleus as it marches to meet Macbeth, other Scots under Mentieth, Caithness, Angus, and Lennox attach themselves. Their military stratagem is well known, as they advance upon the fortress of Dunsinane behind camouflaging boughs from Birnam wood.

It is worth noting that the final confidence of the liberating leaders is consciously placed, neither in armed power nor in strategic skill, but rather in the righteousness of the cause for which they fight. Their plans are made and discussed in terms of such phrases as "an't please heaven," or, "with Him above To ratify the work," and it is their prayers which the Scotch nobles send with Macduff on his mission to England. Macduff himself prays that he may be made the instrument of heaven in working retribution upon Macbeth, while Prince Malcolm declares that

Macbeth
Is ripe for shaking, and the Powers above
Put on their instruments.

Such was the confidence of Malcolm's army as it fought against the "fiend of Scotland" who was Macbeth.

As the forces of the rightful King advance, confident of their place as instruments put on by the "Powers above," what is the opposing faith of Macbeth? It is the pronouncement of the Weird Sisters. We may go even further and say that he relies upon being an instrument supported by the powers below, so sure is his trust in the predictions of his supernatural counselors. Then, with the approach of Malcolm's army, comes the report of a "moving grove," and Macbeth for the first time recognizes the treachery of the demonic:

I pall in resolution, and begin
To doubt th' equivocation of the fiend

Is this not precisely the situation against which Banquo had cautioned in the very beginning of the play, when he warned that the devil would tell truth, and win with honest trifles, so as to betray man "in deepest consequence"? And now, at the very end, Macbeth realizes that he has been betrayed in his reliance upon the diabolic.

In the last moments of his life, when he is called about by the dramatic "Turn, hell-bound, turn" challenge of the just avenger Macduff, Macbeth still relies upon the sole remaining promise of earthly safety, that no man of woman born can defeat him. The false security of this faith Macduff decries:

> Despair thy charm, And let the angel whom thou still hast served
> Tell thee, Macduff was from his mother's womb
> Untimely ripped.

Thus, in the moment of his final extremity, Macbeth discovers that he has been betrayed by the very "angel" in whom he had placed his ultimate trust. His reaction is instantaneous, and comes with the shocking realization that he has been utterly betrayed even in the present life, where all his hopes are placed:

> And by these juggling fiends no more believed,
> That palter with us in a double sense,
> That keep the word of promise to our ear,
> And break it to our hope.

So crushed is the tyrant by this realization, that he refuses to fight until goaded on by Macduff's taunts of exhibition among the spoils of war. Under these threats, Macbeth resolves to "try the last" and meet his death in battle:

> I will not yield
> To kiss the ground before young Malcolm's feet.

In sharp contrast is the humility of the young King Malcolm, with whose speech of reliance upon "the grace of Grace" Shakespeare closes the play.

Nothing could be clearer than that Macbeth pays the wages of sin even in this world, pays them with a living sort of death, a barrenness and dryness which destroys the very minimal values of existence. For Macbeth, before Acheron, life was torture of a mind filled with scorpions; after Acheron, it is a meaningless succession of days filled only with purposeless ennui, boredom, and unrest. Instead of the old internal violence and the raging passion of self-examination, he now is merely "sick at heart" and begins to be "aweary of the sun." He lives in a cheerless, hopeless half-world where time creeps forward in a petty pace from day to day, linking a barren past with a future whose finest promise is no more than dusty death. The more thoughtful among Shakespeare's early audiences must surely have felt that the dramatist was here treating the question, "what shall it profit a man, if he shall gain the whole world, and lose his own soul?" Here, then, is the spiritual framework for Macbeth's great "To-morrow, and to-morrow, and to-morrow" speech. We are not to read these lines, with Santayana, as being Shakespeare's statement of his own view of life, its meaning and purpose. It is rather Shakespeare's statement of that view of life to which Macbeth arrived as the culmination of an existence given up to the "common enemy of man," a view of life which Macbeth accepted on the basis of his own experience of evil.

The understanding of sin and its wages which Shakespeare crowds into this speech (and into the play as a whole) is thoroughly consistent with the Christian thought of his own day. The attitude of the life-wearied Macbeth as he cries,

"Out, out, brief candle," is strikingly similar to that which Shakespeare's younger contemporary, the Rev. Dr. John Donne, ascribed to the man who follows the devil and comes in the end to declare, "I care not though I were dead, it were but a candle blown out, and there were an end of all." When Macbeth proceeds to speak of life as a tale told by an idiot and as a walking shadow, he echoes the Psalmist's descriptions of man who "walketh in a vain shadow" and whose years are spent "as a tale that is told" There is great tragic depth here in Mabeth's final realization that in his bargain with the fiend he has exchanged his eternal jewel for a life which is as brief as a candle and as insubstantial as a shadow.

In the end, he sees it all as "signifying nothing." These words, again, are quite like those of the clergyman Donne as he described the sinner who passes "through this world as a flash, as a lightning of which no man knows the beginning or the ending, as an *ignis fatuus*, in the air, which does not only not give light for any use, but does not so much as portend or signify anything." This quotation from Donne may stand as a gloss upon Macbeth's view of life as "signifying nothing." The very words summarize the estate of spiritual nihilism to which Macbeth degenerates in the course of evil. Set down in a pilgrimage which can lead "to heaven or to hell," Macbeth chooses hell, and finds it even in this life.

From "Macbeth and the Powers of Darkness," *Emory University Quarterly* 8 (1952), 167–74.

*Paul Jorgensen (1971)*

## Macbeth's Soliloquy [editor's title]

In a remarkable soliloquy, Macbeth is compelled not only by his dramatist creator, but by his conscience speaking through his imagination, to recite virtually every heinous feature of the evil toward which he is moving. I know of no other play in which the crime is so nakedly exposed, and I must dwell upon this speech because it has the crucial force we should expect in a drama of crime and punishment and, especially, because without it the punishment and, hence, the sensational artistry of the play would be meaningless.

Although Macbeth almost never speaks without emotion, and although the emotion is almost always given a sense of greater urgency and less control through figurative language, this speech begins with what for Macbeth is relatively literal, logical, and controlled argument. The degree of control is shown by the manner in which he distances himself from the horrible prospect by trying to maintain the namelessness of the deed.

> If it were done, when 'tis done, then 'twere well
> It were done quickly: if th' assassination
> Could trammel up the consequence, and catch
> With his surcease success . . . (1.7.1–4)

He is still, as in his talk with Lady Macbeth, relying upon shrinking words like *it* (four uses) and *do* (three uses). Even here, however, there is a picture-making; and as he proceeds in the speech, even though the careful logic persists for quite a few lines and is never entirely lost, the increasing violence of the imagery attests to the way in which logical comprehension is yielding to emotional apprehension. The very vehemence and painfulness of his imagination during most of the soliloquy are largely due to the horror of what he is picturing; and this picturing in itself becomes a part, in anticipation, of the punishment which he will receive. He will be appropriately, according to the theory of condign punishment, punished through his imagination. He has already had "horrible imaginings" upon his first contemplating the possibility of becoming King, and now he has them in profusion and in a more specifically instructive and penal way than before.

Recognizing that he will have "judgment here," he sees, as the first action of the judgment, the "Bloody instructions which, being taught, return / To plague th' inventor." The murder is the more overt and spectacular aspect of the evil, and the blood resulting from the murder will accurately, being taught, return to punish him. He next refers to "this even-handed Justice" which "Commends th' ingredients of our poison'd chalice / To our own lips." This quality of Justice is at the heart of the play. But the imagery of the poisoned chalice would seem, in terms of sensational punishment, disappointingly unironic here, as it would not have been in *Hamlet*. It does, however, have a possible symbolic reference to the fullest meaning of the crime. Roy Walker sees the chalice as the Eucharist cup, and Macbeth as Judas. "Duncan has almost supped when Macbeth deliberates 'If it were done when 'tis done, then 'twere well / It were done quickly.'" In John's gospel, Walker points out, "it is during the last supper that Jesus says to Judas 'That thou doest, do quickly'" (John 13:27).[1] The archetype, then, is that of the worst betrayal Shakespeare knows, and the poisoned chalice will appropriately return to Macbeth's own life in the form of the most excruciating mental torment known to man, despair.[2]

Such an interpretation runs the calculated risk of further proliferation of Christ figures in Shakespeare. But in view of the Christlike qualities of Duncan to be noted later, and with the understanding that Duncan resembles rather than is Christ, I present this interpretation impenitently. Critics have become needlessly inhibited since the appearance of Roland Mushat Frye's *Shakespeare and Christian Doctrine* (Princeton, 1963). Although Frye's thesis is that critics have read too much Christian symbolism into Shakespeare, his book actually serves the more valuable purpose of pointing out and clarifying the extensive amount of Christian doctrine in the plays which lends itself to symbolic interpretation. Shakespeare's contemporaries indulged guiltlessly in this activity as they did in Biblical allegory, converting history into poetry in Sidneyan fashion; and the Geneva Bible that Shakespeare used was full of marginal notes explaining what a particular Scriptural statement or episode stood for. What the critics must now do is make Christian interpretation as accurate as they can (wherever possible giving Renaissance commentary) and try to demonstrate that the interpretation lends itself to the central dramatic purpose of the play.

As Macbeth proceeds in his vision of the evil, he recognizes its unnaturalness in that Duncan is

> here in double trust:
> First, as I am his kinsman and his subject,
> Strong both against the deed; then, as his host,
> Who should against his murderer shut the door,
> Nor bear the knife myself.

The betrayal is thus made to include that of host to guest and, more important, the killing of kin. The Biblical archetype of killing a kinsman is Cain's murder of Abel, and once again a theological meaning is not only tempting but necessary. Only by associating Macbeth's crime with that of Cain can we, with the help of Renaissance commentary on Genesis, adequately account for much of the subsequent torture of Macbeth, notably the kind of fear that precedes his despair. To the killing of kin is here added that politically supreme form of evil in the Renaissance, the killing of a king; Shakespeare, in earlier plays, had benefited from the fullest kinds of experience in depicting this evil and the impressively condign sort of punishment that awaits the murderer once he is himself king.

In the next portion of the soliloquy, Macbeth contemplates Duncan's innocence, and in doing this his mind is so racked with both pity and horror that imagery takes over almost completely from abstract formulation:

> Besides, this Duncan
> Hath borne his faculties so meek, hath been
> So clear in his great office, that his virtues
> Will plead like angels, trumpet-tongu'd, against
> The deep damnation of his taking-off;
> And Pity, like a naked new-born babe,
> Striding the blast, or heaven's Cherubins, hors'd
> Upon the sightless couriers of the air,
> Shall blow the horrid deed in every eye,
> That tears shall drown the wind.

In their violence of imagery and of feeling, these are the most genuinely sensational lines in the play; and they represent Macbeth suffering in his most characteristic manner. It is his conscience, his Good Angel, crying out with almost its last trumpet-tongued plea. And this outrage against Innocence, as Macbeth correctly foresees, will be avenged by the essential faculty of Innocence itself: Pity. Macbeth even foresees, though not so completely as to rule out irony, that the eye will be a primary victim of the punishment. There is no question but that he fully grasps the ultimate punishment: deep damnation. And his vision of the supernatural violence of reaction against this damnation, and against the unnaturalness of the deed, anticipates its macrocosmic amplification in agitated Nature which will accompany the murder and echo long afterward.

Finally, after a pause of exhaustion from the horrible sensation, he perceives the futility of the deed:

> I have no spur
> To prick the sides of my intent, but only
> Vaulting ambition, which o'erleaps itself
> And falls on th' other—

The inadequacy of his motive is a part of his torment. And in his emotionally drained state, he is able to feel in advance the penalty of ambition, the labor of a nightmare in which one repeatedly leaps only to fall again. This will be the source of much of his physical stress. Ambition, moreover, is later seen as "thriftless" and as "'Gainst nature" (2.4.27–28).

Macbeth's evil is now vividly clear, though of course it will attach to itself the darkly mysterious features of the demonic. It is the worst evil that Shakespeare could imagine. One recent critic even thinks it represents the influence of the worst evil that Dante, the medieval specialist in the abhorrent, could portray and in the order that Dante portrays the separate offences in the ninth circle: against kinsman (Cáina), subject (Antenora), guest (Ptolomaea), and lord (Judecca).[3] Whatever the possible influences of Dante, the only adequate punishment for such an evil requires the most lively features of hell—short of flames—known to Shakespeare.

And Macbeth, to solemnize the espousal of evil, is almost as specific as Lady Macbeth in her conjurations of murdering ministers and the dunnest smoke of hell. After he has yielded to her temptation, Macbeth commits himself, in fullest degree, to the evil which he is compelled to see more clearly than anyone else in the play. This commitment, virtually a pact, comes emphatically at the very end of the first act:

> I am settled, and bend up
> Each corporal agent to this terrible feat.
> Away, and mock the time with fairest show:
> False face must hide what the false heart doth know. (1.7.80–83)

The full meaning intended by Macbeth in thus dedicating his body to evil is to be found in these admonitions by St Paul:

> Neither give ye your membres as weapons of unrighteousnes unto sinne; but
> give your selves unto God, as they that are alive from the dead, and give your

membres as weapons of righteousnes unto God. Knowe ye not, that to whom-
soever ye give your selves as servants to obey, his servantes ye are to whome ye
obey, whether it be of sinne unto death, or of obedience unto righteousness.
(Romans 6:13–16)

Macbeth becomes the servant of Satan and subject to the temporal advantages
and infinite disadvantages which such service entails. In turning from God, he will
be eligible for the pain of loss; and in choosing instead a lesser good (worldly ad-
vancement), he will be eligible, especially since he has so dedicated his body, for
the pain of sense.

## Notes

1   *The Time Is Free. A Study of Macbeth* (London 1949), pp. 53–54.
2   So Clifford Davidson suggests in "Full of Scorpions Is My Mind" (Letter to the
    Editor), *Times Literary Supplement*, Nov. 4, 1965, p. 988.
3   Harry Morris, "*Macbeth*, Dante, and the Greatest Evil," *Tennessee Studies in
    Literature*, 12 (1967), p. 26. Roy Walker had also called attention to the parallel
    with Dante in the abhorrence of traitors (*The Time Is Free*, p. 54).

From *Our Naked Frailties: Sensational Art and Meaning in "Macbeth"* (University of
California Press, 1971), pp. 52–57 abridged. Copyright by the Regents of the University.

*Glynne Wickham (1969)*

## *Macbeth* and Mediaeval Stage-plays

### *(i) Hell castle and its Door-keeper*

Few scenes in Shakespeare can have provoked more laughter in the theatre and
more discomfort in the classroom than *Macbeth*, 2.3. At the centre of this paradox
lies the character of the Porter, and in particular the obscenities which punctuate
his remarks.... Are the references to hell, the devil, drink and lechery to be regarded simply as a rag-bag of swear-words habitual to a coarse, unlettered peasant?
Or are they pointers to the true significance of the scene and its function within
the structure of the play?

I think it may be useful both to the actor and to the teacher to know that anyone familiar with mediaeval religious drama is likely to recognize a correspondence
between the vocabulary of this scene and that of a similar playlet within the English Miracle Cycles, "The Harrowing of Hell." If this story has become unfamiliar, this is partly because it is an aspect of Christian belief which theologians of the
Reformation distorted, and partly because modern Anglican opinion prefers to ig-

nore it. Yet I think it is the story which provided Shakespeare with his model for the particular form in which he chose to cast Act 2, scene 3, of *Macbeth*, and possibly for the play as a whole.

On the mediaeval stage hell was represented as a castle, more particularly as a dungeon or cesspit within a castle, one entrance to which was often depicted as a dragon's mouth. Its gate was guarded by a janitor or porter. Christ, after his crucifixion, but before his resurrection, came to this castle of hell to demand of Lucifer the release of the souls of the patriarchs and prophets. The setting for this play was either the interior of the gatehouse or the courtyard of the castle: Christ's arrival was signalled by a tremendous knocking at this gate and a blast of trumpets. The gate eventually collapses allowing the Saviour-avenger, accompanied by the archangel Michael with his flaming sword, to enter and release the souls held prisoner within. It is in circumstances not unlike these that Macduff knocks at the gate of Macbeth's castle and that Malcolm and Donalbain escape from it in the course of Act 2, scenes 2 and 3.

In *Macbeth*, Macduff enters Macbeth's castle twice, first in 2.3, when Duncan's murder is discovered and Malcolm and Donalbain escape, and again in 5.9, when, as a victorious general, he arrives from the field of battle and addresses Malcolm:

> Hail, King! for so thou art. Behold, where stands
> Th' usurper's cursed head: the time is free. (5.9.20–1)

There is thus no attempt on Shakespeare's part to provide a direct parallel to the Harrowing of Hell within the play of *Macbeth;* but there is ample evidence within the text of the play of a conscious attempt on Shakepeare's part to remind his audience of this ancient and familiar story so that they may discern for themselves the moral meaning of this stage narrative abstracted from the annals of Scottish history. To make this point as forcibly as I think it should be made it is first necessary to reconstruct from the texts and stage directions of the surviving Miracle Cycles the picture of hell and its inhabitants that was familiar to Tudor audiences.

Hell itself was represented as a combination of castle, dungeon and cesspit. Of the four surviving English Cycles, Towneley (Play xxv), "The Deliverance of Souls," follows York (Play 37), "The Saddlers," almost verbatim at times: both are derived in large measure from the Middle-English poetical "Gospel of Nicodemus" of the early fourteenth century.[1] It is from these versions of the play that we learn that hell is equipped with walls and gates like a castle.... In the Towneley "Deliverance" hell is also described as a "pryson" (by Jesus, line 236) and as "that pytt" (by Jesus, line 285) and as "hell pyt" (by Satan, line 360). Prison, pit and dungeon are the words used variously in the Chester cycle to describe hell.

The authors of the Cycles found a door-keeper of hell in the poetical "Gospel of Nicodemus" where, as a character, he already borders on the comic.... In the York and Towneley plays the porter acquires a name; significantly it is Rybald, a word defined by O.E.D. as meaning "Scurrilous, irreverent, profane, indecent" and as derived from the French *ribaut*, menial. A more succinct and apposite description of Macbeth's porter could scarcely be found. In the Towneley play Rybald receives his orders from Belzebub. In *Macbeth*, the porter's first question is,

> Who's ther, i' th'name of Belzebub? (line 4)

We should surely expect him to say "in the name of my master" or possibly "in the name of Macbeth"; but, since Macbeth has just murdered Duncan, "in the name of Belzebub" or "in the devil's name" is just as appropriate. The knocking has at least put the porter in mind of Hell-gate: his comments put it in our minds too.

It is Lady Macbeth who completes the picture. It was she who first heard the knocking at the south gate from the direction of England and it is she who, when the bell starts tolling, says,

> What's the business,
> That such a hideous trumpet calls to parley
> The sleepers of the house? (lines 81–3)

It was Rybald in the Towneley "Deliverance" who cried out to Belzebub on hearing Christ's trumpets at Hell-gate

> . . . come ne,
> ffor hedusly I hard hym call. (lines 118–19)

Thunder, cacophony, screams and groans were the audible emblems of Lucifer and hell on the mediaeval stage. Those same aural emblems colour the whole of 2.3 of *Macbeth* and, juxtaposed as they are with thunderous knocking at a gate attended by a porter deluded into regarding himself as a devil, their relevance to the moral meaning of the play could scarcely have escaped the notice of its first audiences.

In the cyclic plays of the Harrowing of Hell, Satan (or Lucifer) is physically overthrown, bound and either cast into hell pit or sinks into it.

> CHESTER
> (stage direction)    Iaceant tunc Sathanam de sede sua. (line 168)
> TOWNELEY
> *Sathan*                Alas, for doyll and care!
>                         I synk into hell pyt. (lines 359–60)

In the York play the rescued souls leave the stage singing *Laus tibi Domino cum gloria*. Towneley ends with the *Te Deum*. In *Macbeth*, when Macduff has successfully brought Macbeth and his "fiend-like Queen" to justice, it is Malcolm, the new King-elect, who brings the play to its close in joy and thanksgiving.

> Malcolm    So thanks to all at once, and to each one,
>            Whom we invite to see us crown'd at Scone. *Flourish.*
>            *Exeunt.* (5.9.140–1)

Scotland has been purged of a devil who, like Lucifer, aspired to a throne that was not his, committed crime upon crime first to obtain it and then to keep it, and was finally crushed within the refuge of his own castle by a saviour-avenger accompanied by armed archangels. Hell has been harrowed: "the time is free."

### (ii) Out-heroding Herod

When watching a recent performance of the Wakefield Cycle at Bretton Hall it struck me that if the play of the Harrowing of Hell provided Shakespeare with only half of the pattern for the thematic treatment of the story of Macbeth as a dramatic tragedy, the other half was provided by the two plays about Herod the Great—the Visit of the Magi and the Massacre of the Innocents: three wise men, a prophecy of a King in Israel descended from David not Herod, an abortive attempt to frustrate prophecy by murder, the final overthrow and damnation of the butcher-tyrant. This is the story-line of the Herod plays. It also bears a remarkable correspondence to the events depicted in Shakespeare's *Tragedy of Macbeth* from Macbeth's coronation to his execution: three weird sisters, a prophecy of a King in Scotland descended from Banquo not Macbeth, an abortive attempt to frustrate prophecy by murder first of Banquo and Fleance and then of other innocents, the final overthrow of the butcher-tyrant.

In the Cycles Herod's initial, diabolic self-confidence is swiftly shaken by the visit of the Magi, the three wise men with visionary powers who can foretell the future.... Some fifty lines later the three Kings set out for Bethlehem and as soon as they are gone Herod qualifies his anger with sentiments of shame, grief and anxiety.

> For every man may say well this
> that I maynteyne my Realme amisse,
> to let a boy inherit my blisse
> that never was of my blood. (lines 378–81)

Macbeth's fears are more complicated than Herod's since the price that he had to pay for his "fruitless crown" has been a King's murder. Nevertheless his reaction to this situation follows the pattern set by Herod. The prophecy must be thwarted; the innocents must die. Macbeth, like Herod, summons hired assassins to do this work for him.

Like Herod with the Magi, Macbeth adopts a twofold plan. He aims first at Banquo and Fleance; and, when this plan miscarries, he extends his net to cover all potential rivals and strikes down Lady Macduff and her children. The last twenty lines of this scene are imbued with the sharpest possible verbal, visual and emotional echoes of the horrific scene in Bethlehem. Young Siward's image of Macbeth as both tyrant and devil in Act 5 scene 3, and thereby the two complementary images of the religious stage, Herod the tyrant and the Harrowing of Hell, are linked to one another in compressed form to provide the thematic subtext of this Scottish tragedy. Pride and ambition breed tyranny: tyranny breeds violence, a child born of fear and power: but tyrants are by their very nature Lucifer's children and not God's, and as such they are damned. As Christ harrowed hell and released Adam from Satan's dominion, so afflicted subjects of mortal tyranny will find a champion who will release them from fear and bondage. This Macduff does for Scotland; and in due season Fleance, who escaped the murderer's knife just as Jesus did, by flight, will have heirs who become Kings.

## Notes

1    See W. H. Hulme, ed., *The Middle English Harrowing of Hell and Gospel of Nicodemus* (E.E.T.S., 1907), pp. xviii ff.

From *Shakespeare's Dramatic Heritage* (Routledge, 1969), pp. 214–231 abridged. Used by permission.

*Roy Walker (1949)*

# Scotland's Christian Geography [editor's title]

Colme-kill, where Duncan is to be buried, is Iona, one of the Western Isles. The word is said to mean "the cell or chapel of St Columba" by whom Christianity was first preached there in the sixth century. Shakespeare has compressed the facts to get his allusion here. In Holinshed Duncan was first buried at Elgine and afterwards removed to *Colmekill*. We may therefore suppose that Shakespeare had a purpose in bringing in Colme-kill at this point. The allusion seems to be to the return of Duncan's body in honour to the source from whence Christianity was first preached to Scotland by a great saint. This, and the emphasized "sacred storehouse of his predecessors," is the fitting close to the life of "the Lord's anointed temple" broken open by "most sacrilegious murder."

Macduff will go to Fife. Verity informs us that the Saint Colme's Inch of 1.2. is the island of Inchcolm off the coast of Fife, in the Firth of Forth, once occupied by Saint Columba, the first teacher of Christianity to the Picts. On this island are the remains of an abbey dedicated to St Columba (whence Colme derives) and Inch is believed to be the Erse for 'a small island.' Shakespeare may have transcribed Saint Colme's Inch from Holinshed without special dramatic intention— although it is unusual for him to drag into the tragedies a particular and curious place name without some poetic purpose.

If, however, the reference to St Colme's Inch meant anything as poetry rather than as history, it was meant to chime with Colme-kill. Let us first note our impression of Macduff's attitude, ignoring for a moment the reference to Colme-kill. When he says he will not go to Scone but to Fife, we feel he is declaring his loyalty to Duncan and Duncan's cause. In the worldly sense, Duncan's cause is non-existent. Duncan is dead and even Macduff believes for the present that his sons have forfeited all right to the succession by murdering the king and flying in panic from just retribution. Macduff is loyal to Duncan nevertheless, and his loyalty is the growing-point from which it finally revives and triumphs.

Now, if we turn to the chiming references to St Columba, we seem to find that they harmonise with the Macduff music. Duncan has gone to the sacred storehouse of his fathers, to the source from which St Columba preached Christianity to Scotland. Macduff goes sadly home to Fife, not believing that the pomp and ceremony of Macbeth's crowning at Scone is the real continuation of sacred kingship (although we must remember that he has nothing against Macbeth as yet). When Macbeth won Duncan's battle at Saint Colme's Inch in Fife, then he was fighting as a crusader. Now Fife, Macduff's Fife, is the little island of faith in that cause, linked like the little island in the Firth of Forth and its ancient abbey now ruined, with the other island of St Columba—the source of Scotland's knowledge of mercy, pity and peace, where Duncan will lie in the sacred tomb of his fathers, the last of his line (as it now seems) to be a king of Scotland.

A day-dream perhaps! But I cannot now read Macduff's dour words to Ross, who is off to Scone to see the coronation: "No, cousin; I'll to Fife" (2.4.36), and the grieved reserve of his "Well, may you see things well done there:—adieu!—/ Lest our old robes sit easier than our new!" (37–38), without imagining the remains of a ruined abbey on the little island off the coast of Macduff's Fife and the distant sepulchre at Iona where Duncan soon will lie. The closing lines of the Act do not jar upon such thoughts:

> Ross      Farewell, father.
> Old Man   God's benison go with you; and with those
>           That would make good of bad, and friends of foes! (40–1)

I like to think that the first phrase is for Ross, and the rest spoken after the retreating figure of the sorrowing Macduff. To make good of bad at Fife is a harder task than to make foul seem fair at Scone. The heavens are troubled with man's act, but with the man of goodwill God's benison goes still. The old peasant of threescore and ten is nature's spokesman, and supernature's too.

From *The Time Is Free: A Study of "Macbeth"* (London: Andrew Dakers, 1949), pp. 80–82.

*Harry Morris (1985)*

## Hell and Judgment in *Macbeth* [editor's title]

In Canto 33, the last of the *Inferno* but one, Dante meets Friar Alberigo, who tells us:

> Know that the moment any soul betrays,
> As I did, its body is snatched from it
> By a demon, who then dominates it
> Till its allotted time has run out
> And it tumbles down into this cistern. (tr. Bioncolli)

Through the unique punishment of sending the soul to hell before the body dies, Dante emphasizes the utter depravity of murdering one's guests. More than any other, the guest is misled by his betrayer's hypocrisy, by the fair offers and the smiling greeting. Shakespeare does not overlook the added perfidy. His most pointed addition to Holinshed is to place the murder carefully within the doors of Macbeth's castle.

In every respect, Lady Macbeth is as guilty as her husband; all the torments he undergoes or is yet to reap are her portion also. Both merit the punishment of Ptolomaea. Both lose their souls to that region before their bodies die. For those bodies to function, they must be invested by devils, even as Dante describes in the story of Friar Alberigo. Of course, for realistic drama and tragedy based on history, the substitution of devil for soul must be a symbolic or mystical one, an allegorism that Dante would call anagogical. Therefore the substitution is handled symbolically; I know of no play in the Shakespeare canon where the imagery of substitution—or rather investment and possession, as I shall call it—is so prevalent.

Before the crime is committed, we are prepared for the idea of false-covering, the pleasing facade that masks a spotted interior. The eleventh line of the play tells us "Fair is foul, and foul is fair." Duncan, speaking of Cawdor, emphasizes the point: "There's no art / To find the mind's construction in the face" (1.4.11–12). Lady Macbeth informs us clearly that whatever holds sway within her body and her husband's must be replaced. She fears that Macbeth is "too full o' th' milk of human kindness," and that she must pour her spirits into his ear (1.5.17, 26). What are her spirits? We are told through one of the most significant speeches of the play and in the appropriate investment / possession imagery:

> Come, you spirits
> That tend on mortal thoughts, unsex me here,
> And fill me from the crown to the toe top-full
> Of direst cruelty!

The "smoke of hell" surrounds symbolically the spirit that comes to her, because it comes from hell to invest the empty body that her soul, dropping to Ptolomaea, will leave behind.

I believe no one has noticed that Lady Macbeth's invocation is an anti-hymn, paralleling, as a black mass, the *Veni Creator Spiritus* of the Pentecostal service. The Book of Common Prayer, from the first of 1549 to that in use today, has retained one or another English translation of the hymn, always as an adjunct to the order for consecration of priests as well as bishops. The verses pertinent to Lady Macbeth's invocation are as follows:

> Come creator spirit, the hearts of thy faithful visit.
> Fill with heavenly grace, what thou didst create, our hearts.
> . . . .
> Kindle light in our senses, infuse love in our hearts.
> The weaknesses of our bodies with virtue perpetually confirm.

These phrases echo Lady Macbeth's cry that evil spirits come to her, fill her (especially her breasts) with cruelty instead of grace. Furthermore, the light prayed for by the hymnodist is replaced by Lady Macbeth with a call for thick night and smoke of hell. Anti-disciple or anti-priest, she functions as a proselytizer and converts Macbeth to her purpose.

The concept of possession that I trace from Dante's ninth circle was quite familiar to Elizabethans from contemporary sources as well. King James lists, as the third of four kinds of devils that walk the earth, those that "enter within the living and possess them." Those most susceptible to possession are men "guiltie of greevous offences" whom "God punishes by that horrible kinde of scourdge." W. C. Curry says of Macbeth that "The whole drama is discovered to be saturated with the malignant presences of demons or fallen angels; they animate nature and ensnare human souls by means of diabolical persuasion, by hallucination, infernal illusions, and possession."

That the murder of Duncan may be associated immediately with eschatological matters is borne out by the imagery attendant upon the King's death. Although some events such as the supper and the earthquake have been associated with the last days of Christ, others match well with various signs that late medieval writers believed would accompany the last days of the world. Yet in *Macbeth* the association of apocalypse with Duncan's death is even more fitting since immediate damnation for the souls of Macbeth and Lady Macbeth is in reality their judgment day.

As Macduff enters the King's bedchamber where he will discover Duncan's body, Lennox describes the "unruly" night:

> . . . chimneys were blown down, and, as they say,
> Lamentings were heard i' th' air; strange screams of death,
> And prophesying, with accents terrible
> Of dire combustion and confus'd events
> New hatch'd to th' woeful time. The obscure bird
> Clamor'd the livelong night. Some say the earth
> Was feverous and did shake. (2.3.55–61)

Eight separate events are reported by Lennox; seven of them are among the fifteen signs that medieval tradition proclaimed were to forerun judgment day. These signs, by attribution, were first recorded by St Jerome. They have been reproduced by innumerable writers from Bede through Vincent of Beauvais, the authors of the *Legenda Aurea* and the *Cursor Mundi*, to anonymous rimers in many independent lyrics. They are found in thirteenth-century sculpture, stained-glass, and illustrations in Bible picture books such as the *Holkham Bible*. [Morris here provides plate reproductions of each of the 15 signs.]

Immediately after the several signs rehearsed by Lennox, Macduff bursts out of the murder chamber to liken the death of Duncan to "The great doom's image" (2.3.78). Surrounding his words are further evocations of judgment day. Macduff, noting the sleepy confusion of those about him, identifies them with the dead who must arise at the last day:

> Banquo and Donalbain! Malcolm! Awake!
> Shake off this downy sleep, death's counterfeit,
> And look on death itself! Up, up, and see
> The great doom's image! Malcolm! Banquo!
> As from your graves rise up, and walk like sprites,
> To countenance this horror! (2.3.75–80)

Lady Macbeth equates the alarum-bell that Macduff has caused to ring with the horn at judgment day that wakes the dead and summons them to sentence: "What's the business, / That such a hideous trumpet calls to parley / The sleepers of the house?" (81–83).

The porter scene, believed so un-Shakespearean by Coleridge, shows us symbolically, at a moment immediately posterior to the murder of Duncan, the descent into hell of the souls of his slayers. Although Shakespeare must present the porter scene after the murder scene, he causes the knocking to be heard by Macbeth and Lady Macbeth at the moment the murderer cries that his soul is being plucked out through his eyes and the murderess says, "Get on your nightgown" (2.2.68), the moment for each of judgment, punishment, and possession.

The entire porter soliloquy has its analogy to the *Inferno* in general. Just as Dante, by his journey down the terraces to the center of the earth, catalogues sins and sinners, so too the porter lets in first a suicide, then a liar, and last a cheat; but he has broken off because it is too cold; he "had thought to have let in some of all professions that go the primrose way to th' everlasting bonfire" (2.3.17–19). The porter's complaints against the cold are unusually appropriate; for even as he speaks, the souls of Macbeth and Lady Macbeth enter the frozen regions of Cocytus.

From *Last Things in Shakespeare* (Florida State University Press, 1985), excerpts from pp. 168–96 much abridged. Used by permission.

# ANTONY AND CLEOPATRA

## Comment and bibliography

This is a tragedy of lovers who pursue beyond beauties of the eye a hope of a new heaven and a new earth. The hope thus voiced echoes Isaiah's and St John's, but in the play its models of performance reflect the "riggish" religion of Egypt and stoicism's goal of self-transcendence through suicide. Erotic love empowers in Antony and Cleopatra a hyperbole of self-dramatizing showmanship, which some literary critics have praised as a "transcendental Humanism," but others (such as the Arden editor M. R. Ridley) have described as "an *égoisme à deux*" that has "no power to inspire to anything outside itself." Viewed from a realistic perspective, the story provides a marvelous illustration of human vainglory. The worship of "face" which brought about the ruin of ancient Troy is exemplified here in Alexandria, and it is voiced when Eros hails Antony as "that noble countenance / Wherein the worship of the whole world lies" (4.14.85). Such worship indeed *lies* if truthfully judged, however heroic it appears to human fantasy.

From the beginning Cleopatra calls Antony's profession of love an excellent falsehood, yet she caters to it because of her own delight in the sport of make-believe. "Play one scene of excellent dissembling," she chides him, "And make it look like perfect honor" (1.3.78–80). That is a scene she herself plays many times, very notably in 4.13 when she sends Mardian to tell Antony she has slain herself for love of him. It is of course a coquettish pretense, a typical instance of her angling for adulation with dodges and paltering. And it comes just after Antony has learned from sad experience that she was "a boggler ever." He chooses nevertheless to credit her charade of honor and to kill himself to imitate her "courage." Such a response seems born of a desperate self-deception. It indicates in Antony the sealed eyes he himself has said "make us Adore our errors" and strut to our confusion. And at the end of the play Cleopatra's death scene exhibits a similar case of excellent dissembling made to look like honor. Robed like a Queen this quean with crown awry cries out "Husband, I come"—although she has never shown any wifely concern for Antony's welfare. The "immortal longings" in her have always been for her self-image of honor.

A rural clown of homespun wit warns Cleopatra that there is "no goodness" in the worm and not to feed it. But she prefers to illustrate the clown's own observation that a woman he heard of "yesterday" has made a good report of the worm. This clown perhaps is remembering the Septuagint Bible available in Egypt, for he adds that anyone who believes the woman's report will never be "saved" by what such a woman does. Shakespeare expects his audience to recall Eve's acting on the serpent's promise "You shall be like gods" and the spiritual death this brought. Cleopatra's joy is as false as the joy of the worm. And her nursing of this worm, like a baby at her breast, is both madly ludicrous and, for Christian auditors, an upside-down version of true love. When the courtly Charmian cries out in admiration "O Eastern star!" Shakespeare's audience is being prompted to compare such a star with the Virgin Mary, Christianity's *stella maris* and humanity's reversal of Eve.

A surprising amount of imagery in this story is biblical. The fig-leaves with slime on them suggest guilt. Cleopatra's alternation of moods between favor and betrayal is like that of the Bible's Pharaoh, as is her violent treatment of an honest messenger in 2.5. Her feasting accords with Egypt's fleshpots, and her readiness for the sport of "love's soft hours" carried for Elizabethans a pun on hours-whores. Antony's naming her a "Triple-turned whore" is more than a description of her relationship to three Roman princes. For Elizabethans it served to recall the Whore of the book of Revelation, who from her throne on the water captivated and deluded much of the pagan world. When Revelation, chapters 8–11, describes a doomsday signaled by the fall from heaven of a "great star" named "Wormwood," making the waters death-dealing and bringing a darkness on a third of the earth, there is an equivalent of this in Cleopatra's experience when Antony falls from glory and seeks a death which flies from him (Rv 9:6). In Cleopatra's own dying, her "husband" reference unintentionally parodies Rv 22:17, since the heaven she looks forward to is only an enjoying of Antony's lips.

Antony himself in his "hill of Basan" roaring is a parody of the Messiah-figure of Psalm 22. And the phrases Shakespeare gives him during his supper at the end of Act 3 make it a parody of Christ's Last Supper. Later, his "shirt of Nessus" marks him as a sufferer who has forfeited all Herculean virtue. In his hoisting up to Cleopatra his self-wounded body we can recognize a parody of Christ's offering to God a body of holy wounds. When Antony speaks of his shape as "dislimning" and melting, we are reminded of Caesar's earlier characterizing of Antony as "like a vagabond flag upon the stream" that rots itself with lackeying of the varying tide. Tragically, his "chief end" has become Cleopatra's bosom, a goal far different from that of Rome's founder Aeneas. And it lacks the virtue of Octavius, who by his resisting of Cleopatra's lures was able to bring a "time of universal peace" to the three-nooked world of his day.

Our anthology includes commentary from Clifford Davidson, Andrew Fichter, and David Scott Kastan. Davidson sees the play as depicting for Elizabethans the turmoil of paganism that preceded the Christian dispensation. Fichter notices the biblical imagery used by Shakespeare that indicates a quest for divine love that is tragically parodied by Antony and Cleopatra. The play in Fichter's estimate is "a comment on the aimlessness of a universe lacking moral focus from the perspective of one that has achieved coherence through divine revelation." Kastan focuses on the "excellent falsehood" of the lovers that leaves them in the secret house of death, and he comments that "nothing except the intensity of their imagination" validates their faith. Cleopatra's strong toil of grace, Kastan concludes, fails to transcend the tragic; yet by analogy it points the way to God's strong toil of grace which Milton was to hail as the comic imperative of Christian history.

For supplementary reading, the essays by John Alvis and Roy Battenhouse should prove helpful. Alvis notes in the lovers a rhetoric calculated to deify themselves through making a religion of erotic passion; we can see in their fate the waste caused by ignorance of love's proper end. Alvis likens their passion to that De Rougement associated with Tristan and Isolde, a desperate flight from mundane contingency into mystical *askesis*; but its preoccupation with reputation is not a dying to self, simply a suicidal ecstasy. Battenhouse elaborates on the parody-analogy of such love to that of Christian *caritas*. He likens Shakespeare's artistic method to Chaucer's ironic telling of Cleopatra's story, but finds the drama as a whole structured by patterns "figured" in the Book of Revelation. Among other things, that book's use of the number 42 as symbolic of the scope of anti-Christ's reign probably influences Shakespeare's use of 42 scenes in *Antony and Cleopatra*.

Peter Seng has made the pertinent observation that the Bacchanal sung on Pompey's galley in 2.7 parodies the *veni creator spiritus* of Christian hymnody. J. Leeds Barroll has argued that Cleopatra's self-display at Cydnus is that of an icon of Voluptas, making it appropriate that her final act is spoken of as a return to Cydnus.

## Supplementary bibliography

Alvis, John. "The Religion of Eros: A Reinterpretation of *Antony and Cleopatra*," *Renascence* 30 (1978), 185–98.

Barroll, J. Leeds. "Enobarbas' Description of Cleopatra," *Texas Studies in English* 37 (1958), 61–78.

Battenhouse, Roy. *Shakespearean Tragedy* (1969), pp. 161–83.

Cunningham, Dolora. "The Characterization of Shakespeare's Cleopatra," *Shakespeare Quarterly* 6 (1955), 98–117.

Morris, Helen. "Shakespeare and Dürer's Apocolypse," *Shakespeare Studies* 4 (1968), 252–62.

Seaton, Ethel. "*Antony and Cleopatra* and the Book of Revelation," *Review of English Studies* 22 (1946), 219–24.

Seng, Peter. "Shakespearean Hymn Parody?" *Renaissance News* 18 (1965), 4–6.

*Clifford Davidson (1980)*

## Shakespeare's Archetypal Cleopatra [editor's title]

Dante had quite deliberately placed the "voluptuous" queen in the second circle of Hell, along with Dido, Semiramis, Helen, and others noted for their incontinence (*Inferno*, Canto V). "For I am sure," shouts Shakespeare's angry Antony, "though you can guess what temperance should be, / You know not what it is" (3.13.120–22). Cleopatra's witchcraft has brought Mark Antony to subject himself totally to her voluptuousness, but he finds that in battle she only leads him to defeat and disaster. Through her instrumentality, he loses his manhood and gives himself over to blind and irrational Fortune, who then flings him from her wheel.

In a sense, Shakespeare is here, as in *Macbeth*, glancing back at the archetypal woman as she appears at the beginning of time. Eve is man's temptress, deceived by the serpent but nevertheless effective in causing him to fall from any semblance of uprightness. She is the paradigm upon which all later fatal women in myth or literature would, from the Renaissance perspective, seem to be based. Lady Macbeth thus will at a crucial point gain power over her husband's will, causing him to bend all his energies to the terrible deed of regicide in order that he might consummate his desire to be a king—which, for the Renaissance, was to be like a god. However, while Macbeth is stirred to do an act that is illegitimate, Antony is successfully tempted to relax his will in idleness. He who should be Cleopatra's master because of his sex and because of his superior status in the empire, has in his negligence given up "his potent regiment to a trull" (3.6.95). As a result of his submission, he loses his potency.

Egypt is, like the Garden of Eden or the classical paradise as interpreted in the Renaissance, a very fertile place—though it is inhabited by snakes. Because of her function as a temptress, Antony calls Cleopatra his "serpent of old Nile" (1.5.25). Thus she usurps the phallic role, Shakespeare suggests; of course, such usurpation is an attempt to achieve a reversal of the natural order—a reversal that was, after all, the object of the serpent in Eden. While she is thinking amorously about her lover during his absence, Cleopatra therefore feeds herself "With most delicious poison" (1.5.27). She lives in a world that is reminiscent of Spenser's Bower of Bliss and that is fully as poisonous, especially to male visitors from Rome. Antony, once he has drawn himself away from the pleasures of Alexandria in the second act, admits to Caesar that he had "Neglected" his duty "when poisoned hours had bound me up / From mine own knowledge" (2.2.90–91). This poison is obviously to be identified with the great Satanic enemy of life who in the guise of a serpent conveyed death into the fertile Garden of Eden and hence into the whole world of human beings. Not inappropriately, therefore, the asp, the poisonous "worm" that "kills and pains not" (5.2.242–43) helps Cleopatra cross to her own death.

If Cleopatra indeed is playing the role of Eve against Mark Antony's Adam, the extensive food imagery in the play surely underlines a basic element—the forbidden fruit—in the Eden story. Of course, as medieval and Renaissance writers commonly insisted, the deadly sin of gluttony may be a cause of falling into the deadly sin of lechery. Mark Antony and Cleopatra gluttonize in Alexandria and tumble on soft beds. She describes herself as a "morsel" for monarchs (1.5.31). Not surprisingly, it was the first time Antony went to the "feast" as her guest that he paid with his "heart." Unfortunately, however, the meal is an "ordinary"—that is, a public dinner—for Cleopatra is not at this point an untasted "morsel." Later, in his anger in the third act, he reminds her that he found her "as a morsel, cold upon / Dead Caesar's trencher: nay, you were a fragment / Of Gnaeus Pompey's" (3.13.116–18). She stands for excess, since she will not pause at the limits set by nature. As Cleopatra is above shown to be identified with the serpent whose temptation she relays to Adam, so now she is identified with food, the objective sign of the temptation of Adam. It ought not to be forgotten that the Middle Ages had often popularly isolated gluttony as the prime cause of the Fall of Adam and Eve, who thereupon are plunged into amorous desire.

Cleopatra therefore could seem to sum up the destructive and negative side of Eve, for indeed our first mother had her positive side as well which made possible Christ's rescuing of her from the jaws of the underworld at the time of the Harrowing of Hell. Furthermore, it was a commonplace belief of Christian theology during the Renaissance that, as Eve brought sin into the world, so a second Eve would bring redemption into the world. The second Eve is the Blessed Virgin Mary, whose miraculous pregnancy is scheduled by Providence not long after the historical events recounted in Antony and Cleopatra. Cleopatra in one sense appears to be a figure ironically foreshadowing the Blessed Virgin, as, for example, the false king Herod, who also is mentioned in Shakespeare's play but not in Plutarch, foreshadows the true King of Kings. While sacred history is not directly the subject of Shakespeare's drama, he nevertheless is very much aware of the significance of the historical events that he presents on stage. "The time of universal peace is near," Caesar prophetically remarks in the fourth act (6.5). While the New Arden edition of the play does not even have a note on "the time of universal peace," it is perhaps the most significant single line in the play. This will be the "universal Peace through Sea and Land" that, according to Milton's "On the Morning of Christ's Nativity," prepared the scene for "the Prince of Light" to begin "His reign of peace upon the earth." Within a decade after the death of Cleopatra and the establishment of peace throughout the whole world, the Virgin Mary would bring forth a child.

In describing the historic period immediately preceding the first coming of Christ, therefore, it is only appropriate that Shakespeare should draw upon apocalyptic imagery. The old order is coming to a close, and the effect will be to reorient men who believe in the Christian message to the "new heaven" and "new earth" that will be ushered in after the Second Coming. What could be more proper than describing the final conflict of the old order, of the pre-Christian ages, through the visually rich iconography of the Apocalypse itself? Ethel Seaton and Helen Morris demonstrate that Shakespeare's imagery in this play provides many references to the book of Revelation; also, as Miss Morris shows, he was apparently influenced by those passages illustrated by woodcuts imitated from Dürer in certain sixteenth-century Bibles. When the guards discover the fatally wounded Antony, one of them exclaims: "The star is fallen," while the other adds, "And time is at his period" (4.14.106–7). In the Apocalypse, we read: "and there fell a great starre from heaven" (8:10); and "time shuld be no more" (10:6).

One of the most vivid personages depicted in the Apocalypse by John the Divine is the great Whore of Babylon, who brings together in one figure all the negative feminine qualities mentioned above. The biblical writer describes her as having "committed fornication [with] the Kings of the earth" (17:2) in a passage that is echoed by Caesar in Antony and Cleopatra 3.6.66–68: "He hath given his empire / Up to a whore, who now are levying / The kings o'the earth for war." Traditionally, as in Dürer's woodcut, the great Whore of Babylon holds out a cup to the kings before her: it is a cup of sensual pleasure intended to seduce them into bondage to her. Cleopatra has apparently held out the symbolic cup of temptation, if we may speak figuratively, to every king and potentate who has visited the Egyptian court, and she has "committed fornication" at least with Julius Caesar, Pompey the Great, and Antony, though the two earlier recorded affairs were in her "salad days." Furthermore, once Antony's fortunes seem hopelessly falling, we see her attempting to recover her own position in the world by making advances to Caesar through his messenger Thidias. The stoical Caesar, however, refuses to be tempted.

From "*Antony and Cleopatra* and the Whore of Babylon," *Bucknell Review* 25 (1980), 36–39.

*Andrew Fichter (1980)*

## *Antony and Cleopatra* and Christian Quest [editor's title]

The first scene of *Antony and Cleopatra* mirrors the play's thematic movement towards Christian revelation. Antony stands accused by one of his Roman followers, Philo, of a "dotage" that "O'erflows the measure"—words that unmistakably convey the revulsion he feels at the sight of his general's infatuation with Cleopatra.

Antony speaks of his love in terms that alter the tone but retain some of the substance of Philo's remarks:

| Cleopatra | If it be love indeed, tell me how much. |
| Antony | There's beggary in the love that can be reckon'd. |
| Cleopatra | I'll set a bourn how far to be belov'd. |
| Antony | Then must thou needs find out new heaven, new earth. |

Against Philo's Roman sense of propriety and measure Antony asserts a romanticist's impulse to deny limit, finitude and degree, to transgress the boundaries by which a rationalist mind orders its world. The banter with Cleopatra already indicates the inherently tragic disposition of his energy and will. But Antony's words have a prophetic resonance; they refer us to a context in which the quest for "new heaven, new earth" is no longer an expression of will tragically opposed to reality. Antony and Cleopatra are led by their dialogue to what God speaks of to Isaiah and what John sees in his vision of the Day of Judgement:

For lo, I will create new heavens and a new earth: and the former shall not be remembered nor come into mind. (Geneva Bible, Is 45:17)

And I saw a new heaven, and a new earth: for the first heaven, and the first earth were passed away, and there was no more sea. And I John saw the holy city new Jerusalem come down from God out of heaven, prepared as a bride trimmed for her husband. (Rv 21:1–2)

There remains an important difference between Antony's assertion of unbounded love and the divine love of which John speaks. Antony and Cleopatra may pursue the logic of transcendence to the point where it verges on a new perception of the universe, but the vision John records depends on divine intercession rather than heroic romanticism. Antony and Cleopatra come to associate love with eternity, and they approach death as if it were "a lover's bed"; they speak of one another as bride and husband in their final moments, and thereby bring new significance to conventional terms; but the apocalyptic marriage of which John speaks, the final reconciliation between God and humanity, remains beyond their imagination.

Antony is bounded on one side by the Christian visionary tradition to which he cannot attain and on the other by the Roman epic tradition he partly forsakes. His Roman followers see him making the choice that Roman history denies to its first hero, Aeneas. Antony, that is, chooses love over empire, passion over reason, a foreign "marriage" over a Roman one, and thus aligns himself with those forces Roman civilization sees as impediments to its progress. Yet in a sense Antony does not wholly remove himself from epic tradition. He refers to love as though it were another *imperium*, "new heaven, new earth," and he embraces Cleopatra—"Here is my space"—in the spirit of an Aeneas arriving on Italian shores—"hic domus, haec patria est" ["Here is our home, here our country!"]. The love Antony speaks of is both an alternative to empire and an alternative empire.

*Antony and Cleopatra,* then, stands chronologically and metaphysically between the quest traditions of Roman epic and Christianity. On one hand the play looks to Augustan empire as the culmination of historical processes, and on the other hand it conveys the feeling that the energies of its principals are misdirected, that their goals are insufficient to their needs.

The rhythms of *Antony and Cleopatra* are the natural, sexual, and political manifestations of appetite—circular, continuous, and inconclusive. Momentum is ultimately the play's most compelling variable—a giddy inebriation at one extreme, where the rulers of the world are seen dancing the "Egyptian Bacchanals" in a ring (2.7.103ff.), and a feeling of self-strangulation at the other:

> Now all labour
> Mars what it does: yea, very force entangles
> Itself with strength.... (4.14.47–9)

This is perhaps appropriate to a play consciously imitating the to and fro, episodic structure of epic; but it is also a comment on the aimlessness of a universe lacking moral focus from the perspective of one that has achieved coherence through divine revelation.

On one hand we are asked to see Antony's rejection of Roman values as the sufficient cause of his tragic fall; on the other hand that fall, in which Antony and Cleopatra paradoxically envision themselves triumphant and transcendent ironically anticipates Christian redemption. We see Antony in part as an exemplum of moral degradation offered to a Roman audience, a hero debased by his extravagant love for an exotic woman, irrationally bound on a course of self-destruction, simultaneously asserting and undermining his own heroic stature. But Antony may also be judged by the standard of divine love, in which death is, as he imagines, encompassed by an eternity. That his passion for Cleopatra falls short of Christian *caritas,* the movement of the soul towards God, places his tragedy in a different light, making it less an instance of decadent immoderation than one of misdirected love.

Where his behavior seems most disjointed we are referred to Christian myth. Antony's outburst of jealousy when he encounters Thidias kissing Cleopatra's hand, for instance, may be both an overreaction and a potentially comic misdirection of anger—

> O that I were
> Upon the hill of Basan, to outroar
> The horned herd, for I have savage cause— (3.13.126–28)

but the discrepancy disappears when the words are heard in their original context:

> Be not far from me, because trouble is near: for there is none to help me. Many young bulls have compassed me: mighty bulls of Bashan have closed me about. (Ps 22:11–12)

This Old Testament outcry against injustice and betrayal in turn provides the material for the moment Christianity holds to be the ultimate reversal of tragic circumstances, the Crucifixion. It is the psalm from whose beginning Christ quotes as he dies, "My God, my God, why hast thou forsaken me?" transforming despair into hopefulness as he speaks by using these words to confirm himself as the fulfillment of Old Testament messianic prophecies.

In contrast to Christ's deliberate and ultimately redemptive reference to the psalm, Antony's unconscious and contorted allusion confirms him in his tragic posture, outroaring the surrounding herds. Jealousy and grace work radically dissimilar transformations. But at the same time Antony's allusion suggests the frame of reference from which we may finally arrive at more than a morally ambiguous perception of the play.

Two scenes later Antony proposes a final "gaudy night," his Last Supper, as J. Middleton Murry suggests [in *Shakespeare* (1936)], echoes of which may be found both in Plutarch and in the Passion narrative, as the interplay between the Roman and the Christian senses of an ending continues. As in Plutarch Antony asks his followers to fill his cups and make as much of him as they can, but then disheartens them with his gloom:

> Tend me to-night;
> May be it is the period of your duty,
> Haply you shall not see me more, or if,
> A mangled shadow. Perchance to-morrow
> You'll serve another master. I look on you,
> As one that takes his leave. (4.2.24–29)

The words can be found in North's translation of Plutarch, but the tone suggests another reference: Antony's strangely prescient mood and his wavering resolve to accept death are also reminiscent of Christ's agony in the garden at Gethsemane. Like Christ, Antony asks three times that his followers tend him in what he senses are his last hours. The appeal for loyalty subtly draws attention to Enobarbus, who, Judas-like, has by now decided to betray his master. The scene requires of the reader a double vision in which the Christian future is superimposed over the Roman narrative.

Antony's speech is charged with meanings neither he nor his hearers can comprehend. Even his rather awkward attempt to explain himself reinforces our awareness of the central irony:

> Ho, ho, ho!
> Now the witch take me, if I meant it thus!
> Grace grow where those drops fall.... (lines 36–38)

"Grace" is the crux, for were he conscious of the eventual significance of the term Antony's attempts to console his followers by speaking of "another master," a revival of "dying honor" in a mysterious "To-morrow" would not seem so disjointed. It is precisely because he lacks the concept of grace that he can only communicate fatalism to his audience. In the end he returns to a literal and Roman feast rather than a symbolic and Christian one, ironically distorting the meaning of that which his prefigures:

> Let's to supper, come,
> And drown consideration. (lines 44–5)

We can account for the awkwardness of the scene, I think, by seeing in it an implicit juxtaposition of Roman and biblical texts. The coexistence of Christian and Roman perspectives is necessarily unharmonious: Christ's propitiatory self-sacrifice will reverse the fatalistic, Stoic self-conquest Antony envisions. Antony's unmodulated ambivalence is a parody of Christ's agony, a failing show of courage in the face of despair.

[In 4.14] we are on the verge of more than one Christian mystery as Antony envisions a romantic afterlife with Cleopatra, and then metaphorically construes his death as an act of love:

> But I will be
> A bridegroom in my death, and run into't
> As to a lover's bed. (lines 99–101)

As in its other manifestations throughout the play this conceit has both sexual and spiritual overtones. It is Cleopatra's lover speaking, but the words are also reminiscent of John's vision of the New Jerusalem, coming down out of heaven from God, "prepared as a bride trimmed for her husband." Echoes from Revelation continue to be heard as Antony, having thrown himself on his sword without managing to kill himself, pleads with the guardsmen to dispatch him. But once again the allusion underscores Antony's separation from the promise of Christian redemption, as he is compared to "those men which have not the seal of God in their foreheads" when the Apocalypse comes:

> Therefore in those days men shall seek death, and shall not find it, and shall
> desire to die, and death shall flee from them. (Rv 9:6)

If we need a reminder of the sharp discrepancy between Christian apocalypse and Antony's suicide it is provided in the element of mistiming involved in Antony's death. He is at first impatient to die, to "o'ertake" Cleopatra, whom he erroneously believes to be dead: "for now / All length is torture" (lines 45–46). When it is already too late he finds that Cleopatra is still alive. His death is then protracted through a disconcertingly awkward interval, and yet still seems premature when the stage time remaining to the play is considered. Antony's death is a travesty of apocalyptic finality, the end toward which human history is thought to ripen.

Like Antony, Cleopatra presents her audience with a problem of perspective—whether to see in tragedy a diminishment or an aggrandizement of human stature, whether to take death as final and defeating or as a step towards liberation, "that thing that ends all other deeds, / Which shackles accidents, and bolts up change" (5.2.5–6).

Cleopatra at once fulfills the curse of Genesis and prefigures its reversal by speaking of her death as a moment of love, "a lover's pinch, / Which hurts, and is desir'd." Hers are only the reflexes of the flesh, inadequate to convey spiritual insight; but, as Elizabeth Holmes has suggested, we are invited to see beyond the tableau of her death, the grotesque image of Cleopatra nursing the serpent like a baby, to another "eastern star" and another nativity. (*Aspects of Elizabethan Imagery* [1929], p. 50.)

The juxtaposition of these two images—Cleopatra's death and Christ's nativity—is both visually and morally incongruous; but as elsewhere in the play such incongruity is calculated to move us beyond the scope of the tragic universe for a vision of greater substantive reality. From this vantage Cleopatra's death is an inversion of the moment it prefigures.

From "*Antony and Cleopatra*: 'The Time of Universal Peace,'" *Shakespeare Survey* 33 (1980), 99–111, extracts abridged.

*David Scott Kastan (1977)*

## The Ending of *Antony and Cleopatra* [editor's title]

In death the lovers celebrate a marriage, joining the traditional endings of tragedy and comedy. Antony would be "a bridegroom in [his] death" (4.14.100), and Cleopatra dies, magnificently announcing,

> Husband, I come. (5.2.286)

For them, love does overcome death, and all the haunt at last is theirs. They define a world of value beyond time, rising in death, and through death, far

> above
> The element they lived in. (5.2.89–90)

Yet in a real sense the lovers' evaluation of their triumph is an "excellent falsehood" (1.1.40), as Cleopatra herself terms Antony's exuberant vision of love. It is undeniably attractive, but the play does not permit us unequivocal assent. The lovers are self-indulgent and self-dramatizing, and nothing in the play suggests that their consolation is other than imaginary. Antony gives all for the love of a woman who will not risk the safety of her monument as he lies mortally wounded below; and Cleopatra's vision receives little confirmation from a play in which too often he appears "like a doting mallard" (3.10.20). At our harshest, we might feel that their claims of transcendence themselves testify to their moral blindness:

> When we in our viciousness grow hard
> (O misery on't!) the wise gods seel our eyes,

> In our own filth drop our clear judgments, make us
> Adore our errors, laugh at's while we strut
> To our confusion. (3.13.111–15)

Antony and Cleopatra do strut and adore their own errors. Rome will not "in Tiber melt" (1.1.33), and "the strong necessity of time" (1.3.42) demands to be recognized. "If we accept the lovers at their own final evaluation," writes Howard Felperin, "and see their experience from the overview they claim to attain, the play becomes a romance ("The World Well Lost"); yet we must also acknowledge that it is Caesar who remains to deliver the last word."

The central issue is whether Antony has been "beguiled...to the very heart of loss" (4.12.29), which makes the play a moral tragedy, or whether we have the romance action in which his loss is transformed into something rich and strange. In loving Cleopatra has he given "his potent regiment to a trull" (3.6.15), or has he extended his regiment over "new heaven, new earth" (1.1.17)? Clearly the claims of the lovers would frustrate tragic closure as they look to a fulfillment in a time not confined within the formal boundaries of the play. But nothing except the intensity of their imaginations validates this belief, and, while this is a truly significant exception, the play leaves the lovers in "the secret house of death" (4.13.83).

If *Antony and Cleopatra* were actually to be romance rather than to adumbrate it, there could be no ambiguity about the nature of love's triumph. Yet this ambiguity is at the heart of the play, revealed in the very terms in which Caesar himself comes to acknowledge Cleopatra's remarkable power:

> She looks like sleep
> As she would catch another Antony
> In her strong toil of grace. (5.2.344–46)

In the romances the "strong toil of grace" would unambiguously suggest a secular parallel to the miraculous healing action of Divine love; and from the viewpoint of Antony and Cleopatra their love does provide an analogue of the perfect and perfecting love of God that robs death of its victory. But here Caesar's intended meaning cannot be entirely repudiated, for it draws confirmation from Cleopatra's own image:

> I will betray
> Tawny-finned fishes. My bended hook shall pierce
> Their slimy jaws; and as I draw them up,
> I'll think them every one an Antony,
> And say, "Ah ha! Y' are caught!" (2.5.11–15)

Antony has been caught on Cleopatra's hook, and her "strong toil of grace" has betrayed him.

> Egypt, thou knew'st too well
> My heart was to thy rudder tied by th' strings,
> And thou shouldst tow me after. O'er my spirit
> Thy full supremacy thou knew'st, and that

> Thy beck might from the bidding of the gods
> Command me. (3.4.19–20)

And if a kiss repays him for all that he has lost, perhaps it testifies to how completely he has made "his will / Lord of his reason" (3.13.3–4). G. Wilson Knight holds that in the play "man is transfigured by love's orient fire." Even the most moralistic of the Romans would agree to this; but where Knight sees man transfigured "to divine likeness," the moralist, with Philo, sees him "transformed / Into a strumptet's fool" (1.1.12–13). The two perspectives exist simultaneously, each exerting powerful claims upon our sympathies, and we can discover

> no midway
> Twixt these extremes at all. (3.4.19–20)

In *Antony and Cleopatra* there is a distance, as even Antony sees, between Cleopatra's "strong toil of grace" and "the bidding of the gods" which prevents the play from moving convincingly beyond its tragic facts. But if it fails completely to transcend the tragic, it clearly points this way. In the play, the resistance to tragic closure exists in the imaginations of the lovers, while in the romance it exists in the imagination of the playwright; but in both cases it is love that is recognized as the perfecting agent.

The key to the romance vision is the perspective that refuses to see tragic action as a fully realized whole. The field of vision is extended so that tragedy is recognized merely as a component of a more comprehensive action that moves beyond, and through, suffering to clarity and harmony. This is, of course, the commitment of Christianity which insists that the tragic is local and impermanent. In *Paradise Lost*, Adam and Eve must be educated to see beyond the "world of woe" (IX, 11) that their disobedience occasions so that they

> may live, which will be many days,
> Both in one Faith unanimous though sad,
> With cause for evils past, yet much more cheer'd
> With meditation on the happy end. (XII, 602–05)

Milton's "notes" which change to "tragic" in book nine finally echo the comic imperative of Christian history. The "new heaven, new earth" that Antony and Cleopatra want to believe necessary to measure their love is "the happy end" that man is promised. God's strong toil of grace will bring forth

> From the conflagrant mass, purg'd and refin'd,
> New Heav'ns, new Earth, Ages of endless date,
> Founded in righteousness and peace and love,
> To bring forth fruits, Joy and eternal Bliss. (XII, 549–51)

From "More Than History Can Pattern," *Cithara* 17 (1977), 31–33.

# INDEX